WINDOWS VISTA

IN A NUTSHELL

Other Windows resources from O'Reilly

Related titles   Windows Vista Pocket
Reference
Windows Vista: The
Missing Manual
Windows Vista: The
Definitive Guide
Building the Perfect PC
Windows Vista
Annoyances

Word 2007: The Missing
Manual
PowerPoint 2007: The
Missing Manual
Excel 2007: The Missing
Manual
Access 2007: The Missing
Manual

**Networking
Resource Center**   *windows.oreilly.com* is a complete catalog of O'Reilly's
books on networking technologies.

Conferences   O'Reilly brings diverse innovators together to nurture the
ideas that spark revolutionary industries. We specialize in
documenting the latest tools and systems, translating the
innovator's knowledge into useful skills for those in the
trenches. Visit *conferences.oreilly.com* for our upcoming
events.

   Safari Bookshelf (*safari.oreilly.com*) is the premier online
reference library for programmers and IT professionals.
Conduct searches across more than 1,000 books. Sub-
scribers can zero in on answers to time-critical questions
in a matter of seconds. Read the books on your Bookshelf from cover to cover or simply flip to the page you
need. Try it today for free.

WINDOWS
VISTA

IN A NUTSHELL

Preston Gralla

O'REILLY®

Beijing • Cambridge • Farnham • Köln • Paris • Sebastopol • Taipei • Tokyo

Windows Vista in a Nutshell
by Preston Gralla

Copyright © 2007 O'Reilly Media, Inc. All rights reserved.
Printed in the United States of America.

Published by O'Reilly Media, Inc., 1005 Gravenstein Highway North, Sebastopol, CA 95472.

O'Reilly books may be purchased for educational, business, or sales promotional use. Online editions are also available for most titles (*safari.oreilly.com*). For more information, contact our corporate/institutional sales department: (800) 998-9938 or *corporate@oreilly.com*.

Editor: Brian Jepson
Production Editor: Rachel Monaghan
Copyeditor: Audrey Doyle
Proofreader: Rachel Monaghan

Indexer: John Bickelhaupt
Cover Designer: Karen Montgomery
Interior Designer: David Futato
Illustrators: Robert Romano and
Jessamyn Read

Printing History:

December 2006:   First Edition.

 This book uses RepKover™, a durable and flexible lay-flat binding.

ISBN-10: 0-596-52707-1
ISBN-13: 978-0-596-52707-5
[C]   [03/07]

Table of Contents

Part II. Nutshell Reference

Part III. Appendixes

Preface

Windows Vista, the latest product in a long line of operating systems from Microsoft, represents the most dramatic change in Windows since the move from Windows 3.1 to Windows 95. Almost everything about the operating system has been altered, starting with a new look and feel to the desktop and interface featuring transparent, animated windows, to a new Control Panel, improved networking, new versions of Internet Explorer and the email program in Windows, improved security…the list, as you'll see throughout this book, is very long indeed.

Even if you've used a previous version of Windows, you'll find a lot that is new in Windows Vista, and you'll find there's much to learn as well. Windows Explorer looks and works differently, for example, and includes many new ways to access files and folders. The entire interface has gotten a major face-lift. It's easier than ever to set up and manage your own network, including wireless networks. And the new Search feature makes searching lightning-fast, and includes new ways of finding files.

A graphical user interface such as the one in Windows Vista is not a substitute for good, thorough documentation. Naturally, colorful icons and animated windows make the interface more inviting and help uninitiated users stumble through the basics of opening programs and printing documents. There are only so many hours in the day, though, and spending most of them trying to figure out the new networking system and Control Panel, sorting through the thousands of settings in the Registry, discovering all of the hidden tools, or even learning to be productive with the new Windows Movie Maker, is really not a good use of your time.

By taking the undocumented or otherwise hidden features and settings in Windows Vista and placing them in context with more conspicuous and familiar components, this book provides the complete picture necessary to truly understand the operating system and what is involved in completing just about any task.

There are many books on Windows Vista, but most of them get bogged down with elementary tutorials and the scrawniest tasks most of us could perform in our sleep. That's where this book comes in. *Windows Vista in a Nutshell* provides a condensed but thorough reference to Windows Vista, with an organization that helps you get right to the task at hand.

For example, there are literally hundreds of settings and features in Windows Vista, scattered throughout dozens of dialog boxes. Some are plainly accessible through the Start menu or in the Control Panel, and others are hidden under layers of application menus. A few aren't apparent at all without knowledge of hidden features. This book thoroughly documents them all and makes it easy for you to find them by using a simple organization that lets you find a setting, tool, or feature based on the task you want to accomplish.

Considerations and Scope

The focus of this book is on users and their networks and applications, not on large enterprise or corporate systems or network administration. However, the book recognizes that many people run small networks in their homes or in their offices, so it spends a considerable amount of time on network tools, settings, configuration, and troubleshooting. Therefore, in addition to covering the use of Windows Vista on a single PC, the book also covers how to set up a network, how to troubleshoot it, and how to take advantage of Windows Vista's numerous networking features, including file and printer sharing, offline folders, collaboration via Windows Meeting Space, using Remote Desktop Connections, and many other common and not-so-obvious network tasks.

This book also offers you a basic understanding of the deeper levels of network configuration available in large, enterprise-level networks, but specific installation details and detailed configuration information for system and network administrators are largely beyond its scope.

This book has tried to speak universal truths about Windows Vista, but sometimes it is forced to make assumptions about your settings or installed options. Microsoft gives so many configuration options, and computer manufacturers can change some configurations, so the truth is that, for better or worse, each user's machine represents a slightly different installation of Windows Vista. Of all the code and data Microsoft ships on the Windows Vista DVD, only about half is used in any particular user's configuration. What this book says about Windows Vista may or may not be true of your particular installation—although it will be very close.

For example, there's a setting in Windows Explorer Folder Options that instructs Windows to open icons with either a double-click or a single-click, according to your preference. While most users tend to prefer the double-click option, and double-clicking is the default on most systems, your system might be different. Although both setups are clearly defined in Chapter 2, some procedures elsewhere in this book will instruct you to double-click where you may only need to single-click, depending on your system setup. This "knowledge gap" is an unfortunate consequence of the malleable nature of the Windows operating system.

Consider another oddity in Windows Vista: categories in the Control Panel, which split the components of the Control Panel into distinct categories, rather than simply listing them alphabetically. What's more, the Control Panel can be accessed in any of three different ways (as a menu in the Start menu, as a stand-alone folder window, or as an entry in the folder tree in Windows Explorer), and the category interface (which can be disabled completely, if desired) is used in only some cases. This means that it's difficult (and laborious) to predict when you'll need to open the "Appearance and Personalization" category before you can get to the Folder Options dialog. The book compensates for this ambiguity by enclosing the category name in "maybe" brackets, like this: Control Panel → [Appearance and Personalization] → Folder Options.

Also, for all the statements (from Microsoft and others) that Windows Vista is "integrated" and "seamless," the fact is that the system is actually amazingly modular, customizable, and "seamy." This is a good thing. But this almost infinite customizability and modularity of Windows Vista means that there are many different paths you can follow to your goal, and it can be easy to get lost. This book shows you all the paths, picks out the easiest one for you to follow, and includes signposts along the way. Ultimately, Windows Vista is a platform and set of capabilities, not a single, stable product with a fixed set of features. In this book, you get the information you need to tap into all of Windows Vista's capabilities, not just those that are showcased on Microsoft's web site or the Windows Desktop.

Organization of the Book

This book is divided into three parts.

Part I: The Big Picture

This part of the book is designed to give you an overview of Windows Vista and to introduce the concepts used throughout the rest of the book. It consists of two chapters:

Chapter 1, *The Lay of the Land*, gives you a brief guided tour of Windows Vista, highlights all the major changes to the operating system, details its hardware requirements, and offers a comparison of the various versions of Windows Vista and their features.

Chapter 2, *Using Windows Vista*, covers the basics of using Windows, such as starting applications, manipulating files, and getting around the interface. Even if you know your way around previous versions of Windows, this chapter will be helpful, because a lot has changed with Windows Vista.

Part II: Nutshell Reference

This part of the book contains alphabetically organized references for each major element of Windows Vista. To make it easier to find the element, tool, feature, or program you're looking for, it's organized by topics, such as Internet Explorer; Networking, Mobility, and Wireless; and so on. This section is the comprehensive reference that covers all the programs that come with Windows Vista, those listed in the Start menu and Control Panel, and those available only if you know where to look. For GUI-based applications, the book focuses on nonobvious features and provides helpful hints about power-user features and things that will make your life easier. For command-line-based programs, all options are covered, since these programs are not as obviously self-documenting (though many do support the conventional /? command-line option for help).

Chapter 3, *The User Interface*, is a thorough examination of the elements that make up the Windows Vista graphical user interface. It covers in detail new features such as Windows Aero, transparent windows, Windows Flip and Windows Flip 3D, and the Windows Sidebar and associated Gadgets. In addition, it covers the basics of windows, menus, buttons, listboxes, and scroll bars, as well as how to make the most of the Taskbar and how to use any component of Windows with only the keyboard.

Chapter 4, *Working with the Filesystem, Drives, Data, and Search*, covers all aspects of files and the filesystem, including the myriad new features of Windows Explorer. In addition, it covers the new search features of Windows Vista in great detail.

Chapter 5, *Internet Explorer*, details all aspects of the revamped browser in Windows. It covers tabbed browsing, the new antiphishing filter, RSS feeds, the Search Bar, and virtually all of Internet Explorer's other features, tools, and settings.

Chapter 6, *Windows Mail*, puts the spotlight on the email program formerly known as Outlook Express. In Windows Vista, Microsoft has clearly decided to make the email client built into Windows a serious piece of work. The new features extend well beyond merely renaming the program.

Chapter 7, *Networking, Wireless, and Mobility*, covers wired and wireless networks, as well as laptops and mobile computing. Almost everyone these days is a system administrator of some sort, even if it's only for a two-PC home network sharing an Internet connection with a printer attached. So this chapter delves into small networks in some detail, including wireless networks, wireless connections, public hotspots, and similar matters. It also covers the entirely new networking interface, new networking applications such as the collaboration tool Windows Meeting Space, and the Sync Center, which makes it easy to synchronize files among different computers and devices.

Chapter 8, *Security*, covers the myriad new security tools built into Vista, with an emphasis on Internet security. (Windows Vista has a greater emphasis on security than previous versions of Windows, so security gets its own chapter.) Among the topics covered are the Security Center, Windows Defender, User Account Control, System Protection, Network Access Protection, the Windows Firewall, file encryption, and Windows Update. The chapter shows how you can use Windows Vista to make your PC as secure as possible, and includes hidden ways to configure security, such as how to customize the Windows Firewall's outbound port filtering.

Chapter 9, *Working with Hardware*, covers everything about setting up, maintaining, and troubleshooting hardware, including keyboards, mice, monitors, USB devices, input devices, scanners, cameras, sound devices, and printers. It also covers adding, installing, and troubleshooting drivers.

Chapter 10, *Managing Programs, Users, and Your Computer*, covers how user accounts work on Windows Vista, and how to make best use of them. It details Group Policy and user profiles, and it spends a good amount of time on the new User Account Control features, and on the difference between running as a normal user and as an administrator.

Chapter 11, *Performance and Troubleshooting*, covers all of the performance and troubleshooting tools in Windows, including backup, disk defragmentation, System Restore, the Performance Diagnostic Console, Task Manager, system maintenance tools, and much more.

Chapter 12, *Graphics and Multimedia*, covers music and video playing and production, as well as new features that make it easier to connect a variety of multimedia devices to a PC. It includes the new Windows Media Player, the Media Center, connecting to and syncing with MP3 players, making videos with Windows Movie Maker, burning CDs and DVDs, and more.

Chapter 13, *The Registry*, describes the organization of the Windows XP Registry, the central configuration database upon which Windows and all of your applications rely to function and remember your settings. The Registry Editor, the primary interface to the Registry, is covered here, along with some of the more interesting entries scattered throughout this massive database.

Chapter 14, *The Command Prompt*, provides complete documentation on this often overlooked and underestimated part of the operating system. In addition to learning the ins and outs of the Command Prompt application, you can look up commands and find exactly what options they support. Batch files, a quick and easy way to automate repetitive tasks, are also covered.

Part III: Appendixes

This section includes various quick reference lists.

Appendix A, *Installing Windows Vista*, covers everyone's least favorite activity. In addition to documenting the various installers and options, the chapter includes a number of pitfalls and solutions that will apply to nearly every installation.

Appendix B, *Keyboard Shortcuts*, gives a list of keyboard accelerators (also known as *hotkeys*) used in all parts of the Windows interface.

Appendix C, *Keyboard Equivalents for Symbols and International Characters*, explains how to type the symbols and international characters normally accessible only with Character Map.

Appendix D, *Common Filename Extensions*, lists many file types and their descriptions. This appendix is useful when you're trying to figure out how to open a specific file and all you know is the filename extension.

Appendix E, *Services*, lists the background services that come with Windows Vista and their respective filenames. If you need to find a service, or simply need to determine the purpose of a particular program shown to be running in the Windows Task Manager, this appendix will provide the answer.

Conventions Used in This Book

The following typographical conventions are used in this book:

Italic

> Used to introduce new terms, user-defined files and directories, file extensions, filenames, and directory and folder names.

`Constant width`

> Used to indicate command-line computer output and code examples.

`Constant width bold`

> Used to indicate user input.

`Constant width italic`

> Used in code examples and text to show sample text to be replaced with your own values.

[Square brackets]

> Used around an item to show a step or parameter (usually a command-line parameter) that is optional. Include or omit the option as needed. Parameters not shown in square brackets are typically mandatory. See "Path Notation," which follows, for another use of square brackets in this book.

The following symbols are used in this book:

> This symbol indicates a tip.

> This symbol indicates a warning.

Path Notation

Rather than using procedural steps to tell you how to reach a given Windows Vista user interface element or application, I use a shorthand path notation.

For example, the book doesn't say, "Click on the Start menu, then click on All Programs, then on Accessories, and then on Paint." It simply says, Start → All Programs → Accessories → Paint. The book generally doesn't distinguish between menus, dialog boxes, buttons, checkboxes, and so on, unless it's not clear from the context. Just look for a GUI element whose label matches an element in the path.

The path notation is relative to the Desktop or some other well-known location. For example, the following path:

> Start → Control Panel → Security → Windows Firewall

means "Open the Start menu (on the Desktop), then choose Control Panel, then choose Security, and then click Windows Firewall." That is shortened to:

> Control Panel → Security → Windows Firewall

because Control Panel is a "well-known location" and the path can therefore be made less cumbersome. As stated earlier in this preface, the elements of the Control Panel may or may not be divided into categories, depending on the context and settings on your computer. Thus, rather than a cumbersome explanation of this unfortunate design, every time the Control Panel comes up, the following notation is used:

Control Panel → [Security] → Windows Firewall

where the category—"Security," in this case—is shown in square brackets, implying that you may or may not encounter this step.

Paths will typically consist of clickable user interface elements, but they sometimes include text typed in from the keyboard (shown in constant width bold text):

Command Prompt → **mmc**

There is often more than one way to reach a given location in the user interface. I frequently list multiple paths to reach the same location, even though some are longer than others, because it can be helpful to see how multiple paths lead to the same destination.

Using Code Examples

This book is here to help you get your job done. In general, you may use the code in this book in your programs and documentation. You do not need to contact us for permission unless you're reproducing a significant portion of the code. For example, writing a program that uses several chunks of code from this book does not require permission. Selling or distributing a CD-ROM of examples from O'Reilly books *does* require permission. Answering a question by citing this book and quoting example code does not require permission. Incorporating a significant amount of example code from this book into your product's documentation *does* require permission.

We appreciate, but do not require, attribution. An attribution usually includes the title, author, publisher, and ISBN. For example: "*Windows Vista in a Nutshell*, by Preston Gralla. Copyright 2007 O'Reilly Media, Inc., 978-0-596-52707-5."

We'd Like to Hear from You

Please address comments and questions concerning this book to the publisher:

O'Reilly Media, Inc.
1005 Gravenstein Highway North
Sebastopol, CA 95472
800-998-9938 (in U.S. or Canada)
707-829-0515 (international/local)
707-829-0104 (fax)

There is a web page for this book, which lists errata, examples, or any additional information. You can access this page at:

http://www.oreilly.com/catalog/9780596527075

To comment or ask technical questions about this book, send email to:

bookquestions@oreilly.com

For more information about our books, conferences, resource centers, and the O'Reilly Network, see the O'Reilly web site at:

http://www.oreilly.com

Safari® Enabled

 When you see a Safari® Enabled icon on the cover of your favorite technology book, that means the book is available online through the O'Reilly Network Safari Bookshelf.

Safari offers a solution that's better than e-books. It's a virtual library that lets you easily search thousands of top tech books, cut and paste code samples, download chapters, and find quick answers when you need the most accurate, current information. Try it for free at *http://safari.oreilly.com*.

Acknowledgments

This is the fourth *In a Nutshell* book covering a version of Microsoft Windows. Although this book has evolved substantially from its progenitors, *Windows 95 in a Nutshell*, *Windows 98 in a Nutshell*, and *Windows XP in a Nutshell* (as Windows itself has evolved), its existence is due to the hard work of those who worked on those earlier volumes.

Tim O'Reilly developed the original concept for the book; he and Troy Mott were the principal authors of the first edition. Andrew Schulman was also instrumental in helping get the first edition of this book off the ground, and it was he who insisted on the importance of the command line. Walter Glenn was a major contributor to the second edition. The Windows XP edition was developed by David Karp and incorporated some material from his bestselling *Windows Annoyances* series; David offered advice for this edition as well.

For this edition, old friend and Windows guru, Scot Finnie, offered much advice and support, and helped with getting me out of some thorny dual-boot installation problems during early Windows Vista betas. David Pogue offered a variety of tips and suggestions; for his look at Windows Vista, check out *Windows Vista: The Missing Manual* (O'Reilly). Editor of this edition, Brian Jepson, deserves combat pay for extremely fine-grained editing of this book with extensive attention to minute detail, while at the same time managing to get the book out the door on time. His technically astute analysis and overall solid editorial judgment and help made the final book a far better one than when it was begun. Thanks, also, to Rachel Monaghan, production editor and proofreader; Audrey Doyle, copyeditor; and John Bickelhaupt, indexer.

And, of course, most thanks go to my family: my wife Lydia, and my children Gabe and Mia. They reminded me that there is, in fact, a life beyond the keyboard.

The Big Picture

The Lay of the Land

Microsoft spent far longer developing Windows Vista than it did any previous version of Windows, and the results show. Everything you see and use, from the desktop to networking, searching, using the Internet, and beyond, has been overhauled. The interface includes transparent windows and windows animations; the operating system includes a series of Centers, such as the Network and Sharing Center and the Mobility Center, that make it easy to perform your most common tasks and customize how your PC works; and the search function has been baked so deep into the operating system that you need to type only a few letters of what you're looking for and the results start to show up immediately—everything from files to programs to mail to web sites. And there are plenty of other major changes as well, such as a Sidebar brimming with Gadgets that perform common tasks for you.

But it's not just what you see that has been altered, and that's not what took up most of Microsoft's time in developing this new version of Windows. Under the hood, the changes are even more dramatic, mostly having to do with security. In the years leading up to the release of Windows Vista, security had become one of the top, if not *the* top, concerns of most PC users. Spyware, worms, viruses, scammers, crackers, and snoopers had become ubiquitous, and because Windows is by far the most dominant operating system on the planet, it was Windows that they targeted. So Microsoft spent a great deal of effort hardening the operating system against threats. Some of this effort is visible, such as the new Windows Defender antispyware tool, the more powerful firewall, and the phishing filter built into Internet Explorer. But much of it is invisible to you, such as Windows Service Hardening, which stops background Windows services from being used by malware to damage the filesystem, Registry, or network to which the PC is connected.

The result is a new operating system that is more secure than previous versions of Windows, with a more sophisticated interface (some call it more Mac-like) and easier ways to find files and data.

Windows Vista also has heftier hardware requirements than any version of Windows to date, and it is a major enough change that it may take those who use earlier Windows versions some time to relearn how to use the operating system.

There's more to understanding Windows Vista than simply knowing how to open applications and manage your files effectively. This chapter covers what's new in this release and how Windows fits into the big picture. Move on to Chapter 2 for a quick-paced tour of some of the more basic aspects of day-to-day use of the operating system, or skip ahead to the later chapters for meatier content.

The Big Picture

The first few releases of Microsoft Windows in the early 1980s were little more than clunky graphical application launchers that ran on top of the Disk Operating System (DOS) (see Chapter 14 for details). Version 3.*x*, released in the late 1980s, gained popularity due to its improved interface (awful by today's standards) and capability to access all of a computer's memory. Being based on DOS, however, it was not terribly stable, crashed frequently, and had very limited support for networking and no support for multiple user accounts.

Soon thereafter, Windows NT 3.1 ("NT" for New Technology) was released. Although it shared the same interface as Windows 3.1, it was based on a more robust and more secure *kernel*, the underlying code on which the interface and all of the applications run. Among other things, it didn't rely on DOS and was capable of running 32-bit applications (Windows 3.1 could run only more feeble 16-bit applications).* Unfortunately, it was a white elephant of sorts, enjoying limited commercial appeal due to its stiff hardware requirements and scant industry support.

In 1995, Microsoft released Windows 95. Although based on DOS, like Windows 3.*x* (it was known internally as Windows 4.0), it was a 32-bit operating system with a new interface. It was the first step toward bringing the enhanced capability of the Windows NT architecture to the more commercially accepted, albeit less capable, DOS-based Windows line. Soon thereafter, Windows NT 4.0 was released, which brought the new Windows 95-style interface to the NT line. Both of these grand gestures were engineered to further blur the line between these two different Microsoft platforms. Although both operating systems sported the same interface, Windows NT still never garnered the consumer support and commercial success of Windows 95, but it did become popular for use with servers.

As time progressed, the lineage of Microsoft Windows became even less linear. Despite its name, Windows 2000 was *not* the successor to Windows 98 and Windows 95; Windows Me, released at the same time, had that distinction. Instead, Windows 2000 was the next installment of the NT line; it was actually known internally as Windows NT 5.0. Windows 2000 was particularly notable for being the first version of Windows NT to support Plug and Play, which was yet another move to combine the two platforms.

Then came Windows XP, known internally as Windows NT 5.1. Although it was technically merely an incremental upgrade to Windows 2000, it was positioned as

---

* A *bit*, or *binary digit*, is the smallest unit of information storage, capable of holding either a zero or a one. 32-bit operating systems such as Windows NT and Windows 95 were capable of addressing memory in 32-bit (4-byte) chunks, which made them more efficient and powerful than a 16-bit OS such as Windows 3.*x*.

the direct replacement to Windows Me, officially marking the end of the DOS-based Windows 9*x*/Me line. Windows XP unified both lines of Windows, bringing the stability of NT to home and small-business users and the industry support of Windows 9*x*/Me to corporate and power users.

Now Windows Vista has entered the picture, and it makes significant improvements to the user experience, the stability of the operating system, and security. It is the first revision to the unified Windows code, and it overhauls the interface itself as well as the internal workings of the operating system, most notably related to security. It was also developed with mobility and networking in mind, and it makes significant advances in how people can collaborate across networks. In addition, it adds more multimedia capabilities to Windows.

What's New in Windows Vista

Windows Vista is a significant rework of Windows, and although the basics of Windows are the same, much has changed. Here are the most significant additions and changes in Windows Vista compared to Windows XP:

Windows Aero interface

The new interface is the first thing people will notice when they run Windows Vista. It sports customizable, translucent windows (called *Aero Glass*); live Taskbar thumbnails that show a live preview of an underlying window when a mouse is held over the tile; and Windows Flip and Windows Flip 3D, which show thumbnails of open windows as you flip through them. As the name implies, Windows Flip 3D, shown in Figure 1-1, shows the thumbnails in three dimensions. Note that Windows Aero is not available on the least expensive versions of Windows Vista, and that it has special hardware requirements. There are three other levels of the interface that are less sophisticated than Windows Aero: Windows Classic, Basic, and Standard.

Figure 1-1. Using Flip 3D to flip through live previews of open windows

Security

Security has been enhanced at every level of the operating system, in both visible and invisible ways. Windows Defender protects against spyware, and the Windows Firewall now includes outbound as well as inbound protection. Internet Explorer runs by default in Protected Mode, which protects the operating system from assault via the browser, and it includes a phishing filter. Windows Service Hardening stops background Windows services from being used by malware to damage the filesystem, Registry, or network to which the PC is connected. Windows Vista also gives network administrators more control over network and PC security, such as the ability to restrict access to removable storage devices such as Universal Serial Bus (USB) flash drives. Parental Controls allow parents to determine how their children can use the computer and what content they can access. BitLocker Drive Encryption, when used with compatible hardware, locks down a hard disk so that it cannot be accessed if the computer is stolen. Windows Vista also includes User Account Control (UAC), which pops up warnings and asks for passwords when certain setup or customization screens or features are accessed. This enhances security, but it can also mean that you will have to type in a password or click an approval button before you can change certain system features.

Revised Internet Explorer

Internet Explorer, shown in Figure 1-2, has been given its most significant overhaul in years, with the addition of tabs, a redesigned menu system, increased security, Instant Search via an integrated search bar, page zoom, and better printing.

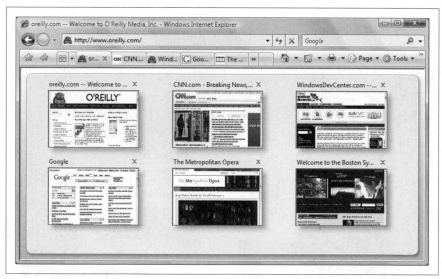

Figure 1-2. A revamped Internet Explorer, featuring tabs and a redesigned menu system

RSS support

Really Simple Syndication (RSS) allows for the delivery of live feeds of web content, news, and web logs. Internet Explorer includes a built-in RSS reader that lets you subscribe to and read RSS feeds.

Windows Sidebar and Gadgets

The new Windows Sidebar, shown in Figure 1-3, puts information and frequently used tasks directly on the desktop. Gadgets that live on the Sidebar perform tasks such as fetching RSS feeds, displaying system information, and showing up-to-date stock information.

Figure 1-3. The Windows Sidebar, which contains gadgets that perform a wide variety of tasks, as well as gather live information

Better search

Search speed has been significantly increased, integrated throughout the operating system, and enhanced with more ways to find files, programs, email, and web information. The Instant Search feature, in Windows Explorer and on the Search menu, finds information the instant you start typing. Instant Search is context-sensitive, so when a search is performed from within a folder, it will search that folder. A new Search Pane adds simple ways to fine-tune and filter searches. In addition, you can create Virtual Folders that are based on search criteria—for example, you can create a Virtual Folder that constantly updates itself and that will display all *.doc* files over a certain size, created after a certain date, and containing certain words.

New "Centers"

Windows Vista organizes common tasks and features into *Centers*, which contain all the information and settings related to the task or feature. For example, the Network and Sharing Center, shown in Figure 1-4, allows you to view information about your current network and connection, see a complete network map, connect to new networks, customize your connections, turn file sharing on or off, change security settings, and so on. Similarly, the Windows Mobility Center includes settings and information related to mobile computing. And the Backup and Restore Center makes it easy for you to back up and restore data as well as the current state of your computer.

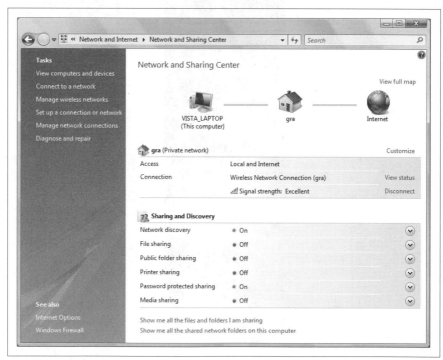

Figure 1-4. The Network and Sharing Center: command central for network information and configuration

New networking features

Collaboration tools make it easy for people to find others with whom to have live meetings over a network. Wireless networking includes support for the WPA2/802.11i security standards. Windows Vista also supports the new IPv6 Transmission Control Protocol/Internet Protocol (TCP/IP) architecture, which expands the number of available IP addresses.

Improved multimedia

Windows Media Center has been overhauled. If a PC has a TV tuner, it will be able to record, watch, and pause live television feeds. Browsing, searching for, and organizing digital media such as photos and music have been improved. See the "Windows Vista Editions" section of this chapter for details on which versions of Vista support these functions. In addition, Windows Media Player 11 features plenty of improvements.

Faster startup and resume

Whenever Windows Vista starts up, it has to run a variety of scripts and services, just as earlier versions of Windows had to do. But with Vista, startup doesn't wait for those scripts and services; instead, it moves ahead and starts, and the scripts run in the background, leading to faster startup. To make Windows Vista start even faster, you can put it into Sleep Mode rather than shutting it down. In Sleep Mode, all your open documents, windows, and programs are saved, but the computer shuts down most of its functions. When you wake it from Sleep Mode, the documents, windows, and programs are restored in exactly the state they were in when your computer went to sleep. Waking from Sleep Mode happens within seconds—faster than it takes for a computer to start up from a shutdown.

SuperFetch

This new technology can improve your PC's performance by watching the programs and data you often use, and then fetching them before you actually need them. That way, the programs and data load and run much faster when you open them. SuperFetch really comes into its own when combined with ReadyBoost, which allows your PC to use a high-speed flash drive for a SuperFetch cache. Flash drives are much less expensive than RAM, so this is an inexpensive way to boost your PC's performance. In addition, some systems, such as laptops, may have limited RAM capacity, so a flash drive is a way to boost those systems' performance.

Restart Manager

Under earlier versions of Windows, you frequently had to reboot your PC whenever you installed a patch to a program because Windows was unable to shut down all the processes associated with that program. With Windows Vista, you will have to reboot far less frequently when applying a patch because Restart Manager can more effectively close down and restart the required processes. (Note that Restart Manager is not an application that you use directly; instead, it's a kind of internal plumbing that works without your intervention.)

Improved stability

Windows Vista includes a variety of new features under the hood to make it more reliable and less prone to crashes than previous versions of Windows. The Startup Repair Tool automatically fixes common startup problems, and all Windows services now have recovery policies that allow Vista to automatically restart a service that has crashed, as well as restart associated services.

Better backup

It's no secret that the backup programs built into Windows XP Home and Professional left much to be desired, and because of that, they were rarely used. Windows Vista's new backup program, Windows Backup, is actually useful and lets you back up to writable discs, USB flash drives, and other removable media, as well as across a network. Backups can be completely automated, and you can also back up an entire system image (what Windows Vista calls a *Complete PC backup*) that saves the current state of your PC so that it can be easily restored in the case of a system failure, or if your PC is stolen. There's also a Backup and Restore Center, shown in Figure 1-5, which provides a central location for all backup and restoration chores.

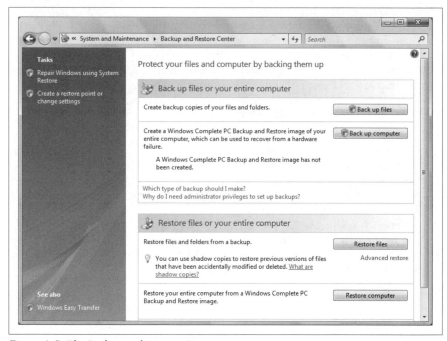

Figure 1-5. The Backup and Restore Center

Windows Vista Editions

Those who were slightly confused by the two different versions of Windows XP—the Home Edition and the Professional Edition—will be flummoxed by the dizzying array of different Windows Vista versions. There are five different core Vista versions, for everyone from users with bare-bones PCs, to home users interested in multimedia, to users who work in large enterprises. As a practical matter, though, most home users will end up with Windows Vista Home Premium; those in many businesses will end up with Windows Vista Business; and those in very large corporations will run Windows Vista Enterprise Edition. Here's the rundown on the five core versions and how they differ:

Windows Vista Home Basic
> As the name implies, this edition offers only bare-bones features. It's designed to run on entry-level PCs and doesn't have the Windows Aero interface, doesn't support creating video DVDs, and lacks Media Center features. It is missing more as well, such as mobility features, and it doesn't support Tablet PCs. Most likely, few people will opt for this version of Windows Vista.

Windows Vista Business
> This version is aimed at users in small to medium-size businesses. It includes Windows Aero, supports Tablet PCs, and has most other Vista features. But it doesn't have a variety of multimedia features, such as the capability to create and burn video DVDs. It does, though, have a variety of features aimed at IT staff, such as wireless network provisioning capabilities, Remote Desktop connections, image-based backup, and other network administration features.

Windows Vista Home Premium
> This has Aero and supports all of the multimedia Vista features, such as creating video DVDs, slide show creation, and the Windows Media Center. It supports basic networking and wireless networking, but it doesn't have network administration tools, wireless network provisioning, or the capability to connect to a domain. It also doesn't have the Encrypting File System (EFS) or image-based backup.

Windows Vista Enterprise Edition
> This one is for large enterprises, and only businesses that have Microsoft Software Assurance or a Microsoft Enterprise Agreement get this version. It offers everything that Windows Vista Business does, and it includes hardware-based encryption, called *BitLocker Drive Encryption*, which employs a physical hardware key and a passcode to secure volumes. This version also comes as a single image that enterprises can deploy from a central location.

Windows Vista Ultimate
> Like the name says, this is the Mother of All Vistas. It has all the features and tools in every other version of Vista—the networking and administrative tools of the various business editions, and the multimedia features of the home editions.

Note that there are actually eight Vista versions. The remaining three versions will be sold only outside the United States. The Windows Vista Starter edition will be sold only on low-end PCs in emerging markets, and two "N" versions of Vista are required to be sold in the European Union. The N versions lack some media-related features.

Table 1-1 provides more detailed information about the different Vista versions, as well as where to turn to learn more.

Table 1-1. Comparing selected features in various versions of Windows Vista

Feature	Home Basic	Home Premium	Business	Enterprise Edition	Ultimate	Chapter providing more information
Windows Aero	No	Yes	Yes	Yes	Yes	3
Parental Controls	Yes	Yes	No	No	Yes	8
Windows DVD Maker	No	Yes	No	No	Yes	12
Tablet PC features	No	Yes	Yes	Yes	Yes	7
Remote Desktop	Client only	Client only	Host and client	Host and client	Host and client	7
Automated backup	No	Yes	Yes	Yes	Yes	11
Back up to a network device or folder	No	Yes	Yes	Yes	Yes	11
Create images of desktops for easy backup and recovery	No	No	Yes	Yes	Yes	11
Windows Shadow Copy (automatically creates copies of files to make it easy to restore deleted or lost files)	No	No	Yes	Yes	Yes	4
Fax and scan	No	No	Yes	Yes	Yes	9
Windows Media Center	No	Yes	No	No	Yes	12
BitLocker Drive Encryption	No	No	No	Yes	Yes	8
Capability to create themed slide shows	No	Yes	No	No	Yes	12
Windows Movie Maker	Yes	Yes	No	No	Yes	12
Wireless network provisioning (allows administrators to set network-side security settings)	No	No	Yes	Yes	Yes	7
Encrypting File System	No	No	Yes	Yes	Yes	8
Network Access Protection (stops nonsecure PCs from connecting to a network)	No	No	Yes	Yes	Yes	8
Windows Anytime Upgrade (automated online upgrades to Windows Vista)	Yes	Yes	Yes	No	No	11

Table 1-1. Comparing selected features in various versions of Windows Vista (continued)

Feature	Home Basic	Home Premium	Business	Enterprise Edition	Ultimate	Chapter providing more information
Network projection (allows connecting to network projectors wirelessly)	No	Yes	Yes	Yes	Yes	7
Windows Meeting Space (allows collaboration over networks)	Can view meetings only	Yes	Yes	Yes	Yes	7
Domain support (allows a PC to join a corporate domain)	No	No	Yes	Yes	Yes	7
Group Policy support (allows administrators to set corporate-wide settings for networking, hardware, and so on)	No	No	Yes	Yes	Yes	10
Offline files and folders (allows users to automatically synchronize with network files and folders)	No	No	Yes	Yes	Yes	4

Hardware Requirements

Windows Vista requires considerable hardware—significantly more than previous versions of Windows. It needs a lot of graphics horsepower to support the full Aero interface, but it is possible to run Windows Vista without running Aero.

Because there are so many different versions of Windows Vista, and because it is possible to run Windows Vista without the Windows Aero interface, the exact hardware requirements are somewhat confusing. To help make things a little less confusing, Microsoft has set two levels of hardware: Windows Vista Capable and Windows Vista Premium Ready. A Windows Vista Capable PC will not be able to run all of the Windows Vista features, notably Windows Aero.

> If you want to run the full Aero interface, make sure you buy a Windows Vista Premium Ready PC, because Windows Vista Capable PCs will not be able to run Aero.

A Windows Vista Capable PC has these minimum hardware requirements:

- An 800 MHz 32-bit (x86) or 64-bit (x64) processor
- 512 MB of RAM
- DirectX 9–capable graphics processor (Windows Display Driver Model [WDDM] driver support recommended) with a minimum of 64 MB of memory, and preferably 128 MB
- 20 GB hard disk, with at least 15 GB free

A Windows Vista Premium Ready PC has these minimum hardware requirements:

- A 1 GHz 32-bit (x86) or 64-bit (x64) processor
- 1 GB of RAM
- DirectX 9–capable graphics processor that supports WDDM driver support, Pixel Shader 2.0, 32 bits per pixel, and a minimum of 128 MB of memory
- 40 GB hard disk, with at least 15 GB free
- DVD-ROM drive

Obviously, more is better, so it's a good idea to exceed these requirements when possible.

Windows System Performance Rating

Windows Vista includes a performance rating system, which may puzzle you at first. After all, your hardware can clearly support Windows Vista if you're able to run the tool, so what is its purpose?

In fact, it's not designed to tell you how well your PC runs Vista, but rather how well it can run other software. The idea is that software makers will assign their software a certain level, and you'll buy only the software that the performance rating system says you can run. The higher the number is, the better the performance.

In theory, that's fine. But it's not clear how well it will work in practice, because software makers, including Microsoft, have yet to rate their software according to this system. And it's also quite mysterious how the performance rating system calculates its ratings. As you can see in Figure 1-6, the individual components of this PC rate relatively high, from a 5 (the top rating) to a 3.7. So why is the overall system rating a 3.7? Windows Vista automatically takes the lowest component rating and uses that as the overall system rating.

Useful or not, you might want to see how Windows Vista rates your hardware. Choose Control Panel → System and Maintenance → Performance Information and Tools.

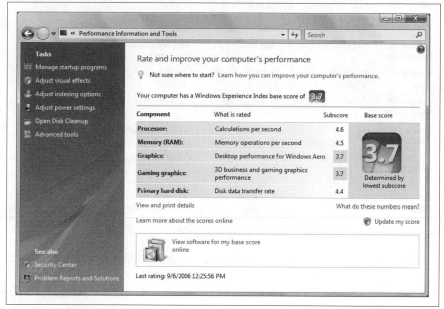

Figure 1-6. Performance rating

Upgrading from Earlier Versions of Windows

When you buy Windows Vista, you buy either a full version of the operating system or an upgrade. Ideally, you'd like to upgrade, because an upgrade is less expensive than buying the full version. Only PCs with Windows XP or Windows 2000 qualify for upgrades; users with PCs running earlier versions of Windows will have to buy the full version.

Users who have Windows XP or Windows 2000 and can upgrade will have one of two choices when they do the Windows Vista installation. They can either perform an in-place upgrade or do a clean install. With an in-place upgrade, you install Windows Vista directly over your previous version of Windows, and you'll keep all of your applications, files, and settings just as they were with your earlier Windows version.

If you can't perform an in-place upgrade, you'll have to back up your files and then do a clean install of Vista—when you do that, you'll wipe out your previous operating system, files, and so on. You will then have to reinstall your applications and copy your files to the PC after the Windows Vista installation is complete.

Whether you're able to do an in-place upgrade depends on your version of Windows XP and Windows 2000, and the version of Windows Vista to which you want to upgrade. Table 1-2 details your upgrade options.

Table 1-2. Upgrade options for Windows Vista

	Home Basic	Home Premium	Business	Ultimate
Windows XP Professional	Clean install	Clean install	In-place installation available	In-place installation available
Windows XP Home	In-place installation available	In-place installation available	In-place installation available	In-place installation available
Windows XP Media Center	Clean install	In-place installation available	Clean install	In-place installation available
Windows XP Tablet PC	Clean install	Clean install	In-place installation available	In-place installation available
Windows XP Professional 64-bit	Clean install	Clean install	Clean install	Clean install
Windows 2000	Clean install	Clean install	Clean install	Clean install

For more information about installing Windows Vista, see Appendix A.

2

Using Windows Vista

This chapter provides a quick overview of the features of the Windows Vista user interface, which should be sufficient to help you become oriented and make the most of the system fairly quickly. Even if you're already familiar with the basic Windows interface, you will learn about the differences between Windows Vista and previous versions, making this chapter worth a read. If you're fairly new to Windows, you should certainly take the time to read this chapter. Concepts that advanced users might consider elementary should prove enlightening. The most important thing is to get a sense of the consistency (or occasionally the lack thereof) in the Windows Vista interface so that you can tackle any new Windows application with ease.

The Desktop

Like most modern operating systems that use graphical user interfaces or GUIs (such as Mac OS X, Unix, and earlier versions of Windows), Windows Vista uses the metaphor of a Desktop with windows and file folders laid out on it. A program called Windows Explorer (*explorer.exe*) provides this Desktop metaphor.

Figure 2-1 shows the main features of the Windows Vista Desktop. The callouts in the figure highlight some of the special-purpose icons and buttons that may appear on the Desktop.

Point-and-Click Operations

Windows Vista offers several settings that affect the way the interface responds to mouse clicks. The default setting (the way it works when you first install Windows Vista) will also be familiar to most users, as it is consistent with the way most operating systems work.

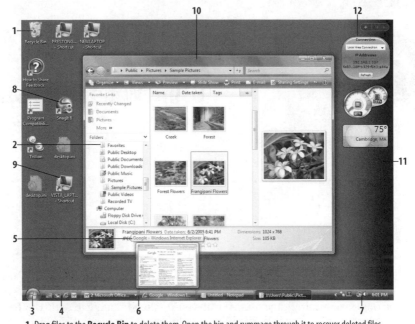

1 Drag files to the **Recycle Bin** to delete them. Open the bin and rummage through it to recover deleted files.
2 A folder lets you organize your files.
3 The **Start** button gives you access to commands and applications on your system.
4 The **Quick Launch** toolbar gives you fast access to frequently used applications.
5 Hover your mouse over a taskbar window icon, and you will see a live thumbnail of its content.
6 The **Taskbar** contains icons for each running application, plus toolbars and the notification area.
7 The **System Tray** (also called the notification area) contains the clock and useful status indicators about programs and services currently running.
8 A shortcut links to a file, folder, or program somewhere else on the system. You can differentiate between shortcuts and regular icons because shortcuts have a curved arrow on them.
9 You can have shortcuts to other computers on your network.
10 An open folder shows its contents in a window.
11 The **Sidebar** is used to display Gadgets.
12 **Gadgets** are mini-applications that can display changing content, such as stock prices or RSS feeds.

Figure 2-1. Windows Vista Desktop features

Depending on your current settings, however, Windows may respond to mouse clicks differently. See the upcoming "Alternate Behavior" section for differences. Later on, you'll see how to choose between the classic behavior and the alternate behavior.

If you are a new computer user who hasn't used a GUI before, here are some things you need to know:

- PCs usually come with a two- or three-button mouse, although there are a variety of alternatives, such as touchpads (common on laptops), trackballs, and styluses. Many mice also include a scroll wheel which, as its name implies, you use to scroll through pages and screens.

- To *click* an object means to move the pointer to the desired screen object and press and release the left mouse button.

- *Double-click* means to click twice in rapid succession with the button on the left. (Clicking twice slowly doesn't accomplish the same thing.)

- *Right-click* means to click with the button on the right.
- If your pointing device has three or more buttons, you should use just the primary buttons on the left and the right, and read the documentation that comes with your pointing device to find out what you can do with the others. (You can often configure the middle button to take over functions such as double-clicking, cut and paste, inserting inflammatory language into emails, and so on.)

Default Behavior

The default setting is consistent with most operating systems, including previous versions of Windows. You can tell whether you have the default style if the captions under the icons on your Desktop are *not* underlined. The alternate behavior (sometimes called the *Web View*) is discussed in the next section. Here is how Windows Vista responds to mouse clicks by default:

- Double-click on any icon on the Desktop to open it. If the icon represents a program, the program is launched (i.e., opened). If the icon represents a datafile, the associated program opens the file. (The associations between files and programs, called *file types* in Windows, are discussed later in this chapter and in Chapter 4.) If the icon represents a folder (such as Documents), a folder window appears, the contents of which are shown as icons within the window.
- When you move your mouse over an icon, it is highlighted but not selected. Single-click on an icon to select it. A selected icon remains highlighted. On the Desktop the icon's text turns white, but in a regular folder window it stays black.
- Single-click on an icon, and then click again (but not so quickly as to suggest a double-click) on the icon's caption to rename it. Type a new caption, and then press the Enter key or simply click elsewhere to confirm the new name. You can also rename by clicking and pressing F2, or by right-clicking and selecting Rename.
- Right-click (click the right mouse button) on any icon to pop up a menu of other actions that can be performed on the object. The contents of this menu vary depending on which object you click, so it is commonly called the *context menu*. The context menu for your garden-variety file includes actions such as Open, Delete, Rename, and Create Shortcut. The context menu for the Desktop itself includes actions such as Refresh and New (to create new empty files or folders). Nearly all objects have a Properties entry, which can be especially useful.
- Click and hold down the left mouse button over an icon while moving the mouse to *drag* the object. Drag a file icon onto a folder icon or into an open folder window to move the file into the folder. Drag a file icon onto a program icon or an open application window (usually) to open the file in that program. Drag an object into your Recycle Bin to dispose of the object. You also can use dragging to rearrange the icons on your Desktop. More drag-and-drop tips are discussed later in this chapter.

- By dragging a file with the right mouse button instead of the left, you can choose what happens when the file is dropped. With the release of the button, a small menu will pop up, providing you with a set of options (Move Here, Copy Here, Create Shortcuts Here) to choose from. Although it is less convenient than left-dragging, it does give you more control.

- Click an icon to select it, and then hold down the Ctrl key while clicking on additional objects—this instructs Windows to remember all your selections so that you can have multiple objects selected simultaneously. This way, for example, you can select a group of files to delete and then drag them all to the Recycle Bin at once.

- Click an item and then hold down Shift while clicking a second item to select both items and all objects that appear between them. What ends up getting selected depends on the arrangement of items to be selected, so this method is more suitable for folder windows that have their contents arranged in a list format. You can use this method in conjunction with the Ctrl method to accomplish elaborate selections.

- You can also select a group of icons without using the keyboard, as shown in Figure 2-2. Draw an imaginary rubber band around the objects you want to select by clicking and holding on a blank area of the Desktop or folder window and dragging it to an opposite corner. Play around with this feature to see how Windows decides which items are included and which are ignored.

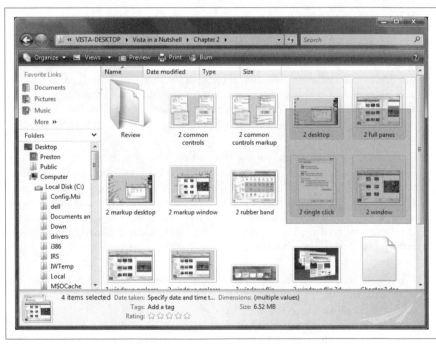

Figure 2-2. Selecting multiple files by dragging a "rubber band"

- Whether you have one icon or many icons selected simultaneously, a single click on another icon or a blank area of the Desktop abandons your selection.
- If you select multiple items simultaneously, they will all behave like a single unit when dragged. For example, if you select 10 file icons, you can drag them all by just grabbing any one of them.
- Press Ctrl-A to select everything in the folder (or on the Desktop, if that's where the focus is). This corresponds to Organize → Select All. (See "Windows and Menus," later in this chapter, if you don't know what I mean by the term *focus*.) See Appendix B for more keyboard shortcuts.

Alternate Behavior

In addition to the default style discussed in the preceding section, Windows also provides a setting that makes the interface work somewhat like a web page. From Windows Explorer's Organize menu, choose Folder and Search Options; if the "Single-click to open an item" option is selected (see Figure 2-3), you're using the settings described here. If you have this setting enabled on your system, clicking and double-clicking will work differently than described in the preceding section, although dragging and right-clicking (as described in the previous section) will remain the same.

Here are the differences between the default and alternate behaviors:

- The whole concept of double-clicking is abolished. Although double-clicking helps prevent icons from being opened accidentally when you're manipulating them, double-clicking can be confusing or awkward for some new users.
- To select an item, simply move the mouse over it.
- To activate (open) an item, click once on it.
- To rename an item, carefully float the mouse pointer over an icon and press F2, or right-click an icon and select Rename.
- You can still select multiple items using the Shift and Ctrl keys.
- Because the default view is, by far, the setting used most frequently, most of the instructions in this book will assume you're using that setting. For example, if you see "Double-click the My Computer icon," and you're using the "Single-click to open" setting, remember that you'll simply be single-clicking the item.

Starting Up Applications

Windows Vista has more ways to launch a program than just about any other operating system:

- Double-click on a program icon in Explorer, on the Desktop.
- Double-click on a file associated with an application to launch that application and open the file.
- Pick the name of a program from the Start menu. (See "Start Menu," in Chapter 3, for details.)

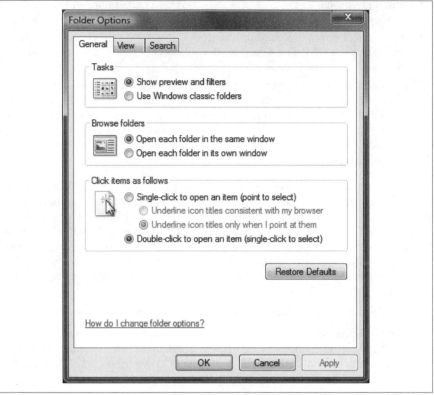

Figure 2-3. Folder options, which specify whether to use a Windows "classic" view or instead display previews and filters, whether folders should open in new windows, and whether double-clicking or single-clicking selects items

- Click on a program's icon in the Quick Launch Toolbar to start it. This tool-bar can include icons for any programs, although by default, it often has icons only for Internet Explorer, the Desktop (click it to go to the Desktop), Switch Between Windows, and Windows Mail after you set up Windows Mail the first time.

 The default icons that appear on the Quick Launch Toolbar often vary from system to system. Computer manufacturers may change what icons appear there or whether Quick Launch even appears at all.

- Right-click on a file, executable, or application icon and choose Open.
- Select (highlight) an icon and press the Enter key.
- Type the filename of a program in the Address Bar, which is displayed above the toolbar in any folder window, in Explorer, in Internet Explorer, or even as part of the Taskbar. You may also have to include the path (the folder and drive names) for some items.

- Type in the filename of a program from the Start Search box and press Enter. You may also have to include the path (the folder and drive names) for some items.

- Type in the first few letters or the entire name of a program (not necessarily the filename) in the Start Search box, choose the program you want to run from the list that appears, and press Enter. For example, if you wanted to run Microsoft Word, you could type **Word**, then select the Microsoft Word icon and press Enter.

 If you're looking to open an application in order to run a specific file, you can search for the file using the Start Search box or other Windows search tools. That way, you can open the file and application in one simple step.

- Open a Command Prompt window and type the name of the program at the prompt. Note that some knowledge of the command prompt, which borrows a lot of syntax and commands from Vista's great-grandfather, the Disk Operating System (DOS), is required—see Chapter 14 for details.

- Create shortcuts to files or applications. A shortcut is a kind of pointer or link—a small file and associated icon that point to a file or program in another location. You can put these shortcuts on the Desktop, in the Start menu, or anywhere else you find convenient. Double-click on a shortcut to launch the program. To launch programs automatically at startup, just place a shortcut in your Startup folder (*C:\Users\username\AppData\Roaming\Microsoft\Windows\Start Menu\Programs\StartUp*).

Some programs are really "in your face." For example, if you install AOL, it often puts an icon on the Desktop, in the Quick Launch Toolbar, and on the All Programs menu, and even shoehorns an icon into the System Tray, which is normally reserved for system status indicators. Other, less obtrusive programs may be more difficult to locate. In fact, you'll probably find several programs mentioned in this book that you never even knew you had!

Windows and Menus

Any open window contains a frame with a series of standard decorations and tools, as shown in Figure 2-4. To move a window from one place to another, click on the title bar and drag. The exact tools and functions available in any window vary according to the application or tool that launches it. Figure 2-4 shows a folder window, which is perhaps the most complicated window in Windows Vista.

Most types of windows are resizable, meaning that you can stretch them horizontally and vertically to make them smaller or larger. Just grab an edge or a corner and start dragging. There are two shortcuts that come in quite handy: maximize and minimize. If you click the maximize button (the middle button in the cluster in the upper right of most windows), the window will be resized to fill the screen. You can't move or resize maximized windows. If you minimize a window (the leftmost button in the cluster), it is shrunk out of sight and appears only as a button on the Taskbar. Minimizing is handy to get windows out of the way without closing them.

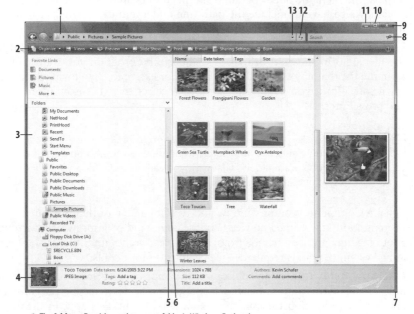

1 The **Address Bar** (shows the current folder in Windows Explorer).
2 Application-specific toolbar.
3 **Navigation pane** (Windows Explorer only).
4 **Details pane** (Windows Explorer only). In many applications, this area is taken up by a status bar that gives information about the content of the window.
5 The scroll bar. Click here to move down one line, or scroll by keeping the mouse button depressed.
6 Drag this to "jump scroll" to a corresponding point in the document.
7 Drag here to resize window.
8 The search bar. It is available in some applications, such as Windows Explorer and Internet Explorer, but not others.
9 Click here to close the window.
10 Click here to maximize the window (make it full screen).
11 Click here to minimize the window (make it into a button on the Taskbar).
12 Refresh the current window. This icon is available in some applications, such as Windows Explorer and Internet Explorer, but not others.
13 Show the history of the current window, such as displaying other folders you've recently visited in Windows Explorer. This icon is available in some applications, such as Windows Explorer and Internet Explorer, but not others.

Figure 2-4. The decorations of a standard window: a title bar, title buttons, a menu, and a scrollable client area

If you hover your mouse over a window that has been minimized to the Taskbar, a preview of the window's content will show up as a thumbnail on top of the Taskbar. (Note that this feature is only available on premium systems with the Aero interface enabled.)

Under certain circumstances, one or two scroll bars might appear along the bottom and far right of a window. These allow you to move the window's view so that you can see all of its contents. This behavior can be counterintuitive for new users because moving the scroll bar in one direction will cause the window's contents to move in the opposite direction. Look at it this way: the scroll bar doesn't move the contents; it moves the *viewport*. Imagine a very long document with very small type. Moving the scroll bars is like moving a magnifying glass—if you move the glass down the document and look through the magnifier, it looks like the document is moving upward.

If multiple windows are open, only one window has the focus. The window with the focus is usually (but not always) the one on top of all the other windows. The Windows Vista Aero Glass interface features transparent edges to windows, so you will be able to see through the edges of the focused window to windows beneath it. It can be difficult in Windows Vista to know which window has focus if several are side by side, because the Aero Glass interface doesn't necessarily make the border and title of the active windows obviously different from the other windows. The window with the focus is the one that responds to keystrokes, although any window will respond to mouse clicks. To give any window the focus, just click on any visible portion of it, and it will pop to the front. Be careful where you click on the intended window, however, as the click may go further than simply activating it (if you click on a button on a window that doesn't have the focus, for example, it will not only activate the window, but press the button as well).

There are three other ways to activate (assign the focus to) a window. You can click on the Taskbar button that corresponds to the window you want to activate, and it will be brought to the front. If it is minimized (shrunk out of sight), it will be brought back (restored) to its original size. Another way is to use a feature called Windows Flip. Hold down the Alt key and press Tab, and you'll see thumbnails of all your open windows. Keep holding down the Alt key and pressing Tab until you highlight the window you want to open, then release the keys, and you'll be sent to that window. Similarly, to use Windows Flip 3D, hold down the Windows logo key and press Tab, and you'll see thumbnails of all your windows in a 3D stack. Scroll through them by continuing to hold the Windows logo key and pressing Tab until you get to the window you want. Figure 2-5 shows Windows Flip in action, and Figure 2-6 shows Windows Flip 3D.

 Windows Flip 3D works only if you're using Windows Aero, not the Windows Vista Basic interface. For more information, see Chapter 1.

Figure 2-5. Switching among windows using Windows Flip

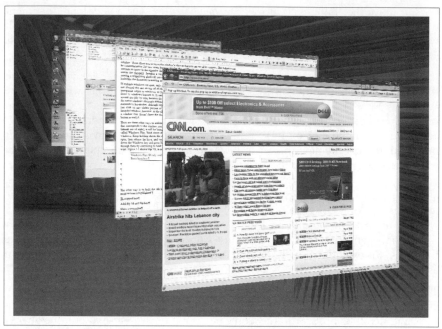

Figure 2-6. Switching among windows using Windows Flip 3D, which works only if you're using Aero

Just as only one window can have the focus at any given time, only one control (text field, button, checkbox, etc.) can have the focus at any given time. Different controls show focus in different ways: pushbuttons and checkboxes have a dotted rectangle, for instance. A text field (edit box) that has the focus will not be visually distinguished from the rest, but it will be the only one with a blinking text cursor (insertion point). To assign the focus to a different control, just click on it or use the Tab key (use Shift-Tab to go backward).

Often, new and veteran users are confused and frustrated when they try to type into a window and nothing happens—this is caused by nothing more than the wrong window having the focus. (I've seen skilled touch-typists complete an entire sentence without looking, only to realize that they forgot to click first.) Even if the desired window is in front, the wrong control (or even the menu) may have the focus.

 If you use the Windows Standard or Windows Classic theme and frequently find yourself mistaking which window has the focus, you can change the colors Windows Vista uses to distinguish the active window by right-clicking the Desktop and choosing Personalize → Window Color and Appearance → Open classic appearance properties for more color options → Advanced → Inactive Title Bar.

You can configure some windows to be "always on top." This means that they will appear on top of other windows, even if they don't have the focus. Floating toolbars, the Taskbar, and some help screens are common examples. If you have two windows that are "always on top," they behave the same as normal windows, because one can cover the other if it is activated, but both will always appear in their own "layer" on top of all the normal windows.

The Desktop is also a special case. Although it can have the focus, it will never appear on top of any other window. To access something on the Desktop, you have two choices: minimize all open windows by holding the Windows logo key and pressing the D key, or press the Show Desktop button on the Quick Launch Toolbar (discussed in Chapter 3) to temporarily hide all running applications. You can also minimize your current window, although in some instances, that only leads you to the next open window you need to minimize, and so on, until you reach the Desktop.

Many windows have a menu bar, commonly containing standard menu items such as File, Edit, View, and Help, as well as application-specific menus. Click on the menu title to drop it down, and then click on an item in the menu to execute it. Any menu item with a small black arrow that points to the right leads to a secondary, cascading menu with more options. Generally, menus drop down and cascading menus open to the right; if there isn't room, Windows pops them up in the opposite direction. If you want to cancel a menu, simply click anywhere outside of the menu bar. See the next section, "Keyboard Accelerators," for details on navigating menus with keys.

Those who are used to previous versions of Windows may be somewhat confused by the absence of menus—which have now been replaced by new toolbars—in Internet Explorer and Windows Explorer. New toolbars take the place of menus in them. However, if you're a fan of the old menus, you can still find them; press the Alt or F10 key and they'll magically appear.

 One thing that is often perplexing to new Windows users is the dynamic nature of its menus. For instance, menu items that appear grayed out are temporarily disabled. (For example, some applications won't let you save if you haven't made any changes.) Also common are context-sensitive menus, which actually change based on what you're doing or what is selected.

Each window also has a Control menu hidden behind the upper-left corner of the title bar (the bar at the top of the window that contains the filename). You can open the menu by clicking on the upper-left corner, by pressing Alt-space, or by right-clicking on a button on the Taskbar. The Control menu duplicates the function of the maximize, minimize, and close buttons at the right end of the title bar, as well as the resizing and moving you can do with the mouse. Using this menu lets you move or resize the window without the mouse (see the next section, "Keyboard Accelerators," for details). The command line (which you can get to by typing **command** at the Search box and pressing Enter to open a Command Prompt window) also has a Control menu, which you can access by right-clicking anywhere in the Command Prompt window. It provides access to the Clipboard for cut, copy, and paste actions, as well as settings for the font size and toolbar (if applicable). However, if you have enabled the Command Prompt's QuickEdit Mode (see Chapter 14), right-clicking will paste the contents of the Clipboard into whatever program happens to be running in the Command Prompt.

Keyboard Accelerators

Windows' primary interface is graphical, meaning that you point and click to interact with it. The problem is that repeated clicking can become very cumbersome, especially for repetitive tasks. Luckily, Windows has an extensive array of *keyboard accelerators* (sometimes called *keyboard shortcuts* or *hot keys*), which provide a simple keyboard alternative to almost every feature normally accessible with the mouse. Some of these keyboard accelerators (such as F1 for help, Ctrl-C to copy, and Ctrl-V to paste) date back more than 20 years and are nearly universal, and others are specific to Windows Vista or a given application.

Appendix B gives a complete list of keyboard accelerators. Some of the most important ones are as follows:

Menu navigation

In any window that has a menu, press the Alt key or the F10 key to activate the menu bar, and use the cursor (arrow) keys to move around. Press Enter to activate the currently selected item or Esc to cancel. (Note: use the Alt or F10 key to turn on the menu in Internet Explorer and Windows Explorer.)

You can also activate specific menus with the keyboard. When you press Alt or F10, each menu item will have a single character that is underlined (such as the *V* in *View*); when you see this character, it means you can press Alt-V (for example) to go directly to that menu. Once that menu has opened, you can activate any specific item by pressing the corresponding key (such as *D* for *Details*); you don't even need to press Alt this time. The abbreviated notation for this is Alt-V+D (which means press Alt and V together, and then press D). You'll notice that it's much faster than using the mouse.

The other way to activate specific menu items is to use the special keyboard shortcuts shown to the right of each menu item (where applicable). For example, open the Edit menu in most windows, and you'll see that Ctrl-Z is a shortcut for Undo, Ctrl-V is a shortcut for Paste, and Ctrl-A is a shortcut for Select All. These are even faster than the navigation hot keys described earlier. Two notes: not all menu items have this type of keyboard shortcut, and these shortcuts work only from within the application that "owns" the menu.

The special case is the Start menu, which you can activate by pressing the Windows logo key (if your keyboard has one) or Ctrl-Esc, regardless of the active window. You can also click the Start button. The Start menu differs from most other menus because you navigate it graphically, although you can also use arrow keys and Return for navigation as well.

Note that once a menu has been activated, you can mix pointer clicks and keystrokes. For example, you could pop up the Start menu by pressing the Windows logo key, and then click on Control Panel.

If there is a conflict and multiple items on a menu have the same accelerator key, pressing the key repeatedly will cycle through the options. You must press Enter when the correct menu item is highlighted to actually make the selection.

Window manipulation without the mouse

The Control menu, described in the preceding section, facilitates the resizing and moving of windows with the keyboard only. Press Alt-Space bar to open the active window's Control menu, and then choose the desired action. If you choose to move the window, the mouse pointer will change to a little four-pointed arrow, which is your cue to use the cursor (arrow) keys to do the actual moving. Likewise, selecting Resize will allow you to stretch any window edge using the cursor keys. In either case, press Enter when you're happy with the result, or press Esc to cancel the operation. If a window can't be resized or minimized, for example, those menu items will not be present. Note that Control menus work just like normal menus, so you could press Alt-Space bar+M to begin moving a window.

Editing

In most applications, Ctrl-X will cut a selected item to an invisible storage area called the Clipboard, Ctrl-C will copy it to the Clipboard, and Ctrl-V will paste it into a new location. Using the Delete key will simply erase the selection (or delete the file). There is a single, system-wide Clipboard that all applications share. This Clipboard lets you copy something from a document in one program and paste it into another document in another program. You can paste the same data repeatedly until new data replaces it on the Clipboard. See Chapter 3 for more information.

Although you probably think of cut-and-paste operations as something you do with selected text or graphics in an application, you can use the same keys for file operations. For example, select a file on the Desktop and press Ctrl-X. Then move to another folder and press Ctrl-V, and Windows will move the file to the new location just as though you dragged and dropped it.

Ctrl-Alt-Delete

In Windows Vista, when you simultaneously press the Ctrl, Alt, and Delete keys, you activate a screen that lets you lock the computer, switch users, log off, change a password, or start the Task Manager, which, among other things, allows you to close crashed applications. You can also click Cancel to go back to what you were doing previously. In Windows XP, pressing Ctrl-Alt-Delete would immediately run the Task Manager.

Alt-Tab and Alt-Esc

Both of these key combinations switch between open windows, albeit in different ways. Alt-Tab runs Windows Flip, which shows thumbnails of all open windows—hold Alt and press Tab repeatedly to move the selection. Alt-Esc has no window; instead, it simply sends the active window to the bottom of the pile and activates the next one in the row. Note that Alt-Tab also includes minimized windows, but Alt-Esc does not. If there's only one open window, Alt-Esc has no effect, although Alt-Tab will show two thumbnails—the open window and the Desktop. Also, neither method activates the Start menu (Ctrl-Esc).

Tab and arrow keys

Within a window, Tab will move the focus from one control to the next; use Shift-Tab to move backward. A control may be a text field, a drop-down list, a pushbutton, or any number of other controls. For example, in a folder window, Tab will cycle between the major components of the window: the Favorite Links, file display area, Search box, folder list, and so on. Use arrow keys in these areas to make a new selection without moving the focus. Sometimes a dialog box will have one or more regions, indicated by a rectangular box within the dialog box. The arrow keys will cycle through buttons or fields only within the current regions. Tab will cross region boundaries and cycle through all the buttons or fields in the dialog box. In addition, some dialog boxes let you cycle through controls with Tab.

If there's only one control, such as in a simple folder window, Tab has no effect. In some applications, such as word processors and spreadsheets, Tab is assigned to a different function (such as indenting).

Common Controls

Many application and system windows use a common set of controls in addition to the ubiquitous title bar, menu bar, Control menu, and scroll bars. This section describes a few of these common controls.

Figure 2-7 shows some of the common controls in Control Panel → Appearance and Personalization → Change screen saver, and some other dialog boxes.

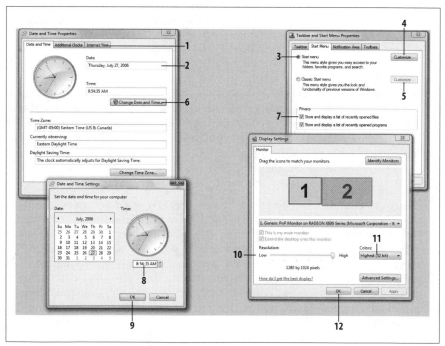

Figure 2-7. Common controls in Windows applications and dialogs

Some of these controls include:

(1) Tabbed dialogs

You can group settings into separate tabbed dialog pages. For example, right-click the Taskbar and choose Properties. Click on any tab to bring that page to the front.

(2) Input boxes

Type text or numbers into these boxes to change their values—for example, to change the date or time.

(3) Radio buttons

You use radio buttons for mutually exclusive settings. Clicking on one causes any other that has been pressed to pop up, just like on an old car radio. The button with the dot in the middle is the one that has been selected. Sometimes you'll see more than one group of buttons, with a separate outline around each group. In this case, you can select one radio button from each group.

(4) Button

Click this to get to another menu that offers another set of options to customize.

(5) Grayed-out (inactive) controls

Any control that is grayed out is disabled because the underlying operation is not currently available. In the dialog box shown in Figure 2-7, the Classic Start menu radio button hasn't been selected, so you cannot customize its features.

(6) Button with User Account Control

Among Windows Vista's new security features is User Account Control (UAC), which protects certain system settings from being changed accidentally or by someone with malicious intent. When you see this icon on a button, it means that it is protected by UAC. When you click it, you'll have to type in an administrator password to proceed (if you're not logged in as a user with administrator privileges), or else you'll get a warning and you'll have to click a button to confirm that you want to proceed with your operation.

(7) Checkboxes

Checkboxes are generally used for on/off settings. A checkmark means the setting is on; an empty box means it's off. Click on the box to turn the labeled setting on or off.

(8) Counters

You can either select the number and type in a new value or click on the up or down arrow to increase or decrease the value.

(9) The default button

When a set of buttons is displayed, the default button (the one that will be activated by pressing the Enter key) is brighter than the other buttons. You can move the focus to another button by hovering your mouse over it, typing the underlined accelerator character in a button or field label, or pressing the Tab or arrow key.

In many dialog boxes, the default button is *hardcoded*—it will always be the same. For example, the OK button is commonly hardcoded to be the default button. To see this in action, right-click on the Taskbar and select Properties. The Taskbar Options tab has the OK button hardcoded as the default. Regardless of which button is the default, pressing Esc always has the same effect as clicking the Cancel button: it cancels the dialog box.

(10) Sliders

Move the slider to change the setting. In this instance, as you move the slider from Low to High (or vice versa), the text beneath the slider changes to show you precise information about each setting along the way.

(11) Drop-down lists

Anytime you see a downward-pointing arrow next to a text field, click on the arrow to drop down a list of other values. Sometimes a drop-down list contains a history of previous entries you've typed into a text entry field. Pressing the first letter will often jump to that place in the list, as long as the list has the focus. The down arrow (or F4) will also drop down the currently selected list. The arrow keys will scroll through the stored entries, even if the list is not already dropped down. Microsoft sometimes calls these lists *Look In Lists*.

(12) OK, Cancel, Apply

Most dialogs will have at least an OK and a Cancel button. Some also have Apply. The difference is that OK accepts the settings and quits the dialog, and Apply accepts the changes but doesn't quit. (This is useful in a dialog with multiple tabs so that you can apply changes before moving to the next tab.) Cancel quits without making any changes. If you click Cancel after clicking Apply, your changes will probably already have been applied and will not revert to their original settings. But don't be surprised if some applications respond differently. Microsoft has never been clear with application developers about the expected behavior of these buttons.

For more information on these various user interface features, see Chapter 3.

Files, Folders, and Disks

Files are the basic unit of long-term storage on a computer. Files are organized into folders, which are stored on disks. (In DOS, Unix, and earlier versions of Windows, folders were more often referred to as *directories*, but both terms are still used.) This section reviews fundamental filesystem concepts, including file- and disk-naming conventions and file types.

Disk Names

Like every version of Windows that preceded it, Windows Vista retains the basic DOS disk-naming conventions. Drives are differentiated by a single letter of the alphabet followed by a colon:

A: Represents the first "floppy" (usually 3.5-inch) disk drive on the system

B: Represents the second floppy disk drive, if present

C: Represents the first hard disk drive or the first partition of the first hard disk drive

D: Often represents a DVD-ROM or CD-ROM drive, but can represent an additional hard disk drive or other removable drive

E: *through Z:*
Represent additional hard disk drives, DVD-ROM or CD-ROM drives, Universal Serial Bus (USB) flash drives, removable cartridges such as ZIP or Jaz drives, or mapped network drives

By default, drive letters are assigned consecutively, but it's possible to change the drive letters for most drives so that you can have a drive N: without having a drive M:. (See Chapter 4 for details.)

Pathnames

Folders, which contain files, are stored hierarchically on a disk and can be nested to any arbitrary level.

The filesystem on any disk begins with the root (top-level) directory, represented as a backslash. Thus, C:\ represents the root directory on the C: drive. Each additional nested directory is simply listed after its "parent," with backslashes used to separate each one. C:\Windows\System\Color means that the Color folder is in the System folder in the Windows folder on the C: drive. Thus, you can express a *path* to any given folder as a single string of folder names.

A path can be *absolute* (always starting with a drive letter) or *relative* (referenced with respect to the current directory). The concept of a *current directory* is somewhat obsolete in Windows Vista, as it was in Windows NT, Windows 2000, and Windows XP, with the exception of commands issued from the command prompt. Each Command Prompt window has an active folder associated with it, to which each command is directed. For example, if the current directory is C:\ *windows*, and you type **DIR** (the directory listing command), you would get a listing of the files in that folder. If you then type **CD cursors**, the current directory would become C:\windows\cursors.

The fact that the entire absolute path was not needed after the CD command is an example of the use of a relative path.

A special type of relative path is made up of one or more dots. The names . and .. refer to the current directory and the parent of that directory, respectively (C:\ *windows* is the parent folder of C:\windows\cursors, for example). Type **CD ..** while in C:*windows*, and the current directory becomes simply C:\. Use of additional dots (such as ...) in some previous versions of Windows is not supported in Windows XP or Vista. The graphical equivalent of .. is the yellow folder icon with the curved arrow, found in common file dialogs.

The left pane (Navigation Pane) in Windows Explorer (by default) contains a hierarchical tree-structured view of the filesystem. The tree structure makes it easier to navigate through all the folders on your system because it provides a graphical overview of the structure. See Chapter 3 for more information on the tree and Chapter 4 for more information on the Windows Explorer application.

Paths to Network Resources

You can refer to files on any shared network via a Universal Naming Convention (UNC) pathname, which is very similar to a path (described in the preceding section). The first element of a UNC pathname is the name of the computer or device that contains the file, prefixed by a double backslash. The second element is the device's share name. What follows is the string of folders leading to the target folder or file.

For example, the UNC path \\shoebox\o\hemp\adriana.txt refers to a file named adriana.txt, located in the hemp folder, located on drive O:, located on a computer named shoebox.

For more information on UNC pathnames and sharing resources on a network, see Chapter 7.

Short Names and Long Names

DOS and Windows 3.1, the Microsoft operating systems that preceded Windows 95 and Windows NT, only supported filenames with a maximum of eight characters, plus a three-character file type extension (e.g., myfile.txt). The maximum length of any path was 80 characters (see "Pathnames," earlier in this chapter, for more information on paths). Legal characters included any combination of letters and numbers, extended ASCII characters with values greater than 127, and the following punctuation characters:

    $ % ^ ' ` - _ @ ~ ! ( ) # &

Spaces were not allowed.

Windows Vista supports long filenames (up to 260 characters), which can include spaces as well as these punctuation characters:

    $ % ^ ' ` - _ @ ~ ! ( ) # & + , ; = [ ] .

For example, a file could be named Picture of my Niece.jpg and could be located in a folder named Family Photos. Furthermore, extensions are no longer limited to three characters; for example, .html is perfectly valid (and distinctly different from .htm). For more information on file types and extensions, see the discussions in the next section and in Appendix D.

The maximum length of any path in Windows Vista depends on the filesystem you're using (NTFS, FAT32, etc.).

File Types and Extensions

Most files have a filename extension, the (usually three) letters that appear after the last dot in any file's name. Here are some common file extensions:

.xls
> An Excel spreadsheet

.txt
> A text file (to be opened with Notepad)

.html

A HyperText Markup Language (HTML) file, commonly known as a web page

.jpg

A JPEG image file, used to store photos

 Windows Vista includes a new document format, called XML Paper Specification (XPS), which uses the *.xps* extension. It is designed so that anyone can view the document, including its fonts, layout, graphics, and so on, even if he doesn't have the application that created it. In that way, it's much like the Adobe Acrobat *.pdf* format. Only those who have Vista or an XPS viewer will be able to view the document.

Although each of these files holds very different types of data, the only way Windows differentiates them is by their filename extensions. How Windows is able to determine a given file's type is important for several reasons, especially because it is the basis for the associations that link documents with the applications that created them. For example, when you double-click on a file named *donkey.html*, Windows looks up the extension in the Registry (see Chapter 13) and then, by default, opens the file in your web browser. Rename the file to *donkey.jpg*, and the association changes as well.

The lesson here is that filename extensions are not a reliable guide to a file's type, despite how heavily Windows Vista relies on them. What can make it even more frustrating is that, by default, known filename extensions are hidden by Windows Vista, but unfamiliar extensions are shown. Rename *donkey.xyz* (an unassociated extension) to *donkey.txt*, and the extension simply disappears in Windows Explorer. Or, try to differentiate *donkey.txt* from *donkey.doc* when the extensions are hidden. To instruct Windows to show all extensions, go to Control Panel → Appearance and Personalization → Folder Options → View, and turn off the "Hide file extensions for known file types" option.

To see all of the configured file extensions on your system, go to Start → Default Programs → Associate a file type or protocol with a program. You'll see a list of all your file types, along with the programs with which they are associated. To change the default program for any file type, highlight the file type, click "Change program," and then select the new program with which the file should be associated.

Using Windows Explorer

Click on a folder icon in Windows Explorer, and you'll see the contents of the folder. Look at the Preview Pane (it's on by default, but if it has been turned off for some reason, turn it on via Organize → Layout) for the number of items in the folder.

Windows Explorer has received a major makeover with Windows Vista, and although the basic function is the same (navigating through your hard disk, viewing and using files, etc.), the layout and features have changed. (For a detailed look at Windows Explorer, see Chapter 4.) Figure 2-8 shows the major features of Windows Explorer.

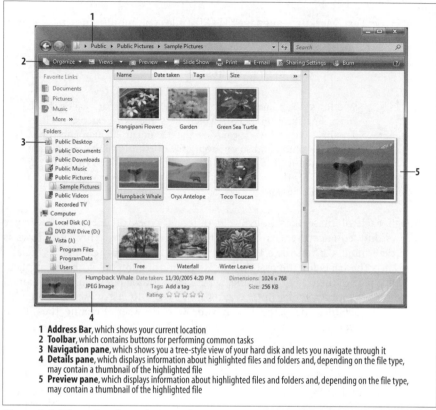

1. **Address Bar**, which shows your current location
2. **Toolbar**, which contains buttons for performing common tasks
3. **Navigation pane**, which shows you a tree-style view of your hard disk and lets you navigate through it
4. **Details pane**, which displays information about highlighted files and folders and, depending on the file type, may contain a thumbnail of the highlighted file
5. **Preview pane**, which displays information about highlighted files and folders and, depending on the file type, may contain a thumbnail of the highlighted file

Figure 2-8. The updated Windows Explorer

You can turn panes on and off by choosing Organize → Layout, and selecting or deselecting the panes you want.

There's another major change to Windows Explorer with Windows Vista—the menus have vanished. To make them appear for a single task, press the Alt key. To keep them on permanently, choose Organize → Folder and Search Options → Layout → View, and check the box next to Always show menus.

Depending on your settings, the files in the folder may be displayed in any of seven different ways: Tiles, Details, List, Small Icons, Medium Icons, Large Icons, and Extra Large Icons. In the Details view, each file is represented by a small icon, and several rows of information are displayed about each file, such as date created, date modified, size, and so on. In the List view, the files are displayed in a single long list. Small Icons, Medium Icons, Large Icons, and Extra Large Icons do exactly what they say: display each file as an icon representation, in whatever size you've chosen. (See Figure 2-9.) Different files will have different icon behaviors. With graphics files, for example, the icons are actual thumbnails of the graphic. But Word files display only the Word icon, not the actual content of the file itself. The Tiles view is a kind of combination of the List and Icon views—it displays the files as tiled icons, without columns of details but with basic information about the file next to each tile, including the name, type, and size of the file.

Figure 2-9. Sort folder listings by clicking on column headers, or change column widths by dragging boundaries between the headers

If you're looking at a folder full of images, any of the icon views will be most useful. The Tiles view is worthwhile if you want to see small icons in addition to basic file information.

If you want to see previews of the actual content of your files, you can turn on the Preview Pane. It appears on the right and shows a thumbnail of the current file you've highlighted. The Preview Pane works in any view. To turn it on, select Organize → Layout → Preview Pane. The icon next to the Preview Pane on the menu will become highlighted in blue, and the pane turns on. To turn it off, select Organize → Layout → Preview Pane, and the highlight around the icon will vanish, as will the pane.

You can change the columns displayed in the Details view. Right-click on any column, and from the list that appears select the file types you want displayed. In addition, you can change the sort order and display of any column by hovering your mouse over the column until a down arrow appears, then clicking the down arrow. You'll be presented with ways in which you can sort and display that column.

In certain instances you can also turn on a Search Pane, which will appear just above the toolbar. The pane works in concert with the Search Bar. Type in a search term, and the Search Pane lets you easily filter your search results by file type—such as Email, Pictures, and so on—by clicking on the appropriate button. To turn the Search Pane on, select Organize → Layout → Search Pane. The Search Pane icon will be highlighted in blue on the menu, and the pane turns on. To turn it off, select Organize → Layout → Search Pane, and the highlight will vanish, as will the pane. However, the Search Pane is only available this way in a few folders, such as Desktop and Computer. If you choose Organize → Layout in other folders, the Search Pane option will not be available. However, in any folder, if you type any text into the Search box, you can make the Search Pane appear by choosing Organize → Layout → Search Pane. But when you delete the text from the Search box, you won't have the option of turning on the Search Pane, except in a few select folders, such as Desktop and Computer.

Windows Vista will remember the view setting for each folder by default and will display it the same way the next time the folder is opened. (If a long time passes before you open a folder again, though, Windows will forget its settings.) You can turn this setting off by selecting Organize → Folder Options → View, unchecking the box next to "Remember each folder's view settings," and then clicking OK.

The Explorer Toolbar, like toolbars in most applications, provides quick access to some of the more frequently used features. The toolbar is *context-sensitive*; that is, it changes according to the content of the folder that you're viewing.

The Address Bar does more than just display your current folder; you also use it for navigation. Either move down the "bread crumb" trail that is displayed there, or else type the path to a folder and press Enter, and the folder's contents will be shown in the current window. This is often faster than navigating with the folder tree or using several consecutive folder windows. See Chapter 3 for details on using the Address Bar.

Although each new folder window you open will appear with Microsoft's default settings, it's possible to modify those defaults. Start by configuring a folder according to your preferences: choose the icon size, the sort order, and so on. Then, go to Organize → Folder Options → View, and click Apply to Folders. The setting will then be used for each new single folder window that is opened.

When you open a new folder, it opens in your existing Windows Explorer window. You can, however, have folders open in new windows instead. Choose Organize → Folder Options → General, select "Open each folder in its own window," and click OK.

Keyboard Accelerators in Folder Windows

Some keyboard accelerators are especially useful in Explorer and folder windows. You can use these in addition to the various keys described in "Point-and-Click Operations," earlier in this chapter.

- Hold the Alt key while double-clicking on a file or folder to view the Properties window for that object.

- Hover your mouse cursor over a file or folder to see basic information about the object, such as size, date modified, and so on.

- Hold the Shift key while double-clicking on a folder to open an Explorer window (with the tree view) at that location. (Be careful when using this because Shift is also used to select multiple files. The best way is to select the file first.)

- Press Backspace in an open folder to go to the parent (containing) folder.

- Hold Alt while pressing the left cursor key to navigate to the previously viewed folder. Note that this is not necessarily the *parent* folder, but rather the last folder opened in Explorer. You can also hold Alt while pressing the right cursor key to move in the opposite direction (i.e., forward); this is similar to the Back and Next buttons in Internet Explorer, respectively. Windows Explorer also has Back and Next buttons.

- Hold the Shift key while clicking on the close button (the *x* in the upper-right corner of the window on the menu bar) to close *all* open folders that were used to get to that folder. (This, of course, makes sense only in the single-folder view and with the "Open each folder in its own window" option turned on.)

- Press Ctrl-A to quickly select all contents of a folder—both files and folders.

- In Explorer or any single-folder window, press a letter key to quickly jump to the first file or folder starting with that letter. Continue typing to jump further. For example, pressing the N key in your *Windows* folder will jump to *nap*. Press N again to jump to the next object that starts with *N*. Or, press N and then quickly press O to skip through the *N*s and jump to *notepad.exe*. If there's enough of a delay between the N and the O keys, Explorer will forget about the *N*, and you'll jump to the first entry that starts with *O*.

Advanced Drag-and-Drop Techniques

Some of the basics of drag-and-drop are discussed in "Point-and-Click Operations," earlier in this chapter, but you can use some advanced techniques to have more control when you're dragging and dropping items. Naturally, it's important to be able to anticipate what will happen when you drag and drop an item before you actually do the dropping. The problem is that drag-and-drop is handled differently in various situations, so sometimes you'll need to modify your behavior to achieve the desired result. Here are the rules that Windows follows when determining how dropped files are handled:

- If you drag an object from one place to another on the same physical drive (*c:\docs* to *c:\files*), the object is moved.

- If you drag an object from one physical drive to another physical or network drive (*c:\docs* to *d:\files*), the object is copied, resulting in two identical files on your system.

- If you drag an object from one physical or network drive to another and then back to the first drive, but in a different folder (*c:\docs* to *d:\files* to *c:\stuff*), you'll end up with three copies of the object.

- If you drag an application executable (an EXE file), the same rules apply to it that apply to other objects, except that if you drag it into any portion of your Start menu or into any subfolder of your Start Menu folder, Windows will create a shortcut to the file. Dragging other file types (documents, script files, or other shortcuts) to the Start menu will simply move or copy them there, according to the preceding rules.

- If you drag a system object (such as an item in the My Computer window or the Control Panel) anywhere, a shortcut to the item is created. This, of course, is a consequence of the fact that these objects aren't actually files and can't be duplicated or removed from their original locations.

- If you drag system icons or items that appear within system folders, such as Documents, Internet Explorer, or the Recycle Bin, any number of things can happen, depending on the specific capabilities of the object. For example, if you drag a recently deleted file from the Recycle Bin, it will always be moved, because making a copy of, or a shortcut to, a deleted file makes no sense.

If you have trouble remembering these rules, or if you run into a confusing situation, you can always fall back on the information Windows provides you while you're dragging, in the form of the mouse cursor. A blue right-pointing arrow appears next to the pointer when copying, and a curved arrow appears when creating a shortcut. If you see no symbol, the object will be moved. This visual feedback is very important; it can eliminate a lot of mistakes if you pay attention to it.

Here's how to control what happens when you drag and drop an item:

- To copy an object in any situation, hold the Ctrl key while dragging. Of course, this won't work for system objects such as Control Panel items—a shortcut will be created regardless. Using the Ctrl key in this way will also work when dragging a file from one part of a folder to another part of the same folder, which is an easy way to duplicate a file or folder.

- To move an object in any situation, hold the Shift key while dragging. This also won't work for system objects such as Control Panel items—a shortcut will be created regardless.

- To create a shortcut to an object in any situation, hold the Ctrl and Shift keys simultaneously while dragging. If you try to make a shortcut that points to another shortcut, the shortcut will simply be copied (duplicated).

- To choose what happens to dragged files each time without having to press any keys, drag your files with the right mouse button, and a special menu will appear when the files are dropped. This context menu is especially helpful because it will display only options appropriate to the type of object you're dragging and the place where you've dropped it.

The Command Line

Many people who are new to computers will never have heard of the command line, also known as the command prompt, and sometimes (but incorrectly) called the DOS prompt. (DOS was the operating system used by most PCs before Windows became ubiquitous. The command line in DOS was the only way to start programs and manage files, and the command prompt in Windows borrows many of the command names from DOS but with vastly improved capabilities.) Users of older PCs may remember the command line, but they may be under the impression that it's purely a thing of the past. Advanced users, on the other hand—whether they remember the old days of the DOS command line or not—have probably learned the advantages of the command-line interface, even when using Windows Vista on a day-to-day basis.

You can perform many tasks faster by typing one or more commands into the Command Prompt window. In addition, some of the programs in Windows Vista are command-line-based tools, and you can run them from the command prompt as well as from the GUI. For full documentation on the command line and the Command Prompt application, see Chapter 14.

At the command prompt, you can get help on the available command-line options by typing:

```
commandname /?
```

You can see a list of all built-in command-line utilities by typing **help** and pressing Return.

 When you run some command-line programs, such as openfiles, which displays all currently open files, you may get an error message similar to this: ERROR: Logged-on user does not have administrative privilege. You may get this message even if you are using an administrator account. There is a workaround: type **cmd** at the Start Search box on the Start menu (don't press Enter), right-click the "cmd" entry that appears at the top of the search results, and then choose Run as Administrator. You'll now be able to run any command-line program, such as openfiles, that gives you that error message.

Here are a few examples that show how you can use the command line as an alternative to the GUI:

- To create a folder called *sample* in the root directory of your hard disk and then copy all the files from another folder into the new folder, for example, it can be quicker and easier to type:

```
C:\>mkdir \sample
C:\>copy d:\stuff\*.* \sample
```

than to open Windows Explorer, navigate to your *d:\stuff* folder, select all the files, click File → Copy (or Ctrl-C), navigate to the new location, click New → Folder, type the folder name, open the new folder, and then click Edit → Paste (or Ctrl-V) to copy in the files. That's a heck of a sentence, and a heck of a lot of steps for what you can accomplish with the two simple commands shown here.

- Once you learn the actual filename of a program rather than its Start menu shortcut name, it can be quicker to start it from the Run prompt or the Address Bar than it is to navigate the Start menu hierarchy. Which is really easier? Clicking your way through these menus:

    Start → Programs → Accessories → System Tools → Character Map

or typing:

```
charmap
```

into the Start menu's Search box or Explorer's Address Bar and pressing the Enter key? Typing a command is much faster than carefully dragging the mouse through cascading menus, where an unintentional slip of the mouse can get you somewhere entirely different from what you planned.

- Finally, many useful programs don't appear on any menu in the Start menu. Once you know what you're doing, you can put shortcuts to such programs in the Start menu or on the Desktop—but once you know what you're doing, you might also find it easier to just type the program name.

Online Help

Many windows have some degree of online documentation in the form of a Help system that you can access by clicking the small question mark icon in the upper-righthand portion of the screen. The help is context-sensitive and will be relevant to the window from which you've accessed it.

In addition, you can press F1 at almost any time to display help. In some situations, pressing F1 will display only a tiny yellow message (known as a *tool tip*) with a brief description of the item with the focus; at other times, F1 will launch an online index of help topics. Sometimes F1 will have no effect whatsoever.

Furthermore, if you hold the pointer over many screen objects (such as a window's toolbar), a tool tip may appear. A tool tip may display nothing more than the name of the object to which you're pointing, but in other cases, it may provide additional information. For example, placing the pointer on the system clock pops up the date. You can turn tool tips off in the Windows interface by going to Control Panel → Appearance and Personalization → Folder Options → View and turning off the option "Show pop-up description for folder and Desktop items." Note that this won't necessarily turn off tool tips in other applications—only Explorer.

Shutting Down

You shouldn't just turn off the power to a Windows Vista machine, because it caches a lot of data in memory and needs to write it out before shutting down. See the section "Shut Down," in Chapter 3, for additional details.

Nutshell Reference

3

The User Interface

One of the responsibilities of a graphical operating system such as Windows Vista is to provide a common set of interface controls not only for itself, but also for all the applications that run on it. This chapter provides an alphabetical reference to the elements of the Windows Vista user interface, how to use them, and what tricks you can perform with them. Also included are the building blocks of the Windows Vista shell (commonly known as *Explorer*), such as the Desktop and the various toolbars.

In addition to imposing a certain level of user interface consistency, these common elements allow programmers to quickly piece together the interfaces for their applications with a "toolbox" of parts. Although these interface elements are available to all applications, some application designers choose instead to implement their own custom controls and interface paradigms. Sometimes this can lead to an innovative and clever design, but more often than not, it just results in a mess. A poor result typically comes not so much from the choice not to use Windows common controls, but from a failure to follow the rules of good user interface design.

The following are a few guidelines that apply to all elements of the Windows interface, which should provide some understanding of why certain elements are designed the way they are in Windows Vista. Even if you're familiar with previous versions of Windows, you'd do well to review these elements, because Windows Vista's richer visual experience alters some basic ways that Windows previously ran.

Visual clues

One of the most basic advantages of a graphical operating system is that the elements of the interface contain visual clues on how they're used. For example, buttons have a 3D look, implying that you're supposed to click them. Folder icons look like actual yellow folders you'd see in a file cabinet, reinforcing the notion that they are containers that hold your documents. Folder icons in Windows Vista let you actually look inside those folders by showing a preview of the contents within—for example, so you can see that one folder holds photographs and another contains Word documents, as shown in Figure 3-1.

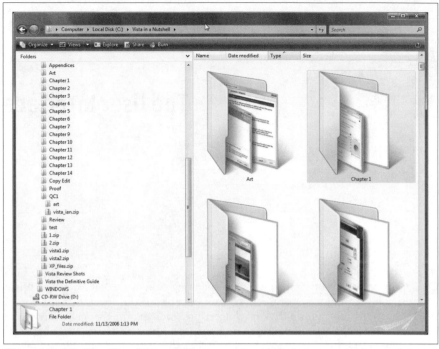

Figure 3-1. Windows Vista folders displaying previews of their contents so that you know the kinds of files inside without having to open the folders

Folders also light up when you're dragging items over them, signaling that they can accept dropped objects. Even the mouse pointer provides visual feedback, changing to a resize arrow when it's over the edge of the window, or changing to a circle with a line through it when you're dragging over an object that can't accept the object you're holding. (Don Norman, author of *The Design of Everyday Things* [Doubleday], calls these *visual clues* and says they are intended to recall the way the physical world affords opportunities to interact with objects, or "perceived affordances.") These clues are present in nearly every aspect of the Windows interface; learn to recognize them, and you will quickly find even the most unfamiliar interface more intuitive and easier to use.

Constraints

Many controls have limits, or *constraints*, that permit you to enter only certain values. Scroll bars have a maximum and a minimum limit, for instance, so you can't scroll past the end of a document.

Grayed-out (inactive) controls

Any control that appears "grayed out" is disabled because the underlying operation is not currently available. For example, in the dialog box shown in Figure 3-2, you need to select "Single-click to open an item" before you can choose the Underline button.

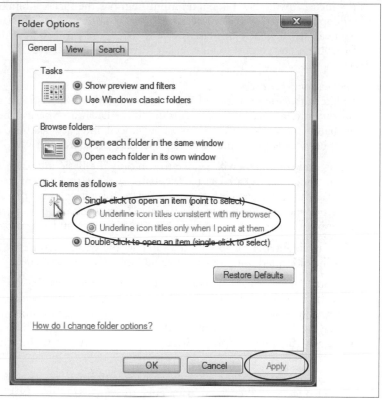

Figure 3-2. Disabled (grayed out) options, indicating that they're unavailable or not applicable

Gray items typically don't respond at all when clicked, and sometimes it's not obvious what action must be taken in order to "un-gray" a menu item. If you're stuck, try to imagine the context in which the menu item is used, and then try to put the application in the correct state for that menu item to be appropriate. For example, some menu items in your word processor will be grayed out when graphics are selected, or if the spellchecker is open.

Ellipses (…)

You'll commonly see ellipses on menu items and command buttons, and occasionally on other interface elements. This notation implies that a new window will appear when the control is activated.

Focus

The focus (explained in greater detail in Chapter 2) is the visual highlighting of a single control, identifying which element will receive input from the keyboard. Because there's only one keyboard, only one control can have focus at a time, and because only one window can be active at a time, you should always be able to determine what will happen when you press keys on the keyboard by simply looking for the focus. For example, if a button has the focus, it will glow blue; if an input field has the focus, a blinking cursor will appear where text is to be typed (this is known as the *insertion point*). You can usually click an item to give it focus, use the Tab key to move the focus from one control to another, or hover your mouse over the item (such as a button).

Different visual experiences

Unlike with earlier versions of Windows, with Windows Vista the fine points of your interface may change according to the hardware you use, because not all hardware supports Vista's most advanced interface features. Windows Vista has four levels of interface: Basic, Classic, Standard, and Windows Aero.

Entry-level computers will be able to run only the Basic interface. Basic does not include sophisticated visual elements such as transparent windows, or live Taskbar thumbnails that show previews of windows on the Taskbar. It does, however, use the same basic overall organization and interface as all versions of Windows Vista, such as new folder views, and so on.

The Classic interface is exactly the same as the Basic interface except that it uses the old square windows and overall look of Windows 2000.

The Standard interface includes the features of the Basic interface but also uses the new Windows Display Driver Model (WDDM), which makes for faster and smoother screen and window redraws, no time lags when displaying content, and an end to the "tearing" effect you sometimes had in Windows XP, when a dragged window would leave traces of itself all across your screen.

Windows Aero, the most advanced interface, features transparent windows (and also lets you alter the transparency to your taste), live Taskbar thumbnails, and Windows Flip 3D for switching among open applications, as well as other features. When most people think of Windows Vista, they think of Windows Aero; it's what gives the operating system its distinctive look and feel, and it's the interface that the vast majority of Windows Vista users run.

Styles

In Windows Vista, the style of all your windows and interface elements is determined by the actual Windows Vista interface you're running (Basic, Classic, Standard, or Windows Aero). However, there is a way to change the style of all your windows and interface elements, no matter which interface you're running. You can choose another style by going to Control Panel → Appearance and Personalization → Personalization → Window Color and Appearance. (If you are running the Windows Aero user interface, you'll need to also click "Open Classic appearance properties.") Click on Advanced, and you'll be able to choose the look and feel of all of Windows Vista's controls, including title bars, buttons, scroll bars, and much more (see Figure 3-3).

The Appearance Settings dialog box lets you choose to run a different Windows Vista interface than the one you're currently running. So, for example, if you're running Windows Aero and you want to switch to Windows Basic, you can do that. However, it will not let you run an interface your hardware won't support. So if your hardware won't support Windows Aero, you won't be able to switch to it from this dialog box.

Figure 3-3. The Appearance Settings dialog, which allows you to choose among the visual styles available in Windows Vista

Controlling the Interface

This chapter doesn't cover only the building blocks of the interface, it also covers all the elements of the interface itself—including all the applets, controls, and features that make up the interface and let you customize it, such as the Control Panel, Windows Aero, the Windows Sidebar, and Gadgets. In addition, it discusses how to personalize your Desktop, the Taskbar, and the System Tray. Windows Vista offers a richer visual experience than previous versions of

Windows, and its interface is far more open to customizing and tweaking. This chapter will show you all the ways you can control Windows Vista to your heart's content—everything from customizing the transparency of windows to changing the system font size to displaying Gadgets, and more.

 In this chapter, you will see some steps listed in brackets, as in Control Panel → [Appearance and Personalization] → Personalization. If you are using Control Panel categories, include the step in brackets; if you have categories turned off, ignore the bracketed step. For more information on categories, see the "Control Panel" section, later in this chapter.

Here is an alphabetical reference of entries in this chapter:

Address Bar	Font Viewer	Shortcuts
Bread Crumbs	Fonts Folder	Shut Down
Buttons	Gadgets	Start Menu
Change Your Color Scheme	Icons	Start Search
Checkboxes	Input Fields	Status Bar
Clipboard	Labels	System Tray
Combo Boxes	Listboxes	Tabbed Dialogs
Computer	Live Taskbar Thumbnails	Taskbar
Context Menus	Log Off	Taskbar and Start Menu Properties
Control Menus	Menus	Text Boxes
Control Panel	Network	Theme Settings
Date and Time Properties	Notification Area	Title Bars
Desktop	Personalization	Toolbars
Desktop Background	Progress Indicators	Tray
Desktop Icons	Properties	Trees
Details	Radio Buttons	Turn Off Computer
Dialog Boxes	Recycle Bin	User Account Control Buttons
Display Settings	Regional and Language Options	Windows
Drop-Down Listboxes	Screen Saver	Windows Aero
Ease of Access Center	Scroll Bars	Windows Flip and Windows Flip 3D
File Open/Save Dialogs	Send To	Windows Sidebar and Gadgets

Address Bar

The Address Bar (see Figure 3-4) is a special toolbar with an input field and (optionally) an arrow. It appears in Internet Explorer, Windows Explorer, and, if you've right-clicked on the Taskbar and selected Address from the Toolbars menu, on the Taskbar. When you type an Internet address, the name of a program, or the path of a folder, and then press Enter, the Address Bar will respond in one of many ways, depending on its location and your system's settings.

Figure 3-4. The Address Bar, shown here on the Windows Taskbar

Although the Address Bar's main purpose is to make it easy to type in a web address and point your browser to that address, or to navigate through folders on your hard disk, you also can use it to type a command or application to launch, just like typing it into the Start Search box on the Start menu or the command line. This means that you can easily choose between point-and-click and command-line operations—whichever is easier for completing a given task.

One major difference between the Start Search box and the Address Bar is how they treat an unknown address or command. The Address Bar in Internet Explorer assumes that any unknown text string is a web search. So, for example, typing **oreilly** in the Address Bar will launch an Internet search, using your default search engine. In Windows Explorer, if you type in a text string, the Address Bar appends an *http://* in front of it, and a / to the back of it. So typing **oreilly.com** will bring you to *http://oreilly.com*, which is a legitimate web address, but typing **oreilly** will bring you to *http://oreilly/*, which is not a legitimate web address and will display an error message.

If you type the same string at the Start Search box, you'll get a list of all documents, files, and folders that include *oreilly* in them, as well as any web sites you've visited with that word in them. You can, however, also use the Start Search box to search the Web. Type in the term and select Search the Internet, and it will perform an Internet search, using your default search engine.

If you type text, such as **oreilly**, and press Ctrl-Enter, an *http://www.*.com* will be added to the address so that you can quickly go to the web site.

The Address Bar features a drop-down list containing the history of all recently entered URLs and command lines. Click the down arrow at the far right of the Address Bar for the list. Pick an item from the drop-down list to re-execute the command or revisit the specified web site.

Although it is useful for running command-line programs, the Address Bar does have one drawback when you use it in this fashion. When you issue a command, the command opens in a new window. Once the command has finished, that window closes instantly. If you are issuing a command that does not normally leave the window open, but you need to see a response (such as *ping* or *dir*), you'll have to have very fast eyes. For these types of commands, you're better off using the command prompt.

There is a workaround if you want to use the Address Bar for running command-line programs: prefix the command with cmd /k—for example, cmd /k ping oreilly.com.

Bread Crumbs

Windows Explorer now includes bread crumb navigation along the top, which shows you the complete path to your current location, as shown in Figure 3-5. Click on any spot back along the path, and you'll navigate directly there. Click the arrow next to any spot on the path, and you'll see a drop-down list of all the subfolders under that location.

See also

"Address Bar"

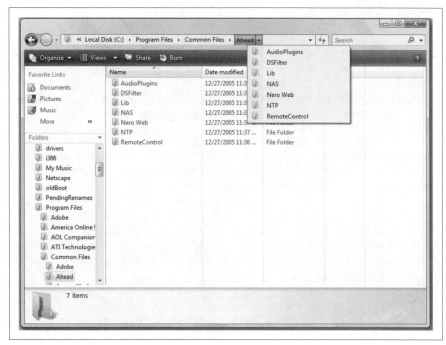

Figure 3-5. Bread crumb navigation

Buttons

Just click a button to make it do what its label says. In Figure 3-6, the Browse button is typically used to display a file dialog box. When you choose a file and click OK, the name and location (also known as the path) of the file are automatically entered into the text field. This synergy of controls is common, saves typing, and prevents typos. Some applications place a small folder icon next to a text field rather than the full-size text field, but the usage is the same.

If the button has the focus, press the Space bar, press Enter, or click the button with the mouse to activate it. In dialogs with more than one button, often one of them has a color that fades in and out (usually the OK button)—this is the "default" button and you can activate it by pressing Enter, regardless of which control has the focus. Similarly, there is usually a cancel button (typically labeled "Cancel") that responds to the Esc key but has no visual distinction. If in doubt, use Tab to cycle through the buttons and then press the Space bar.

Some button behavior is different in Windows Vista than in earlier versions of Windows—notably, that the default button is highlighted in a color that fades in and out.

Figure 3-6. The Browse button marked with ellipses (…), implying that another window will appear when it is clicked

Following is a more detailed explanation of buttons and their uses:

Toggle buttons
> Some buttons, typically custom controls or buttons on toolbars, are used to change a setting and will simply stay pushed in until you click them a second time. There's no rule that makes these buttons look different from standard buttons, so you'll have to rely on experience to determine which are "toggles." For example, the **B** and *I* buttons (corresponding to **bold** and *italic*, respectively) commonly found on word processor toolbars are toggles, but the Save and Print buttons are traditional buttons, and you use them to carry out a command rather than to change a setting.

The default button
> When a set of buttons is displayed—typically at the bottom of a dialog box—one button will be the "default," meaning that it will be the one activated by the Enter key. Its color will be highlighted and will fade in and out (do not confuse this with the dotted rectangle signifying the focus, discussed at the beginning of this chapter). Not all dialog boxes have a default button, but when it's there, it's usually the OK button.

The Cancel button

Much like the default button, a single button is often set as the Cancel button, meaning that it will be activated when the Esc key is pressed (regardless of which control has the focus). The Cancel button has no visual distinction from any other buttons.

OK, Cancel, Apply

Most dialogs will have at least an OK and a Cancel button, and many also have an Apply button. Typically, OK is the "default button" and Cancel is the "cancel button." Both the OK and Apply buttons accept whatever settings you've entered, but the OK button closes the window and Apply leaves it open, allowing you to make more changes. Finally, Cancel closes the window without applying your settings.

What may be confusing is what happens when you click Apply and then Cancel. The assumption is that the settings that were "applied" are not lost; instead, any that were made *after* you clicked Apply are ignored. Theoretically, the behavior should be the same as though you clicked OK, then reopened the dialog, and then clicked Cancel. But don't be surprised if some applications respond differently; Microsoft has never been clear with application developers about the expected behavior in this situation.

Change Your Color Scheme

Change the color and "glassiness" of windows, the Start menu, and the Taskbar.

To open

Control Panel → [Appearance and Personalization] → Personalization → Window Color and Appearance

Right-click the Desktop and choose Personalize → Window Color and Appearance

Description

One of the most notable changes in Windows Vista compared to earlier versions of Windows is its transparent windows, courtesy of Windows Aero. You can change their colors and transparency from the Window Color and Appearance page, shown in Figure 3-7.

Click a color to choose a new color. If you want to further customize the colors, click "Show color mixer," and controls will let you choose the precise colors of your windows. To change the transparency of windows, use the Color intensity slider. Move the slider to the left to make windows more transparent and to the right to make them less transparent. To change the colors and fonts of all screen elements in pretty much any way you'd like, click "Open classic appearance properties for more color options," and you'll open a dialog box from Windows Vista that lets you customize all elements of your screen.

 If you aren't using Windows Aero, choosing Window Color and Appearance leads you to a different screen—Appearance Settings, a holdover from Windows XP that lets you choose a color scheme but doesn't let you set the transparency of windows.

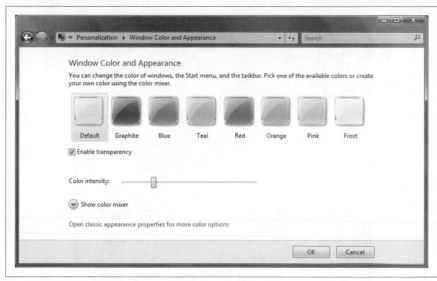

Figure 3-7. The Window Color and Appearance page, where you can customize Windows Aero's transparency and colors

Checkboxes

Checkboxes are generally used for on/off settings. A checkmark means the setting is on; an empty box means it's off. Click on the box to turn the labeled setting on or off.

In some instances, instead of a checkmark in the box, the box will be a solid blue. This means that the value is neither on nor off. Here's an example: select some files in Explorer or on your Desktop, right-click on one of them, select Properties, and you'll get a dialog similar to Figure 3-8. The checkmark is missing for the Hidden attributes, but the box is a solid blue for the Read-Only attribute because some of the selected files have it enabled, and others don't.

Clipboard

A shared, system-wide storage area for temporarily holding and moving data.

To open

Edit → Cut (Ctrl-X)

Edit → Copy (Ctrl-C)

Edit → Paste (Ctrl-V)

Description

The Clipboard is an invisible portion of memory, used to temporarily hold data as it's moved or copied from one application to another. Although you will never "see" the Clipboard, it's used every time you cut, copy, or paste something.

Using the Clipboard is easy. Select a portion of text in your word processor, an image in your graphics program, or a file in Explorer, and then select Cut from the Edit

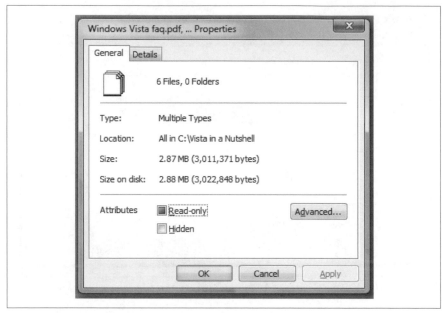

Figure 3-8. Checkboxes, for turning settings on or off

menu; the selected object(s) will disappear and be stored in the Clipboard. (Use Copy instead of Cut if you don't want the original data erased.) Then, move to another location and select Paste from the Edit menu to place a copy of the object on the Clipboard in that location. You can paste the data as many times as you like.

 If you use Microsoft Office, don't confuse the Windows Clipboard with the Office Clipboard. The Office Clipboard springs into action and pops up on the right side of your screen at apparently random times, but there is some method to the madness. If you copy or cut two different items consecutively in the same program; or copy an item, paste the item, and then copy another item in the same program; or copy one item twice in succession, the Office Clipboard will annoyingly appear on-screen. But there is no relationship between the Office Clipboard and the Windows Clipboard.

Notes

- The Clipboard works like the penalty box in hockey; it holds only one item at a time. If you place new data in the Clipboard, its previous contents are erased. If you never got around to pasting the previous data, it's lost for good. However, you may be able to switch back to the program that you cut from and select Undo (Ctrl-Z) to get it back.

- You can paste only data that an application is prepared to receive. For example, you cannot paste an image into some applications that recognize only text (such as the Command Prompt or Notepad).

- Even without an Edit menu, you can usually still access the Clipboard using either keyboard shortcuts or the right mouse button. For example, web browsers have a

Copy command in the Edit menu, but this command is used only for copying portions of the currently displayed web page to the Clipboard. To cut, copy, or paste text in the Address Bar, just right-click on the text or use Ctrl-X, Ctrl-C, or Ctrl-V.

- See Chapter 14 for help with copying and pasting data with the Command Prompt window.

- The keyboard shortcuts (Ctrl-X, Ctrl-C, and Ctrl-V) may not be intuitive at first, but when you consider that they appear together on the keyboard and are located very close to the Ctrl key, the decision to use these keys becomes clear. As a hold-over from earlier versions of Windows, you also can use Shift-Delete, Ctrl-Ins, and Shift-Ins for Cut, Copy, and Paste, respectively.

- A variation on the Clipboard theme is the Snipping Tool utility. It's a clever new Windows Vista applet that lets you copy any portion of any screen, annotate it, and then send it via email, copy it to the Clipboard as a graphic, or save it as an HTML or graphics file. It's a great way to capture and annotate screenshots, or information or graphics you find on the Web, and then share them with others. For details, see "Snipping Tool," in Chapter 12.

Combo Boxes

See "Listboxes," later in this chapter.

Computer

In Vista, the Computer icon in Windows Explorer and the Computer link on the Start menu have replaced the My Computer icon used in Windows XP. It is solely a navigational icon and has no program associated with it. Right-click it and choose Properties, and you'll open the System Control Panel applet. (You can also get to the applet by choosing Control Panel → System and Maintenance → System.) This applet, shown in Figure 3-9, shows you basic information about your system and includes links to many other applets, controls, and menus that let you customize the use of your computer.

Notes

- Double-click the Computer icon to open Windows Explorer at the topmost level—at your computer, with all its drives listed beneath it.

Context Menus

In Figure 3-10, I've right-clicked on the Recycle Bin icon to display its context menu, which is a list of special actions or commands that affect only that object. The idea is that the options available for any given object in Windows depend upon the *context*, the set of circumstances under which you're operating. The Empty Recycle Bin option is shown here, because it is relevant to the context of the Recycle Bin. (If the Recycle Bin were empty, the option would be grayed out [disabled].) Nearly all objects in Windows have their own context menus, which are almost always accessible with the right mouse button. See "Windows Explorer," in Chapter 4, for details on customizing the context menus for your files, folders, and certain Desktop items, and see Chapter 12 for details on the way Windows stores file type information.

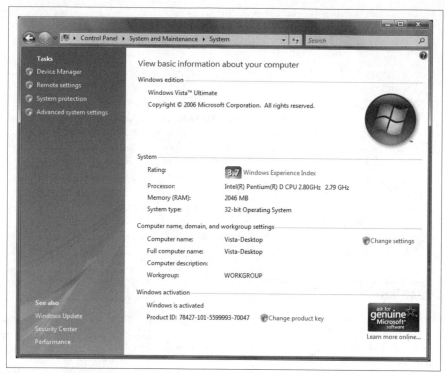

Figure 3-9. The System Control Panel applet

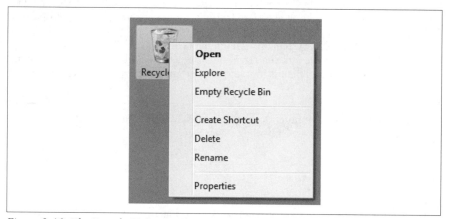

Figure 3-10. The Recycle Bin's context menu

When a file or other object is selected (highlighted), press Shift-F10 to display the context menu. If you have a special Windows keyboard, there is a special key for this purpose, usually located to the right of the Space bar. The most frequently used item in most context menus is Properties, which you can access quickly by pressing Alt-Enter. Other shortcuts for context menu items include the Delete key, F2, Ctrl-X, Ctrl-C, and Ctrl-V for Delete, Rename, Cut, Copy, and Paste, respectively.

Notes

- The bold item (usually, but not always, at the top of any given context menu) is the default action, carried out when you double-click.

- Most new keyboards also include a context key (which looks like a menu with a pointer on it) that will open the context menu of any selected item.

- Context menus exist for all major interface elements—files, folders (including system folders such as the Recycle Bin), the Desktop, the Taskbar, the System Tray, and so on—but they often also exist for elements within an application window or dialog. If you're ever stuck, try right-clicking on a user-interface element and see whether anything helpful pops up.

- In other cases, the context menu is quite extensive. For example, right-clicking on the files on your Desktop (or even on an empty area of the Desktop) provides access to the features that would otherwise be unavailable due to the absence of a standard menu. Of particular use is the New entry, which allows you to create a new folder, shortcut, or empty file of certain types (a text document, compressed folder, Office document, and more).

- Right-clicking on the title bar or the Taskbar button for an open application displays the context menu for the window, commonly known as the Control menu, which is also accessible by clicking on the upper-left icon or upper-left corner (see "Windows," later in this chapter). Oddly enough, some windows don't have an icon, but you can still click there. Right-clicking in the body of the window gives you the context menu for the application or the selected element within the application, if one exists. Note that this is different from the context menu that you get by clicking on the program's shortcut icon when it is not running.

- See "Send To," later in this chapter, for details on the Send To command found in the context menu for files and folders.

Control Menus

See "Windows," later in this chapter.

Control Panel   *\windows\system32\control.exe*

The central interface for most of the preferences, hardware configurations, and other settings in Windows Vista.

To open

Start → Control Panel

Windows Explorer → navigate to the *Desktop\Control Panel* folder (it's not available in the *\Users\username\Desktop* folder, however)

Search box or Command Prompt → **Control**

Search box or Command Prompt → *filename.cpl*

Usage

```
control [filename.cpl] [applet_name]
control [keyword]
filename.cpl
```

Description

The Control Panel has no settings of its own; it's merely a container for any number of option windows (commonly called applets or *Control Panel extensions*), most of which you can access without even opening the Control Panel folder. Unfortunately, the Control Panel can look vastly different from one computer to another, based on preferences scattered throughout several dialog boxes. Furthermore, the default settings vary, depending on how Windows Vista was installed (see Figure 3-11). To simplify notation in this book, I'm making certain assumptions about your preferences. It's best to familiarize yourself with the various options described here so that you won't be confused when a setting in the Control Panel is referenced.

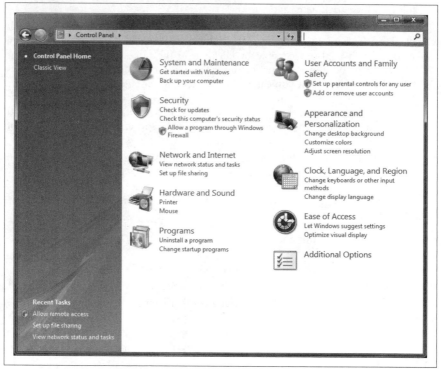

Figure 3-11. The normal view of the Control Panel

The Control Panel has two views: the normal view and the "Classic" view. In the normal view, you see major categories and click through to subcategories until you find the setting or applet you're looking for. Windows Vista changes Control Panel behavior to a certain extent compared to Windows XP, because even at the category level, there are applets you can click without having to drill down. The Classic view, by way of contrast, presents a simple, alphabetical listing of all Control Panel applets.

Figure 3-11 shows the normal view, and Figure 3-12 shows the Classic view. To switch from the normal view to the Classic view, click the Classic View link. To switch from the Classic View to the normal view, click Control Panel Home.

Figure 3-12. The Classic view of the Control Panel

There are several different ways to access the Control Panel and its contents:

Start menu

The way the Control Panel appears in the Start menu depends on several different settings, resulting in no fewer than five different possibilities.

If you're using the normal Vista Start menu, right click on the Start button and select Properties. On the Start Menu tab, make sure that Start Menu is selected (if you've got Classic Start Menu selected, skip ahead a couple of paragraphs), then click Customize next to Start Menu. In the Control Panel area, there are three possibilities for display of the Control Panel. "Display as a link" opens the normal Control Panel when clicked. If you choose "Display as a menu," a right arrow will appear next to the Control Panel on the Start menu; click the arrow, and a list of all Control Panel applets appears as a menu. "Don't display this item" hides it on the Start menu altogether.

If enabled, the Control Panel entry appears in the second column in the Start menu. Figure 3-13 shows the normal view, and Figure 3-14 shows it as a cascading menu.

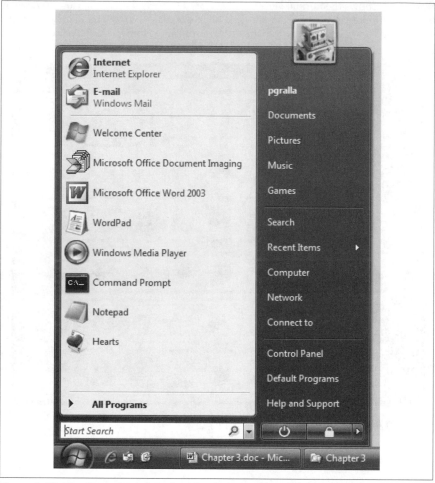

Figure 3-13. The Control Panel displayed in the normal view

If you're using the Classic Start menu, get to the Control Panel by selecting Start → Settings → Control Panel. The Control Panel will then appear in Classic View. You can instead have a cascading menu appear, with a list of all applets, when you select Start → Settings → Control Panel. To do this, when you're using the Classic Start menu, right-click on the Start button and select Properties. On the Start Menu tab, make sure that Classic Start Menu is selected, then click Customize next to Classic Start Menu. In the Advanced Start Menu options area, check the box next to Expand Control Panel. Then click OK, and click OK again.

Explorer

The Control Panel appears as another folder under the Desktop branch. Double-click the folder to display the Control Panel.

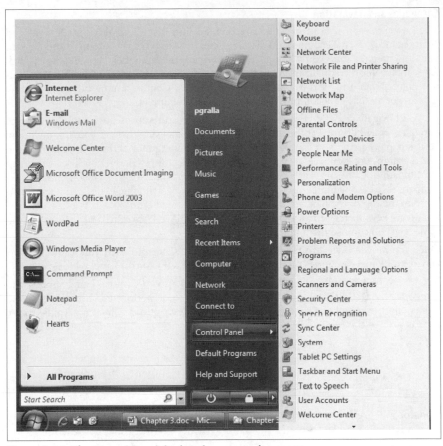

Figure 3-14. The Control Panel displayed as a cascading menu

Command prompt

At any command prompt or the Start menu's Search box, type **control** to open the Control Panel. See the upcoming "Command-line usage" section for information on opening specific Control Panel applets from the command prompt.

Shortcuts

In addition to accessing a particular entry by first opening the Control Panel, it's possible to open a specific applet directly, either with a standard Windows shortcut or with one of the many links built into the Windows interface. For example, Folder Options is also available in the Organize menu of Windows Explorer, and Internet Options is available in the Tools menu of Internet Explorer. To create a standard Windows shortcut to a Control Panel applet, simply drag the desired icon from the Control Panel folder onto your Desktop or into any folder. Then double-click the icon to open the applet, skipping the Control Panel folder altogether.

Categories and navigation

The contents of the Control Panel are divided into discrete categories (System and Maintenance; User Accounts and Family Safety; Network and Internet; and so on). Click a category and you'll come to a group of subcategories. For example, click Appearance and Personalization, and you'll come to subcategories including Personalization, Taskbar and Start Menu, and Ease of Access Center, among others. Click any subcategory to either accomplish a task or see a list of applets.

As you navigate up and down through categories and subcategories in the Control Panel, the bread crumbs at the top of the Control Panel show where you are, including your complete path. You can jump anywhere back along that path by clicking it in the bread crumb. For example, if you're in the Personalization section, you'll see the bread crumb path of Control Panel → Appearance and Personalization → Personalization. To jump back to Appearance and Personalization, click it in the bread crumb trail; to jump to the top of the Control Panel, click it in the bread crumb trail. You can also use the arrow keys to the left of the bread crumbs to move backward and forward in the same way you can use them in Internet Explorer.

Once you move down into the category level in the Control Panel, you'll find links to all Control Panel categories on the lefthand side of each Control Panel window.

In addition to containing the icons for most of the standard Control Panel applets, the categories have additional links based on the task to be performed. Essentially, these links point to the same icons, only using different descriptions. The same holds true at the top level of the Control Panel.

 The Control Panel keeps track of which applets you've recently used, and displays links to the ones you've used most recently, on the bottom lefthand side.

Some people prefer the Classic view to the normal category view, because the applets are always presented consistently, no matter how the Control Panel is opened.

Regardless of the setting you prefer, it's important to understand the notation adopted throughout this book. For example, the following instruction shows the category name in square brackets (commonly used to denote an optional step or parameter):

Go to Control Panel → [Appearance and Themes] → Display

If you are using Control Panel categories, include the step in brackets; if you have categories turned off, ignore the bracketed step.

Control Panel changes in Vista

The Control Panel has been given a thoroughgoing redesign in Windows Vista. Categories have been added, taken away, and altered; navigation has changed with the addition of bread crumbs; it's now easy to jump from any level of the Control Panel to get directly to an applet; and the Control Panel offers a much more comprehensive way to perform tasks and customize Windows Vista.

That's the good news. The bad news is that under the hood, the Control Panel is now something of a mess. It's made up of a collection of category pages and applets that have accumulated through various versions of Windows. As you'll see shortly, in "Command-line usage," in some cases you can run an applet directly from the command line by typing the name of the applet itself. In other cases you can run an applet by typing in **Control** and then a keyword, such as **telephony**. And in yet other cases you can't run an applet from the command line at all. Making matters more confusing is that in some instances, running an applet from the command line leads to a traditional dialog box (such as *main.cpl* for the Mouse Properties dialog box), but in other instances it leads to a subcategory that is actually a folder along the Control Panel bread crumb path (such as *powercfg.cpl*, which leads to the folder/subcategory Control Panel → Hardware and Sound → Power Options). The upshot? Like it or not, it may be easier to use the Control Panel itself rather than the command line for running applets.

Command-line usage

This section explains how to use *control.exe* from the command line. By *command line*, I mean the Address Bar or Start Search box as well—both will accept commands. And you can also use filenames for creating Windows shortcuts to specific Control Panel applets.

 The simplest way to create a Windows shortcut to a Control Panel applet is to drag the applet from the Control Panel onto the Desktop. When you do that, a shortcut will be automatically created. In this way, you can create a shortcut to any applet, even if the applet cannot be run from the command line.

Note that you cannot launch all applets from the command line; see the upcoming "Notes" section for a workaround. *Control.exe* supports two command-line methods (see "Usage," at the beginning of this section), but no method covers all applets.

Control.exe accepts the following parameters:

filename.cpl
> The filename of the *.cpl* file (found in *\Windows\System32*) containing the applet you want to open. For example, type:
>
>   control main.cpl
>
> to open the Mouse Properties dialog. If more than one Control Panel applet is contained in the *.cpl* file, and the one you want is not the default, you'll need to specify the *applet_name* (discussed next) to open it.

 Note that you don't have to use *control.exe* in order to run any applet that is a *.cpl* file; just type in the name of the file, such as *main.cpl*. You can also use the applet name, like this: *main.cpl Keyboard*.

applet_name, tab
> The formal name of the applet you want to launch, spelled and capitalized exactly as described in Table 3-1. This parameter is necessary only if more than one applet is contained in a given *.cpl* file. If you omit *applet_name*, the default applet in the specified *.cpl* file will be used. For example, type:
>
>   control main.cpl Keyboard
>
> to open the Keyboard Properties dialog. Note that the *main.cpl* file is the same file as the one in the previous example, but the use of *applet_name* allows applets other than the default to be opened.

For some tabbed dialogs, you can also specify the tab to open by including a space and then a comma after the *.cpl* filename (the preceding space is required), and then a number. Specify 0 for the first tab (or omit the tab completely), 1 for the second, and so on. This technique will even work for applets that lead to a User Account Control (UAC) prompt. For example, if you type **control sysdm.cpl ,3** to try to open the System Properties window to the Advanced tab, you'll first have to go through a UAC prompt.

keyword

Keyword is an alternate way of opening a specific Control Panel applet from the command line. Instead of using *filename.cpl* and *applet_name*, simply include one of the following names: admintools, color, date/time, desktop, folders, fonts, international, keyboard, mouse, printers, schedtasks, system, telephony, or userpasswords.

See Table 3-1 for a list of Control Panel applets that you can run directly from the command line, and the category in which you can find them. Not listed are applets that you cannot run from the command line.

Table 3-1. Control Panel applets

Applet name	Category	What to type at the command line
Add Hardware	N/A (see "Notes," later in this section)	control hdwwiz.cpl
Add or Remove Programs	Programs	control appwiz.cpl
Administrative Tools	System and Maintenance	control admintools
Appearance Settings	Appearance and Personalization	control color
Audio Devices and Sound Themes	Hardware and Sound	control mmsys.cpl
Date and Time	Clock, Language, and Regions	control timedate.cpl or control date/time
Display Settings	Appearance and Personalization	control desk.cpl or control desktop
Firewall	Security	control firewall.cpl
Folder Options	Appearance and Personalization	control folders
Fonts	Appearance and Personalization	Explorer "\windows\fonts" or control fonts
Game Controllers	Hardware and Sound	control joy.cpl
Infocard	N/A (see "Notes," later in this section)	control infocardcpl.cpl
iSCSI Initiator	N/A (see "Notes," later in this section)	control iscsicpl.cpl
Internet Options	Network and Internet	control inetcpl.cpl
Keyboard	Hardware and Sound	control main.cpl Keyboard or control keyboard

Table 3-1. Control Panel applets (continued)

Applet name	Category	What to type at the command line
Mouse	Hardware and Sound	control main.cpl or control mouse
Network Connections	Network and Internet	control ncpa.cpl or control netconnections
Pen and Input Devices	Hardware and Sound	control tabletpc.pcl
People Near Me	Network and Internet	control collab.pcl
Phone and Modem Options	Printers and Other Hardware	control telephon.cpl or control telephony
Power Options	Hardware and Sound	control powercfg.cpl
Printers and Faxes	Hardware and Sound	control printers
Regional and Language Options	Clock, Language, and Regions	control intl.cpl or control international
Scanners and Cameras	Hardware and Sound	control sticpl.cpl
Windows Security Center	Security	control wscui.cpl
Task Scheduler	System and Maintenance	control schedtasks
Text to Speech	Ease of Access	control speech
System	System and Maintenance	control sysdm.cpl
User Accounts	User Accounts and Family Safety	control nusrmgr.cpl or control userpasswords or control userpasswords2

Notes

- The Control Panel has many more applets than those listed in Table 3-1, but the ones in the table are the only ones that you can launch directly from the command line.

- Many applets in the Control Panel can't be launched from the command line using *control.exe* or by typing in the applet's filename. However, it's still possible to launch these (and any other) applets from the command line using a Windows shortcut. (Obviously, you can also launch the shortcuts by double-clicking them.) Simply drag the desired icon onto your Desktop or into a folder to create a shortcut. Then, to launch the shortcut from the command line, just type its full path and filename, including the *.lnk* filename extension. For example, to launch a shortcut named "Taskbar and Start Menu" (presumably linked to the applet of the same name), stored in your Stuff folder, type the following:

  ```
  \stuff\Taskbar and Start Menu.lnk
  ```

- Add Hardware, Infocard, and iSCSI Initiator are not listed in any category. Add Hardware launches the Add Hardware Wizard; Infocard opens an applet that lets you create an Infocard that will automatically log you into web sites; and the iSCSI Initiator lets you configure storage devices that use iSCSI connections. These applets are typically automatically launched by Windows Vista when you initiate a task that requires them—for example, adding new hardware.

- Some applications, software drivers, and hardware drivers come with their own applets, so you may have additional applets in your Control Panel that are not listed here. Also, depending on your version of Windows Vista, and any installed optional components, some of the items listed here might not be present in your Control Panel. See the specific entries elsewhere in this chapter for details on each applet mentioned here.

Date and Time Properties

\windows\system\timedate.cpl

Set your system's clock, choose a time zone, and enable Internet time synchronization.

To open

Control Panel → [Clock, Language, and Region] → Date and Time

Right-click on the time in the notification area, and select Adjust Date/Time.

Command Prompt → **timedate.cpl**

Command Prompt → **control date/time**

Description

The Date and Time dialog is pretty straightforward. Set your system's clock and time zone with the Date and Time tab, add additional clocks with the Additional Clocks tab, and automatically synchronize your PC clock to the true time over the Internet with the Internet Time tab.

The Date and Time tab is as simple as it gets: click "Change date and time" or "Change time zone" to make your changes.

The Additional Clocks tab, shown in Figure 3-15, lets you add up to two additional clocks, both of which can be from many places throughout the world. The "Enter display name" field lets you type in a name for your clock—for example, *Gabe's time*. The clock will then display that label. By default, the names for the two clocks are Clock1 and Clock2. If you delete the names, the clocks will not display any labels.

Hover your mouse over the time, and the time of your additional clocks pops up in a small display. Click the time for a fuller display, shown in Figure 3-16.

The Internet Time tab allows you to synchronize your PC's clock with one of several Internet time servers automatically. If you turn on the "Synchronize with an Internet time server" option, Windows will synchronize your clock once a week. Naturally, you must be connected to the Internet for this option to work; if you're not connected when Windows attempts to connect to the time server, it will just try again next week. Also, your time zone and daylight savings settings must be set properly; otherwise, the time synchronization will set the wrong time.

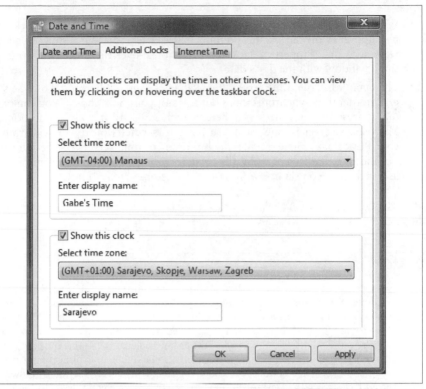

Figure 3-15. The Additional Clocks feature in Windows Vista, which lets you display up to two additional clocks from throughout the world

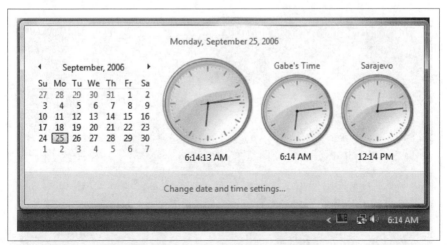

Figure 3-16. The full display of the additional clocks you've added

Notes

- When you click on the time in the notification area, a calendar and clock will pop up, set to the day's date and time. Click Date and Time Settings to get to Date and Time Properties. Hovering the mouse over the time will pop up a small window with the day's date.

- The default Internet time server, *time.windows.com*, is Microsoft's own server for Internet time synchronization, but it is not your only choice. You can type the address of any time server here, which is useful if your connection to Microsoft's server is slow or if you get errors when you try to synchronize your PC's clock. There are literally hundreds of time servers on the Internet. To find one that is geographically close to you, find an Internet Time Server list, such as the one at *http://tf.nist.gov/service/time-servers.html*.

See also

"Control Panel"

Desktop

The Desktop is the basis for the modern graphical user interface (GUI) paradigm. It is considered a container for all other resources on your computer, as well as a backdrop for your Windows workspace. The Desktop is always underneath any open windows—to access it if it's covered, you need to minimize or close any open windows. Press the Windows logo key and the D key to accomplish this quickly. If the Desktop icon is visible in the Quick Launch area, clicking that will accomplish the same thing. Both of these actions work like toggles, so you can use them to switch back and forth between the Desktop and your open window or windows.

As shown in Figure 3-17, the Desktop contains two types of icons: *namespace icons* and *file icons*.

Figure 3-17. Namespace icons and file icons

File icons can be files or folders (actually located in your \Users\username\Desktop\ folder on your hard disk). You can drag and drop a file icon to and from the Desktop as though it were any other ordinary folder. The Desktop is a good place to store newly downloaded files from the Internet, email attachments, items from floppies, and other files you're currently working on.

Namespace icons, on the other hand, such as the Recycle Bin, aren't files but rather specific resources built into Windows. You can rename and hide all of these icons. As a general rule, to rename a namespace icon, right-click it, choose Rename, and then type in the new name you want to appear. To hide it or make it appear, use the Personalization Control Panel applet. (See "Personalization," later in this chapter, for details.)

As with most other components of the Windows interface, the Desktop has properties you can customize. Right-click on an empty portion of the Desktop and click Personalize to change the wallpaper, color, screensaver, settings for the display, and more. (This is the same applet that you will get by choosing Control Panel → [Appearance and Personalization] → Personalization.)

You can also change the appearance, size, and display order of the Desktop icons. Right-click the Desktop and choose View to change the size of the icons as well as how they should be arranged on the Desktop. From the View options, select Align to Grid if you want the icons to go into neat rows automatically; unselect it if you want to be able to drag them anywhere on the Desktop. When the Desktop is full, Align to Grid stops working.

To change the order in which the icons appear, right-click the Desktop and choose View → Auto Arrange. Now right-click the Desktop again and select "Sort by." You'll be able to arrange the icons by name, size, date modified, and file extension.

Notes

- You can also change the size of the fonts used on the Desktop. Right-click the Desktop, choose Personalize, and click Adjust Font Size (dpi). You can choose from several preset font sizes, or else select a size of your own. To select one of your own, click Custom DPI and fill out the screen. You'll have to reboot in order for the changes to take effect. The changes will be made system-wide, not just to your Desktop.

- The actual icons that are displayed by default on your Desktop may vary according to your computer manufacturer.

See also

"Control Panel," "Personalization," and "Taskbar"

Desktop Background

Change the background of your Desktop (sometimes called *wallpaper*).

To open

Control Panel → [Appearance and Personalization] → Personalization → Desktop Background

Description

Desktop Background (Figure 3-18) allows you to select a background image, or color. The background image (also called *wallpaper*) can be centered (displayed in its actual size in the middle, surrounded by the background color if it's not big enough), tiled (repeated so that it fills the screen), or stretched (displayed once, but enlarged or shrunk so that it fits the screen exactly). Windows Vista comes with a wide variety of backgrounds; select a category from the drop-down box, browse to the one you want, and click it to choose it.

Figure 3-18. Choosing a background for your Desktop

You're not bound to the background listed here; you can use any picture on your PC in the *.bmp*, *.gif*, *.jpg*, *.jpeg*, *.dib*, or *.png* format. Click the Browse button, and use Windows Explorer to select a new picture.

Notes

- You can use any picture you find on the Web to be your Desktop background. In Internet Explorer, right-click the picture and select Set as Background.

See also

"Control Panel" and "Personalization"

Desktop Icons

Select which Desktop icons to display.

To open

Control Panel → [Appearance and Personalization] → Personalization → Change desktop icons (located in the task list on the left)

Description

When you install Windows Vista, the Recycle Bin is the only system Desktop icon displayed on the Desktop. You can, however, choose to display any system Desktop icon, and even change which icon is displayed for it, using the Desktop Icons setting page (Figure 3-19).

Figure 3-19. Selecting which Desktop icons to display, and which to hide

Check the boxes next to the icons you want to display; uncheck the boxes next to those you want to hide. To change the icon associated with any of the objects, click it, select Change Icon, and choose which to use. For more details about changing icons, see "Icons," later in this chapter.

See also

"Icons"

Details

See "Listboxes," later in this chapter.

Dialog Boxes

Dialog boxes are temporary windows that applications use to request your attention or input. Dialog boxes usually don't have a resizable border (although File Open/Save dialogs do), and they often have OK, Cancel, and Apply buttons. They are usually *modal*, which means that when they're open, you can't use any other part of the owning application until they're closed. See "Windows," later in this chapter, for more information.

There are several different kinds of dialog boxes in Windows. Many dialog boxes offer help with configuration—for example, using the Internet Options dialog box to select from a variety of options from inside Internet Explorer. These have the OK, Cancel, and Apply buttons.

Another kind of dialog box appears when you need to take an action of some kind—for example, if you want to save changes to a file. In Windows Vista, Microsoft has introduced a new style of dialog box for this, designed to provide more information to help you decide which action to take. In past versions of Windows, dialog boxes have not always been a paragon of clarity, and have at times confused users about the consequences of choosing different actions. The new-style dialog boxes introduced in Windows Vista use up more screen real estate to explain the consequences of each action more clearly. They sometimes also recommend which action to take.

Figures 3-20 and 3-21 show the difference between the old- and new-style dialog boxes.

Figure 3-20. Old-style dialog boxes, which offered no information to help you understand the consequences of taking actions

Windows Vista itself uses the new-style dialog boxes. But applications written by third parties do not necessarily use the new-style dialog boxes. Any application written before the release of Windows Vista, for example, will use the old-style dialog boxes. And even applications written after the release of Windows Vista may use the old-style dialog boxes as well; which style to use is entirely up to the developers themselves. Microsoft encourages the use of new-style dialog boxes, but doesn't require them.

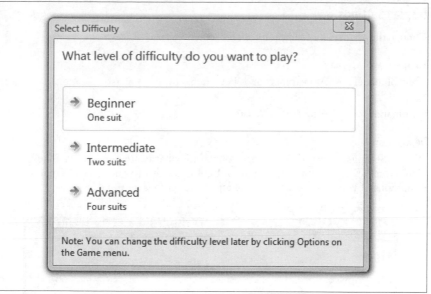

Figure 3-21. New-style dialog boxes, which offer more information to help you understand the consequences of actions you take

The new-style dialog boxes include multiple areas that programmers can use to provide information to help you decide what action to take:

- Main Instruction Area
- Content Area
- Progress Area
- Radio Button Area
- Command Link Area
- Command Area
- Footer Area
- Expanded Information Area

For more information, see *http://shellrevealed.com/blogs/shellblog/archive/2006/09/19/So-long-MessageBox-and-thanks-for-all-the-memories.aspx*.

Display Settings

Change the settings for your monitor and screen.

To open

Control Panel → [Appearance and Personalization] → Personalization → Display Settings

Command Prompt → `control desk.cpl`

Description

Display Settings allows you to change your display hardware settings (see Figure 3-22). Here, you can choose the resolution and color depth of your screen. There are two limitations of your video card that may affect the settings here.

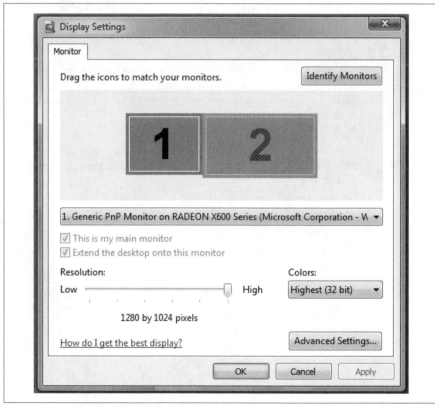

Figure 3-22. Display Settings, where you can choose your screen resolution, color depth, and multiple-monitor setup

First, the amount of memory on your video card dictates the maximum color depth and resolution you can use. As you adjust your color depth, Windows may automatically adjust other settings depending on your card's capabilities. If you increase your color depth, your resolution might automatically decrease; likewise, if you raise the resolution, your color depth might go down.

If you are using a CRT (glass) monitor, the second limitation that may affect your available settings is the refresh rate that your card will be able to generate (LCD panels generally operate at a 60 Hz refresh rate no matter what resolution they are set to). Although the maximum refresh rate does not depend on the amount of memory your card has, you may have to lower your resolution to achieve the desired rate. Windows should automatically adjust your refresh rate to the highest setting your card and monitor support, but this is not always the case. If you notice that your display appears to be flickering, especially under fluorescent lights, you'll need to raise your refresh rate either by adjusting the refresh rate setting directly or by lowering your resolution or color depth. (Note that this does not apply to LCD and laptop displays, which never flicker.)

If you hear a slight whine from your monitor, it means your refresh rate is too high (if you hear a whine even at reasonable resolutions, your monitor needs repair). The minimum refresh rate you are likely to tolerate is around 72 Hz at 1024×768 (higher resolutions will need a higher refresh rate). People with corrective lenses seem to be more sensitive and might require a higher setting to be comfortable. Most cards available today support refresh rates of 75 Hz and higher, so this is usually not a problem. Click Advanced Settings and choose the Adapter tab. If your display driver supports it, you can adjust your refresh rate with the Refresh Rate setting. If the setting is not there, you'll need to either obtain a more recent video driver from Windows Update or the manufacturer of the card, reduce your resolution or color depth, or get yourself a better video card or monitor.

If you have more than one monitor, using either two separate video cards or a single video card that supports two monitors, all configured screens will be shown in the preview area. Click any screen icon to activate it; the settings below the icon apply only to the selected monitor. You can even drag and drop monitor icons to rearrange them so that, for example, a different monitor assumes the role of the one pictured on the upper-left part of the screen. Click Identify Monitors if you're not sure which monitor is #1 and which is #2.

The Advanced Settings button allows you to view the hardware properties for your video adapter(s) and monitor(s). You'll never really need to adjust these settings unless you're updating a driver for your monitor or display adapter, adjusting your refresh rate (as discussed earlier), configuring color profiles (for matching the color output of your printer with your scanner and monitor), or tweaking advanced 3D settings for your card. If you use some video cards, such as those made by NVIDIA and ATI, you may also see additional settings or tabs.

Drop-Down Listboxes

See "Listboxes," later in this chapter.

Ease of Access Center

Make it easier to access your computer.

To open
Control Panel → [Appearance and Personalization] → Ease of Access Center

Description

If you have problems with your vision, or other issues that make it difficult to interact with your computer, the Control Panel's Ease of Access Center (Figure 3-23) will let you change your settings to make it easier to use your PC.

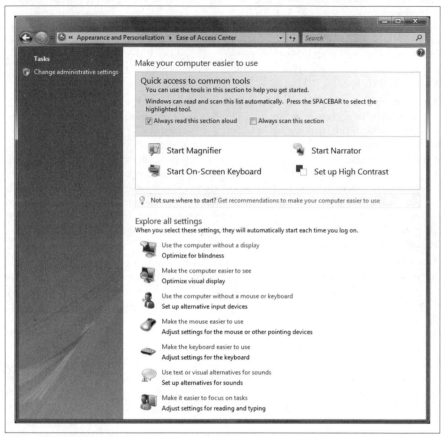

Figure 3-23. The Ease of Access Center, which makes it easier for you to use your PC if you have problems with your vision, or other issues that make it difficult to use your PC

The center offers these settings. Select any of them, and they will automatically be turned on when you boot up your PC:

Start Magnifier
Lets you enlarge sections of the screen to make them easier to see

Start On-Screen Keyboard
Lets you use a mouse or other pointing device to type by clicking on keys on an on-screen keyboard

Start Narrator
Turns on the Narrator, which reads text aloud from the screen

Set Up High Contrast
Turns on extremely high contrast to reduce eyestrain and make the screen easier to see

Perhaps the most useful part of the Ease of Access Center is the links that appear at the bottom of the screen: "Use the computer without a display," "Make the computer easier to see," and "Use the computer without a mouse or keyboard." Click any of these links, and you'll come to a constellation of settings for each purpose. For example, "Use the computer without a display" optimizes Windows Vista for users who are blind.

Notes

- Select Start → All Programs → Accessories → Ease of Access to display or run the various Ease of Access applets.

File Open/Save Dialogs

There's a reason why File Open and File Save dialogs look the same in nearly all applications; they're common dialogs provided by Windows. Strangely, one of the few applications that doesn't use these common dialogs is Microsoft Office, which instead employs custom dialogs that actually have more limited functionality than their standard counterparts.

The main part of the standard file dialog is really just a folder window, as shown in Figure 3-24; you can even drag and drop items into and out of this window, as well as display the contents in the same Tiles, Details, and variously sized Icons views found in Windows Explorer. That's because the dialog box is, in essence, Windows Explorer.

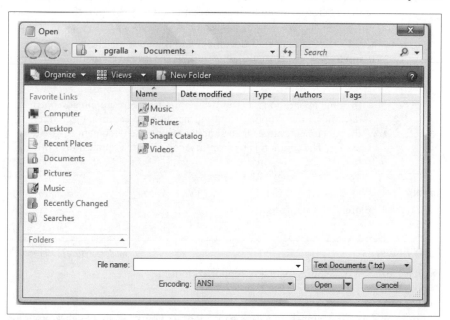

Figure 3-24. Standard File → Open, File → Save, and Browse dialogs

Another standard component in file dialogs is the list of folders and objects on the left side, called Favorite Links. Here, eight (or more) shortcuts to special system folders are shown; click an icon to quickly jump to the corresponding location. You can also display a list of all of your folders, beneath those Favorite Links, by clicking the small up arrow next to the word *Folders*. Better yet, you can add any folder or object to your Favorite Links by displaying your folders, then dragging any folder or object to the Favorite Links list. A shortcut to the folder or object will then appear in Favorite Links.

Navigating to find or save files in the dialog boxes works exactly like it does in Windows Explorer. Use the "bread crumbs" navigation at the top to quickly jump to parent folders, and click the down arrow next to the bread crumb trail to drop down a list of folders you've used recently. Windows Vista also solves a problem with past Windows versions in that the full path of the current folder is shown in the bread crumb trail—something you didn't see in previous Windows versions.

You can type any filename into the "File name" box, including the full path desired, to open or save. Directly to the right of the "File name" box is a list used to filter the display of files in the main listing. This is often the most confusing part of this window for new users, because in most cases, only certain file types are shown—those that match the file types that can be opened by the application you're using. So, for example, in Notepad you'll see only *.txt* files, but in WordPad you'll see a wider variety of files, including *.rtf*, *.wri*, *.txt*, and *.doc*. If the file you're looking for does not match the file type selection, it won't show up at all. Typically, the last entry in this list is All Files (*.*); choose this item to turn off the filter and display all files, regardless of type.

Notes

- Like most dialog boxes, File Open/Save dialogs are modal, which means that you must close them before you can use another part of the application.

- An alternative to opening an application and then using File → Open is to navigate to the folder containing your document and then double-click it to open it in its default application. You can also drag and drop a document icon into an open application window to open the file in that program.

 In some applications, if you drop a file icon into an already open document, the dropped icon will be inserted as an "object" into that document, rather than simply opening the document as you'd expect. The solution is to drop the icon onto the application's title bar.

See also
"Windows Explorer," in Chapter 4

Font Viewer
\windows\system32\fontview.exe

Display a preview and summary of any supported font file.

To open
Control Panel → [Appearance and Personalization] → Fonts → Double-click any font file

Usage
```
fontview [/p] filename
```

Description

It's easiest to use Font Viewer by double-clicking on a font file (see Figure 3-25). You can view any font formats normally supported by Windows Vista, including True-Type fonts (*.ttf*), bitmap fonts (*.fon*), and Type 1 fonts (*.pfm*).

In addition to the font name and summary information displayed at the top of the report, a preview of the font is shown with the full alphabet in upper- and lowercase, the full set of numbers, a few symbols, and the phrase "the quick brown fox jumps over the lazy dog. 1234567890" in several different sizes.

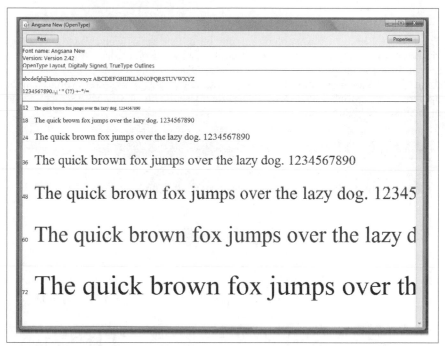

Figure 3-25. Double-clicking on a font file to view a preview

To run Font Viewer from the command line, you must specify the full path and file-name of the font file, including its extension (such as *.fon* or *.ttf*). To send the report to the printer, use the /p option (which is the same as clicking the Print button in the Font Viewer window).

Notes

- Windows Vista typically keeps its installed font files in *Windows**Fonts*, which is easiest to access by going to Control Panel → Fonts.
- Although Adobe Type 1 fonts are actually stored in the font binaries (*.pfb*), Font Viewer works only with the font metrics (*.pfm*).
- Font Viewer does not display every character in the font, only the predefined subset described earlier. To display every character in the font, use Character Map. (However, Character Map works only on installed fonts.)

See also

"Fonts Folder," discussed next, and "Character Map," in Chapter 10

Fonts Folder

Display all the installed fonts.

To open

Control Panel → [Appearance and Personalization] → Fonts

Command Prompt → `control fonts`

Command Prompt → `explorer \windows\fonts`

Description

The Fonts folder is merely a folder on your hard disk (specifically, *\Windows\fonts*). However, when viewed in Explorer, it's configured to display a list of installed fonts instead of a list of the contents of the folder. (The two aren't necessarily the same thing.) Select View → Details for a view that, among other things, allows you to match up a font name with the file in which it's stored. Use the Preview Pane to see a preview of the font (see Figure 3-26).

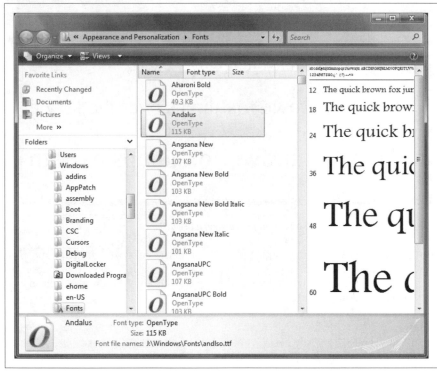

Figure 3-26. The Details view of the Fonts folder, which shows the relationships between your font names and font filenames

Right-click a font file and select Properties to see additional information pertaining to the font, such as hinting and font-smoothing properties, copyright information, font vendor information, and whether such fonts can be embedded.

To view a preview of an installed font in large size, just double-click its name; see "Font Viewer," earlier in this chapter, for more information. To delete a font, delete it as you'd delete any file (press the Delete key or drag and drop it into the Recycle Bin).

To install a font (as long as it's one of the supported types), just drag and drop it into the Fonts folder. Supported typeface formats include TrueType (*.ttf*), Adobe Type 1 (*.pfm* and *.pfb*), OpenType (also known as TrueType v2), and ugly old raster fonts (*.fon*) used in early versions of Windows.

Notes

- If a font file icon has a shortcut arrow (see "Shortcuts," later in this chapter), it means the font is installed but not actually stored in the *Windows**Fonts* folder.

- Windows Vista comes with built-in support for Adobe Type 1 fonts, so a product such as Adobe Type Manager is no longer needed.

- If you're sharing documents with other users, you may need to send them copies of the font files you've used as well. If you drag and drop the desired files from the Fonts folder onto, say, your Desktop, make sure to hold the Ctrl key (or drag with the right mouse button and select Copy Here) so that the font file is copied and not moved (which would uninstall it). Keep in mind that some fonts are licensed products, and copying them would be a copyright violation.

- With Windows Vista, Microsoft has introduced the new XML Paper Specification (XPS) file format, which stores files in the *.xps* format. It lets you share documents that can be printed and viewed, without needing the program that created them, but it retains all the formatting and layout information of the document, including the fonts. In this way, you can share documents without having to share the fonts. See "XPS Document Viewer," in Chapter 9, for details. The recipient will have to use Windows Vista or have an XPS file viewer.

- Adobe Acrobat (not the free reader application, but the full version available at *http://www.adobe.com*) also allows you to share documents without having to share the fonts used. However, the recipient must have a copy of either the free reader application or the full program. Windows Vista does not ship with the Acrobat reader.

- Any nonfont files that, for whatever reason, have been stored in the Fonts folder, will not show up at all, nor will they appear in any search results. To display a normal listing of the files in the Fonts folder, use the dir command at the command prompt (see Chapter 14).

- To change the font size for icons, menus, and other screen elements, go to Control Panel → [Appearance and Personalization] → Personalization → Adjust Font Size (dpi).

See also

"Control Panel"

Gadgets

See "Windows Sidebar and Gadgets," later in this chapter.

Icons

Strictly speaking, an icon is any small picture used to symbolize an object or a function in the interface. Icons commonly appear in menus and on toolbars, but the term is most often used to describe the objects that represent files and folders on your Desktop and in Windows Explorer.

Chapter 2 covers the basic use of icons, especially in the way you can open, move, copy, and delete them. Right-click any icon to display its context menu. (See "Context Menus," earlier in this chapter.)

The image used for a given icon depends on the type of object it represents, as does the procedure for customizing that icon. For example, you can customize the icons for My Computer, Recycle Bin, and other Desktop namespace objects by right-clicking on an empty area of the Desktop and going to Personalize → Change desktop icons (this option is in the Tasks list on the left side of the Control Panel). From there, you'll be able to determine which to display on the Desktop and which to hide, as well as which icon to use for each individual namespace object. For details, see "Personalization," later in this chapter.

The icon used for a document depends on its type; all *.txt* files use the same icon, all *.jpg* files use the same icon, and so on. In Windows Explorer, though, with many file types, you'll see an actual thumbnail of the file itself rather than its icon, particularly when the file is a graphics file.

You can change the icon for any Windows or Internet shortcut by right-clicking and selecting Properties → Shortcut → Change Icon. If the shortcut is for a program that's been installed on your Desktop, the Change Icon dialog box usually points to a location specified by the installation program. If it's a Windows shortcut, by default the Change Icon dialog box for a shortcut usually points to *\Windows\System32\shell32.dll*, which contains more than 200 different icons, including the standard icons for folders, disks, and so on (see Figure 3-27).

A Browse button in the Change Icon dialog box lets you search for other sources of icons, but where do you browse? You can store icons in a variety of files, including *.exe* and *.dll* files (program components) as well as *.ico* files (standalone icon files). You can even use *.bmp* (Windows bitmap) files for icons. Browsing for icons can be time-consuming, though, because the Change Icon dialog can look inside only one file at a time. The alternative is to use Explorer; the standard file icon for *.ico* files is the actual icon it contains, making it easy to peruse an entire folder full of icon files (you'll have to use any of the Icons views or the Tiles view to see thumbnails of your *.bmp* files).

Although other Windows files (such as *\windows\explorer.exe*) have additional icons, you may want to look on the Web for decent icons to decorate your workspace; there's no end to web sites that contain freely downloadable icon libraries.

 Some sites with downloadable icons and icon libraries may host spyware on the site itself, as well as with any installation program for the icons, so take care before you visit and download. Make sure to keep Windows Defender running.

Figure 3-27. To find icons to use on the Desktop, browse to \Windows\System32\shell32.dll, which contains more than 200 different icons

Notes

- Paint, the rudimentary image editor included with Windows Vista (and every version of Windows since the 1980s), allows you to create and modify *.bmp* files, but it doesn't support the *.ico* format. Furthermore, its tools for doing detail work (essential when creating the tiny images used for icons) are pretty lousy. The Microangelo package, available from *http://www.microangelo.us*, is about the best icon editor you'll find.

See also

"Personalization"

Input Fields

As the name suggests, input fields are small controls (usually found in a dialog box in which you provide required information; see Figure 3-28). A text box is one of the most common forms of input field. Essentially a miniature word processor, the text box is used for entering text. Most input fields allow only a single line of text (such as the Address Bar or the Filename field in File Open/Save dialogs), but some allow multiple lines. You can almost always right-click in a text box to display a quick menu for Cut, Copy, Paste, Delete, and Select All (see "Clipboard," earlier in this chapter). The menu also offers other options, such as inserting special characters and even changing the reading order from left to right to right to left.

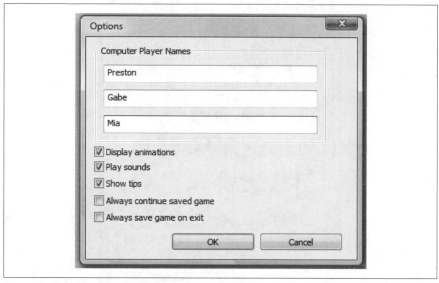

Figure 3-28. A simple input field (text box), which allows you to type a small bit of text; right-click to display Cut, Copy, Paste, Delete, and Select All

There are four common variations of input fields. The first type includes input fields made to look like labels (see the next section, "Labels"). The second is combo boxes (see "Listboxes," later in this chapter). The third is known as *counters*, which are simply input fields with up and down arrows to the right, allowing you to increment and decrement a numeric value without typing (some even have a tiny divider between the arrows, allowing you to quickly "scroll" to any value). Finally, we have password fields (Figure 3-29), which look and act just like standard input boxes except that their contents are masked with asterisks or dots to hide them from prying eyes.

Notes

- Right-click in an input field to display additional options. In addition to the Clipboard operations (Cut, Copy, and Paste), you'll see Select All, Right to Left Reading Order (to make the text right-justified), and two options for using Unicode characters (useful primarily for programmers).

- Some nonstandard input fields allow formatting (bold, italics, font selection, etc.). These "rich text" fields typically work the same as standard input fields, although they often have additional features specific to the application.

Labels

Labels are basically noninteractive pieces of text placed on dialogs used to describe a control (such as the sliders shown in Figure 3-30) that doesn't have a place for a description. Clicking labels usually has no effect.

Some labels contain a single underlined letter. Holding Alt and pressing the key for that letter will send the focus to the next control. This is useful because the input field in this example doesn't have a shortcut key of its own.

Figure 3-29. Password fields, which work like standard input fields except that the characters you type are masked with asterisks

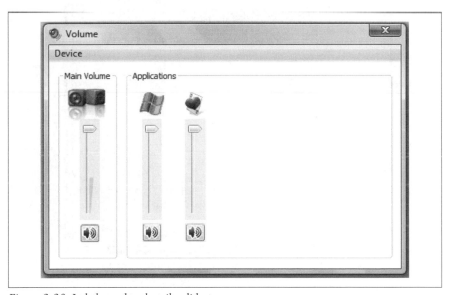

Figure 3-30. Labels used to describe sliders

Notes

- Some labels allow you to select and copy text and are distinguished because the mouse pointer changes to an "I-beam" when over the label. Strictly speaking, these are just standard input fields (without borders) that have been made to look like labels. You can see examples of this type of field by right-clicking on a file and selecting Properties.

Listboxes

A listbox is a list from which you can choose one item or many. There are four common types of listboxes:

Standard listbox

A standard listbox (see Figure 3-31) is a rectangular control that contains one or more entries. If there are more entries than can be displayed in the space allotted, scroll bars will appear as well. Click an entry to select it. If the listbox allows multiple items to be selected simultaneously, hold down the Ctrl key while clicking or pressing the Space bar to select additional items one by one, or use Shift-click to select a range of items.

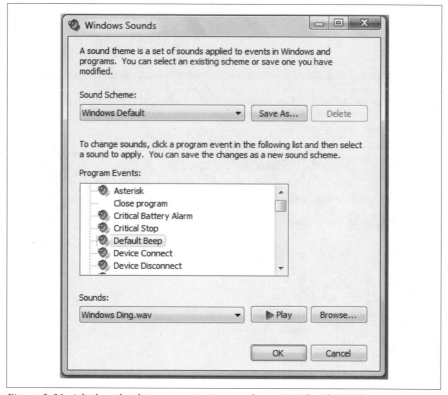

Figure 3-31. A listbox that lets you customize sounds associated with Windows events

Use the arrow keys to move up and down the list. Type a letter to jump to the first entry that begins with that letter; if there are a lot of items, you can type several letters quickly in succession to jump to the first item that begins with those letters.

Drop-down listbox

A drop-down listbox (see Figure 3-32) works much like a standard listbox, except that only the currently selected entry is shown. Click the down arrow to open the list and choose another item. Drop-down listboxes never allow multiple selections.

Figure 3-32. Drop-down listboxes, which work much like standard listboxes except that they consume less screen real estate

With the focus on a drop-down listbox, press the down arrow key to open the list, the arrow keys to navigate, and then the Tab key to jump to the next control, which will close the list automatically (press the Esc key to close the list without selecting a new item). If you press Enter to commit your selection, though, it might activate the default button (see "Buttons," earlier in this chapter).

Combo box

A combo box is a hybrid between an input field and a drop-down listbox. You can type just like in an ordinary input field, or you can click the down arrow to choose an item from the list. If you click an item, that item's caption will be placed into the text field, at which point you can edit or move on. Often, a drop-down list contains a history of previous entries you've made into a text entry field; the Address Bar is essentially a glorified combo box.

The keyboard shortcuts are the same as for drop-down listboxes and input fields (discussed earlier in this chapter). Additionally, you can begin typing and then press the down arrow, and the first entry in the list that matches what you've typed (if any) will be selected automatically.

ListView (commonly known as Details)

An enhanced version of the standard listbox, the ListView control is what appears in folder windows and File Open/Save dialogs. It's commonly used to display lists of files, but it's not unusual to see this presentation for other types of data as well (see Figure 3-33).

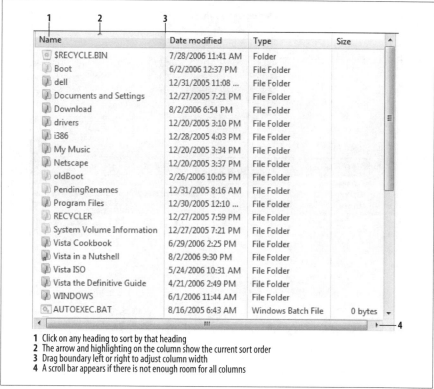

1 Click on any heading to sort by that heading
2 The arrow and highlighting on the column show the current sort order
3 Drag boundary left or right to adjust column width
4 A scroll bar appears if there is not enough room for all columns

Figure 3-33. ListView controls

The main advantage of this control is that it supports multiple, resizable columns, each of which has a header that you can usually click to sort the contents of the list (click again to reverse the sort order). In some instances, you can sort the contents of a column in multiple ways; if that's the case, when you hover your mouse over the column header, an arrow will appear. Click the arrow to reveal the multiple ways you can sort the column, and then make your choice. Drag the lines dividing the headers to resize the width of columns, or drag the headers to rearrange them.

See Chapter 2 for more information on working with the folder window. Because folders use the common ListView control, almost anything that works with a folder will work with other ListView controls. For example, in addition to selecting multiple items with Ctrl and Shift, as described for standard listboxes, you can usually select multiple items by drawing a rubber band with your mouse.

Live Taskbar Thumbnails

This feature of Windows Aero displays a thumbnail of the contents of any window on the Taskbar when the mouse hovers over the window. Above the thumbnail is the name of the application and open file. The thumbnail is actually live, as it shows what is currently happening in that window, unless the window is currently minimized. So if a video is playing, you'll see the video playing in the thumbnail, as shown in Figure 3-34. Live Taskbar thumbnails work only when your PC uses Windows Aero.

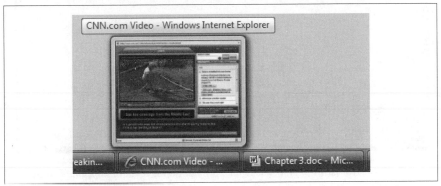

Figure 3-34. Live Taskbar thumbnails, which show you the content of any window and even the video playing inside it

See also

"Windows Aero" and "Taskbar"

Log Off

Logs off the current user.

To open

Start → [Click the right arrow] → Log Off

Ctrl-Alt-Delete → Log Off

See Chapter 10 for more information on logging on, logging off, and managing multiple users.

Menus

The menu is a place where you can cram all the functionality of a program. Rather than all of the available commands littering your screen, they are categorically arranged into cascading lists, as shown in Figure 3-35. Modern applications have become so elaborate, however, that menus are often very complex, making it a pain to have to sift through them all to find the command you want. Thus, designers invented toolbars (discussed later in this chapter) as shortcuts for the items we actually use. It makes us wonder, then, why we need menus in the first place.

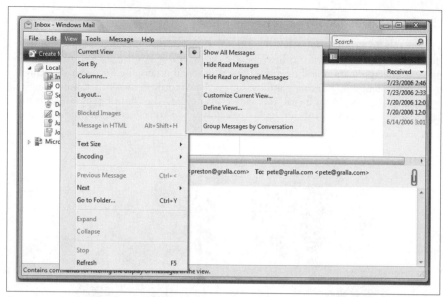

Figure 3-35. Nested (cascading) menus, which provide access to all options and features of an application

Microsoft has apparently wondered the same thing, because it has done away with menus in two of its most important applications in Windows Vista: Windows Explorer and Internet Explorer, shown in Figure 3-36. In both instances, toolbars replace menus, although if you're the kind of person who really does like menus, you can still make them appear by pressing the Alt key.

Figure 3-36. Internet Explorer and Windows Explorer use toolbars instead of menus

However, menus remain in other Windows Vista applications, and in other applications as well. If you ever get lost, menus tend to be pretty consistent across applications. For example, you can almost always find Open, Save, Print, and Exit in the File menu, just as Cut, Copy, Paste, and Undo are always in the Edit menu.

See Chapter 2 for more information on using menus. See "Context Menus," earlier in this chapter, for details on the menu that appears when you right-click on something.

Press F10 or Alt (by itself) to enter the menu, use the cursor keys to navigate, and press Enter to select an item. Once you're in the menus, press the underlined letter of a menu item to quickly jump to that item, or if no letter is underlined, press the first letter of the item's caption. You can also jump right to a specific menu from anywhere else in the application by pressing the key of the underlined letter while holding Alt. Look to the right of many menu items for additional keyboard shortcuts. For example, open the Edit menu in most applications and you'll see Ctrl-X, Ctrl-C, and Ctrl-V alongside the Cut, Copy, and Paste commands, respectively.

See also

"Windows Explorer," in Chapter 4, and "Internet Explorer," in Chapter 5

Network

The Network icon in Windows Explorer has replaced the My Network Places icon used in Windows XP. Click it and you'll see a list of all the computers connected to your network.

Notes

- Double-click the Computer icon to open Windows Explorer at the topmost level—at your computer, with all its drives listed beneath it.

See also

"Network and Sharing Center," in Chapter 7

Notification Area

The notification area, commonly known as the *Tray*, is the small area at the far right (or bottom) of the Taskbar that, by default, holds the clock and the tiny, yellow speaker icon, among other possible icons. With the exception of the clock, the purpose of the tray is to hold status icons (see Figure 3-37) placed there by Windows and other running applications. Hold the mouse cursor over the clock to see the date temporarily or click it to see a full clock. Right-click on an empty area of the Taskbar and click Properties to turn the clock on or off and to change other settings (for more details, see "Taskbar," later in this chapter).

Figure 3-37. The notification area (Tray), which holds the clock and icons for some running processes

The Tray can be a convenient place for applications to display information and provide quick access to certain features, but there is little standardization among Tray icons. Some icons are clicked, others are double-clicked, others require a right-click, and some don't get clicked at all. Some flash, some don't. You can disable most of them, but some just won't go away. Most support tool tips, so you can find out what each icon does by holding the mouse over it for a second or two.

The notification area also often has a small arrow at its extreme left. If the arrow points to the left, it means that you can display additional icons by clicking on it. If it points to the right, it means that you can hide some of the icons by clicking on it.

You can customize which icons will be displayed.

The only way to turn off the notification area completely is to hide each icon (and the clock) individually. However, you can selectively hide icons by right-clicking the Taskbar and choosing Properties → Notification Area tab. See "Taskbar and Start Menu Properties," later in this chapter, for more information.

Notes

- Right-click on the clock and select Adjust Date/Time to adjust the system date and time.

- The Notification Area is available to any application that chooses to use—or misuse—it. For example, both AOL and RealPlayer install a startup icon in the Notification Area (as well as just about anywhere else they can put one), which is a clear abuse of the intended purpose.

- The power status indicator is generally useful only on laptops. It shows a plug when the system is connected to AC power, and a battery when the system is running on the battery. The height of the color in the battery gives a rough idea of how much power is left; to get a more precise estimate, hold the pointer over the indicator until a notification pops up showing the percentage of the remaining charge.

See also

"Date and Time Properties," "Taskbar," and "Taskbar and Start Menu Properties"

Personalization

Personalize Windows Vista's appearance.

To open

Control Panel → [Appearance and Personalization] → Personalization

Command Prompt → `control desktop`

Description

This Control Panel category (see Figure 3-38) serves as the central location for customizing the way your Desktop and Windows Vista look and sound, and it contains a variety of applets that let you change everything from your desktop background to your display settings, font size, and more.

See also

"Control Panel," "Display Settings," "Change Your Color Scheme," "Desktop Background," "Screen Saver," and "Theme Settings"

Figure 3-38. Command central for personalizing your Desktop and Windows Vista

Progress Indicators

The progress indicator is a linear gauge that graphically shows the progress of a particular task, allowing you to roughly estimate the time to completion. In some cases, the indicator doesn't actually show the estimated time to completion but merely shows that it's searching (see Figure 3-39). The annoying part is that the accuracy of progress indicators is typically not very good; the value (0 to 100 percent) displayed by an indicator is based entirely on approximations the application has made. What's worse is that some programs, especially application installers, often have several consecutive progress indicators; unfortunately, these display only the progress of a particular task rather than the entire process, which obviously is not terribly helpful.

Properties

The Properties window (sometimes called the *Properties sheet*) is a dialog box that serves a very specific purpose: to display and allow changes to the settings associated with a file, folder, or other object in Windows. Most objects have Properties sheets, which are almost always accessible by right-clicking and selecting Properties, as shown in Figure 3-40. (You can also display Properties by holding Alt and double-clicking, or if the item is already highlighted, by pressing Alt-Enter.) You can access some items in the Control Panel quickly by right-clicking on various interface elements and selecting Properties. For example:

- Computer icon → Properties points to System Properties
- Taskbar or Start button → Properties points to Taskbar and Start Menu Properties

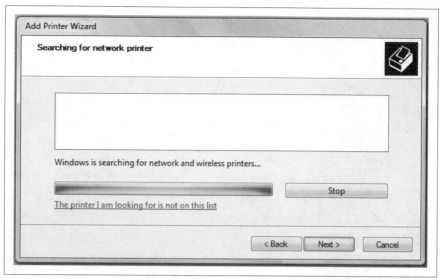

Figure 3-39. A progress indicator

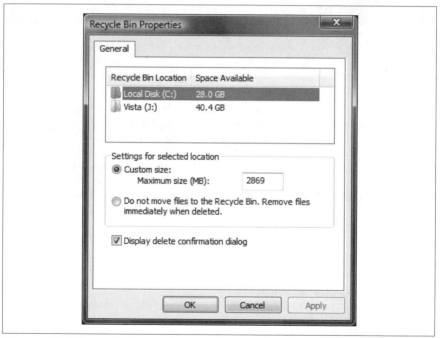

Figure 3-40. A Properties sheet—often a good place to find extra features and settings

At minimum, most Properties sheets will have a General tab, but most have more. Note that the particular information and settings available depend entirely on the object that was clicked.

Notes

- Folders, printers, and disk drives have a second property tab called Sharing. See Chapter 7 for details. Shortcuts to MS-DOS and older command-line-based programs have additional settings for legacy support such as EMS and XMS memory emulation. All command-line programs, even 32-bit applications such as the Command Prompt, have additional settings for font settings and mouse behavior.

- To see the amount of disk space used by a group of files, select them and then view the Properties entry for the selected list. On the first tab, you'll see the size of the whole group. Change any of the attributes, and the change will be applied to all of the files in the selected group. (If any of the files in the selected group has a different attribute from other files in the group, it will look different, indicating that the files have different settings and that if you change it, you will apply the change to all of them. This poor user interface design was discussed in "Combo Boxes," earlier in this chapter.)

- Certain types of files, such as Microsoft Word files, will have additional property pages that are generated by the application that created them. Word files, for example, have pages that let you summarize and view the statistics for documents.

- Among the settings in a Properties sheet for files are the Attributes (Read-only, Hidden, and Archive). See "Attrib," in Chapter 14, for details.

Radio Buttons

Radio buttons are used for mutually exclusive settings. Clicking on one causes any other that has been pressed to pop up, just like on an old car radio. The button with the dot in the middle is the one that has been selected (see Figure 3-41). Sometimes you'll see more than one group of buttons, with a separate outline around each group. In this case, you can select one radio button from each group. Functionally, a group of radio buttons works like a standard listbox.

Navigating radio buttons with the keyboard can be confusing. When using the Tab key to jump between controls, Windows considers a group of radio buttons to be a single control. When the Tab key places the focus on a single radio button, you'll need to use the arrow keys to select a different one; otherwise, another press of the Tab key will jump to a different control, seemingly skipping a whole bunch of radio buttons.

Recycle Bin

In the early days of computing, once you deleted a file it was gone. An unerase tool (available as part of Norton Utilities) was commonly used to recover accidentally deleted files. Microsoft caught on, though, and a while back gave Windows its own Recycle Bin—a feature that gives nearly every file a second chance, so to speak.

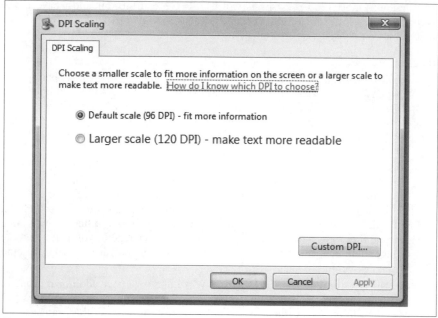

Figure 3-41. Two radio buttons are used to allow you to choose only one of the available options

Drag any item from the Desktop to the Recycle Bin icon to delete it, as shown in Figure 3-42. When you drag the item and hold it over the Recycle Bin, an arrow appears next to the item. Drop it in the bin and the item disappears. Selecting File → Delete on the menu bar of a folder also moves items to the Recycle Bin, as does selecting the item and then pressing the Delete key. By default, files are not deleted immediately but are stored until the Recycle Bin runs out of space, at which point they are deleted, oldest first, to make space. Until that time, you can retrieve them by double-clicking on the Recycle Bin icon, browsing through the contents of the Recycle Bin window, and dragging or sending the file elsewhere.

Figure 3-42. Dragging an icon onto the Recycle Bin deletes the icon

When you open the Recycle Bin by double-clicking it, you'll see that it's a specialized version of Windows Explorer, shown in Figure 3-43. Buttons let you empty the entire bin at once or restore all items at once. You can also right-click any file and select Restore.

To access the Recycle Bin with the keyboard, it's easiest to simply open Windows Explorer and navigate to Desktop → Recycle Bin.

Figure 3-43. A specialized version of Windows Explorer, with buttons for emptying the Recycle Bin and restoring all items

Files dragged to the Recycle Bin (or that are otherwise deleted) from floppies, network drives, or other external drives such as ZIP drives will not be stored in the Recycle Bin. They are simply deleted.

Each user account has its own Recycle Bin. So if there are two accounts on a Windows Vista PC, one named Gabe and the other Mia, when Gabe is logged in he'll see files that he's deleted but not ones that Mia has deleted, and vice versa.

The Recycle Bin's Properties window has one tab, General. This tab has entries for the current user as well as for local volumes, as you can see in Figure 3-44.

The General tab lets you customize how the Recycle Bin works in the following ways:

- Highlight any entry and you can specify how much of the available storage for that entry you can allocate to the Recycle Bin. Select Custom Size and then type in the amount of space, in megabytes, you want devoted to the Recycle Bin. The amount of space that the files in the Recycle Bin actually use is displayed in the Bin's status bar when you open it.

- Highlight any entry and you can specify that deleted files are not to be stored in the Recycle Bin for that entry, but instead are to be removed immediately from the disk. Make this selection if you don't want to have to remember to empty your Recycle Bin to delete files, although it can be rather dangerous if you're careless with the Delete key.

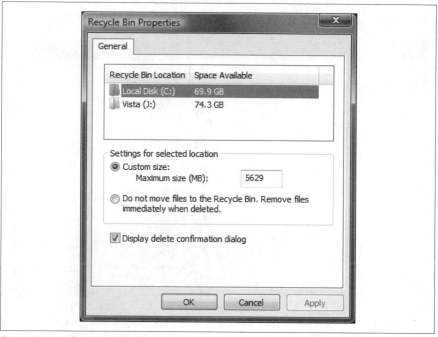

Figure 3-44. The General Tab of the Recycle Bin Properties sheet, which shows you recycle bins for the current account as well as local volumes

- A checkbox asks whether you want to display a delete confirmation dialog. This checkbox affects all Recycle Bin entries. You can have the delete confirmation turned off at the same time that the "Do not move files to the Recycle Bin" setting is turned on. This means that it's possible to permanently delete files without any warnings at all.

> To delete a single file without sending it to the Recycle Bin, use Shift-Delete in Windows Explorer or the del command at the command prompt.

Notes

- With the Details or Tiles view, you can sort the contents of the Recycle Bin by name, by original location (useful in case you want to put something back where it was), by the date deleted, by type, by size, or by the date the file was last modified. Click on any of the headings to sort contents by that heading. Click again on the same heading to reverse the order of the sort.

- You can delete the entire contents of a floppy disk by dragging the disk icon to the Recycle Bin. You will be prompted for confirmation. You cannot drag a hard disk (such as C:) to the Recycle Bin, however, nor can you drag key components of the user interface, such as the Control Panel, to it. (Well, you can drag them there, but they won't go in.) Note that you can remove some of these Desktop items by right-clicking and selecting Delete.

Regional and Language Options

Language and localization settings affecting the display of numbers, currency, times, and dates.

To open

Control Panel → [Clock, Language, and Region] → Regional and Language Options

Command Prompt → `intl.cpl`

Command Prompt → `control international`

Description

Numbers, times, dates, and currency are displayed differently in different parts of the world, and the Regional and Language Options dialog (see Figure 3-45) allows you to choose your display preferences in painful detail.

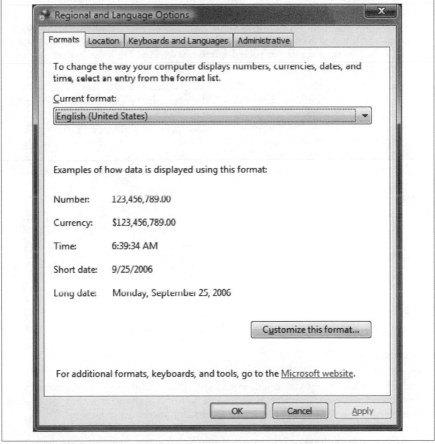

Figure 3-45. Choosing the way dates, times, and currency are displayed with the Regional and Language Options dialog

This dialog has the following tabs:

Formats

Select your language from the list. If you want to further customize any language setting, click "Customize this format." The settings in this dialog are fairly self-explanatory, although it's important to realize that the entries in the language list are not "themes." That is, if you customize your settings and then change the language in the list, those customized settings will be lost. Note that this setting affects dates, times, currency, and so on, but not the actual character set of the language. To add or change a character set, use the Keyboards and Languages tab.

Location

Choose your location. This won't affect the format of dates, time, currency, and so on, but it will tell any external services you subscribe to over the Internet your location so that they will deliver the right news to you.

Keyboards and Languages

Click Manage Languages if you want to add support for additional languages or remove support from languages already on your system. Click Settings if you want to change your input language. If more than one language is installed, the Language Bar and Key Settings features will be available, which you can use to easily switch between the installed languages with a Desktop bar or keyboard shortcut, respectively.

Administrative

Most programs should be able to detect the preferred language, and if supported, adjust their interfaces accordingly. You use the "Language for non-Unicode programs" option to add support for older programs that don't recognize the settings made in the Languages tab. Click Change System Locale to do that. If you want to apply the changes you've made in the Regional and Language Options dialog box to other accounts on your system, click "Copy to reserved accounts."

See also

"Control Panel"

Screen Saver

Choose a screensaver and change its behavior.

To open

Control Panel → [Appearance and Personalization] → Personalization → Screen Saver

Description

Years ago, monochrome monitors, when left on for long periods of time, would be ruined when the images displayed would get "burned in." So, screensavers were invented to blank the screen after a certain period of inactivity. It wasn't long before screensavers started showing animations instead of just a blank screen. Today, the concept of monitor burn-in is obsolete, but screensavers are still fun and can even provide security from prying eyes by obscuring the screen when you walk away from your computer. Choose from one of the available screensavers here and click Settings to configure it or Preview to see it in action (see Figure 3-46).

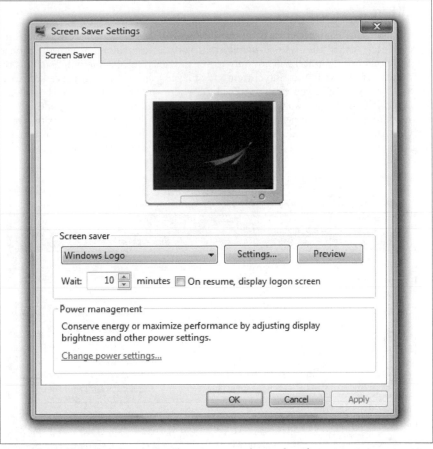

Figure 3-46. The Screen Saver tab, where you can select and configure a screensaver

Choose the length of inactivity before the selected screensaver is activated. A computer is considered inactive if no mouse or keyboard entry is received; updates to the screen, such as progress indicators or animations, don't count and won't stop a screensaver from being invoked. Use the "On resume, display logon screen" feature to lock up access to the computer once a screensaver has been invoked.

Click Settings to configure how the screensaver will run. In many instances, you won't be able to configure the screensaver, but in others you may be able to change things such as its motion and speed.

Note that the screensaver can interfere with some programs, so you may want to temporarily disable it if you're experiencing a problem backing up to tape or burning a CD, for example.

You also can start any particular screensaver from the command line or from Windows Explorer by launching the corresponding *.scr* file.

See also

"Control Panel," "Display Settings," "Change Your Color Scheme," "Desktop Background," and "Personalization"

Scroll Bars

A scroll bar (see Figure 3-47) is a vertical or horizontal bar on a window with a little box inside it (called the *slider* or *thumb*) that you can drag along it with the mouse. Applications use the scroll bar not only to set the position of something (such as the text cursor in a text box or the currently displayed page of a word processor document), but also to give you visual feedback of where you are and how much stuff you can't see. The thumb shows you where you are in the entire piece of text, and the size of the thumb shows what percentage you're viewing. (A large thumb means that most of what's there is visible and a small thumb means that there's a lot you can't see.) The scroll bar usually becomes disabled (grayed out) if there's no scrolling to be done.

Figure 3-47. The scroll bar, which lets you view all of the items in a folder when the folder window is not sufficiently large

Click the up or down arrow to move the scroll bar incrementally, or drag the thumb with the mouse to move to the desired position. You can also click in the gray areas between the arrows and the thumb to move up or down a page at a time.

It is possible to use the cursor keys and PgUp/PgDn keys to control the scroll bar if it has the focus. If the scroll bar is part of another control, it cannot receive the focus to receive keyboard input directly. Instead, use the cursor keys to navigate in the listbox or input field with which the scroll bar is associated. The thumb blinks if it has the focus.

Send To

Send a selected item to a program, disk drive, folder, or email recipient.

To open

File or folder's context menu → Send To

Description

Right-click on any file or folder and select Send To to send it to any one of several locations, people, or programs—including any disk drive, any folder, an email recipient, or a fax recipient—as well as create a shortcut to it on the Desktop or compress it in a ZIP archive. For example, if the destination is an application, the application will be started and the selected file(s) will be opened. If the destination is a folder or a drive, the item(s) will be copied or moved (depending on several circumstances described in Chapter 2). When you install a new program, it may install an entry in the Send To menu so that you can right-click any file and select the new program's entry in Send To, and that program will open the selected file. Figure 3-48 shows the Send To menu.

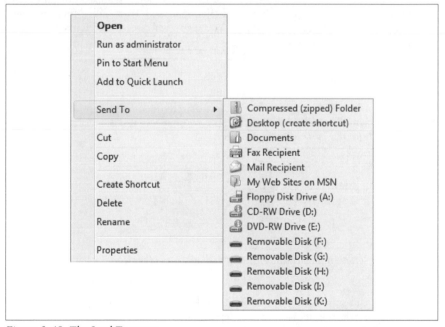

Figure 3-48. The Send To menu

When you select an item from the Send To menu, you're in fact sending it to one of the shortcuts in your Send To folder, located in *\Users\username\SendTo*. The result of using Send To is the same as dragging and dropping the icon onto the shortcut, but of course, it's far more convenient to use Send To than to have to drag items to that folder.

Notes

- The options that appear in the Send To menu are determined by the contents of the *\Users\username\SendTo* folder. To add another Send To recipient, create a shortcut in that folder. For example, if you put a shortcut to *notepad.exe* into that folder (which I find extremely handy), you could easily open any file in Notepad, regardless of the file type.

Send To works a bit differently depending on the destination. Sending to a folder (including the Recycle Bin) actually moves the file there (or copies it if the source and destination are on different drives); sending to a program simply opens the file. You can use Send To on shortcuts with impunity, but when you use it on an original file, remember that you may actually be moving the file.

- If you place a shortcut to your Send To folder in your Send To folder, you can create new Send To destinations simply by sending them to the Send To folder! (Say that five times fast.)
- Place shortcuts to folders in Send To for an easy way to organize your files. You can work on files on the Desktop and then use Send To to move them to their storage location when you're done. You can even create shortcuts to shared folders on other machines.

Shortcuts

A shortcut is a link to a program, file, folder, drive, system object, printer, or URL. Shortcuts are actually small files that come in two flavors: Windows shortcuts (*.lnk*) and Internet shortcuts (*.url*). (See Figure 3-49.)

Figure 3-49. A standard shortcut icon, distinguishable from other icons by the little curved arrow

Although you can start a program or open a folder by double-clicking on its icon on the Desktop or selecting its icon in the Start menu, odds are that the application is stored elsewhere and you're using a shortcut only to access the application executable. If you find that there's a program, document, folder, or web site you use often, it's easy to create a shortcut to the object.

There are several ways to create a shortcut:

- Use the Explorer to navigate to the directory where the program's executable (*.exe*) is stored; if the program is a Windows component, its executable is probably in the *\Windows\System32* folder. Otherwise, the executable is probably located in a subfolder of *Program Files*. Once you've located the *.exe* file, use the right mouse button to drag it to the location of your choice (typically the Desktop or the Start menu) and select "Create shortcut here" from the context menu that appears. The same procedure works for folders, drives, and documents as well. You can find more information on right-dragging in Chapter 2.

- Right-click on an empty area of the Desktop (or any folder) and select New → Shortcut. This two-page wizard prompts you for only two pieces of information: the full path of the object and the name of the resulting shortcut. This procedure is more laborious than the others listed here, but it does have the advantage of allowing you to create a shortcut to a program with command-line parameters.

- A quick way to create a shortcut to a folder (or drive) is to open the folder and then drag the control icon (the small icon at the left of the Address Bar) onto the Desktop or other destination. If you instead drag the folder itself, you'll create a copy of the folder on the Desktop, independent of the original folder.

- Right-click any file or system object (such as an item in the Control Panel or the Printers and Faxes folder) and select Create Shortcut. A shortcut to the selected object will be created in the same folder. Once the shortcut has been created, you can move it anywhere you like.

- Open any web page in Internet Explorer and click the Add to Favorites (+) button to add it to the Internet Explorer Favorites Center. (For details, see Chapter 5.)

- Open any web page in Internet Explorer and drag the little icon in the Address Bar (immediately to the left of the *http://*) onto the Desktop or other destination.

Users commonly place shortcuts on the Desktop and Start menu for quick access to programs and documents, but you can really place them anywhere. One of the purposes of having a central Documents folder is to enforce the notion that you should arrange documents and personal files by project, not by application. This means that you might place Internet shortcuts and Windows shortcuts in the same folder as WordPerfect and Excel documents, making it easy to group all the resources for a particular project together and decreasing the time spent repeatedly trying to locate files and data.

You can also create a shortcut to a local or network printer. Dragging a file onto the shortcut sends that file to the printer without requiring you to open the associated program, which is handy if you do a lot of printing. Putting printer shortcuts in your Send To menu lets you conveniently send files to printers other than your default printer.

Shortcut properties

Shortcuts have a small curved arrow superimposed on the lower left of their icon, and the label "Shortcut" is added after the name of the object (for example, *Budget.doc – Shortcut*). This arrow helps distinguish shortcuts from the files to which they're linked.

To get more information about a shortcut, go to its Properties sheet (right-click it and select Properties). Figure 3-50 shows an example of the second page of a shortcut's properties. The sheet will vary slightly, depending on the object for which a shortcut has been created. For example, a program's shortcut Properties sheet contains a tab that a file's sheet doesn't—the Compatibility tab, which lets you change how earlier programs run to ensure that they will run properly in Windows Vista.

Figure 3-50. The second page of a Windows shortcut's properties

Here are the options available for a shortcut:

Target

> This field appears in the Properties sheet of Windows shortcuts (see the "URL" entry, later in this list, for its counterpart in Internet shortcuts). If the shortcut is to an executable with a command-line equivalent (including, but not limited to, Command Prompt programs), or even to a folder, the full command line required to activate the target is specified here.

> If it's a shortcut to Notepad, you'll see just *Notepad.exe* here. If it's a shortcut to Adobe Photoshop, it'll look like *c:\Program Files\Adobe\Photoshop\Photoshop.exe*. Note that the full path is required for Photoshop, but not for Notepad because Notepad is already in a folder in the system path (described in Chapter 6).

> This field is also convenient for adding command-line parameters that are typically used to pass options to the target program, so you don't have to do it manually every time it's started. For example, instead of creating an ordinary shortcut to *Explorer.exe*, create a shortcut to *Explorer.exe /n,/e,/select,c:* to launch Explorer rooted at My Computer with drive *C:* selected. See "Windows Explorer," in Chapter 4, for details on this syntax.

Start in

> If the shortcut is to a program, this option specifies the working folder in which the program will first look for files to open or save.

Shortcut key

You can map a keyboard sequence to open or execute the shortcut (sometimes called a *keyboard accelerator*), allowing you to activate the shortcut without having to hunt for the shortcut icon. For instance, you might want to map the keys Ctrl-Alt-E to a shortcut to Explorer.

Press any key on the keyboard here and you will see Ctrl-Alt-*key* appear as the shortcut key sequence. Type that sequence to launch the shortcut without clicking on it. You should check Appendix B to make sure you aren't creating conflicts with any existing keyboard accelerator.

Run

A drop-down list allows you to specify whether the target application should run in its normal window, be maximized, or be minimized. The Minimized option can be useful for applications you'd like to have started automatically when Windows starts (see "Notes," later in this section). The Maximized option can be useful for applications you'd like to run in full-screen mode, but don't automatically remember their window state from session to session.

Open File Location

Click this button to open the folder containing the original file to which this shortcut links. The original file will be selected in the folder window.

Change Icon

By default, the icon used for the shortcut is the same as its target; in the case of Internet shortcuts, the icon is simply an Internet Explorer logo. See "Icons," earlier in this chapter, for more information on customizing icons.

Advanced

If the shortcut is to a program, this will allow you to run the program as an administrator. There's also an option for running the program in a separate memory space.

URL

The URL field is the Internet shortcut counterpart to the Target field, described earlier. It simply contains the full address (URL) of the page to which it's linked.

Compatibility tab

The Compatibility tab appears only in shortcuts to programs and is not available for Windows components or applications that Windows knows to be fully compatible with Windows Vista. Generally, you'll never need to mess with these settings, unless you're using an older Windows or DOS program that behaves strangely in Windows Vista. You'll probably need to experiment with these settings, or possibly contact the manufacturer of the application for suggestions, to get the program to work most reliably.

 If you have problems running older DOS programs in Vista, try the open source DOSBox (*http://dosbox.sourceforge.net*). It does a remarkable job of running legacy DOS programs and games—it can even emulate a Sound Blaster card for legacy DOS games.

Options, Font, Layout, and Colors

Shortcuts to Command Prompt applications have four additional tabs—Options, Font, Layout, and Colors—that are all used to control the options of the command prompt environment in which the program will run. The settings in these extra tabs are described in Chapter 10 and are also available from the control menu of the Command Prompt window.

Notes

- Because shortcuts are merely links to applications and not the applications them-selves, you can delete shortcuts without fear of any permanent damage. If you want to actually delete an application, use Add or Remove Programs, and the associated shortcuts will probably be removed as part of the uninstall process.

- To have one or more shortcuts launched automatically when Windows starts, place them in your Start → Programs → Startup menu. See "Start Menu," later in this chapter, for details.

Shut Down

Shut down the system, restart the computer, log off, switch to another user account, lock the computer, or put it into a power-saving mode.

To open

Start → Click one of the Shut Off buttons, or the right arrow next to them

Description

You should never simply turn off a Windows Vista machine, because the system caches data in memory and needs time to write it out to disk before it is turned off. Always use a Shut Down option before you turn off the power.

Windows Vista has significantly changed the way you turn off your computer, and it may at first be disconcerting to those who are used to the simpler Windows XP shut-down procedure. Click the Start button, and on the far right two buttons and a right arrow appear, as shown in Figure 3-51.

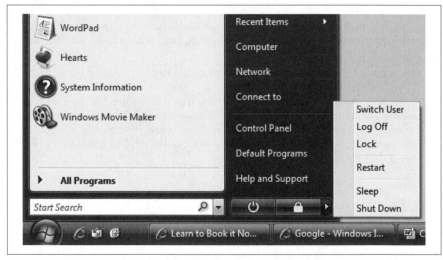

Figure 3-51. Windows Vista's new shutdown options

Here are your shutdown options:

Sleep

The Sleep button puts your PC into a new power-saving *hybrid sleep* mode that combines Windows XP's standby and hibernate modes. It puts your PC into a low-power mode so that it appears to be shut off, and it uses very little power but saves all of your work to your hard disk—including not only the programs and files you were using, but also window locations and sizes. In other words, it saves the precise state of your computer. To wake your PC out of sleep, press the Power button and it quickly comes back to life—far more quickly than if it had been shut off. You'll have to unlock it by supplying your password, at which point the PC will resume its previous state.

Lock

This locks your PC and displays the logon screen. Return to the Desktop by entering your password. If you set up your account without a password, you'll be able to return to the Desktop by clicking the account name on the screen.

The logon screen also lets you switch to another account. Click the Switch User button, select the account you want, and log on.

Arrow menu

Click the arrow and you'll be able to switch users, log off, lock your computer, restart, put your PC to sleep, or completely shut it down. If you have a laptop, you'll have an additional item here, Hibernate, which is similar to Sleep, except the power is completely shut off and the state is saved to the hard disk (in Sleep the power is mostly, but not completely, shut off). It takes slightly longer to revive a PC from Hibernate than it does from Sleep (if you shut off the power to your computer while it is in Sleep mode, it is effectively in Hibernate mode because of the new hybrid sleep feature).

Start Menu

The central location for your application shortcuts and many Windows features.

To open

Desktop → Start

Press the Windows logo key, if you've got one.

Ctrl-Esc

Description

The Start menu was one of Microsoft's answers to the growing size and complexity of the Windows operating system when it was introduced in Windows 95. Since then, other features have been introduced to compensate for the Start menu's inadequacies, such as the Quick Launch Toolbar, the new Windows Vista–style Start menu, and the new Start Search input box.

One of the subtler changes to the Start menu is that when you're using Aero Glass, the menu is slightly transparent (translucent, really) so that you can see the content underneath it in a hazy kind of way.

Here is a quick rundown of the items you'll find in the Start menu, shown in Figure 3-52. Note that some of these items may be hidden as a result of changing the Start Menu settings.

Figure 3-52. The basic, unadorned Windows Start menu

All Programs

While the Desktop is commonly used to hold icons for the most frequently used programs, the All Programs menu is designed to hold icons for every program installed on your computer. Hold your mouse over the arrow or click it to see a list of all the programs installed on your PC. Some programs are listed directly on the All Programs menu when you click it, and others are organized in folders (Games, Microsoft Office, etc.). The Windows Vista All Programs menu differs significantly from the Windows XP All Programs menu. The Windows XP All Programs menu cascaded; the Windows Vista All Programs menu shows the programs directly on the Start menu itself. Figure 3-53 appears when you click All Programs, and Figure 3-54 appears when you then click the Games folder.

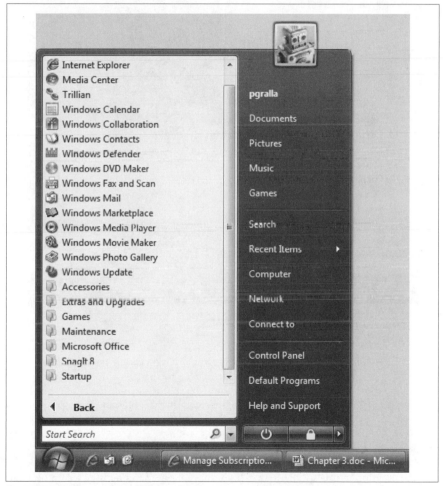

Figure 3-53. The result of clicking All Programs

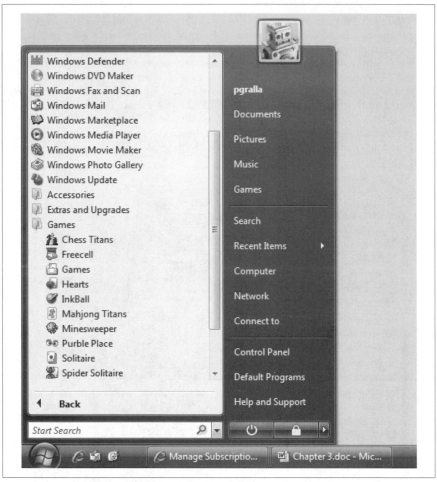

Figure 3-54. The result of clicking the Games folder

You can drag and drop programs to any location on the All Programs menu, including inside folders, to change the location where it appears. When you do this, you're not moving the actual program itself, but instead a shortcut to the program. (See "Shortcuts," earlier in this chapter, for details about how shortcuts work.)

All Programs → Startup

To have a program run automatically when Windows starts, place a shortcut to the program in this special folder. If you have more than one user set up on your computer, you'll want to control whether the program starts up automatically for just you or for all users, so instead of dropping it right in your Start menu, right-click on the Start button, choose Open All Users or Explore All Users, click Programs, and then click Startup. From that folder you come to, you can add or delete shortcuts for startup programs.

Recently Used Programs
Located just above All Programs, this is a list of the programs you've most recently used. Click any icon to run the program. For security reasons, you may want to disable this menu. To do so, right-click on the Taskbar and choose Properties → Start Menu, uncheck the box next to "Store and display a list of recently opened programs," and then click OK.

Internet, Email
These two items are user-customizable links to your favorite web browser and email program, respectively. By default, they're set to Internet Explorer and Windows Mail, but you can replace them with any programs properly registered as web browsers and email clients. See "Taskbar and Start Menu Properties," later in this chapter, for details on how to change what's displayed here.

User Account
At the top of the Start menu is your user account icon. Click it to manage your user account. Clicking this icon brings you to the same Control Panel applet as if you followed the path Control Panel → User Accounts and Family Safety → User Accounts.

 For advanced options for controlling user accounts, at a command prompt type **control userpasswords2**, and use the resulting dialog box.

username Button
Just below the User Account icon is a button which, when clicked, opens Windows Explorer to the *username* folder, which contains personal documents, Desktop settings, Favorites, and personal information for the currently logged-on user.

Documents, Pictures, Music
Clicking any of these buttons brings you to the corresponding folders for the current user account—*username\Documents*, *username\Pictures*, and *username\ Music*.

Games
This button leads you to the Games folder, which has a list of installed games. It's the same list you'll find if you choose All Programs → Games.

Search
This brings you to Search. For details, see "Search," in Chapter 4.

Recent Items
This is a list of automatically generated links to the last dozen or so documents that were opened. Click the links to open the documents in their default applications. For security reasons, you may want to disable this menu. To do so, right-click on the Taskbar and choose Properties → Start Menu, uncheck the box next to "Store and display a list of recently opened files," and then click OK.

Favorites
This is a mirror of the current user's Favorites folder (*\Users\username\Favorites*) and the All Users' Favorites folder (*\Users\All Users\Favorites*). Although this is the same menu you'll see in Windows Explorer and Internet Explorer, the shortcuts in this menu will launch whatever browser is currently registered as the default. By default, this menu is not displayed. To turn it on, right-click on the Taskbar and choose Properties → Start Menu, click Customize, check the box next to "Favorites menu," and click OK.

If you're a fan of the Run box from Windows XP, you can have it displayed on the Start menu. Right-click on the Taskbar and choose Properties → Start Menu, click Customize, check the box next to "Run command," and click OK. As a practical matter, there's no real need for this box, though, because the Start Search box does everything that Run does, and more.

Shut Down
> See "Shut Down," earlier in this chapter.

Log Off
> See "Log Off," earlier in this chapter.

Start Search
> This lets you do a quick search for files, folders, programs, and sites you've visited. See "Start Search," later in this chapter.

Computer
> This opens Windows Explorer to the Computer view of your PC, the topmost level of Windows Explorer, and displays all of your drives.

Network
> See "Network," earlier in this chapter.

Connect To
> This opens the Connect to a Network dialog box, which lets you connect to wireless, dial-up, and Virtual Private Network (VPN) networks. For details, see Chapter 7.

Control Panel
> See "Control Panel," earlier in this chapter.

Default Programs
> Opens the Default Programs Control Panel applet, which lets you change a variety of settings related to how you run programs in Windows Vista, such as choosing your default programs for email, browsing the Web, and playing music. You can get to this applet via the Control Panel by going to Control Panel → Programs → Default Programs. For more details, see Chapter 10.

Help and Support
> This opens the Windows Help and Support Center, where you can search for help, launch troubleshooters, and get help online.

Notes

- If you want to place a new shortcut in your Start menu, remove an existing shortcut from your Start menu, or rearrange your Start menu shortcuts, you can drag and drop shortcuts in your Start menu almost as easily as you can in Explorer or on your Desktop. When you start dragging, an insertion line will appear where you can drop the shortcut; if the mouse pointer changes to a circle with a line through it, you're over a portion of the Start menu that you can't customize. To drag new shortcuts into the Start menu, start dragging and hover the mouse cursor over the Start button for a second or two; it will open automatically, allowing you to complete your drag. Finally, you can right-click any shortcut in your Start menu, allowing you to delete it, change its properties, or even rename it in place. I frequently use this feature to make certain application shortcuts more accessible by placing items on the Desktop that otherwise would be buried many menus deep.

- If you're a fan of the Windows 2000–style Start menu, you can use that instead of the Windows Vista one. Right-click the Taskbar, select Properties → Start Menu → Classic Start menu, and click OK.

- You can also add programs and folders to the top of the Start menu, to the Default Programs list, by dragging and dropping their icons onto the Start button. In addition, you can instead drag them to *C:\Users\username\AppData\Roaming\Microsoft\Windows\Start Menu*. You should do this only for programs that you use fairly often. Good programs to add there might be the Explorer and the Command Prompt. Adding folders at this level is a great way to organize all of your programs into categories. Once you have created new folders, you can move the program shortcuts from the Start Menu → Programs folders into your own folders and leave all the other shortcuts (uninstalls, READMEs, etc.) behind.

- By default, dragging any files or other objects directly into the Start menu will create shortcuts to those items, which is inconsistent with the way Windows handles drag and drop elsewhere (see Chapter 2). If you're dragging an existing shortcut or a folder full of shortcuts into the Start menu, hold the Shift key to force Windows to move (or the Ctrl key to copy) the items, rather than create shortcuts to them.

- Start → All Programs can get fairly cluttered, because most programs add shortcuts to this menu as part of their installation process. Don't be afraid to rearrange and consolidate your shortcuts here; you probably never use most of them anyway.

- To bypass the programs in the Startup folder, hold down the Shift key while the system is booting. Keep holding it down until the Desktop has completely loaded.

- Shortcuts that appear in Start → All Programs and Start → Favorites are saved for the currently logged-on user, as noted several times throughout this section. If you have more than one user configured on your machine and you want any of these items to appear for all of those users (everyone may want to use the installed word processor, for example), open Explorer and navigate to the *C:\ProgramData\Microsoft\Windows\Start Menu* folder. There's also a folder for each configured user in *C:\Users\username\Start Menu*, as well as a Default User folder (a template for subsequently added users) in *C:\Users\Default*. You may want to delegate shortcuts to these various folders, depending on their use. Note that if a shortcut is listed in a user's personal Start Menu folder as well as the ProgramData Start Menu folder, it will appear twice in that user's Start menu. The same goes for the Desktop and Send To folders (both discussed earlier in this chapter).

See also

"Taskbar and Start Menu Properties," "Start Search," "Log Off," "Control Panel," and "Network," in this chapter, and "Search," in Chapter 4

Start Search

Windows Vista integrates its search directly into the user interface itself, through the Start Search input box that appears when you click the Start button (see the preceding section, "Start Menu"). Type in the first few letters of the term you're searching for, and a list will appear of matching objects, organized by category: Programs, Favorites and History, Files (which includes folders), and Communications (which includes email and newsgroup posts). As you type in more letters of your term, your search narrows. Click the file, folder, program, or communication you want to run or open. Figure 3-55 shows a typical example of a search.

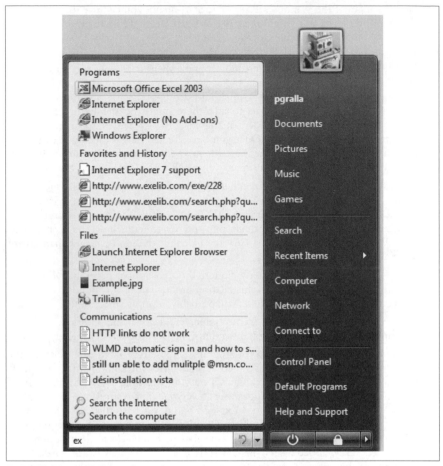

Figure 3-55. Typical search results

When you use the Start Search box, you also have the choice of searching the Internet or the index on your PC. Choose Search the Internet, or Search Everywhere. For details about the index and searching, see Chapter 4.

The Start Search input box has obvious uses for finding files and emails, but don't overlook its capability to help you run programs as well. The Start menu lists many common Windows Vista applications and accessories, plus any third-party applications you've installed. It is far from complete, though, and navigating to the program you want is often fairly tedious. The Start Search box can cut through that tedium.

Ironically, the increasing complexity of the system pushes even the most graphically oriented user back in the direction of the command line. Just about the quickest way to run any program that isn't already on your Desktop is to type the name of the program at the command line. Windows Vista offers two different command lines: the Address Bar and the Command Prompt window. You can use the Start Search box on the Start menu as a quick and convenient command prompt as well.

If you keep an Address Bar visible at all times (see "Address Bar," earlier in this chapter), it is by far the most convenient of the three command lines. The Start Search box is a close second. However, if you are a heavy user of command-line utilities, you may still find a Command Prompt window most useful. The Command Prompt window has an advantage in that it provides useful file management commands such as dir, del, copy, and so on.

For the most part, though, you can use the three command lines interchangeably. If you type the name of a Windows GUI application, it will launch in its own window. If you type the name of a text-based program (for example, *ping*) it will display its output in the current Command Prompt window or, if issued from the Address Bar or Run dialog, will launch its own Command Prompt window, which will last only as long as the command itself executes.

If you use the Start Search box to run programs from a command line, you won't have to type their full names. Just type the first few letters, and a list of matching programs, files, folders, and web sites you've visited will appear. Click the program you want to run, and press Enter.

Notes

- One important difference between the one-line prompts (Address or Start Search) and a Command Prompt window is the context in which commands run. A command interpreter, or shell, always has a particular context, or environment, in which it runs. This environment can create significant differences in the results when you type a command name.
- A number of commands can be issued only at a Command Prompt window (documented in Chapter 14), and all of them are unavailable from the Run prompt or Address Bar.

See also

"Address Bar," earlier in this chapter, and "Search," in Chapter 4

Status Bar

The Status Bar is a panel at the bottom of each window (part of the same frame that contains the title bar) that gives information about the contents of the window. The standard Status Bar shown in Figure 3-56 has several sections, each of which is used to show a relevant statistic or setting.

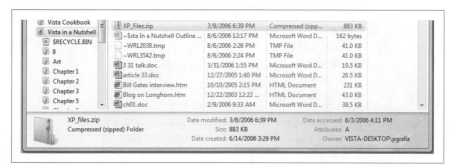

Figure 3-56. The Status Bar, which often shows useful information

Some elements of the Status Bar respond to clicks and double-clicks, although there's no standard for any user interaction. If an application has a Status Bar, you can usually hide it or make it visible as an entry in the View menu. Some programs even let you configure the Status Bar with the information that is important to you. (Try right-clicking on the Status Bar for configuration options.)

The Status Bar changes according to the program or application in use. The Status Bar in Windows Explorer also changes according to what object is currently highlighted. For a file, for example, it shows name, date modified, file size, date created, and so on. For a folder, it displays the number of items.

System Tray

See "Notification Area," earlier in this chapter.

Tabbed Dialogs

Tabs are used in dialog boxes when there are too many settings to fit on the same page (see Figure 3-57).

Figure 3-57. Tabbed dialogs

Activate a tab by clicking on it. The active tab (or page) is visibly more prominent than the rest, and the displayed settings typically fall within the category depicted by the caption of the selected tab.

When changing settings in a dialog box, the rule is that all settings behave as though they were on the same page. That is, if you change a setting under one tab, switch to another tab and change a setting there, and then click OK, both settings will be implemented. Unfortunately, some application developers don't follow these rules. Sometimes the tab selection itself is a setting; in the example just given, this means that only one of these settings would be implemented and the other would be lost. The other problem occurs when settings are saved when you flip between tabs.

Press Ctrl-Tab to move to the next tabbed page or Shift-Ctrl-Tab to move in reverse.

Taskbar

The Taskbar, shown in Figure 3-58, contains the Start Menu button, buttons representing all open application windows, the notification area (also known as the Tray, discussed earlier in this chapter), and any optional toolbars (see "Toolbars," later in this chapter).

Figure 3-58. The Taskbar, with buttons that appear for each open window

The Start button isn't terribly complicated: just click on it to open the Start menu (discussed earlier in this chapter).

You can keep track of all running applications by looking in the portion of the Taskbar between the Start button and the Tray. Nearly every currently open window is represented by a button on your Taskbar. Click the button of a corresponding window to bring that window to the top (if it happens to be obscured) and shift focus to that window. If the window is currently active, clicking its Taskbar button will minimize (hide) it. The currently active window appears pushed in, and any others appear as normal buttons. If a window has been minimized (see "Windows," later in this chapter), it will also appear as a normal button, indistinguishable from those for visible windows. Right-click on a Taskbar button to access the window's control menu (also covered in "Windows"), allowing you, among other things, to close a window without first having to restore it.

A notable change in the Taskbar with Windows Vista is what Microsoft calls live Taskbar thumbnails (you need to be running Aero for this to work). Hover your mouse over an active window in the Taskbar and a thumbnail of the window appears, with the name of the file or windows showing above it, as shown in Figure 3-59. These thumbnails really are "live"—if the window is performing an action, such as playing a video, for example, the thumbnail will display the live contents of the screen. Thumbnails are not updated for minimized applications.

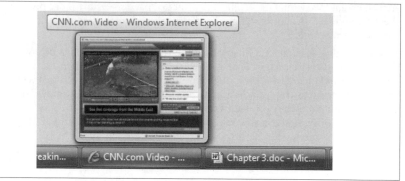

Figure 3-59. Hover your mouse over a button for the open window, and a thumbnail appears above it

If an application is busy, clicking a Taskbar icon sometimes won't activate the window. If this happens, try right-clicking on the Taskbar icon and selecting Restore. If an application has crashed and you're unable to shut it down gracefully, you can often close it by right-clicking its Taskbar button and selecting Close. Although this doesn't always work, it is much quicker and more convenient than using the Windows Task Manager (discussed in Chapter 11).

By default, the Taskbar appears at the bottom of the screen, but you can drag it to the top or to either side by grabbing any empty portion of the Taskbar with the mouse (unless it's locked; see the upcoming discussion). You can also resize the Taskbar by grabbing its edge.

Right-click on an empty area of the Taskbar to pop up its context menu. Here are the available options:

Toolbars
> Show or hide any of the Taskbar toolbars (discussed later in this chapter) or the Address Bar (discussed earlier in this chapter).

Cascade Windows
> Arrange all windows (except those that are minimized) so that they appear "cascaded"; the window on the bottom of the pile will be moved to the upper left of your Desktop, the next will appear just slightly lower and to the right, and so on.

Show Windows Stacked
> Arrange all windows (except those that are minimized) so that they don't overlap and are stacked on top of one another to fill the screen.

Show Windows Side by Side
> Arrange all windows (except those that are minimized) so that they don't overlap and are stacked next to one another to fill the screen. Side-by-side tiling results in wider windows and stacked tiling results in taller, narrower windows.

Show the Desktop
> Bring the Desktop to the top of the pile, covering all open windows. This has the same effect as minimizing all open windows, except that you can then use Show Open Windows to quickly drop the Desktop back down to the bottom and

restore all windows to their previous states. Note that the Minimize All Windows option found here in versions of Windows previous to XP is still absent, but you can still quickly minimize all open windows by holding the Windows logo key and pressing D.

Task Manager

Open the Windows Task Manager (see Chapter 11).

Lock the Taskbar

If you lock the Taskbar, you won't be able to move or resize it, nor will you be able to move or resize any Taskbar toolbars that happen to be docked. If you find yourself accidentally messing up the Taskbar, locking it will eliminate the problem. You can lock most toolbars in Windows in this way. Note also that locking the toolbar will hide the resize handles, giving you a little more Taskbar real estate for your task buttons.

Properties

This is the same as Control Panel → [Appearance and Personalization] → Taskbar and Start Menu, and it's the same as right-clicking the Start button and selecting Properties. See "Taskbar and Start Menu Properties," later in this chapter, for details on these settings.

Notes

- To activate the Taskbar buttons with the keyboard, from the Desktop press Tab to send focus to the task buttons. Use the cursor keys to navigate from button to button, and press the Space bar to activate a window or Shift-F10 to display its control menu. It's usually preferable to simply use Windows Flip (Alt-Tab or Shift-Alt-Tab to go in reverse) or Windows Flip 3D, both covered in this chapter, to cycle through the open windows rather than this elaborate procedure. While we're at it, you can also press Alt-Esc to send a window to the bottom of the pile (an alternative to minimizing it).

- Some applications have icons in the notification area (also known as the Tray, discussed earlier in this chapter) instead of Taskbar buttons. A few applications have both, and some have neither. If an application window has no Taskbar button, it will not be accessible when you press Alt-Tab (used to switch between running applications).

- By default, the Taskbar "groups" similar task buttons together. But what does this mean? Most applications are capable of opening several documents simultaneously without having several separate instances of the application   a design known as multiple document interface (MDI) design. This not only saves screen real estate, but it also makes comparing documents side by side and sharing information among multiple documents much easier. In Office 2000, and now Office XP, Microsoft unfortunately tried to abolish MDI in favor of separate single document interface (SDI) windows. The consequence was increased clutter on the Taskbar, so Microsoft came up with task button grouping, which consolidates all of the open documents of an SDI application into a single button. To enable or disable this option, go to Control Panel → [Appearance and Personalization] → Taskbar and Start Menu → Taskbar tab.

- See the next section, "Taskbar and Start Menu Properties," for more settings that affect the Taskbar. Among the more useful are the "Auto-hide the Taskbar" and "Keep the Taskbar on top of other windows" options.

Taskbar and Start Menu Properties

Change the appearance and behavior of the Taskbar, notification area, and Start menu (see Figure 3-60).

Figure 3-60. Use Taskbar and Start Menu Properties to specify your preferences for your Start menu, Taskbar, and notification area (Tray)

To open

Control Panel → [Appearance and Personalization] → Taskbar and Start Menu

Right-click on an empty portion of the Taskbar → Properties

Right-click on the Start button → Properties

Start → Settings → Taskbar and Start Menu (Classic Start menu only)

Description

The Taskbar is the bar, typically appearing along the bottom edge of your screen, that holds the Start button, the notification area (commonly known as the Tray), and the task buttons (one for each open application window). It has four tabs: Taskbar, Start Menu, Notification Area, and Toolbars. The settings for each tab are as follows.

Taskbar

Lock the Taskbar

Lock the Taskbar to prevent it from being accidentally (or intentionally) resized or moved, or to prevent resizing or removal of any Taskbar toolbars. The Taskbar is locked by default.

Auto-hide the Taskbar

Enable this feature to have the Taskbar drop out of sight when it's not being used. Move the mouse to the bottom of the screen (or to the sides or the top, if that's where you have your Taskbar) to make the Taskbar pop up. You can also press Ctrl-Esc (or the Windows logo key, if you have one) to pop up the Taskbar and open the Start menu.

Keep the Taskbar on top of other windows

Enable this feature to prevent other windows from covering the Taskbar. Although similarly named features appear in some other applications (such as the Task Manager), this one is somewhat different because in addition to having the Taskbar appear "always on top," this option actually shrinks the Desktop and space available for applications. For example, if you maximize an application, its outer edge will become flush with the Taskbar. See "Windows," later in this chapter, for more information.

Group similar Taskbar buttons

See "Taskbar," earlier in this chapter, for more information on task button grouping.

Show Quick Launch

See "Toolbars," later in this chapter, for more information on the Quick Launch Toolbar.

Show window previews (thumbnails)

Allow the thumbnail preview of each window on the Taskbar when the mouse hovers over its Taskbar button. See "Taskbar" for more information.

Start menu

Start menu versus Classic Start menu

This setting changes the arrangement of the items in your Start menu. The Classic Start menu is a single-column menu, similar to the one found in Windows 2000 and Windows 9x/Me. All of your installed programs are listed in the Programs menu.

The Start menu in Windows Vista is a more complex menu with all the same options as the Classic Start menu, plus links to the most frequently used applications, as well as your favorite web browser and email program. All of your installed programs are listed in the All Programs menu. (For more details, see "Start Menu," earlier in this chapter.)

Note that this setting has no effect on the "style" of the Start button or Taskbar. Use Control Panel → [Appearance and Personalization] → Change the Theme to change the style.

Don't be alarmed if some of your Desktop icons disappear and then appear when you switch between the Start menu and the Classic Start menu; whether these icons are shown or hidden is saved with the customization of each Start menu selection, as described next in "Customize." The default for the Windows Vista Start menu is to show only the Recycle Bin icon out of all available system objects, while the Classic Start menu shows the Control Panel, Network, and Computer in addition to the Recycle Bin.

Customize

The Customize button, available with either Start menu type, allows you to selectively show or hide certain items in the Start menu, as well as control the appearance and functioning of the Start menu. Figure 3-61 shows the dialog for customizing the Vista Start menu.

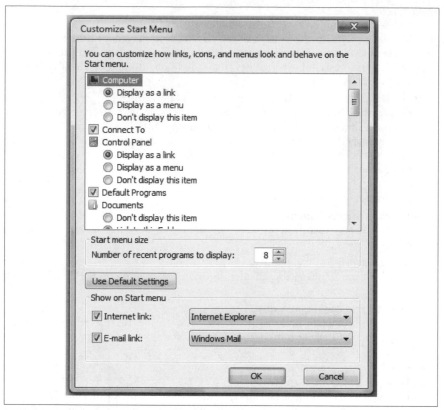

Figure 3-61. The dialog for customizing the Vista Start menu

You'll be able to control whether to display items such as Computer, Network, Recycle Bin, and so on. You'll also determine whether to display them as cascading menu items or instead only as a link. Figure 3-62 shows Computer displayed only as a link; Figure 3-63 shows it displayed as a cascading menu.

In addition, you can control how the Start Search box functions: you can have it search only the current user's files or the entire index, and specify whether it should search Favorites and History as well as your email and other communications. (See Chapter 4 for more details.) You can also choose whether to use large icons (the default) or smaller icons. Customize also allows you to have the All Programs menu sorted by the name of the programs. In previous versions of Windows, programs started off being sorted by name, but new programs were added to the bottom of the list. Customize offers a variety of other options as well, such as whether newly installed programs should be highlighted.

Customize also lets you determine whether to display your browser and email programs on the Start menu, and it lets you change which of them to display.

Privacy

This section lets you turn off the display of recently opened files and recently used programs. See "Start Menu," earlier in this chapter, for details.

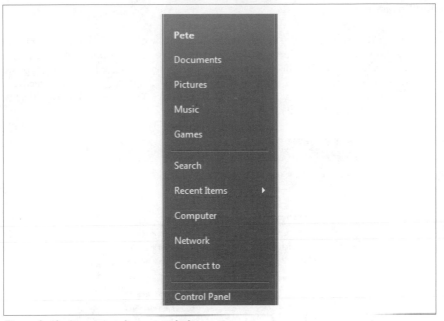

Figure 3-62. Computer, shown as a link

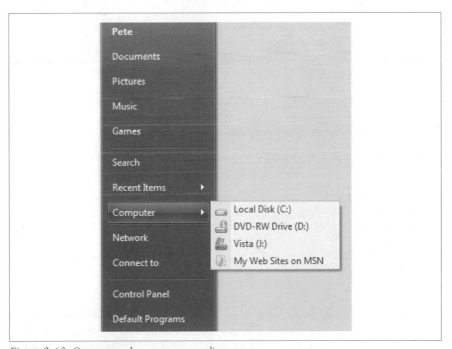

Figure 3-63. Computer, shown as a cascading menu

Notification area

Hide inactive icons

Windows keeps a history of the status icons that various applications display in the notification area. Turn on the "Hide inactive icons" option and then click Customize to display the Customize Notifications dialog, which allows you to selectively show or hide icons that are currently displayed—or have ever been displayed—in the notification area (see Figure 3-64). Here the term *inactive* means currently not displayed.

Figure 3-64. Selectively hiding unwanted Tray icons with the Customize Notifications dialog

If you want to hide an icon, try the settings in the application that owns the icon first. Only if there is no such setting, or if the setting doesn't work, should you resort to the Customize Notifications dialog. If no icons are shown in the notification area and if the clock is disabled (as discussed earlier), the notification area disappears entirely. If one or more icons are hidden with the Customize Notifications dialog, however, a small arrow appears, allowing you to show or hide any such icons.

System Icons

This displays or hides the clock, Network icon, Power icon, and volume controls for your sound device in the notification area. Hold the mouse pointer over any of the icons in the notification area to display relevant information—for example, the current state of your battery for the Power icon. Click any icon to get more information and ways to customize that setting.

See also

"Control Panel" and "Taskbar"

Text Boxes

See "Input Fields," earlier in this chapter.

Theme Settings

Choose a theme.

To open

Control Panel → [Appearance and Personalization] → Personalization → Theme

Description

A *theme* is a name under which a collection of display settings is saved, including menus, icons, backgrounds, screensavers, sounds, and mouse pointers. After you've selected these preferences through the various applets in the Personalization Control Panel category, go to Theme Settings (Figure 3-65) and click Save As to create a new theme. Then, if you ever make a subsequent change, you can easily revert to your saved preferences by selecting the desired theme from the Theme list.

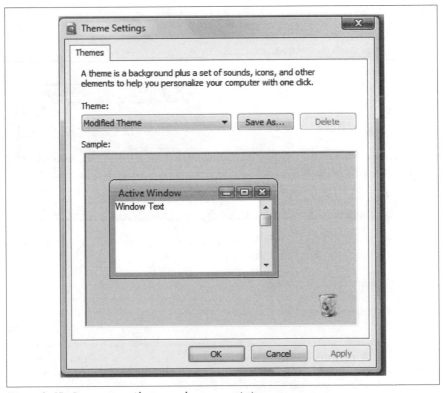

Figure 3-65. Create a new theme or choose an existing one

Saving your theme is a good idea, as it will allow you to restore your settings easily if they're ever changed. It also allows you to quickly switch among multiple groups of settings, which is useful, for example, if you use two different monitors. When you click Save As, you'll be prompted to enter a filename with the *.theme* filename extension. However, the default folder for these files is *My Documents*, which is not where Windows looks for themes when it populates the Theme drop-down listbox. To have your theme listed in the Theme list, save your *.theme* file in the *\Windows\Resources\Themes* folder.

You can also select existing themes from the Theme Settings tab, including the Windows Vista theme and, for those who prefer the retro look, the Windows Classic theme.

See also

"Control Panel," "Display Settings," "Change Your Color Scheme," "Desktop Background," and "Personalization"

Title Bars

See "Windows," later in this chapter.

Toolbars

Toolbars are used to provide quick access to frequently used functions in a program. Windows comes with several toolbars, including those found in Windows Explorer, Internet Explorer, WordPad (and other applications), and the Quick Launch Toolbar on the Taskbar (see Figure 3-66).

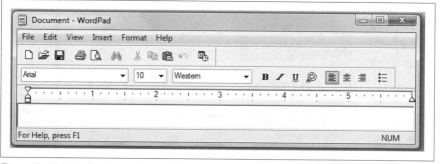

Figure 3-66. WordPad's toolbar, which provides access to 11 of the most commonly used functions, such as Open, Save, Print, and Find

In some programs, the buttons in a toolbar don't provide any functionality that isn't otherwise accessible through the menus or via a keystroke or two. Toolbars are almost exclusively mouse-oriented, so a toolbar that works with the keyboard is a rare occurrence.

Windows Explorer and Internet Explorer have received new toolbars with Windows Vista, and these toolbars are the primary way that you interact with both programs— so much so that the traditional menus have been done away with, although you can make them appear by pressing the Alt key.

The toolbars in most modern applications are configurable; that is, you can rearrange the tools to your liking, add new items, and remove the ones you don't use. It's definitely worth taking a few minutes to configure the toolbar with the features you use the most, especially because the default toolbars in most applications are set up to showcase the most marketable features of the product rather than to make the program easier to use.

The configuration and features of a particular toolbar are typically the responsibility of the application that owns it, although most modern applications use Microsoft's toolbar controls, which afford a good degree of consistency.

You can often right-click on an empty portion of a toolbar to change its properties or to add or remove buttons. You can usually "dock" toolbars to the top, bottom, or sides of an application, or they can float. Play around with toolbars to get a feel for how they respond to being dragged and resized; there's no substitute for 30 seconds of fooling around. You can "lock" some newer toolbars so that you can't accidentally move, resize, or close them.

Many larger applications, such as Microsoft Office, support multiple toolbars, including custom toolbars you can create as needed. You can typically rearrange these toolbars by dragging them around, although you may not get any visual feedback until you let go. To hide a toolbar, try right-clicking on it, or just drag it (if it's docked) so that it floats and then click the Close button in the toolbar's title bar.

 A quick way to customize the buttons on toolbars is to hold the Alt key while dragging or right-clicking (to move a button or change its properties, respectively). Pressing the Alt key puts the toolbar into "edit" mode temporarily; in fact, you can even drag buttons from one toolbar to another with this method. Note that Taskbar toolbars (discussed next) are always in edit mode, so the Alt key is not needed.

Toolbars on the Taskbar

In addition to the Desktop and Start menu, you also can place shortcuts to frequently used programs in configurable toolbars that are either docked on the Taskbar (discussed earlier in this chapter) or allowed to float.

By default, there are six Taskbar toolbars. Right-click an empty area of the Taskbar and select Toolbars to show or hide any of them. The six toolbars are as follows:

Address
> The Address Bar on the Taskbar lets you run programs and visit web sites. See "Address Bar," earlier in this chapter, for details.

Windows Media Player
> This installs a toolbar and puts the Windows Media Player icon in the Quick Launch Toolbar (I cover Quick Launch in more detail shortly). Click the icon to launch Windows Media Player.

Tablet PC Input Panel
> This doesn't install a toolbar, but instead puts an icon for the Tablet PC Input Panel in the notification area. The panel works with a Tablet PC to perform handwriting recognition.

Links
> The Links toolbar is designed to hold your favorite Favorites or, more specifically, links (Internet shortcuts) to your favorite web sites. This is the same toolbar as the Links toolbar in Internet Explorer (see "Internet Explorer," in Chapter 5). Shortcuts displayed on this toolbar are stored in \Users\username\Favorites\Links.

Quick Launch

The Quick Launch Toolbar shows any number of shortcuts to your most frequently used programs; it's yet one more way to quickly launch a program.

The Quick Launch Toolbar, as well as any other custom toolbars you create (except Desktop, discussed next), are mirrors of folders on your hard disk. For example, the contents of the Quick Launch Toolbar are stored in *\Users\username\ AppData\Roaming\Microsoft\Internet Explorer\Quick Launch.* You can get there quickly by right-clicking on an empty portion of the Quick Launch Toolbar and selecting Open Folder (I discuss other items on this menu shortly).

 One of the niftiest icons on the Quick Launch Toolbar is the Show Desktop icon. Don't delete this one; it's not a shortcut but rather a Windows Explorer command (*.scf*) file. It has the same effect as right-clicking on the Taskbar and selecting Show Desktop (see "Taskbar," earlier in this chapter, for details); it pops the Desktop on top of all other windows, allowing you to access Desktop icons without having to minimize anything. It's far superior to displaying the Desktop Toolbar.

Desktop

The Desktop Toolbar was intended as a handy way to get at the contents of your Desktop when it's covered with open windows. It's really just another custom toolbar (like Quick Launch), except that it mirrors the contents of your Desktop folder. Of course, if you have a lot of things on your Desktop, this toolbar can itself get pretty unwieldy, so I don't find it too useful. Your mileage may vary. You'll probably prefer to just use Show Desktop (either the button in the Quick Launch Toolbar or the entry on the Taskbar's context menu) for quick access to items on your Desktop.

You can create your own custom toolbars by right-clicking on the Taskbar and selecting Toolbars → New Toolbar. Simply specify an existing folder whose contents you want made into a toolbar (such as Control Panel, Dial-Up Networking, or one of the folders in your Start menu), or click Make New Folder if you want to start with a blank toolbar.

One limitation of custom toolbars is that if they're ever closed, Windows won't display them on the list of available toolbars, as with the preconfigured toolbars discussed here. If you ever close a custom toolbar, you'll have to start over and go through the New Toolbar process to get it back (though all your shortcuts will still be there).

Once a toolbar is enabled, you can right-click on an empty portion to display a context menu with several options. (Right-clicking one of the toolbar buttons is the same as right-clicking the corresponding shortcut in Explorer.) In addition to the standard entries on the Taskbar context menu (see "Taskbar," earlier in this chapter), you'll find the following. Note that not every toolbar has all of these options, and the exact options available to you vary from toolbar to toolbar. Also, you may be able to see all these options only if you first unlock the Taskbar by right-clicking it and unchecking Lock the Taskbar.

View → Large Icons, View → Small Icons
> Allows you to display either large (32×32) or small (16×16) icons. Neither choice is perfect; small icons can be very difficult to see and distinguish, and large icons take up too much space and offer little advantage over Desktop icons. Choose whichever icons best suit your needs.

Open Folder
> Opens the folder to which the toolbar is linked. When customizing a toolbar, it's often easier to deal with the actual shortcuts in a real folder than it is to mess with the buttons on the toolbar.

Show Text
> Displays a text label next to each icon. This is useful if you have a toolbar containing icons of the same type, and if you've got room on your Taskbar to spare. It's the default setting for the Links Toolbar, but not for the Quick Launch Toolbar.

Show Title
> Shows the name of the toolbar when it is docked on the Taskbar. It's really a waste of space for the standard toolbars, but perhaps it is useful if you set up a lot of custom toolbars. You also can use the title as a handle.

Close Toolbar
> Closes the toolbar. As stated earlier, closed custom toolbars do not remain on the Toolbars list.

Notes

- If a Taskbar toolbar doesn't seem to allow dragging or resizing, right-click on an empty portion of the Taskbar and turn off the "Lock the Taskbar" option.

Tray

See "Notification Area," earlier in this chapter.

Trees

Many different parts of the Windows Vista interface are represented by hierarchical trees, such as the one in Figure 3-67. You can find this collapsible tree interface in the Registry Editor (representing Registry keys) and in the Device Manager (representing installed devices). Windows Explorer uses a modified version of the collapsible tree interface as well. (This is a change with Windows Vista; in every version of Windows up until now, Windows Explorer used the same tree representation used by the Registry Editor and Device Manager.)

In most cases, displaying all entries in all branches of a tree would take too much time and would certainly be unwieldy. Instead, branches are "collapsed" and only the top levels are shown; you can expand any branch by clicking the plus sign (+), and then collapse any branch by clicking the corresponding minus sign (–). You can also double-click any branch to expand it, and again to collapse it. If no + sign appears, the entry has no "children" and cannot be expanded further.

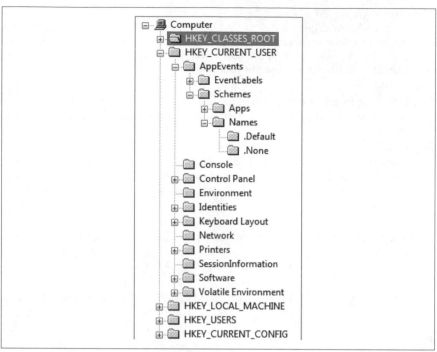

Figure 3-67. The Folder Tree, an efficient and useful way to visualize and navigate a hierarchy, as seen here in the Registry Editor

In Windows Explorer, the + and – signs have been done away with. It uses small, hollow, right-facing triangles for + signs. When you click one to reveal the folders beneath, the triangle turns solid and faces at a downward 45-degree angle. And when you move the mouse away, the triangles fade away (see Figure 3-68).

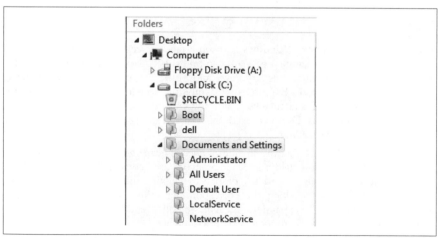

Figure 3-68. Windows Explorer's slightly modified version of the hierarchical tree for browsing

Navigating trees with the keyboard is often more convenient than using the mouse. As with listboxes (discussed earlier in this chapter), you can jump to any branch by typing the first letter (or first few letters) of its name. This works regardless of the depth of the entry, but only on entries that are currently visible. Use the right arrow key to expand the currently selected branch, or the left arrow key to collapse it; if the branch is already collapsed, the left arrow key jumps to the parent. The Backspace key also jumps to the parent, but it never collapses branches.

Turn Off Computer

See "Shut Down," earlier in this chapter.

User Account Control Buttons

On many buttons throughout Windows Vista, you will see a small shield next to many settings. The shield means that the setting is protected by a User Account Control (UAC), which pops up warnings and asks for passwords when certain setup or customization screens or features are accessed. For more information, see "User Account Control," in Chapter 8.

The User Interface

Windows

The window is the basis for the GUI. This style of interface was first popularized by Apple and later by Microsoft, but Xerox developed the first graphical windowing operating system more than a decade before the first Mac or Windows computer ever saw daylight.

Most windows are rectangular, but irregular shapes are allowed, too. Standard windows have a title bar across the top that, in addition to identifying the window and the currently open document (if applicable), is used as a handle with which to move the window around the screen (see Figure 3-69). The title bar also shows which window is currently active; in the active window, the text is darker than in other windows. (Small floating toolbars in some applications ignore this rule, always appearing either inactive or active.)

Windows Vista brings one big change to the appearance of windows. When you use Windows Aero, the title bar as well as the entire outside border of each window is slightly transparent so that you can see through to whatever is underneath. This doesn't really serve any useful purpose, but it is a very pleasing piece of eye candy and makes the operating system more enjoyable to use. You can change the color and transparency (which Windows Vista calls *glassiness*) of windows by going to Control Panel → Appearance and Personalization → Personalization → Window Color and Appearance.

 Windows will be transparent only if you're using the Windows Aero interface. Windows Aero is not available in Windows Vista Home Basic, and it will run only if you have the proper graphics hardware. (See Chapter 1 for details.) You can turn Windows Aero on and off, even if you have hardware capable of running it. For details, see "Windows Aero," later in this chapter.

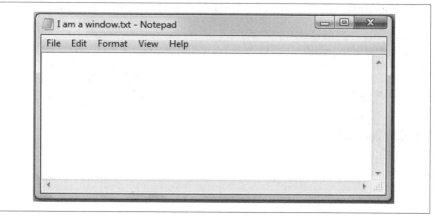

Figure 3-69. A garden-variety window, complete with title, menu, and client area

In addition, in Windows Aero and Vista Basic, when you hover your mouse over a button in a window, the button illuminates so that you know the button has the focus. In Windows Aero, the Minimize and Maximize buttons glow blue, and the Close button glows red. When you hover your mouse over an item in a window that is live—that is, one that will perform an action when clicked upon—the item will be highlighted in blue.

The elements commonly found on window title bars are described in the following list (any or all might be missing, depending on the type of window):

Control Menu

Click the icon on the upper-left corner of a window or press Alt-Space bar to display the control menu, which duplicates the Minimize, Maximize, and Close buttons and provides Move and Resize options (discussed shortly). Double-click the control menu icon to close the window.

Dialog boxes don't typically have control menu icons, but the menu is still there and you can access it with Alt-Space bar. The standard entries in the control menu are present to make it possible to move, resize, minimize, maximize, and close the window with the keyboard. For example, press Alt-Space bar and then S to resize a window with the cursor keys.

Some windows have additional functions in this menu, especially if those applications don't have full-blown menus. If you see two control menus, one on top of the other, you're using an application (such as a word processor) that can have one or more document windows open simultaneously; see the description of multiple document interface, provided shortly.

Minimize

Click Minimize to hide a window so that only its task button on the Taskbar is visible. See "Taskbar," earlier in this chapter, for details.

Maximize/Restore

Maximize a window to have it fill the screen. Click the Maximize button again to restore it to its free-floating position and size. You can also double-click the title bar to maximize and restore a window.

Close

Close a window. This is usually the same as selecting File → Close or File → Exit, or at least it's supposed to be. Double-clicking the control menu icon also closes windows, as does pressing Alt-F4.

You can resize most windows by grabbing any edge with the mouse and dragging. Some windows have an additional resize handle on the lower-right corner, which can be a little easier to get a purchase on than the edges.

Multiple document interface (MDI) applications have windows within windows, usually allowing multiple documents to be open simultaneously. The MDI parent window, the container of the document windows, usually has a Window menu that allows you to switch to any open documents and provides some features to arrange the documents visually (Cascade, Tile, etc.). Some applications (Corel's WordPerfect and Qualcomm's Eudora, to name a couple) have incorporated a clever Taskbar for their MDI applications, making it easy for you to manage several documents without having to use the somewhat awkward Window menu.

See "Taskbar," earlier in this chapter, for more information on MDI applications and how some newer Microsoft applications are abandoning this design.

Here are some keyboard shortcuts for working with windows:

- Windows logo key-Tab uses Windows Flip 3D (if you're using Aero Glass) to switch between windows. See "Windows Flip and Windows Flip 3D," later in this chapter, for details.

- Alt-Tab switches among open application windows. Hold Shift to go in reverse.

- Press Alt-Tab and release the Tab button to see thumbnails of all your open windows. Then use Alt-Tab to switch to the one you want.

- Ctrl Tab (or Ctrl-F6) switches among open documents in an MDI application window. Again, hold Shift to go in reverse.

- Alt-Esc sends the current window to the bottom of the pile and activates the next one in line.

- Alt-F4 closes the current application window. Ctrl-F4 closes the current document in an MDI application window.

- If a window has multiple panes (such as Microsoft Word), use F6 or Ctrl-Tab to switch among them.

- Internet Explorer uses tabs so that you can keep multiple web sites open at once. But you can also have multiple instances of Internet Explorer open at once, each with multiple tabs, which can make navigation among all the sites quite confusing. When possible, use tabs in Internet Explorer rather than opening multiple instances of the browser.

Notes

- You can usually move some "more stylish" (read "weird") windows without title bars by clicking on any empty area of the window.

- Technically, the Desktop is a window, although it's always at the bottom of the pile (called the *Z-order*). Conversely, you can set some windows (and even the Taskbar) to "always on top," which means that they're always on top of the pile and can't be covered by other windows (except by other "always on top" windows). When you use Windows Flip or Windows Flip 3D, you'll be able to see the Desktop as its own window.

See also

"Menus," "Taskbar," "Windows Aero," and "Windows Flip and Windows Flip 3D"

Windows Aero

Windows Aero (sometimes referred to as *Aero Glass*) represents a significant change in the Windows interface. It adds a variety of new features, including transparent windows, live Taskbar thumbnails, and Windows Flip and Windows Flip 3D, some of which are designed to make it easier to navigate and find useful information (live Taskbar thumbnails and Windows Flip 3D) and others that are designed to make the overall experience more visually pleasing (transparent windows and animation).

You don't have to run Windows Aero when you run Windows Vista; you can run Windows Classic, Basic, or Standard instead. (For details, see Chapter 1.) But the vast majority of people will use Windows Aero. Following are its primary features:

- The Start menu and parts of windows are transparent. In windows, the title bar and window borders are transparent, as are the edges of dialog boxes. (See Figure 3-70.)

- Windows and dialog boxes have drop shadows. (See Figure 3-70.)

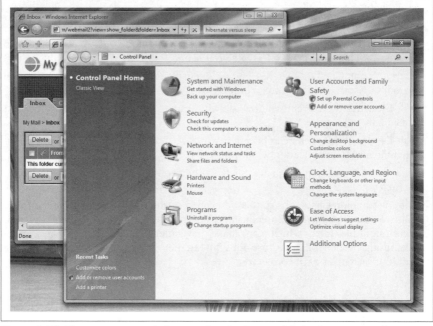

Figure 3-70. The transparent title bar, window borders, and dialog boxes in Windows Aero

- When you hover your mouse over a button in a window, the button illuminates so that you know the button has the focus. The Minimize and Maximize buttons glow blue, and the Close button glows red.

- Windows actions are subtly animated. When you minimize a window, you can watch it "whoosh" down to the Taskbar. Similarly, a window "whooshes" back up when you maximize it. When you close a window, it fades from view instead of suddenly vanishing.

- Windows Aero displays a thumbnail of the contents of any window on the Taskbar when the mouse hovers over the window. (See Figure 3-71.) It also shows the name of the application and open file. See "Live Taskbar Thumbnails," earlier in this chapter, for more details.

Figure 3-71. Live Taskbar thumbnails, which show you previews of a window when you hover your mouse over one on the Taskbar

- With Windows Aero, there is a new way to switch among your windows—Windows Flip and Windows Flip 3D. Both let you see thumbnails of your windows as you switch among them, with Windows Flip showing them side by side and Windows Flip 3D showing them stacked in three dimensions. You activate Windows Flip by using Alt-Tab, and Windows Flip 3D works by using the Windows logo key-Tab combination. See "Windows Flip and Windows Flip 3D," later in this chapter.

Notes

- Windows Aero has higher-end hardware requirements than previous versions of Windows and is not available in Windows Vista Basic, although it is available in all the other versions of Windows Vista. But even if you have a version of Windows Vista that includes Windows Aero, that doesn't mean you can run Windows Aero, because your PC will still need to meet those hardware requirements. In order to run it, you'll need a PC with a 1 GHz 32-bit (x86) or 64-bit (x64) processor; 1 GB of RAM; and a DirectX 9–capable graphics processor that supports WDDM, 32 bits per pixel, and Pixel Shader 2.0, and has a minimum of 128 MB of memory. (For more details about Windows Vista hardware requirements, see Chapter 1.)

- Windows Aero uses the new WDDM and the new Desktop Compositing Engine (DCE). One significant benefit of DCE is that it eliminates the display issues that sometimes happened with previous versions of Windows when you dragged a window on your desktop—for example, the window leaving traces of itself as you drag.

- You can turn off transparent effects, or customize them by changing the color and transparency of windows. Choose Control Panel → Appearance and Personalization → Personalization → Window Color and Appearance. For more details, see "Personalization," earlier in this chapter.

See also

"Windows Flip and Windows Flip 3D," "Live Taskbar Thumbnails," and "Personalization"

Windows Flip and Windows Flip 3D

Preview open windows and switch among them.

To open

Alt → Tab (Windows Flip)

Windows logo key → Tab (Windows Flip 3D)

Click the Windows Flip 3D icon in the Quick Launch area

Description

The old Alt-Tab method of switching among windows in Windows XP has been replaced by the far more useful Windows Flip and Windows Flip 3D in Windows Vista. They each let you see thumbnails of your windows before you switch among them, making it easier to decide which window you want to switch to. Windows Flip shows the thumbnails side by side (see Figure 3-72), and Windows Flip 3D shows the thumbnails stacked in three dimensions (see Figure 3-73).

Figure 3-72. Windows Flip, which shows thumbnails side by side

You activate Windows Flip by using Alt-Tab. In addition to showing you thumbnails of all your windows, it also shows your Desktop; if you switch to your Desktop using Windows Flip, all of your windows will be automatically minimized. Switch among your windows by pressing the Tab key as you hold down the Alt key or by clicking on one of the windows with your mouse.

You activate Windows Flip 3D by using the Windows logo Key-Tab combination. Press the combination once and remove your hands from the keys, and the windows stay stacked; switch among them using the mouse's scroll wheel or by using the arrow keys. You can also switch among windows by holding down the Windows logo key while you press the Tab key.

You also can activate Windows Flip 3D by clicking the Windows Flip 3D icon in the Quick Launch area. It's located to the right of the Show Desktop icon.

Notes

- Windows Flip and Windows Flip 3D are available only with Windows Aero.
- Sometimes the Windows logo key-Tab combination will not freeze your stacked windows so that you can scroll among them; instead, it will switch to the next window. If this happens, use the Windows logo key-Ctrl-Tab combination.

Figure 3-73. Windows Flip 3D, which shows thumbnails stacked in three dimensions

- Some manufacturers may add a Windows Flip 3D key to their keyboards so that instead of using a keyboard combination, you can activate Windows Flip 3D by pressing a single key.

See also
"Windows Aero"

Windows Sidebar and Gadgets

Gadgets perform automated tasks and display information; they live in the Windows Sidebar on the Desktop.

To open
Double-click the Windows Sidebar icon in the notification area.

Control Panel → [Appearance and Personalization] → Windows Sidebar Properties → Start Sidebar when Windows starts

Start → All Programs → Accessories → Windows Sidebar

Description

One of Windows Vista's most useful new features is the Windows Sidebar and the Gadgets that live there. Gadgets are mini-applications that automatically perform a variety of useful tasks or display helpful information; many of them are designed to connect to the Internet in order to grab information for you. For example, they can fetch and display current stock information, news, and traffic reports. They can also play live slideshows of pictures on your PC and display information about how your system is currently performing. And they can integrate with your applications to give you a quick way to interact with them, for example, by displaying Really Simple Syndication (RSS) feeds from Internet Explorer, or displaying recent emails. (For more information, see "RSS Feeds," in Chapter 5.)

Gadgets live in the Windows Sidebar on the right side of the screen, although you can move the Sidebar to the left. Make the Sidebar and Gadgets appear by double-clicking the Windows Sidebar icon in the notification area or by right-clicking the icon and choosing Bring Gadgets to Front. (Make them disappear by double-clicking the icon again.) Choose new Gadgets by clicking the + sign at the top of the Sidebar, and a gallery of available Gadgets appears. Drag a Gadget to the place on the Sidebar where you want it to appear. Figure 3-74 shows the Windows Sidebar, along with a gallery of Gadgets.

Figure 3-74. The Windows Sidebar and Gadget gallery

The Gadgets that ship with Windows Vista are only a few of the Gadgets that are ultimately expected to be available. Click "Get more gadgets online" at the bottom of the Gadget gallery, and you'll be sent to a web page with a list of more Gadgets you can download and use.

Two types of Gadgets are available from Microsoft's web site, but only one of them is designed to work with Windows Vista and the Windows Sidebar. One type of Gadget lives on the Microsoft Windows Live site, and you can use this type only when visiting the site in your browser. You won't be able to put these Gadgets on the Windows Sidebar. The other type is designed to work on the Windows Sidebar.

To remove a Gadget from the sidebar, hover your mouse over it and click the X that appears just above it. To customize how the Gadget works, click the checkmark, and a dialog box appears, like the one shown in Figure 3-75. This box will vary from Gadget to Gadget, depending on each Gadget's function.

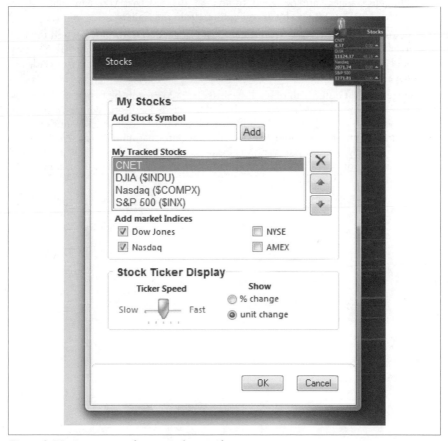

Figure 3-75. Customizing how a Gadget works

Via the Windows Sidebar Control Panel applet, you have some basic control over how the Windows Sidebar works. Choose Control Panel → Windows Sidebar, or right-click the Windows Sidebar icon, and choose Properties. The applet will let you control whether the Windows Sidebar should automatically display every time you start Windows, whether to always keep the Windows Sidebar on top of other windows, whether to display the Windows Sidebar on the right side of the screen (the default) or the left, and, if you use more than one monitor, it will let you determine on which monitor the Windows Sidebar should be displayed. There's also a View list of running Gadgets button that will show you a list of all the Gadgets currently on the Windows Sidebar, and let you remove any. (Removing one removes it only from the Windows Sidebar, not from your PC.)

Notes

- Although Gadgets are designed to live in the Sidebar, you can place them anywhere on the Desktop by dragging them from the Gallery.

- Microsoft is expected to extend the idea of Gadgets even further, beyond the PC. Other devices that use Windows may get Gadgets built into them as well, which could be shown in displays. A phone, for example, may have a variety of Gadgets, such as one showing the five most recent phone calls.

- Gadgets are an outgrowth of an ill-begotten idea Microsoft first tried in Windows 98. Windows 98 had a feature called the Active Desktop, which turned the Desktop into a live area on which information could be displayed from the Web, and mini-applications could live and display information. The Active Desktop was extremely confusing to use, was exceedingly slow, could crash PCs, and was not particularly well designed. It was rarely used, and Microsoft abandoned it in later versions of Windows.

4

Working with the Filesystem, Drives, Data, and Search

At the heart of Windows Vista are the filesystem and the files in it; without files, there's no reason to use a computer, after all. When Windows Vista was first announced, Microsoft had big plans for a completely redone filesystem, along with powerful search tools, all built on top of a new filesystem database.

Reality intruded, and those plans had to be curtailed. Still, despite that, the ways to navigate your hard disk and find files have been dramatically upgraded compared to previous versions of Windows. Windows Explorer has gotten a face-lift, along with new capabilities for filtering and viewing files. And the new Search is one of Windows Vista's best new features. Not only is it available almost everywhere, but it's also lightning fast and includes considerable new ways to search, including the ability to save searches for future use. This chapter covers that, along with all other aspects of the filesystem, Windows Explorer, and Search.

Here is an alphabetical reference of entries in this chapter:

Explorer

See "Windows Explorer," later in this chapter.

File Compare (comp)   *\windows\system32\comp.exe*

Compare the contents of two files (or sets of files) byte by byte and display the differences between them.

To open

Command Prompt → **comp**

Usage

```
comp [file1] [file2] [/n=number] [/c] [/offline] [/d] [/a] [/l]
```

Description

File Compare (*comp.exe*) compares two files (or more, using wildcards) and reports whether the files are identical. If the files are identical, *comp.exe* will report Files compare OK. If the files are the same size but have different contents, *comp.exe* displays the differences, character by character, by reporting Compare Error at OFFSET *n* (where *n* is the *byte offset*, or the location of the difference, in characters, from the beginning of the file). If the files are different sizes, *comp.exe* reports Files are different sizes, and the comparison stops there.

Here are the options for *comp.exe*:

file1, file2
> Specify the filenames of the files to compare. For any files that aren't in the current directory, you'll need to include the full path. If *file1* includes a wildcard, all matching files are compared to *file2*. Likewise, if *file2* includes a wildcard, each matching file is compared to *file1*. If one or both of these parameters are omitted, *comp.exe* will prompt you for the files to be compared.

/n=number
> Include the /n option to compare only the first specified number of lines in the files, or omit it to compare the files in their entirety. For example, specify /n=5 to check on the first five lines in each file.

/c
> Disregard the case of ASCII characters; upper- and lowercase letters are treated as identical.

/offline
> *comp.exe* normally skips files marked as "offline." Specify /offline (or just /off) to include offline files as well. (See "Sync Center," in Chapter 7, for more information on offline files.)

/d
> Display differences in decimal format.

/a
> Display differences in ASCII characters. The /a option is the default, so specifying it has no effect.

/l
> Include line numbers in any output.

Notes

- Windows Vista actually comes with two file comparison utilities: *comp.exe* (this one) and *fc.exe* (discussed in the next section). *comp.exe* performs a character-by-character comparison, but displays differences only if the files are exactly the same size. *fc.exe* performs a line-by-line comparison and works regardless of the file sizes. For most users, *fc.exe* will be the tool of choice, as it displays the differences between the files and doesn't have any prompts, so you can use it from a WSH script or batch file.

- You can also use File Compare in interactive mode, without first typing filenames. Type **comp** at the command prompt, and you'll be asked for the names of files to compare, along with any options for comparing.
- Regardless of the outcome of the comparison, *comp.exe* will ask whether you want to perform another comparison. Although there's no way to disable this prompt, you can use the following workaround to bypass it:

```
echo n | comp file1 file2
```

File Compare (fc)   *\windows\system32\fc.exe*

Compare the contents of two files (or sets of files) line by line and display the differences between them.

To open
Command Prompt → **fc**

Usage
```
fc file1 file2 [/a] [/c] [/lbn] [/n] [/t] [/w] [/offline] [/nnn]
[/l]
fc /b filename1 filename2
```

Description
File Compare (*fc.exe*) compares the contents of two files (or more, using wildcards) and displays the differences (if any). If the files are identical, *fc.exe* will report FC: no differences encountered. If the files are different, *fc.exe* lists the differing lines. Here's an example of how to use *fc.exe*.

Start with an ordinary text file—say, *Bill.txt*. Open it in Notepad, change one line, and save it into a new filename—say, *Marty.txt*. Then open a Command Prompt window, make sure you're in the same directory as the two files, and type the following:

```
fc bill.txt marty.txt
```

The output will look something like this:

```
Comparing files Bill.txt and Marty.txt
***** Bill.txt
Way down Louisiana close to New Orleans
Way back up in the woods among the evergreens
There stood a log cabin made of earth and wood
***** Marty.txt
Way down Louisiana close to New Orleans
Way back up in the woods among the antihistamines
There stood a log cabin made of earth and wood
*****
```

For each line or sequence of lines that differs in the two files, *fc.exe* prints out a pair of excerpts from each file. The first and last lines in each excerpt are what the two files have in common and are included for context. The lines in between (only a single line in this example) show the differences. The report will include one pair of excerpts for each difference found; if there are three nonconsecutive differing lines, there will be six excerpts. Here are the options for *fc.exe*:

file1, file2

> Specify the filenames of the files to compare. For any files that aren't in the current directory, you'll need to include the full path. If *file1* includes a wildcard, all matching files are compared to *file2*. Likewise, if *file2* includes a wildcard, each matching file is compared to *file1*. Both parameters are required.

/a

> Display only the first and last lines for each set of differences, as opposed to the default of every different line. This option is applicable only if a single sequence of differing lines (resulting in a single excerpt pair) is three lines or longer; otherwise, /a has no effect.

/c

> Disregard the case of ASCII characters; upper- and lowercase letters are treated as identical.

/lb*n*

> Specify the maximum consecutive mismatches; /lb17 will list only the first 17 differing lines. If omitted, the default is 100 maximum mismatches.

/n

> Include line numbers in the report.

/t

> Preserve any tabs in the files being compared. By default, tabs are treated as spaces, with one tab equal to eight spaces.

/w

> Compress whitespace (tabs and spaces) to a single space for comparison. This is possibly useful when comparing *.html* files, as web browsers will eliminate redundant tabs in spaces as well.

/offline

> *fc.exe* normally skips files marked as "offline." Specify /offline (or simply /off) to include offline files as well. (See "Sync Center," in Chapter 7, for more information on offline files.)

/*nnn*

> Specify the number of consecutive lines that must match after a mismatch. For example, if you specify /4, a mismatched line followed by three matching lines, followed by one or more mismatched lines, is treated as though it were a single sequence of mismatched lines in the report.

/l

> Treat the files as ASCII (plain text). Because /l is the default, it has no effect.

/u

> Treat the files as Unicode text.

/b

> Treat the files as binary and perform the comparison on a byte-by-byte basis (similar to *comp.exe*, the other file comparison utility). Differing bytes are displayed in parallel columns, instead of in the pairs of excerpts explained earlier. A binary comparison is typically appropriate only for files of the same sizes, but unlike *comp.exe*, the comparison will still be performed if they are different sizes. You can't use the /b option in conjunction with any of the other options.

Notes

- Windows Vista actually comes with two file comparison utilities: *comp.exe* (discussed in the preceding section) and *fc.exe* (this one). *comp.exe* performs a character-by-character comparison, but displays differences only if the files are exactly the same size. *fc.exe* performs a line-by-line comparison and works regardless of the file sizes. For most users, *fc.exe* will be the tool of choice, as it displays the differences between the files and doesn't have any prompts, so you can use it from a WSH script or batch file.

- *fc.exe* is most useful when comparing two different but similar text files. For example, you can compare two Registry patches (because *.reg* files are plain-text files) made at two different times to see what changes have been made. See Chapter 13 for more information on Registry patches.

- Although *fc.exe* can compare two binary files, if you try to compare two word processor documents (*.doc* and *.wpd* files are binary files), the results won't be terribly helpful. Try converting the documents to an ASCII-based format, such as *.rtf* or *.html*, and then perform an ASCII comparison. Naturally, most modern word processors have their own document comparison tools, but they can often be limited; although word processors may miss subtle formatting changes, *fc.exe* will catch every single difference.

- If you just want to see whether two files are different, you can redirect the differences to the nul: device and use the fact that *fc.exe* sets an ERRORLEVEL of 1 when the files differ:

  ```
  fc file1 file2 > nul:
  if ERRORLEVEL 1 (echo Different) ELSE (echo Same)
  ```

  This will also let you compare two binary files without your command prompt beeping at you while you press Ctrl-C in a desperate attempt to halt the stream of non-ASCII characters flooding your screen.

File Expansion Utility
\windows\system32\expand.exe

Extract one or more compressed files from a cabinet (*.cab*) file.

To open

Command Prompt → **expand**

Usage

```
expand -d source.cab [-f:files]
expand [-r] source.cab [destination]
expand source.cab -f:files destination
```

Description

A *cabinet file* is a compressed archive commonly used to package application installation files. You use the File Expansion Utility to extract files embedded in these cabinet files. The utility takes the following options:

source.cab

The name of the cabinet (*.cab*) file from which to extract the files.

destination

The name of the folder in which to place the extracted files, a new filename to use for the extracted files, or a combination of the two. If using the -f option, *destination* is mandatory and must include a filename (with or without wildcards).

-d

Display (list) the contents of the specified cabinet file.

-r

Specify -r (recursive) without *destination* to extract all the files contained in the specified cabinet file. For example:

```
expand -r package.cab
```

Specify -r along with *destination* to rename the files according to the file specification included in *destination*. For example, the following extracts all the files in *package.cab* and renames their file extensions to *.txt*:

```
expand -r package.cab *.txt
```

-f:*files*

Use the -f option to specify one or more files to extract; use this if you don't want to extract all the files from the cabinet file. For example, the following extracts the file *uno.txt* from *package.cab*:

```
expand package.cab -f:uno.txt uno.txt
```

Note that the *destination* parameter is mandatory when using the -f option and is used to specify the target filename. In this example, as well as most times this program will be used, *files* and *destination* will be the same.

Notes

- The easiest method for extracting files from cabinets is to simply double-click the *.cab* file in Explorer and then drag the desired file(s) out. You can also use it when installing or repairing Windows Vista when Explorer isn't available.

See also

"Cabinet (CAB) Maker," in Chapter 10

File Properties

View and change the properties of files.

To open

Right-click a file → Properties

Click a file → Organize → Properties

Description

The File Properties window has four tabs:

General

This tab (Figure 4-1) displays basic information about the file, including its location, type, size, and size on disk; the date it was created, modified, and last accessed; and its attributes. You can change the program that opens it by clicking the Change button, and you can change the file attributes by selecting Read-only or Hidden. The Advanced button lets you compress and/or encrypt the file, add or take away the file from the index for searching, and add or take away the Archive bit (for use in backups).

Why are there two listings for file size—one for size, and one for size on disk? There are two cases where the file size and size on disk are different:

- The *cluster size* of your NTFS filesystem dictates the size of the chunks that are set aside for files. On an NTFS filesystem with 4 KB clusters, a 1 KB file would use up 4 KB of disk space, and a 5 KB file would use up 8 KB.

- If a file has been compressed, the size listing shows its uncompressed size, and the size on disk shows its actual size on your hard disk.

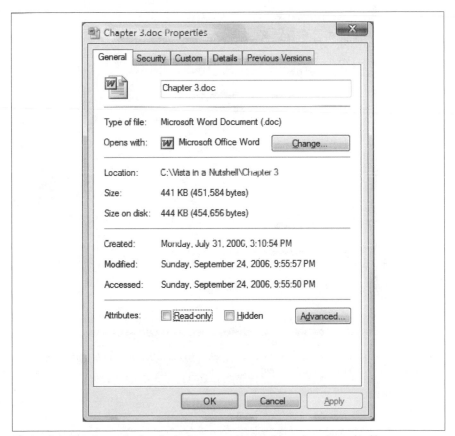

Figure 4-1. The General tab, which shows you basic information about the file

Security

This tab (Figure 4-2) shows you who has access to read and modify the file and its attributes, and lets you change those permissions. Click each group and user-name and you'll be shown the rights that person or group has to the file—whether they can read the file, modify the file, and so on. You can modify the permissions for each person or group, add new groups or people and set their permissions, and delete people or groups, which means they would have no access to the file.

The various file permission options and their meanings are quite complex, and beyond the scope of this book. However, if you want more details about the available options, go to the Microsoft Knowledge Base article at *http://support.microsoft.com/kb/308419/en-us*.

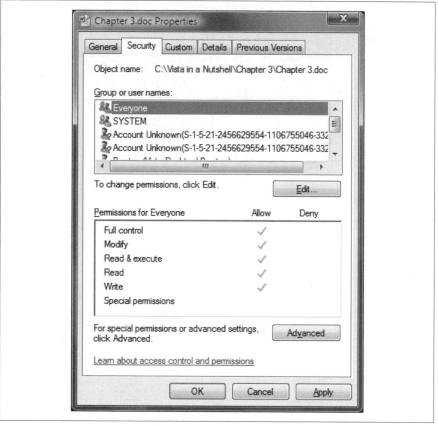

Figure 4-2. The Security tab, which lets you see what rights different people and groups have to the file—and lets you alter them

Details

This tab (Figure 4-3) displays the metatags associated with the file, as well as a wide variety of other information, including the basic file information shown in the General tab. It also has a great deal of program-specific information. For example, a Word document will display what template was used to create the file, the number of pages in the file, the word count, the character count, the line count, the paragraph count, the total length of time during which the file has been edited, and so on. You can also remove metatags and properties from the file by clicking the Remove Properties and Personal Information link. The details for each file type are quite different from one another. Graphics files, for example, include resolution, bit depth, width and height, and other similar information, as well as a quality rating that users can apply to the file.

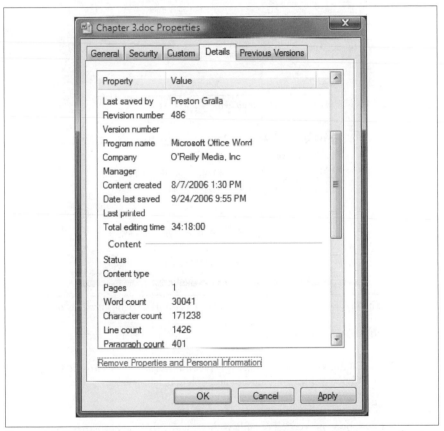

Figure 4-3. The Details tab, which displays metatags and other useful information about the file

Previous Versions

This tab (Figure 4-4) lets you view, save, or restore a previous version of a file, if such a version is available. Two types of previous versions may be available: those from a backup and those from what Windows Vista calls *shadow copies*. A shadow copy is a copy of a file made when Windows creates a restore point. (See "System Protection and System Restore," in Chapter 11, for details.) Different files and types of folders have differing options for how you handle previous versions, but in general, you'll be able to open and save the previous version of a file to a different location, or restore it over the existing files.

Figure 4-4. The Previous Versions tab, which lets you restore previous versions of the file

Microsoft Office files may have another tab in addition to the standard four:

Custom

This tab (Figure 4-5) displays custom information about Microsoft Office files. You can add new values, and modify and delete existing values.

Notes

• To restore a previous version of a file without using the File Properties screen, right-click the file in Windows Explorer and select "Restore previous versions." You'll receive a warning before you overwrite the existing folder with the previous one.

• Some file types may have other tabs in addition to the ones mentioned here, depending on whether the program that created it created those additional tabs.

• Music files include a great deal of detailed information, including the artist, album, year of release, genre, bit rate, and so on.

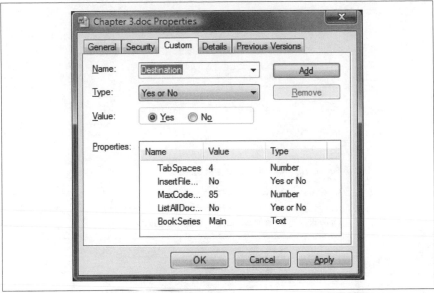

Figure 4-5. The Custom tab, which is for Microsoft Office files

See also

"Folder Properties," discussed next, "System Protection and System Restore," in Chapter 11, and "Sharing Resources and Files," in Chapter 7

Folder Properties

View and change the properties of folders.

To open

Right-click a folder → Properties

Click a folder → Organize → Properties

Description

The Folder Properties window has five tabs:

General

This tab (Figure 4-6) displays basic information about the folder, including its parent folder, size, size on disk, date and time created, and number of files and subfolders contained within. The Advanced button lets you compress and/or encrypt the folder, add or take away the folder from the index for searching, and add or take away the Archive bit (for use in backups).

Why are there two listings for folder size—one for size, and one for size on disk? If a folder has been compressed, the size listing shows its uncompressed size, and the size on disk shows its actual size on your hard disk.

Figure 4-6. The General tab, which shows you basic information about the folder

Sharing

This tab (Figure 4-7) lets you set sharing options for the folder. Click Share to share the folder, or change sharing options if the folder is already shared. Click Advanced Sharing if you want to give it a shared name in addition to its existing folder name. You would do this if you wanted to make it easier for someone to find the folder.

Security

This tab (Figure 4-8) shows you who has access to read and modify the folder and its attributes, and lets you change those permissions. Click each group and username and you'll be shown the rights that person or group has to the folder—whether they can read it, modify it, and so on. You can modify the permissions for each person or group, add new groups or people and set their permissions, and delete people or groups, which means they would have no access to the folder. The Advanced button gives you additional ways to edit permissions, as well as a way to change who has ownership of the folder.

> The various file permission options and their meanings are quite complex, and beyond the scope of this book. However, if you want more details about the available options, go to the Microsoft Knowledge Base article at *http://support.microsoft.com/kb/308419/en-us*.

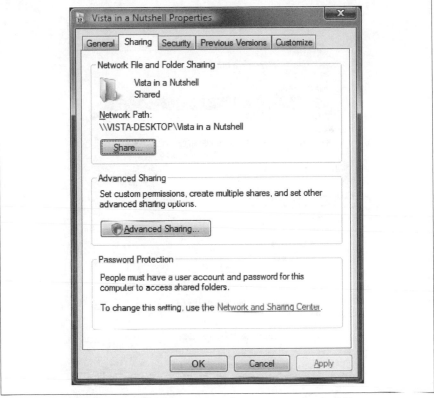

Figure 4-7. The Sharing tab, which lets you set sharing options for the folder

Previous Versions

This tab (Figure 4-9) lets you view, save, or restore a previous version of a folder, if such a version is available. Two types of previous versions may be available: those from a backup and those from what Windows Vista calls shadow copies. As explained earlier, a shadow copy of a folder is a copy of a file made when Windows creates a restore point. (See "System Protection and System Restore," in Chapter 11, for details.) Different files and types of folders have differing options for how you handle previous versions, but in general, you'll be able to open and save the previous version of the folder to a different location, or restore it over the existing folder.

Customize

This tab (Figure 4-10) lets you customize how the folder looks and acts. You can choose the kind of folder it is (All Items, Documents, Pictures and Videos, Music Details, or Music Icons). Based on what type of folder it is, the documents in it will be displayed differently, and different features will be available. For example, if a folder is a Pictures and Videos folder, the details it will display about each file include the date taken, tags, size, and rating, and the folder toolbar will include a Slide Show button so that you can display a slide show of the files in the folder. If the folder is a Documents folder, the details it will display are the date modified, type, size, and tags, but no Slide Show button will appear on the toolbar.

The tab also lets you choose a file that will be displayed on the folder's icon in Windows Explorer, and lets you choose a different icon than the default.

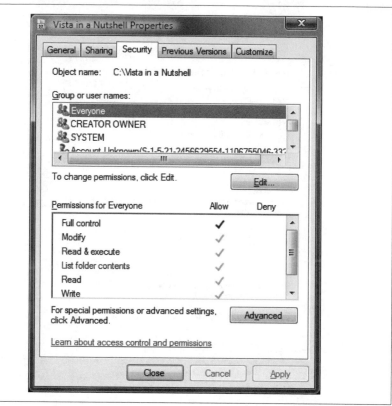

Figure 4-8. The Security tab, which lets you see what rights different people and groups have to the folder—and lets you alter them

Notes

- To restore a previous version of a folder without using the Folder Properties screen, right-click the folder in Windows Explorer and select "Restore previous versions." You'll receive a warning before you overwrite the existing file with the previous one.

See also

"File Properties," earlier in this chapter, "Sharing Resources and Files," in Chapter 7, and "System Protection and System Restore," in Chapter 11

Folder and Search Options

Control the way folders appear in Explorer and configure Search.

To open

Control Panel → [Appearance and Personalization] → Folder Options

Windows Explorer → Organize → Folder and Search Options

Command Prompt → `control folders`

Figure 4-9. The Previous Versions tab, which lets you restore previous versions of the folder

Description

The Folder Options window has three tabs (General, View, and Search):

General

Of the three settings on this page, the one people find most confusing is the Tasks section (see Figure 4-11). If you select "Show preview and filters," the Details and Preview panes will appear in all folders. In Windows classic folders, your other choice, the Details and Preview panes, will not be displayed. It will give you more room to display files because those panes are missing, but you'll see less information about each file.

View

After you've selected all your preferences in the General and View tabs, click Apply to Folders to make your settings the default. Otherwise, all your settings will be lost as soon as you switch to a different folder.

The Advanced settings in the View tab (Figure 4-12) here are quite important, and they give you a great deal of control over the way you work with Windows. Some of the default settings, in fact, can make Windows more difficult to use. Many of these settings are self-explanatory; some of the more interesting and useful ones follow:

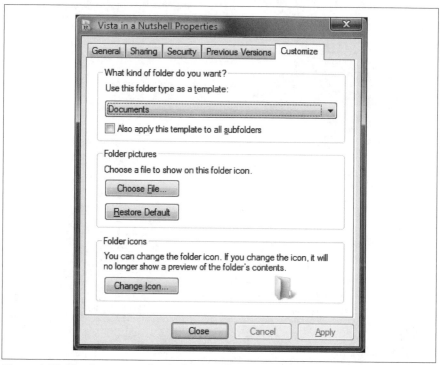

Figure 4-10. The Customize tab, which lets you change how the folder looks and acts

Always show icons, never thumbnails

A thumbnail is a visual representation of a file's actual contents (for example, you'll see a thumbnail-size picture of a graphics file), and an icon is a generic, static representation of a file type. Thumbnails are more useful, but if previews slow down your system or Windows Explorer, choose this setting so that only icons will be used.

Always show menus

Windows Vista has done away with menus in Windows Explorer—sort of. In fact, the classic Windows menus are still there, waiting to be sprung into action. Press the Alt key and they'll be visible just above the toolbar. If you'd like them to be visible all the time, choose this setting.

Display simple folder view in Navigation pane

This rather oddly named option simply shows or hides the dotted lines in the collapsible folder tree (see "Trees," in Chapter 3) in Windows Explorer. The default is on, but if you turn it off, the tree appears more like it did in earlier versions of Windows. In my opinion, the lines make the tree a little clearer and easier to use, so I recommend turning this option off.

Hidden files and folders

By default, Windows doesn't show hidden files in Explorer. Change this option if you need to access them. As a general rule, if you do any kind of system customization or troubleshooting, you should show hidden files and folders.

Figure 4-11. The General tab, which lets you turn off the Details and Preview panes in folder windows, among other options

Hide extensions for known file types

In one of Microsoft's biggest blunders, this option has been turned on, by default, since Windows 95. By hiding file extensions, Microsoft hoped to make Windows easier to use—a plan that backfired for several reasons. Because only the extensions of registered files are hidden, the extensions of files that aren't yet in the File Types database are still shown. What's even more confusing is that when an application finally claims a certain file type, it can appear to the inexperienced user as though all of the old files of that type have been renamed. It also creates a "knowledge gap" between those who understand file types and those who don't. (Try telling someone whose computer still has hidden extensions to find *Readme.txt* in a directory full of files.) Other problems have arisen, such as trying to differentiate *Excel.exe* and *Excel.xls* in Explorer when the extensions are hidden; one file is an application and the other is a document, but they may have the same icon. The upshot is that it's not a good idea to hide extensions for known file types.

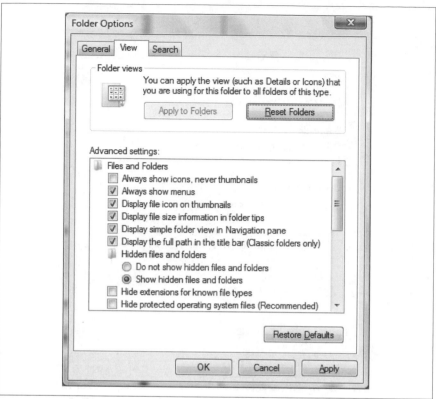

Figure 4-12. The Folder Options' View tab, which contains many settings that affect the display of folders and files

There's another reason you should not hide file extensions: doing so can be a security hazard. Windows allows you to create files with several file extensions—for example, you can create an executable file named *kittenpictures.jpg.exe*. When you hide file extensions, only the last extension is hidden. So if you hide file extensions and you are sent the file *kittenpictures.jpg.exe* in an email, the file will appear as *kittenpictures.jpg*. You would assume that the file contains pictures of kittens, but in fact it is an executable file—one that could be a Trojan or a virus. If you didn't hide file extensions, you would see the entire filename, *kittenpictures.jpg.exe*, and you would know that it was a potentially dangerous executable file, not a picture.

Hide protected operating system files
By default, this option is checked. It is another attempt by Microsoft to protect you against yourself so that you don't accidentally delete or harm important Windows Vista files. But hiding these files makes troubleshooting and customizing much more difficult, so consider unhiding them.

Launch folder windows in a separate process
> Turn on this option to start a new instance of the Windows Explorer application tion every time you open a new folder window.

Remember each folder's view settings
> If this option is enabled and you use Explorer's View menu to alter the display of a particular folder, those settings will be saved with that folder for the next time it's opened. If you're looking for a way to save your View settings as the default for all folders, this option won't do it; instead, use the Apply to Folders button.

Restore previous folder windows at logon
> If you select this option, when you start your computer this will open the folders you were using the last time you shut down Windows.

Show encrypted or compressed NTFS files in color
> If you've encrypted or compressed NTFS files, this will show them in a color to distinguish them from files that haven't been encrypted or compressed.

Show preview handlers in preview pane
> Good luck translating this option into English. Here's what it means, though: if you deselect it, the contents of your files will never be shown in the Preview pane. Why use this option if displaying previews slows down your system?

Use check boxes to select items
> Normally, in Windows, you can select several files at once by holding down the Ctrl key while you click the files. If you'd instead prefer that checkboxes show up next to files so that you can select them that way, use this option.

Use Sharing Wizard
> Windows Vista includes a new wizard to help you share files with others on your PC. If you prefer to walk through the file-sharing process manually, uncheck this selection.

Search
> This tab (Figure 4-13) controls the basic features of Search. (For more details, see "Search," later in this chapter.) It includes these sections:

What to search
> This section controls how Search handles filenames and file contents. In some circumstances it searches through the actual names of files, and in other circumstances it searches through the names of files as well as through their contents. By default, it searches filenames and contents in indexed locations, and filenames only in nonindexed locations. This section, however, lets you change that behavior. Keep in mind that if you choose to always search through filenames and contents of nonindexed files, it may slow your search considerably, because searching nonindexed files can be sluggish.

How to search
> This controls a variety of search behavior. You can include or not include subfolders when typing in the Search box, find or not find partial matches, and choose not to use the index when searching (doing this will slow down the search process considerably, but it casts a wider net).

> In addition, it lets you use what is called *natural language search*. Windows Vista's Search is an extremely powerful tool, but it can be confusing to use because it often requires very strict and specific syntax in order to work. If

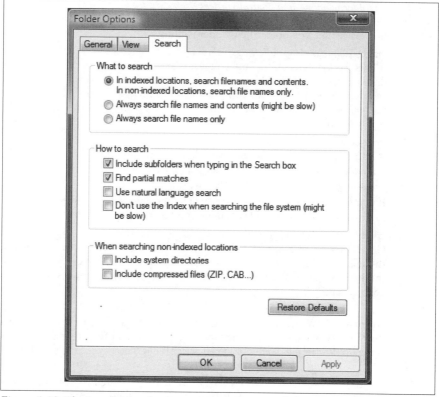

Figure 4-13. The Search tab, where you can customize many Search functions

you'd prefer to use plain English commands (music by Gluck and Salieri) rather than kind: music artist: (Gluck AND Salieri), turn on natural language search. See "Search," later in this chapter, for more details about natural language search.

When searching non-indexed locations
You can choose to include or not include system directories and compressed files when searching through nonindexed areas. Including them will slow down search performance but will result in a broader search.

Notes

- Windows XP had another useful tab, File Types, but it has been taken away in Windows Vista. The File Types tab let you create and change file associations, and customize various actions associated with files. For example, in Windows XP, you could set multiple associations for files, as well as customize precisely what actions a program should take when it opens a file. You could, for example, set one program to play a file type by default, but a different program to edit the file by default. In Windows Vista, you can change file associations, but nothing else. To change file associations, you choose Start → Default Programs → Associate a file type or protocol with a program. See "Default Programs Control Panel," in Chapter 10, for details.

- You can add a nonindexed area, such as Universal Serial Bus (USB) flash drives, flash memory cards, network drives, and nonindexed portions of your hard disk, to your index so that you'll be able to search them faster. For details, see "Search," later in this chapter.

See also
"Search" and "Windows Explorer," later in this chapter, and "Default Programs Control Panel," in Chapter 10

Indexing Options

Configure and customize the index for searching.

To open
Control Panel ‣ System and Maintenance] → Indexing Options

Windows Explorer → Search Tools → Modify Index Locations (the Search Tools icon appears when you type text into the Search box, but it is otherwise invisible)

Description
The Indexing Options screen (Figure 4-14) shows you what folders are included in your index and lets you add or remove folders. The index is used to speed up searches in Windows Vista.

Figure 4-14. The Indexing Options screen, where you set your indexing options

The Advanced button leads to two tabs: Index Settings and File Types. The Index Settings tab (Figure 4-15) lets you index encrypted files, control how accented characters are treated, rebuild the index, and change the location of the index. It also lets you tell the index how to handle two words that are otherwise identical, except that one has an accent mark (known as a *diacritic*) and the other doesn't. You can tell the index to treat them as separate words or as the same word (the default). The File Types button lets you set which file types should be indexed, and choose for each file type whether the contents and properties of the file should be indexed, or just the properties.

Figure 4-15. The Advanced button, where you set advanced indexing options

To remove existing folders or to add new folders, from the Indexing Options screen choose Modify → Show all locations. Then expand the drives you see. Folders with checkboxes are included in the index; those without checkboxes are not included. Check or uncheck the checkboxes as appropriate.

Notes

- File properties include not only filenames, but also tags, such as date created, date modified, and so on.

- If you discover that when you search, you're not finding files that you know are in your index, the index may have been damaged. To solve the problem you'll need to rebuild the index. Select Advanced → Index Settings → Rebuild.

Label

Change the label of any hard disk, floppy disk, or removable media.

To open
Command Prompt → **label**

Usage
```
label [drive:] [label]
```

Description
Every disk has a label—the name shown in Explorer next to the drive letter (Explorer doesn't show the label for floppies). To change the label for any disk, right-click on its icon in Explorer (or the My Computer window), select Properties, and type a new name in the unlabeled field at the top of the Properties window. The Label tool duplicates this functionality from the command line. For example, to change the label of drive *c:* to "shoebox," type:

```
label c: shoebox
```

If you omit *label*, you will be prompted to enter a new label. If you omit *drive*, *label* will use the current drive.

Notes
- A disk's label has no effect on the operation of the disk; for hard disks, it's purely decorative. For CDs and other removable media, it's used to quickly identify what's in the drive.
- You can also set a label for a drive using the Disk and Volume Properties dialog. For details, see "Disk and Volume Properties," in Chapter 9.

NTFS Compression Utility

View or configure the automatic file compression on NTFS drives.

To open
Command Prompt → **compact**

Usage
```
compact [/c | /u] [/s[:dir]] [/a] [/i] [/f] [/q] [filename]
```

Description
One of the features of the NTFS filesystem (see "FAT to NTFS Conversion Utility," in Chapter 11) is its support for automatic compression of individual files; older files can be optionally compressed to take up less disk space at the expense of speed to access them.

Right-click on any file or folder, select Properties, and then click the Advanced button. The "Compress contents to save disk space" option is used to instruct Windows to compress the selected item. If a folder is selected, all of its contents will be compressed (you'll be prompted about any subfolders); furthermore, any files added to that folder will be automatically compressed as well.

The NTFS Compression Utility is the command-line equivalent of this setting, useful for automating the compression or decompression of several files with the help of a WSH script or batch file. The NTFS Compression Utility takes the following options:

filename
:   Specifies a file, folder, or group of files (using wildcards) to compress or uncompress.

/c
:   Compresses the specified file(s). If a folder is specified for *filename*, the folder will be marked so that subsequent files added to the folder will be compressed automatically. Include the /s parameter to compress files already in the folder.

/u
:   Uncompresses the specified file(s). If a folder is specified for *filename*, the folder will be marked so that subsequent files added to it will not be compressed automatically. Include the /s parameter to uncompress files already in the folder.

/s
:   If a folder is specified for *filename*, the /c and /u parameters will act only on new files added to the folder. Include the /s parameter as well to compress or uncompress files already in the folder. If *filename* is omitted, use the /s option to act on all files in the current folder.

/a
:   Includes files with hidden or system attributes set; otherwise, ignored by *compact. exe*.

/i
:   Ignores errors; otherwise, *compact.exe* will stop when the first errors are encountered.

/f
:   Forces compression on all specified files; otherwise, files that are already compressed will be skipped.

/q
:   Quiet mode; use this option to report only the most essential information.

If you run the NTFS Compression Utility without any options, it will display the compression settings for the current directory and all of its contents.

Notes

- This type of file compression is supported on NTFS drives only.
- Go to Windows Explorer → Organize → Folder and Search Options → View tab and turn on the "Show encrypted or compressed NTFS files in color" option to visually differentiate such files from unencrypted, uncompressed files.
- For tangible proof that a given folder or file is actually compressed, right-click on it in Explorer and select Properties. If the "Size on disk" value is less than the "Size" value, the item is compressed.

See also

"FAT to NTFS Conversion Utility," in Chapter 11

OpenFiles
\windows\system32\openfiles.exe

List all currently open files, either shared and accessed by other users on a network or (optionally) opened locally.

To open
Start → type **command** into the Search field → right-click on Command Prompt → Run as Administrator

Usage
```
openfiles /local [ on | off ]
openfiles /query [/s system [/u user [/p [pass]]]]
 [/fo format] [/nh] [/v]
openfiles /disconnect [/s system [/u user [/p [pass]]]]
 {[/id id] [/a accessedby] [/o openmode]} [/op openfile]
```

Description
The OpenFiles tool lets you view a list of all the shared files that are currently open across the network and, optionally, files that are opened locally. You can use this to avoid deleting or changing a document that a remote user is working on.

Type **openfiles** without any options to display a report such as this:

```
Files Opened Remotely via local share points:
-----------------------------------------------
ID Accessed By Type Open File (Path\executable)
===== ============= ========== ====================================
98 LOU Windows C:\Stuff to Eat\frittatas.txt
101 EDDIE Windows C:\Stuff to Drink\milkshakes.txt
107 CLANCY Windows C:\Stuff to Eat\pork chops.txt
```

OpenFiles accepts one of three primary commands, each of which has a range of parameters:

/local [*parameters*]
> Turn on or off the inclusion of local files in reports. Type:
>
> > openfiles /local on
>
> to turn on the "maintain objects list" global flag; this setting is turned off by default and requires Windows to be restarted when changed. Note that turning on this setting may slightly reduce performance.

/query [*parameters*]
> Display a list of opened files and folders; specify /query for more flexibility than using openfiles without any options, such as the ability to connect to a different machine. Type **openfiles /query /?** for more information on the available parameters.

/disconnect [*parameters*]
> Selectively disconnect files and folders that have been opened remotely. When viewing the list of open files, each entry has an ID; you can use that ID to close open files. Type **openfiles /disconnect /?** for more information on the available parameters.

Notes
- OpenFiles is available only to a user with administrator privileges.

See also
"Net," in Chapter 7

Search

Search for files.

To open

Start → Search

Start → Enter text in Start Search

Enter text in Search box in Windows Explorer.

Description

Search has been embedded so deeply into Windows Vista and Windows Explorer that at first it can be difficult to know where to begin. Should you use the Search box inside Windows Explorer? The one inside Internet Explorer? The Start Search box that appears when you click the Start button? How about choosing Start → Search to go straight to the Search Folder and Advanced Search screen?

Table 4-1 shows the major ways you can perform a search in Windows Vista and recommendations on when to use which.

Table 4-1. Different ways to search

Search method	When to use it
Search box in Windows Explorer	Best for searching inside individual folders and subfolders, because it searches only the current folder and subfolders. Also best for searching on filenames.
Start → Search (leads to Search folder and Advanced Search)	Best for performing complex searches across multiple folders and for when you want to save a search for future use.
Start Search box on the Start menu	Best for quick searches across multiple folders or for searching the Internet. Not good for searching for filenames.
Search box in Internet Explorer	Best for searching the Internet.

Windows Vista performs a search while you type your search term into a Search box. So as you type the letters *vis*, for example, it will display all files that have *vis* in them and will narrow the search as you type more letters into the box.

Understanding searching and the index

When you search for a file on your computer, you aren't actually searching your entire hard disk. Instead, you're searching the Windows Vista index, which makes searching lightning fast.

Sometimes you will search outside the index. For example, when you perform a search inside a folder, you also search the filenames inside the folder, not just the index. And, as explained later, you can also expand your search to nonindexed locations when you want.

Although the index makes searching lightning fast, it can cause some confusion, as well. By default, your entire PC is not indexed, because doing that would defeat the purpose of the index—it would get so large that it would slow down your search.

By default, the following are indexed:

- Your user folder (\Users\username), which contains your Documents, Music, Pictures, and Videos folders, as well as Contacts, Favorites, and the hidden AppData folder, which contains your Windows Mail messages.

- Offline files, which are files stored on a server or network drive that you have configured to be available offline. For details, see "Offline Files," in Chapter 7.

- The contents of your Start menu.

That's well and good, but what happens if you don't store files and folders underneath your user folder? What if you store them in other places on your hard disk? Then you won't find them when you perform a search, unless you specifically search for them outside the index, which of course defeats the purpose of the index.

There is a solution, however. You can add any folders you want to the index (and take them away, as well). For details, see "Indexing Options," earlier in this chapter. A simple way to get to the Indexing Options screen is from Windows Explorer, by choosing Search Tools → Modify Index Locations. (The Search Tools icon appears only after you type text into the Search box.)

The Windows Explorer Search box

The Search box in Windows Explorer searches only within the current folder and subfolders beneath it. It searches the index and the names of files in the folder and subfolders, and displays results directly in Windows Explorer, as you can see in Figure 4-16.

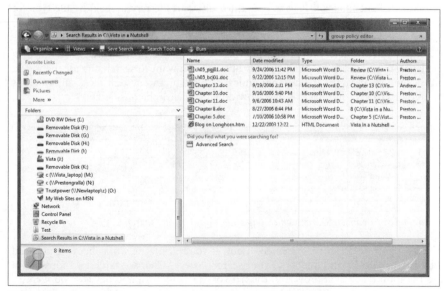

Figure 4-16. Results when searching from a folder in Windows Explorer

You can sort, filter, group, and stack the results, as you can normally with Windows Explorer. (For details, see "Windows Explorer," later in this chapter.)

At the bottom of your results, you'll see a "Did you find what you were searching for?" heading. Beneath that, you will see an Advanced Search link, which will launch an advanced search when clicked. (See the next section, "The Search Pane and Advanced Search," for details.) If the folder you've searched through hasn't been indexed, you'll also see a link to "Search in File Contents," which will search the actual contents of the files in the folder, rather than just the filenames.

The Search Pane and Advanced Search

To make it easier to search in a folder, you can turn on the Search Pane (Figure 4-17), by selecting Organize → Layout → Search Pane.

Figure 4-17. The Search Pane in Windows Explorer, which makes it easy to search for specific file types

 The Search Pane is not normally available as an option from Organize → Layout. However, as soon as you type text into the Search box, the option will be available. Delete the search or move your cursor out of the box, and the Search Pane will no longer be available. However, the option is always available from the Computer and Desktop folders.

The Search Pane makes it easy to search for different file types; click the file type for which you want to search, and then perform your search.

The Search Pane also displays an Advanced Search button at the far right of the screen. Click it, and Advanced Search appears (Figure 4-18). Use of Advanced Search is self-explanatory and needs no further clarification. If you want to search outside the index, check the box next to "Include non-indexed, hidden, and system files," although as Windows Vista warns you, this may slow down your search considerably.

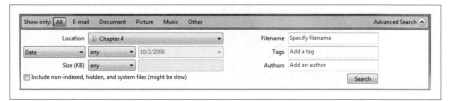

Figure 4-18. Advanced Search, which lets you fine-tune your searches

The Location field can be extremely useful if you're on a network, because you can add network drives and folders to your search. Select "Choose search locations" from the Location field, then browse to the network PCs, folders, and devices you want to search (Figure 4-19) and include them in the search.

Figure 4-19. Adding network locations to your search

The Start Search box

The Start Search box on the Start menu works much like the Search box in Windows Explorer, with some differences. It searches your entire PC, not just within an individual folder and subfolders. As you type, it shows you these results, grouped according to the types listed here (and shown in Figure 4-20):

- Programs (includes utilities and Control Panel applets as well as programs)
- Favorites and History (from the Internet)
- Files (includes folders and shortcuts)
- Communications (email and chat transcripts)

Click any result to view it, open it, or launch it. To see all results in Windows Explorer, click "See all results." To search the Internet using your default search engine, click "Search the Internet," and a search will be launched using your default browser.

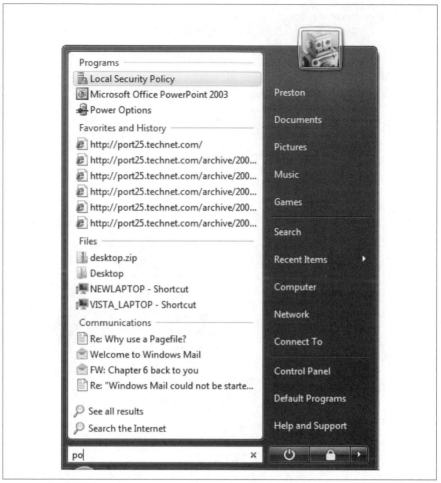

Figure 4-20. Searching from the Start menu

The Search folder and saving searches

When you choose Start → Search, you're sent to the Search Results folder (*Users\ username\Search Results*), which starts as a blank Windows Explorer screen, with the Search Pane turned on. You can do a basic Windows Explorer search from here, or turn on Advanced Search in the usual way. Even starting in the *Users\username\Search Results* folder, though, you'll do a search of your entire PC, not just the individual folder.

To save a search, click Save Search. From the screen that appears (Figure 4-21), give the search a name. File extensions for searches are *.search-ms*, and by default, they are saved in the *\Users\username\Searches* folder, but you can save them to any folder.

There are many ways to return to a saved search. You can navigate to the *.search-ms* file and double-click it. There's a faster way, though: in the Navigation Pane, click More under Favorite Links, and choose Searches. You'll be sent to the *\Users\username\ Searches* folder, and a list of all saved searches will appear—not just those that you've created, but also those that Windows Vista has already created for you, including searches for all recent documents, recent email, recent music, and more.

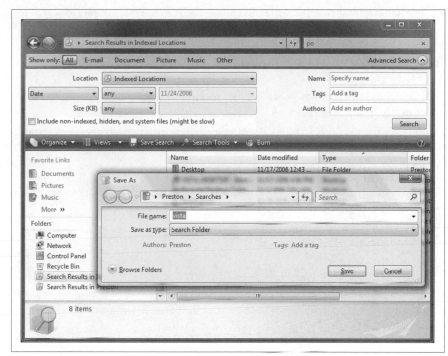

Figure 4-21. Saving a search so that you can later return to it

Note that you can save searches not only when you use Start → Search, but also when you're inside any folder in Windows Explorer. Your searches will be saved by default to your Search folder, no matter where you start your search.

Using Search Properties and syntax

The Windows Explorer Search box (and other search boxes also) lets you search using file properties, as well as a specialized syntax that makes finding files easier. You can search on any metadata associated with any files as a quick way to find what you want. Table 4-2 shows you some of the more common properties you can search on and how to search using them.

Table 4-2. Search properties

Property	Property description	How to search for it
Filename	The name of the file.	Type part or all of the filename. To find a file named *budget.xls*, you could type **budg** or **.xls**.
Kind of file	A description of the file, such as Document, Picture, Video, or Music.	Type the kind of file—for example, **Music** for any music files.
File extension	The file extension, such as *.xls*, *.doc*, *.jpg*, and so on.	Type the filename extension. You can also use wildcards—for example, ***.mp3**.
Tags	Words or phrases you or others added to the files to describe them.	Type a tag to see a list of files that have the matching tag.
Author	The person who created the file.	Type the name of the author.

Use properties with the proper syntax to narrow the search. For example, to search for files that have the name "budget" in them, you would type this:

```
Name:budget
```

To search for files with the tag of "budget" you would type:

```
Tag:budget
```

To find files modified on November 7, 2006, you would type:

```
Modified:11/07/2006
```

You can also use the Boolean filters AND, NOT, and OR; the comparison operators > and <; and grouping syntax, such as " " and ( ). Furthermore, you can combine them with searching for file properties.

If you want to forgo complex searches and having to remember search syntax, you can also use natural language search, which, as explained earlier, is the ability to search for files using plain English rather than complex syntax.

For example, instead of typing:

```
Kind:music artist:(Gluck or Salieri)
```

you could type:

```
Music by Gluck or Salieri
```

If you want to do that, you'll have to turn on natural language search, using the Search tab of the Folder Options window. See "Folder and Search Options," earlier in this chapter, for details.

Notes

- When using Boolean filters, you have to capitalize AND, NOT, and OR.
- To modify how and where to search—for example, whether to include subfolders in searches, when and how to use the index, and so on—use the Search tab of the Folder Options screen. For details, see "Folder and Search Options."

See also

"Windows Explorer," "Folder and Search Options," and "Indexing Options"

Shadow Copies

Shadow copies are made every time Windows Vista creates a restore point, and they can be used to restore previous versions of files. See "System Protection and System Restore," in Chapter 11, and "File Properties," in this chapter, for details.

Subst

\windows\system32\subst.exe

Create a new drive letter that is linked to a folder on your hard disk.

To open

Command Prompt → **subst**

Usage

```
subst [drive:] [path | /d ]
```

Description

Subst is a neat little utility that creates a new drive letter and actively links it to an existing folder on your hard disk. For example, type:

```
subst z: c:\opera\Cecilia Bartoli
```

to create a new drive letter, *z:*, and link it to the folder *c:\opera\Cecilia Bartoli*. When you open drive *z:* in Explorer, you'll see the contents of the linked folder. This is very useful if you access a particular folder frequently but find Windows shortcuts too limiting. For example, a drive created with Subst allows you to access a file in the folder, like this: *z:\ Se mai senti.mp3*. To disconnect a Subst'd drive, type:

```
subst z: /d
```

Notes

- Any drive letters created with Subst are forgotten when the computer shuts down.

Windows Explorer   *\windows\explorer.exe*

The default Windows interface, including the Start menu, the Desktop, the Taskbar, the Search tool, the Windows Explorer window, and all folder windows.

To open

Start → All Programs → Accessories → Windows Explorer

Command Prompt ▸ **explorer**

Double-click any folder icon on the Desktop or in any folder window.

Windows Key-E

Usage

```
explorer.exe [/n] [,/root,object] [[/select],subobject]
```

Description

The Explorer is the default Windows shell (see Figure 4-22). When run without any command-line parameters, it opens a two-paned window (commonly referred to simply as Explorer) in which you can navigate through all of the files, folders, and other resources on your computer.

See Chapter 2 for basic navigation and file management principles, and Chapter 3 for discussions of the visual elements.

Explorer accepts the following command-line options (note the mandatory commas):

/n Forces Explorer to open a new window (even if the specified folder is already open somewhere).

/select],subobject
   Include *subobject* to specify the file or folder to be initially highlighted or expanded when the folder is opened. If *subobject* is a folder, it will be expanded in the tree. If you also include the /select parameter (not valid without *subobject*), the parent of the specified folder is highlighted on the tree, no branches are initially expanded, and *subobject* will be highlighted in the right pane.

,/root,object
   By default, Explorer opens with the Desktop as the root folder. Use ,/root,object to specify a different root. The *object* parameter can be a folder name or a class ID.

Figure 4-22. Windows Explorer, the primary means of file and folder management in Windows Vista

For example, if you want Explorer to open to the Computer folder so that no drive branches are initially expanded (which is handy if you have several drives), type the following:

```
explorer.exe /n, /select, c:\
```

To open an Explorer window rooted at the Documents folder, type:

```
explorer.exe /root,c:\Documents and Settings\username\Documents
```

where *username* is the username of the owner of the Documents folder.

The Windows Explorer Toolbar

Depending on the type of folder you're viewing, the Windows Explorer Toolbar changes to offer context-sensitive buttons, although it always has the basic Organize and Views buttons. For example, when viewing the Computer folder (Figure 4-23), there are icons for viewing file and object properties, viewing system properties, uninstalling or changing a program, mapping a network drive, and opening the Control Panel.

If the folder you're viewing is filled with music, a different toolbar appears and includes buttons for playing music and burning a CD. A folder with pictures and videos, meanwhile, would include buttons for playing a slide show and burning a CD. You can customize your view of folders using the Customize tab of the Folder Options dialog box. (See "Folder and Search Options," earlier in this chapter.)

If the folder has pictures in it, you can play a slide show that displays the pictures one by one, using the Slide Show button. For details, see "Slide show," in Chapter 12.

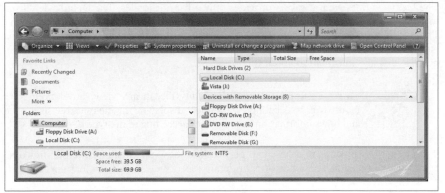

Figure 4-23. The Windows Explorer Toolbar for the Computer folder

Windows Explorer views

The Views button on Windows Explorer pops up a menu (Figure 4-24) that lets you choose among seven different folder views:

- Extra Large Icons
- Large Icons
- Medium Icons
- Small Icons
- List
- Details
- Tiles

Figure 4-24. The Views menu in Windows Explorer

The four icon views are self-explanatory. Windows Explorer folder icons are "live"—that is, they will display live thumbnails of the contents within them so that you can see thumbnails of pictures contained in the folder. The larger the icon, the easier it is to see these live thumbnails.

The List view does what it says—provides only a list of the files. The Details view lists the files and displays information about each, such as file size, date created, and so on. The information displayed about each will vary according to the folder type. The Tiles view is a combination of an icon view and a List view; it shows thumbnails of each file but also displays information about them.

To see basic information about any file, in any view, hover your mouse over it. A balloon will appear displaying the file type, file size, and other information that changes according to the type of file.

If the folder has pictures in it, you can play a slide show that displays the pictures one by one, using the Slide Show button. For details, see "Slide show," in Chapter 12.

Windows Explorer panes

Windows Explorer has four main panes that you can turn on and off by choosing Organize → Layout:

Search Pane
Displays the Search toolbar (see "Search," earlier in this chapter, for details)

The Search Pane option appears only when you type text into the Search box. If you delete the text, the Search Pane will no longer be available as an option. However, it is available as an option from the Desktop and Computer folders.

Details Pane
Shows, at the bottom of the screen, information about the object currently highlighted

Preview Pane
Shows, on the righthand side, a preview of the file currently highlighted

Navigation Pane
Shows folders and objects on the lefthand side of the screen in tree-style view for navigating

Figure 4-25 shows Windows Explorer with the panes labeled.

Stacking and sorting

Windows Vista introduces new ways to filter and display files in Windows Explorer by grouping and stacking files based on their metadata. In Windows Explorer, if you click in the right side of any property header (Name, Size, Rating, and so on), a down arrow appears, along with a drop-down list that includes buttons labeled Sort, Group, and Stack. The Sort button is the default for Windows Explorer. The Group button displays files in separate groups, according to the value of the property—for example, by rating, as shown in Figure 4-26.

You can collapse and expand any group by double-clicking the group title—for example, 3 Stars. In addition, you can display only some groups and not others. In the example in Figure 4-26, if you selected 3 Stars instead of Group, you would display only files that were rated three stars.

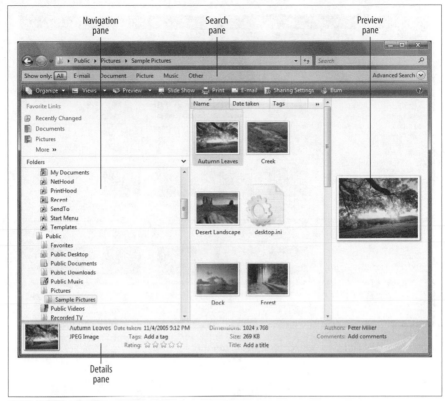

Figure 4-25. The four panes in Windows Explorer

If you instead chose Stack, it would organize the files into what look like subfolders in our example, by three stars, four stars, and five stars. To see the files in any stack, double-click the stack.

Modifying file tags and properties

Every file on your system has tags and properties associated with it, and these are displayed in several places in Windows Explorer—on the righthand side of the screen when using Details or Tiles views, when hovering a mouse over the file, and in the Details Pane. They're also shown inside many applications. And when you do a search for files, those tags and properties are searched through as well.

You often can modify tags and properties using the program that created the file, but you can also use Windows Explorer to modify them. Turn on the Details Pane, then highlight the file whose property you want to change. In the Details Pane, click the property you want to change, edit what's there or add new text, and click Save.

To add tags, type them directly into the Tags field; separate multiple tags with semicolons, as shown in Figure 4-27.

Figure 4-26. Stacking files based on rating metadata

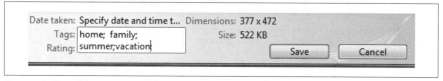

Figure 4-27. Adding tags to a file using the Details Pane

 Certain properties that are inherent to the file itself can't be changed, such as file size and dimensions.

Windows Explorer Address Bar

The Address Bar is covered in some detail in Chapter 3, so there is no need to go into detail about it here. However, there is one unique, often overlooked aspect of Windows Explorer's Address Bar—the menu that appears when you right-click it (Figure 4-28).

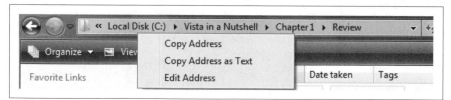

Figure 4-28. The little-known Address Bar menu

You can use it to copy the address to the Clipboard. The Edit Address choice turns the Address Bar into a text menu that lets you type in text. Figure 4-29 shows you how the Address Bar changes when you edit it as text.

Figure 4-29. Using text in the Address Bar

Using ZIP archives in Windows Explorer

Using Windows Explorer, you can compress files and put them into packages using the *.zip* format, or simply compress individual files. In addition, Windows Explorer lets you look inside *.zip* archives and uncompress them.

In Windows Explorer, select the file or files that you want to compress, right-click them, and choose Send to → Compressed (zip) folder. A ZIP file will be created in the current folder, with the name of the file or the first file in the group, and ending in the *.zip* extension. You can rename it to what you want.

You can view files inside *.zip* archives just as you can any other folder. But if you double-click a file in the folder, you'll open a read-only copy. To make changes to the file, choose File → Save As and save it on your hard drive. You can instead extract the files from the archive, and then work with them after they've been extracted. Right-click the *.zip* file, select "Extract all," and then extract the files to any location.

CD burning

You can "burn" data directly to a CD or DVD using Windows Explorer. Click the Burn button and follow the directions. But keep in mind that this burns only a data disc—that is, it merely copies files from your PC to the disc. You won't be able to play it in a CD player that plays only music CDs. To burn a music CD, you need to use Windows Media Player. See "Windows Media Player," in Chapter 12, for details.

Notes

- Some folders in Windows Vista are *junctions*, which means that they don't actually exist and are only pointers to another folder. These junctions are used to preserve holdovers from earlier versions of Windows, and they are there so that programs written for earlier versions of Windows can continue to function properly. For example, the Documents and Settings folder is a junction, and if you try to access it in Windows Explorer, you will get the error message "Documents and Settings is not available." If you look at the Documents and Settings folder, you'll see that it's actually a shortcut; it has the shortcut icon on the folder itself. It points to the *\Users* folder, which has replaced it.
- If you turn on the Search Pane in a folder and use it to do a search, you will search only in that folder, not across your entire computer.

See also

"Folder Properties," "File Properties," and "Search," in this chapter, and "Internet Explorer," in Chapter 5

5

Internet Explorer

Internet Explorer has long been the most popular browser in the world, but before the launch of Windows Vista, it had became the most maligned browser in the world as well. There's good reason for that. Although newer browsers such as Firefox continually added new features such as tabbed browsing and security help, Internet Explorer changed little from version to version. It began to look down at the heels—and worse, it was becoming less useful than Firefox and other browsers.

The launch of Windows Vista changed all that. Microsoft took the opportunity to give Internet Explorer a thoroughgoing makeover, and it is a success. The Vista-based browser now includes tabbed browsing, plenty of security features, and a more modern, streamlined interface, making it easier than ever to use.

This chapter offers a guide to all of Internet Explorer's most valuable features and shows you how to customize them. It doesn't, however, cover general Internet features, such as adding a new connection or troubleshooting connections. For that, turn to Chapter 7.

Here is an alphabetical reference of entries in this chapter:

Add-On Manager	Internet Options	Pop-Up Blocker
Alt Menu	Internet Options Privacy Tab	Print Preview
Content Tab and Content Adviser	Internet Options Security Tab	RSS Feeds
Delete Browsing History	Page Menu	Search Bar
Favorites Center	Phishing Filter	Tab Options
Internet Explorer		

Internet Explorer

\program files\internet explorer\iexplore.exe

A web browser used to view web content.

To open

Start → All Programs → Internet Explorer

Use the Internet Explorer icon on the Start menu or on the Quick Launch Toolbar.

Command Prompt → **iexplore**

Usage

```
iexplore [-nohome] [url]
```

Description

Internet Explorer is a full-featured web browser that you can use to navigate the Web, as well as view web content on your local network or hard drive. Web content is typically in the form of web pages (*.html*), but it can also be images (*.gif*, *.png*, and *.jpg*), FTP sites, or even streaming video or audio (via Windows Media Player) (see Figure 5-1).

Figure 5-1. Internet Explorer 7.0, the default web browser in Windows Vista

You navigate in Internet Explorer by clicking hyperlinks in web pages or by typing addresses in Internet Explorer's Address Bar. You can "bookmark" frequently visited sites by creating Internet shortcuts (similar to Windows shortcuts), stored in your Favorites folder, your Desktop, or anywhere else on your hard disk.

Use the Back and Next buttons (as well as the Alt-left arrow and Alt-right arrow, respectively) to navigate through the history, which is empty in each new Internet Explorer window or tab that you open. Use the Stop button (or press the Esc key) to stop the loading of a page, and use the Refresh button (or press F5) to reload the page, displaying any changes that might have been made or displaying an updated version of a dynamically generated page.

The Home button loads the currently configured *home page(s)* into the browser window. The home page is merely a shortcut to a single web site, and you can change it by going to Tools → Internet Options.

If you start Internet Explorer from the command line or Start box, you can use either of the following options:

-nohome

Starts Internet Explorer without loading the home page (blank). You can also configure Internet Explorer to use a blank page (*about:blank*) as its home page, effectively causing Internet Explorer to always start without loading a home page.

url

The *Uniform Resource Locator*, which is the address of a page to load. If you omit *url*, Internet Explorer will display the home page.

Here are descriptions of some of the features of Internet Explorer:

Windows Update

Updates to Internet Explorer are frequently made available on the Windows Update site. Windows Vista comes with Internet Explorer 7, but subsequent versions will add support for new standards, new features, bug fixes, and probably a few new bugs. If you're upgrading to a new major release, always take advantage of the feature that saves the old system files, allowing the new version to be uninstalled in case you run into a problem or incompatibility.

AutoComplete

Internet Explorer has an auto-completion feature, which encompasses several features to help reduce typing. While you're typing web addresses, Internet Explorer checks your browser history for any matches and displays them below the Address Bar. The more characters you type in the Address Bar, the narrower the list of suggestions will be, until the list disappears. To choose a URL from the list, just use the arrow keys on your keyboard and press Enter, or use your mouse.

You can also type an address without the *http://* prefix, the *.com* extension, and even *www* (if applicable) in your addresses, and the site will still be found and loaded, as long as it is in the *.com*, *.edu*, or *.org* domain. To add new domains to be included in AutoComplete, use the Registry Editor to add them to *HKEY_LOCAL_MACHINE\SOFTWARE\Microsoft\InternetExplorer\Main\UrlTemplate*.

AutoComplete goes further to remember usernames, passwords, and even some form data. Be careful when having Internet Explorer "remember" sensitive data, as others will be able to access it as well. For example, don't store your bank PIN or credit card number if others have access to your computer. You can configure the AutoComplete options by going to Tools → Internet Options → Content → AutoComplete → Settings.

The AutoSearch feature extends AutoComplete by allowing you to initiate web searches from the Address Bar. To use AutoSearch, start by typing a keyword into the Address Bar (such as **bozo**). Internet Explorer will perform a search using your default search site. The default is MSN Search, but you can change it by clicking the down arrow next to the Search Bar and selecting Change Search Defaults.

Search Bar

You can also do searches from the Search Bar. Type in a term, and it will perform a search using your default search site. You can add multiple providers by clicking the down arrow next to the Search Bar and selecting Find More Providers. From the page that appears, choose another provider. To use a provider other than your default, click the down arrow next to the Search Bar, and select the provider you want to use for that search. You can also change the search default by clicking the down arrow next to the Search Bar and selecting Change Search Defaults.

Cookies

Cookies, first introduced by Netscape, allow a web site to store specific information on your hard disk. For example, if you visit an online store that has a shopping cart, that web site will be able to keep track of who you are by storing one or more cookies on your computer. This allows thousands of people to simultaneously access a site yet have their own separate and distinct shopping carts. Cookies are often the target of privacy advocates, because it's possible for web site administrators to use cookies to track which pages certain visitors view at their site. However, cookies are available only to the sites that assign them (a cookie defined at Amazon.com cannot be read by any other web site), so the actual risk is minimal. You can adjust how Internet Explorer handles cookies by going to Tools → Internet Options → Privacy tab.

The Information Bar

Whenever anything untoward happens when you browse the Web—an ActiveX control tries to download, a web site tries to get around Internet Explorer's security settings, etc.—the yellow Information Bar appears just below Internet Explorer's address bar with a Security Warning. Clicking the Information Bar provides more information and a context menu with possible actions, from giving your OK to switching off any future alerts. This toolbar is usually hidden, appearing only when a security "event" occurs.

Pop-Up Blocker

Pop-up ads are among the Web's most annoying annoyances, and Internet Explorer can block them, making web surfing much more enjoyable and clutter-free. You'll find its full options in the Tools menu (Tools → Pop-up Blocker, shown in Figure 5-2), or by clicking the Information Bar when it blocks an offender.

Figure 5-2. The Pop-Up Blocker, which makes surfing the Internet much more enjoyable

The Pop-Up Blocker is automatically activated, although you can switch it off. When it blocks a pop up, a yellow bar appears at the top of the current page. Click the bar and you can 1) temporarily allow pop ups during your visit to the site and see exactly what each pop up is (for instance, an urgent news post or logon screen), 2) give the web site permission to display pop ups whenever you visit; or 3) open the Pop-Up Blocker settings window. From here, you can choose to block every pop-up window you encounter except for those you OK on the spot, switch off the blocker entirely, or have the blocker determine which pop ups to suppress and which to let through.

Download Blocker

By default, Internet Explorer stops all downloads. That may be overkill, but even careful users occasionally click the wrong box or get tricked by a misleading message. In the bad old days before the Download Blocker was baked into Internet Explorer, it was also annoying to have to constantly swat down requests to install ActiveX components with names such as "uber1337 Password Manager 1.843 by clicking this you agree to let us show you a million ads watch your movements and dial porn sites in Paraguay." These requests are now blocked by default. You'll find the full settings list by clicking Tools → Internet Options, the Security tab, and the Custom Level button.

The Download Blocker stops any program that tries to install anything without your permission and flashes a warning via the Information Bar. Ignore the warning, and nothing will be downloaded. However, click the Information Bar to display download options and further information about exactly what the site is trying to send you.

If you trust the web site (say, Macromedia) and you know you need to accept the download (say, the latest Shockwave player), you can give the site a permanent thumbs up by selecting "Always install software from *companyname*" (Internet Explorer fills in the company name for you). If the site is totally untrustworthy, you can click "Never install software from *companyname*" and blacklist it forever.

In most cases, however, you'll probably choose the middle ground and select "Ask me every time" so that you can make the decision about any potential download on a case-by-case basis.

Make sure you confirm what a component does before disabling it, or you could lose important Internet Explorer functionality. If the name doesn't supply enough details (for example, Shockwave ActiveX Control), search Google for the add-on's name, or search the add-on publisher's site for information.

The Add-on Manager

In the course of your web travels, all sorts of "enhancements" to Internet Explorer may be added by the web sites you visit—ActiveX components and browser extensions that add features, browser helper objects that display flash and PDF files, and so on. If an add-on has been installed by accident, or you simply want it out of your hair, the new Manage Add-ons screen lets you turn it off like a light bulb. To actually uninstall software, you still must use the Add or Remove Programs control panel. To access this control, select Tools → Manage Add-ons → Enable or Disable Add-ons. You'll see a list of any add-on components you've allowed onto your system (see Figure 5-3). To enable or disable an add-on that's on your system, just select it in the list, then click the Enable or Disable radio button below and click OK.

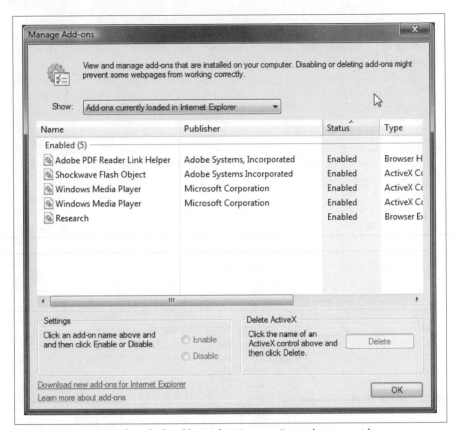

Figure 5-3. Managing those little add-ons that "improve" your browser without your knowledge

Notes

- If Internet Explorer is the default browser, you can also go to Start → Start Search and type any web address to open the page at that address. However, you can set any browser as the default. Typically, during installation of another browser, such as Firefox (*http://www.mozilla.com/firefox*) or Opera (*http://www.opera.com*), there will be an option to make that browser the default. Once you have installed one of these other browsers, the procedure to make it the default varies. In Internet Explorer, go to Tools → Internet Options → Programs tab, and turn on the "Tell me if Internet Explorer is not the default web browser" option. Then, after closing all open Internet Explorer windows, open a new Internet Explorer window; when prompted, verify that you want to make Internet Explorer the default.

Another way to specify whether Internet Explorer should be your default browser is to choose Start → Default Programs → Set your default programs, to change whether Internet Explorer should be your default browser.

- Go to Tools → Internet Options (see "Internet Options," later in this chapter) to set the various options relating to the display of web pages, security on the Internet, related Internet applications, and other, more technical Internet-related settings.

- The files that make up web pages, *.html* files, are simply plain-text files and can be viewed or modified with a plain-text editor, such as Notepad. In fact, if you select Page → View Source, Internet Explorer will display the code for the current page in a new Notepad window. However, if you're not familiar with HyperText Markup Language (HTML) code, you can use any modern word processor to create and modify web pages. Most Internet service providers (ISPs) will even host your pages for you, effectively giving you your own web site.

- When you type the name of a folder on your hard disk into Internet Explorer's Address Bar, Windows Explorer will open in a new window and the contents of the folder will be displayed. (You'll get a security warning that says, "A website wants to open web content using this program on your computer." Click Allow to continue.) Likewise, if you type an Internet address into the Address Bar of an Explorer window or a single folder window, the window will be replaced with Internet Explorer and the page will load.

- If you find the text size on any page to be too small, go to Page → Text Size and choose the text size to your liking.

See also

"Manage Network Connections," in Chapter 7, "Windows Explorer," in Chapter 4, and "Internet Options," "Tab Options," "Phishing Filter," "Print Preview," and "RSS Feeds," in this chapter

What's new in Vista

With Windows Vista, Microsoft gave Internet Explorer one of its biggest face-lifts in years. In fact, it gave it more than just a face-lift—it also added significant new security features, both ones you see and ones you don't see. Before the development of Windows Vista, Internet Explorer was looking long in the tooth and had become inferior to competing browsers; it didn't allow tabbed browsing, for example, and it was notoriously insecure. With the release of Windows Vista, though, all of that has changed. Here are the highlights of what's new in Windows Vista:

Tabbed browsing
> The most noticeable change in Internet Explorer is that you can open multiple web pages, each in its own tab, as shown in Figure 5-4. To open a new tab, click the small tab to the far right, and a blank tab will open. When you click a link on a page, it will open as it normally would—in the current tab, or in a separate window if the HTML on the web page has told it to do so. But if you want, you can have any link open in a new tab instead. Simply right-click the link and choose Open in New Tab. To control how tabs operate, go to Tools → Internet Options and click Settings next to Tabs on the General page.

No more menus
> Use Internet Explorer for a short time, and you'll notice something odd: the familiar menus have vanished and have been replaced with a new set of menus on the far-right portion of the page. If you want to use the old familiar menus, press the Alt key and they will magically appear.

Figure 5-4. Internet Explorer tabs

Phishing filter

Phishing has become the newest scourge of the Internet. In a phishing attack, you're sent an email that purports to be from a legitimate financial site, such as your bank, PayPal, or eBay. You're asked to click a link to log in to the site, and often you're told you need to log in as a way to guarantee your security. When you click to the site, it looks legitimate, but it is in fact from a scammer, who steals your password and login and proceeds to empty your back account or use your account in other nefarious ways.

Internet Explorer's phishing filter solves the problem by stopping you in your tracks when you visit what it believes to be a phishing site. A page warns you that you are about to head to a "reported phishing website." You then have the choice of closing the web site, or ignoring the Microsoft recommendation and visiting it.

If the filter instead detects what it says is only a *suspected* phishing site, you're let through, but a yellow button appears next to the Address Bar and labels the site a "Suspicious website." You can then decide whether to stay at the site or head away.

RSS feeds

With Really Simple Syndication (RSS), you can get news and weblogs (blogs) delivered straight to your PC. You get a preview of the content available on the blog or web site, or you receive the full content, depending on how the site set up its feed. If you get a preview and you want to read the full post or news item, you click on the feed and are sent to the site or blog.

Vista's Internet Explorer includes an RSS reader for subscribing to and reading RSS feeds, shown in Figure 5-5. When you're on a page that has an RSS feed, the RSS icon on the Internet Explorer toolbar turns orange. Click the icon to read the feed using Internet Explorer's built-in RSS reader.

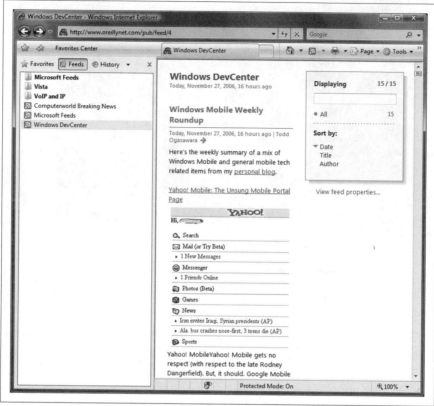

Figure 5-5. Reading RSS feeds with Internet Explorer

The reader lets you sort items by date, title, and author. A search box lets you search through all the feeds. To configure how Internet Explorer's RSS reader works, choose Tools → Internet Options → Content, and in the Feeds section, click Settings.

Protected Mode

Internet Explorer has long been a target of malware writers. Partly that's because it's the most popular browser on the planet. But part of the reason is that Internet Explorer includes hooks directly into Windows itself, and so a hacker can wreak havoc on Windows using Internet Explorer.

In Windows Vista, Microsoft has taken a big step toward solving that problem. It runs in Protected Mode, which shields your filesystem and Registry from any actions taken by Internet Explorer or any Internet Explorer add-ins. So even if a piece of malware breaks through all of Internet Explorer's security features, it can't do harm to your PC, because Protected Mode in essence locks Internet Explorer in a safe box.

Internet Explorer hot keys

Many people like using the mouse, but those who are more keyboard oriented are always looking for fast ways to access Internet Explorer features. That's where hot key combinations come in; rather than having to mouse around, you can press a simple key combination, such as Ctrl-D, to add a site to your Favorites. Table 5-1 lists Internet Explorer hot keys. For hot keys related to tabs, see "Tab Options," later in this chapter.

Table 5-1. Internet Explorer hot keys

Key combination	Action
Alt-left arrow	Go to the preceding page.
Alt-right arrow	Go to the next page.
Ctrl-Tab/Shift-Ctrl-Tab	Go to the next/previous tab.
Escape (Esc)	Stop the page from loading.
F5 or Ctrl-F5	Refresh the page.
Alt-Home	Go to your home page.
Alt-D	Give focus to the Address Bar.
Ctrl-Enter	Add "www." and ".com" to what you typed in the Address Bar, then navigate to the site.
Space bar/Shift-Space bar	Scroll down/up the web page.
Alt-F4	Close Internet Explorer.
Alt-M	Activate the Home button on the Command Bar.
Alt-J	Activate the Feeds button on the Command Bar.
Alt-O	Activate the Tools button on the Command Bar.
Alt-L	Activate the Help button on the Command Bar.
Alt-C	Open the Favorites Center set to display favorites.
Ctrl-Shift-Q	Bring up a list of open tabs.
Ctrl-D	Add sites to Favorites.
Shift-click	Open a link in a new window.
Shift F10	Open the right-click context menu for the currently selected item.
Ctrl-mouse wheel up/down	Zoom in/out by 10 percent.
Ctrl-(+)	Increase zoom by 10 percent.
Ctrl-(–)	Decrease zoom by 10 percent.
Ctrl-0 (zero)	Go back to the original size.
Ctrl-E	Go to the Toolbar Search Box.
Alt-Enter	Open your search query in a new tab.
Ctrl-down arrow	Display the search provider menu.
Ctrl-I	Open the Favorites Center to your favorites.
Ctrl-H	Open the Favorites Center to your history.
Ctrl-J	Open the Favorites Center to your feeds.

Alt Menu

Brings back the pre-Internet Explorer 7 menus.

To open

In Internet Explorer, press the Alt key.

Description

One of the biggest changes to the Internet Explorer interface in Vista and Internet Explorer 7 is that the menus just beneath the Address Bar seem to have vanished. In fact, though, they haven't vanished; they've just been hidden. You can make them appear again by pressing the Alt key. The items on the menu are available somewhere else in the Internet Explorer interface. For example, the Favorites menu gives you access to features that are more easily accessible in the Favorites Center. But if you're one of those people who enjoys the traditional Internet Explorer menus, you can always get to them by a simple press of the Alt key.

Notes

- Once you get used to the new Internet Explorer interface, you most likely won't need to rely on the old menus. But if you're having trouble finding a particular feature, they're worth turning on (select Tools → Menu Bar to keep them on permanently).

Content Tab and Content Advisor

Controls content you can view and use in Internet Explorer.

To open

Internet Explorer → Tools → Internet Options → Content

Description

This tab on the Internet Options dialog box controls a variety of miscellaneous content-related settings, including the Content Advisor, which can control the kind of web sites users of the PC are allowed to visit. It includes the tabs shown in Figure 5-6.

The following is a list of what is available on the Content tab:

Parental Controls
> Clicking this button brings you to the Parental Controls Control Panel applet that lets you decide how children can use the computer and Internet. It lets you set time limits on computer use, as well as control what sites they can visit, what games they play, and what programs they use. For more details, see "Parental Controls," in Chapter 8.

Content Advisor
> This section lets you use a ratings system to control the kind of Internet content that can be viewed on the computer. It's questionable how useful the Content Advisor is, because it depends on a system in which sites rate themselves for violence, nudity, sex, and profanity—and very few sites actually do the rating. And, of course, because the site does its own ratings, it may not rate itself accurately. The Internet Content Rating Association (ICRA) (*http://www.icra.org*)

Figure 5-6. The Content tab, which lets you configure how Internet Explorer should handle a variety of miscellaneous content

oversees the rating system. Click Enable under the Content Advisor, and you'll come to the tabbed dialog box shown in Figure 5-7.

Following are details about each of the tabs:

Ratings

This lists a variety of objectionable content—for example, "Depiction of drug use," "Violence," and "Sexual material." Highlight each and then move the slider to specify how the content may be viewed on a scale starting with "None" and ending with "Unrestricted."

Approved sites

This tab lets you specify sites that you want to either always block or always allow to be viewed.

General

This lets you customize a variety of Content Advisor settings, such as whether to allow users to view web sites that have no ratings. It also lets you add other rating systems and create a supervisor password that can be used to allow users to view restricted content.

Figure 5-7. The Content Advisor, which lets you fine-tune what content can be viewed on the Web

Advanced

This lets you consult rating bureaus for every page you visit, or use the Platform for Internet Content Selection Rules (PICSRules), which is a series of rules created by the PICS rating system that you can apply to determine which site can be visited, and which blocked. This is an old ratings system that doesn't appear to be used much, if at all.

Certificates

It's fairly easy for one site to masquerade as another. Digital certificates, which use cryptography to create unique identifiers that can't be forged, can be used by sites that want to prove their identity to you. Here, you can identify which certificate authorities (certificate issuers) you want to trust. If Internet Explorer receives a certificate by an authority it doesn't know about, it will either display a warning or not display the associated web page at all, depending on your settings. Companies sometimes self-certify their pages, especially in an intranet context, and you will get a warning when you try to connect to one of these sites.

AutoComplete

Internet Explorer's AutoComplete feature remembers text you've typed into your browser, including web site addresses, names, passwords, usernames, and forms data. Click Settings, and a dialog box appears that lets you determine whether to use AutoComplete for each of those, or whether to turn off AutoComplete completely. See "Internet Explorer," earlier in this chapter, for more details.

Feeds

Click Settings to control how Internet Explorer handles RSS subscriptions. You can control whether it should automatically check for feeds, and if so how often, as well as whether to play a sound when a feed is found and whether to use the special RSS reading pane. For more information, see "RSS Feeds," later in this chapter.

Notes

- It's questionable how useful the Content Advisor is. Rating systems have been proposed since at least as far back as 1997, but none has really caught on, and they are rarely used. If you're a parent and you worry about your children's use of the Internet, using the Parental Controls feature is a much better choice.

See also

"RSS Feeds," later in this chapter, and "Parental Controls," in Chapter 8

Favorites Center

Revisit your favorite web sites and read RSS feeds.

To open

Click the Favorites Center icon in Internet Explorer.

Press Alt-C when using Internet Explorer.

Description

The Web is a massive, chaotic place, and it is difficult to remember all of your favorite web sites, much less be able to navigate quickly to them. That's where the Favorites Center, shown in Figure 5-8, comes in. It lets you organize all your favorite sites in a logical fashion, in folders, so that you can revisit them. It also lets you organize and read RSS feeds.

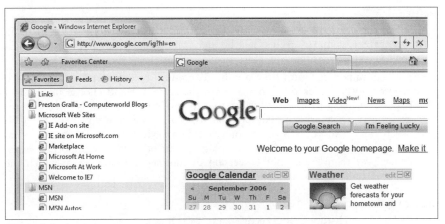

Figure 5-8. Organizing your favorite web sites using the Favorites Center

To open the Favorites Center, click the Favorites Center icon (it looks like a star). It opens to the leftmost portion of Internet Explorer, and it overlays the web page you're viewing so that it hides the leftmost portion of it. To pin the Favorites Center so that it stays in place and the page underneath resizes so that no portion of the page is hidden, click the arrow on the upper right of the Favorites Center.

Pages are organized in folders, or you can put them in the top level of Favorites. To navigate to a web site inside a folder, click the folder, and then the site. To read RSS feeds, click the RSS icon, and select the feed you want to read.

You can also browse to pages that you've visited previously but haven't necessarily put into the Favorites Center. Click the History button in the Favorites Center to view a list of the sites you've previously visited. When you click the button, a menu appears that lets you list the sites by date, site name, sites you've visited most often, or sites you've visited today. You can also search through your history by choosing Search History from the menu.

When you're on a site that you want to add to your Favorites Center, click the + button, click Add to Favorites, and from the dialog box that appears, choose which folder to put it in (or create a new folder and put it there), and then click Add.

You can also add Tab Groups to the Favorites Center. First create a Tab Group by opening all the sites in their own tabs, as outlined in "Tab Options," later in this chapter. Then click the + button, and click Add Tab Group to Favorites. Give the group a folder name, then click Add.

To open the Tab Group in the Favorites Center, click the Favorites Center button, then click the folder that you want to open. Next, click the arrow to the right of the folder name. The Tab Group will now open, with each site in its own separate tab.

You can organize your favorites in several different ways. You can drag folders and sites to new locations within the Favorites Center, or you can instead click the + button, select Organize Favorites, and from the screen that appears, use tools to organize them. When moving a favorite from one folder to another, it's fastest to do it from directly inside the Favorites Center, but if you're going to be doing a lot of work, it's worth using the tools.

Notes

- When you clear your History, as outlined in "Delete Browsing History," later in this chapter, your History list will be blank. It automatically populates itself as soon as you start visiting sites after you clear it out.

- You can import favorites from another computer, or export favorites to it. To export favorites, click the + button with the star on it and choose Import and Export. The Import/Export Wizard appears. Follow the wizard's directions for exporting your favorites. Make sure that you save it to a location where the PC to which you'll import it has access, or save it to a device such as a Universal Serial Bus (USB) flash drive, which you can plug into the other PC. To import favorites, first export them from another version of Internet Explorer, then launch the Import/Export Wizard and follow the directions for importing them.

See also

"Delete Browsing History," "RSS Feeds," and "Tab Options"

Internet Options

Change the settings that affect Internet Explorer and your dial-up Internet connection.

To open

Control Panel → [Network and Internet] → Internet Options

Command Prompt → `inetcpl.cpl`

Internet Explorer → Tools → Internet Options

Description

The Internet Options dialog is a densely packed dialog with every conceivable option for Internet Explorer. Settings are divided into the following tabs:

General

The General tab is shown in Figure 5-9. The "Home page" section allows you to choose the pages that load automatically whenever an Internet Explorer window is opened, as well as pages linked to the Home button on the toolbar. In the Vista version of Internet Explorer 7, you can have multiple home pages so that whenever you click the Home button, each home page will open in its own tab. To set multiple home pages, type each on its own line in the "Home page" section. Press Enter at the end of a line to move to the next line. Make sure to include the *http://* in front of each page you want to load as your home page.

The Browsing history section lets you delete your browsing history, temporary Internet files, cookies, saved passwords, and information you've typed into web forms. Temporary Internet files, also known as your *browser cache*, are stored in a folder on your hard disk that stores copies of recently visited web pages for quicker access the next time they're visited. The Temporary Internet Files folder is located at *C:\Users\username\AppData\Local\Microsoft\Windows\Temporary Internet Files* by default (to open this folder, click Settings in the "Browsing history" section, then click "View files"). Cookies, a feature unrelated to Temporary Internet files, are pieces of information stored on your computer to allow certain web sites to remember your identity or preferences; click Delete Cookies to clear all cookies stored on your computer. To selectively remove cookies, open the *C:\Users\ username\AppData\Roaming\Microsoft\Windows\Cookies* folder in Windows Explorer. See "Internet Options Privacy Tab," in the "Security" section of this chapter, for more cookie settings.

Internet Explorer keeps track of pages you've visited and displays links to those pages in a different color (purple by default, as opposed to the standard blue for links to pages you haven't yet visited). Items in your History are also accessed with the AutoComplete feature discussed in "Internet Explorer," earlier in this chapter. For details on how to control the length of time before pages are removed from Internet Explorer's history, and how to change your cache settings, see "Delete Browsing History," in this section of the chapter. For more information about clearing your Browsing history, see "Internet Options Privacy Tab," in the "Security" section of this chapter.

The Search section lets you remove search providers and set your default provider. Click the Settings button, and from the dialog box that appears you'll see a list of all your search providers. To remove one, highlight it and click Remove, then click OK. To make one of them the default search provider, highlight it and click Set Default, then click OK. Note that for some odd reason, you

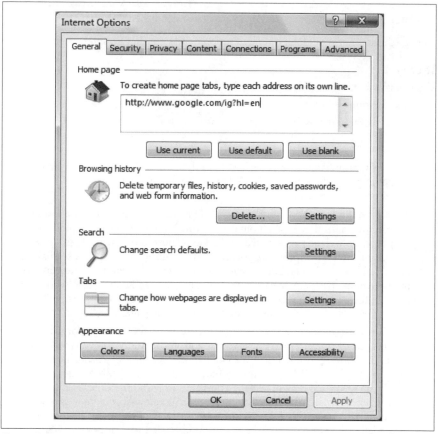

Figure 5-9. Internet Options' General tab, which lets you choose a default home page, change or add search providers, control how tabs work, and clear out your web browsing traces

can't add search providers from this dialog box. Instead, you have to add providers via a menu that drops down from the Search Bar itself. For details, see the discussion of the Search Bar, earlier in this chapter.

The Tabs section lets you control how tabs appear and function. You're given a great deal of control over how they work, including whether they should even be used. For details, see "Tab Options," later in this chapter.

The remaining buttons allow you to control the default colors, fonts, and languages in which pages are shown. The Accessibility button essentially limits the control web pages have over their appearance.

Security

This tab lets you specify the security settings for different predefined zones of Internet content. There are four basic zones: Internet, Intranet, Trusted, and Restricted. By default, all sites are placed into one of the first two zones. All sites found on your local network are placed into the Intranet zone. All other sites are placed into the Internet zone. You can manually add sites to the Trusted and Restricted zones. Security settings for each zone are preset, but you can change these settings if you want. For each zone, you can specify High, Medium, Low, or Custom security settings. Security settings govern such things as whether ActiveX controls, Java applets, and JavaScript programs are used, how files are downloaded, and how user authentication takes place. For details, see "Internet Options Security Tab," in the "Security" section of this chapter.

Privacy

The Privacy tab controls when and how Internet Explorer accepts cookies, and allows you to customize the Pop-Up Blocker. Play around with the slider to choose among six different preconfigured privacy policies, or click Advanced to choose your own settings. The Medium or Low policy should be suitable for most users. You can also click Edit in the Web Sites section to selectively choose which web sites can store and retrieve cookies, and which cannot. You can view the cookies currently stored on your hard disk by opening the *C:\Users\username\AppData\Roaming\Microsoft\Windows\Cookies* folder in Windows Explorer. For details, see "Internet Options Privacy Tab," in the "Security" section of this chapter.

Content

The Content tab contains a number of miscellaneous functions that allow you to control what Internet Explorer can and cannot view. It also controls how Auto-Complete functions, and how Internet Explorer handles RSS feeds. Many of the features in the Content Advisor section are not widely used and still have a few kinks to be worked out. For details about this tab, see "Content Tab and Content Advisor," earlier in this chapter. Additionally, this tab lets you go to Parental Controls to control how children can use the computer and Internet. For details about Parental Controls, see Chapter 8.

Connections

The Connections tab allows you to choose to have your dial-up or cellular data connection dialed automatically. If you're not using a dial-up or cellular connection but rather DSL, cable, or a direct LAN connection, most of this page will be of no use to you. The exception is the LAN Settings dialog, which lets you configure your proxy (if you have one). In addition, the Add VPN button lets you create a Virtual Private Network (VPN) connection. A VPN connection lets you create a secure, encrypted connection that in essence lets you use the Internet as though it were a private, secure network. You can use VPNs to connect from home to a corporate network, or to establish a secure connection at a public wireless hot spot. For details, see "Virtual Private Network Connection," in Chapter 8.

If you have one or more dial-up connections, they will be listed here. If you have two or more connections and you want to use the Auto Dial feature, choose one and click Set Default. Then, click either "Dial whenever a network connection is not present" or "Always dial my default connection," whichever you prefer.

Select a connection and then click Settings → Advanced to choose how many times Windows will dial before giving up, and whether it should disconnect automatically if it detects that the connection is no longer needed.

The Setup button starts the New Connection Wizard. See Chapter 7 for more information on setting up new Internet connections.

Programs

The settings in the Programs tab let you choose settings for Internet-related programs. For the most part, when you click to change a setting, you're sent to another part of Vista to finish making the change. One exception is the "Default web browser" section, which lets you decide whether to use Internet Explorer as the default browser. If the "Tell me if Internet Explorer is not the default browser" box is checked, anytime you start up Internet Explorer (as long as it isn't already your default browser), it will ask you whether you want to make it your default browser. Thus, this setting is really just a shortcut to change file/program associations.

The Manage Add-Ons section is just a frontend to the Add-On Manager. See the discussion of the Add-On Manager, earlier in this chapter, for details.

The "HTML editing" section lets you choose which program you want to use to edit HTML files that create web pages. Choose any from the drop-down list and click OK.

The "Set programs" button in the Internet programs section is just a frontend to the Default Programs Control Panel applet. (See the discussion of the Default Programs Control Panel applet, in Chapter 3, for details.) The applet lets you set your default programs not only for Internet use, but also for all programs on your PC. Oddly enough, Excel is listed as a possible HTML editor, even though you can't really use it for that purpose.

Advanced

Advanced contains myriad Internet Explorer settings in a hierarchical tree (see Figure 5-10). They cover everything from accessibility to security, general browsing, multimedia, and printing. Many of these settings are rarely used and most are self-explanatory. Useful settings include:

Notify when downloads complete

Normally, a message pops up when a download is complete, interrupting whatever you are doing. Disabling this feature is particularly helpful when you perform multiple downloads at once.

Use smooth scrolling

This specifies whether a page slides gradually when you click the scroll bar, a feature that can be especially distracting.

Underline links

This specifies whether links on pages should be underlined always, never, or only when you hover your mouse pointer over them.

Multimedia

Multimedia can be a great part of the web experience, but it can also slow down the delivery of web pages. The multimedia section lets you control whether certain multimedia elements, such as pictures, videos, and sounds, are downloaded for display. Thankfully, all those awful sounds in web pages can be silenced for good! This section also lets you turn on and off Always Use ClearType for HTML, which makes for better viewing on laptop displays and LCDs. However, ClearType can actually make the displays on traditional CRT monitors worse, so if you use a CRT monitor, turn off ClearType. (Note that if you change your ClearType setting, you'll have to restart Internet Explorer for it to take effect.)

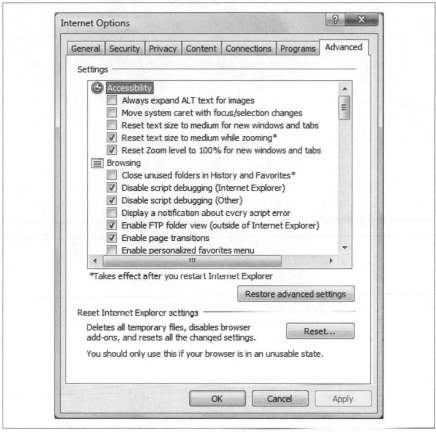

Figure 5-10. The Advanced tab, which contains many settings that affect all aspects of web browsing with Internet Explorer

Printing
> This enables or disables the printing of background colors and images when you print a web page. You can increase print speed considerably with this option disabled.

Security
> It's best to leave the default security settings for Internet Explorer. There's one exception: you might want to check the box next to "Empty Temporary Internet files when browser is closed." When you do that, all your temporary files are deleted whenever you close Internet Explorer. It may slightly slow down initial browsing to web sites you've already visited, but it also will make for extra security. The Security section also includes turning the phishing filter on and off. For details, see the earlier discussion pertaining to the phishing filter. Finally, note that you can find the settings that control Java and JavaScript in Security → Custom Level.

Notes

- The settings in the Connections tab affect only your dial-up Internet connection (if you have one), which affects all of your Internet applications. All the other tabs affect only the Internet Explorer application. You can find settings that control the security and privacy features of other browsers, such as Firefox and Opera, in those applications' options windows.

See also

"Control Panel," in Chapter 3, "Search," in Chapter 4, and "Content Tab and Content Advisor,""Internet Explorer," and "Tab Options," in this chapter

---

Page Menu

Performs a variety of functions on the current web page, including sending the page via email, changing the text size on the page, and copying text from the page.

To open

Internet Explorer → Page

Description

The Page menu, shown in Figure 5-11, is a catchall for letting you perform a wide variety of functions on the web page you're currently visiting. The topmost choices are self-explanatory and follow basic Vista conventions for copying, cutting, and pasting text, as well as opening a new window. (Note that when you open a new window, you're opening an entire new instance of Internet Explorer, not just a new tab. The new instance will be opened to the current web page.)

Here are the other options on the menu:

Save As
> Saves the current web page to your hard disk so that you can view it or edit it locally. You have several choices for saving. If you're not planning to edit the HTML of the file, your best bet is to save it as a "Web Archive, single file (*.mht*)." That way, you won't clutter up your hard disk with extra folders and files stored in different locations; everything is saved to a single file. Saving it as a "Web Page, complete" stores the HTML file, as well as associated graphics, in a folder structure. Saving it as a "Web Page, HTML" will save just the HTML file itself, with no associated graphics and no folder structure. You can also save it as a text file, but if you do, expect to spend time cleaning it up because it saves all the text on the page, often in an unstructured way. To read the page after you've saved it to your disk, press Ctrl-O, browse to the directory where you've saved the page, and open it.

Send Page by E-mail
> This opens a wizard that takes you through a step-by-step process to send the page via email.

Send Link by E-mail
> This opens a wizard that takes you through a step-by-step process to send the link via email.

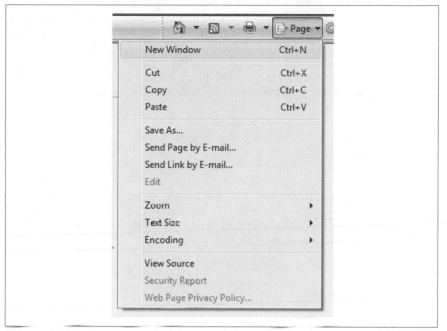

Figure 5-11. The Page menu, which lets you perform a variety of tasks on the current web page

Edit
> This opens the HTML file of the web page in Notepad (or another program listed here), which you can then use to edit the file. You'll have to save the new HTML file locally. Note that if you use an HTML editor and you've associated that editor with HTML files, the page will open in that editor rather than in Notepad.

Zoom
> This lets you set the zoom level to a maximum of 1,000 percent.

Text Size
> This lets you change the text size. There are five sizes from which you can choose.

Encoding
> This selects the type of text encoding to use; use it when you need to display text in another language.

View Source
> This opens the web page in Notepad so that you can view it.

Security Report
> If you are on a web site that uses encryption, choosing this option will open a page telling you whether the connection you have to the site really is encrypted, and giving you the name of the site. Click View Certificates, and you'll come to a dialog box that provides details about the security certificate used to encrypt the connection and the certifying authority that issued the certificate. There is also more detailed information, including descriptions and technical information about the encryption keys.

Web Page Privacy Policy

This lets you see the privacy policy of the current web page. But that requires that the current web page posts its privacy policy in a way that hooks into Internet Explorer. Many of the most popular sites on the Web don't do this. For example, Google and Amazon don't, so you can't view their privacy policies. Microsoft and Yahoo! do, so you can view theirs. This option will also tell you whether Internet Explorer has blocked any cookies from the site, based on your privacy settings.

Notes

- You can also change the Zoom level by using the Change Zoom Level icon in the lower-righthand portion of the page. And you can zoom in and out in increments of 10 percent by pressing Ctrl- + (plus) to zoom in, and Ctrl- – (minus) to zoom out.

- If you want to open a web page for editing and the page was created with frames, you have to right-click on each frame and choose View Source. If you want to see the source for the overall frame that contains the individual windows, press Alt-V to display the View menu, and then click Source.

See also

"Parental Controls," in Chapter 8

Print Preview

Preview your page before it prints and customize the printing.

To open

Internet Explorer → Print Menu → Print Preview

Description

For the most part, you print in Internet Explorer in the same way you print anywhere else in Vista—by pressing Ctrl-P or clicking the Print icon. But that is somewhat misleading, because Internet Explorer 7 solves web page printing woes and offers quite advanced printing features.

As anyone who has ever printed out a web page knows, you'll often encounter serious problems when you need to print. Web pages were designed for viewing on the Web, not for printing. So frequently, text will be cut off on the right side of the page. The Vista version of Internet Explorer automatically fixes these problems by shrinking web pages so that they are not cut off on the right margin.

If you want, though, you can control printing well beyond that, and do things such as turning headers and footers on and off. To do that, use Internet Explorer's Print Preview feature, shown in Figure 5-12.

To use the feature, click the down arrow next to the Print icon and choose Print Preview. Icons at the top of the page let you customize how you print and how you preview your pages. The icons are a bit confusing, because some control your preview of the page and others control how the page will actually print. For example, the Show Multiple Pages drop-down box lets you preview one, two, three, six, or twelve pages at a time, but it won't affect how the pages actually print, only how you look at them on your screen. The Shrink to Fit drop-down box, on the other hand, controls how the pages will actually be printed.

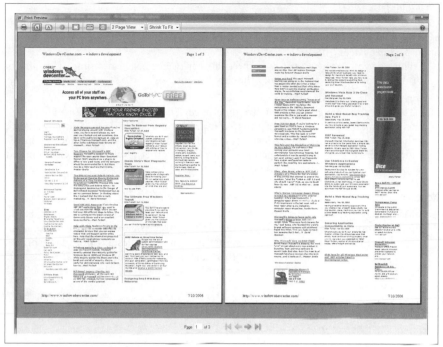

Figure 5-12. Internet Explorer's new Print Preview feature, which lets you control many aspects of printing web pages

Following is a description of each icon, from left to right, along with its shortcut keys for each. Note that the shortcut keys work only when you are in Print Preview—they won't work outside this window.

Print Document (Alt-P)
This prints your page. Click this button after you've customized your page, and it will print it according to your choices.

Portrait (Alt-O)
This prints the page in portrait mode (vertically oriented).

Landscape (Alt-L)
This prints the page in landscape mode (horizontally oriented).

Page Setup (Alt-U)
This brings you to the familiar Print Page Setup page, the same one you see throughout Vista when you print.

Turn headers and footers on or off (Alt-E)
This will toggle the page headers and footers on or off. The header includes the name of the web site from which you're printing, the page number, and the total number of pages. The footer includes the exact URL of the page you're printing and the date. This toggle works not just for display; the option you choose here will actually be printed.

View Full Width (Alt-W)
This allows the width of the web page to cover the entire width of your screen, so you will not be able to see the bottom of the page unless you scroll. This affects only the display of the page, not the way it prints.

View Full Page (Alt-1)
> This displays the entire page so that you can see it on one screen, without scrolling. This affects only the display of the page, not the way it prints.

Show Multiple Pages (Alt-N)
> This lets you preview one, two, three, six, or twelve pages at a time. This affects only the display of the page, not the way it prints.

Change Print Size (Alt-S)
> This lets you change the print size on a page. The default is Shrink to Fit, which will shrink the print size to ensure that it prints on a single page. You can change the print size to any preset level in the drop-down list, which ranges in increments between 30 and 200 percent. To print at other levels, select Custom and enter any number between 1 and 999 percent.

Notes

- Many web sites include a Print this Page feature that automatically reformats the page for optimal printing. If you come across a web page with this feature, it's a good idea to use it, even though Internet Explorer includes a feature that shrinks text to fit on the page. The Print this Page feature usually eliminates ads and prints text from multiple pages if an article goes across multiple pages, so it is quite useful.

See also

"Printers," in Chapter 9

RSS Feeds

Receive live feeds of web content, news, and weblogs (blogs).

To open

Internet Explorer → Tools → Internet Options → Content → Feeds (to configure feeds)

Click the Feeds button in the Internet Explorer toolbar (to subscribe to feeds).

Click the Favorites Center in Internet Explorer, and choose the Feeds tab (to read feeds).

Description

RSS refers to a family of formats for web feeds that deliver information straight to your PC over the Internet. Many blogs use RSS feeds, but so do news sites. In fact, any web site that so desires can easily add an RSS feed to its offerings.

When you receive an RSS feed, you either get a preview of the content available on the blog or web site, or receive the full content, depending on how the site set up its feed. If you get a preview and want to read the full post or news item, click on the feed and you are sent to the site or blog.

Internet Explorer 7, built into Vista, includes an RSS reader for subscribing to and reading RSS feeds. When you're on a page that has an RSS feed, the RSS icon on the Internet Explorer toolbar turns orange. Click the icon to read the feed using Internet Explorer's built-in RSS reader, as shown in Figure 5-13. In some cases, a web site has more than one feed on it. Click the inverted triangle next to the RSS icon and you'll see a list of all feeds on the site. Click the one you want to read.

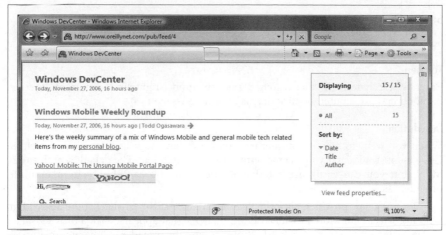

Figure 5-13. Reading a feed using the RSS reader

The reader lets you sort items by date, title, and author. A search box lets you search through all the feeds.

To subscribe to a feed, click the + button (the same button you use to add a favorite) at the top of the toolbar, or click the Subscribe to this Feed link in the feed itself. When you subscribe to a feed, it is automatically downloaded to your PC, without your intervention. To view all the feeds to which you've subscribed, click the Favorites Center icon on the Internet Explorer toolbar (it's a star) and click the Feeds tab, and you'll come to a list of your feeds. Click on one to read it.

Internet Explorer's RSS reader also gives you basic control over how you want it to work. To configure it, choose Tools → Internet Options → Content, and in the Feeds section, click Settings. Check the box next to "Automatically check feeds for updates" if you want Internet Explorer to check your feeds without your intervention, and then select the frequency at which you want the feeds checked (choices range from once every 15 minutes to once a week). You can also specify whether Internet Explorer plays a sound when a new feed is found, and whether you want to turn off the feed reading view. If you turn it off, feeds will appear as plain web pages without controls for sorting and filtering the feeds.

Notes

- An excellent way to see when there is new information in an RSS feed is to use the Feed Watcher or Feed Viewer Gadget in the Vista Sidebar. The Gadgets let you preview feeds, but in slightly different ways. The Feed Watcher lists each individual feed and shows you how many new items each feed has. Click a feed and you're sent to Internet Explorer's RSS reader. The Feed Viewer instead displays each individual new post for all of your feeds, one at a time, including a synopsis. Click any post to read it.

See also

"Internet Options," earlier in this chapter, and "Windows Sidebar and Gadgets," in Chapter 3

Search Bar

Searches the Internet using a variety of search providers.

To open

Enter a search term in the Search Bar in the upper-righthand corner of Internet Explorer and press Enter, or click the magnifying glass icon.

Description

When you want to search the Internet, you don't have to visit a search site such as Google—instead, enter your search term into the Search Bar. The default search site is MSN, but you can easily use a different one. And you can choose from multiple providers as well:

- To add a new provider, click the inverted triangle at the far right of the Search Bar and select Find More Providers. From the page that appears, click a provider link. A dialog box appears. Click Add Provider, and the provider will be put on a list at the top of the menu that appeared when you clicked the inverted triangle (Figure 5-14). To search using the provider, type in the term, select the provider, and press Enter.

Figure 5-14. Configuring your search providers

- To change your default provider, click the inverted triangle at the far right of the Search Bar and select Change Search Defaults. Select the provider you want to be the default, click Set Default, and then click OK. To remove a provider, highlight it, click Remove, and then click OK.

Notes

- Anyone can write a script that will allow her site's search engine to be used by the Internet Explorer Search Bar. For details, go to *http://msdn.microsoft.com/library/ default.asp?url=/workshop/browser/external/overview/ie7_opensearch_ext.asp*.

See also

"Search," in Chapter 4

Tab Options

Control how Internet Explorer uses tabs.

To open

Internet Explorer → Tools → Internet Options → General, then click Settings in the Tabs section

Description

Probably the biggest visible change in the Vista version of Internet Explorer (and Internet Explorer 7 in XP) is the addition of tabs that allow you to browse multiple web sites simultaneously, each in its own tab. The Tab Options dialog box, shown in Figure 5-15, lets you control how Internet Explorer handles tabbed browsing.

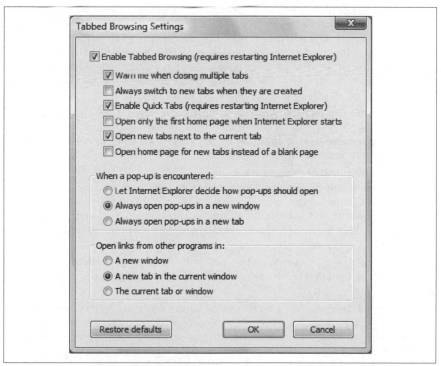

Figure 5-15. The Tab Options dialog box, which controls how Internet Explorer handles tabs

The dialog box has these options:

Enable Tabbed Browsing
> This is the default. If it is unchecked, you won't be able to use tabs. When you uncheck it (or check it after it has been unchecked), you'll have to restart Internet Explorer for the new setting to take effect. The settings are as follows:

Warn me when closing multiple tabs
> Normally, if you have multiple tabs open and you close Internet Explorer, you first get a warning, alerting you to the number of tabs you have open and asking whether you want to close them all down and exit. Check this box if you want that warning to appear. Keep in mind that although the warning may be annoying at times, it's useful because sometimes you might mean to close only a single tab, not all of them, and if you don't check this box, you'll mistakenly close Internet Explorer rather than an individual tab.

Always switch to new tabs when they are created
> When Internet Explorer opens a new tab for some reason—for example, when you've right-clicked a link and selected Open in New Tab—that tab normally opens in the background; that is, you stay in your original tab. Check this box if you instead want to be sent to each new tab as it opens. Note that when you create a new tab by clicking the New Tab tab or by pressing Ctrl-T, you will always be sent to your new tab, regardless of this setting.

Enable Quick Tabs
> In the left portion of the Internet Explorer toolbar, you'll see an icon with four tabs on it: the Quick Tabs icon. Click the icon and you'll see thumbnail sketches of all your open tabs. Click any thumbnail to switch to it. If you don't want this Quick Tabs feature enabled, uncheck this box. When you uncheck it (or check it after it has been unchecked), you'll have to restart Internet Explorer for the new setting to take effect.

Open only the first home page when Internet Explorer starts
> Internet Explorer lets you set multiple home pages. Check this box if you want only your primary one to load when Internet Explorer starts. If the box is unchecked (the default), each home page loads in its own tab every time you start Internet Explorer.

Open new tabs next to the current tab
> When you open a new tab by right-clicking a link and selecting Open in New Tab, or by clicking a link that opens a new tab, it normally opens directly to the right of your live tab. If you uncheck this box, the new tab will open to the right of the rightmost tab, instead of to the right of the current live tab.

Open home page for new tabs instead of a blank page
> When you click the New Tab tab, a blank page normally opens. If you instead want that tab to have your home page, check this box.

When a pop-up is encountered
> This section controls how tabs handle legitimate pop ups—that is, pop ups that serve a purpose and that the Pop-Up Blocker doesn't block. You can choose to have pop ups always open in a new window or always open in a new tab, or let Internet Explorer decide whether they should be opened in a new window or tab. Be aware that the Pop-Up Blocker is not perfect, and sometimes undesirable pop ups will make it through.

Open links from other programs in

Many programs, such as Windows Mail and Office applications, can automatically open links in Internet Explorer. This section controls whether those links should open in a new window (in other words, a new instance of Internet Explorer), or instead in a new tab in the current window (that is, the current instance of Internet Explorer), or instead in the current tab or window.

Tab groups

What if there is a group of sites you often open in concert with one another—for example, a group of your favorite news sites, or your favorite blogs? You can create Tab Groups that will allow you to open all the sites into their own tabs with a single click.

To create a Tab Group, first open all the sites in their own tabs. Then click the Add/Subscribe button, and click Add Tab Group to Favorites. Give the group a folder name, and then click Add.

To open the Tab Group, click the Favorites Center button and then click the folder that you want to open. Next, click the arrow to the right of the folder name. The Tab Group will now open, with each site in its own separate tab.

Tab shortcuts

Internet Explorer has several shortcut keys for handling tabs, as shown in Table 5-2.

Table 5-2. Tab shortcut keys

Key combination	Action
Ctrl-T	Open a new tab in the foreground.
Ctrl-W	Close the current tab.
Ctrl-Tab; Ctrl-Shift-Tab	Switch between tabs.
Ctrl-Q	Open Quick Tabs.
Ctrl-Alt-F4	Close all tabs except for the current tab.
Alt-Enter in the Address Bar	Open a new tab in the foreground; open to the URL of the current tab.
Ctrl-N	Switch to the *n*th tab (*n* can be a number from 1 to 8; tab number 1 is the leftmost tab, tab 2 is directly to its right, and so on).
Ctrl-9	Switch to the last tab—the rightmost one.
Ctrl-click	Open a link into a new tab in the background.
Ctrl-Shift-click	Open a link into a new tab in the foreground.

Notes

- To close the current tab, click on the X in the upper right of the tab. To close any other tab, right-click it and choose Close.

- To see a list of all of your current tabs, click the down arrow to the left of your first tab. A list of all your tabs appears, with a checkbox next to the current one. To jump to any tab, select it from the list.

See also

"Pop-Up Blocker"

Security

Internet Explorer has long been one of the most insecure parts of Windows, but with Windows Vista, Microsoft finally turned its attention to plugging many of those security holes. New to Vista are a phishing filter that can cut down on Internet scams, and Protected Mode, in which Internet Explorer is segregated from the rest of the operating system. Vista also includes previous security features such as cookie handling, and a Pop-Up Blocker tool as well.

As you'll see in this section, there is no single location in Internet Explorer that lets you handle security, so you'll have to try the various locations listed here. This chapter covers security-related features found directly inside Internet Explorer. In addition to what's here, Vista has other Internet-related security and privacy tools, such as Windows Defender, Parental Controls, and the Windows Firewall. Turn to Chapter 8 for details about these and other security features.

Add-On Manager

See what ActiveX controls and add-ons are running in Internet Explorer, and disable or enable them.

To open

Internet Explorer → Tools → Manage Add-ons

Description

Internet Explorer allows a variety of add-ons and ActiveX controls to run inside it. Many of these are required for the basic operation of the browser, but many others add extra functions, such as the Google Toolbar, which lets you search Google from directly within Internet Explorer. Unfortunately, spyware and other malware may also run as add-ons. In addition, sometimes add-ons conflict with one another.

The Add-On Manager lets you take control of your add-ons and disable or delete any that are dangerous. It lets you view all of the ActiveX controls and add-ons running in Internet Explorer, and disable or delete ones you don't want to run, as well as enable ones you do want to run if they've been disabled for some reason.

Select Tools → Manage Add-ons → Enable or Disable Add-ons, and the screen shown in Figure 5-16 appears.

You'll see a list of all the add-ons currently running in Internet Explorer. Included are the name, publisher, status (enabled or disabled), type (for example, a toolbar, ActiveX control, Browser Helper Object, and so on), and actual filename of the add-on.

To disable an add-on, highlight it, select Disable, and click OK. To enable one that has been disabled, highlight it, select Enable, and click OK. The changes may not take effect until you restart Internet Explorer. You can do this for ActiveX controls as well as add-ons. To delete an ActiveX control, highlight it and click the Delete ActiveX button. The changes might not take effect until you disable Internet Explorer. (You can't delete add-ons in this way, only disable them. To delete an add-on, go to Control Panel → Programs → Uninstall a Program.)

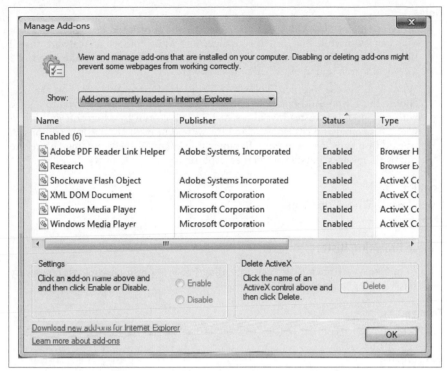

Figure 5-16. The Add-On Manager, with a list of add-ons currently running in Internet Explorer

You can display more than just the add-ons currently running in Internet Explorer. From the Show drop-down list, you can make these choices:

Add-ons that have been used by Internet Explorer
As the name implies, this displays the add-ons that Internet Explorer has used in the current session. (Note: this won't list the add-ons that Internet Explorer must run for its basic operations.)

Add-ons currently loaded in Internet Explorer
This displays add-ons currently being used by Internet Explorer. (Note: this won't list the add-ons that Internet Explorer must run for its basic operations.)

Add-ons that run without requiring permission
These are add-ons that Internet Explorer has determined are safe. They typically are required for the basic operation of Internet Explorer.

Downloaded ActiveX Controls (32-bit)
These are ActiveX controls that you have downloaded from the Internet.

Although the Add-On Manager lets you disable add-ons and ActiveX controls, there's one thing it doesn't do—tell you which are likely to be safe, and which aren't. So how can you know which to disable? Your best bet is to type the filename into Google. From there, you'll be able to easily determine whether it's safe or not.

Notes

- Browser Helper Objects (BHOs) are a specific kind of Internet Explorer add-on that can be useful, but also very dangerous. Many pieces of malware install themselves as BHOs. So when you see anything listed as a BHO, make sure to do a Google search to find out whether it's malware.

- When you choose Internet Explorer → Tools → Manage Add-ons, you can also choose Find More Add-ons. That, however, does not actually lead you to a page with true add-ons. Instead, you're sent to a site co-run by Microsoft and *http://www.cnet.com* that has shareware and freeware, but most are not true add-ons. A true add-on runs inside Internet Explorer, but many of the programs on the site run by themselves, outside of Internet Explorer.

See also
"Windows Defender," in Chapter 8

Delete Browsing History

Clean out traces of your Internet use, including browsing history, cookies, temporary files, passwords, and forms data.

To open
Internet Explorer → Tools → Delete Browsing History

Description

When you browse the Web, sites that you visit can potentially gather a surprising amount of your personal information because of the browsing traces you carry with you. Similarly, intruders can also potentially view these browsing traces as well. These traces include a history of sites you've visited, cookies, files from the Internet temporarily stored on your PC, passwords, and information you've typed into web forms.

You can delete any and all of this information using the Delete Browsing History dialog box, shown in Figure 5-17.

The dialog box offers the following options:

Delete files
> This deletes all the temporary files that Internet Explorer stores on your hard disk to speed up browsing, including graphics files, multimedia files, and web pages. Note that deleting these files may temporarily slow down browsing to sites that you've already visited.

Delete cookies
> This deletes all the cookies on your hard disk. Keep in mind that cookies can automatically log you into web sites and customize sites for you, so if you delete them, you will lose those abilities. (For information on how to handle cookies and protect your privacy, see "Internet Options Privacy Tab," later in this chapter.)

Figure 5-17. The Delete Browsing History dialog box, where you can delete traces of your Internet activities

Delete history
> This deletes the list of the web sites that you've recently visited.

Delete forms
> This deletes information you've typed into web forms, such as your address, name, phone number, and so on.

Delete passwords
> This deletes all the passwords you've typed in order to get into web sites.

Delete all
> This deletes files, cookies, history, forms, and passwords.

Notes

• When you delete all of your files, cookies, history, forms, and passwords, your Favorites and subscribed feeds are not affected and will not be deleted.

See also

"Internet Options Privacy Tab"

Internet Options Privacy Tab

Lets you take control over your privacy by controlling the way you manage cookies.

To open

Internet Explorer → Tools Panel → Internet Options → Privacy

Command Prompt or Search Box → *inetcpl.cpl*, then click the Privacy tab

Description

This tab lets you control how Internet Explorer handles cookies, small text files that web sites put on your hard disk to personalize the site for you or to track and record your activities on the site. As a means of site customization, they're a great way of helping you get the most out of the Web. They can also carry information about login names and passwords, which is a timesaver because you won't have to log in to each site every time you visit. If you delete all your cookies, you won't automatically get your Amazon wish list the next time you visit that site.

But cookies are controversial, because they can also be used to track your online activities and identify you. Information about you, based on what cookies gather, can be put in a database, and profiles of you and your surfing habits can be created.

Internet Explorer, via the Internet Options Privacy tab, lets you restrict how web sites place and use cookies on your PC. Before understanding how to use the tab, you need to understand three cookie-related terms:

First-party cookie
> A cookie created by the site you're currently visiting. Sites often use these cookies to let you log on automatically—without having to type in your username and password—and customize how you use the site. Typically, these kinds of cookies are not invasive.

Third-party cookie
> A cookie created by a site other than the one you're currently visiting. Frequently, advertisers or advertising networks use third-party cookies. Some people (including me) consider these kinds of cookies invasive.

Compact privacy statement
> A publicly posted policy that describes the details of how cookies are used on a site—for example, detailing the purpose of cookies, how they're used, their source, and how long they will stay on your PC. (Some cookies are automatically deleted when you leave a web site, and others stay valid until a specified date.)

To protect your privacy, you also need to know the difference between *implicit consent* and *explicit consent*. Explicit consent means you have specifically told a site it can use personally identifiable information about you. It's the same as opting in. Implicit consent means you haven't specifically told a site not to use personally identifiable information. It's the same as not having opted out, or not specifically requesting to be taken off a list.

Internet Explorer lets you customize how it handles cookies. You can choose from six levels of privacy settings, from Accept All Cookies to Block All Cookies. Some sites won't function well or at all at the higher privacy settings, particularly if you choose to reject all cookies. By default, Internet Explorer chooses a Medium setting.

On the tab shown in Figure 5-18, move the slider to your desired level of privacy.

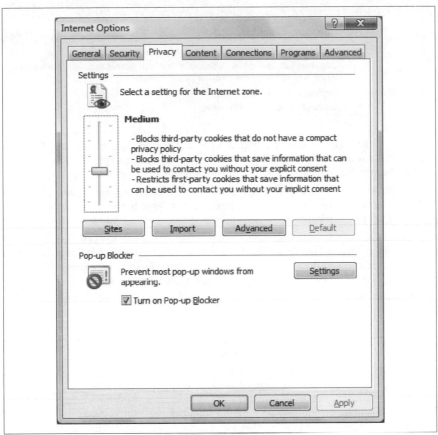

Figure 5-18. Customizing cookie settings in Internet Explorer

Table 5-3 shows how each setting affects Internet Explorer's cookie handling.

Table 5-3. Internet Explorer's privacy settings and your privacy

Setting	How the setting affects your privacy
Block All Cookies	Blocks all cookies, without exception.
	Does not allow web sites to read existing cookies.
High	Blocks cookies from all web sites that don't have a compact privacy policy.
	Blocks all cookies that use personally identifiable information without your explicit consent.
Medium High	Blocks third-party cookies from sites that don't have a compact privacy policy.
	Blocks third-party cookies that use personally identifiable information without your explicit consent.
	Blocks first-party cookies that use personally identifiable information without your implicit consent.
Medium (Default)	Blocks third-party cookies from sites that don't have a compact privacy policy.
	Blocks third-party cookies that use personally identifiable information without your implicit consent.
	Accepts first-party cookies that use personally identifiable information without your implicit consent, but deletes them when you close Internet Explorer.

Table 5-3. Internet Explorer's privacy settings and your privacy (continued)

Setting	How the setting affects your privacy
Low	Blocks third-party cookies from sites that don't have a compact privacy policy.
	Accepts third-party cookies that use personally identifiable information without your implicit consent, but deletes them when you close Internet Explorer.
Accept All Cookies	Accepts all cookies, without exception.
	Allows web sites to read existing cookies.

You're not locked into Internet Explorer's preset levels of cookie handling. You can customize how it handles cookies so that you can, for example, accept or reject cookies from individual sites, or accept or reject all first-party and third-party cookies.

To accept or reject all cookies from a specific site, click the Sites button on the Privacy tab. The Per Site Privacy Actions dialog box appears. Type in the name of the site you want to accept or block cookies from, and click either Block or Allow.

To customize how you handle first- and third-party cookies, click the Advanced button on the Privacy tab. Check the "Override automatic cookie handling" box. You can accept or reject all first- or third-party cookies, or choose to be prompted whether to accept them. You can also decide to always allow *session cookies*, or cookies that last only as long as you're on a specific web site and are deleted once you leave the site.

Notes

- Note that the Privacy tab also controls Pop-Up Blocker settings. For details, see "Pop-Up Blocker," later in this chapter.

- If your cookies are accidentally deleted, you won't be able to automatically log in to web sites, and your customized settings at many sites will be lost. As a safety precaution, you can back up your cookies and then restore them. To export or back up cookies from Internet Explorer, first press the Alt key to make the menus appear. Then choose File → Import and Export. The Import/Export Wizard will launch. Choose Export Cookies and follow the directions. A single text file containing all your cookies will be created in your Documents folder, though you can choose a different location for them. To import cookies, launch the Import/ Export Wizard, choose Import Cookies, and browse to the location where the cookie file has been stored.

- You can examine and delete individual cookies from inside Vista. Each cookie is stored as an individual file in *C:\Users\username\AppData\Roaming\Microsoft\ Windows\Cookies*. Open the folder in Windows Explorer, and you'll see a list of individual cookies in this format: *your name@abcnews.com[1].txt*. As a general rule, the name of the web site or ad network will be after the @, but not always— sometimes it will merely be a number. Open the file as you would any other text file (in Notepad, WordPad, or another text editor). Usually, there will be a list of numbers and letters inside, though you might find other useful information in there—for example, your username and password for the web site. If you don't want the cookie on your hard disk, simply delete it as you would any other text file.

- You can check whether the web site you've visited in your current session has placed any cookies on your hard disk. Press Page → Web Page Privacy Policy. You'll see a list of the sites you've visited, and whether any have placed a cookie on your disk.

See also
"Delete Browsing History"

Internet Options Security Tab

Controls overall Internet Explorer security settings.

To open

Internet Explorer → Tools Panel → Internet Options → Security

Command Prompt or Search Box → *inetcpl.cpl*, then click the Security tab

Description

In the real world, it's usually obvious which are the seedier, more dangerous parts of town, and most people know what streets to avoid after dark. But that isn't always true on the Web. An attractive, respectable home page may disguise a site that wants to do you harm.

To help protect you, Internet Explorer uses different security zones for web sites, depending on whether it believes they can be trusted. It applies a different level of security to each of the zones, as follows:

- Internet (medium security)
- Local intranet (medium-low security)
- Trusted sites (medium security)
- Restricted sites (high security)

Each zone has a specific security setting associated with it that determines how Explorer handles web pages in that zone—for example, whether it allows file downloads or runs certain types of web programs, such as Java applets and ActiveX controls.

What Is Protected Mode?

Protected Mode is a new Vista feature designed to protect your PC against Internet-borne attacks. For all zones except for Trusted sites, Internet Explorer runs in Protected Mode as a default. Protected Mode shields your filesystem and Registry from the actions taken by Internet Explorer or any add-ons to Internet Explorer. It works in concert with User Account Control (UAC) and only allows Internet Explorer to run at a privilege level for surfing the Web, and not much more. In that way, even if a piece of malware managed to break through all of Internet Explorer's security features, it couldn't do harm to your PC because Protected Mode in essence locks it in a safe box. To find out whether you're in Protected Mode, look at the bottom righthand side of your Internet Explorer window. If you are in Protected Mode, it will read "Protected Mode: On."

If you're not happy with the security levels Microsoft has set for each zone, you can overrule those settings using the Internet Options Security tab, shown in Figure 5-19.

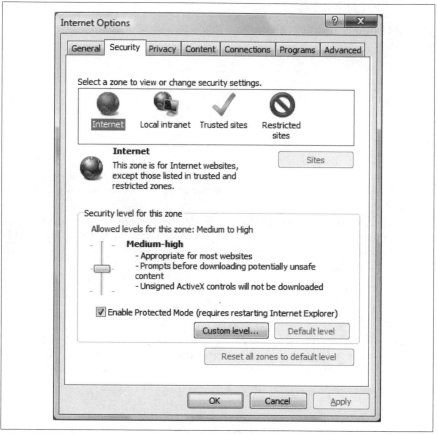

Figure 5-19. The Internet Options Security tab, which lets you control Internet Explorer's security settings for browsing the Web

For instance, if you don't want Explorer to treat the Internet zone with medium security, but rather a more trusting medium-low security, you can make that change using the Internet Options Security Tab. Depending on the zone whose level you want to change, you do things slightly differently. For Local intranet and Trusted sites, click the zone and then drag the slider to the security setting you want that zone to have, then click OK. For Internet and Restricted Sites, click the zone and select Custom Level, and the Security Settings dialog box appears. From the "Reset to" drop-down box at the bottom of the screen, select the security level you want to apply to that zone and click OK.

Table 5-4 tells you how each setting affects security.

Table 5-4. Internet Explorer's security settings

Security level setting	How the setting affects security
High	Disables most features including ActiveX controls, Java and Java applets, and downloads.
Medium	Pops up a box when an ActiveX control tries to run, and asks whether you want to run it. Prompts you before running signed ActiveX controls; disables unsigned ActiveX controls and certain other ActiveX controls; enables downloads and Java applets; and prompts you before downloading potentially unsafe content. (Note: unsigned ActiveX controls are those that have not been digitally "signed" by a site, so you can't absolutely know who created those controls.)
Medium-Low	Most settings are the same as Medium, except that it will allow some active content to run without first popping up messages asking whether you want to run it.
Low	Runs all active content such as ActiveX controls; has the minimum number of safeguards and prompts so that you won't be prompted whether you want to run an ActiveX control, for example.

You can also further customize the security setting for any zone by picking and choosing from a variety of security options, rather than relying on the High, Medium, Medium-Low, and Low levels. Click any zone and then select Custom Level. The Security Settings dialog box appears. Pick and choose your options, such as whether a site should be allowed to install desktop items, how to handle ActiveX controls, and so on. Then click OK.

You don't have to rely on Microsoft's judgment about which web sites belong in which zones—you can classify them yourself. For example, if you know and trust a web site, you can put it in the Trusted Sites zone.

To assign a web site to a particular zone, select a zone, click Sites, and from the dialog box that appears, click Advanced. In the next dialog box that appears, type in the site URL and click Add. To remove sites from the zone, highlight them and click Remove.

Notes

- Although it's not recommended, you can turn off Protected Mode for any zone. Highlight the zone, uncheck the box next to Enable Protected Mode, and click OK.

- For maximum security, you can run Internet Explorer without any third-party add-ons, extensions, toolbars, or ActiveX controls. To do so, choose Start → All Programs → Accessories → System Tools → Internet Explorer (No Add-Ons).

See also

"Internet Options Privacy Tab" and "Delete Browsing History"

Phishing Filter

Protect yourself against online scams and spoofs.

To open

Internet Explorer → Tools → Phishing Filter

Description

One of the greatest dangers you face online is a so-called "phishing" attack, in which you're sent an email that appears to be from a bank, financial institution, eBay, or other web site that has personal, financial information about you. You're told to click a link to go to a web site and log in to your account. The link sends you to what appears to be a legitimate site but is instead a scam. When you enter your password and login information, the scammer steals it and can empty your bank account.

It can be hard to distinguish real sites from phishing sites, because phishing sites duplicate the exact look and feel of the real thing. Internet Explorer's phishing filter, though, protects you from attacks.

With Internet Explorer's phishing filter, when you try to visit what Microsoft deems a phishing site, Internet Explorer stops you in your tracks with a page warning you that you are about to head to a "reported phishing website." You then have the choice of closing the web site or ignoring the Microsoft recommendation and visiting it.

If the filter instead detects only a *suspected* phishing site, you're let through, but a yellow button appears next to the Address Bar that labels the site a "Suspicious website," as shown in Figure 5-20. You can then decide whether to stay at the site or head away.

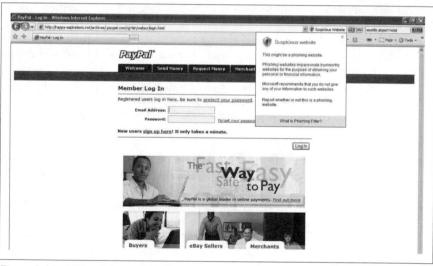

Figure 5-20. A "Suspicious website"

Internet Explorer uses three methods to determine whether a site is legitimate or a phishing site. As a first line of defense, Microsoft compiles a database of known phishing sites, and Internet Explorer compares sites you visit against that database. The database is compiled from several data providers, including Cyota, Internet Identity, and MarkMonitor, as well as from direct user feedback. The information in that database is stored locally on your computer; whenever you visit a site, Internet Explorer looks at that local database to see whether the site you're visiting is a phishing site.

Second, Internet Explorer uses heuristics that compare characteristics of the site you're visiting against common phishing web site characteristics to decide whether the site is legitimate. The heuristics tool is particularly important, because you may stumble across a phishing site before it is included in the database of known culprits.

Finally, Internet Explorer sends addresses of some of the sites you visit to Microsoft, which checks them against a frequently updated list of reported phishing web sites.

The phishing filter isn't particularly customizable, but you can change several of its options. To do so, in Internet Explorer, choose Tools → Phishing Filter. These are your choices from the menu that appears:

Check this Website
> This sends the URL of the site you're currently visiting to Microsoft, which then checks the site's validity and reports back to you whether it is suspicious, a known phishing site, or a legitimate site. Figure 5-21 shows the alert you receive when the site is legitimate.

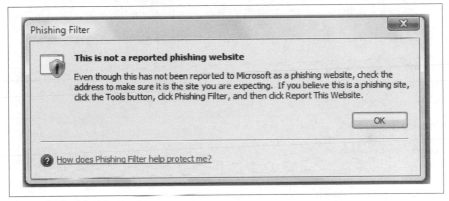

Figure 5-21. A legitimate site

Turn Off/On Automatic Website Checking
> This turns off the feature that sends some web site addresses to Microsoft to check its most recent database and determine whether the site is legitimate. If you turn off this feature, the phishing filter will still work; it will use your local database, and heuristics. But it won't send web site addresses to Microsoft for checking. Users who believe that Microsoft may invade their privacy may want to turn off automatic checking, although Microsoft says that the information is not saved or tracked personally.

Report this Website
> If you're visiting a site that you believe to be a phishing site, choose this option. A new browser window will open. To report a site, check the box next to "I think this is a phishing website," choose the language used by the site, and click Submit.

Phishing Filter Settings
> This is a somewhat confusing way to change your phishing filter settings. When you select this option, the Advanced Internet Options dialog box opens, which has dozens of Internet Explorer settings covering virtually every aspect of the browser, from accessibility to general browsing, security, printing, multimedia settings, and more. You won't see the phishing filter settings. To get to them, scroll toward the bottom of the dialog box. Near the bottom, you'll find the phishing filter settings. Choose "Disable Phishing Filter" to turn it off entirely; choose "Turn off automatic website checking" to stop sending addresses to Microsoft to check; and choose "Turn on automatic website checking" to send addresses to Microsoft to check. These last two options accomplish the same thing that the Turn Off/On Automatic Website Checking menu does.

Notes

- When you use automatic web site checking, the phishing filter sends more than just the address of the web site you're visiting. It also sends other information, including your computer's IP address, browser type, and phishing filter version number. To make sure that information can't be intercepted by anyone except Microsoft, the information is encrypted using SSL. Any information that might be associated with the web site address you're currently visiting—such as search terms you've used, information you've entered into forms, or cookies—is not sent.

- A web site that is flagged as suspicious has some of the characteristics typical of phishing web sites, and it is neither on the list of legitimate web sites that is stored on your computer nor on the online list of reported phishing web sites. The web site might actually be legitimate, but you should not submit any personal or financial information to it unless you are certain that the site is trustworthy.

See also

"Windows Defender," in Chapter 8, and "Pop-Up Blocker," discussed next

---

Pop-Up Blocker

Blocks pop-up windows.

To open

Internet Explorer → Tools → Pop-Up Blocker

Description

Small windows that pop up on the Web with messages or ads are one of the most annoying things about being online. But pop ups are more than merely annoying—they can be dangerous as well. Pop-up ads are one of the most common ways that spyware infects people's PCs. Click a pop up, and software may silently install on your PC without your knowledge. Or the pop up may purport to serve a legitimate purpose—perhaps asking you to participate in a survey—but in fact, when you click, spyware will be installed.

Internet Explorer includes a pop-up blocker that blocks most pop ups and makes browsing safer and more enjoyable. When you visit a web site and a pop up is blocked, you'll get the message shown in Figure 5-22 in Internet Explorer's Information Bar.

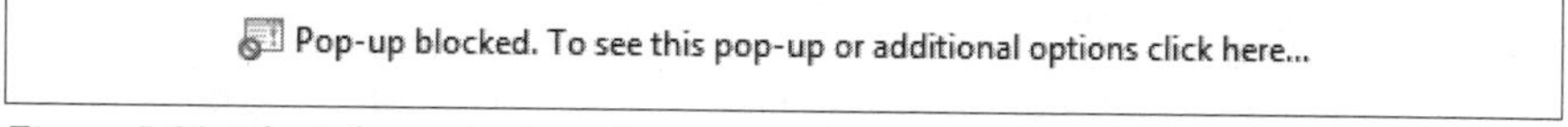

> 🔲 Pop-up blocked. To see this pop-up or additional options click here...

Figure 5-22. The Information Bar alerting you that a pop up has been blocked

Click the Information Bar, and a menu will appear that lets you manage pop ups from the site:

- Click Temporarily Allows Pop-ups to allow pop ups from the site for just this browsing session.
- Click Always Allow Pop-ups from This Site to always allow pop ups.

- Click Settings, and a menu appears to let you further configure the Pop-Up Blocker. From the menu, select Turn Off Pop-Up Blocker to turn off the Pop-Up Blocker. Unselect Show Information Bar for Pop-ups if you do not want the Information Bar to appear when a pop up is blocked. Select More Settings, and a screen appears that lets you always allow or block pop ups from a specific site, as detailed later in this section.

In addition, when a pop up is blocked, the screen in Figure 5-23 will appear over Internet Explorer. If you do not want to see the screen every time a pop up is blocked, click "Don't show this message again" and then click OK. You'll still get the yellow Information Bar.

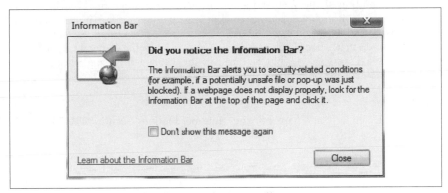

Figure 5-23. An annoying alert that's worth turning off

You don't have to wait until you get a pop up if you want to configure the Pop-Up Blocker. In Internet Explorer, select Tools → Pop-Up Blocker, and a menu appears with two choices. Turn Off Pop-Up Blocker, and Pop-Up Blocker Settings. Click Turn Off Pop-Up Blocker, and pop ups will no longer be blocked. Click Pop-Up Blocker Settings, and a screen appears that lets you configure the Pop-Up Blocker in several different ways. Here are your options:

Exceptions
This top part of the screen lets you allow pop ups from specific sites. Use this when the feature of a site requires the use of pop ups. To allow a pop up from a specific site, type the site URL into the "Address of website to allow" box and click Add. It will be added to your list of Allowed sites. To remove a site from the list, highlight it and click Remove. To remove all sites, click Remove All.

Notifications and Filter Level
This middle portion of the screen controls whether and how you're notified in case of pop ups, and how aggressively the filter blocks them. Check the box next to "Play a sound when a pop-up is blocked," to hear a small "pop" sound every time a pop up is blocked. Check the box next to "Show Information Bar when a pop-up is blocked" to display the Information Bar notification that a pop up was blocked.

Filter Level
This final portion of the screen is a drop-down list that lets you determine how aggressively pop ups should be blocked. The High level blocks all pop ups, even if Internet Explorer determines that the pop up is needed for the site to run properly. The Medium level (which is the default level) blocks most pop ups but allows those required for the proper running of a site. The Low level allows all pop ups for sites that Internet Explorer determines to be safe.

Notes

- The Pop-Up Blocker, in its default level, allows some pop ups to be displayed. There are several reasons this may happen. If you have spyware on your PC, pop ups may appear because the Pop-Up Blocker isn't designed to block spyware pop ups. Additionally, the blocker will allow some pop ups with "active content"—for example, ActiveX controls and browser add-ons that include features that are integral to the proper functioning of a web site, or that add a feature to a web site. In addition, the blocker will not block pop ups from web sites in your Local intranet or Trusted sites content zones. To block pop ups from these sites, you'll have to remove them from the zones.

- When you browse the Web and a pop up makes it through the Pop-Up Blocker (for example, if it contains active content), the pop up appears in its own small, separate window. If you want, though, you can have pop ups appear in their own tabs. To do that, select Tools → Internet Options, click the General tab, and then, under the Tabs section, click Settings. In the Tabbed Browsing Settings dialog box, click "Always open pop-ups in a new tab," and then click OK.

See also

"Windows Defender," in Chapter 8, and "Internet Options Security Tab," earlier in this chapter

6

Windows Mail

Windows Mail, the mail reader built into Windows Vista, is the successor to Outlook Express, which was built into previous versions of Windows. There have been some cosmetic and feature changes between Outlook Express and Windows Mail, but to a great extent, the basic operations of the mail program have remained the same.

Microsoft may have named the mail client *Windows Mail* because of the confusion between Outlook and Outlook Express. Outlook, shipped with Microsoft Office, is a more full-featured mail reader and includes a built-in calendar, task list, and other tools, so it's possible that Microsoft renamed Outlook Express to better differentiate the two programs. This is somewhat ironic, because Microsoft decided to name the email program *Outlook Express* in the first place to imply that it was a "lite" version of Outlook, even though there was really no relationship between the programs.

Even though Outlook offers more features, Windows Mail is a powerful email program. It includes spam filtering, good searching features, the capability to create rules to automatically handle incoming mail, and more.

Although Windows Mail is much like Outlook Express, there have been a number of changes, deletions, and additions to the program:

New toolbar
> A new toolbar has been added, just below the menu, that gives access to Windows Mail's most commonly used features, such as creating, replying to, and forwarding mail; sending mail; printing mail; deleting mail; and searching.

Junk email filtering
> Windows Mail includes what Microsoft calls *SmartScreen technology* to filter out spam; Outlook Express didn't include built-in junk mail filtering.

Quick search
> In the upper-right corner of the main screen in Windows Mail is a Search box, much like the one in Internet Explorer, that lets you do a quick search through all of your messages.

Windows Mail communities

> Windows Mail lets you rate the usefulness of newsgroup postings and view the ratings that others give to postings.

Elimination of identities

> Outlook Express allowed for the creation of multiple identities, a feature that let more than one person use Outlook Express on the same PC with their own accounts, settings, and mail. Windows Mail eliminates identities. In Windows Vista, you'll have to create separate user accounts to accomplish the same thing. If you install Windows Vista over a previous version of Windows that had Outlook Express with multiple identities, Windows Mail will automatically launch a wizard to guide you through the process of importing previous email identities into your current user account. The wizard will launch every time you start Windows Mail until you import or delete all the identities.

Here is an alphabetical reference of entries in this chapter:

Columns	New Message	Watch Conversation
Find	Newsgroups	Windows Contacts
Internet Accounts	Read Options	Windows Mail
Junk E-mail	Signatures	Windows Mail Options
Message Rules	Stationery	Windows Mail Security

Windows Mail

\Program Files\Windows Mail\WinMail.exe

An Internet email client and newsgroup reader.

To open

Start → All Programs → Windows Mail

Double-click the Windows Mail icon on the Desktop, if it's been enabled.

Command Prompt → `winmail`

Description

Windows Mail (see Figure 6-1) uses a familiar Explorer-like tree interface to manage the folders into which email and newsgroup messages are organized. Highlight any folder name to display its messages; the currently highlighted message is then shown in the preview pane. Double-click the message to open it in a new window for easier reading and other options.

Newly received messages are stored in the Inbox folder. Files queued to be sent are stored in the Outbox folder, and are then moved to the Sent Items folder when they have been sent. The Deleted Items folder is like the Recycle Bin because it stores deleted messages until it is emptied manually. The Drafts folder stores messages as they're being composed. To add a new folder, select Local Folders in the tree and go to File → New → Folder. You can move messages from folder to folder by dragging and dropping them.

The first time you open Windows Mail, a wizard walks you through setting up your first account. An account in Windows Mail is not actually an email account, but rather an entry in Tools → Accounts that connects to an existing email account. Windows Mail uses either the Post Office Protocol 3 (POP3) or the Internet Message Access Protocol 4 (IMAP4) Internet mail protocol to receive mail, and the Simple Mail

Message list

Folders

Preview pane

Figure 6-1. Windows Mail, the email application that comes with Windows

Transfer Protocol (SMTP) to send mail. Nearly all Internet service providers (ISPs) and many online services (such as AOL and MSN) use POP3 and SMTP for mail transfer.

In addition to mail accounts, you can set up Directory Service accounts, which allow you to look up contact information using any of several online global contact lists. Windows Mail also functions as a newsreader for participating in Internet newsgroups; you'll need to add a News Account to Windows Mail before you can read any newsgroups (contact your ISP for details). Note, though, that it includes a built-in setup for participating in newsgroups on Microsoft's public NNTP server. Click on Microsoft Communities and it will walk you through the process of setting up access.

Windows Mail hot keys

Many people like using the mouse, but those who are more keyboard-oriented are always looking for fast ways to access Windows Mail features. That's where hot key combinations come in; rather than having to mouse around, you can press a simple key combination. Table 6-1 lists Windows Mail hot keys.

Table 6-1. Windows Mail keyboard shortcuts

Key combination	Action
In Main window, View Message window, and Send Message window	
F1	Open Help.
Ctrl-A	Select all messages or all text within a single message.
In Main window and View Message window	
Ctrl-M	Send and receive email.
Ctrl-N	Open or post a new message.
Ctrl-Shift-B	Open Contacts.
Delete or Ctrl-D	Delete an email message.
Ctrl-R	Reply to the message author.

Table 6-1. Windows Mail keyboard shortcuts (continued)

Key combination	Action
Ctrl-Shift-R or Ctrl-G (newsgroups only)	Reply to all.
Ctrl-F	Forward a message.
Ctrl-Shift-F	Find a message.
Ctrl-P	Print the selected message.
Ctrl->	Go to the next message in the list.
Ctrl-<	Go to the preceding message in the list.
Alt-Enter	View the selected message's properties.
Ctrl-U	Go to the next unread email message.
Ctrl-Shift-U	Go to the next unread newsgroup conversation.
In Main window	
Ctrl-O or Enter	Open a selected message.
Ctrl-Enter or Ctrl-Q	Mark a message as read.
Tab	Move among the message list, Folders list (if on), and Preview pane.
Ctrl-W	Go to a newsgroup.
Left arrow or plus sign (+)	Expand a newsgroup conversation (show all responses).
Right arrow or minus sign (–)	Collapse a newsgroup conversation (hide responses).
Ctrl-Shift-A	Mark all newsgroup messages as read.
Ctrl-J	Go to the next unread newsgroup or folder.
Ctrl-Shift-M	Download newsgroup messages for offline reading.
Ctrl-I	Go to your Inbox.
Ctrl-Y	Go to a folder.
F5	Refresh newsgroup messages and headers.
In Message window: viewing or sending	
Esc	Close a message.
F3 or Ctrl-Shift-F	Find text.
In Message window: sending only	
F7	Check spelling.
Ctrl-Shift-S	Insert a signature.
Ctrl-Enter or Alt-S	Send a message or post it to a newsgroup.
Ctrl-Tab	Switch among the Edit, Source, and Preview tabs when working in Source Edit view.

Notes

- Alternatives to Windows Mail include the popular Eudora Email (*http://www. eudora.com*) by QUALCOMM, and web-based email services such as Hotmail (*http://www.hotmail.com*) by Microsoft, Gmail (*http://www.gmail.com*) from Google, and PINE for those die-hard Unix users. Another alternative is the excellent Mozilla Thunderbird (*http://www.mozilla.org/products/thunderbird*), which offers plenty of customizability in the form of third-party plug-ins.

- Because it is an integrated component of Windows, Windows Mail may become the target of virus and Trojan horse attacks, in the same way that its predecessor, Outlook Express, was and that Outlook still is. A number of viruses exploited the vulnerabilities in Outlook Express to replicate themselves, sending a virus-infested attachment to everyone in your Contacts. Sadly, this isn't going to stop anytime soon. Given the dominance of Windows Mail and Outlook Express (and that of its big sister, Outlook), it's always going to be the virus writer's favorite target. On the bright side, though, Windows Mail has been made "leaner" than Outlook and Outlook Express, so it may present less of a target to malware authors.

- If you want to use Windows Mail Express when you're not connected to the Internet, go to File → Work Offline. If you are using a dial-up connection, you may even want to further reduce online time by configuring Windows Mail to hang up after sending and receiving messages. To do this, go to Tools → Options → Connection tab and turn on the "Hang up after sending and receiving" option. If autodial is enabled, Windows Mail will reconnect automatically when you go to Tools → Send and Receive.

- To send a file along with an email message, go to Insert → File Attachment in the message composition window, or just drag the file from your Desktop or Explorer into the body of the message. If Windows Mail is your default email program, you can also send a file as an email attachment by right-clicking it and selecting Send To → Mail Recipient. This opens a new, blank message with the file attachment included.

Columns

Changes the display of columns in the Message List.

To open
View → Columns

Right-click the top of any column in the message list and choose Columns.

Description
The message list in Windows Mail displays information about each message in columns. By default, those columns are labeled From, Subject, Received, Flag, Attachment, and Priority. But there are other columns you can display as well. To add columns to or remove columns from the display, choose View → Columns, and Figure 6-2 appears.

Check the box next to any columns you want displayed; uncheck the box next to those you don't want displayed. In addition to the default columns, you can display these:

- Size (shows the size of the message)
- Sent (shows whether a message was sent)
- To (shows the recipient of a message)
- Watch/Ignore (shows whether a message is being watched or ignored)

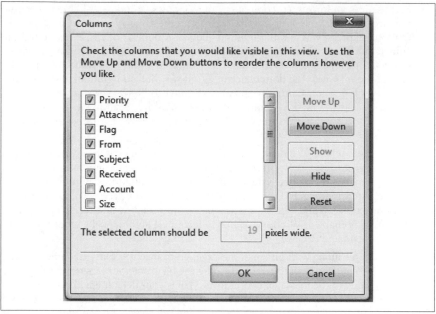

Figure 6-2. Adding and removing columns from the message list

To change the order of columns, highlight an entry and click Move Up or Move Down. When you move a column "up," it will be moved to the left in the message list; moving it "down" moves it to the right.

You can also change the width of any column by highlighting it and typing the new width (in pixels) in the box near the bottom of the screen.

Notes

• By default, messages are displayed in descending order by date (the newest messages are on top). To change that to ascending order, click the Received column. To switch it back, click the Received column again. To sort by any column other than the Received column, right-click the top of the column and choose either Ascending or Descending, depending on the order in which you want them displayed.

See also

"Watch Conversation"

Find

Search for messages, people, and text.

To open

Edit → Find

Click the Find icon on the toolbar.

Description

One of the biggest problem that many people have with email is finding messages that they've sent or received. Windows Mail's Find feature does a very good job of helping you find messages. Find lets you perform three different kinds of searches: for messages, for people, and for text within a message. To choose among the three, click the down arrow next to the Find icon and select what you're looking for. (If you click the icon itself, you'll launch a search for messages.) Similarly, when you select Edit → Find, you'll have the choice of which Find feature to use.

When you choose to search for messages, the screen shown in Figure 6-3 appears. You'll be able to specify which folder to search; whether to search the From:, To:, Subject:, or message text field; whether the message has an attachment or has been flagged; and a date range to search within.

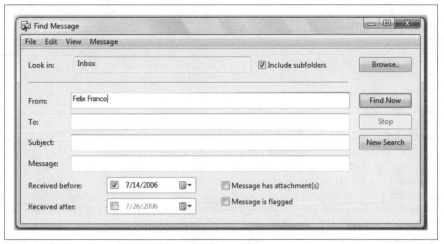

Figure 6-3. The Find Message feature, which gives you multiple options for searching for messages

When you do a search, the results show in a pane beneath the Find Message screen.

When you search for people, a screen appears that lets you search by name, email address, street address, phone number, and freeform text. If you're in a corporation that uses Active Directory, you can search for people in your corporation by choosing Active Directory from the Look In drop-down list. Similarly, if your corporation subscribes to the Verisign Internet Directory Service, you can search for people outside your business. Choose Verisign Internet Directory Service from the Look In drop-down list.

To search for text within a message, highlight the message and choose the "Text in this message" option.

Notes

- The hot key combination for doing a search—Ctrl-Shift-F—may confuse you because it's context-sensitive. If you're reading a message in a separate window (double-click on a message in the message list to open a separate window), that hot key launches a dialog box for finding text inside your message. If you're in the main Windows Mail screen instead, it will launch a dialog box for finding messages.

- Windows Mail also has a Quick Search feature, the search bar in the upper-right-hand corner of the screen. It does an immediate text-only search of messages in the current folder, so you won't be able to search by date, specific fields, attachments and flags, and so on.

- If you're looking for more robust search features than those that are built into Windows Mail, use the Search feature in Windows, which offers more searching flexibility and searches through emails and documents simultaneously. It also allows you to save searches so that you don't need to reformulate them after you've run them once.

See also
"Search" and "Indexing Options," both in Chapter 4

Internet Accounts

Sets up, customizes, and manages email accounts, newsgroup subscriptions, and Internet Directories.

To open
Tools → Accounts

Description
To send or receive email, you need to set up an account in Windows Mail. The first time you open Windows Mail, a wizard walks you through setting up your first account. An account in Windows Mail works with an existing email account that you have with a mail provider, such as your ISP, employer, or school. Windows Mail uses either the POP3 or the IMAP4 Internet mail protocol to receive mail, and SMTP to send mail. Nearly all ISPs use POP3 and SMTP for mail transfer.

Before setting up an account in Windows Mail, you'll need to get the POP3, IMAP4, or SMTP settings from your mail provider. The wizard will ask you for those settings, as well as your username and password, in order to set up your account. Make sure that you get all the details of the settings—not only the address itself (such as *smtp.comcast.net* or *pop.isp.net*), but also whether the servers require authentication.

The Internet Accounts dialog box, shown in Figure 6-4, lists all of your email accounts; lets you add, edit, or remove existing accounts; and lets you set up newsgroup accounts and Internet Directory Servers (LDAP) as well. (An Internet Directory Server makes it easy to find people's email addresses.) To add a new account, click Add and follow the wizard. It's the same wizard you'll encounter the first time you start Windows Mail. Unfortunately, the only way to set up a new account entry is to use the cumbersome wizard.

If you have more than one mail account, you can choose the default by highlighting it and clicking Set as Default. Thereafter, that account will be used as your return address when sending outgoing email (unless you change it on a per-message basis).

The Set Order button, which lets you choose the search order when looking up contacts in your Directory Services, may be a little confusing at first. Because only an entry is shown, there's nothing to rearrange; to include more entries in Set Order, double-click each entry and turn on the "Include this account when receiving mail or synchronizing" option on the General tab.

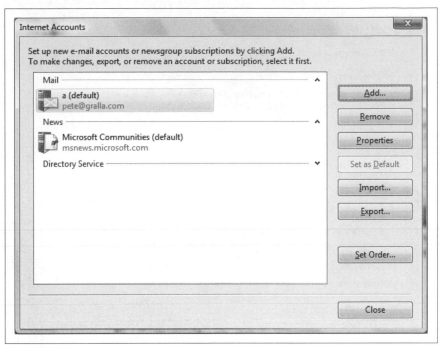

Figure 6-4. The Internet Accounts dialog box, which puts all of your email, newsgroups, and Internet Directory accounts into one location

  Most problems encountered when sending or receiving email are caused by improper settings in the Internet Accounts screen.

Not uncommonly, when you're setting up a new account, there will be problems with it. Perhaps you mistyped the POP3 server address, or you didn't realize that your server required authentication. And sometimes your ISP may change a server address. Perhaps you've changed your username and password. And for some accounts, you may need to set some of the more advanced options, such as whether to automatically check mail from this account, whether to leave copies of your mail on the server, or whether to use a different email address when replying to messages sent to this account.

To change information about any account, you'll need to use the Properties window to enter information. To get to the Properties window, highlight an account and select Properties, or double-click the account. The screen shown in Figure 6-5 appears.

Following is what each tab does:

General

This tab includes basic information about the account, including the account name, user information, and email address. Note that the tab allows you to have a separate email address for sending and receiving. So you can send with the email address for the account, but when someone replies to the mail, it can go to a separate address. If you want both addresses to be the same, leave the Reply address blank, and all replies will go to the account's sending email address. This tab also

Figure 6-5. The Properties window, which lets you change options for each of your accounts

lets you decide whether the account should always be included when you send and receive mail. To ensure that it does, check the box next to "Include this account when receiving mail or synchronizing."

Servers

This contains information your POP3, IMAP (both are used for receiving mail), and SMTP (used for sending mail) servers. More often than not, if you have trouble setting up an account, here's where your problems will lie. Make sure that you type in the exact server address given to you by your ISP (or, if you are connecting to your email at work or at school, your system administrator). Also, you have to know whether you need Secure Password Authentication for incoming mail, or username and password authentication for outgoing mail.

Connection

In most cases, you'll never have to use this tab. You'll need it only if the mail account for some reason requires that you connect to it only via a specific dial-up or other Internet connection. If it does, check the box next to "Always connect to this account using" and then select the account from the drop-down list.

Security

If you want to digitally sign messages with this account, here's where you enter the information.

Advanced

Here's where you enter detailed information about each server, including port numbers, whether the servers require secure SSL connections, whether you need to account for server timeouts, and whether to leave copies of messages on the server even after you've downloaded or sent them. If you are connecting to an SMTP server at work or school, you may need to use a different port number for outgoing mail. This is because many ISPs block outgoing access on port 25 to all but their own SMTP servers (this is a security measure to reduce the likelihood that home computers will be used as spam-spewing zombies). Port 587 is often a working alternative, but consult with your system administrator for details.

IMAP

Use this tab to specify the root folder of your IMAP server, as well as which IMAP folders to use for sent items, drafts, deleted items, and junk mail.

Notes

* Some free web-based email providers let you use an email client such as Windows Mail to send and receive mail. As of this writing, Gmail does, MSN Hotmail doesn't, and Yahoo! does—but only if you pay $19.99 a year for Yahoo! Mail Plus. Problems encountered when sending or receiving email are caused by improper settings in this window. If you want to use Gmail with Windows Mail, read the Gmail Help document about it, because it requires a very specific setup.

* If you use a mail provider other than your own ISP, you may run into problems sending mail. Let's say, for example, that you own the domain *yournamehere.com* and your ISP is *bigisp.net*. You want to use mail servers of *yournamehere.com* so that your email address is your last name, like this: *yourname@yournamehere.com*. But when you use the *yournamehere.com* SMTP server, mail refuses to send. If your mail provider can't offer access on an alternate port (see "Advanced," earlier in this section), you'll need to use *yournamehere.com* for your account, but the *bigisp.net* SMTP servers. You'll set up all that on the Server Properties screen. Even this, though, may run you into trouble if your ISP doesn't want to relay on behalf of *yournamehere.com*, or if recipients (or their email programs) conclude that your email is forged because the sending domain and relay domain don't match.

* If you access the same account from two different computers, you may want to set up one computer to download messages, but not delete them from the server. Set up your other system to delete messages after downloading them. This way, one system always has a complete set of messages. Do this by using Tools → Accounts → *any account* → Properties → Advanced tab → Leave a copy of messages on server. If you use IMAP for your email, all of your message folders reside on the server, so you won't need to use this feature (Windows Mail will download copies of messages only in order to index them and make them available offline).

* If you have multiple accounts set up and do not want one included when you click Send and Receive, go to Tools → Accounts → *any account* → Properties → General tab and deselect "Include this account when receiving mail or synchronizing." For IMAP accounts, you can also set sync settings on a per-folder basis. To get to these settings, click on the top-level folder for your IMAP account, and the sync settings will take over the righthand pane where you'll be able to choose from Don't Synchronize, All Messages, New Messages Only, and Headers Only.

Windows Mail

- If you have more than one account set up in Windows Mail, only one account can be the default at any time. Although you can choose a From account each time you compose outgoing mail, the default account is the one that is used if you don't make a choice. Unfortunately, there's no way to set up a Message Rule to change the default account used when responding to incoming messages; for that, you'll need a more full-featured email program such as Eudora.

See also
"Message Rules"

Junk E-mail

Filters out spam and junk email from your inbox.

To open
Tools → Junk E-mail Options

Description

To use email is to be bedeviled by spam. Offers to get rich quick, enlarge certain body parts, buy authentic Rolex watches for $4.99…these, and more, come in an unending stream, 24 hours a day.

Spam is more than a nuisance; it can be dangerous as well. Many scams are launched via email, including the notorious Nigerian scam, also called the 419 scam, in which you are apparently enlisted in a scheme to get millions of dollars—except that it's your bank account that is emptied. Phishing attacks, in which you are lured to a site posing as a financial site such as your bank, are launched via email as well.

To help get spam under control, Windows Mail includes a way to block and filter junk mail. By default, this spam control is turned on. Windows Mail's junk mail filter examines all incoming mail, and if it suspects that it is junk mail, it automatically forwards it to the Junk E-mail folder. From there you can examine the mail and delete any you don't want. If the filter makes a mistake, you can move the mail to your inbox and tell Windows Mail not to consider mail from that sender as junk in the future. You can also add email addresses manually to a Blocked Senders list, and the filter will always consider mail from them as spam. Plus, you can add email addresses manually to a Safe Senders list and the filter will never consider mail from them as spam.

 As a way to protect you from malicious spam, when mail is in the Junk E-mail folder the links in the mail won't work. But what if the filter has made a mistake and you need to click a link on mail in the folder? Simply move the mail out to another folder, and the links will work; they won't function only when they're in the Junk E-mail folder. If you want the filter to recognize in the future that the sender isn't sending spam, mark the message as not junk.

There are a number of ways you can customize how the junk mail filter works, as well as make it more effective. To get to them, use the Junk E-mail Options dialog box, shown in Figure 6-6.

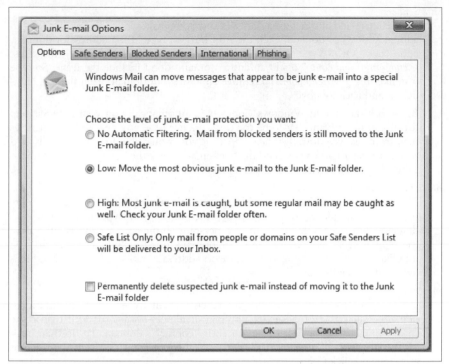

Figure 6-6. Customizing Junk E-mail Options

Following are details about the use of each tab:

Options

This lets you choose how aggressively you want the filter to handle spam; it lets you choose your level of protection:

No Automatic Filtering

This will not automatically check for spam, although it will move mail to your Junk E-mail folder from anyone on your Blocked Senders list.

Low

This is the default level. It catches only the most obvious spam. It will let spam through, but it also usually won't incorrectly move legitimate mail to your Junk E-mail folder.

High

This more aggressive level will catch more spam than Low, but it will also sometimes move legitimate mail to your Junk E-mail folder.

Safe List Only

This will consider all mail as spam, unless it is from someone on your Safe Senders list.

This tab also gives you the option of having Windows Mail automatically delete spam instead of moving it to the Junk E-mail folder. This is a dangerous option to choose. The junk mail filter is not perfect, and at times it will consider some legitimate mail as junk. So if you choose this option, you may delete important mail without ever seeing it.

Safe Senders

This lets you add and remove addresses and domains to your Safe Senders list. To add an address or domain, click the Add button, type in the address or domain, and click OK. Type in the person's entire email address, like this: *friend@myfriend.com*. To add an entire domain, don't include the *www*. So type it in like this: *myfriend.com*. To remove an address or domain from the list, highlight it and click Remove.

By default, anyone in Windows Contacts is automatically on your Safe Senders list. If you don't want that to be the case, uncheck the box next to "Also trust e-mail from my Windows Contacts." And if you would like to automatically add people to the list when you send them an email, check the box next to "Automatically add people I e-mail to the Safe Senders List."

Blocked Senders

This lets you add and remove addresses and domains to your Blocked Senders list. To add an address or domain, click the Add button, type in the address or domain, and click OK. Type in the person's entire email address, like this: *friend@myenemy.com*. To add an entire domain, don't include the *www*. So type it in like this: *myenemy.com*. To remove an address or domain from the list, highlight it and click Remove.

International

You may notice that whenever you receive email from certain international domains (such as *.ru* for Russia), the mail is almost always spam. If that is the case, you can filter out mail from an entire country's domain. To do that, click Blocked Top-Level Domain List, select a country or countries from the list that appears, and click OK.

Similarly, you may notice that when you receive email in a foreign language with foreign characters, that mail is almost always spam. To filter out email with foreign character sets, click Blocked Encoding List, select the language or languages from the list that appears, and click OK.

Phishing

The junk mail filter also checks whether incoming mail is likely to be a phishing attempt. But it handles potential phishing attacks in a confusing manner. If it believes an email to be a phishing attack, it doesn't move the mail to the Junk E-mail folder, but it does deactivate the links in the mail. The Phishing tab lets you change that behavior. If you want the filter to deactivate the links and move the suspicious mail to the Junk E-mail folder, check the box next to "Move phishing E-mail to the Junk Mail folder." If you want to turn off antiphishing checking entirely, uncheck the box next to "Protect my inbox from messages with potential phishing links."

 If the junk mail filter doesn't block a phishing attempt, Internet Explorer will still use its phishing filter to help ensure that you don't fall prey to a phishing attack.

There's another way to work with the junk mail filter—on a message-by-message basis—and you'll most likely work with it that way rather than using the dialog box. Select any email and then select Junk E-mail. A menu appears that allows you to add the mail sender or domain to the Safe Senders list or Blocked Senders list, unblock the mail, or mark the mail as not junk. When you mark the mail as not junk, it is moved to your inbox, but the sender isn't added to your Safe Senders list, so the next time he sends you an email, it will be considered junk. If you want all subsequent email from him to be considered legitimate, you should instead choose Add Sender to Safe Senders List.

Notes

- If you don't think that the Windows Mail filter is doing an adequate job of fighting spam, you can buy any of a number of antispam programs that purport to do a better job. Companies such as Symantec and Cloudmark sell antispam software.

- You may be flooded with spam, but more spam than you actually see is being sent to you. Your mail provider has spam filters as well, and it filters out much spam before you ever even see it. But because spam has become such a problem, some of these filters are overly aggressive and filter out legitimate mail. That means that you may be sent legitimate mail that you never receive. If someone tells you he's sent you mail, and you've never received it, contact your mail provider, give the provider the email address of the person, and ask that spam from him not be filtered. Your mail provider may or may not do this; some are notorious for not responding to requests.

- Microsoft continues to update its Junk Mail filter with new addresses of known spammers. They will be delivered via Windows Update.

See also

"Phishing Filter," in Chapter 5, and "Windows Defender" and "Windows Update," in Chapter 8

Message Rules

Create rules to take action on incoming mail, such as routing it to a specific folder or automatically responding to it.

To open

Tools → Message Rules

Description

You can set up Windows to automatically handle incoming mail in a number of ways. For example, you can set up rules instructing Windows Mail to store all email retrieved from your business account in a certain folder, all email retrieved from your personal account in a different folder, and all junk mail (spam) in the trash. Furthermore, you can have Windows Mail automatically respond to certain messages and mark some messages as urgent and others as potentially annoying.

Go to Tools → Message Rules → Mail to view the mail rules currently in effect. If you haven't yet set up any rules, you would be prompted to do so now; otherwise, click New to create a new rule (see Figure 6-7).

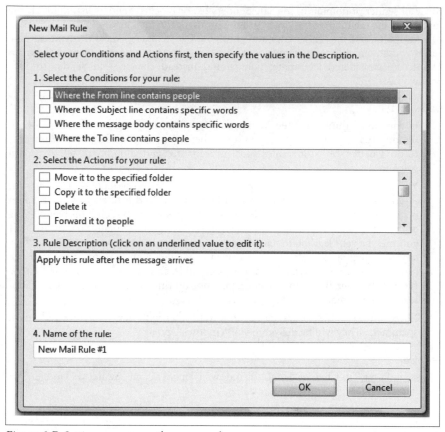

New Mail Rule

Select your Conditions and Actions first, then specify the values in the Description.

1. Select the Conditions for your rule:

- [ ] Where the From line contains people
- [ ] Where the Subject line contains specific words
- [ ] Where the message body contains specific words
- [ ] Where the To line contains people

2. Select the Actions for your rule:

- [ ] Move it to the specified folder
- [ ] Copy it to the specified folder
- [ ] Delete it
- [ ] Forward it to people

3. Rule Description (click on an underlined value to edit it):

Apply this rule after the message arrives

4. Name of the rule:

New Mail Rule #1

OK   Cancel

Figure 6-7. Setting up your email message rules

Each rule is set up as follows:

Select the Conditions for your rule

Choose one or more conditions that, when met, will instruct Windows Mail to take the desired action. For example, to create a rule that applies to all email from Grandma, place a checkmark next to "Where the From line contains people."

Select the Actions for your rule

After you've chosen one or more conditions, these options allow you to decide what to do with messages that meet those conditions. For example, you may want to place all of Grandma's email in a certain folder, in which case you would place a checkmark next to "Move it to the specified folder." On the other hand, if Grandma drives you nuts, you may want to place a checkmark next to "Delete it."

Rule Description

The third box displays a summary of the conditions and actions you've chosen, and allows you to input the specifics. For example, if you've chosen to move all of Grandma's email into a certain folder, the phrase "contains people" will be underlined and hyperlinked, as will the word "specified." Before you can complete this rule, you must click each of these links; in the case of "contains people," you would type Grandma's email address. Likewise, in the case of "specified," you would select the path of the folder in which to store Grandma's email.

Name of the rule

Finally, choose a label for the rule; although the name makes no difference, it will allow you to easily identify and differentiate the rules.

Don't expect to get all your rules right the first time. After creating a new rule, scrutinize its performance as new mail is retrieved.

You can also create new rules on the fly, using some of the context-based tools in Windows Mail. Start by opening a message, and then go to Message → Create Rule from Message. Here, the familiar rule dialog box is shown, but some fields have been filled in with information from the selected message.

Notes

- Don't try to use Message Rules to block spam; instead, it's a much better idea to use Windows Mail's Junk E-mail features. See "Junk E-mail," earlier in this chapter.

- You can use Message Rules to act on newsgroup messages as well as email. Choose Tools → Message Rules → News, and follow the same steps as you would to create rules for mail. You will be able to take different actions on newsgroup messages than you can on email messages. For example, with newsgroup messages, you can flag messages, mark them as read, highlight them with color, and delete them.

See also

"Junk E-mail"

New Message

Create a new email message in Windows Mail.

To open

File → New → Mail Message

Click the Create Mail icon.

Press Ctrl-N.

Description

When you create a new mail message, as shown in Figure 6-8, you use several sets of menus, toolbars, and icons. Addressing the message is simple: type an email address into the To: and Cc: fields, or click the Contacts icon and select a contact. Then type a subject into the Subject line, type in your message, and send the message by clicking the Send icon. (You can also select File → Send, or press Alt-S.)

The top menu bar and the toolbar beneath it are somewhat redundant because they offer similar functions—for example, you can copy text by clicking the Copy icon on the toolbar, or instead choose Edit → Copy from the toolbar. But many functions are available only from the menu bar, and a few functions are available only from the toolbar. The toolbar has on it what Microsoft believes are the most common tasks you'll want to accomplish.

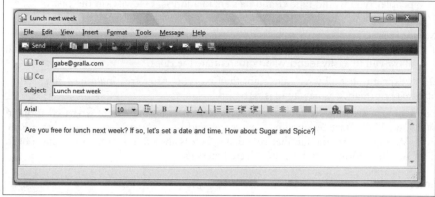

Figure 6-8. Creating a new message with Windows Mail

The ribbon bar just above the box where you type the text of your message lets you format your text by changing the font, size, and so on. It works exactly like similar features in word processors.

> If you prefer to send mail in plain-text format (or your recipients prefer to receive it in that format), you can easily do so. Select Tools → Options → Send, and select Plain Text under Mail Sending Format. If you want to primarily send mail in HTML format and send plain text occasionally, select HTML from that setting, but when you compose a new email, choose Format → Plain Text in the message window.

The menu bar

Following are the main purposes for the menu bar:

File

This menu lets you create, send, copy, delete, and save messages, as well as perform related tasks. In addition, it lets you save a message as a template for stationery (see "Stationery," later in this chapter, for details.)

Edit

This familiar menu, like most Edit menus throughout Windows Vista and in Windows applications, lets you cut, copy, and paste text, as well as perform similar tasks. It also lets you search for messages across all folders, and search for text within a message. In addition, it lets you remove hyperlinks in a message. Normally, when you type text, such as *www.oreilly.com*, Windows Mail will automatically turn it into a hyperlink. Choosing the Remove Hyperlink option from the Edit menu will remove any selected hyperlinks.

Insert

This lets you insert an attachment, picture, horizontal line, business card, signature, hyperlink, and text from a file.

Format

This lets you format the text of your message; choose a background picture, color, or sound; choose to send as plain text or HTML; and apply stationery.

Tools

This lets you check the spelling in your email, request a "read" or "secure" receipt, check whether the names of recipients are found in Windows Contacts, encrypt a message, and digitally sign a message. It also can launch Windows Contacts and Windows Calendar.

Message

This lets you create another message, create one using a specific kind of stationery, and set delivery priority for your message (low, medium, or high).

The toolbar

The toolbar lets you perform common tasks on your outgoing email messages by clicking the appropriate icon. Most of these tasks are self-explanatory, such as sending the message; cutting, copying, and pasting text; inserting an attachment; setting message priority; and so on.

However, several icons let you perform less common tasks, and they are not always self-explanatory:

Check names

Click this icon, and Windows Mail checks the addresses you've typed into the To: and Cc: fields, looks for incorrect syntax, and if it finds any, looks to see whether there are any near matches in Windows Contacts. You can then choose the correct name from Windows Contacts.

Digitally sign message

This allows you to "sign" the message using a digital signature that will guarantee to the reader of the message that you are who you say you are. To use this feature, you'll have to first install a digital certificate, also called a *Digital ID*. Some corporations give their employees Digital IDs, and in that case, Windows Mail may already be set up to use one. If your company does provide a Digital ID, but for some reason it hasn't been set up yet, you can install it yourself. First, find out where the ID is located. Then in Windows Mail, select Tools → Options → Security. Under Secure Mail, click Digital IDs. Click Import, and then follow the instructions to import your Digital ID.

Encrypt message

This allows you to encrypt the message so that only the recipient can read it. To use this feature, you'll have to first install each recipient's digital certificate.

Notes

- You can also create a new newsgroup message, by choosing File → New → News Message. When you do this, most of your options for creating messages will be the same, but there will be a few differences. For example, there will be no ribbon bar for formatting text. Instead, you will see options for choosing the type of newsgroup post you want it to be: comment, question, or suggestion.

- If you've chosen plain text as your mail sending format (Tools → Options → Send → Mail Sending Format), you won't see the ribbon bar for formatting text.

Windows Mail

- Beware when sending pictures in your email, because some servers have a limit on message sizes—sometimes as small as 1 MB per message. You can, however, have Vista shrink the size of pictures before you send them, using the Windows Photo Gallery. You'll have to open the picture in the Windows Photo Gallery first, resize it using the built-in tools, and then use a built-in Windows Photo Gallery feature for sending the picture via email. See "Windows Photo Gallery," in Chapter 12, for details.

See also

"Windows Photo Gallery," in Chapter 12

Newsgroups

Participate in discussion groups.

To open

Tools → Newsgroups

Ctrl-W

Click the newsgroup icon in the toolbar.

Description

Newsgroups are world-spanning discussion groups that cover every topic imaginable. They predate the World Wide Web, and even though community sites on the Web such as MySpace have become exceedingly popular, millions of people all over the world still participate in newsgroups.

Before you can participate in newsgroups, you first need to set up an account. For details on how to do it, see "Internet Accounts," earlier in this chapter. For server information you'll need in order to set up an account, check with your ISP. By default, Windows Mail comes with an account already set up for Microsoft support newsgroups.

Newsgroups open up in the main Windows Mail screen, as shown in Figure 6-9. Each newsgroup server appears as a separate server; beneath that server are newsgroups to which you have subscribed (more on that a little later). You read posts in the same way as you do mail; information about each post—such as the subject, sender, and so on—appears in the message list, and the content of the post appears in the preview pane.

To a great extent, you use Windows Mail in much the same way for reading newsgroups as you do for sending and receiving mail. However, there are a number of differences:

Subscribe to newsgroups

When you choose Tools → Newsgroups or press Ctrl-W, you'll be sent to the Newsgroups Subscriptions screen (shown in Figure 6-10), which lists all of your newsgroup servers on the left. Click any, and you'll see the list of newsgroups in which you can participate in the All tab. To read any newsgroup, double-click it, or highlight it and click the "Go to" button. You can subscribe to newsgroups in which you want to participate regularly. That way, the newsgroups will always show up in your folders in the main Windows Mail screen for quick access. To subscribe to groups, highlight them (you can highlight multiple ones at the same time using the familiar Windows Shift-click or Ctrl-click selection method), and

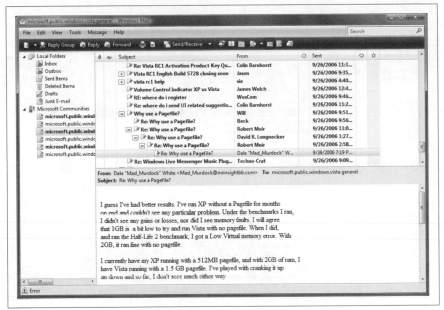

Figure 6-9. Reading newsgroups in Windows Mail

then click Subscribe. The groups will now show up in your folders, as well as on the Subscribed tab in the Newsgroups Subscriptions screen. To unsubscribe to a newsgroup, highlight it in the Subscribed tab and click the Unsubscribe button. You can unsubscribe to multiple newsgroups at the same time, in the same way that you can subscribe to them.

Search

There are many thousands of newsgroups, and it can be difficult to scroll through them all to find the ones you're interested in. At the top of the Newsgroups Subscriptions screen is a search box that helps you search for newsgroups in which you'd like to participate. The search can work in one of two ways: it can either search only the names of newsgroups (such as *microsoft.public.br.vfp*), or it can search the names and descriptions of newsgroups. Newsgroup names aren't always particularly descriptive, so it's a good idea to search names and descriptions. By default, it searches only by names, because it first needs to download the descriptions of the newsgroups from the server if you want to search by description as well. To search through descriptions, check the box next to "Also search descriptions." If you haven't yet downloaded the descriptions, you'll be prompted to do so before you search.

Communities

As a way to help you better know if other people's newsgroup posts are useful, Windows Mail uses Microsoft Communities, which lets participants rate the usefulness of other people's newsgroup posts. The rating of each post then shows up in the Rating column, which is denoted by a star at the top. Only users who are signed into Microsoft Communities can rate or see the ratings. (You can rate them on the Web as well. The communities are available online via a web-based mail reader at *http://www.microsoft.com/communities/newsgroups/en-us/default.aspx*.) To rate any post you're reading, select a rating from the Rate drop-down list in the Rate this

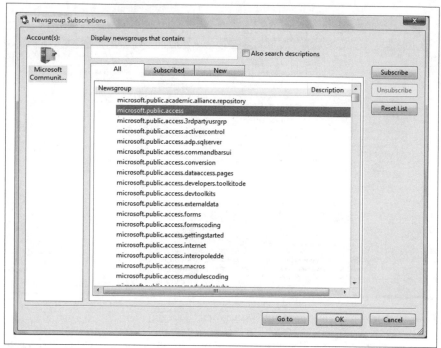

Figure 6-10. The Newsgroups Subscriptions screen

Post section. If you haven't yet logged in using Windows Live or Windows Passport, you'll be prompted to enter that Live login information. (If you don't have a Windows Live login, you'll have to create one first.) You can then rate the post as either useful or not useful.

Downloaded messages

Many newsgroups have tens of thousands of posts, and it could take an extremely long time to download all of the posts of every newsgroup in which you want to participate. So Windows Mail downloads only the headers of the most recent 300 messages to your PC. When you click any message, the message itself is then downloaded to your PC, where you read it. If you want to see more headers than just the most recent ones, select Tools → Get Next 300 Headers.

Notes

- Newsgroups can contain objectionable and pornographic material, including pictures and videos as well as messages, so be forewarned before participating in any you don't know about.

- Not all newsgroup servers allow access to all newsgroups. The servers for the Microsoft support newsgroups, for example, have only newsgroups for Microsoft support. So your ISP may not give you access to all newsgroups. There are a number of free newsgroup servers you can use; search for "free newsgroup server" or conduct another similar search on Google or Live Search to find them. A popular one is *freenews.netfront.net*. The site *http://freeusenetnews.com* has a list of many free ones.

- Some web sites let you read newsgroups directly from the Web, without having to use a client such as Windows Mail. The best-known one is Google Groups at *http://groups.google.com*, and Microsoft makes its public newsgroups available at *http://www.microsoft.com/communities/newsgroups/default.mspx*.

- It can be annoying to wade through the thousands of messages that can exist in a single newsgroup. Custom views work like Rules (discussed earlier) and let you weed out some of the extraneous messages. For example, you can hide messages that are written by certain users (in Usenet parlance, this is referred to as a "bozo filter"), contain certain words in the subject, are over a certain length, or are over a certain age. Go to View → Current View → Customize Current View to set your preferences.

- Some newsgroup messages are scrambled as a way to hide offensive or sensitive material. Windows Mail doesn't let you scramble messages, but it does let you unscramble them to make them readable. Often, a scrambled message has the characters *ROT13* near the beginning of the message. ROT13 scrambles messages by replacing every character in the message with one that appears 13 characters later in the alphabet. You can unscramble a message by first opening it, and then choosing Message → Unscramble (ROT13).

See also
"Internet Accounts"

Read Options

Set options for displaying and reading message in Windows Mail.

To open
Tools → Options → Read tab

Description
This dialog box, shown in Figure 6-11, lets you change how Windows Mail displays messages, and how you read them.

The box has three sections:

Reading Messages

This section customizes basic mail reading and display. Some of the options here are self-explanatory, such as how long it takes for a message to be marked as read after you highlight it (the default is five seconds) and whether to automatically expand grouped messages (the default is no). Perhaps the most important option in this section is "Read all messages in plain text." If you select this, all formatting will be stripped from your HTML email, and it will most likely be very difficult to read. By default, this option is turned off. This section also lets you choose the color for watched messages.

The most baffling option in this section is "Show ToolTips in the message list for clipped items," which is turned on by default. When the subject line of a message is too long to be displayed in the subject column, the subject line appears "clipped"—that is, three dots (...) appear at the end. With this option turned on, when you hover the mouse pointer over the subject line, the entire subject line will appear in a tool tip.

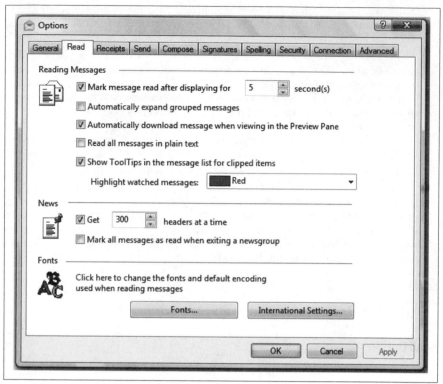

Figure 6-11. Changing your options for reading mail using the Read Options dialog box

News

This section lets you change how many newsgroup headers should be downloaded from individual newsgroups when you view any. The default is 300. The section also lets you mark all messages as being read (when they're read, they change from boldface to plain text) when you exit a newsgroup. The default is not to mark them as read when you exit.

Fonts

This lets you change the font and default encoding for reading messages. It lets you change the language, as well as the specific font, size, and so on.

Notes

- For maximum safety, choose the "Read all messages in plain text" option, because it will turn off HTML, which can prove to be dangerous. On the other hand, then you won't be able to view graphics, fonts, and so on. And some messages that are composed in HTML may be unreadable as plain text.

See also

"Watch Conversation" and "Newsgroups"

Signatures

Automatically include text or HTML at the bottom of all of your outgoing messages.

To open

Tools → Options → Signatures

Description

You may want to have text or HTML appended to the bottom of all your outgoing messages—for example, your contact information, or a pithy quote that sums up your views about life, love, and whether the Red Sox will ever win the World Series again.

The Signatures dialog box, shown in Figure 6-12, lets you create and assign signatures to your different accounts. To create a new signature, click New, type in a distinctive name for it, and then type the text into the Edit Signature section. If you already have a signature in a text file, click File in the Edit Signature section, browse to the file, and click OK. If you want to use an HTML signature, first create it as an HTML file, then browse to it and click OK.

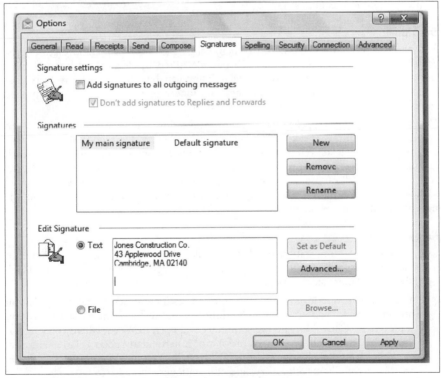

Figure 6-12. Creating your signatures

Windows Mail lets you use different signatures for different accounts. To do it, highlight the signature you want to assign to an account, click Advanced in the Edit Signature section, choose the account, and click OK.

Notes

- You can use plain-text characters (called ASCII characters) to create pictures for your signatures. Plenty of web sites include art that you can save to a text file and then use to create a signature. In Google, search for "ASCII art" or "ASCII signature."

- A signature is different from stationery. Stationery is background colors, graphics, and multimedia that you use as a background for outgoing messages; a signature is text or HTML appended to the bottom of outgoing messages.

See also

"Stationery"

Stationery

Use backgrounds colors and graphics for your email.

To open

Tools → Options → Compose tab

Description

Stationery imposes a visual style on your message, including colors and even images. Stationery files are just *.html* files (web pages), stored by default in *\Program Files\ Common Files\Microsoft Shared\Stationery*. They can be edited with any web page editor or plain-text editor. To create new stationery or to use one of the supplied templates, first go to Tools → Options → Compose tab.

To create new stationery, click Create New, and follow the wizard's instructions. To use existing stationery, check the box next to either Mail or News, depending on your purpose for creating stationery. Unfortunately, you can't set default stationery for each account separately (something Eudora lets you do), so whatever stationery you choose will be used for all of your email or newsgroup accounts. However, you can choose stationery on a per-message basis by going to Format → Apply Stationery in the message composition window (see Figure 6-13).

Notes

- To download more stationery, click Download More in the Stationery section of the Compose tab. You'll be brought to a web page in your web browser. Click "Download more stationery here."

- You can edit Windows Mail's presupplied stationery. Select stationery as you normally would, and in the Select Stationery window, highlight the stationery you want to edit. Click Edit, and the stationery will open in Word, where you can edit the HTML stationery file. But Word is not a particularly good HTML editor. A better bet is to launch your favorite HTML editor, go to *\Program Files\Common Files\Microsoft Shared\Stationery*, and edit stationery there.

See also

"Signatures"

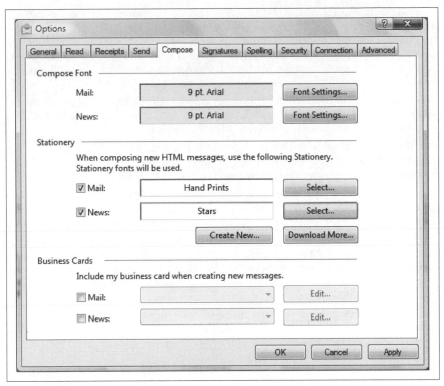

Figure 6-13. Choosing and creating stationery

Watch Conversation

Keep track of discussions and message threads in email and newsgroups.

To open

Highlight or open the mail or newsgroup post you want to watch, and choose Message → Watch Conversation.

To ignore a conversation, highlight or open the mail or newsgroup post you want to watch, and choose Message → Ignore Conversation.

Description

A *conversation* is a continuous series of email or newsgroup messages, often called a *thread*. For example, if you were to write an email with the subject "Propane Elaine," it might spark a series of messages between you and the recipient, all of which would have the subject "Re: Propane Elaine." This thread of messages is called a conversation in Outlook Express, and there are tools included for dealing with it.

You can "watch" a conversation that is of interest to you by highlighting a message and going to Message → Watch Conversation. Likewise, you can "ignore" a conversation by going to Message → Ignore Conversation. Either of these will place an icon in the Watch/Ignore column: eyeglasses or a red circle with a line through it, respectively. Click the icon to toggle among Watch, Ignore, and nothing.

The first time you choose to watch or ignore a conversation, you'll get a message asking whether you want to turn on a new column in the message list. If you turn on the column, the Watch/Ignore column appears on the far-left side of the message list, denoted at the top by a small pair of eyeglasses. An eyeglasses symbol appears in that column next to every message in every conversation you watch. In addition, the messages you are watching appear in color.

When you choose instead to ignore a conversation, the messages in the conversations you've chosen to ignore appear grayed out, and a "no" symbol (a circle with a diagonal line through it) appears in the Watch/Ignore column.

For the most part, this is merely a decorative setting; it doesn't affect the way Windows Mail handles these messages. However, you can choose to highlight watched conversations and hide ignored conversations, as follows.

Customize the color of messages in watched conversations by going to Tools → Options → Read tab → Highlight watched messages.

To hide all messages in a conversation marked as Ignored, go to View → Current View → Hide Read or Ignored Messages. Then, go to View → Current View → Customize Current View, remove the checkmark next to "Where the message has been read," and click the links in the bottom screen so that the description reads: "Where the message is ignored, Hide the message." (For more details about creating rules, see "Message Rules," earlier in this chapter.)

Finally, if you select View → Current View → Group Messages by Conversation, messages in conversations will be grouped in expandable branches, like the folders in Explorer.

Notes

- Beware of watching too many conversations, because that defeats the purpose of this feature. If you watch many conversations, all of your mail will appear in color, and all will have the eyeglasses next to them in the Watch/Ignore list, so there will be no way to differentiate important conversations from unimportant ones.

See also

"Columns"

Windows Contacts

Keep track of people's names, email addresses, phone numbers, and other personal information.

To open

Tools → Windows Contacts

Ctrl-Shift-C (works only when you are in Windows Mail)

Start → All Programs → Windows Contacts

Description

Windows Contacts replaces the old Windows Address Book, but it serves the same function. Rather than being in a familiar, Address Book–style format, it looks and works much like any other folder, as shown in Figure 6-14—so much so that it includes the familiar toolbar across the top.

Figure 6-14. Windows Contacts, which replaces the old Windows Address Book

Windows Contacts works in a straightforward way, like any other similar address book. Click New Contact to add a new contact, then fill out as much information as you can on the various tabs, including names, email addresses, phone numbers, street addresses, web site addresses, and personal information such as a contact's spouse, children, gender, birthday, and anniversary. You can add a picture as well.

If you frequently send out email to a group of people, you'll find the Contact Group feature useful. Click the New Contact Group icon on the toolbar, type in a name for the group, click the Select Members button, and then add contacts to the group. Send an email to the group name, and it will be delivered to every contact in the group.

Sharing contacts

Previous to Windows Vista, a common way for people to share contact information was to send a *vCard* via email. The vCard is a contact in a format that could be directly imported into Outlook Express, the Windows Address Book, or Outlook, and it would show up as a contact.

Windows Vista and Windows Mail still support vCards, but they have a preferred, different method for sharing contacts. If you want to share your information with someone else who uses Windows Vista, you attach your contact information to an email message. Attach the contact as you would any other file. You'll find your contacts in *C:\Users\username\Contacts*. All your contacts will be listed, followed by a *.contact* extension, such as *Preston.Gralla.contact*. You can share any contact in this way, not just your own information. If the person uses Vista and is on the same network as you are, open Windows Contacts, right-click the contact you want to share, click Share, and follow the instructions.

To share contact information with someone who doesn't use Vista, right-click the contact and click Send Contact (vCard), and a vCard will be automatically created and attached to a new mail message. Send the message as you would any other message.

When you receive a message with a vCard attached, double-click the vCard and the contact will be added to Windows Contacts.

Notes

- Windows Contacts uses an XML-based file format in which every contact is actually a separate *.contact* file. Microsoft also has built APIs for it so that in theory, it should be much easier to integrate it with other applications.

- You can import contacts from, or export them to, another contact program. Click either the Import or the Export button, and follow the simple wizards.

- If you upgrade to Windows Vista from Windows XP, the contacts from your Windows Address Book will be automatically converted to contacts in Windows Contacts. If you don't upgrade, or if you used a different program than the Windows Address Book, you can import contacts into Windows Contacts. In the program that has the contacts you want to import, export the contacts as a comma-separated value (*.csv*) file or a Windows Address Book (*.wab*) file. Copy it to a disk, or directly to the Vista PC where you will import the contacts. Then in Windows Contacts, click the Import button, choose the file format that you'll be importing, browse to the location that has the file, and import it. Similarly, you can export contacts from Windows Contacts by clicking the Export button and following the directions.

- By default, every person to whom you send a reply is added to Windows Contacts. To change this behavior, use the Tools → Options → Send tab.

Windows Mail Options

The central location for setting all major Windows Mail options and preferences.

To open
Tools → Options

Description
The most important Windows Mail options are available from this multitabbed dialog box. It should be the first place you look when you want to change an option or a preference. Following are the tabs and what you need to know about each:

General
> This tab, shown in Figure 6-15, covers several basic operations of Windows Mail. The General section of the tab is more for newsgroups than email, and it lets you set whether you want to be notified when new newsgroups are available on the newsgroup server to which you connect. The tab also lets you use a new feature introduced with Windows Mail: Microsoft Communities, which lets you rate and view ratings of the usefulness of other people's newsgroup posts. Check the box next to "Use newsgroup message rating features" if you want to participate.

Read
> This tab controls all your options for reading mail and newsgroup messages. For example, it lets you determine what colors you want "watched" messages to be displayed in, and whether to read all messages in plain text rather than HTML. It also lets you change the font of messages. For more details about these options, see "Read Options."

Receipts
> This tab lets you control options related to requests that a receipt be sent to you when someone reads a message you send. It also governs how Windows Mail

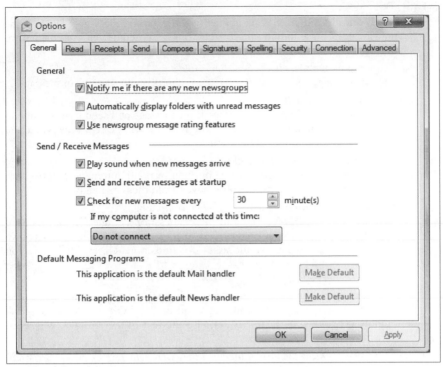

Figure 6-15. The General tab, which governs overall mail features, such as how frequently to check for messages

handles return receipt requests that are attached to incoming mail messages. Check the box next to "Request a read receipt for all sent messages" if you want all mail to be sent with a return receipt.

Just because you request that a receipt be sent to you when someone reads your mail is no guarantee that you'll actually get the receipt. The recipient is notified that you want a receipt, but can block that receipt from being sent.

In the Returning Read Receipts section, you control how Windows Mail handles mail sent to you with return receipts. You can have Windows Mail never send back a return receipt, always send back a return receipt, or notify you when one is requested so you can choose on a case-by-case basis.

The tab also lets you control how Secure Receipts should be handled. A Secure Receipt is like a normal Read Receipt, except that it covers mail sent with Digital IDs, which verify the identity of the sender of the mail. Click the Secure Receipts button, and you'll be able to request that you be sent secure receipts for all messages you send. You can also control how you want to handle when people send you mail with secure receipts requested—always send them, never send them, or notify and let you decide on a case-by-case basis.

Send

This tab controls options that are applied when you send messages. The Sending section includes these important global settings. By default, all are enabled; to disable any, uncheck the box next to it and click OK:

Save copy of sent messages in the Sent Items folder

This is a straightforward setting; it keeps copies of all of your sent messages.

Send messages immediately

If you select this, as soon as you finish the message and send it, it is immediately sent. If you uncheck the box, the message will be sent only when you choose to send and receive all messages.

Automatically put people I reply to in my Contacts list

Select this, and every person to whom you respond automatically goes into your Contacts list; otherwise, you'll have to add them manually.

Automatically complete e-mail addresses when composing

With this selected, as you type in the Address: or Cc: lines, Windows Mail will look through your Contacts and history of people with whom you've corresponded, and suggest addresses if it finds a match. Highlight any you want to use and press Enter.

Include message in reply

Select this, and the previous message will be inserted into the message. At the top of the inserted previous message will be "----- Original Message -----", followed by addressing information and the text of the message, with each line preceded by a > and a space.

Reply to messages using the format in which they were sent

With this option, when you're sent a text message, your reply will be in text; if you're sent an HTML message, the reply will be in HTML. Otherwise, the reply will be in the global setting you've chosen for all mail—which you choose from the Mail Sending Format section of the Send tab.

The tab also includes options for choosing your mail- and newsgroup-sending formats. You can choose text or HTML, as well as encoding or MIME settings for messages.

Compose

This lets you choose the font you want to use for new messages, both for mail and for newsgroups. In addition, it lets you choose background stationery. For details, see "Stationery," earlier in this chapter. You can also choose to send an electronic business card containing your contact information with each message.

Signatures

This lets you create a signature to append to the bottom of your messages. You can create multiple signatures and use different ones for different accounts. For details about how to create signatures, see "Signatures," earlier in this chapter.

Spelling

If you want a spellchecker to check each message before you send it, check the box next to "Always check spelling before sending." (By default, it's turned off.) The rest of the tab lets you choose spellchecking options, including whether to ignore words in all uppercase, whether to ignore words with numbers in them, whether to ignore Internet addresses, and whether it should check the original text in messages you reply to or forward. You can also choose the language you want to use (your choices are English, French, German, and Spanish).

Security

This tab lets you choose from a variety of security options, such as blocking certain attachments from being opened, using Digital IDs, and encrypting messages. For details, see "Windows Mail Security," later in this chapter.

Connection

This is a largely useless tab. By default, Windows Mail shares Internet connection information with Internet Explorer, so you don't need to do any connection setup here. If you click the Change button, though, you'll be sent to the Connections dialog box, which will let you change your connection for Internet Explorer and Windows Mail. In addition, this tab will be of use to people who use dial-up (or cellular data) rather than broadband connections. If you use a dial-up connection, you can have the connection automatically hang up after sending and receiving, and be alerted before Windows Mail switches from one of your dial-up connections to another.

Advanced

Go here for some fairly esoteric settings. If you send out a business card with your messages, you can choose to send it in the vCard format or the Windows Contact format. Those who use IMAP servers can choose whether to use the server's Deleted Items folder. For message threads, you can choose to automatically mark message threads you start as Watched. When you reply to or forward messages, you can choose whether your reply should be at the top or bottom of the original message, and whether your signature should be inserted at the bottom of the reply.

Click the Maintenance button for choosing how to handle deleted messages (for example, whether to empty messages from the Deleted Items folder when you exit). It also lets you choose how frequently your database of messages should be compacted, which will save disk space, and it lets you change the location of your message store.

Notes

- Be careful when using the Receipts tab to have all mail automatically sent with the return receipt option. Many people do not like receiving mail that is sent with return receipts, and feel that it is an invasion of their privacy. In addition, if you choose to have all mail sent using return receipts, your mailbox will quickly become overrun with the receipts.

See also

"Read Options," "Stationery," "Signatures," "Windows Mail Security," and "Watch Conversation"

Windows Mail Security

Protects your PC against email-borne threats.

To open

Tools → Options → Security

Description

Email has become one of the primary ways that PCs are attacked, and Windows Mail's Security Options tab, shown in Figure 6-16, lets you customize how you protect yourself.

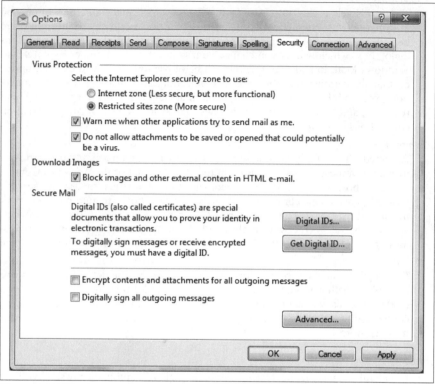

Figure 6-16. Windows Mail's Security Options tab, which lets you customize how to protect yourself when handling mail

Here are each of the tab's sections, and what they do:

Virus Protection

This lets you customize Windows Mail's antivirus, antiworm, and antispyware protection. Windows Mail shares Internet Explorer's security settings. (See "Internet Options Security Tab," in Chapter 5.) By default, Windows Mail uses the Restricted sites zone, which offers the highest level of security and disables most features that could harm your computer, including turning off ActiveX controls, Java and Java applets, and downloads. You can, if you choose, override this and tell Windows Mail to use the Internet zone so that it will run that kind of active content, but unless there are specific reasons why you might want to do that, it's best to leave the default.

By default, Windows Mail will also notify you if another application on your PC tries to send mail with your identity. This is to protect against Trojans and other malware from using your PC as a spam or phishing engine; some malware in essence hijacks your PC and uses it to send out that kind of mail in the background, without your knowledge. If you want, you can turn off this notification by unchecking the box next to "Warn me when other applications try to send mail as me." But unless you have a specific reason for turning this off, don't do it.

The final option in the Virus Protection section is a bit more problematic. By default, Windows Mail will not allow you to save or open a wide variety of attachments that could potentially harbor malware or harm your PC. So, for example, *.exe* files are blocked, as are *.vb* (VBScript) files, because both can be dangerous. But it also blocks Microsoft Access project files (*.adp*), Microsoft Visual FoxPro programs (*.prg*), and other files you might want to be able to receive via mail. To allow Windows Mail to receive and open blocked files, uncheck the box next to "Do not allow attachments to be saved or opened that could potentially be a virus." Keep in mind that if you do this, you are opening your PC to potential dangers.

 The attachment setting is an all-or-nothing proposition—you can't allow some attachments through but block others. However, if you know that you are going to receive a blocked attachment that you want to be able to open, you can uncheck the box, receive the mail, and then afterward, check the box again so that future attachments are blocked. There is a workaround, however. Ask the sender to put the file into a *.zip* file, and send the *.zip* file as an attachment. Windows Mail considers *.zip* files as safe, so it allows them through.

Download Images
Images in HTML email can harbor a variety of dangers. Notably, they can contain "web bugs" that can, in essence, be used to detect whether you read the message. In addition, if you click on images, they may lead to malware downloads or send you to dangerous sites. HTML mail can contain other content, such as streaming media, that can be dangerous as well. By default, Windows Mail blocks images and external content. If you feel that you can safely view and use that kind of content, uncheck the box in this section.

Secure Mail
This lets you find and install Digital IDs, digital certificates that can be used to guarantee to recipients that you are who you say you are. If your business has given you a Digital ID, Windows Mail may already be set up to use one. If your company does provide a Digital ID, but for some reason it hasn't been set up yet, you can install it yourself. First, find out where the ID is located. Then click Digital IDs in this tab. Click Import, and then follow the instructions to import your Digital ID. The tab also lets you automatically encrypt, and digitally sign, all outgoing messages with the Digital ID.

Notes
* If a Trojan or other malware has been installed on a PC without the owner's knowledge, and it is used to send out spam or phishing attacks, that PC is commonly called a *zombie* or a *bot*. Malware writers can command vast fleets of tens of thousands of zombies, which they rent out to spammers and phishers. In fact, security researchers say that many spam and phishing attacks are sent via these zombies.

See also
"Internet Options Security Tab," in Chapter 5

7

Networking, Wireless, and Mobility

Windows Vista is the first version of Windows developed at a time when networking, via home networks, corporate networks, and the Internet, has become truly ubiquitous. Because of that, it was designed from the ground up with networking in mind. In addition, Windows Vista has many built-in features designed for mobile computing, which is particularly important because laptop computers have become as common as desktops.

This chapter covers all aspects of networking and mobility, from basic networking terminology and setup to configuring and managing wired and wireless networks, sharing files and resources, using Windows Vista's built-in networking applications such as Windows Meeting Space, using mobile features, and finally, using Windows Vista's many useful command-line networking tools.

Here is an alphabetical reference of entries in this chapter:

Networking 101

A *network* allows two or more computers to connect to each other to share files and printers, exchange data, and share an Internet connection. Networks have been common in large companies for decades, are ubiquitous in small businesses, and have become extremely common in homes as well. Home networks have become inexpensive and easy to set up, and as more homes have multiple PCs, networks are commonly used to share a broadband Internet connection, such as a DSL or cable modem.

Among the things you can do with a simple network are the following:

File sharing
> Documents and even some applications stored on one computer can be accessed by another computer on the network, as though they were on the remote computer's hard disk.

File synchronization
> Files can be automatically synchronized between several computers—for example, between a PC and a laptop. When the laptop is disconnected from the network—for example, to take on a trip—the files can be altered on the laptop, and when it plugs into the network, those files are automatically copied to the PC, where they can be worked on.

Device sharing
> Printers connected to one computer can be used by any other computer on the network. The same goes for many scanners, backup devices, and high-speed Internet devices, such as DSL and cable modems.

Online gaming
> Networkable games can be played against other users on your local network or even over the Internet; after all, it's more fun blowing up your friends than computer-generated characters.

Communication and collaboration
> Send and receive email, chat, and even videoconference across the room or across the country in seconds, over any type of network connection. Windows Vista includes a slew of new collaboration features, including the ability to give live presentations over a network.

Web exploration
> The Web has become ubiquitous. Using Internet Explorer or the web browser of your choice, you can retrieve information from the other side of the world as easily as you can from the other side of town.

Data collaboration
> A network connection allows two or more users to simultaneously access the same database, which is useful for patient tracking in a doctor's office, parallel development of an application in a software company, or keeping track of bills and expenses at home.

Administration

Maintain and troubleshoot multiple computers over a network more easily. Using Remote Desktop sharing (or a third-party alternative), control a remote computer as though you were sitting in front of it. Rather than spending several hours over the phone helping someone far away fix a problem with his computer, fix it yourself in a few minutes.

The ability to perform these tasks depends only on your software and the speed of your connection. Because Windows Vista includes built-in support for networking, as well as starter applications that provide all of the functionality just described, all you have left to do is to set it up.

It's important to note at this point that when you connect your computer to a network, you can dramatically increase its exposure to hackers and viruses. See the "Implementing Network Security" section, later in this chapter, as well as the security advice in Chapter 8, for more information on safeguarding your computer.

Networking Terminology

Understanding networking terminology is essential to making sense of the software and hardware used to assemble a network. The following terms are used throughout this chapter, as well as in just about any conversation about networking:

Bandwidth

The capacity of a network connection to move information. If a network is capable of transferring data at 100 Mbps (megabits per second) and two users are simultaneously transferring large files, they will have only about 50 Mbps of bandwidth apiece at their disposal. See "Hubs and switches," later in this list, for limitations.

Bluetooth

A short-range radio frequency (RF) wireless standard used to connect handheld devices and peripherals at speeds from 1 to 2 Mbps. It has mostly shown up in mobile phones, although Bluetooth-capable GPS units, printers, mice, keyboards, and other devices that need to transmit modest amounts of data over short distances are on the market and gaining in popularity. Windows Vista supports Bluetooth natively.

Bluetooth devices use a *passkey* to connect to your computer. This is usually used only when two devices meet (the "handshake") for the first time. During this time, the two devices set up a trust relationship based on stronger security keys than the short password used for the initial handshaking procedure. From that point on, the computer and Bluetooth device can be sure of each other's identity, which is why your mouse won't suddenly start controlling your office mate's cursor. One security measure: before you connect any Bluetooth device to your PC, you must check the "Allow Bluetooth devices to find this computer" box in the Bluetooth Control Panel and then configure your Bluetooth device to be "discoverable." Once you add the new device, it can connect to your PC at any time, even if the "Allow Bluetooth devices to find this computer" box is later unchecked.

Your connections can be encrypted—if your applications and drivers provide it. Due to Bluetooth's relatively short range, there's not a lot that passersby can do, although hackers have risen to the challenge with *bluejacking*, or sending usually harmless messages to victims' phones (there are rarer activities in which malicious hackers use specially crafted messages to exploit vulnerabilities in certain models of phones). You can limit your exposure to unwanted messages by turning off discovery mode, thereby ensuring that only devices you've specifically configured to work with your device can talk to it.

Dynamic Host Configuration Protocol (DHCP)

A protocol used to assign a unique Internet Protocol (IP) address to each computer on a network. The IP address is assigned dynamically every time a PC connects to the network so that the PC may receive a different IP address every time it connects. A PC that has a static IP address, on the other hand, has the same IP address every time it connects, and a DHCP server does not need to assign it the address. Windows Vista lets you configure PCs for either dynamically assigned addresses or static addresses. (See "Network Connection Properties (Includes Wired and Wireless Connections)," later in this chapter, for details.)

Domain

A network that uses the client/server model so that one or more servers provide central resources for the network, such as file sharing, printer serving, and email. PCs (called *clients*) connect to servers in order to connect to the network. Domains are common in large organizations, and multiple LANs, spread across the globe, can be connected to a single domain. Don't confuse these domains with Internet domain names (such as *oreilly.com*).

Ethernet

The technology upon which the vast majority of LANs are built. A basic Ethernet connection is capable of transferring data at a maximum of 10 Mbps, and a Fast Ethernet connection can transfer data at 100 Mbps. A device capable of communicating at both speeds is typically labeled "10/100." There are also gigabit Ethernet connections, which, as the name suggests, transfer data at 1 Gbps.

Firewall

A layer of protection that permits or denies network communication based on a predefined set of rules. You can use a firewall to restrict unauthorized access from intruders, close backdoors opened by viruses and other malicious applications, and eliminate wasted bandwidth by blocking certain types of network applications. Windows Vista includes a firewall. For details, see Chapter 8.

Gateway

A piece of hardware that ties together two networks that use different protocols or connects two IP networks. For example, a gateway may connect a local wireless or wired network to the Internet. Gateways are commonly built into home routers, which allow PCs in a home to communicate with one another and connect to the Internet.

Hubs and switches

Devices on your network to which multiple Ethernet connections (called *nodes*) are made. See Figure 7-2 for an example. The main difference between a hub and a switch is a matter of performance (and cost). A switch is capable of handling multiple, simultaneous, full-bandwidth connections, and the less expensive hub throttles all connections such that, for example, three simultaneous connections can each use only one-third of the total bandwidth.

Hotspot

A public wireless network, available at many cafes, coffee shops, libraries, airports, and other locations. It allows anyone to connect to the network using WiFi in order to get Internet access. Some hotspots are for-pay, and others are free. Some cities have turned entire downtown areas into giant hotspots so that anyone can connect, often for free. For hotspots near you, check out *http://www.wi-fihotspotlist.com*. For a list of free hotspots, see *http://free-hotspot.jiwire.com*. Note, though, that hotspots often appear and disappear frequently, so those sites may be out-of-date.

IP address

A number composed of four bytes (e.g., 207.46.230.218) corresponding to a single computer or device on a Transmission Control Protocol/Internet Protocol (TCP/IP) network. No two computers on a single network can have the same IP address, but a single computer can have multiple IP addresses (for example, a gateway server has two IP addresses: one for each network that it bridges). Most elements of the address can range from 0 to 255, providing approximately 256^4 or nearly 4.3 billion possible combinations. Network Address Translation (NAT) is used to translate an address from one network to another. This is useful, for example, when a firewalled LAN is connected to the Internet (for example, this translation is what makes it possible for web servers to send responses back to the correct machine on your network, even though all the Internet traffic is funneled through a single cable or DSL modem).

On the Internet, dedicated machines called *nameservers* are used to translate named hosts, such as *www.microsoft.com*, to their respective numerical IP addresses. See "Windows IP Configuration" and "NSLookup," later in this chapter, for more information.

The four-byte addressing scheme is employed by the currently used version of networking, called IPv4. But Windows Vista also supports IPv6, which greatly expands the number of IP addresses available, as well as adds security and Quality of Service (QoS) features. An IPv6 address looks like this: fe80::28ff:b329:f8b3:a44e. IPv6 is not yet in widespread use; when it is, it will be used more for large corporate networks than for home or small-business networks.

LAN

Local area network, a designation typically referring to a network contained in a single room or building.

Mbps

Megabits per second, the unit of measure used to describe the speed of a network connection. Ethernet-based networks can commonly transfer data either up to 10 or 100 Mbps, although now gigabit networks (1,000 Mbps) are becoming common as well. High-speed leased-line, DSL, and cable modem connections typically transfer data at up to 15 Mbps and faster; the fastest analog modems communicate at a glacial 56 kbps, or 0.056 Mbps.

Because there are eight bits to a byte, you can determine the theoretical maximum data transfer rate of a connection by simply dividing by 8. For example, a 384 kbps connection transfers 384 / 8 = 48 KB of data per second, which should allow you to transfer a 1 MB file in a little more than 20 seconds. However, more is going on than just data transfer (such as error correction), so actual performance will always be slower than the theoretical maximum.

NIC

Network interface card, commonly known as an Ethernet adapter or network adapter. If your computer doesn't have built-in Ethernet, you'll need a NIC to connect your computer to a network. For desktops, your NIC should be built into your motherboard; for laptops, your NIC should also be built-in, but it may also be a PCMCIA (PC Card) card. Most laptops also include built-in WiFi NICs. Universal Serial Bus (USB)–based NICs can also be used with both desktops and laptops.

Peer-to-peer network

A network in which there is no central server, and PCs communicate directly with one another and share their resources. Home networks, such as those built on home routers bought from retail stores or online, are peer-to-peer networks, as are many small-business networks. Larger networks commonly use central servers instead of peer-to-peer networking. The term *peer-to-peer* is sometimes used in another sense, to refer to applications, such as BitTorrent, that directly connect computers over the Internet or a network to allow them to share files.

Ports

A number representing the type of communication to initiate. For example, web browsers typically use port 80 to download web pages, so web servers must be "listening" at port 80. Other commonly used ports include port 25 for sending email (SMTP), port 110 for retrieving email (POP3), port 443 for accessing secure web pages, port 21 for FTP, port 23 for Telnet, port 22 for SSH, port 53 for Domain Name System (DNS), port 119 for newsgroups, and port 6699 for peer-to-peer file-sharing applications.

PPP

Point-to-Point Protocol, a protocol used to facilitate a TCP/IP connection over long distances. Windows uses PPP to provide an Internet connection over ordinary phone lines using an analog modem. Some DSL connections use PPPoE, a related technology.

PPPoE

Point-to-Point Protocol over Ethernet, which encapsulates PPP frames inside Ethernet, is used primarily for DSL modems.

Protocol

A protocol is the language, so to speak, that your computer uses to communicate with other computers on the network. The TCP/IP set of protocols is the de facto standard for LANs and WANs and is required for Internet connections.

Router

Transfers data packets among networks and inside a network, as well as routes the packets to their proper locations. A router, for example, handles the work of examining data packets on a network, seeing their destination, and then sending them on their way. On the Internet, routers commonly send data packets to other routers, which send them to other routers, until the packets reach their final destination. Many people confuse routers with switches. A switch is a passive device that connects devices to form a network, and a router actively routes packets.

A home or small-business router actually has more hardware in it than just a router, and it typically includes a hub (or a switch) and a gateway so that a single device can form the basis of an entire network. If you use the Network Map feature of Windows Vista to map your home wireless router, it will show a switch, the router itself, and a gateway as separate devices (see Figure 7-1), even though they are all combined into a single piece of hardware. You can create your own network map by opening Control Panel → Network and Internet → Network and Sharing Center and then clicking "View full map."

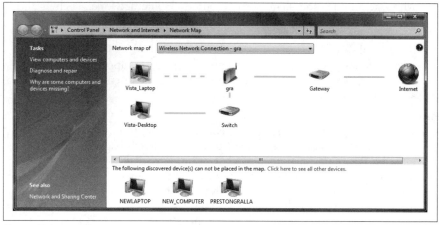

Figure 7-1. Windows Vista's Network Map, which shows a switch, router, and gateway on a home wireless network

Server

A computer in a network that performs a service of some kind, such as handling email, storing and serving files, running a database or other application, and so on. Home networks commonly do not use servers, and corporate networks do.

Service set identifier (SSID)

A name that identifies your wireless network. Routers come preconfigured with SSIDs (for example, Linksys routers all have the SSID "Linksys"), but you can (and should) change them in the router's setup software.

TCP/IP

Shorthand notation for the collection of protocols that includes Transmission Control Protocol (TCP), Internet Protocol (IP), User Datagram Protocol (UDP), and Internet Control Message Protocol (ICMP). TCP/IP is required for all Internet connections and is the standard protocol for most types of modern LANs.

Topology

The physical layout of your network. See the next section, "Planning Your Network," for more information on how topology comes into play.

Virtual Private Network (VPN)

A virtual network that allows private, encrypted information to be sent across the Internet. Companies often use VPNs to allow their employees to connect to a corporate network remotely from home or while traveling. Employees use the Internet to connect to the corporate network, but all of their communications are encrypted and travel inside a virtual "tunnel" so that they are private and secure. Windows Vista includes built-in capabilities to create VPN connections. For details, see "Set Up a Connection or Network," later in this chapter.

WAN

Wide area network, or a network formed by connecting computers over long distances. The Internet is an example of a WAN. On a home router, several ports are typically used to connect computers to the home network, and a single WAN port connects the home network to the Internet.

WiFi (802.11x)

The current standard(s) for wireless networking. The 802.11x series isn't one technology, but several. But when we talk about WiFi connections, we usually mean 802.11g—the current worldwide standard, especially for home networks, which offers transmission speeds up to 54 Mbps (with typical throughput of 20 Mbps). The previous commonly used WiFi standard was 802.11b, which offers speeds of 11 Mbps (5.5 Mbps real-world speed). Many public hotspots still use 802.11b rather than 802.11g, and older networks use 802.11b as well. 802.11g networking gear is backward-compatible with 802.11b networks and can connect to them, although obviously at the lower network speeds.

The next generation of WiFi, 802.11n, is just being introduced and can theoretically offer speeds of up to 540 Mbps, although as a practical matter in the real world it will rarely, if ever, give that real speed. In fact, wireless networks do not transmit data at their maximum possible speeds because of interference, distances between transmitters and receivers, and so on.

(Also on the market is 802.11a, although its limited range and lack of compatibility with the "b" and "g" standards generally make it a poor choice. It is not in widespread use.)

These standards include encryption to keep your data secure and to make sure that only authorized computers are able to connect. The most common methods are WiFi Protected Access (WPA), WPA2 (also known as 802.11i), and the older Wired Equivalent Privacy (WEP). WPA2 is the most secure, WPA is the second most secure, and WEP is the least secure. Your hardware needs to be compatible with the encryption standards in order to use them. Older equipment may not be compatible with WPA2, and in some instances very old equipment will not be compatible with WPA. A driver or firmware upgrade may solve the problem; if not, you will need to purchase new hardware.

A wireless network typically consists of a wireless router (the access point) connected to the Internet via broadband, and one or more computers that can tap into the router. (You can have a wireless network without a wireless router using "ad hoc" mode, but only between two computers at a time.) Most new laptops come with WiFi support built in, although desktop PCs may require a wireless PCI card or USB adapter.

Windows Vista can access any WiFi connection out of the box if you have the necessary hardware.

Workgroup
A group of computers that are connected via a peer-to-peer network and share resources such as printers and files. Most people confuse a workgroup with a network. A single network can have multiple workgroups in it, and you can add and delete workgroups to the network. When you set up a network in Windows Vista, Windows automatically creates a workgroup for it and gives it a name. You can, however, change the workgroup's name and add new workgroups to the network. Workgroups are peer-to-peer, and in Windows Vista you can easily change the workgroup to which your PC is attached. See "Change Workgroup or Domain," later in this chapter, for details.

If you're using a Mac OS X or Linux system to exchange files with your Vista system using Windows file sharing, you may want to edit the */etc/smb.conf* file (you'll need to have root access to do this) to use the same workgroup as your Windows PCs.

Planning Your Network

There are many types of networks, but for the purposes of this chapter, we will be focusing on three basic categories:

Peer-to-peer LAN
A LAN is the connection of two or more computers in close proximity, typically in the same building or room. The term *peer-to-peer* implies that each computer on the network will have pretty much the same role. This is in contrast to a client/server setup, in which certain computers are intended solely to store data, handle printing, or manage user accounts.

Wireless networking

Wireless networking typically refers to 802.11*x* , or WiFi for short. The most common variety used in home networks is 802.11g, although many people with older networks still use the older and slower 802.11b standard. Increasingly, the faster 802.11n standard is being used in home networks as well.

Connection to the Internet

By connecting your computer to the Internet, you are networking your machine to the world's largest WAN.

As far as Windows Vista is concerned, there is very little difference among these three types of network connections. The distinction is made primarily to help you visualize the topology of your environment. See Figures 7-2, 7-3, and 7-4 for some example setups.

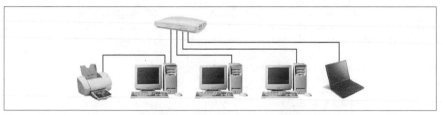

Figure 7-2. A simple network with four computers connected with a hub (or switch), one printer connected to one of the computers, and no Internet connection

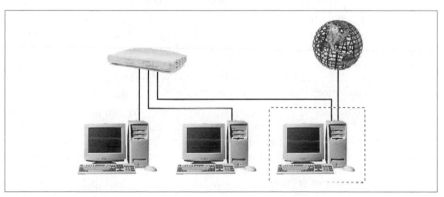

Figure 7-3. A simple network with three computers, one of which has an Internet connection that can be shared

An especially interesting application of these technologies is how you can mix and match them. For example, you can connect your LAN to the Internet, giving Internet access to everyone on your local network. In fact, that is the primary reason (even more than sharing computer resources) that many people buy home network hardware. Or you can simulate a LAN over an Internet connection using a VPN.

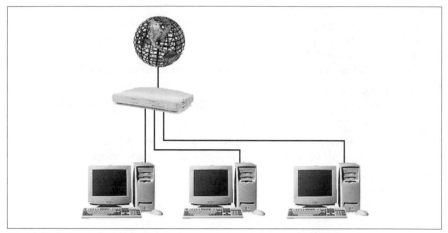

Figure 7-4. A simple network with three computers connected to a hub or router

Here are some things to consider when planning your network:

- If you're building a wired network, wiring can be time-consuming and frustrating. Drawing a diagram of the physical layout of the computers and devices on your network can help you visualize the topology and plan the cables, hubs, and other devices required. For example, if two or more users will share a printer, make sure the printer is in a convenient, central location.

- As a practical matter, wireless networking is the best choice for home users and small-business users. Setup is relatively simple and equipment is inexpensive, although interference can sometimes slow down wireless networks or cause connection problems (because 802.11a operates in the less crowded 5 GHz range, as opposed to the 2.4 GHz range used by 802.11b and 802.11g, it is a popular choice in environments with a lot of interference).

- It's also important to realize that you don't have to commit solely to one technology or another. For instance, you can mix and match wireless and wired networks, which may mean purchasing wireless equipment only for laptops or computers that would otherwise be very difficult to wire. Home routers and small-business routers typically come with multiple Ethernet ports in addition to their wireless capabilities, so you can plug several computers into the router itself, while offering wireless access to other computers located in other parts of the house or building.

- When assigning roles to different computers, think about how often they'll be used. For example, a computer hosting a shared printer will need to be turned on, and a computer hosting shared files should have adequate hard-disk capacity.

- Windows Vista includes Internet connection-sharing functionality right out of the box, but it is limited compared to buying a home router; as a practical matter, you should avoid it.

- You can hook up some printers directly to the network, eliminating the need for a dedicated computer to host them. You can connect them via an Ethernet connection or wirelessly. Although this typically adds cost, it means that any computer on the network can print without you first having to turn on another computer. If this option is not available for your printer, you can still hook it up to a separate print-server device. Some small-office or home network routers include a built-in print server.

Setting Up a Network

Setting up a peer-to-peer network in Windows Vista is quite straightforward. This section assumes that you have a broadband connection (such as a DSL or cable modem) and that you want several PCs to share that Internet connection as well as to share resources with one another.

You'll need to buy a router, which is commonly available for between $50 and $100, depending on its capabilities. Your best bet is to buy a wireless router, as described earlier in this chapter. Wireless routers include Ethernet ports (most commonly four) so that you can use them to network both wired and wireless PCs.

Make sure that each PC has a wired or wireless network adapter. (See the entry for "NIC," in the "Networking Terminology" section, earlier in this chapter.) Virtually any desktop PC you buy should already have an Ethernet adapter built in, and laptop PCs almost always include both built-in wireless and Ethernet adapters. If not, though, you can buy wireless adapters as PC cards for laptops, PCI cards for desktops, and USB adapters for either desktops or laptops. If you're buying new adapters, make sure that your wireless router and all the wireless adapters follow the newer, faster 802.11g wireless standard, not the older, slower 802.11b standard.

Keep your eye on the 802.11n standard. If it ever gets final certification from the body that governs WiFi connections, it is worth considering because of its high speed. However, steer clear of any equipment labeled "pre-n" because that means it has been built before the standard has been formally ratified, and it may not be compatible with the standard, or with other 802.11n equipment, when the standard is finally approved.

Follow the instructions of the router manufacturer for installing the network. Take note of the IP address range used by your router (such as 192.168.0.x, where x is between 1 and 254). As a general rule, though, you need to first install all the adapters or wireless adapters on all the PCs. Then connect the router to your DSL or cable modem using an Ethernet cable. Make sure you use the correct port on the router. It may be labeled as "Internet" or "WAN," and it may be set apart from the other ports on the router in some way. For example, in some Linksys routers, the port for connecting to a DSL or cable modem is outlined in blue, and the ports for connecting to PCs are outlined in yellow.

Next, connect one of your PCs via an Ethernet cable to the router. This will be used to configure the router. Follow the manufacturer's instructions for doing so.

Many routers come with an extra CD or installation disk. Keep the disk handy, but note that you don't always need this disk in order to set up your router. Not uncommonly, the disk comes with trial versions of firewalls, antivirus software, and other software that will install automatically on the PC that you are using to set up the router. Install from the CD only the software you know you want to use.

After that, configure each individual PC to connect to the network, either via Ethernet cables or wirelessly. Details on how to do that are covered in "Connect to a Network," later in this chapter.

Once you've configured the PCs, they should all have Internet and network access. It's a good idea to test each PC's connection using Ping (see "Ping," later in this chapter). By default, your router will assign IP addresses in the following way: the first computer will be 192.168.0.2 (.1 is usually reserved for the router), the second will be 192.168.0.3, and so on.

 The first three bytes of the numbers may vary from router to router (see "Understanding Private and Public IP Addresses," later in this chapter), but the last byte will progress in the same manner. So, you may need to replace the 192.168.0 portion with the numbers from the IP address range you noted when you set up your router. See "Network Connection Status," later in this chapter, to figure out your current IP address.

Assuming your network is similar, pick a computer (or your router), go to a command prompt, and type **ping *address***, where ***address*** is the IP address of the other computer. For example, from the 192.168.0.2 computer, you would type:

```
ping 192.168.0.1
```

If the network is working, you'll get something like this:

```
Pinging 192.168.0.1 with 32 bytes of data:
Reply from 192.168.0.1: bytes=32 time=7ms TTL=128
Reply from 192.168.0.1: bytes=32 time=1 TTL=128
```

On the other hand, if you get this result:

```
Pinging 192.168.0.1 with 32 bytes of data:
Request timed out.
Request timed out.
```

it means the network is not functioning.

If your network is functioning, you can proceed to set up the various services you need, such as file sharing, printer sharing, and so on. You can also use ping to test your connection to the Internet, for example, by typing:

```
ping www.oreilly.com
```

If you receive a Request timed out response, try pinging another web site, because the issue could be caused by the web site rather than your own network.

What to Do If Your Connection Doesn't Work

If all goes well, you should be able to set up a network without problems. But if you do run into trouble, follow these tips to help you get around most of the common hurdles you'll encounter when setting up a LAN:

- If you're setting up a wireless network, a number of things may cause connection problems. Your PCs may be too far away from the router, or they may be in a "dead spot" that gets bad reception. Try moving your PCs or your router until you get better reception. Try placing the router in a central place in your house or business or extending your wireless network's range with multiple access points configured for Wireless Distribution System (WDS) operation.

- Some home devices can interfere with wireless networks, such as microwave ovens and cordless phones. Try turning them off to see if that solves any interference problems.

- If the problem is with wired PCs, check your cables and make sure the appropriate lights are on. If you're unsure which lights to look for, try unplugging a cable from a device. If a light on the device goes out and then goes back on when the cable is plugged in, that's the light you're concerned with. Such lights are often labeled "Link."

- If you can ping the PCs on your network but you do not have Internet access, it means that your network is working properly but there is a problem with its connection to the Internet. Make sure that your cable or DSL provider has turned on your Internet connection and that it is visible to them.

- Run the Diagnose and Repair Wizard (Control Panel → Network and Internet → Network and Sharing Center → Diagnose and repair). That should track down the cause of the problem and fix any issues, or recommend fixes.

- Try restarting (power down, wait one minute, and power on) your router and your cable or DSL modem. Sometimes for reasons beyond the comprehension of mortals, this will fix connection problems.

- Windows Vista is designed to implement most changes to the network without restarting. However, if you encounter problems, try restarting one or all of your machines to force them to recognize the new network.

- Make sure no two computers on your network are attempting to use the same computer name or IP address.

- Make sure you have the latest drivers for your network adapter or, if you have a built-in network adapter, for your motherboard or PC; check with the manufacturer for details.

- Right-click the connection icon in the Network Connections window and select Diagnose.

These instructions assume the network settings for your connections haven't been tampered with. If you suspect that your settings might be wrong, open Device Manager, right-click the entry corresponding to your network adapter, and select Uninstall. (Note that it's not necessary to physically remove the device from your system.) When you restart Windows, the adapter will be redetected and the drivers will be reinstalled.

Understanding Private and Public IP Addresses

Any computer on the Internet or a LAN must have an IP address in order to be connected and to use all its services. (An exception is if you are connected to an older-style network that is not based on IP, but this is extremely rare these days.) But because of the explosion of the Internet and networks, including home and small-office networks, there are not enough IP addresses to go around for everyone who wants to connect.

To solve that problem, home networks and small-office networks use a technique called *Network Address Translation* (NAT). With NAT, each PC on the network receives its own private IP address that can be used only for communicating internally on the network. The network, as a whole, has a single public IP address used on the Internet. So a PC on the internal network may have an IP address of 192.168.1.103, but to the Internet, its IP address may be 66.30.117.9.

How does this magic happen? The home router has the IP address of 66.30.117.9. Every PC that connects to the Internet uses that IP address. But inside the network, the router uses DHCP to assign each PC an internal, private IP address, such as 192.168.1.100, 192.168.1.101, and so on.

Several blocks of IP addresses are assigned to be private IP addresses, including 192.168.0.0 to 192.168.255.255, which are the private IP addresses commonly used by home and small-office routers. That means the PCs on your network can use any IP address in that range, and your neighbor's PC can use any IP address in that range—in fact, anyone with a private network can use any IP address in that range. There will not be a conflict between you and others using the same IP address because those IP addresses are internal to the networks, are private, and are not used on the public Internet.

Other private IP addresses include 10.0.0.0 to 10.255.255.255, 172.16.0.0 to 172.31.255.255, and 169.254.0.0 to 169.254.255.255.

 NAT also provides some Internet security. It makes it more difficult for malicious users to directly connect to or attack a PC on a network that uses NAT because the PC's IP address is not a public IP address, making direct "end-to-end" connections more difficult.

Networking Windows Vista with Windows XP and Other Windows Versions

If you have a network that combines Windows Vista PCs with PCs that have earlier versions of Windows, you may notice anomalies and problems. Windows Vista includes new technologies that make networking easier than previous Windows versions, notably the new Link Layer Topology Discovery (LLTD). LLTD allows Windows Vista to automatically detect wired and wireless devices attached to the network, obtain and display information about those devices, and diagnose problems with them, such as low bandwidth in home networks or weak wireless signals.

The devices have to support LLTD, but many existing devices are upgradeable via firmware, and many new devices include built-in LLTD support.

The problem, though, is that older versions of Windows do not include LLTD. So those PCs are not supported as well as Windows Vista-based PCs. For example, when you view a network map (see "Network Map," later in this chapter, for details), the PCs may take a very long time to show up on the map—even as long as 15 minutes. In addition, they generally appear at the bottom of the screen, but not as part of the map itself.

At the launch of Windows Vista, Microsoft was slated to issue a patch that will add LLTD capabilities to Windows XP PCs. But it currently has no plans to add LLTD to any other earlier versions of Windows.

Implementing Network Security

Security is a very real concern for any computer connected to a network or the Internet. There are three main categories of security threats:

A deliberate, targeted attack through your network connection
> It's possible for a so-called hacker to obtain access to your computer, either through your Internet connection or from another computer on your local network. Ironically, this is the type of attack most people fear, but realistically, it is the least likely to occur—at least where home and small-office networks are concerned.

An automated invasion by a virus or robot
> A virus is simply a computer program that is designed to duplicate itself with the purpose of infecting as many computers as possible. If your computer is infected by a virus, it may use your network connection to infect other computers; likewise, if another computer on your network is infected, your computer is vulnerable to infection. The same goes for Internet connections, although the method of transport is typically an infected email message or an application that has been downloaded from a malicious source. This is why you need to be careful about what you get from peer-to-peer file-sharing systems; some attackers will share a file claiming to be one thing, while it's actually malicious software in disguise.

> There also exist so-called robots, programs that are designed to scan large groups of IP addresses and look for vulnerabilities. The motive for such a program can be anything from exploitation of credit card numbers or other sensitive information to the hijacking of computers for the purpose of distributing spam or viruses.

A deliberate attack by a person sitting at your computer
> A person who sits down at your computer can easily gain access to sensitive information, including your documents, email, and even various passwords stored by your web browser. An intruder can be anyone, from the person who steals your computer to a coworker casually walking by your unattended desk. Naturally, it's up to you to determine the actual likelihood of such a threat and to take the appropriate measures.

There are a variety of ways to protect your network from attack, including using the Windows Firewall, Windows Defender, the Security Center, and more. For details, see Chapter 8, in particular the "Internet Security" section.

Setting Up Wireless Encryption

If you have a wireless network, it's a good idea to use encryption to protect it. If your network isn't protected by encryption, passersby may be able to easily connect to it or use a network "sniffer" to read all of its traffic.

Setting up wireless encryption is a two-step process. First, you enable wireless encryption on your wireless router, and then you configure every wirelessly equipped PC on your network to use that encryption.

 If you have a network that includes both wired and wireless PCs, you won't need to configure your wired PCs to use encryption—they don't use encryption because their data is not sent out over the air.

Every router manufacturer has a different method for configuring wireless encryption, and it even varies from model to model of the same manufacturer. So read your router's documentation for how to configure yours. The instructions that follow are for the Linksys SRX400 router.

First, log in to your administrators screen, then select Wireless → Wireless Security. From the Security Mode drop-down menu, select the encryption method you want to use. WPA/WPA2 Personal is a good choice for a home or small network. WEP is a less powerful encryption method and is not as good a choice.

 To use WPA/WPA2 Enterprise encryption, you'll need a separate authentication server called a RADIUS server.

Fill out the form that appears (Figure 7-5). Enable WPA and WPA2, and choose the kind of encryption algorithm you want to use. Then type in a personal "key," which is a password between 8 and 63 characters long. The longer the key, the more secure the network. Write down the password, because you'll need it in order to configure encryption on each of your wireless PCs. Click Save Settings when you're done.

Now you have to go to each of your wirelessly equipped PCs and match their encryption information and key to the routers. Go to Control Panel → [Network and Internet] → Network and Sharing Center → View status, and click Wireless Properties. Click the Security tab. The screen shown in Figure 7-6 will appear.

Select the Security type and Encryption type that match the types you chose on your router, and in the Network Security key field, type in your password. Click OK. Your PC will now be able to connect to the router using encryption.

Sharing an Internet Connection with Internet Connection Sharing

There is a way to share a single Internet connection among multiple PCs without using a router to connect to the Internet. It's called Internet Connection Sharing (ICS). In ICS, a single computer with an Internet connection acts as a gateway,

Figure 7-5. Setting up encryption on a Linksys router

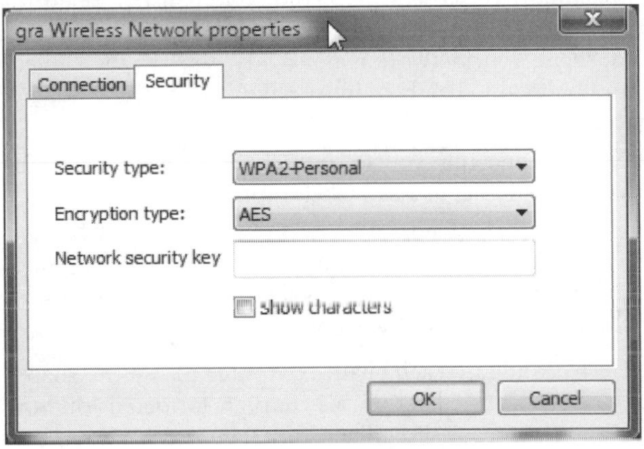

Figure 7-6. Setting up encryption on your PC

allowing other computers on the LAN to use the connection. The computer that is connected directly to the Internet is called the *host*; all the other computers are called *clients*. It's usually best to use a router to provide shared Internet access, but if you prefer, you can set up a network using two PCs, one of which (the host PC) is connected to a broadband connection (such as a cable/DSL modem or an Ethernet connection in a hotel room). That PC can share the broadband connection to a second PC using a second Ethernet port or its wireless card.

To get ICS to work, you'll need the following:

- At least two computers, each with an Ethernet or WiFi adapter properly installed and functioning. It is assumed you've already set up your local network, as described in "Setting Up a LAN," earlier in this chapter. If you connect the host PC to a hub instead of directly to another PC, your Internet connection can be shared with as many clients as your LAN will support.

- One of the computers must have an Internet connection properly set up. The instructions that follow assume that the computer handling the Internet connection is running Windows Vista.

- If your Internet connection is provided by a router or you've allocated multiple IP addresses, you don't need ICS.

- If you're sharing a DSL, cable modem, or other high-speed, Ethernet-based Internet connection, the computer with the Internet connection must have two Ethernet adapters or one Ethernet and one WiFi adapter. See Figure 7-3 for a diagram of this setup.

The first step in setting up ICS is to configure the host, the computer with the Internet connection that will be shared:

1. Open the Network Connections window (Control Panel → Network and Internet → Network and Sharing Center → Manage network connections). Here, you should have at least two connections listed: one for your Internet connection and one for the Ethernet adapter connected to your LAN. If they're not there, your network is not ready; refer to the earlier topics in this chapter and try again. The host must have two working adapters, so if a PC has only one adapter, it cannot be a host.

2. Right-click the connection you want to share. (It will be the adapter that will be used for your Internet access.) Click Properties.

3. Select the Sharing tab (Figure 7-7), and then check the box next to "Allow other network users to connect through this computer's Internet connection." You can also allow other network users to control or disable the shared Internet connection. Click OK when you're done.

The next step is to configure each client computer to use the shared connection. See "Connect to a Network," later in this chapter, for details on how to set up an Internet connection for each PC. They must be set up to get an IP address automatically.

Setting Up a Bluetooth Device

Bluetooth is a wireless networking technology used primarily to connect devices and PCs over short distances. It is commonly used in cell phones, PDAs, and even mice, keyboards, and printers.

To set up a Bluetooth device, you'll need a Bluetooth adapter for your PC. The adapter will allow your PC to wirelessly connect with a Bluetooth device. If you don't have a Bluetooth adapter already, buy one and plug it into your USB port. Windows Vista will recognize the adapter and install it via a wizard.

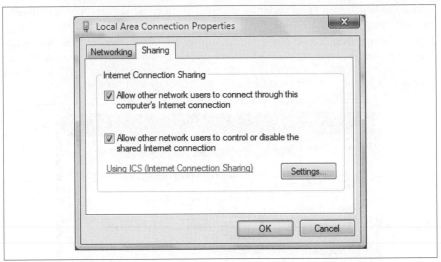

Figure 7-7. Enabling Internet Connection Sharing via the Sharing tab of a network connection's properties

Next, turn on the Bluetooth device and make it discoverable. Doing this will allow it to communicate with your PC. The way you make a device discoverable varies from device to device, so check the device's documentation or the manufacturer's web site.

Now go to Control Panel → [Hardware and Sound] → Bluetooth devices. Click Add, and follow the directions for connecting the device to your PC.

Wired and Wireless Connections, Management, and Configuration

Windows Vista includes many tools, screens, and features for setting up, connecting to, managing, and configuring networks. This section covers all of Windows Vista's features for doing that, and it includes basic information for setting up and connecting to networks and network connections.

Change Workgroup or Domain

Change the workgroup or domain to which a PC is attached.

To open
Control Panel → [System and Maintenance] → System → Change Settings → Computer Name tab

Description
The Networking and Internet Control Panel and the Network and Sharing Center both have one surprising shortcoming: they do not offer a way to change the workgroup or

domain to which your PC is currently attached, or to easily connect to a new domain or workgroup. So you may think that there is no way to perform both tasks.

In fact, though, they're both easy to do, as long as you know where to look. And you'll have to look in a surprising place—on the Computer Name tab of the System Properties dialog box (Figure 7-8). You can also reach it via Control Panel → [Network and Internet] → Network and Sharing Center → Network Discovery → Change Settings.

Figure 7-8. The System Properties dialog box, which lets you connect to a domain or workgroup and change your domain or workgroup

Click Network ID to launch a wizard that will allow you to join an existing domain or workgroup. Click Change and the dialog box shown in Figure 7-9 appears. Select either Domain or Workgroup, and enter the name of the domain or workgroup to switch to a new one.

Connect to a Network

Connect to a network or the Internet.

To open

Click the network icon in the System Tray → Connect or disconnect

Control Panel → [Network and Internet] → Connect to a network

Control Panel → [Network and Internet] → Network and Sharing Center → Connect to a network

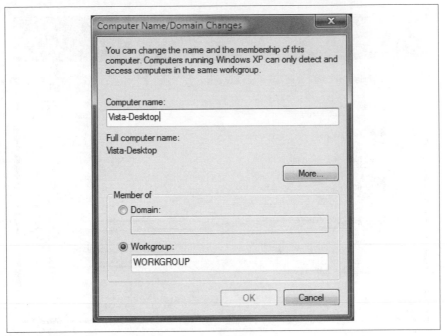

Figure 7-9. Switching to a new domain or workgroup

Description

Once you've set up a network connection (see "Set Up a Connection or Network," later in this chapter), use the "Connect to a network" screen (Figure 7-10) to connect to any network—wired, wireless, VPN, or dial-up.

Connecting is straightforward: double-click the network to which you want to connect, or highlight it and click Connect. When you're connected to a network, disconnect from it by clicking Disconnect.

This screen is primarily designed for wireless, dial-up, and VPN connections. If your only connection to a network is via an Ethernet cable, you won't even get to the screen shown in Figure 7-10 when you choose to connect. Instead, you'll be told that you're already connected to the network. Want to disconnect? There's a simple, physical solution for you—unplug your Ethernet cable.

Making the wireless connection

The "Connect to a network" screen has really been designed for wireless connections, not wired ones. It's a way to quickly and easily make a connection to a wireless network, not only when you're at home or work, but also when you're at a public hotspot.

To connect to a wireless network, click the network icon in the System Tray and you'll see the screen shown in Figure 7-11.

Click "Connect to a network," and a list of all nearby wireless networks will appear, as shown in Figure 7-12. You may see multiple networks on the "Connect to a network" screen that are unfamiliar to you. That's because Windows Vista finds any wireless networks within range. For each wireless network, in addition to seeing the name of

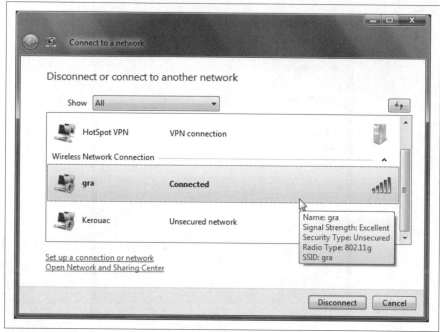

Figure 7-10. Choosing a network to which you want to connect

Figure 7-11. Screen indicating that wireless networks are available

the network, you'll also see whether it is secure and protected by encryption, or unsecured. At the far right of the listing for each network, you'll also see the strength of the network's wireless signal. For more details about any network, hover your mouse over it. You'll be shown, for example, whether the network is 802.11b, 802.11g, or some other WiFi standard.

To connect to a network, highlight it and click Connect. If it's not protected by encryption, you'll see a warning. If you want to connect anyway, click Connect Anyway. Once you make the connection, you'll be asked whether you want to save the network, and if so, whether you want to connect to it automatically whenever you're in range (Figure 7-13). If it's a network to which you often connect, it's a good idea to save it and connect to it automatically. Later on, you'll also be able to manage this wireless network, if you save it now. (For details, see "Manage Wireless Networks," later in this chapter.)

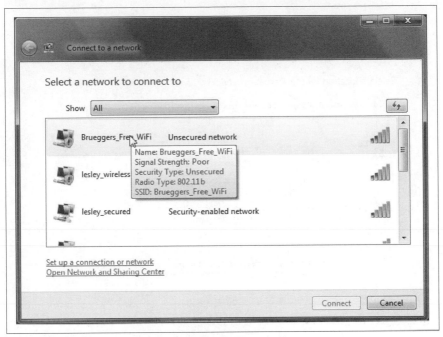

Figure 7-12. Browsing through the list of available networks

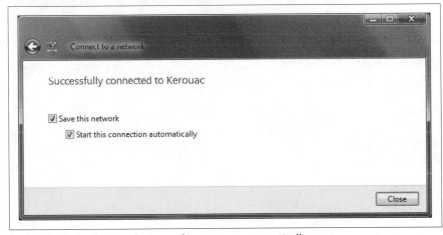

Figure 7-13. Configuring the network to connect automatically

Next, a screen appears, asking you what type of settings should be applied to the network—whether it is a home, work, or public location (see Figure 7-14). This will determine the kind of security that will be applied to the network; home and work network connections require less security than public connections.

Choose which type of network it is (you can always change this later; see the upcoming section, "Manage Wireless Networks"). You're now connected, and you can use the network.

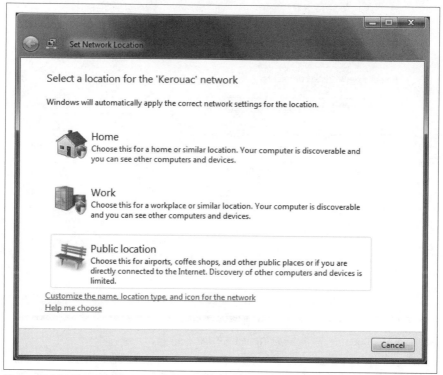

Figure 7-14. Choosing the type of network

Manage Network Connections

\windows\system\ncpa.cpl

Configure and manage your network connections.

To open

Control Panel → [Network and Internet] → Network and Sharing Center → Manage network connections

Command prompt → **ncpa.cpl**

Description

Manage Network Connections (Figure 7-15) is actually a specialized folder that lists and provides details about all of your network connections, and lets you configure and manage them. Click any network connection and a toolbar appears that lets you take a variety of actions on the connection, including connecting it, disabling the network device, renaming the connection, viewing the status of the connection, changing the connection's settings, and diagnosing problems with the connection.

You can also right-click any connection to perform several of those tasks, or delete the connection, rename it, and create a shortcut to it.

The folder is also useful for bridging separate networks. When you do this, you allow data to be transferred between two (or more) different networks. In effect, a bridge turns your computer into a hub of sorts, but with the advantage of allowing you to

Figure 7-15. Manage Network Connections, a specialized folder that lets you configure and manage all your network connections

combine two otherwise incompatible networks. Select at least two connection icons, right-click, and select Bridge Connections to create a network bridge between the connections.

Notes

- You can't bridge any network connection that Internet Connection Sharing is using to share an Internet connection with several PCs.
- You can create only one network bridge on your PC, but you can add multiple networks to a single bridge.

See also

"Manage Wireless Networks"

Manage Wireless Networks

Configure and manage wireless networks.

To open

Control Panel → [Network and Internet] → Network and Sharing Center → Manage wireless networks

Description

Many people regularly connect to more than one wireless network—one at home, one at work, and possibly more than one public hotspot. When you create a wireless connection, you have the option of saving that network as a connection; any networks that you've saved will show up on the Manage Wireless Networks screen (Figure 7-16).

Manage and configure your networks using the toolbar. Clicking Add will let you add a new network—either within or outside your wireless range. If it's inside your wireless range, follow the usual steps for adding a wireless connection. (See "Connect to a Network," earlier in this chapter, for details.) If it's outside your wireless range, you can manually create a network profile so that the next time you're near that network, you can automatically connect to it. To do this, you'll need to know the network name (SSID), and its security key if it uses security. You can also create an ad hoc network, a temporary direct connection with another nearby wirelessly equipped PC, rather than with an access-point-based network.

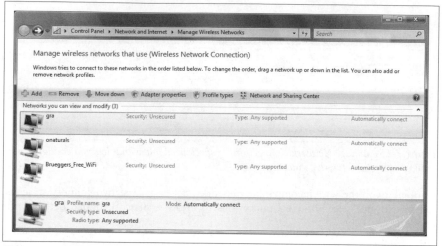

Figure 7-16. Managing multiple wireless networks

The network list shows you the order in which Windows Vista will attempt to connect. So if you have two or more networks within range of each other, move your preferred network to the top of the list, your least preferred network to the bottom, and so on. To move a network up and down the list, highlight it and choose either "Move up" or "Move down."

Click "Adapter properties" to launch the Wireless Network Connection Properties dialog box, which lists all the services and protocols associated with a network and lets you add, configure, or remove more protocols and services. (See the next section, "Network Connection Properties (Includes Wired and Wireless Connections)," for details.)

Profile Types lets you choose whether the networks can be accessed by anyone using the PC, or whether you want to allow each user to create her own connections. By default, all accounts can access the networks. If you change that to a per-user basis, the PC may lose network connectivity when users log off or when switching user accounts.

See also
"Manage Network Connections"

Network Connection Properties (Includes Wired and Wireless Connections)

Configure network services associated with a network connection.

To open
Control Panel → [Network and Internet] → Network and Sharing Center → View Status → Properties

Description

The Network Connection Properties screen (Figure 7-17) lists all the installed protocols and services associated with a network connection (both wired and wireless). It provides you with basic information about your wireless connection to help with troubleshooting, and it helps you configure your network and its connection. You can selectively choose which protocols and services are supported by any specific connection by using the checkboxes in the list.

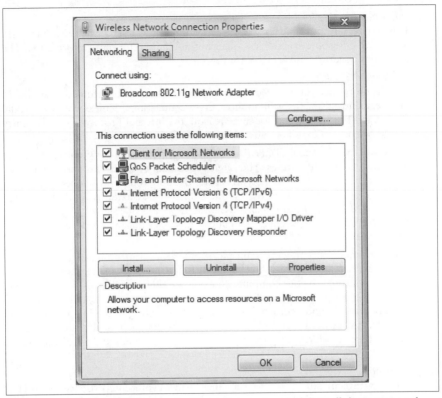

Figure 7-17. The Network Connection Properties screen, which lists all the services and protocols associated with a network connection

If you need to add support for a protocol or service not shown on the list, click Install to add it. If a protocol or service is shown but you're certain it's not used by any of your connections, you can uninstall it by clicking Uninstall. If you install or uninstall a protocol or service, the change will take effect for all existing connections.

Probably the most useful button, however, is Properties. Depending on the service or protocol currently selected, Properties allows you to set many of the advanced options for a connection. The following list shows common services and protocols available in Windows Vista:

Client for Microsoft Networks

This is an essential component for connecting to a Microsoft Network. This entry should always be present and enabled, unless you specifically need to connect to a non-Microsoft network (such as an older NetWare network). Most users will have no need to modify it via its Properties window.

QoS Packet Scheduler

This protocol allows network traffic to be optimized and controlled, including prioritizing certain services over others.

File and Printer Sharing for Microsoft Networks

This service is responsible for sharing files and printers over a Microsoft Network; see "Sharing Resources and Files," later in this chapter, for more information. The Properties window is unavailable for this entry.

Internet Protocol (TCP/IPv4)

TCP/IP, introduced in the beginning of this chapter, is the protocol used by all Internet connections, as well as most LAN connections. Unless you specifically don't want TCP/IP support for some reason, the Internet Protocol (TCP/IP) entry should be enabled for all of your connections.

Select Internet Protocol (TCP/IP) and click Properties to view and change the connection's TCP/IP settings. The Internet Protocol (TCP/IP) Properties window, shown in Figure 7-18, is where you set the IP address of your connection (if you have a static IP address), as well as the subnet mask, gateway, and DNS server addresses. If the connection has a dynamic IP address (assigned by your router/ gateway every time you connect), choose the "Obtain an IP address automatically" option.

Click Advanced to configure multiple IP addresses and multiple gateways, use more than two DNS servers, and set up WINS. Choose the Alternate Configuration tab to configure your computer to use more than one network. For example, if you bring a laptop back and forth between home and work, and you use one network at home and another at work, you can use this tab to configure a second network. If your home network uses DHCP to be assigned an IP address, but you have a static IP address at your work network, you could configure your laptop for both networks.

Internet Protocol (TCP/IPv6)

These settings are similar to those for IPv4. Unless your enterprise uses IPv6 (and most enterprises do not), you won't need to touch this setting.

Link-Layer Topology Discovery Mapper I/O Driver

This discovers and locates other PCs, devices, and network hardware. You can also use it to measure network bandwidth, and the Network and Sharing Center uses it to map your network (see "Network Map," later in this chapter). The Properties window is unavailable for this entry.

Link-Layer Topology Discovery Responder

This allows the PC to be discovered by other PCs and devices on the network. The Properties window is unavailable for this entry.

Some connections may have a Sharing tab in addition to the Networking tab. The Sharing tab lets you use the connection for ICS (see "Sharing an Internet Connection with Internet Connection Sharing," earlier in this chapter) to share a single Internet connection with multiple PCs.

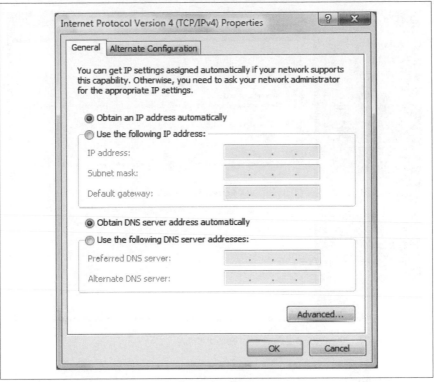

Figure 7-18. The Internet Protocol Properties window

Dial-up connections and VPN connections have additional tabs for dialing options and, in the case of a VPN connection, for security settings.

Network and Internet Control Panel

Quick access to Windows Vista's networking and Internet features.

To open
Control Panel → [Network and Internet]

Description
This control panel (Figure 7-19) gives you access to all of the networking and Internet features in Windows. As with other control panels, you can drill down to further subcategories or click links to perform common tasks, such as adding a device to the network or allowing a program through the Windows Firewall.

See also
"Network and Sharing Center"

Networking
and Mobility

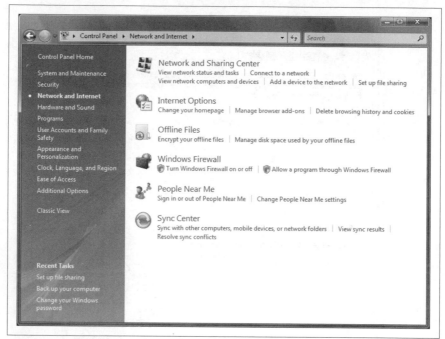

Figure 7-19. The Network and Internet Control Panel

Network Map

Display a "live" map of your network.

To open

Control Panel → [Network and Internet] → Network and Sharing Center → View full map

Description

The Network Map feature (Figure 7-20) shows a detailed schematic of your network and all the devices connected to it. The map is "live"—that is, the icons are not merely representations, but also perform actions and provide information. Hover your mouse over a device and you'll get information about that device; for example, hover your mouse over a gateway to see its IP address and MAC address (a MAC address is a unique identifier for network hardware, a kind of serial number). Click a PC, and you'll connect to it and see all the shared network files and folders in Windows Explorer. Click the Internet icon, and you'll launch your default browser to your home page.

The Network Map may not display all of the devices on your network, or if it does display them, it may not be able to place them on the map and may instead place them at the bottom of the screen. PCs with older versions of Windows will not be able to be placed on the map and may not be recognized at all. Printers and devices attached to those PCs may not be recognized as well.

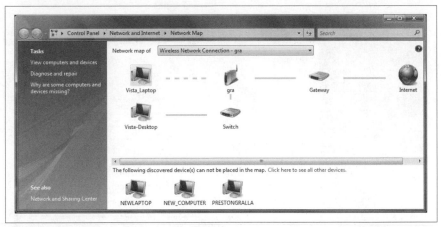

Figure 7-20. Network Map displaying all the devices on a network

Notes

- Windows Vista introduced a new technology to make it easier to recognize network devices—Link Layer Topology Discovery (LLTD). With LLTD Windows Vista can automatically obtain and display information about devices and diagnose problems with them. But hardware has to be LLTD-compliant. Older hardware may be upgradeable via firmware, and many new devices include built-in LLTD support. Older versions of Windows do not include LLTD, which is why they might not be able to be placed on the Network Map. As of this writing, Microsoft is working to create a patch that will add LLTD capabilities to Windows XP PCs. But it currently has no plans to add LLTD to earlier versions of Windows.

See also

"Network and Sharing Center"

Network and Sharing Center

Configure, customize, and access network and collaboration tools.

To open

Control Panel → [Network and Internet] → Network and Sharing Center

Description

The Network and Sharing Center (Figure 7-21) lets you configure, access, and troubleshoot a wide variety of network features. You'll most likely find that it's the primary place you'll turn for handling network issues, configuring networks, troubleshooting networks, and performing other network-related tasks.

Front and center is a brief diagram of your network, showing your computer name and how it connects to your local network, and then to the Internet. Think of it as a kind of "you-are-here" diagram, because you'll see the words "This computer" underneath your computer. The diagram is so basic that at first it appears it may be useless, but in

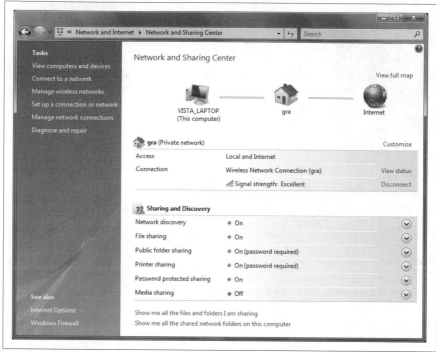

Figure 7-21. The Network and Sharing Center

fact, you'll find it surprisingly useful. The diagram is "live" so that if there's a problem with your network or Internet connection, you'll be notified here. In addition, you can click on the icons representing the different portions of your network and connect to them. For example, click your computer's icon, and you'll open Windows Explorer to your Computer folder. Click the Network icon to open Windows Explorer to the Network folder, which lists all of the computers on your network. Click Internet to open Internet Explorer to your home page.

To see a fuller diagram of your network, including all the computers and devices attached to it, such as routers, switches, and gateways, click "View full map." That diagram will be live as well, and it allows you to get more detail about any device by hovering your mouse over it. For more details, see the preceding section, "Network Map."

The screen is divided into the following areas:

Network

You'll find this area just beneath the diagram of your network. It displays your network's name and whether it is private or public. (For details about private and public networks, see "Connect to a Network," earlier in this chapter.) To customize your network's name, whether it's private or public, and similar details, click Customize. The "Customize network settings" screen appears (Figure 7-22). Here you can change your network's name and icon, as well as change the network from private to public, and vice versa. If your PC is connected to several networks and you want to merge them into a larger, single network, click "Merge or delete network location." The screen that appears lets you delete the network location, as well as merge networks.

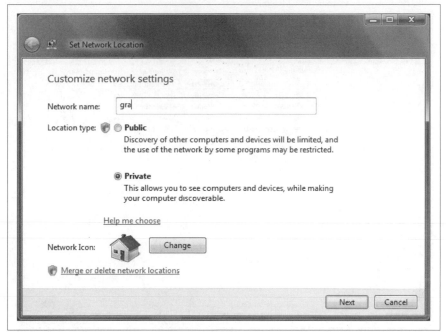

Figure 7-22. The "Customize network settings" screen, where you can change your network's name and whether it's private or public

Next to Access, you'll see displayed the current status of your network connectivity—whether you have local access, Internet access, or both. Next to Connection, you'll see your connection type—for example, "Wireless Network Connection." Click the "View status" link for details about the connection, including the connection speed, how long you've been connected, and more. (For more information, see "Network Connection Status," later in this chapter.)

Sharing and Discovery

This section lets you share files, folders, printers, and media among computers, and it allows you to control sharing settings. For more details, see the upcoming section, "Sharing Resources and Files."

Tasks

The links listed here let you perform common and useful network-related tasks. Click "View computers and devices" to open Windows Explorer to the Network folder, *Desktop\Network* (Figure 7-23), which lists all the computers and devices attached to your network.

This is more than just an ordinary Windows Explorer folder. For each device, it lists not only the name, but also its category (computer or printer, for example), as well as its workgroup within your network and the network to which it is attached. In addition, the toolbar includes icons for adding a printer, adding a wireless device, and opening the Network and Sharing Center.

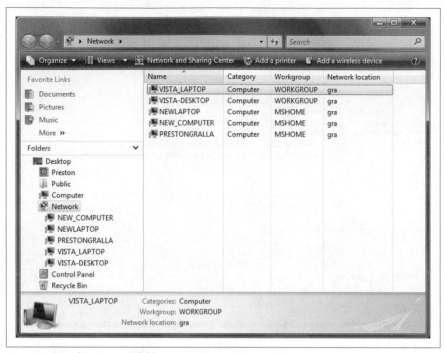

Figure 7-23. The Network folder, a Windows Explorer folder with network-specific features

The tasks also let you do the following:

- Connect to a wired or wireless network. The Connect to a Network Wizard launches and walks you through connecting to a network. (See "Connect to a Network," earlier in this chapter, for details.)

- Set up a connection or network. The Set Up a Connection or Network Wizard launches and walks you through setting up a network. (See "Set Up a Connection or Network," later in this chapter, for details.)

- Manage your network connections. The Network Connection folder launches. (See "Manage Network Connections," earlier in this chapter, for details.)

- Diagnose and repair problems with your network or Internet connection. (See "Network Connection Status," later in this chapter, for details.)

Notes

- If you have a mixed network of PCs with Windows Vista and other versions of Windows, you may run into some anomalies. Non-Windows Vista PCs might show up properly on the network, or they may show up at some points and not others. For example, they may not show up on the Network Map, but they may show up in the Network folder. Microsoft is working on software that can be installed on Windows XP that will make it work better with networks that have Windows Vista PCs.

- Devices such as printers attached to Windows XP computers may not show up on the Network Map, in the Network folder, or anywhere else in Windows Vista networking.
- The screens and options you see in the Network and Sharing Center and throughout Windows Vista networking may differ depending on whether you are connected to a workgroup (a peer-to-peer network) or to a domain (a server-based network in use at corporations).

See also

"Network Map," "Connect to a Network," and "Manage Network Connections"

Phone Dialer
\Windows\System32\dialer.exe

Make voice calls, video calls, and conference calls using a phone line or Internet connection.

To open

Command Prompt → `dialer`

Description

Few people know that this simple dialing program (Figure 7-24) exists. Use it to make calls through your modem. Dial a number by typing it into the input box or clicking numbers on the on-screen number pad and then clicking "dial." Choose from past numbers using the drop-down list. You can put numbers on the speed-dial list by clicking any number on the list and filling out a form.

Figure 7-24. The Phone Dialer, which lets you dial a phone using a modem

See also

"Phone and Modem Options"

Phone and Modem Options
\windows\system32\telephon.cpl

Configure your modem and telephony devices, and choose dialing preferences.

To open

Control Panel → [Hardware and Sound] → Phone and Modem Options

Command Prompt → `telephon.cpl`

Command Prompt → `control telephony`

Description

Although DSL and cable Internet access is rapidly making dial-up modems obsolete, a good number of people still use traditional modems to connect to the Internet. And if you get online through your cell phone or a cellular data card, you may need to use Phone and Modem Options to make some configuration changes.

When you first run Phone and Modem Options, you'll have to answer a series of questions, including the country you're dialing from, your area code, whether you use tone dialing or pulse dialing, and similar information. Once you've done that, your modem will be set up to work. You can change your phone and modem configuration by running Phone and Modem Options again, using the following tabs:

Dialing Rules

Assuming your modem is properly installed (see the Modems tab), Windows will use these settings to determine how to dial. Click Edit to change the dialing rules for the selected location (see Figure 7-25). You can configure multiple locations if you have a portable computer and need to dial out from within different area codes or from varying phone numbers with different dialing requirements.

As you undoubtedly know, if you dial a phone number in your own area code, you usually don't need to include the area code. For this reason, Windows needs to know which area code it's in, as well as any special numbers that are required to dial outside lines, place international calls, place calling-card calls, or disable call waiting (so that you won't be interrupted by incoming calls).

Modems

Before you can use a modem with Network Connections or with Microsoft's fax service, you must configure it here. The items listed here are the same as those listed in the Modems branch in Device Manager (discussed earlier in this chapter), so if Windows has detected your modem through Plug and Play, there's probably nothing left to do here. If your modem doesn't show up in the list, it's probably not Plug and Play–compliant; you'll have to click Add to start the Add Hardware Wizard (discussed in Chapter 9) to scan your system and install the appropriate drivers.

Select your modem from the list and click Properties to view the device's Properties sheet, which is the same as the one in Device Manager. Of special interest here is the Diagnostics tab, which will communicate with your modem and provide troubleshooting data, and the Advanced tab, which allows you to specify a modem initialization string (refer to your modem's documentation). Don't waste your time trying to get an old modem to work with Windows Vista; brand-new Plug and Play PCI modems are ridiculously cheap and extremely easy to install.

Advanced

The Advanced tab lists the telephony drivers currently installed on your system. You can add, remove, or configure drivers here. Note that unless you use a telephony application, you'll never need to touch these settings.

Figure 7-25. Configuring multiple locations for dialing

Notes

- All of the settings in this dialog are also covered in Chapter 9.

See also

"Phone Dialer," earlier in this chapter, and "Windows Fax and Scan," in Chapter 10

Set Up a Connection or Network

Set up a new network or Internet connection.

To open

Control Panel → [Network and Internet] → Network and Sharing Center → Set up a connection or network

Description

One of the reasons that networking in Windows Vista is so much easier than working in previous Windows versions is this wizard (Figure 7-26). Answer a series of questions, and you can set up a new network or connection in minutes.

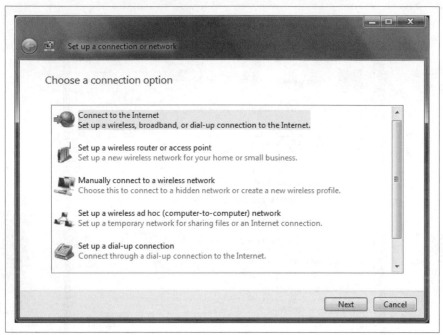

Figure 7-26. The Network Connections window, which allows you to connect your computer to a local network or to the Internet

You have six choices for creating a new connection or network:

Connect to the Internet

Choose this option to set up a direct connection to the Internet, via a cable modem, DSL modem, or dial-up modem. If you are already connected to a home network, small-business network, or corporate network, you shouldn't make this choice, because your network already provides you with Internet connectivity.

If you choose to connect via a DSL or cable modem that requires you to enter a username and password, select Broadband (PPPoE). You'll see a screen like that pictured in Figure 7-27. Fill out the information and click Connect. If you're going to allow other PCs on the network to share the Internet connection, check the box next to "Allow other people to use this connection." If later on, you decide you want others to share the connection, you can set that up; see "Sharing an Internet Connection with Internet Connection Sharing," earlier in this chapter, for details.

 You most likely will not need to use the Set Up a Connection Wizard if you're connecting via a cable modem, and you may not need it if you connect via a DSL modem, either. Connect your PC to your cable or DSL modem; after a few minutes, the connection may be made automatically. You'll mainly need to use the Connect to the Internet Wizard if your ISP requires that you enter a username and password in order to connect. PPPoE generally requires that a username and password be used, and DSL connections often use PPPoE, so use the wizard if you use PPPoE and your ISP requires a username and password.

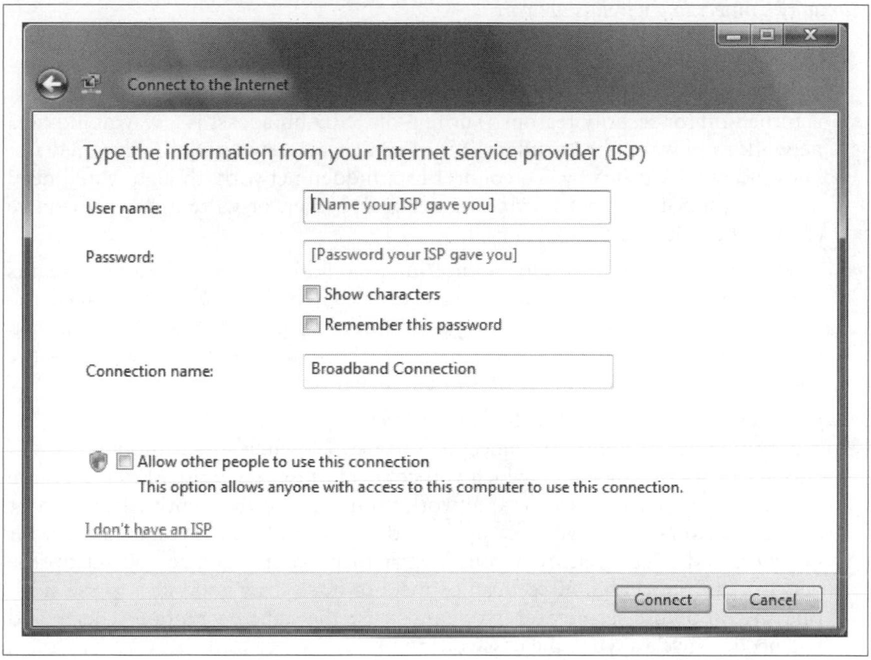

![Connect to the Internet dialog box]

Connect to the Internet

Type the information from your Internet service provider (ISP)

User name: [Name your ISP gave you]

Password: [Password your ISP gave you]

               ☐ Show characters
               ☐ Remember this password

Connection name: Broadband Connection

    🛡 ☐ Allow other people to use this connection
          This option allows anyone with access to this computer to use this connection.

I don't have an ISP

Connect   Cancel

Figure 7-27. Making a connection using a broadband modem that requires a password and username

If you instead connect via dial-up modem or ISDN, make that selection from the wizard. The screen is very similar to that shown in Figure 7-27, except that you also have to fill in a phone number, and you can create a set of dialing rules that includes information such as whether you need to dial a prefix to reach an outside line.

Set up a wireless router or access point

This wizard will find and configure your wireless router or access point, set up file and printer sharing, make the network a private one (this controls what services Vista offers over the network; it doesn't have any effect on the security or configuration of the network itself), and offer instructions for how to connect other devices to the network. In some cases, it will be able to do the router or access point configuration automatically, but often it will not. When it can't do automatic configuration, it will open the device's configuration page, and you'll have to do the configuration yourself, based on the hardware's documentation.

You don't necessarily have to run the wizard in order to set up a wireless network. Usually, you can do it yourself relatively easily by following the manufacturer's advice or by using the setup program or wizard provided by the manufacturer.

If you have a wireless router that supports configuration via USB flash drives, you can instead have the wizard create the settings and save them to a USB flash drive, which you can then plug into the wireless router for automatic configuration.

Manually connect to a wireless network

Use this option if you are going to connect to a *hidden* wireless network, or you want to create a connection to a wireless network even if you are not within range of the network at the moment. A hidden network is one in which SSID broadcast is turned off for security reasons. Turning off SSID broadcast is a way of hiding a network from would-be intruders; if they can't see a network SSID, they may not know a network is nearby. To connect to a hidden network, though, you'll need to know the SSID, so get it from the network owner, or write it down if you've created the hidden network yourself.

After you launch the wizard for connecting to a hidden network, or to one that is not currently within range, you'll have to fill in the network SSID (called the *network name*), any security or encryption information, and so on. You can then connect to the network, or you can close the dialog after you've set up the connection, and connect to the network at a later time.

Set up a wireless ad hoc (computer-to-computer) network

This option lets you directly connect to a nearby PC wirelessly, without the use of a router or server. The PC to which you connect must be within 30 feet. If you're already connected to a wireless network, you may be disconnected from your current network when you set up an ad hoc connection. You'll name your network, and select security if you want it to be secure. (Once you set up the network, anyone within 30 feet can connect to it, so it's a good idea to use security.) If you do use security, everyone must use the same encryption scheme and you need to give everyone the password to use it.

Set up a dial-up connection

This is the same screen you'll come to if you choose Connect to the Internet and then choose Dial-up from the screen that appears.

Connect to a workplace

Many businesses allow workers to remotely access their corporate networks, either directly over the Internet or by dialing in to a modem-equipped PC or server. Most commonly, you'll have to set up a VPN connection in order to do this. In a VPN, your connection with the corporate network is done over any public Internet connection, but all communications and data are encrypted and travel inside a virtual "tunnel" that is private and secure.

 In some instances, you won't be able to use Vista's built-in VPN feature to connect to your corporate network via a VPN. Some VPN connections require special software or hardware, which a system administrator will provide to you.

If you're connecting via a VPN, choose "Use my Internet connection (VPN)" when the wizard launches. The screen shown in Figure 7-28 will appear. Type in the address of the VPN server, as provided to you by your system administrator. It can be in IPv4 format (157.54.0.1, for example) or IPv6 format (3ffe:1234::1111, for example), or it can be the server name (*mycorpvpn.com*, for example). You can also choose to share the connection with others on your network, and to set up the connection now but not connect to it. If your VPN requires the use of a smart card for security, check the appropriate box.

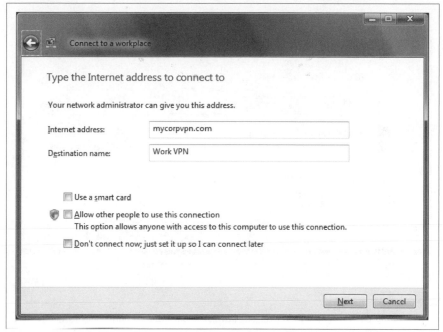

Figure 7-28. Creating a VPN connection to connect to your corporate network securely over the Internet

In the next screen, type in your username and password, and your domain if one is required. Then click Create, and you'll create the VPN and connect to it, if you want to connect now. The VPN does not actually give you Internet access, so before you can use it, you have to be connected to the Internet.

Once you're connected to the Internet, you can launch your VPN in several different ways. The simplest is to click on the network icon in the System Tray and select "Connect to a network." The screen shown in Figure 7-29 appears. Select the VPN connection and click Connect.

You can also connect by choosing "Connect to a network" from the Network and Sharing Center, as outlined in "Connect to a Network," earlier in this chapter, or by going to the Network Connections Folder and double-clicking the connection or highlighting it and choosing "Start this connection." (See "Network and Sharing Center," earlier in this chapter, for details.)

If you instead want to connect to your workplace via a direct dial-up connection, when the wizard launches, choose Dial Directly and you'll fill out a form and follow instructions similar to the ones you followed on the VPN form, except that it will ask for a phone number rather than a VPN server address. Use the dial-up connection in the same way you make any other network connection, as outlined in the previous paragraph.

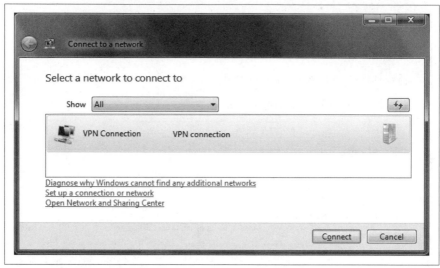

Figure 7-29. Connecting to a VPN

Notes

- In many cases, Windows Vista will automatically detect and set up a network or network connection, so you may not need to run the wizard.

- VPNs have a use in addition to connecting to a workplace—they can provide security when you use a public wireless hotspot to connect to the Internet. Hotspots are nonsecure and use no encryption, so someone may be able to examine your Internet traffic when you're on it. You can use a for-pay VPN service to encrypt all your wireless communications when you're at a hotspot. Set up this kind of VPN in the same way you do a corporate VPN; the VPN provider will give you server information, the username, the password, and so on. A good one to try is HotSpotVPN at *http://www.hotspotvpn.com*.

See also

"Network and Sharing Center" and "Connect to a Network"

Virtual Private Network

See "Set Up a Connection or Network," earlier in this chapter.

Windows Firewall

See "Windows Firewall," in Chapter 8.

Windows Defender

See "Windows Defender," in Chapter 8.

Network Connection Status

Get details about a network connection.

To open

Control Panel → [Network and Internet] → Network and Sharing Center → View Status

Control Panel → [Network and Internet] → Network and Sharing Center → Manage network connections → Right-click a connection and select Status

Description

You can use this screen for wired and wireless networks, although it will be used more frequently for wireless networks because wireless connections require more care and handling than wired connections. They are more apt to be slow because of interference problems, and to disconnect due to interference and other problems. And you're likely to have multiple wireless connections set up on your PC—one for work, one for home, and several for your favorite hotspots.

The Network Connection Status screen (Figure 7-30) provides you with basic information about your connection to help with troubleshooting, and to help you configure your network and its connection.

Figure 7-30. The Network Connection Status screen, which provides detailed information about each connection

The screen varies slightly, according to whether you're examining a wired or wireless connection. But overall, no matter the network, it provides basic information, including the SSID of the connection (the SSID is, in essence, the network name of the wireless network; wired networks don't have SSIDs), the speed, the signal quality, the duration of the connection, and similar information. It also shows the amount of data sent and received between your PC and the network, measured in bytes.

The screen also contains a number of buttons that either provide more information or accomplish tasks:

Details

> This provides an exceptional amount of detail about the wireless connection (Figure 7-31), in particular related to network infrastructure, including IPv4 and IPv6 IP addresses, DNS information, the default gateway, the DHCP server, DNS servers, when the IP lease was obtained, when it is scheduled to expire, and so on. It also shows the MAC address of the adapter (which the screen calls the Physical Address), which is a unique identifier that a piece of networking hardware has, something like a serial number.

 For a quick way to find out your IP address—whether you're on a wired or a wireless network—click the Details button.

Figure 7-31. Details, which provides an exceptional amount of detail about a wireless connection, particularly related to IP and network infrastructure

Wireless properties (only for wireless networks)

This screen has two tabs: Connection and Security. The Connection tab (Figure 7-32) lets you configure how Windows Vista should handle the wireless connection. You can have your PC automatically connect whenever the network is within its range, which is very useful for when you frequently connect to the same wireless network—for example, at home or at work. That way, you don't need to do anything when you're nearby; just turn on your PC, and Windows Vista will automatically connect.

Figure 7-32. The Connection tab, which lets you configure the way Windows handles the wireless connection

You may run into a situation where you are near two wireless networks to which you frequently connect. This tab lets you determine which one should get preference. For the network that gets the highest preference, uncheck the box next to "Connect to a more preferred network if available." For other networks, make sure the box is checked. That way, you'll tell Windows Vista which network it should connect to first, in case you're within range of both.

 There's an even better way to tell Windows Vista the order of preference for connecting to wireless networks. You can order them, from most preferred to least preferred. See "Manage Wireless Networks," earlier in this chapter, for more details.

The tab also has a security feature. One way to protect your wireless network from intruders is to tell it not to broadcast its SSID. That will make it harder for other users to know your network exists, and to connect to it. But how can your PC connect to the network if the network doesn't broadcast its SSID? Check the box next to "Connect even if the network is not broadcasting."

The Security tab lets you use network encryption to keep your network safe from intruders and snoopers. For details, see "Setting Up Wireless Encryption."

Properties

Brings up the Network Connection Properties dialog box, which has detailed config-uration information relating to services and protocols used by the network. For details, and to learn more about how to configure this screen, see "Network Connec-tion Properties (Includes Wired and Wireless Connections)," earlier in this chapter.

Disable

Be very careful before clicking this button. Instead of disconnecting you from the network, it disables the network adapter so that it no longer works. You will no longer be able to connect to any network, because your adapter will be disabled. (Of course, if you disable a wireless adapter, you can still connect to a wired network, and if you disable a wired adapter, you can still connect to a wireless network.) Windows Vista will not recognize the hardware. If this happens, however, you can have Windows Vista re-enable the hardware. From the Network and Sharing Center, choose "Diagnose and repair," and it will turn the hardware back on.

Diagnose

If you run into a problem with your connection, click this, and it will diagnose the problem and repair it or suggest a way to repair it.

See also

"Manage Wireless Networks" and "Setting Up Wireless Encryption"

Sharing Resources and Files

There's little point in setting up a network with multiple computers if you don't take advantage of the connection by sharing files and printers. Once you've established a network connection with another Windows computer and verified that the connec-tion is working, you can set up resources to be shared over your network.

A shared resource is a folder on your hard disk, a printer physically attached to your computer, or some other device that you would like to share with other computers on your network. If you share a printer, others on your network can print to it; if you share a folder, others on your network can access the files and folders contained therein as though they were stored on their own hard disks.

Whenever you share a resource, you are opening a backdoor to your computer. It's important to keep security in mind at all times, especially if you're connected to the Internet. Otherwise, you may be unwittingly exposing your personal data to intruders looking for anything they can use and abuse. Furthermore, an insecure system is more vulnerable to viruses and other malicious programs.

To start sharing resources, you first need to enable sharing on your PC. Open the Network and Sharing Center (Figure 7-33) by choosing Control Panel → Set up file sharing, or Control Panel → [Network and Internet] → Network and Sharing Center.

Set up sharing in the Sharing and Discovery section. Here are your options:

Network discovery

Turn network discovery on; if you don't, you won't be able to see other network computers and devices, your PC won't be visible to other network computers and devices, and sharing will be impossible.

File sharing

Turn this on if you want to be able to share files and folders from your PC with other network users.

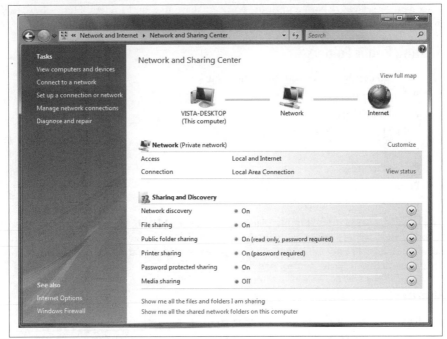

Figure 7-33. The first step to sharing resources—configuring the Network and Sharing Center properly

Public folder sharing

This lets you share files in your Public folder with other network users. You can do this kind of sharing in concert with file sharing, as detailed earlier, or by itself. When you share files via the Public folder, you have to move files and folders into the Public folder in order for other people to get access to them. When you turn on this type of file sharing, the Public folder will show up on other computers on the network. To get it on your network, open Windows Explorer and go to the Public folder (*c:\Users\Public*). Drag files and folders into that folder to share them.

With Public folder sharing, you have three choices:

- Allow anyone with network access to view files but not change or create files in the Public folder.
- Allow anyone with network access to view, change, and create files.
- Stop sharing the Public folder. Other accounts on your computer will still be able to access the folder, though.

Password-protected sharing

If you turn this on, only people who have an account on your computer can access shared files and printers in the Public folder and in other folders. If you turn it off, no account or password will be needed. Note that if neither file sharing nor public folder sharing is turned on, this option will have no effect.

Media sharing

This allows people and devices on the network to share music, pictures, and videos on your PC, and for you to access other people's shared media.

Once you've set your sharing options, you can share files and folders. Here's how to do it for Public folders, as well as any files and folders on your system.

Sharing Public Folders

The Public folder, by default, contains these subfolders:

- Public Documents
- Public Downloads
- Public Favorites (Hidden)
- Public Music
- Public Pictures
- Public Videos
- Public Desktop (Hidden)

The subfolders are empty. Simply place any folders or files in the appropriate folders, or make new folders and put them there. They'll now be available to anyone with network access. At any point, you can change access rights to those folders by going to the Network and Internet control panel.

Sharing Other Folders

To share a folder not in the Public folder, right-click it, select Share, and choose the appropriate options from the screen that appears, as shown in Figure 7-34.

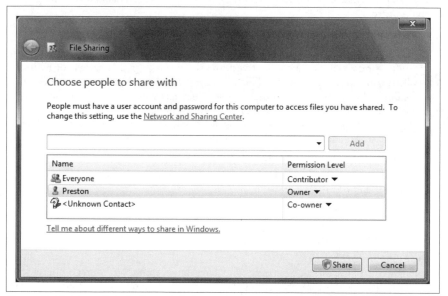

Figure 7-34. Using the File Sharing dialog to share a folder and set its access privileges

You'll see accounts and account groups listed, and next to each account, its permission level. Here are the choices, and what each means:

Reader
> The person or group can only view files.

Contributor
> The person or group can view files, add files, and change or delete the files that they add. They cannot, however, change or delete files that others have added.

Co-owner
> The person or group can view files, add files, and change and delete all files in the folder, even those created by others.

Owner
> As with the co-owner, the person or group can view files, add files, and change and delete all files in the folder, even those created by others. Only the person who actually created the folder will be listed as an owner.

Configure each account and account group. The Everyone group, as the name implies, covers everyone who connects to your PC, except for other users you specifically configure on this screen. Permissions are inherited, which means if you configure the permissions for a folder, those permissions will be active for all subfolders and their contents. However, you can set rather liberal permissions for, say, a drive, and then selectively restrict access for the more sensitive folders contained therein.

If you want to add new accounts or groups to let them access your shared folders, click the down arrow in the input box next to the Add button, choose from the list that appears, and click Add. Choose "Create a new user" and follow the prompts if you want to create a new user account for accessing your folders.

When you're done, click the Share button, and the folder will be shared with the permissions you specified. You'll see the notification shown in Figure 7-35, which shows you the shared name and location of the folder.

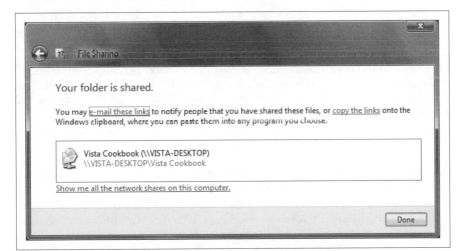

Figure 7-35. The notification showing you the folder's shared name and location

Note that if you've turned on password-protected sharing, only people who have a user account and password on your PC will be able to access the shared folder. This means that you need to make sure that your user accounts are in order before others on your network are able to access your shared resources. With password-protected sharing, every user who wants to access data on your computer remotely (that is, through the network connection) must have a user account on your computer. For example, if you're logged in as "Lenny," you'll be able to access resources only on other computers that also have an account called "Lenny" and that have the same password configured for that account. If you have two Windows Vista machines, one with a "Lenny" account and one with a "Lenny" and a "Karl" account, a user logged in as "Karl" will be able to access resources only on the second machine. Of course, if you turn off password-protected sharing, anyone on the network will be able to access data from your PC remotely.

 If you have a network that mixes Windows Vista and Windows XP PCs and/or Windows 2000 PCs, your Windows XP and 2000 PCs may have a difficult time accessing shared files and folders on your Vista PC. The problem may be caused because the Windows XP and Windows 2000 PCs are on a different workgroup than the Windows Vista PCs. Different versions of Windows use different default names for workgroups, so you may need to change them so that they match. In fact, if you've renamed your workgroups, you can run into the same problem even if you have a Vista-only network. To solve the problem in Windows XP, change the workgroup for each XP-based PC. In Windows XP, right-click My Computer, select Properties, and select the Computer Name tab. In the Workgroup area, click Change, and type in the name of the workgroup to which the Windows Vista PC belongs, then click OK. You should be able to gain access to folders and files on the Windows Vista PC now. To change the workgroup name in Windows Vista, see "Change Workgroup or Domain," earlier in this chapter.

Once a folder has been shared, and assuming the user accounts are set up properly, you can access the folder from another computer via the Network and Sharing Center, in particular from the Network Map (click "View full map" from the Network and Sharing Center), as shown in Figure 7-36.

Click any computer on the network, and you'll see all the folders and devices it shares, as you can see in Figure 7-37. This shows several shared folders on the computer called VISTA-DESKTOP. Note that several of the folders have small circular icons beneath them. That means that those are offline folders that synchronize between two PCs. For details, see "Sync Center," later in this chapter.

Note that you don't have to go through the Network and Sharing Center in order to connect to other shared folders on your network. You can also open Windows Explorer and click Network in the Folders area, and you'll see a list of all PCs connected to your network, as you can see in Figure 7-38. Open them to browse to their shared folders.

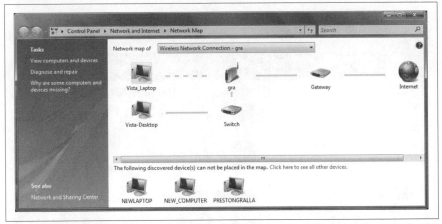

Figure 7-36. The Network Map, which shows you all the devices on your network and gives you access to them

Figure 7-37. Connecting to another PC on the network and seeing its shared folders and devices

Networking
and Mobility

Figure 7-38. Viewing other PCs on the network via Windows Explorer

Don't confuse file synchronization with sharing folders. When you synchronize (sync) a file, you keep an identical copy of it in several locations. When changes are made to one of those copies, they are automatically applied to the other one as well. When you share a file, other people on the same network can access that file, but the file is available only in that one location.

The full path to a network resource (called a UNC path, for Universal Naming Convention) looks a little different from a standard path. For example, the path to a shared folder called *Budget2007*, located on a computer called *Barney*, will look like this:

```
\\Barney\Budget2007
```

Sharing Printers

Printers are shared in much the same way that folders are. First, on the computer to which the printer is attached, go to the Network and Sharing Center and turn on Printer sharing. Then go to the PC on which you want to use that shared printer and choose Control Panel → Hardware and Sound → Add a printer, and follow the wizard for adding a printer. For details, see "Add Printer," in Chapter 9.

Mapping Drives

Don't like to use multiple clicks to connect to a shared folder or networked PCs? You can instead have folders or PCs show up in Windows Explorer as drives. They'll appear in the Network Locations area, as well as in the Folders area, as you can see in Figure 7-39. Connect to them as you would any other folder.

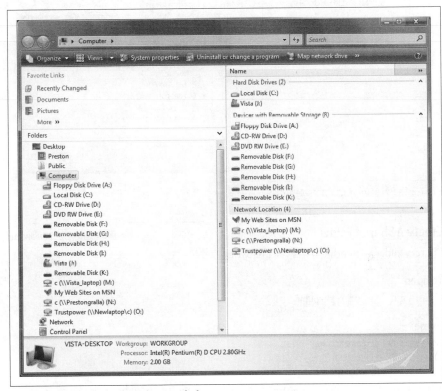

Figure 7-39. Several mapped network drives

To map a drive, click Map Network Drive on the Windows Explorer toolbar. The Map Network Drive dialog appears. Click Browse and then double-click the Network icon that appears. A list of the PCs on your network appears. (See Figure 7-40.) Choose the PC or folder on a PC that you want to map, click OK, and from the Map Network Drive dialog, select the drive letter. Click Finish. If you want to automatically reconnect to the network drives whenever you log on, keep the box checked next to "Reconnect at logon."

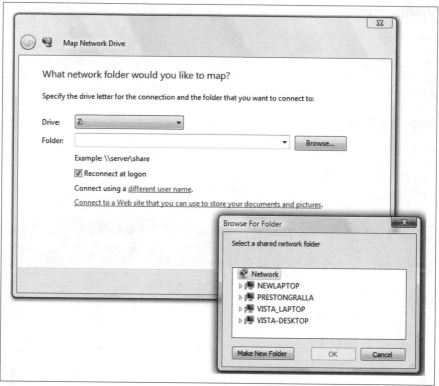

Figure 7-40. Mapping a network drive

Create A Shared Folder

\windows\system32\shrpubw.exe

Share a folder with other users on a network.

To open

Command Prompt → **shrpubw**

Usage

```
shrpubw [\foldername]
```

Description

The easiest way to begin sharing a folder or drive is to right-click on its icon in Explorer, select Share, and fill in the file-sharing form. But if you want to create a new folder and share it in a single step, a better bet is the Create A Shared Folder Wizard (Figure 7-41), which you can invoke with the shrpubw command.

The interface is extremely simple. Below the Computer field (which can't be changed once the program has started), there are three other fields:

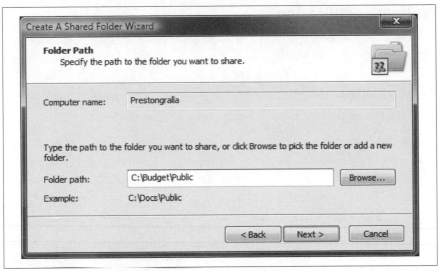

Figure 7-11. The Create A Shared Folder Wizard, which provides an alternate way to share any folder on your hard disk with other computers on your network

Folder to share

Enter the full path of the folder you want to begin sharing (e.g., `c:\my stuff\`) or click Browse to navigate the folder tree. You can also create a new folder here.

Share name

Enter the name under which the folder will be known on the network (e.g., `my stuff`).

Share description

The description is optional, but a quick note describing the purpose of the folder can be very helpful, especially in large organizations. For example: `Lenny's Stuff`.

When you're done, click Next to view the second and final page. Here, you can specify the security options for the share, such as which users will be able to read and/or modify the data in the shared folder. Click Finish when you're done.

Notes

- The wizard also allows you to create shared folders on other computers attached to the network, as long as you have administrative rights to them, by using the syntax `shrpubw /s computer_name` where *computer_name* is the name of the computer on which you want to share or create a folder.

See also

"User Accounts," in Chapter 10

Network Applications

Windows Vista includes several new network applications, notably those for collaboration. This section details each.

Network Projector

\Windows\System32\NetProj.exe

Give a presentation over a projector attached to your network.

To open

Start → All Programs → Accessories → Connect to a network projector

Windows Meeting Space → Options → Connect to a network projector

Command Prompt → **netproj**

Description

A network projector is a projection device, like a standard projector, with one important difference: it's connected to a network. You can use Windows Vista to give presentations over the projector. When you give a presentation, whatever is on your screen will be displayed by the projector.

When you run Network Projector, a wizard launches that helps you find a network projector. The wizard can automatically find all projectors attached to the network, or it will let you type in the address of a projector, if you happen to know it. You can use either Internet or network addresses—for example, *http://BigServer/projectors/fancyprojector* or *\\BigServer\projectors\fancyprojector*.

 In order to connect to a network projector in Windows Meeting Space, a meeting needs to be underway; people will have to be in your meeting. If you launch Windows Meeting Space and you don't invite people to a meeting, or no one attends the meeting, you won't be able to use Network Projector.

When you see a list of projectors, icons next to each projector indicate whether it is secured (requiring a password) or unsecured (allowing anyone to connect to it without a password). When you make the connection, you have the option of having the projector mirror exactly what is on your display, or using the projector as an extension of your display—in other words, you will be able to drag windows between the projector and your own desktop.

When you use the projector, the Network Presentation dialog box lets you pause and resume your presentation, as well as disconnect from the projector.

See also

"Windows Meeting Space"

People Near Me

\Windows\System32\p2phost.exe
\Windows\System32\collab.cpl

Identifies nearby network users with whom you can collaborate using tools such as Windows Meeting Space.

To open

Control Panel → [Network and Internet] → People Near Me

Command Prompt → **Control Collab.cpl**

Command Prompt → **p2phost** (logs in automatically)

Description

Windows Vista, for the first time, introduces the idea of "presence" to the world of Windows networking. Presence lets other network users know about your availability online so that they can work with you online, using Windows Meeting Space.

People Near Me allows other network users to know that you are online and available for Windows Meeting Space. In addition, if you want to start a Windows Meeting Space session, you'll first have to sign in to People Near Me.

The first time you sign in to People Near Me, you'll see the screen shown in Figure 7-42.

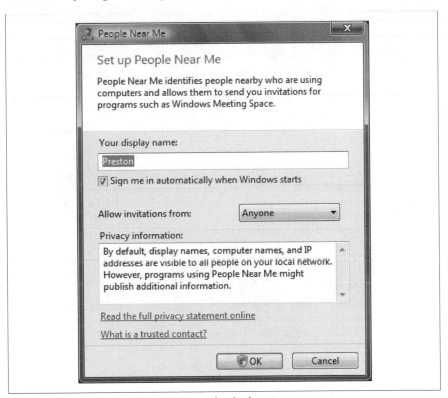

Figure 7-42. Signing in to People Near Me for the first time

Your display name—the name that other people see—is the same as your Windows Vista account name by default, although you can change that. Pay attention to the "Allow invitations from" drop-down box; this will determine who is allowed to see your availability. You can choose to have anyone see you, only Trusted Contacts, or no one. Although the default is to have anyone, for maximum privacy you should choose Trusted Contacts. That will cut down on the inevitable spam that presence brings. This is particularly important when you are on a public network, such as a hotspot.

On the other hand, if you are on a secure network, such as your own home network or a corporate network, choosing Anyone is a good bet. That will allow any business associates to see your presence, even if you haven't yet established a trusted relationship with them.

 A Trusted Contact is someone who has sent you his contact information vie email, or on a disk, USB flash drive, or other removable media. Trusted Contact information includes a certificate to confirm that contacts are who they say they are; that's why they are trusted.

When first signing in to People Near Me, you also have the option of signing in to it automatically whenever Windows starts.

After you sign in, you'll see a small People Near Me icon in the System Tray. You can sign out by right-clicking the icon and choosing Sign Out. Once you sign in, you're available to be contacted for Windows Meeting Space sessions.

 A Trusted Contact will be able to see a variety of information about you when you sign in to People Near Me, such as your username, display name, and IP address.

After you've set up People Near Me, you can change your options by right-clicking the icon in the System Tray and choosing Properties, or by going to Control Panel → [Network and Internet] → People Near Me → Change People Near Me settings. You'll find the following tabs:

Settings
> This lets you change the name that other people see. In addition, it lets you use a picture of yourself so that others will see your picture when collaborating with you. The picture, by default, is your user account picture. But you can choose to use any picture you want, including a photograph of you. Click Change Picture, and you'll be sent to the User Accounts → Change Your Picture screen. Choose a new picture as you normally would for changing a user account picture. (See Chapter 10 for details.) Keep in mind, though, that when you change your picture for People Near Me, you're also changing it for your user account; there's no way to have separate pictures for each.

> This tab also lets you change who can see you in People Near Me, and whether to sign in automatically when Windows starts. In addition, it lets you decide whether to display a notification when you've received an invitation.

Sign in
> This screen signs you in to or out of People Near Me.

Notes
- To find out whether a contact is trusted, select it in the Windows Contacts folder. If the person is a trusted contact, the words "Trusted Contact" will appear below the contact's display name.
- People Near Me works on any network, including public networks such as hotspots. For maximum security, don't use the feature on a public network, unless you specifically want to collaborate with others on that network. For example, if you and coworkers want to set up a Windows Meeting Space session at a public hotspot, you would use People Near Me.

- When you sign in to People Near Me, you won't actually be visible to others until they initiate a Windows Meeting Space session. The opposite holds true as well; you won't be able to see others until you initiate a Windows Meeting Space session.

- When you right-click the People Near Me icon and choose Properties, you'll notice there is one option for signing out and another option for exiting. When you sign out, you're still running People Near Me, but you've signed out of the service. To sign back in, right-click the icon again and choose Sign In. If you instead exit, you'll stop running People Near Me. To sign in, you'll have to go to Control Panel → [Network and Internet] → People Near Me.

See also

"Windows Meeting Space"

Remote Desktop Connection   \windows\system32\mstsc.exe

Access another computer remotely and use it as though you are sitting in front of it.

To open

Start → All Programs → Accessories → Remote Desktop Connection

Command Prompt → `mstsc`

Description

Remote Desktop Connection allows you to connect to another computer (or allows someone else to connect to your computer) and use it as though you were sitting in front of it. Much more than simply a remote command prompt (like SSH or Telnet), Remote Desktop Connection allows you to see a full Desktop, complete with icons and the Start menu, and even run programs on the remote computer (see Figure 7-43 for configuring a connection).

To configure a computer to accept incoming connections via Remote Desktop Connection, go to Control Panel ▸ [System and Maintenance] ▸ System ▸ Remote Settings → Remote Desktop, and turn on "Allow connections from computers running any version of Remote Desktop (less secure)" or "Allow connections only from computers running Remote Desktop with Network Level Authentication (more secure)." By default, all users with administrator privileges always have access, but you can enable access for other users as well by clicking Select Users.

Once a computer has been set up, you can connect to it by opening Remote Desktop Connection and typing that computer's name (if connected on a local network) or that computer's IP address (if connected to the Internet). Click Options to specify a username, password, and domain (only for Windows Server domains), and even to save your connection settings to a file so that you can connect more easily later.

To make a Remote Desktop Connection, you need a user account on the computer to which you're connecting. You can't use the user account on the computer from which you're connecting, unless that account has the same user ID and password as the computer to which you're connecting.

Figure 7-43. Connecting to another Windows Vista computer using a Remote Desktop Connection

The Display tab lets you choose the size of the windows in which you want to run a Remote Desktop connection, as well as the color quality. The Local Resources tab lets you choose whether sounds generated by the remote computer are played locally (which can slow the connection), whether certain keystroke combinations are interpreted locally or sent to the remote computer, and whether to automatically connect you to the remote computer's disks, printers, or serial ports. Choose the Programs tab to set up a program to start automatically when a connection has been established. The Experience tab allows you to turn on or off features that will affect performance; depending on your connection, for example, you may want to enable or disable the remote computer's background wallpaper or windows animations. The Advanced tab configures what should happen if your authentication on the remote PC fails (retry, do not connect, or receive a warning), and lets you configure the use of a Terminal Services Gateway (TSG) if you need to connect to users on a corporate network using a public Internet connection. Figure 7-44 shows a Remote Desktop Connection.

You can save the connection profile for a particular connection by clicking Save As. This will create a Remote Desktop Profile (.*rdp*) file, which you can double-click to start the connection without having to retype the connection information. Right-click any .*rdp* file and select Edit to return to the Properties dialog for the profile. (By default, the files are saved in your Documents folder.)

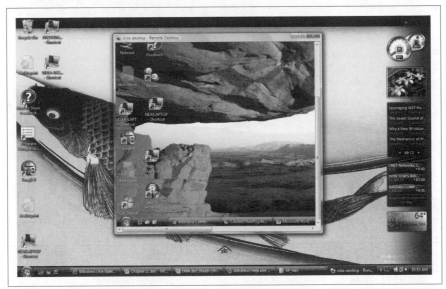

Figure 7-44. A Remote Desktop Connection with the remote desktop running inside a window

Notes

- Remote Desktop Connection differs from Remote Assistance, even though in both cases, a connection is being made to a remote PC. With a Remote Desktop Connection, you access the resources of another PC, but you don't perform troubleshooting tasks.

- When you make a Remote Desktop Connection, you're logging on to a remote PC using your account on it. If someone on the PC logs on, your remote connection will be terminated.

- To end the connection, close the window in which the connection is being made.

See also

"Remote Assistance," in Chapter 11

Windows Meeting Space   *\Program Files\Windows Collaboration\WinCollab.exe*

Share documents, programs, and your desktop with others.

To open

Start → All Programs → Windows Meeting Space

Command Prompt → `wincollab`

Description

Windows Meeting Space is Windows Vista's tool for allowing people to collaborate in online meetings by sharing presentations and files. When you first run Windows Meeting Space, a wizard configures the Windows Firewall to allow communications through. The wizard also enables file replication, because Windows Meeting Space allows people to share files across a network.

You can use Windows Meeting Space to create online meetings on a private network, such as at a business or home, but you can also use it in public spaces, such as hotspots.

Windows Meeting Space works closely in concert with People Near Me. (For details, see "People Near Me.") In fact, People Near Me's only real purpose is to make it easier for people to connect to Windows Meeting Space.

To start a meeting, click "Start a new meeting" and type in the meeting name and a password for the meeting (Figure 7-45). You have the option of allowing those logged in to People Near Me to see the meeting without you having to alert them, or to hide the meeting from them.

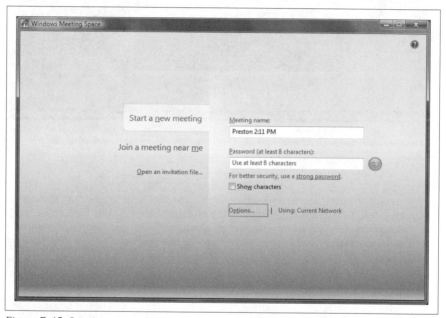

Figure 7-45. Starting a new meeting

Once you've created the meeting, click Invite People. A list of those who are signed in to People Near Me will appear. Check the boxes next to the names of people you want to invite, and click "Send invitations." If you want to invite people who are not on the list, click Invite Others, and you'll be able to send an invitation via email or create an invitation file that you can send via instant messaging, or use some other means of file transfer.

When you directly invite someone (in other words, not via email or instant messaging), she'll get a notification (Figure 7-46), including your name and the name of the meeting. She'll be told whether the invitation is from someone who is one of her trusted contacts. (Trusted contacts are contacts in Windows Contacts who have provided a certificate proving that they are who they say they are.) She can accept or decline the invitation. In order to join the meeting, she needs to have the meeting password. So you will have to find some way to provide her with a password for the meeting—for example, by phone, instant messaging, or email.

If you want to allow people to join your meeting without requiring a password, when you fill out the "Invite people" form, uncheck the box next to "Require participants to type the meeting password."

Figure 7-46. A Windows Meeting Space invitation

Once you've set up a meeting, you can do the following:

Share a program or your desktop

This lets you share either your entire desktop or a single program or file. "Sharing" means that other meeting participants can see exactly what you're doing on-screen. So, for example, you can give a PowerPoint presentation, display a spreadsheet or other document, and so on. As you move your cursor, type, minimize and maximize programs, and so on, the participants will see exactly what you do. If you share only a program, they will see only that program.

 When you share your desktop or a program with other participants, you may all revert to the Windows Basic interface because there may be incompatibilities between your desktop settings and theirs.

You spend the meeting not in the Windows Meeting Space window itself, but rather using your program or desktop as you would normally. You use the Windows Meeting Space window only when you want to take additional Windows Meeting Space options, such as creating handouts (covered in the next section).

A bar also appears at the top of your desktop or program, depending on which you are sharing. The bar includes buttons for stopping sharing, pausing sharing, giving control to another user so that he has control of the meeting, showing the Windows Meeting Space window, and connecting to a network projector. A network projector is a specialized projector connected to your network that will allow you to make presentations over the network using Windows Meeting Space. In that way, you can connect to a distant physical projector to make a presentation.

The Windows Meeting Space window itself doesn't change when you're sharing your desktop, but if you'd like, you can see what others are seeing as you share your desktop or programs. Be aware, though, that this can be a bit like looking in a fun house mirror, because you'll see your desktop mirrored multiple times—first is your desktop itself, then inside that is the Windows Meeting Space window in which you see your desktop mirrored on someone else's PC, and in that desktop there is a Windows Meeting Space window with a mirror of the desktop, and so on. Figure 7-47 is an example.

Figure 7-47. Lost in the funhouse

Add a handout

This lets you create a "handout" that appears on everyone's screen. You don't actually create a new handout. Instead, you send a file of any type to everyone—a Word document, an Excel spreadsheet, a PowerPoint file, a graphics file, and so on—so that everyone can view it on her screen. Everyone can then mark up the handout. That markup, however, does not alter the handout itself; the original stays untouched. Only one person at a time can mark up and change the document, however. In order for a person to mark up the document, the current owner of the meeting has to turn ownership over to that person. Anyone in the meeting can add handouts at any time, though; the owner does not need to give permission. Indicated underneath each handout is the name of the person who added it. You can list multiple handouts for each meeting, as you can see in Figure 7-48.

Figure 7-48. Each handout showing who added it to the meeting

Send a note

Windows Meeting Space includes a very rudimentary instant messaging component. Double-click the person to whom you want to send a note, and a small
window pops up, shown in Figure 7-49. Type in a message, or if you prefer, click
the Ink button, and you can instead draw something and send the note.

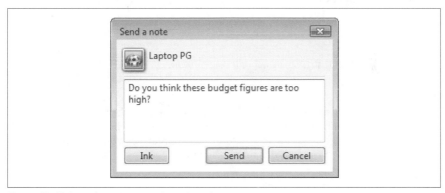

Figure 7-49. Windows Meeting Space's rudimentary instant messaging component

The instant messaging component is about as bare-bones a feature as you can
imagine. Send the note, and it vanishes from your screen so that when someone
sends you a reply, you won't see the note that you sent. As a result, there's no
conversation thread to follow.

Along the top of the Windows Meeting Space window is a toolbar that lets you leave
the meeting, exit the Windows Meeting Space program, save the handouts from the
meeting, invite others to the meeting, share applications, and add handouts.

Notes

- When you're in a meeting, if someone else has control and you would like to be in control, click the button on the top right of the Windows Meeting Space Toolbar (it will list who is currently in control of the meeting) and select Request Control.

- When you send an invitation to someone via email, he'll have to open the attachment, which will launch Windows Meeting Space. He'll still need to know the meeting password. The same holds true for when you send an invitation file via instant messaging or some other means. Invitation files and attachments are in the *.wcinv* format.

- When you use Windows Meeting Space, you may notice some flickering in your applications or desktop, or when starting up or exiting the program.

- When you exit a meeting, you can save all the handouts, even if other people created them.

See also

"People Near Me" and "Network Projector"

Mobile Computing

Windows Vista includes numerous features for mobile computing, as well as for synchronizing files between mobile PCs and a network or other computers. For wireless topics related to mobile computing, see the "Wired and Wireless Connections, Management, and Configuration" section, earlier in this chapter.

Mobile PC Control Panel

Links to mobility settings.

To open

Control Panel → Mobile PC

Description

The Mobile PC Control Panel (Figure 7-50) provides a central place for all of your mobile settings. As with many other Control Panels, it primarily links to other Control Panel applets, although links directly below those applets let you accomplish some tasks without first going through the individual applets.

See also

"Windows Mobility Center," "Power Options," "Tablet PC," "Pen and Input Devices," and "Sync Center"

Offline Files

Work with files stored on a network when you're not connected to it.

To open

Control Panel → [Network and Internet] → Offline Files

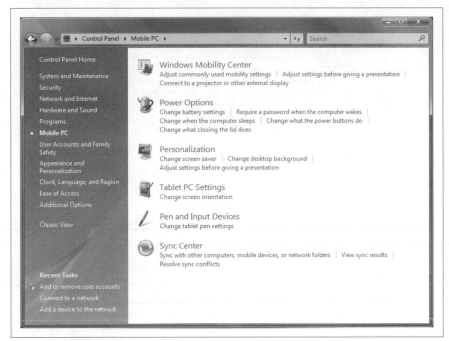

Figure 7-50. The Mobile PC Control Panel, which provides a central location for all of your mobile settings

Description

The Offline Files dialog (Figure 7-51) lets you turn on (and off) and configure Windows Vista's Offline Files feature, which allows you to work with files stored on a network (either server-based or peer-to-peer), when you're not actually connected to the network. Windows XP also had the capability to work with offline files, but it was so confusing to use and configure that people rarely used it. In Windows Vista, the Offline Files dialog and the Sync Center make the use of offline files far easier. If you use a laptop to connect to your network and would like the ability to work with those files when you're not connected, it's an extremely useful feature.

Offline files seems like a bit of magic—after all, how can you work with network files when you're not on a network? But the term is somewhat misleading. When files are made available offline, they are actually copied onto your PC and kept synchronized with network files while you're attached to the network. So when those files are changed on the network, they're also changed on your PC. When you disconnect from the network, those offline files are available locally on your PC, where you can work on them. When you connect with the network, your local offline files are synchronized with the network files. Any changes you make (including deleting and adding files) will be made back to the network files; any changes on the network files will be made back to your PC (including deleting and adding files). If a file has been changed in both places, you'll be prompted to decide which file should be used. (For more information about how synchronization works, see "Sync Center," later in this chapter.)

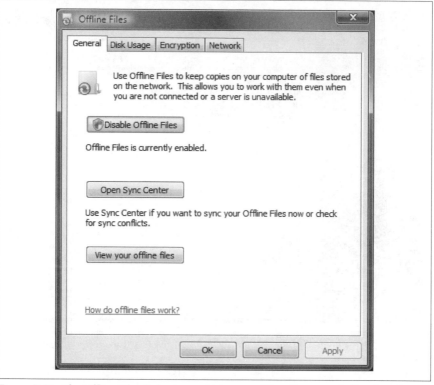

Figure 7-51. The Offline Files dialog box, which turns offline files on and off and configures offline file usage

To make files available offline, first click Enable Offline Files on the General tab of the Offline Files dialog box, then right-click the folders and files you want to make available offline and select Always Available Offline. They'll be synchronized to your local PC. (For more details, see "Sync Center.")

The Offline Files dialog has these tabs for customizing the way Offline Files works:

General

This lets you turn on and off offline files, open the Sync Center, and view your offline files. When you click the "View your offline files" button, Windows Explorer will display any mapped network drives, servers, computers, and personal folders that have offline files in them. Open each to view your offline files.

Disk usage

Shows you how much disk space offline files take up on your PC (Figure 7-52). To ensure that they don't take up too much space, Windows Vista puts a limit on the amount of space devoted to offline files. You can change that limit from this tab.

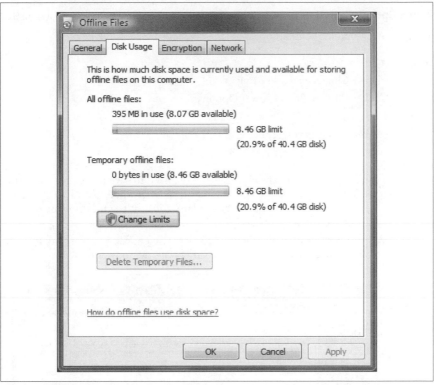

Figure 7-52. Setting the maximum amount of space to use for offline files

Encryption
Lets you encrypt (or unencrypt) your offline files. If they contain sensitive information, consider encrypting them. This encryption works separately from Windows Vista's normal NTFS encryption. (For details, see the "Encryption" section in Chapter 8.)

Network
A slow network connection can cause problems with offline files, because synchronization may fail or be exceedingly slow. This tab lets you automatically work offline if you are on a slow network connection (the default), or work online even if the connection is slow. You can also tell Windows Vista how frequently to check whether the connection is slow; that way, it can reconnect you after a certain amount of time if the network connection is speedier.

Notes
- A folder needs to be shared before files in it can be turned into offline files. For details, see "Sharing Resources and Files," earlier in this chapter.

See also
"Sync Center" and "Sharing Resources and Files"

Power Options

\windows\system\powercfg.cpl

Select a power plan for your laptop.

To open

Control Panel → Change battery settings

Control Panel → [Mobile PC] → Power Options

Right-click the battery icon → Power Options

Command Prompt → **powercfg.cpl**

Description

When you use a laptop, you're always balancing the need to save power against laptop performance. You want to use the computer as long as possible on a battery charge (for example, if you're on a cross-country airplane trip), but you also want to be as productive as possible when using it.

The Power Options Control Panel (Figure 7-53) lets you choose a power plan for your laptop, customize power plans, and change a variety of other power options.

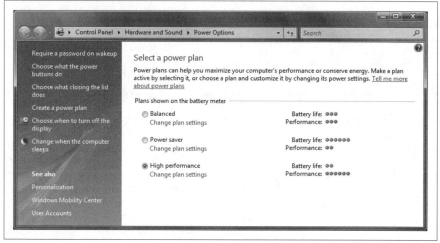

Figure 7-53. The Power Options window, which lets you configure the various power-saving features of your computer

To understand power plans, you need to understand the two power-saving modes available in Windows Vista: sleep and hibernation. They are similar enough so that they may cause confusion. In sleep mode, all your work and the state of your computer are saved to memory and to your hard disk. Your computer is put into a power-saving state that requires practically no power. When you wake your computer from sleep, its state and all your programs and files will be back on-screen in seconds, and you can continue working.

In hibernation mode, your work is saved to memory and to your hard disk, and Windows Vista then turns off the display, hard disk, and computer. When you restart, Windows will restore your desktop and work exactly as you left it.

So what's the difference between the two? In sleep mode, your PC never actually shuts down, so it comes back to life within seconds rather than having to go through the entire startup procedure. It does use a very small amount of power, though. In hibernation mode, your PC actually shuts down, so you have to go through a shortened version of the usual Windows startup procedure when you restart. Hibernation uses no power.

With that as a background, you'll be better able to understand power plans. Each power plan has two settings, one for when the laptop is plugged in and one for when it's on battery power. A power plan is a constellation of settings governing how the laptop handles when to turn off the hard disk, when to turn off the display, when to sleep, and so on. What's not obvious about each power plan, though, is that settings also determine how much of the processor power to use. So the Power Saver plan, for example, uses only a percentage of the processor's capabilities, the High Performance plan uses all of the processor's capabilities, and the Balanced plan falls between the two.

There are three preset power plans from which you can choose:

Balanced
> This plan offers a compromise between performance and battery life. When the laptop is on a battery, it turns off the display after 5 minutes of nonuse and puts the computer to sleep after 15 minutes of nonuse. When the laptop is plugged in or on a desktop PC, it turns off the display after 20 minutes of nonuse and puts the computer to sleep after 1 hour of nonuse.

Power Saver
> This plan saves the maximum amount of power at the expense of performance. When the laptop is on a battery, it turns off the display after 3 minutes of nonuse and puts the computer to sleep after 15 minutes of nonuse. When the laptop is plugged in or on a desktop PC, it turns off the display after 20 minutes of nonuse and puts the computer to sleep after 1 hour of nonuse.

High Performance
> This plan always delivers the highest possible performance at the expense of battery life. When the laptop is on a battery, it turns off the display after 20 minutes of nonuse and puts the computer to sleep after 1 hour of nonuse. When the laptop is plugged in or on a desktop PC, it turns off the display after 20 minutes of nonuse and never puts the computer to sleep.

To see the current state of your battery, look at its icon in the System Tray. Hover your mouse over it, and you'll see how much power you have left, as well as your current power plan. Click the icon, and a small window pops up that lets you choose a different power plan from the one you're currently using. If you're running a desktop PC, you won't see the battery icon in the notification area, but you can still check your plan by going to Control Panel → Hardware and Sound → Power Options.

Customizing and creating power plans

There are several ways you can customize existing power plans and create new ones. To customize an existing plan, click "Change plan settings" beneath the plan you want to customize, and the Edit Plan Settings screen appears (Figure 7-54). You'll be able to customize only the very basics of the plan—when to turn off the display and when to put the computer to sleep. You can, however, customize far more about each plan than what you see on the screen. Click "Change advanced power settings," and you can customize far more about the plan, including how much processor power to use for it, the amount of power to use for PCI cards and wireless adapters, how to handle sleep, and so on.

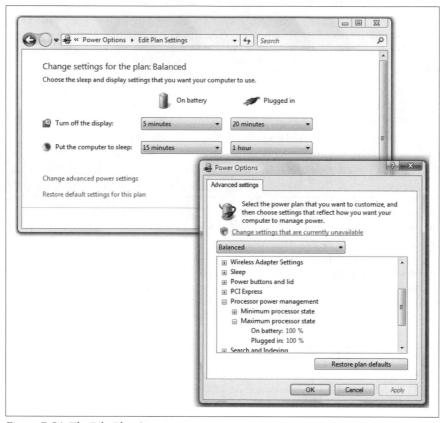

Figure 7-54. The Edit Plan Settings screen

You can also create your own power plan from scratch. On the left side of the Power Options Control Panel, click "Create a power plan" and follow the wizard. Note that the wizard will create only the most basic plan—when to turn off the display and when to put the computer to sleep. But once you've created the plan, it will show up on the Power Options Control Panel, and you can customize it using advanced options, as you can any other power plan.

You can also apply global changes to all of your power plans. For example, let's say that when you close the lid of your laptop, you want it to go into hibernation. You can make that change apply globally to all of your power plans. You can make several of these kinds of global changes to your power plan; links to them are on the left side of the Power Options Control Panel. You can make global changes to the following using those links:

- Require a password on wake-up.
- Choose what the power buttons do.
- Choose what closing the lid does.

 The preceding three links bring you to the same dialog.

- Choose when to turn off the display.
- Change when the computer sleeps.

Notes

- If you have trouble with sleep and hibernation modes—for example, if your laptop won't awake from them—it may be because your PC's video card doesn't support sleep or hibernation. Update the drivers, and check the manufacturer's web site for details.
- Sometimes sleep or hibernation mode causes problems with laptops because those power-saving modes are turned off in the laptop's BIOS. Check your system's documentation for how to access the BIOS setup, and then use that setup to enable power-saving modes.

See also

"Windows Mobility Center"

Presentation Settings   *\Windows\System32\PresentationSettings.exe*

Customize settings for giving a public presentation when using a laptop.

To open

Control Panel ▸ Mobile PC → Adjust settings before giving a presentation

Command Prompt → **presentationsettings**

Description

If you've ever had your screen go black or a screensaver start up in the middle of a presentation, you'll appreciate this dialog box (Figure 7-55). It lets you turn off the screensaver, set the volume control, and show and customize a specific background. You can also browse for any displays to which you're currently connected and set any of them as the default display. Customize your settings, and then before you give a presentation, come back to this screen and turn the settings on; when the presentation is done, return again and turn them off.

See also

"Network Projector"

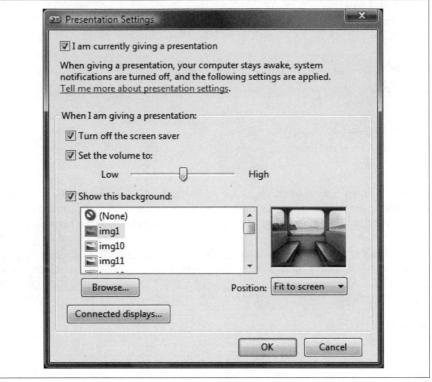

Figure 7-55. Configuring your PC for giving mobile presentations

Sync Center   *\windows\system32\mobsync.exe*

Synchronize files and folders with devices and network folders.

To open
Control Panel → [Mobile PC] → Sync Center

Control Panel → [Network and Internet] → Sync Center

Command → **mobsync**

Description
If you have multimedia devices such as MP3 players and iPods, have portable storage devices such as USB flash drives, or work on files on multiple PCs, you know how hard it is to keep all your files in sync on those devices and computers. The Sync Center (Figure 7-56) is Windows Vista's answer. It's the central location for syncing all your devices and network folders.

When devices and network folders are synced, Windows Vista copies and updates files and folders in both locations. So, for example, if you've made changes to files on both your PC and the device, Windows Vista will perform actions on both of them so that they have identical files and folders.

You can also use the Sync Center for synchronizing files across a network, via offline files. With offline files, you can get access to files on a shared network folder, even if

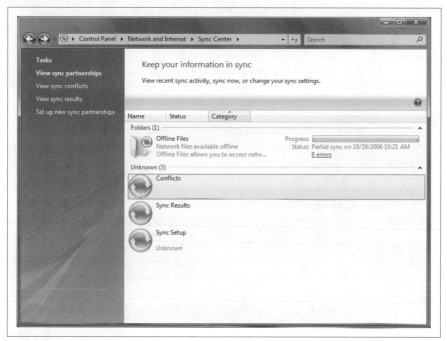

Figure 7-56. The Sync Center, which shows all of your sync partnerships and displays the progress of any current sync activity

your laptop is not currently connected to the network. Offline files allow you to open files, work on them when you're disconnected, and then update them at a later time when the connection has been reestablished.

When you make a shared network folder available offline, you actually save those files to your own PC. When you make changes to them on your own PC or the shared network folders, they are kept in sync. Naturally, you could just save remote files on your own hard disk manually, edit them, and then transfer them manually to their original locations, replacing older versions where necessary. However, Windows Vista's support for offline files is much more convenient.

Here are the rules that Windows Vista follows when you sync files between a PC and a device, or among PCs:

- If the files are different, the Sync Center decides which version of each file to keep and then copies that version of the file to the other location and overwrites the version there. Unless you have set up the sync partnership differently, it keeps the most recent version and overwrites the older version.

- If a file has changed in both locations, the Sync Center flags it as a sync conflict and then asks you which version to keep.

- If the files are identical in both locations, the Sync Center takes no action.

- If you have added a new file to one location but not to the other, the Sync Center will copy the file to the other location.

- If you have deleted a file from one location but not from the other, the Sync Center will delete the file from the other location.

The offline folders feature is not available in Windows Vista Home Basic and Windows Vista Home Premium.

When you open the Sync Center it will display any sync partnerships you've set up and report on the most recent activity of each. The Sync Center lets you accomplish these tasks:

View sync partnerships

This is the main screen, which displays all the sync partnerships, including recent activity.

View sync conflicts

If files cannot be synced because differences can't be reconciled among the different versions stored on different devices or shared folders, the conflicts will be listed here, along with any details about the conflicts. For example, if you've changed a document on your PC since the last sync, and a different change was made to the same document on an offline folder or mobile device, that will be listed as a conflict. Select the conflict, click Resolve, and the Resolve Conflict dialog box opens (Figure 7-57), which lets you determine which version of the file to keep, or whether to keep both, under different file names.

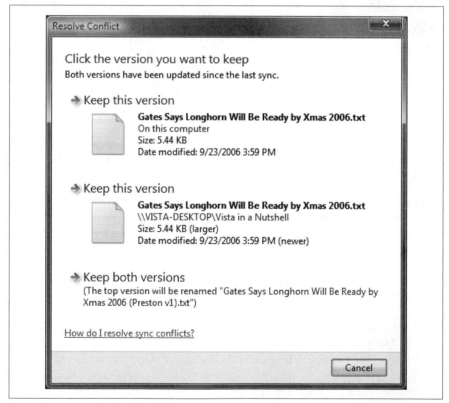

Figure 7-57. Resolving a sync conflict

View sync results

This displays the history of your syncs. In addition to showing you successful syncs, as shown in Figure 7-58, errors and warnings will be displayed here.

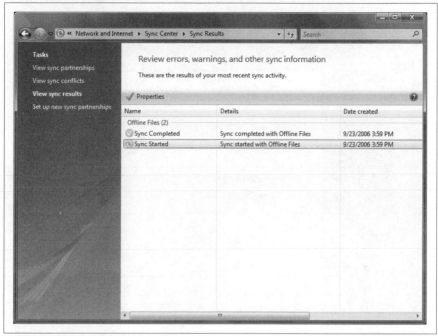

Figure 7-58. Reviewing sync history

Set up new sync partnerships

This screen shows any devices available for synchronizing. Before you can perform a sync, you first need to set up a partnership from this screen. Click the device or folders for which you want to set up a sync partnership, and then click "Set up" and follow the directions.

Syncing portable music players

The Sync Center has some confusing aspects to it, notably the way it handles (or more precisely, doesn't handle) syncing with portable music players and USB flash drives. If you have a USB flash drive or portable music player such as an iPod or MP3 player, it will show up as a device in the "Set up new sync partnership" screen. But you can't actually set up a sync partnership with that device in the Sync Center or perform a sync to it in the Sync Center. Instead, you have to do it using Windows Media Player, which includes syncing capabilities. (For details, see "Windows Media Player," in Chapter 12.) In addition, if you go to the View sync results screen, you won't see the histories of your syncs with those devices.

Working with offline files

The Sync Center is best suited for handling syncing offline files. The feature works only with shared network folders—and it works only with folders that you have specifically turned into offline folders. To do that, right-click a folder or file that you want to be available offline, and select Always Available Offline.

When you do that, there's no need to set up a sync partnership; making folders available offline automatically creates that partnership. From the front page of the Sync Center ("View sync partnerships"), you'll see an entry for "Offline files" (Figure 7-59). Double-click it and you'll see a list of all of your offline folders, along with information about the last time each folder was synchronized.

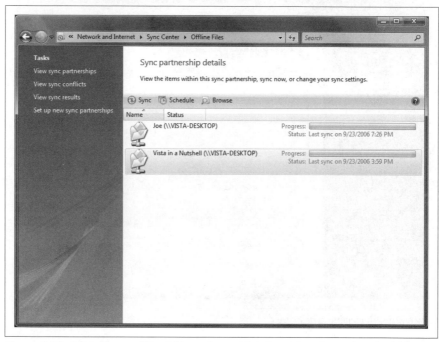

Figure 7-59. A list of your offline folders, along with information about when the folders were last synchronized

To sync any folder, highlight it and select Sync. You can also create a schedule for synchronizing files, based not only on time but also on system events. Highlight the folder for which you want a schedule, and click Schedule. From the wizard that appears, select the folder or folders for which you want to create a schedule. Click Next. At this point, the wizard branches; you can choose to sync either at a scheduled time or based on an event or an action—when you log on, when your computer is idle for a specified amount of time, when you lock or unlock Windows, or many other events or actions.

You can also work with files in your offline folders. Open any folder by double-clicking it, and you'll connect to the folder on the remote PC. As you can see in Figure 7-60, small icons show you that the files are part of a sync partnership.

At this point, you're actually connected to the folder on the remote PC. So if you open any of those files, you're opening them there, not on your own PC. If you weren't connected to the remote PC, though, you would be able to work with the files on your own PC because they would be available as offline files. After you work on them offline, when you connect back to the network you can sync them. You can also

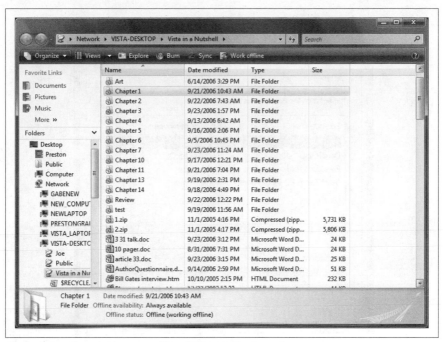

Figure 7-60. Connecting to an offline folder via the Sync Center

manually disconnect from the remote PC so that you can work with the files on your own PC. To work on offline files on your own PC, even if you're connected to the network, click Work Offline in the folder's toolbar. To reconnect, click Work Online.

Notes

- You can also sync offline files without having to go through the Sync Center. Select the offline file or folder you want to sync, and select Sync.

See also
"Offline Files"

Pen and Input Devices

\windows\system32\TabletPC.cpl

Configure pens and similar input devices.

To open
Control Panel → Mobile PC → Pen and Input Devices

Command Prompt → `tabletpc.cpl`

Description
The Pen and Input Devices dialog (Figure 7-61) customizes your pen or similar input device.

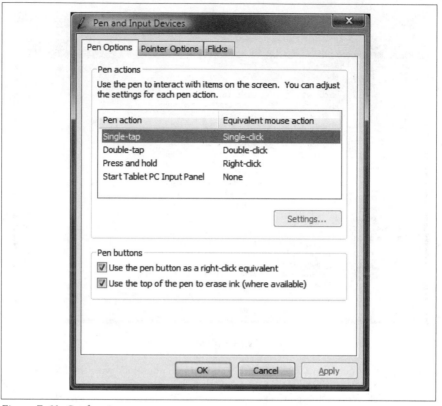

Figure 7-61. Configuring a pen

It includes these tabs:

Pen Options

> Sets how the pen interacts with the screen—for example, what actions a single tap, a double tap, a press and hold, and so on, should perform. It also allows you to configure a pen button as a right-click equivalent, and to use the top of the pen to erase "ink."

Pointer Options

> Sets the visual feedback received for single taps, double taps, pressing the pen button, and pressing and then tapping the pen button. Also can show the pen cursor instead of the mouse cursor when the pen is being used.

Flicks

> Sets pen motions to be recognized as "flicks" for navigation and editing, and sets the sensitivity of the flicks.

See also

"Tablet PC"

Tablet PC

Change settings for your Tablet PC.

To open

Control Panel → Mobile PC → Tablet PC Settings

Description

Tablet PC Settings (Figure 7-62) customizes Tablet PCs for use, including turning on automatic learning for handwriting recognition, changing the orientation of the tablet, and more.

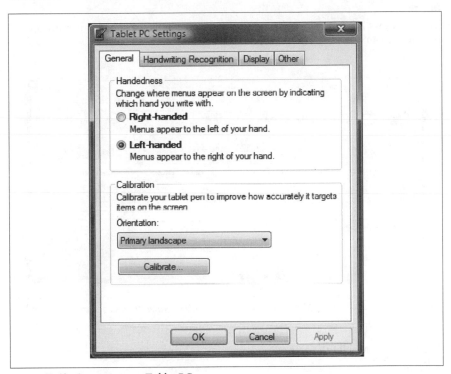

Figure 7-62. Customizing a Tablet PC

It includes these tabs:

General
> Configures the tablet for someone who is right-handed or left-handed, sets the tablet orientation, and calibrates the pen.

Handwriting Recognition
> Lets you turn on (or off) automatic learning, in which handwriting recognition learns from you, for more accurate recognition.

Display
> Sets your orientation and lets you change the order in which your screen rotates.

Other
> This tab may be used by different Tablet PC manufacturers for their own purposes. It also links to the Pen and Input Devices dialog for configuring the pen.

See also

"Pen and Input Devices"

Windows Mobility Center

Control commonly used mobility settings.

To open

Control Panel → Mobile PC → Windows Mobility Center

Description

The Windows Mobility Center Panel (Figure 7-63) offers quick access to turn on and off and customize a variety of commonly used mobility settings.

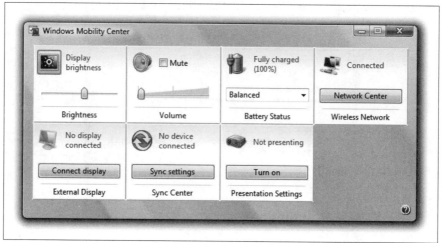

Figure 7-63. The Windows Mobility Center, which offers quick access to commonly used mobility-related settings

The Windows Mobility Center offers control over these settings:

Brightness
Lets you adjust the brightness of your display.

Volume
Lets you turn the volume up or down, or mute it.

Battery Status
Shows the state of your battery charge and lets you choose from a different power plan (see "Power Options," earlier in this chapter, for details about power plans).

Wireless Network
Takes you to the Network Center.

External Display
Lets you connect to or disconnect from an external display—for example, when giving a presentation or when you want to use another display with your laptop.

Sync Center
> Links to the Sync Center for syncing with devices, viewing sync activity, or changing your sync settings. (See "Sync Center," earlier in this chapter, for more details.)

Presentation Settings
> Lets you turn presentation settings on and off. (See "Presentation Settings," earlier in this chapter, for more details.)

See also

"Windows Mobility Center," "Power Options," "Sync Center," and "Presentation Settings"

Networking and Internet Command-Line Tools

For many networking and troubleshooting tasks, your best bet is to use command-line tools. This section covers the networking command-line tools built into Vista.

Connection Manager Profile Installer   *\windows\system32\cmstp.exe*

An automated connection profile installation utility.

To open

Command Prompt → **cmstp**

Description

You use the Connection Manager Profile Installer to automate the installation (or removal) of connection profiles. For example, an ISP or network administrator may build an *.inf* file containing all the necessary information to connect to another computer or service, and then use the Connection Manager Profile Installer to integrate the information into a particular computer. Type **cmstp** at any prompt for information on its usage.

Finger   *\windows\system32\finger.exe*

Display information about a user account.

To open

Command Prompt → **finger**

Usage

```
finger [-l] [user][@host]
```

Description

The Finger client uses a standard protocol to retrieve publicly available information from any networked computer that is running the Finger daemon. Let's say you want to find out about the username "Woodrow" on your own system; you would simply type:

```
finger woodrow
```

Finger accepts the following options:

user

> The username you want to query. Omit to list all the users currently logged in on the specified host.

@host

> The target machine containing the user account(s) you want to query. Omit to query the local machine (localhost).

-l

> Displays information in a long list format.

The Finger protocol has been around for a long time, and all versions of Windows NT, Windows 2000, Windows XP, Windows Vista, Unix, Solaris, and other platforms support it. The output from a Finger request varies widely (if you get a response at all); it depends on the operating system running on the specified host and the specific settings imposed by that machine's administrator.

Finger, when it works, commonly retrieves a report that looks something like this:

```
Login: woodrow Name: Gordie Howe
Directory: /usr/local/home/woodrow Shell: /bin/csh
Never logged in.
New mail received Mon Oct 1 23:35 2001 (PDT)
 Unread since Wed Nov 20 11:54 1996 (PDT)
No Plan.
```

Although most of the information included in this simple report is self-evident, the last line mentions a *plan*. The plan is a text file to be shown when one's account is fingered. It might contain contact information, office hours, personal statistics, or anything else the user wants.

Notes

- The Finger daemon is the service responsible for responding to finger requests. This service is disabled by default, but you can enable or otherwise configure it using the services component of the Microsoft Management Console. Note that enabling the service on your computer may pose a security hazard, allowing outsiders to gain some information about one or more users on your system.

- As more users and administrators become security-savvy, you'll find fewer occasions when a Finger request actually gets a response. Typically, you'll receive a "connection refused" message.

FTP

\windows\system32\ftp.exe

File Transfer Protocol; transfer files between two computers, typically across the Internet.

To open

Command Prompt → **ftp**

Usage

```
ftp url
ftp [-v] [-d] [-i] [-n] [-g] [-s:filename] [-a] [-A] [-w:size] [host]
```

Description

You use FTP to transfer files to and from a remote computer, typically on the Internet. Like many Internet applications, FTP is a client application that requires a corresponding FTP server to work. When you start FTP, you are connecting to a remote host and then issuing commands to instruct the host to send or receive files, display directory listings, and so on.

Although each FTP session requires a username and password, there's a very common workaround that allows anonymous connections. Typically, one enters **anonymous** or **ftp** as the username and an email address (or, frankly, any bogus text ending in @) as the password to log in (assuming anonymous access is allowed on the server at all).

Once you've logged in, you issue commands by typing in the prompt; the complete list of FTP commands is documented later in this section. The exception is when FTP is run in noninteractive mode using the *url* option.

Command-line parameters for FTP are as follows:

url
> A web-style address (URL) to a specific file located on an anonymous FTP server, which looks something like this:
>
>   ftp://example.com/path/file
>
> If you specify a complete URL, FTP will download the file and then quit automatically, rather than going into interactive mode.

host
> Specify the hostname or IP address of the remote host (server) to connect to. If you omit it, you can enter it once FTP has started by using the open command. For example:
>
>   ftp ftp.microsoft.com
>
> Note that the common ftp. prefix, although not mandatory with FTP, is merely a hostname that signifies a specific machine, often solely devoted to serving FTP requests.

-v
> Suppress the display of remote server responses to commands—useful if you're running FTP from a script.

-n
> Suppress auto-login upon initial connection. To connect, you'll need to use the user command once FTP is running.

-i
> Turn off interactive prompting during multiple file transfers when using the mget and mput FTP commands.

-d
> Enable debugging—displaying all FTP commands passed between the client and server (for troubleshooting purposes).

-g
> Disable filename globbing, which permits the use of wildcard characters in local file- and pathnames. (See the FTP glob command in the list that follows.)

-s:*filename*
> Specify an FTP script, a plain-text file containing sequential FTP commands, one per line. The commands are issued as though they were typed at the keyboard.

-a

Use any local interface when establishing a connection.

-A

Log in as anonymous (note the capital A). This is the same as logging in normally and manually typing in anonymous as the username and an email address as the password.

-w:*size*

Override the default transfer buffer size of 4,096. Change only if you encounter performance problems.

Note that you can start FTP without any command-line parameters to enter interactive mode, but you won't be able to use most of the commands until you log in with the open command (see the following list).

FTP commands

The following list shows the commands available once FTP is running. Most require that a connection has been established and not all will work with every FTP server. The most important commands to know are put, get, mput, mget, cd, lcd, dir, and bye. If you are transferring binary files across platforms (from a Unix host to a Windows-based client, for example), be sure to use the binary command first, or the files may be corrupted in transit.

! [*command*]

Run the specified command (e.g., cd) on the local computer, as though you temporarily jumped out of FTP, ran a command, and then jumped back in—all without disconnecting. Naturally, you could just open a second Command Prompt window, but some contextual commands, such as cd (see Chapter 14), require the use of the ! command to be effective. Type ! by itself to start a mini-Command Prompt session in which you can type multiple commands; type **EXIT** to return to the active FTP session.

? [*command*]

Same as help.

append

Append a local file to a file on the remote computer.

ascii

Set the file transfer type to ASCII (plain text), the default (except in noninteractive mode). ASCII mode is useful if you're transferring plain-text files between Unix and Windows systems, as line-ending translation must be performed on these types of files. Note that this translation will almost always corrupt binary files such as ZIP archives or Word documents, so you should use the binary command if you're not transferring ASCII files.

bell

Turn on or off the beep after each file transfer command is completed. By default, the bell is off.

binary

Set the file transfer type to binary, a crucial step for transferring nontext files (such as *.zip*, *.gif*, and *.doc*) between Unix and Windows-based machines. Although it's not necessary if the server is also a Windows system, it's a good idea to get into the habit of typing **binary** (or simply **bin**) every time you use FTP. Note that binary is the default in noninteractive mode, when used with the *url* command-line parameter. See also "ascii," earlier in this list.

bye

End the FTP session and, if necessary, disconnect from the remote computer. The standard Command Prompt exit command won't work here, but quit will.

cd [*directory*]

Change the working directory on the remote computer (to cd on the local machine, use ! cd or lcd).

close

Disconnect from the remote computer without exiting FTP. Use open to connect to a different FTP server or bye to exit FTP.

debug

Toggle debugging. When debugging is on, each internal command sent to the remote computer is displayed, preceded by the string --->. By default, debugging is off.

delete *remote_file*

Delete a file on the remote computer. You can delete only a single file at a time with delete (no wildcards are allowed); use mdelete to delete multiple files at once.

dir

Display a list of the contents of the working directory on the remote computer, with details. Use ls for a simple listing. Occasionally, directory listings for anonymous users may be disabled, in which case dir will not work; if you want to download, you'll need to know the particular filename(s) beforehand.

disconnect

Same as close.

get *remote_file* [*local_file*]

Transfer *remote_file* from the server to the local machine. If *local_file* is not specified, the local file will be given the same name as the original. The file will be placed in the local working directory; to choose a different destination, use lcd. You can download only a single file at a time with get (no wildcards are allowed); use mget to transfer multiple files at once. If transferring binary (nontext) files, use the binary command first.

glob

Toggle filename globbing. Globbing permits use of wildcard characters in local file- or pathnames. By default, globbing is on. You also can disable globbing with the -g command-line parameter.

hash

Turn on or off FTP's crude progress bar for file transfers. A hash mark (#) character is displayed for each 2 KB of data transferred, so large files will have longer progress bars than small files. By default, hash mark printing is off.

help [*command*]

Display all the available commands. Include *command* to get help with a single command (e.g., help get). Same as ?.

lcd [*directory*]

Change the working directory on the local computer. Enter a full path as *directory* (e.g., *c:\downloads*) to effectively instruct FTP to place downloaded files there. Omit *directory* to simply display the current working directory. By default, the working directory is in use when FTP is started; if FTP is opened from Start → Run, the working directory is *c:\Users\username*.

literal *command_line*

Send so-called "arbitrary" commands to the remote FTP server (such as retr, stor, pasv, and port). A single FTP reply code is expected in return. Typical use of FTP does not involve using literal, but it can provide access to some advanced functions; among the more interesting is the ability to transfer files between two remote computers without having to first transfer them to the local machine.

ls

Display an abbreviated list of a remote directory's files and subdirectories. This is useful when a directory contains a lot of files. Type **ls -l** (or use **dir**) to show the "long" listing, including file details. Occasionally, you can disable directory listings for anonymous users, in which case ls will not work; if you want to download, you'll need to know the particular filename(s) beforehand.

mdelete [*files*]

Delete multiple files on remote computers. Unlike with delete, you can use wildcards (e.g., *.txt for all *.txt* files).

mdir *remote_files local_file*

Store a listing of the remote working directory's contents (with details) into a file; both parameters are required. You use the *remote_files* parameter to modify the listing, either by specifying a wildcard (use * to list all files) or by specifying the name of another directory. *local_file* is the target filename in which the directory listing is stored.

mget *remote_files*

Transfer one or more remote files to the local computer. Unlike with get, you can use wildcards (e.g., *.txt for all *.txt* files). You will be asked to confirm each transfer unless you turn off prompting with the prompt command. Local files will be given the same names as their remote counterparts. If transferring binary (nontext) files, use the binary command first.

mkdir *directory*

Create a remote directory. Note that anonymous users are usually not permitted to create directories on remote systems.

mls *remote_dir local_file*

Same as mdir, except that a short listing (no details) is stored.

mput *local_files*

Transfer one or more local files to the remote computer. Unlike with put, you can use wildcards (e.g., *.txt for all *.txt* files). You will be asked to confirm each transfer unless you turn off prompting with the prompt command. Remote files will be given the same names as their local counterparts. If transferring binary (nontext) files, use the binary command first.

open *hostname or IP address*

Connect to the specified FTP server. This is the same as specifying a server in the FTP command line; use open if you omitted the host parameter. You can use open whenever there's no current connection, either if you disconnected using disconnect or close, or if the initial connection attempt was unsuccessful.

prompt

Turn on or off prompting for multiple file transfers. When you use the mput or mget command, FTP will prompt you before transferring each file. By default, prompt is turned on; type **prompt** before using mput or mget to transfer multiple files without being prompted.

put *local_file* [*remote_file*]

Transfer *local_file* from the local machine to the server. If you do not specify *remote_file*, the remote file will be given the same name as the original. The file will be placed in the remote working directory; to choose a different destination, use cd. You can upload only a single file at a time with put (no wildcards are allowed); use mput to transfer multiple files at once. If transferring binary (nontext) files, use the binary command first.

pwd

Print Working Directory (PWD) displays the remote working directory; use cd to change to a different remote directory.

quit

End the FTP session with the remote computer and exit FTP.

quote [*command line*]

Same as literal.

recv *remote_file* [*local_file*]

Same as get.

remotehelp [*command*]

Display help for remote commands supported by the server. This is probably similar to the commands available on the client, but may not be identical. As with ? and help, supplying no arguments returns a list of command names. Use remotehelp *command* to get more information on each command.

rename *from_name to_name*

Rename a remote file. Note that anonymous users are usually not permitted to rename files on remote systems.

rmdir *remote_directory*

Delete a remote directory. Note that anonymous users are usually not permitted to delete directories on remote systems.

send *local_file* [*remote_file*]

Same as put.

status

Display the current status of the connection and the current settings of options such as prompt, verbose, and ascii|binary.

trace

Turn on or off packet tracing, which displays the route of each packet when executing an FTP command. By default, trace is off.

type [*type*]

Display whether transfers are performed in binary or ascii mode. Use type binary (or just binary) to transfer binary files.

user *username* [*password*]

Specify the username on the remote computer; if you do not specify a password, you will be prompted for one. Typically, FTP prompts for the username and password when a connection is first established; however, if you type an incorrect username and password, you can try again with the user command without having to reconnect.

verbose

Turn on or off verbose mode. If verbose is on (the default), all FTP responses are displayed, such as when a file transfer completes and any statistics regarding the efficiency of the transfer.

Examples

To copy the file *preface.doc* from the directory */pub/nutshell* on a remote computer to *\temp\docs* on your local computer, once you're logged on to a server, you would perform the following from the command prompt (note that cd within *ftp* is for the remote computer):

```
C:\>cd \temp\docs
C:\temp\docs>ftp remote_computer username password
ftp>binary
ftp>cd /pub/nutshell
ftp>get preface.doc
```

Run a script containing ftp commands:

```
C:\>ftp -s:myfile.scr
```

This will load *ftp* and run *myfile.scr*, executing any ftp commands in the file.

Notes

- Most web browsers support the *ftp://* protocol, which provides limited FTP functionality without having to use an FTP client. For example, you can retrieve a single file from an anonymous FTP server by opening this address in any web browser: *ftp://example.com/path/filename.ext*.

- Furthermore, you can specify a username and (optionally) a password, like this: *ftp://username:password@example.com/path/filename.ext*.

- Some browsers will even let you upload files when connected to an FTP server (assuming the server permits you to do so). In Internet Explorer, you can simply drag and drop files into an FTP window as though it were a folder on your hard disk.

- You can abbreviate all ftp command names to their first four letters, sometimes fewer.

- If you omit any nonoptional arguments from most FTP commands, you'll be prompted for them.

- When using the get or mget command, transferred files will be placed in whatever directory was the working directory when you launched FTP. Once an FTP session has begun, you can change the working directory with the lcd command: to switch from the local *C:* drive to the *A:* drive, for example, you would type:

  ```
  ftp>lcd a:/
  ```

- In FTP, to maintain consistency with its Unix heritage, you must use the forward slash (/) instead of the backslash (\) when specifying pathnames. Furthermore, directory and filenames are case-sensitive when connecting to a Unix FTP server; *readme.txt* is a different file than *Readme.TXT*.

- Many FTP servers impose an "idle timeout" on FTP connections; that is, if you open an FTP connection and let it sit for several minutes without typing any commands, the FTP server will disconnect you.

Msg

\windows\system32\msg.exe

Send a text message to one or all local users.

To open

Command Prompt → **msg**

Usage

```
msg recipient [/server:name] [/time:sec] [/v] [/w] [message]
```

Description

You use Msg to send a text message to a user currently logged in to the local computer; you also can use it to send a message simultaneously to all logged-in users.

Note that Msg is not intended to send messages to other computers, but to users remotely logged in to your computer. The exception is a user on another machine currently logged in to your machine (or the machine specified by /server), assuming that machine is set up as a Terminal Server. To send a message to another computer, use an instant messaging program such as MSN Messenger or Chat (or just send an email).

Msg accepts the following options:

message
> The text message to send. If you omit it, Msg prompts for it. Also can read from standard input; see Chapter 14.

recipient
> *Recipient* can be a username, a session name, a session ID, or a filename (pointing to a file containing a list of usernames, session names, or session IDs). Or, specify an asterisk (*) to send a message to all sessions on the specified server.

/server:name
> Specifies /server:*name* to send the message to users on another machine, where *name* is the name of a Terminal Server (see "Services," in the "Microsoft Management Console" section in Chapter 10, for details).

/time:sec
> Indicates the amount of time, in seconds, to wait for the recipient to acknowledge the message being sent.

/v

> Verbose mode; displays additional information about the actions being performed.

/w
> Waits for a response from the recipient; useful with /v.

Net

\windows\system32\net.exe

Display, modify, and troubleshoot your current workgroup settings.

To open

Command Prompt → **net**

Usage

```
net command [parameters]
```

Description

Net is a general-purpose diagnostic tool used to configure, control, and troubleshoot the networking settings on a Windows Vista system. The Net tool will appeal most to more advanced users or those who need to control network settings from the command line.

To use Net, you must specify one of the following 21 commands, followed by any of the applicable parameters. To get more information about any of these commands, use the help command, like this:

```
net help command
```

Here are the commands used with Net:

accounts

Use net accounts to update the user accounts database and modify password and logon requirements for all accounts. If used without parameters, the current settings for password, logon limitations, and domain information are displayed.

computer

Use net computer to add or delete computers from a domain database; it is available only on Windows Server.

config

The net config command displays configuration information about the workstation or server service. See the "Example" section at the end of this list.

continue

Type net continue to reactivate a Windows service that has been suspended by net pause.

file

net file closes a shared file and removes any file locks. When you use it without options, net file lists the open files on a server. The listing includes the ID number, location, number of locks, and user currently accessing the file.

group

net group adds, displays, or modifies global groups on servers. When you use it without options, net group displays a list of the groups on the server.

help

net help displays more information about any command. When you use it without options, net help displays all the available commands.

helpmsg

The net helpmsg command displays information about error, warning, and alert messages relating to a Windows network. For example, type **net helpmsg 2181** to display an explanation of error #2181 and any possible remedies.

localgroup

net localgroup modifies local groups on computers. When you use it without options, net localgroup displays a list of the groups on the server.

name

The net name command adds or deletes a messaging name, an alias to which messages are sent (via net send). When you use it without options, a list of names accepting messages at the computer is displayed.

pause

Use net pause to temporarily suspend a Windows service or resource, and use net continue to reactivate it when you're ready.

print

The net print command displays print jobs and shared printer queues.

session

net session lists or disconnects sessions between the computer and other computers on the network.

share
: The net share command makes a server's resources available to network users. When you use it without options, it lists information about all resources being shared. See also "Create A Shared Folder," earlier in this chapter.

start
: Use net start to start a service. When you use it without options, it lists services that have already been started.

statistics
: net statistics displays the statistics log for the local workstation or server service. When you use it without parameters, net statistics displays the services for which statistics are available.

stop
: Use net stop to stop a service that has been started with net start. Note that stopping some services will cause others to be stopped, and some services cannot be stopped at all.

time
: Probably the most interesting command in the bunch, net time is used to synchronize the computer's clock with that of another computer or domain. You can also use net time to set the NTP timeserver for the computer.

use
: The net use command connects (or disconnects) a computer to a shared resource (shared with net share). When you use it without options, it lists the computer's active connections.

user
: net user creates and modifies user accounts. When you use it without options, net user lists the user accounts for the computer. The user account information is stored in the same user accounts database used by Control Panel → User Accounts; see "User Accounts," in Chapter 10.

view
: net view displays a list of resources being shared on a remote computer. When you use it without options, it displays a list of computers in the current domain or network.

Example

To display your computer's current workgroup settings, type this:

```
C:\>net config workstation
Computer name \\Vista-Desktop
Full Computer name Vista-Desktop
User name Preston

Workstation active on
        NetbiosSmb (000000000000)
        NetBT_Tcpip_{BB30432A-962C-4AB4-806D-35A14EE4E36C} (00123F7DD66F)

Software version Windows Vista (TM) Ultimate

Workstation domain WORKGROUP
Logon domain Vista-Desktop
```

```
COM Open Timeout (sec) 0
COM Send Count (byte) 16
COM Send Timeout (msec) 250
The command completed successfully.
```

Netsh

\windows\system32\netsh.exe

Wide-ranging command-line tool with an extremely large number of available commands.

To open

Command Prompt → **netsh**

Usage

```
netsh command [parameters]
```

Description

The netsh command contains many, many dozens of commands and useful features; to list them all is well beyond the scope of this book. Suffice it to say that if there's some networking information you want to get from the command line, or a task you want to perform, there's a reasonable chance that netsh can help. Many levels and sublevels of commands are available.

There are many categories of commands used with netsh; type this command:

```
Netsh command ?
```

to get the primary list, which follows:

Dhcpclient
> Diagnostic and configuration tools relating to clients that use DHCP

Firewall
> Diagnostic and configuration tools relating to your firewall

ipsec
> Diagnostic and configuration tools relating to IPsec security

lan
> Diagnostic and configuration tools for your LAN

Wlan
> Diagnostic and configuration tools related to the WAN to which you're connected

Example

To display the current configuration of your firewall, type this:

```
C:\> Netsh firewall show config
Domain profile configuration:
-------------------------------------------------------------------
Operational mode                    = Enable
Exception mode                      = Enable
Multicast/broadcast response mode   = Enable
Notification mode                   = Enable

Allowed programs configuration for Domain profile:
Mode     Traffic direction    Name / Program
-------------------------------------------------------------------
```

```
Port configuration for Domain profile:
Port   Protocol Mode     Traffic direction     Name
--------------------------------------------------------------------


Standard profile configuration (current):
--------------------------------------------------------------------

Operational mode                   = Enable
Exception mode                     = Enable
Multicast/broadcast response mode  = Enable
Notification mode                  = Enable

Service configuration for Standard profile:
Mode    Customized   Name
--------------------------------------------------------------------

Enable  No           File and Printer Sharing
Enable  No           Network Discovery

Allowed programs configuration for Standard profile:
Mode    Traffic direction    Name / Program
--------------------------------------------------------------------


Port configuration for Standard profile:
Port   Protocol Mode     Traffic direction     Name
--------------------------------------------------------------------


ICMP configuration for Standard profile:
Mode     Type Description
--------------------------------------------------------------------

Enable   8    Allow inbound echo request

Log configuration:
--------------------------------------------------------------------
File location   = J:\Windows\system32\LogFiles\Firewall\pfirewall.log
Max file size   = 4096 KB
Dropped packets = Disable
Connections     = Disable
```

NSLookup
\windows\system32\nslookup.exe

Perform a DNS lookup; used to convert domain names to IP addresses and vice versa.

To open
Command Prompt → **nslookup**

Usage
nslookup *address*

Description
When you type a web address into a browser's address bar and press Enter, Windows looks up the server name to determine the corresponding IP address. Then the IP address is used to initiate communication with the server. If the lookup fails, either because the name servers (the machines containing the DNS lookup tables) are down or because the specified domain does not exist, the connection attempt will fail as well.

NSLookup is a simple tool that allows you to look up the IP address of any domain name or server name, as well as find the server name associated with any particular IP address. To use NSLookup, just specify the domain name at the prompt, like this:

```
c:\> nslookup annoyances.org
Name: annoyances.org
Address: 209.133.53.130
```

Likewise, you can specify an IP address, and NSLookup will report the associated domain (called a *reverse lookup*):

```
c:\> nslookup 209.204.146.22
Name: www.oreilly.com
Address: 209.204.146.22
```

Notes

- Every time you initiate communication with a server, there will be a delay while Windows performs an NSLookup. To eliminate the delay, use NSLookup to determine the IP address and then replace the reference with the IP address. However, take care to do this only with IP addresses that you know will not change; it is not unusual for web and mail servers to occasionally change IP addresses (and some servers have multiple IP addresses).

- Most ISPs employ at least two nameservers, which are used for lookups for all of their customers. If one goes down, the other takes up the slack. However, if both nameservers are down for some reason, or even are just performing poorly, it can disable most Internet communication. If, however, you use IP addresses as described in the preceding note, you eliminate your susceptibility to this problem.

- Because NSLookup and the automatic lookups performed behind the scenes depend on your ISP's nameservers, they are susceptible to receiving outdated information. If you're having trouble accessing a particular server, you can use an NSLookup gateway to double-check your findings. An NSLookup gateway is simply a web-enabled version of NSLookup. You also can use it to perform lookups; however, if the gateway site is outside your ISP, it will use its own nameservers and therefore may provide more up-to-date information. To find such a site, perform a web search for "NSLookup gateway."

- NSLookup also performs a lookup of the IP address of your local computer and displays it before performing the requested lookup. In many cases, though, it will fail, which means that you may see an error message every time you run NSLookup (such as "Can't find server name..."). However, this won't interfere with NSLookup's primary function.

- Windows caches some lookups, which means that you may see outdated information. To flush the cache, type **ipconfig /flushdns** at the command prompt. See "Windows IP Configuration," later in this chapter, for more information.

See also

"Ping," "Tracert," and "Windows IP Configuration"

Ping
\windows\system32\ping.exe

Test the "reachability" of another computer on the network or across the Internet.

To open
Command Prompt → **ping**

Usage
```
ping target [-t] [-a] [-n count] [-l size] [-f] [-w timeout]
 [-r count] [-s count] [-j host_list | -k host_list]
 [-i ttl] [-v tos]
```

Description
The primary function of Ping is to see whether another computer is "alive" and reachable. Ping works on local networks and across Internet connections. For example, type the following at a command prompt:

```
ping oreilly.com
```

and you'll get a report that looks something like this:

```
Pinging oreilly.com [209.204.146.22] with 32 bytes of data:
Reply from 209.204.146.22: bytes=32 time=78ms TTL=238
Reply from 209.204.146.22: bytes=32 time=31ms TTL=238
Reply from 209.204.146.22: bytes=32 time=15ms TTL=238
Reply from 209.204.146.22: bytes=32 time=78ms TTL=238
Ping statistics for 209.204.146.22:
 Packets: Sent = 4, Received = 4, Lost = 0 (0% loss),
Approximate round trip times in milli-seconds:
 Minimum - 15ms, Maximum = 78ms, Average = 50ms
```

Here, Ping sent out four pings (the default), reported the time it took for them to return (in milliseconds), and then displayed various statistics about the session. Ping is especially useful if you're having trouble contacting a server and you want to see whether the server is alive (running and accepting connections). If the server does not reply (meaning that it is down, the connection has been severed, or the server is ignoring Ping messages for security reasons), you'll see Request timed out. Ping accepts the following options:

target
> The machine to ping; it can be the name of a computer on your network, an IP address (e.g., 209.204.146.22), or an Internet address (e.g., *oreilly.com*).

-t
> Normally, Ping sends out four pings and then quits. Include the -t option to ping continually until you interrupt Ping by pressing Ctrl-C. Press Ctrl-Break to display statistics without interrupting.

-a
> Resolve addresses to hostnames.

-n *count*
> The number of pings to send; the default is four.

-l *size*
> The size of the packets to send, in bytes; the default is 32 bytes.

-f
> Turn on the "Don't Fragment" flag in packet.

-w *timeout*
> The amount of time to wait, in milliseconds, before Ping gives up and displays Request timed out; the default is 500 milliseconds (half a second).

-r *count*
> Display the route taken to reach the server (see "Tracert," later in this chapter). The *count* is the maximum number of hops to record and can range from one to nine.

-s *count*
> Display a timestamp for *count* hops.

-j *host_list*
> Impose a "loose" route (see the -r option) along which to ping.

-k *host-list*
> Impose a "strict" route (see the -r option) along which to ping.

-i *ttl*
> Specify the Time to Live (TTL); valid range is from 0 to 255.

-v *tos*
> Specify the Type of Service (TOS); valid range is from 0 to 255.

-R

> Use routing header to test reverse route also (IPv6 only).

-S *srcaddr*
> Source address to use (IPv6 only).

-4

> Force using IPv4.

-6

> Force using IPv6.

Notes

- The word *ping* comes from submarine lingo, when sonar was used to detect nearby objects, such as ships and other submarines. Pulses of sound were sent through the water; those that returned indicated the existence of an object off which the pulses were reflected. *ping.exe* works very similarly, except it sends packets rather than sonic pulses.

See also

"Tracert" and "NSLookup"

Route

\windows\system32\route.exe

Manipulate the TCP/IP routing table for the local computer.

To open

Command Prompt → **route**

Usage

```
route [-f] [-p] [command] [destination] [gateway]
[mask netmask] [metric metric] [if interface]
```

Description

Routing tables provide information necessary to connect to other computers on a network or the Internet. Route accepts the following options:

command
> Specifies one of four commands:
>
> print
>> Prints a route (similar to netstat -r). The route print command is useful if you are having a problem (e.g., "Host unreachable" or "Request timed out") with the routes on your computer, because it will display all the different fields in the active route (see the example).
>
> add
>> Adds a route to the routing table; used until the computer is shut down (unless the -p option is specified).
>
> delete
>> Deletes a route from the routing table.
>
> change
>> Modifies an existing route in the routing table.

destination
> The remote computer that is reachable via *gateway*.

-f
> Frees (clears) the routing tables of all gateway entries. If you use this in conjunction with one of the commands listed earlier, the tables are cleared prior to running the command.

-p
> When you use this with the add command, -p makes a route persistent across boots of the system. If you don't specify -p, any route you add will be valid only until the computer is restarted. The -p option has no effect on other commands, as they're all persistent.

gateway
> The gateway computer to be used for traffic going to *destination*. It is possible to use a hostname for the gateway, but it is safer to use an IP address because a hostname may resolve to multiple IP addresses. For example, you might type the following:
>
>> route add 0.0.0.0 10.0.0.200

mask *netmask*
> Specifies the subnet mask for a *destination*. If you do not specify it, a mask of 255.255.255.255 is used (i.e., a "host route" to a single host, not a network).

metric *metric*
> Specifies the metric or "hop count" for this route. The metric indicates which route is preferred when multiple routes to a *destination* exist and signifies the number of hops or gateways between the local computer and the *gateway*. The route with the lowest metric is used unless it is unavailable, in which case the route with the next lowest metric takes over.

if *interface*
> Specifies the interface number for the specified route.

If you type **route print** at the command prompt, you'll get something that looks like this:

```
=========================================================================
Interface List
 8 ...00 12 3f 7d d6 6f ...... Intel(R) PRO/1000 PL Network Connection
 1 ......................... Software Loopback Interface 1
 9 ...02 00 54 55 4e 01 ..... Teredo Tunneling Pseudo-Interface
10 ...00 00 00 00 00 00 00 e0  isatap.hsd1.ma.comcast.net.
=========================================================================

IPv4 Route Table
=========================================================================
Active Routes:
Network Destination        Netmask          Gateway       Interface  Metric
          0.0.0.0          0.0.0.0      192.168.1.1   192.168.1.107      20
        127.0.0.0        255.0.0.0          On-link       127.0.0.1     306
        127.0.0.1  255.255.255.255          On-link       127.0.0.1     306
  127.255.255.255  255.255.255.255          On-link       127.0.0.1     306
      192.168.1.0    255.255.255.0          On-link   192.168.1.107     276
    192.168.1.107  255.255.255.255          On-link   192.168.1.107     276
    192.168.1.255  255.255.255.255          On-link   192.168.1.107     276
        224.0.0.0        240.0.0.0          On-link       127.0.0.1     306
        224.0.0.0        240.0.0.0          On-link   192.168.1.107     276
  255.255.255.255  255.255.255.255          On-link       127.0.0.1     306
  255.255.255.255  255.255.255.255          On-link   192.168.1.107     276
=========================================================================
Persistent Routes:
  None

IPv6 Route Table
=========================================================================
Active Routes:
 If Metric Network Destination      Gateway
  9     18 ::/0                      On-link
  1    306 ::1/128                   On-link
  9     18 2001::/32                 On-link
  9    266 2001:0:4136:e378:1c9f:3624:3f57:fe94/128
                                     On-link
  8    276 fe80::/64                 On-link
  9    266 fe80::/64                 On-link
 10    281 fe80::5efe:192.168.1.107/128
                                     On-link
  8    276 fe80::1c84:e9d0:6b05:c9d5/128
                                     On-link
  9    266 fe80::1c9f:3624:3f57:fe94/128
                                     On-link
  1    306 ff00::/8                  On-link
  9    266 ff00::/8                  On-link
  8    276 ff00::/8                  On-link
=========================================================================
Persistent Routes:
  None
```

The fields in this printout are as follows:

Gateway
> The IP address of the gateway for the route. The gateway will know what to do with traffic for the specified network address.

Interface
> The IP address of the network interface that the route will use when leaving the local computer.

Metric
> The hop count or number of gateways between the local computer and the gateway.

Netmask
> The mask to be applied to the network address. If the mask is 255.255.255.255, the route is a host route and refers to a single machine, not a network.

Network Address
> Any network matched by this address should use this route. The default route is all zeros and is used if no other route is found.

Notes

- If the command is print or delete, you may use wildcards for the destination and gateway, or you may omit the gateway argument.

See also

"Tracert"

Tracert
\windows\system32\tracert.exe

Trace the route of communication across the Internet.

To open

Command Prompt ▸ **tracert**

Usage

```
tracert [-d] [-h max_hops] [-j list] [-w timeout] target
```

Description

The Internet is a decentralized interconnection of computers. This means that there is rarely, if ever, a direct connection between two computers on the Internet. Instead, information is transferred across several computers, if not dozens, to make it from one place to another. The further the geographical distance between two machines, the greater the likelihood that there will be more hubs and other intermediate computers along the way. You use Tracert to list all the computers encountered on the journey from one computer to another.

Type the following at a command prompt (while connected to the Internet) to trace the route from your computer to *microsoft.com*:

```
tracert microsoft.com
```

Tracert accepts the following options:

target
> The name or IP address of the computer to contact.

-d
> If you specify an IP address, Tracert will attempt to resolve the hostname (using DNS, which could slow things down). Include the -d option to skip this step.

-h *max_hops*
> Specifies the maximum number of "hops" (servers along the route) to display before giving up; the default is 30 hops.

-j *host-list*
> Loosely imposes a route to follow, where *list* is a list of hosts (IPv4 only).

-w *timeout*
> Sets the amount of time to wait (in milliseconds) for each reply.

-R
> Traces the round-trip path (IPv6 only).

-S *scaddr*
> Specifies the source address to use (IPv6 only).

-4
> Forces it to use IPv4.

-6
> Forces it to use IPv6.

Notes
- Tracert has many uses, but probably the most valuable on a day-to-day basis is troubleshooting. For example, if you are trying to contact a web server, email server, or any other machine on the Internet, and it does not appear to be responding, you can perform a Tracert to see whether it is the fault of the actual machine or one of the hosts along the way. If it turns out to be one of the hosts along the way, your network administrator or ISP may be able to use your Tracert report to help solve the problem.

See also
"NSLookup" and "Ping"

Windows IP Configuration   *\windows\system32\ipconfig.exe*

Display the current IP address(es) of the active connection(s).

To open
Command Prompt → **ipconfig**

Usage
> ipconfig [*/command*] [*adapter*]

Description
The Windows IP Configuration tool, used without any options, displays your computer's current IP address, subnet mask, and default gateway. Knowing your

---

computer's IP address is important for many reasons, such as allowing other users to connect to you by using Remote Desktop Connection or calling you with Microsoft NetMeeting.

Windows IP Configuration takes the following parameters:

adapter
> Used with some of the commands in this list, *adapter* specifies the name of a network connection (see "Manage Network Connections," earlier in this chapter) on which to act. *Adapter* can contain wildcards, such as *. Omit *adapter* (if allowed) to act on the default connection.

/all
> Displays all available configuration information.

/allcompartments
> Displays detailed information about all compartments.

/release [*adapter*]
> Releases the IPv4 address(es) for the specified connection, effectively disconnecting that connection from all network communication. Use /renew to reestablish communication.

/release6 [*adapter*]
> Releases the IPv6 address(es) for the specified connection, effectively disconnecting that connection from all network communication. Use /renew6 to reestablish communication.

/renew [*adapter*]
> Renews the IPv4 address for the specified adapter, effectively reestablishing communication for the connection.

/renew6 [*adapter*]
> Renews the IPv6 address for the specified adapter, effectively reestablishing communication for the connection.

/flushdns
> Purges the DNS Resolver cache. See "NSLookup," earlier in this chapter, for details. See the entry in this list for /displaydns to show the contents of the DNS cache.

/registerdns
> Refreshes all DHCP leases and reregisters DNS names.

/displaydns
> Displays the contents of the DNS Resolver Cache (see /flushdns).

/showclassid *adapter*
> Displays all the DHCP class IDs allowed for *adapter*.

/setclassid *adapter* [*classid*]
> Modifies the DHCP class ID for *adapter*.

Notes

- Windows Vista supports IPv6 and its longer IP address format, and reports to you both the IPv4 and IPv6 addresses.
- The IP address of any given network connection is also shown in the connection's Status window, which you can view by double-clicking the connection in the Network Connections window. See "Manage Network Connections," earlier in this chapter, for details.

8

Security

One of Microsoft's primary goals for Windows Vista was to make it more secure than previous versions of Windows, so not surprisingly, Microsoft made many changes and additions in the name of security. For example, Windows Vista includes a two-way firewall, built-in antispyware, hardware-based encryption, Parental Control features, antiphishing tools, a pop-up killer, and User Account Control (UAC), which forces you to confront pop-up warnings before you take certain actions.

This chapter covers these changes and more. But Microsoft has done at least as much work under the hood to make sure Windows Vista is as secure as possible. You won't see these changes, because they take place without you having to take any action, and there's no way for you to turn them off or customize them. Here are some of the new built-in security features you don't see, but that protect you every time you use your PC:

Windows Service Hardening
> This prevents malicious software from doing damage by stopping abnormal activity from taking place in the filesystem, Registry, and network to which the PC is attached.

Network Access Protection (NAP)
> This stops an infected computer from making a connection to a network so that it cannot spread its infection to other computers.

File and Registry virtualization
> In some instances, Windows Vista creates virtual folders and Registry keys so that when changes are made or new software is installed, changes are not made to the actual system but instead are made first to these virtual areas for safety purposes.

For the changes that you *can* see—and can do something about—peruse this chapter. Here is an alphabetical reference of entries in this chapter:

BitLocker Drive Encryption	Parental Controls	User Account Control
Certificate Manager	Phishing Filter	Virtual Private Network Connection
Encrypting File System (EFS)	Pop-Up Blocker	Windows Defender
Internet Explorer Protected Mode	Security Center	Windows Firewall
Local Security Policy	Security Control Panel Category	Windows Update
NTFS Encryption Utility	Security File and Folder Properties	Windows Update Standalone Installer

General Security

Windows Vista includes many new general security tools, as well as holdovers from Windows XP. It also includes an entirely new way to access security settings, via Security in the Control Panel. This section of the chapter covers general security settings and tools. Note that there is some overlap between this section and the "Internet Security" section later on; for example, Parental Controls are covered in this section because they control access to applications and time spent on the computer, even though a major purpose of Parental Controls is to control how children can use the Internet.

Local Security Policy

\windows\system32\secpol.msc

Sets local policies for security. See "Microsoft Management Console," in Chapter 10.

Parental Controls

Controls the way children can use the computer and the Internet.

To open

Control Panel → [User Accounts and Family Safety] → Parental Controls

Control Panel → [User Accounts and Family Safety] → Set up parental controls for any user

Control Panel → Set up parental controls for any user

Control Panel → [Security] → Parental Controls

Control Panel → [Security] → Set up parental controls for any user

Description

Many parents are justifiably worried about how their children use computers and the Internet. The Internet can be a dangerous place for children—particularly young children, preteens, and even teens. They may inadvertently come across pornography, violent images, or other unsuitable content, and they could even be targeted by predators.

But it's not just the Internet and its dangers that parents worry about. Computers themselves may be a problem as well. Some children may spend inordinate amounts of time using a computer—by playing games, for example—and parents may want to ensure that their children do not spend too much time using a PC. An increasing number of games are violent, portray drug use, and include sexual situations, and parents may want to block access to those games.

Security

In addition, parents may want to block access to certain programs on a shared PC—giving children access to your personal finance software, for example, could prove to be disastrous.

To help parents, Windows Vista offers a new feature, Parental Controls, which lets parents limit the web sites their children visit, set time limits on using the computer, control the games they play, and block access to specific programs. It also logs children's activity so that parents can see what their children are doing on the computer and online.

Before setting up Parental Controls, you first need to set up a new user account. (For details, see Chapter 10.) Once you do that, you can turn on Parental Controls in a variety of ways; the most direct way is by selecting Control Panel → Set up Parental Controls. You'll come to a screen with all the user accounts on the PC listed. Click the one for which you want to set up Parental Controls. Select "On, enforce current settings," and you'll see the screen pictured in Figure 8-1.

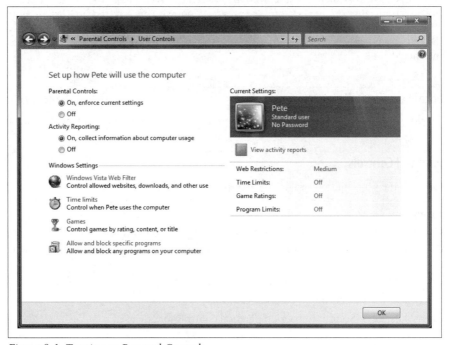

Figure 8-1. Turning on Parental Controls

When you first turn on Parental Controls for an account, there are no limits in place. The screen in Figure 8-1 lets you control the user of the PC for the account in the following ways:

Activity Reporting
> This tracks how the child uses the computer, including web sites visited, games played, instant messenger programs used, and so on. It creates a report, which is viewable using the Activity Report setting, described later on in this section.

Windows Vista Web Filter
> This allows parents to control what types of web sites their children can visit, and it can even limit visits to specific sites only. Click it, and on the screen that appears (Figure 8-2) select "Block some websites or content." In the "Block web

content automatically" area, choose the restriction level you want to apply. Each level has a different set of categories it blocks, which are listed below the selection. To create your own custom level, select Custom, and then select the categories you want to block. Parental Controls cannot rate every single site on the Web, particularly new ones, so you can also tell it to block access to sites that have not been rated.

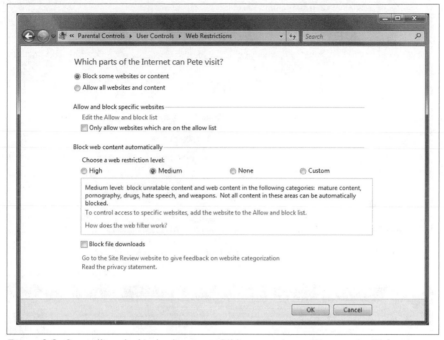

Figure 8-2. Controlling the kinds of content children can view and use on the Web

When a child tries to access a web site that has been filtered, he will get the message shown in Figure 8-3.

You also allow or block access to specific web sites by clicking "Allow and block specific web sites" and filling out the form. Doing this overrides the categories you've chosen. So, for example, if you've found a site that the filtering blocks but that you want your children to be able to access, include that site. Alternatively, if there's a site that you want blocked but Parental Controls doesn't block it, you can add it.

The screen also lets you block file downloads from the Internet.

Time limits

This lets you specify what hours of each day and week you want to block children from using the computer. Click the link, and you'll come to a page that lets you easily block out the time, as shown in Figure 8-4.

Games

This lets you entirely block a child from using games, block or allow specific games, and choose a level of game a child can play, ranging from Early Childhood all the way up to Adults Only. You can also block games with specific kinds of content in them—for example, games with references to drugs, that contain intense violence, and even that depict blood.

Figure 8-3. The message a child receives when he tries to visit a blocked site

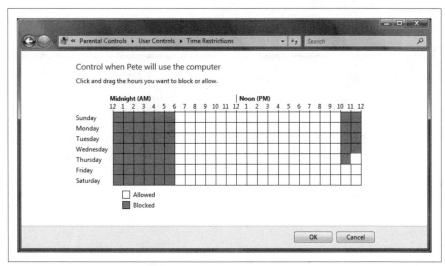

Figure 8-4. Setting up a schedule of when a child can use the computer

Allow and block specific programs

This lets you select specific programs that the child can or cannot use.

View Activity reports

This shows you information about how your child has used the computer, including a list of web sites blocked, the most popular web sites visited, games played, applications run, instant messenger conversations held, emails sent and received, and more. (See Figure 8-5.)

In addition, there's a useful feature that has nothing to do with Parental Controls. You can view information about the entire system, including any changes made to system settings and user accounts, any failed logon attempts, and any changes to the system clock.

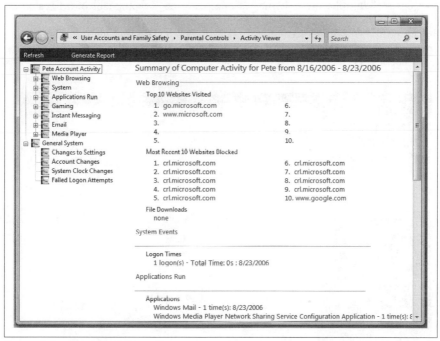

Figure 8-5. The Parental Controls activity report

Notes

- When you set up a new user account, you'll come to a screen that lets you set up Parental Controls. When creating user accounts for children, it's a good idea to immediately turn on and configure Parental Controls at that point.

- The Entertainment Software Rating Board (ESRB) provides the game categories. The actual ratings of each game are provided by a number of systems, including the ESRB.

- Parental Controls is no substitute for teaching your children the right way to use computers and the Internet. Many sites offer advice on how to do this, including *http://www.safekids.com* and *http://www.staysafe.org*.

- If you set up or change Parental Controls when the child is logged on to the computer, the changes may not be applied until he logs off and then on again.

Security

Security Center

Provides easy access to the Windows Firewall, antivirus and antimalware settings, Windows Update, and other security settings.

To open

Control Panel → Security → Security Center

Command Prompt → **wscui.cpl**

Description

The Security Center (Figure 8-6) doesn't actually provide any additional security, but it does act as a control center for your existing software—keeping tabs on what's on or off and what needs updating or replacing, and providing impossible-to-miss warnings that erupt from the Windows notification area. You'll get a warning from the System Tray if the Security Center detects that something is amiss with your security; otherwise, the Security Center won't appear there.

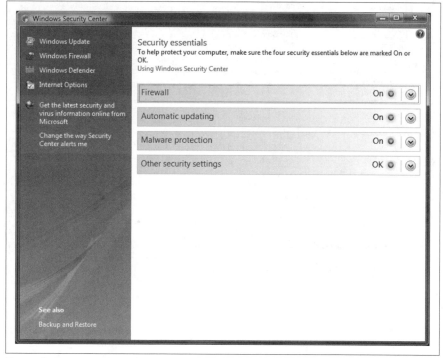

Figure 8-6. A computer with solid security protection, according to the Security Center

Don't confuse the Security Center with the Security Control Panel category. The Security Control Panel category includes links to a wider variety of security settings and controls than does the Security Center. The Security Center's main purpose is to issue alerts and warnings about your security settings, not to provide a front door to every security feature in Windows Vista—for example, it doesn't link to BitLocker Encryption and Parental Controls like the Security Control Panel category does.

The Security Center keeps an eye on firewalls (Windows Vista's own or any Windows Vista–compliant third-party program), your antivirus software, your antispyware software, your Internet security settings, UAC, and the Automatic Updates feature in Windows. The Center will pop up an alert if it thinks there's a problem in any of these areas. You can turn off monitoring by clicking the "Change the way Security Center alerts me" link in the main Security Center window. Note that the Security Center monitors your software only for activation and updates—it doesn't actually provide any security itself.

The main part of the screen, the righthand side with the green or red buttons, serves only to alert you to whether security features are turned on or off (green for on; red for off). You can't actually turn on or customize security features by clicking the red or green buttons. Click the button, and a message drops down, telling you the state of that particular security option. For example, if the Firewall button is green, click it and you'll get a message telling you that the Windows Firewall is on and working. Clicking the button again makes the message go away. You can perform the same function via the up and down arrows to the right of each button.

The Security Center monitors the status not only of built-in Windows Vista security software and features, but also of third-party software. The Security Center monitors these security features:

Windows Firewall
   It checks whether the Windows Firewall is running. If you use a different firewall, though, it will monitor that as well.

Automatic updating
   It checks to make sure that Windows Update is turned on for automatic updates.

Malware protection
   It checks to see whether the antispyware program, Windows Defender, is running. If you use a different piece of antispyware, it will monitor that as well. It also checks to make sure that you're running antivirus software. Windows Vista doesn't ship with antivirus software, but it checks to make sure you're running a third-party antivirus program.

Before installing antivirus software, make sure that it's designed to work with Windows Vista. Older antivirus software written for Windows XP usually will not work with Windows Vista, so make sure to get the latest version of your antivirus software before installing it on Windows Vista.

Other security settings
> This checks to make sure that your Internet security options are set to a safe, recommended level, and that UAC is turned on. (For more details about Internet security options see Chapter 5, and for information about UAC, see the "User Account Control" section, later in this chapter.)

That main part of the screen monitors your security, but it won't let you actually do anything about your settings. If you want to make changes to your security settings, you need to use the links on the left side of the screen. Here's what each setting does:

Windows Update
> By default, Windows Vista automatically downloads and installs all high-priority (aka critical) updates to the operating system at a set time each day. This happens in the background, without any intervention by (or notification to) you. (The exception is when an update requires a reboot.) This is the easiest way to keep your system up-to-date, but it's not compulsory. Clicking this button lets you customize how Windows Update works. (For details, see "Windows Update," later in this chapter.)

Windows Firewall
> This link leads to a tabbed dialog box that lets you configure Windows Vista's firewall. It will also monitor most third-party programs.

Windows Defender
> This leads to the main screen for the Windows Defender antispyware software.

Internet Options
> This leads to the Security tab of the Internet Properties dialog box.

See also

"Windows Firewall," "Windows Defender," and "Windows Update"

Security Control Panel Category

Provides easy access to all the major security features and settings of Windows Vista, including Windows Firewall, Windows Update, Windows Defender, Internet Options, Parental Controls, and BitLocker Drive Encryption.

To open

Control Panel → Security

Description

The single best place to get access to all of Windows Vista's security features is the Security Control Panel category, shown in Figure 8-7. This is a new Control Panel category. In previous versions of Windows, no such category existed; there was only the Security Center.

> Don't confuse the Security Control Panel category with the Security Center. The Security Control Panel category includes links to a wider variety of security settings and controls than does the Security Center (although it doesn't issue security alerts like the Security Center does).

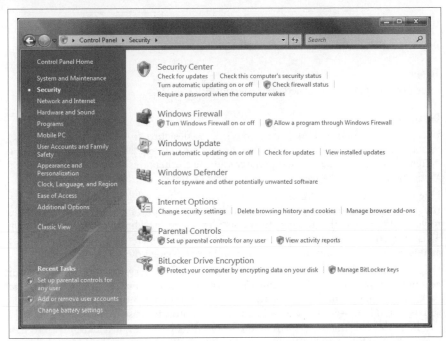

Figure 8-7. The Security Control Panel category, command central for all of your security settings

Particularly useful is that the Security Control Panel includes more than just links to Windows Vista's major security features; it also lets you directly perform actions. For example, there are links on the panel to turn the Windows Firewall on or off, to initiate spyware scans, to check for automatic updates, and so on.

Notes

- BitLocker Drive Encryption is available only with the Enterprise and Ultimate editions of Windows Vista.

See also

"Security Center," "Windows Firewall," "Windows Defender," "Windows Update," "Parental Controls," and "BitLocker Drive Encryption"

Security File and Folder Properties

Set permissions on a file or folder.

To open

Right-click a file or folder and select Properties → Security.

Description

See "File Properties," in Chapter 4, for details.

User Account Control

Protects users against threats by controlling access to important settings.

To open

User Account Control is turned on by default.

Description

User Account Control (UAC), new to Vista, is designed to protect users against a variety of threats, but it is by far the most controversial change to the operating system. The feature caused enough outcry during the beta (testing) phase of Windows Vista that Microsoft changed how it works several times.

Like it or not, though, UAC is here to stay, and it offers substantially increased security over previous versions of Windows. It is designed to prevent unauthorized changes to your computer so that the system and its files cannot be damaged or tampered with. This protection is designed not only against external threats and malware, but also against users of the computer who accidentally make dangerous changes.

UAC relies on there being two types of accounts on a system: an administrator account and a standard user account. The administrator can perform many tasks and make many changes that the standard user cannot. For maximum security, you should run as a standard user rather than as an administrator, because unauthorized changes can be more easily made when you run as an administrator—for example, a piece of malware set loose on a PC running with an administrator account can wreak far more havoc than a piece of malware loose on a PC running with a standard user account.

There is a great deal of confusion about administrator accounts in Windows Vista, and justifiably so. There are, in fact, two different types of administrator accounts: the single, all-powerful Administrator account (which is disabled by default), and the accounts that are part of the Administrators group. The Administrator account can do anything on the computer, and members of the Administrators group run much as standard users, except that they can elevate their privileges by clicking a Continue button in a dialog box when prompted. The single, overall Administrator, on the other hand, will not be prompted by dialog boxes.

Under UAC, standard users can perform most common tasks, such as using applications and email, surfing the Internet, and so on. But when they try to change a setting that requires administrator privileges—for example, a setting that affects other users or is dangerous, or that wants to install new software—they'll get a prompt, asking them to type in the password of an administrator's account. If multiple administrators are set up on the computer, the prompt will include a list of all the administrators. The user will have to type the password underneath the right administrator account.

In most instances, a standard user will know ahead of time that the prompt will appear, because the setting will have an icon of a shield next to it, as shown in Figure 8-8.

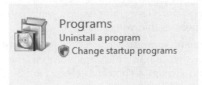

Figure 8-8. Shield icon signifying that the setting is protected by UAC

Once the user types in the administrator password, he can continue making the change.

Administrators will also receive prompts when they want to make a change, but because they're already logged in, they won't have to retype their passwords. So the prompt doesn't ask for a password; instead, the administrator only has to click the Continue button in order to proceed.

 When the prompt appears for either an administrator or a user, Windows Vista will switch to secure desktop mode, in which everything on the screen darkens except for the prompt. While in secure desktop mode, all you can do in Windows Vista is type in the password, click Continue, or cancel the operation.

Understanding and elevating privileges

UAC can be somewhat confusing, so to help you get a better handle on its use, you should know a little bit about the guiding principle behind it—the *least-privileged user*. In this principle, an account is set up that has only the minimum amount of privileges (the ability to make changes) needed in order to run the computer for most tasks. A standard user, in Windows Vista, is this least-privileged user.

When a change needs to be made that can affect the overall operation or security of the operating system, the privilege needs to be elevated—that is, someone with greater privileges than the least-privileged user must make the change. That's why a standard user will need to type in an administrator password to make a change, and it's why an administrator will have to confirm that she wants to make a change.

An administrator can allow standard users to run certain applications without having to type in administrator credentials. To do this, the administrator can "elevate" the privileges of the application—in other words, have it always run with elevated privileges so that no password need be typed in to run it.

To do this, an administrator right-clicks the application, selects the Compatibility tab, and under Privilege Level selects "Run this program as an administrator." Then she clicks OK.

Customizing UAC

You can use the Local Security Policy Microsoft Management Console to change how UAC behaves on your PC. (See "Local Security Policy," earlier in this chapter, and "Microsoft Management Console," in Chapter 10, for details.)

Security

Run Local Security Policy (*\windows\system32\secpol.msc*) and go to *Security Settings/ Local Policies/Security Options*. (This utility is not available in the Home versions of Vista.) You'll find these policies that you can edit:

User Account Control: Admin Approval Mode for the Built-In Administrator Account
This determines whether the Administrator account (the single account, not part of the Administrators Group) is subject to UAC. Enabling it means that UAC will treat the account like any other administrator, and the user must click Continue in dialog boxes when prompted. If it is not enabled, no prompt will appear for the account.

User Account Control: Behavior of the elevation prompt for administrators in Admin Approval Mode
This determines what prompt appears for administrators (members of the Administrators Group, not the built-in Administrator account). The default is Prompt for Consent, in which the administrator needs to click Continue or Cancel. You can also choose Prompt for Credentials, in which case the administrator password will have to be typed in. Choosing No Prompt will not allow administrators to elevate their privileges—in other words, they won't be able to make the change.

User Account Control: Behavior of the elevation prompt for standard users
This determines what prompt appears for standard users. The choices are Prompt for Consent, Prompt for Credentials, and No Prompt. The default is Prompt for Credentials in the Home editions, but No Prompt for the Enterprise edition, as a way to reduce calls to the Help Desk.

User Account Control: Detect application installations and prompt for elevation
By default, this is enabled in Home editions, so before software can be installed, UAC will ask for a prompt or a password. Disabling it allows software to be installed without that prompt. In Enterprise editions, it is disabled because enterprise-level installation technologies handle security on their own.

User Account Control: Only elevate executables that are signed and validated
When enabled, this will only allow users to install programs that have been properly signed and validated by their creators. If you try to install an unsigned application, you will get an error message instead of a UAC prompt.

User Account Control: Only elevate UIAccess applications that are installed in secure locations
UIAccess applications are those that require a higher degree of security than normal because of their capability to change system settings. This setting controls whether UIAccess applications must be run from a secure area of the operating system, or whether they can instead be run from any area. Secure areas are *C:\ Program Files* and *C:\Windows*. Enabled means that UIAccess applications will launch only if they are in secure areas; disabled means that the applications will launch wherever they are located. The default is enabled.

 For more information about these settings, see the article "Understanding and Configuring User Account Control in Windows Vista," at *http://www.microsoft.com/technet/windowsvista/library/ 00d04415-2b2f-422c-b70e-b18ff918c281.mspx*.

User Account Control: Run all administrators in Admin Approval Mode
This rather murky-sounding setting can essentially turn UAC on or off. By default, it is enabled, which means that UAC is turned on. If you disable it to turn off UAC, you will have to perform a system reboot before it takes effect.

User Account Control: Switch to the secure desktop when prompting for elevation
This determines whether Windows Vista will switch to the secure desktop when the prompt appears. By default, it is enabled.

User Account Control: Virtualize file and Registry write failures to per-user locations
This controls whether changes to the Registry made by standard users should be written to a special, virtual area, rather than directly to the Registry. This protects the Registry. By default, it is enabled.

Turning off UAC

There are several ways to turn off UAC, although it's not recommended. One way is to use the MSCONFIG tool. (For details about MSCONFIG, see "System Configuration Utility," in Chapter 11.) First, run MSCONFIG by typing **MSCONFIG** at the command line or in the Search box. When the tool runs, click the Tools tab and scroll down until you see Disable UAC. Highlight it and click the Launch button, then reboot. To turn it back on again, follow the same steps, except choose Enable UAC instead.

You can also disable UAC using the Registry Editor. Launch the Registry Editor (see Chapter 13 for details). Go to HKEY_LOCAL_MACHINE\SOFTWARE\Microsoft\Windows\ CurrentVersion\Policies\System\EnableLUA and give it a value of 0. You may need to reboot in order for the change to take effect.

You can also go to Control Panel → [User Accounts and Family Safety] → User Accounts → Turn User Account Control on or off. And as outlined in the preceding section, you can disable the "User Account Control: Run all administrators in Admin Approval Mode" option.

Notes

- When a user is asked to type in an administrator password, that is called *credential prompting*; when an administrator is asked to allow an action to proceed, that is called *consent prompting*.

See also

"Microsoft Management Console," in Chapter 10

Windows Update Standalone Installer   *\windows\system32\wusa.exe*

Install Windows Updates from the command line.

To open

Command Prompt → **wusa**

Usage

```
Wusa update [/quiet] [/norestart] [filename]
```

Security

Description

If you prefer to install updates manually rather than having Windows Vista download and install them, you can use the Windows Update Standalone Installer. It also comes in handy if for some reason, Windows Update refuses to automatically update or work properly.

To use it, first download the update, which will end in the extension *.msu*. Then run the Windows Update Standalone Installer from the command line. It takes the following options:

filename
> Specifies an update file with the extension *.msu*.

/quiet
> Quiet mode; requires no interaction on the part of the user, will reboot automatically if needed, and won't reboot if not needed.

/norestart
> When combined with /quiet, no reboot will be done. If you use it alone, without /quiet, it will be ignored.

See also

"Windows Update"

Windows Update

Automatically downloads and installs updates to Windows Vista over the Internet.

To open

Control Panel → [Security] → Windows Update

Control Panel → Check for Updates

Start → All Programs → Windows Update

Description

Windows Update (Figure 8-9) downloads and installs updates to Windows Vista quickly and easily. These updates are important because they often contain security patches that plug holes found in the operating system.

By default, Windows Update is turned on in Windows Vista. Windows Vista checks for new updates daily. It categorizes three types of updates: important updates, recommended updates, and optional updates. Important updates include security and critical performance updates. Recommended updates are those that help fix or prevent problems. Optional updates are less important updates, such as new or updated drivers. Optional updates are not automatically installed, but Windows Update will list any available and let you download and install them if you want.

Windows Update includes links to these features:

Check for updates
> This checks whether any updates are available, reports which are ready, and downloads and installs them if you want.

Change settings
> This screen, shown in Figure 8-10, lets you customize how updates are downloaded and installed. You can have Windows Update check for updates one day a

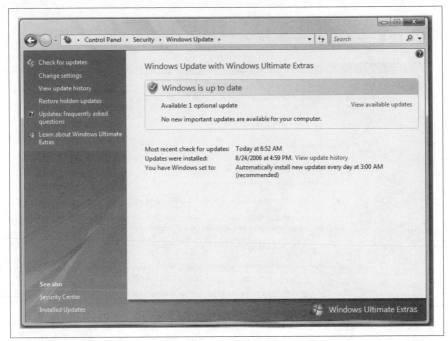

Figure 8-9. The Windows Update tool, which you can use to make sure you have the latest bug fixes and security patches

week (and specify that day and time) instead of daily, you can turn off automatic updating (not recommended), you can have updates automatically downloaded but not installed (you'd then pick which ones to install), or you can have Windows Update check for updates but then let you choose which to download and install. In addition, you can turn off the download of recommended updates and have only important updates downloaded and installed.

View update history

As the name says, this displays a list of all updates that have been downloaded and installed. You'll be shown the date of each update, whether it was successful, the type of update, and its purpose. Double-click any to get more details about the update.

Restore hidden updates

This lets you install updates that you have previously decided you don't want installed on your PC and so have "hidden." For details, see the next section, "Removing updates."

Get updates for more products

This link, at the bottom of the screen, sends you to the Microsoft Update site, which downloads an installer onto your system that will allow you to download updates to Microsoft Office products, including patches, service packs, and add-ons. The installer integrates directly into Windows Update on Windows Vista, so it will always be available from there, rather than you having to visit Microsoft Update. Note that after the installer integrates into Windows Vista, the link will no longer appear on the bottom of the screen.

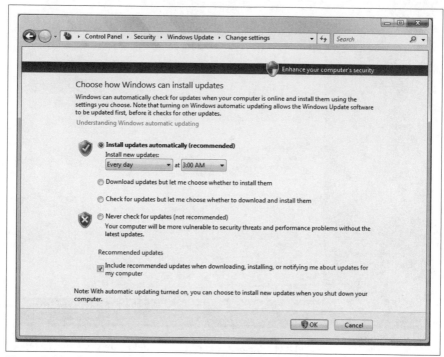

Figure 8-10. Changing the way Windows handles automatic updates

Removing updates

If an update is causing a problem, you can remove it by going to Control Panel →
Programs → View Installed Updates, right-clicking on an update, and then selecting
Remove. You won't be able to remove all updates; many security-related ones cannot
be removed.

If you have set your system to automatically install updates, however, the update you
removed will be automatically installed the next time Windows Update does its job.
One way around the problem is to change Windows Update settings so that you must
first review all downloaded updates or which updates to download. There's another
way around the problem, though. You can "hide" the update so that it isn't downloaded and installed, even if Windows Update is set to automatically download and
install all updates. Open Windows Update, click "Check for updates," and after
Windows finds updates, click "View available updates." Right-click the update you
don't want downloaded and installed, and select "Hide update." Windows Update
will ignore the update from now on. If at some point later, you decide you want to
install the update, go to Windows Update, click "Restore hidden updates," select the
update you want installed, and click Restore.

Notes

- Your update history also includes spyware definition updates for Windows
  Defender. It doesn't, however, include antivirus definition updates, because those
  are done via a third-party program rather than directly through Windows Vista.

- You can also visit the Microsoft Automatic Updates site at *http://corporate.windowsupdate.microsoft.com* to update Windows. It requires the use of Windows Explorer and will not work with other browsers.
- If you use the old-style menus in Internet Explorer (see Chapter 5 for details), you can open Windows Update by selecting Tools → Windows Update.
- Be careful when Windows Update discovers an optional update for a hardware driver. It sometimes offers an older version of the driver than is available from the vendor, unless the driver update is for a Microsoft product such as a mouse, keyboard, or game controller. Your best bet is to check at the manufacturer's web site rather than going through Windows Update for these drivers.

See also
"Internet Explorer Protected Mode"

Internet Security

The greatest danger to your PC comes from when you connect to the Internet, and because of that Windows Vista includes a substantial amount of online and network protection. For more details about online security, such as how to use Internet Explorer's phishing filter and how to handle online privacy, see Chapter 5. For details about fighting spam, see Chapter 6. For information about how to use encryption on wireless networks, see Chapter 7.

Internet Explorer Protected Mode

Protects a PC by isolating Internet Explorer from the rest of the operating system; it only allows certain changes to be made if it first asks permission.

To open
By default, Protected Mode is turned on.

To turn it off, in Internet Explorer choose Tools → Internet Options → Security, and uncheck the box next to Enable Protected Mode.

Description
Protected Mode, one of Internet Explorer's new security features, is also tied to Windows Vista's new UAC. It is designed to stop spyware and other malware from being installed without your knowledge—for example, via *drive-by downloads*, which are downloads initiated by web sites or pop-up ads of which you might not be aware. It does more than that, though. Under Protected Mode, a user cannot install software and modify Internet Explorer files without first going through UAC warnings, shown in Figure 8-11. Under Protected Mode, Internet Explorer can write data only to the Temporary Internet Files folder, and if it wants to write elsewhere, it must first ask for permission.

By default, Protected Mode is turned on, and you're told that it's turned on via a notification at the bottom right of Internet Explorer (Figure 8-12). You can turn it off by double-clicking the notification and unchecking the box next to Enable Protected Mode. You can also turn it off by choosing Tools → Internet Options → Security, and unchecking the box next to Enable Protected Mode. You can do this on a per-zone basis so that you can turn it on for some zones and off for others.

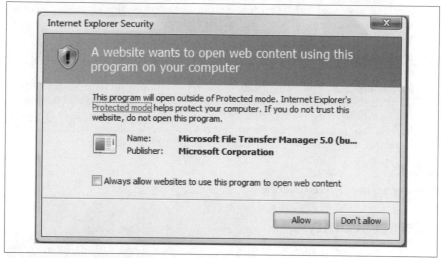

Figure 8-11. The warning that Internet Explorer's Protected Mode issues when a web site tries to install software on your PC

Figure 8-12. Protected Mode turned on

Notes

- Just because you can turn off Protected Mode doesn't mean you should. Unless you have a good reason for turning it off (and it's hard to imagine what that reason would be), you should always use Protected Mode.

Phishing Filter

See "Phishing Filter," in Chapter 5.

Pop-Up Blocker

See "Pop-Up Blocker," in Chapter 5.

Virtual Private Network Connection

Make a secure, encrypted connection over the Internet to your workplace.

To open

Control Panel → [Network and Internet] → [Network and Sharing Center] → Set up a connection or network

Description

More and more people need to connect to their corporate networks when they are away from the office. The least expensive and safest way to do this is via a Virtual Private Network (VPN), which in essence creates a secure tunnel through the public Internet. On each end of the tunnel—at your PC and at your corporate network—data is encrypted and put inside a normal Internet packet. Because the data inside the packet is encrypted, no one can see it, but because it is also wrapped in a normal Internet packet, it can use the public Internet rather than requiring an expensive, private connection.

A network administrator needs to set up a VPN server at the workplace. When he does, he then gives you the IP address or name of the server, and your username and password. Armed with that, you can create a VPN connection so that you can securely connect to the network from home, a wireless hotspot, a hotel room, or any other place where you can get Internet access.

Set up a VPN connection as you do other new network connections. (See Chapter 7 for details.) When you choose "Set up a connection or network" from the Network Center, choose "Connect to a Workplace." When prompted, choose the VPN connection option, and you'll be asked for more information (Figure 8-13). Enter the address or name of the VPN server, give it a name, click Next, and fill out the username, password, and domain information.

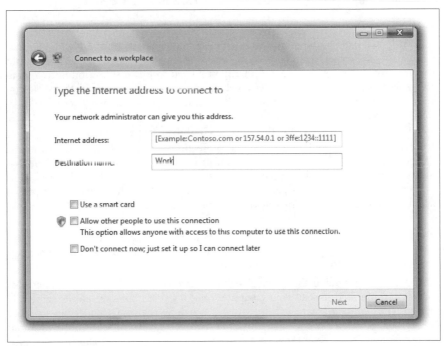

Figure 8-13. Setting up a VPN

When you're done, click Connect, and you'll make the connection. From now on, to connect to the VPN, make the connection from the Network Center by clicking "Connect to" and selecting the VPN connection you created.

Notes

- VPNs can also protect you when you're at a public hotspot. For-pay VPN services will encrypt all of your data when you're at the hotspot so that the information cannot be snooped upon. An example of such a service is HotSpotVPN (*http://www.hotspotvpn.com*), which charges $8.88 per month for access. Set up a VPN connection to this kind of service in the same way you would create a VPN connection to your workplace. The service will give you the server, username, and password information that you need to set up the connection.

See also

- "Group Policy Object Editor," in Chapter 10

Windows Defender
\Program Files\Windows Defender\MSASCui.exe

Protect your PC against spyware, home-page hijackers, and other threats.

To open

Start → Control Panel → Security → Windows Defender

Double-click the Windows Defender icon in the System Tray

Command Prompt → **\Program Files\Windows Defender\MSASCui.exe**

Description

Windows Defender is the antispyware software included with Windows Vista (see Figure 8-14). It protects against spyware, home-page hijackers, and similar threats, but it won't protect against viruses. For that, you'll need to buy a subscription to a security service such as Windows OneCare Live, or antivirus software such as Norton AntiVirus (*http://www.symantec.com*), PC-Cillin (*http://www.trendmicro.com*), or avast! antivirus (*http://www.avast.com*), which is free for personal use. Before installing an antivirus program, make sure that it's the Windows Vista version.

Windows Defender offers you automatic protection against spyware. It runs in the background as you use your computer, and it is designed to stop spyware before it infects your computer. When a piece of spyware attempts to install itself, hijack your home page, or do other damage, Windows Defender deletes the software and puts it into a quarantine area, where you can examine it later on. Should you decide that Windows Defender deleted the software in error, you can restore it.

In instances where there has been a threat to your PC but there's no software to quarantine—for example, in an instance where a web site tried to hijack your home page by resetting it—Windows Defender stops the action.

In addition to providing this kind of real-time protection, Windows Defender also comes preconfigured to scan your computer once a day for spyware, in the same way that antivirus software scans PCs for viruses. When Windows Defender finds a piece of malware, it deletes it and quarantines it. You can go to the quarantine area and restore the software if you believe that Windows Defender deleted the file in error.

New spyware is constantly being released, so Windows Defender regularly downloads definition updates to help protect your PC against the newest threats. Different pieces of spyware exhibit different patterns of unique behavior, called *definitions*. By constantly updating its definitions, Windows Defender can protect you against emerging threats.

Figure 8-14. Windows Defender, which protects your PC against spyware but not viruses

Doing a scan

Windows Defender, by default, scans your system for spyware once a day, but anytime you want it to scan, just click Scan at the top of the Windows Defender screen. That performs a full scan—that is, it scans all your files and folders. If you want to perform a more abbreviated scan, click the down arrow to the right of the Scan icon and choose Quick Scan. That will perform a scan of only the areas of your PC that are most liable to be infected—specifically, the Windows folder and subfolders, the Program Files folder and subfolders, and the Registry. To customize which files and folders to scan, click the down arrow to the right of the Scan icon, select Custom Scan, click "Scan selected drives and folders," and then select the drives and folders you want to scan and click Scan Now.

Viewing your history

Click History at the top of the screen and you'll view the history of all actions that Windows Defender has taken, including issuing alerts, putting files into quarantine, and so on.

Customizing the settings

Although Windows Defender comes preconfigured to protect you, you can also customize it in numerous ways. From the Windows Defender main screen, click Tools, and you'll be able to change these settings:

Options

Here's where you set your scan schedule, the default actions Windows Defender takes when it comes across spyware, and your real-time protection options. (This is pictured in Figure 8-15.) In the "Automatic scanning" section, select the scan frequency (either daily, or choose a day of the week), the time you want the scan to be performed, and the type of scan (Quick scan, Full scan, or Custom scan). Also choose whether to automatically download the newest definitions before scanning and whether to scan inside archives, such as *.zip* archives.

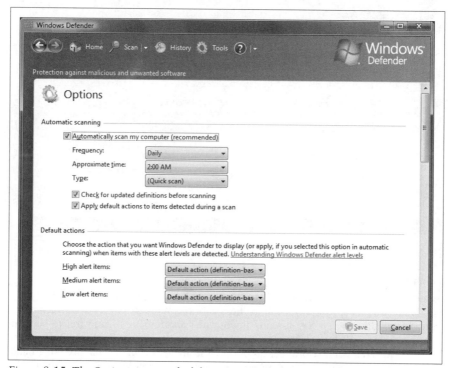

Figure 8-15. The Options screen, which lets you customize most aspects of Windows Defender

You also choose the action that Windows Defender should take when it comes across a piece of spyware, in the "Default actions" section. You can choose to remove it, ignore it, or follow the "Default action." In that case, the definition itself will determine whether to remove or ignore the software. For example, a dangerous piece of spyware would be removed, but a piece of adware might be ignored.

The "Real-time protection options" section determines which kind of real-time shields the program should put up against spyware. The details of all of them are too lengthy to go into here, but by default, they're all selected—and you should leave them that way. This section also lets you determine when Windows Defender should notify you when a piece of software wants to make a system change. You then have the option of allowing or disallowing the change. By default, you're notified only when software that Windows Defender has not yet classified as safe tries to make a change. If you want to be notified when even "allowed" software makes a change—in other words, software that is known to be safe—check the box next to "When changes are detected from allowed software."

The Administrator section lets you determine whether only administrators, or anyone who uses the system, can start a scan and remove spyware. By default, anyone can. To change the option, uncheck the box.

Microsoft SpyNet

This is one of the ways that Windows Defender determines what is spyware and what isn't. When you click Microsoft SpyNet, you're brought to a screen that lets you join it. When you join, every time you delete a program using Windows Defender because you believe it's spyware, that information is sent to Microsoft. Information from everyone is collated, and this helps Windows Defender decide what is spyware. You can become a basic or advanced member of SpyNet, or not join at all. With a basic membership, only information about your actions is sent to SpyNet. With an advanced membership, information about your actions, plus additional information, is sent, possibly including personal information. Note that you don't have to join in order to use Windows Defender, so choosing not to join won't affect how the program works.

Quarantined items

Click on this icon, and you're brought to a screen that displays all of the items that Windows Defender has deleted and put into quarantine. For each item, you'll see the name of the file or program, the alert level assigned to it, and the date it was quarantined. To take an item out of quarantine, highlight it and click Restore. To delete an item permanently, highlight it and click Remove. Unless you absolutely know a file is safe, don't remove it from quarantine.

Software Explorer

Whenever you run your PC, programs and services run in the background. The Software Explorer section of Windows Defender (Figure 8-16) lists them all for you and lets you terminate any that may be dangerous. When you get to the page, choose Startup Programs from the drop-down list and you'll see a list of programs that automatically start when you turn on your PC. Click on any to see details about it, such as the publisher, filename, file size, whether it ships with the operating system, and so on. Also included is a SpyNet Voting section, which shows you whether other people consider the file to be spyware. To stop a program from running on startup, highlight it and click Disable. The Show for All Users button at the bottom of the screen displays all software and services running for all users of the PC and lets you click Remove/Enable/Disable for programs and services that are running with elevated privileges.

When you choose Currently Running Programs from the drop-down list, you'll see all the services and files that are running on your system. Again, highlight any for details about it, and click End Process to end it.

When you choose Network Connected Programs from the drop-down list, you'll see the list of Internet-related services and programs currently running. Highlight any for details. To end one, highlight it and click End Process. You can also keep a service running but block it from receiving any incoming data. You might want to do this if you suspect a Trojan or other rogue program, but you're not sure whether it is dangerous and you don't want to terminate it. Highlight the program and click Block Incoming Connections.

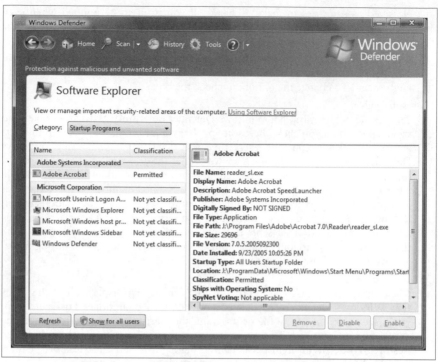

Figure 8-16. The Software Explorer, which lets you get details about any piece of software currently running on your PC

Choosing Winsock Service Providers from the list shows you what Winsock Layered Service Providers are running. Winsock Layered Service Providers are services required for network and Internet communications. Most Service Providers are necessary for your system, but some spyware authors write malicious Winsock Layered Service Providers. However, Windows Defender gives you no way to distinguish the good from the bad and no way to halt the bad. This section is mainly for informational purposes.

Allowed items

Windows Defender automatically creates a list of programs that it considers safe. To see the list, click "Allowed items." If you think any are not safe, highlight them and click Remove.

Windows Defender web site

Click here to go to the Windows Defender web site and get the latest news, information, and help about Windows Defender and about spyware in general.

Notes

- Windows Defender protects against spyware but not against other malware such as viruses and Trojans. So you'll need an antivirus program in addition to Windows Defender to be fully protected against malware.

- Spyware may be installed on your computer when you click on pop-up ads, or when a "drive-by download" installs itself without your knowledge. Internet Explorer includes built-in tools for preventing against these and other dangers. See Chapter 5 for details.

- The complex nature of spyware means that no single antispyware program is capable of protecting you against all spyware threats. So it's a good idea to use another piece of antispyware software in addition to Windows Defender. Good free ones are Ad-Aware (*http://www.lavasoft.com*) and Spybot Search & Destroy (*http://www.safer-networking.org*).

See also

"Windows Firewall," discussed next, and "Pop-Up Blocker," in Chapter 5

Windows Firewall

\windows\system32\firewall.cpl
(Windows Firewall Control Panel applet—basic features)
\windows\system32\wf.msc
(Windows Firewall with Advanced Security Group Policy—advanced features)

Protects against Internet-based and network-based threats.

To open

Control Panel → [Security] → Windows Firewall

Control Panel → [Network and Internet] → Windows Firewall

Command Prompt → **firewall.cpl** (Windows Firewall Control Panel applet)

Command Prompt › **wf.msc** (Windows Firewall with Advanced Security Group Policy)

Description

The Windows Firewall protects your PC against Internet threats by acting as a gatekeeper of sorts between you and the Internet, allowing only nonmalicious traffic through. It permits or denies network communication based on a predefined set of rules. These rules restrict communication so that only certain applications are permitted to use your network connection, or only certain network ports may be used. This effectively closes backdoors to your computer that viruses, hackers, and other malicious applications might otherwise exploit.

Windows Vista's firewall is a significant upgrade over the Windows XP firewall because it filters both inbound and outbound connections. (The Windows XP firewall blocked only inbound connections.) The addition of outbound filtering is important because some spyware, Trojans, and malicious software "phone home"—that is, they live on your PC, silently, and then make an outbound connection to someone who uses that connection for malicious purposes. The Windows Vista Firewall, however, blocks those outbound connections.

By default, both outbound and inbound protection are turned on when you install Windows Vista.

Windows Vista offers an exceptional amount of control over how the Windows Firewall runs. You can block or allow specific applications from making inbound or outbound connections; you can block or allow specific inbound and outbound ports; you can customize how certain applications access the Internet; and more.

Turning the Windows Firewall on and off is simple; select Control Panel → [Security] → Turn Windows Firewall on or off, and on the General tab select On, then click OK.

The primary way to control the Windows Firewall is via the Windows Firewall Control Panel applet, which is the only obvious way of doing it. That applet, though, gives you control over inbound connections only; you can't use it to customize outbound connections. To customize outbound connections, you'll instead have to use Windows Firewall with Advanced Security in Group Policy. Windows Firewall with Advanced Security in Group Policy also gives you far more control over every aspect of the Windows Firewall.

For most purposes, the Control Panel applet works fine, but for fine-grained control and to customize outbound connections, you'll have to turn to the Windows Firewall with Advanced Security in Group Policy.

Windows Firewall Control Panel

The Windows Firewall Control Panel applet has the following three tabs:

General
> In this tab you can switch the firewall on and off (see Figure 8-17). You can also use this tab to completely block any program from accessing the Internet. Check "Block all incoming connections" if you have a laptop with a wireless adapter, you're in a public location, and you don't want anyone to connect to your computer.

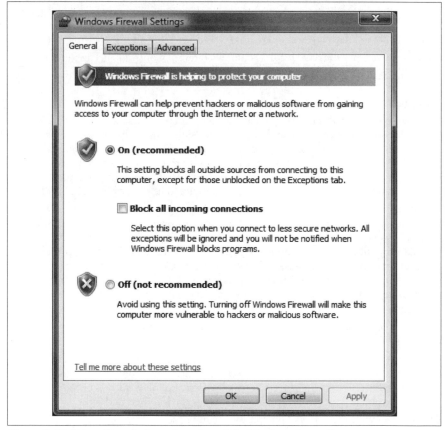

Figure 8-17. Controlling the basic functions of the Windows Firewall

You should never have more than one firewall running at one time, so if you're using a third-party firewall, such as ZoneAlarm or Norton Personal Firewall, you should turn off your Windows Firewall. Most third-party firewalls will turn off the Windows Firewall, but it's a good idea to check, just in case.

Exceptions

This tab lists programs or services that have attempted to make an Internet connection, as well as some services and programs that have not yet attempted to make a connection. Those with ticked checkboxes have been granted access; the rest are currently blocked. To grant access to one that is currently blocked, check the box next to it; to take away access from any, uncheck the box. For details about any program on the list, highlight it and click Properties.

To add a new program to the list, click the Add Program button to display a list of your installed software and double-click any application that you want to block or unblock. The Browse button on this dialog box lets you track down individual executables that don't appear on the list. The Add Port button lets you grant or deny access to a specific port by name and port number. Both the Add Program and Add Port buttons lead to dialog boxes with a "Change scope" button, where you can restrict the exception to just your network, a set of IP addresses and subnets that you specify, or any computer on the Internet (the default).

For details about any program on the Exceptions list, highlight it and click Properties. You'll get a brief description of the program, as well as a "How do I view and edit all properties?" link that leads to the Windows Vista help system. Don't bother to click the link; it leads to generic help about the Windows Firewall. However, if you dig deep enough, you'll find out that if you want to change the properties of how the firewall treats any program on the Exceptions list, you'll have to use the Windows Firewall with Advanced Security Group Policy. For details about how to use it, see the next section.

Advanced

This tab controls the level of access that each connection has to network services such as web servers, FTP servers, and remote desktop functions. The Restore Defaults button returns Windows Firewall to its factory settings.

Windows Firewall with Advanced Security

Group Policy gives you a great deal of control over how the Windows Firewall runs. You can run the Windows Firewall with Advanced Security by running the file *wf.msc* in *C:\Windows\System32* (Figure 8-18).

This is a very powerful tool, and detailing every way you can customize the Windows Firewall with it is beyond the scope of this book. These, though, are the tool's most useful features:

Windows Firewall Properties

Click this link to customize how the Windows Firewall works on domains, public networks, and private networks (Figure 8-19). For each, you can choose to have the firewall turned on or off (off on a domain, for example, and on when on a public network), and you can fine-tune it by outbound and inbound connections. You can also control whether the firewall will send messages when it blocks a connection, and you can configure IPsec security settings.

Figure 8-18. This powerful tool lets you customize almost every aspect of how the Windows Firewall works

Inbound Rules and Outbound Rules

Click this link to fine-tune how the Windows Firewall handles the way specific programs make inbound or outbound connections. This section is particularly relevant for network administrators, because it will allow them to customize how specific users and computers can access network connections and applications. The Outbound Rules link is the only way you can customize how the Windows Firewall handles outbound connections. Apart from that, however, you'll use these links only if you're a network administrator.

Notes

- There are third-party firewall solutions available that might provide a higher level of security or more options, but the Windows Firewall should provide an adequate level of protection for most home and small-office computers and networks.
- By default, Windows Vista does not log communication blocked by the Windows Firewall. To enable firewall logging, go to the Overview section of Windows Firewall with Advanced Security in Group Policy, select Windows Firewall Properties, and on the Domain Profile, Private Profile, and Public Profile tabs, click Customize in the logging section, then select On for both "Log dropped packets" and "Log successful connections." The default location of the log is *\Windows\pfirewall.log*, which is a text file that you can open in Notepad.

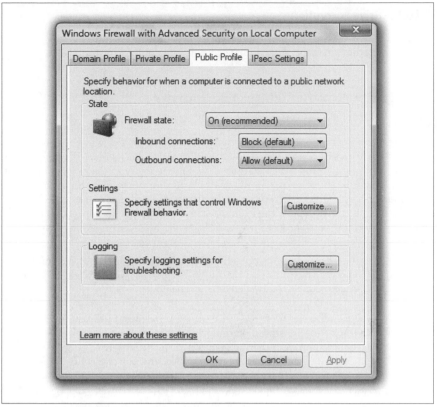

Figure 8-19. Configuring how the Windows Firewall works on domains, as well as on public and private networks

- If you find that a particular program no longer works, the problem may be that the Windows Firewall is blocking it for some reason. Verify that the firewall is causing the problem by temporarily disabling it and trying again. If the firewall is indeed the culprit, add a new rule to permit the program to communicate over your Internet connection.

See also

"Group Policy Object Editor," in Chapter 10

Encryption

If you want to make sure that no one can read your files or folders without your permission, your best bet is to use one of Windows Vista's encryption schemes, which scrambles data so that only those with the proper keys or passwords can read or use it.

Windows Vista has two types of encryption. The Encrypting File System (EFS) is a holdover from Windows XP, and it lets you encrypt individual files and folders. BitLocker Drive Encryption, new with Windows Vista, lets you lock down an entire computer so that only you can use it. In fact, if someone steals your laptop and you've encrypted it with BitLocker Drive Encryption, he won't even be able to start it up, much less read the files on it.

BitLocker Drive Encryption

Encrypts entire drives so that data can't be read, even if your computer is stolen (available only with the Enterprise and Ultimate editions of Windows Vista).

To open
Control Panel → [Security] → BitLocker Drive Encryption

Description
BitLocker Drive Encryption, new to Windows Vista, is the best way to keep all of your files safe from others. It works even if you have a laptop and it's stolen. It's designed so that your laptop or PC won't even start up without your encryption key, so a thief will not even be able to boot your PC, much less read any of its files. BitLocker Drive Encryption encrypts all files on a drive, including those needed for startup and logon. By doing this, it ensures that a thief cannot start your system, log on to it, and then steal your encrypting password as a way to decrypt and read your files.

The EFS can encrypt individual files and folders, but it cannot encrypt an entire startup drive (Windows won't work if you encrypted the files needed for startup and logon).

BitLocker encrypts all new files you add to your protected drive. The files are encrypted only when they are stored on the drive you've encrypted. If you copy them to another drive or computer, they are automatically decrypted. Shared files are encrypted when they are stored on the encrypted drive, and any user who has access to BitLocker-protected shared files will be able to use them as she would normally.

To turn on BitLocker Drive Encryption, choose Control Panel → [Security] → BitLocker Drive Encryption (see Figure 8-20) and click Turn on BitLocker. Alternatively, you can choose Control Panel → [Security] → BitLocker Drive Encryption. Follow the wizard that appears for turning it on; the instructions are straightforward. You'll be prompted to save a startup key to a removable Universal Serial Bus (USB) device, unless you have the Trusted Platform Module (TPM) version 1.2 or higher. (See the next section, "BitLocker hardware requirements," for details.) From then on, you'll have to insert the USB device into your computer in order for it to start. In addition, you'll create a recovery key or password so that you can always unlock BitLocker, in case you have problems starting up your PC.

Make sure not to skip the step for creating a recovery key or password—if you don't create one, you could lock up your PC so that you can't start it or recover any of your files.

BitLocker hardware requirements
BitLocker has specialized hardware requirements, which means that you may not be able to use it. It stores its encryption and decryption key in a device separate from your hard disk. Because of this, you'll need one of the following in order to use BitLocker:

- A computer that has TPM version 1.2 or higher. (TPM is a microchip in some new computers that supports advanced security features.) If you have hardware with TPM 1.2 or higher, BitLocker Drive Encryption will store its key on the chip.

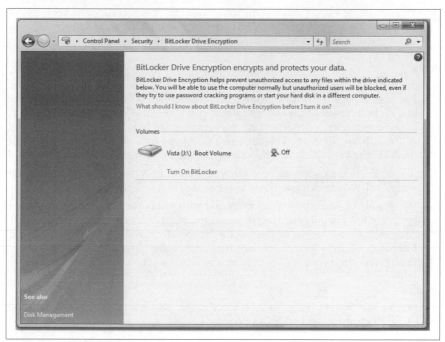

Figure 8-20. Turning on BitLocker Drive Encryption

- A removable USB flash drive. In this case, BitLocker Drive Encryption will store its key on the removable drive. Keep in mind, though, that you'll need to have the removable drive attached to your computer in order to use BitLocker Drive Encryption.

 Although Microsoft mentions that you can use BitLocker if you have a USB flash drive, you do need to go through some steps to get this to work. See *http://www.microsoft.com/technet/windowsvista/ library/c61f2a12-8ae6-4957-b031-97b4d762cf31.mspx* for details.

Even if you have one of the two aforementioned devices, though, you may not be able to use BitLocker Drive Encryption. You'll also need to meet the following requirements:

- You must have at least two partitions on your hard disk—one for the Windows Vista operating system (usually the *C:* drive), which BitLocker will encrypt, and another partition, which must remain unencrypted in order for your PC to start. This second partition needs to be both a primary partition and the active boot partition. If you have only one partition, you'll need to create a second one with these properties. As of this writing, the only way to do this is to perform a clean install of Vista and use "Repair Your Computer" to run *diskpart.exe*, then partition a small (at least 1.5 GB) primary and active partition that appears before your *C:* drive. Microsoft may release a tool in the future to repartition an existing drive.

- Your disk must be formatted with the NTFS filesystem. If it is formatted with FAT32, you can convert it to NTFS. See "FAT to NTFS Conversion Utility," in Chapter 11.

- You must have a BIOS that is compatible with the TPM and supports USB devices during computer startup. If you don't have one, you'll have to update the BIOS. If this is not the case, you will need to update the BIOS before using BitLocker.

Notes
- To find out whether your hardware supports TPM, check the BitLocker Drive Encryption page (shown in Figure 8-20). There should be a TPM administrator link in the left pane. If the link isn't there, you'll need a USB flash drive. However, in some instances, a BIOS problem may prevent the link from appearing, even if your hardware supports TPM. If you think your hardware supports TPM but don't see the link, check your documentation or the manufacturer's web site.
- If your PC doesn't support TPM but you have a USB flash drive, the BitLocker wizard will require that you create a startup key that will be stored on the drive.
- When your PC starts up and it's protected with BitLocker, BitLocker checks your hardware for potential security risks—for example, changes to startup files, BIOS changes, or disk errors. If this occurs, it will lock your drive. You'll need a BitLocker recovery key or password to unlock the drive. That's all the more reason to create a recovery key or password when you first turn on BitLocker.

See also
"Encrypting File System (EFS)" and "NTFS Encryption Utility," in this chapter, and "FAT to NTFS Conversion Utility," in Chapter 11

Certificate Manager   \windows\system32\certmgr.msc

Manages encryption and other certificates. See "Microsoft Management Console," in Chapter 10.

Encrypting File System (EFS)

Encrypt files and folders on NTFS drives (Business edition and higher only).

To open
Right-click a file or folder → Properties → General → Advanced

Description
You use the Encrypting File System (EFS) to prevent unauthorized access to your data, and one of the features of the NTFS filesystem is its built-in support for automatic encryption of files and folders using "public key cryptography." NTFS encryption is invisible, and encrypted files are opened as easily as decrypted files. The difference is that other users, either those who access your computer remotely or those who also log in to your computer under a different user account, will not be able to open or read encrypted files on your system.

Right-click on any file or folder, select Properties, and then click the Advanced button. The "Encrypt contents to secure data" option (shown in Figure 8-21) is used to instruct Windows to encrypt the selected item. If a folder is selected, all of its contents will be encrypted (you'll be prompted about any subfolders); furthermore, any files added to that folder will be automatically encrypted as well.

Figure 8-21. Encrypting a file or folder

The names of encrypted files show up in Windows Explorer in green rather than in the default black. (Compressed files show up blue.)

Notes

- NTFS drives support both encryption and compression, but you cannot compress and encrypt a given file at the same time. If you attempt to encrypt a compressed file, Windows will first uncompress the file.

- When you move an encrypted file to a nonencrypted folder on an NTFS drive, the file will remain encrypted.

- If you encrypt some or all of the files on your drive and your hard disk crashes, or you encounter some other program that requires Windows to be reinstalled, you may not be able to access your previously encrypted files (assuming they're still intact). You can avoid this by using the /r parameter of the NTFS Encryption Utility to generate a "recovery agent key," a cryptographic key that you can use to unlock files in the event of an emergency. You should be able to use this key to subsequently gain access to your encrypted files when necessary. For more information, go to Start → Help and Support and search for "cryptography." See "NTFS Encryption Utility," later in this chapter, for details.

- This type of file encryption is supported on NTFS drives only. If you want to encrypt files on a non-NTFS drive, you can either upgrade to NTFS or use a third-party file encryption utility such as TrueCrypt (*http://www.truecrypt.org*).

- If you don't want encrypted files to show up in green, open Windows Explorer and choose Organize → Folder Options → View tab and uncheck the "Show encrypted or compressed NTFS files in color" option.

See also

"NTFS Encryption Utility" and "BitLocker Drive Encryption"

NTFS Encryption Utility   \windows\system32\cipher.exe

View or configure the automatic file encryption on NTFS drives.

To open

Command Prompt → **cipher**

Usage

```
cipher [/e|/d|/c] [/b] [/s] [/a] [/f] [/q] [/h] [filename]
cipher /k
cipher /x [filename]
cipher /r:efs_file
cipher /w:dir
cipher /u [/n]
cipher /y
cipher /adduser [/CERTHASH:hash | /CERTFILE:filename]
cipher /removeuser /CERTHASH:hash
cipher /rekey
```

Description

The NTFS Encryption Utility is the command-line equivalent of encrypting files using
Windows Explorer. (See the preceding section, "Encrypting File System (EFS)," for
details.) However, it adds several powerful features not normally available through
Explorer. It's also useful for automating the encryption or decryption of several files
with the help of a batch file. The NTFS Encryption Utility takes the following options:

filename

Specifies a file, folder, or group of files (using wildcards) to compress or uncompress. Omit *filename* to act on the current directory.

/e

Encrypts the specified file(s). If a folder is specified for *filename*, the folder will be
marked so that subsequent files added to it will be encrypted automatically.
Include the /a parameter to encrypt files already in the folder and the /s parameter to act on subdirectories as well.

/d

Decrypts the specified file(s). If a folder is specified for *filename*, the folder will be
marked so that subsequent files added to the folder will be decrypted automatically. Include the /a parameter to decrypt files already in the folder and the /s
parameter to act on subdirectories as well.

/s

By default, if *filename* is a directory, the /e or /d option acts on the specified
directory but not on any subdirectories. Include /s to include all subdirectories as
well. Use the /a option to encrypt the files stored in these directories.

/a

Operates on files as well as folders. If folders and files are not *both* marked to be
encrypted, it's possible for an encrypted file to become decrypted when it is modified if its parent folder is not encrypted.

/b

Aborts if an error occurs. Cipher normally continues to execute, even if it encounters errors.

/h

Includes files with hidden or system attributes set; otherwise, ignored by *cipher.exe*.

/k

Generates and displays a new file encryption key (certificate thumbprint) for the current user. You cannot use the /k option with any other options.

/r:*efs_file*

Generates an EFS recovery agent key and certificate, and then writes them to *efs_file.pfx* (containing the certificate and private key) and *efs_file.cer* (containing only the certificate). Because the /r option will automatically add the appropriate file extensions, all you need to specify are the path and file prefixes for *efs_file*. See "Notes," later in this section, for more information.

/w:*dir*

"Wipes" the drive containing the directory *dir*. When a file is deleted in Windows, only that file's entry in the filesystem table is deleted; the actual data contained in the file remains on the hard disk until it is overwritten with another file. Wiping a drive writes over all unused portions of the disk, possibly containing deleted files so that previously deleted data cannot be recovered. The /w option does not harm existing data, nor does it affect any files currently stored in the Recycle Bin. This is an extreme form of data security, and you should use it on a regular basis if security is a big concern.

/u

Updates all encrypted files on all local drives. Use /u to ensure that your file encryption key or recovery agent key is current. You cannot use the /u option with any other options, except for /n.

/n

Modifies /u so that encrypted files are only listed, not updated. Type **cipher /u /n** to list all the encrypted files on your system. You can use the /n option only in conjunction with /u.

/x

Backs up the EFS certificate and keys into a file. If *efs_file* is provided, the current user's certificate(s) used to encrypt the file will be backed up. If not, the user's current EFS certificate and keys will be backed up.

/y

Displays your current EFS certificate thumbnail.

/adduser

Adds a user to the specified encrypted file(s). If CERTHASH is provided, cipher will search for a certificate with the hash SHA1. If CERTFILE is provided, cipher will extract the certificate from the file.

/rekey

Updates the specified encrypted file(s) to use the configured EFS key.

/removeuser

Removes a user from the specified file(s). CERTHASH must be the SHA1 hash of the certificate.

If you run the NTFS Encryption Utility without any options, it will display the encryption settings for the current directory and all of its contents.

Security

Notes

- If you encrypt some or all of the files on your drive and your hard disk crashes, or if you encounter some other program that requires Windows to be reinstalled, you may not be able to access your previously encrypted files (assuming they're still intact). You can avoid this by using the /r parameter to generate a "recovery agent key," a cryptographic key that you can use to unlock files in the event of an emergency. You should be able to use this key to subsequently gain access to your encrypted files when necessary. For more information, go to Start → Help and Support and search for "cryptography."

- The /w option, used to wipe unused data on a drive, isn't strictly a form of encryption, and you can use it regardless of whether you employ Windows Vista's built-in encryption.

- Although *cipher.exe* is available on the Home editions of Vista, it will return an error ("The request is not supported") if you try to encrypt a file with it.

See also

"BitLocker Drive Encryption"

9

Working with Hardware

Windows Vista makes quick work of managing your hardware; to a great extent, once you plug in a device, the operating system automatically recognizes it and either finishes the installation itself or prompts you to install a disk with the proper driver.

But that's not always the case, of course. And even if it does recognize your hardware properly, you need to manage the hardware, customize the way it runs, or troubleshoot any problems with it.

This chapter covers all the ways Windows Vista works with hardware of any kind. It details the tools, screens, and options for handling hardware. Note that some troubleshooting and maintenance tools are covered in Chapter 11, and mobile-related options, such as Power Options, are covered in Chapter 7.

Here is an alphabetical reference of entries in this chapter:

Add Hardware Wizard	DriverQuery	Signature Verification Tool
Add Printer	Game Controllers	Sound
AutoPlay	Keyboard Properties	Sound Recorder
Color Management	Mouse Properties	System Information
Computer Management	Pen and Input Devices	System Properties
Device Manager	Phone and Modem Options	Tablet PC Settings
DirectX Management Tool	Power Options	Volume Mixer
Disk and Volume Properties	Printers	Windows Update Driver Settings
Display Settings	ReadyBoost	XPS Document Viewer
Driver Verifier Manager	Scanners and Cameras	

Add Hardware Wizard

\windows\system\hdwwiz.cpl

Detect non-Plug and Play devices and install the appropriate drivers.

To open

Control Panel → Add Hardware (in Classic view)

Command Prompt → **hdwwiz.cpl**

Description

When you turn on your computer, Windows automatically scans for newly added Plug and Play (PnP) devices and installs drivers for any that it finds. If you're trying to install a device that isn't detected automatically, you'll need to run the Add Hardware Wizard (see Figure 9-1).

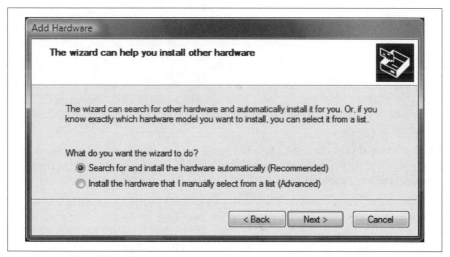

Figure 9-1. The Add Hardware Wizard

When you start the Add Hardware Wizard and click Next, it goes through the following steps:

1. You're asked whether to have the wizard search for and install the hardware automatically, or whether you want to choose the hardware from a list. It's best to have the wizard search automatically.

2. The wizard scans your system for any newly attached PnP devices. If one or more devices are found, the appropriate drivers are located and installed.

3. If no new devices are found in step 2 (or if you decide in step 1 to choose hardware from a list), you'll be asked to click Next to choose your hardware from a list.

4. The wizard displays a list of hardware categories from which you can choose ("Display adapters," "Imaging devices," "All devices," and so on). Select a category. A list of manufacturers appears. Select the manufacturer.

5. If you have the drivers for the device on either a floppy, a CD, or your hard disk, click Have Disk at this point. Otherwise, choose the specific model number from the list on the right. If your device doesn't show up here, drivers for it aren't included with Windows Vista.

6. The last steps involve copying and installing the drivers, and then prompting you to restart (if applicable).

Notes

- Some devices have specific installation procedures that you must follow. For example, you may need to install the included software first and then connect the device. When Windows detects the device, the drivers are already in place and installation proceeds without a hitch. Make sure you review the installation instructions before you resort to the Add Hardware Wizard.

- If your hardware comes with an installation CD, it's best to first try to install the hardware using the installation routine on the CD before launching the Add Hardware Wizard.

- If you don't have the driver on disk, go to the manufacturer's web site, download the driver, and use that driver when you click Have Disk. The manufacturer's web site also may have an installation program. If it does, download and use that rather than the Add Hardware Wizard.

- When Windows discovers new hardware, either during startup or when using the Add Hardware Wizard, you'll usually be prompted to specify a driver. The Install Software Automatically option is usually the best choice, as it will attempt to use one of the built-in drivers in Windows. If no compatible driver can be found, you'll be prompted to insert a disk or point to a folder containing appropriate drivers, either shipped with the hardware product or downloaded from the manufacturer's web site, respectively.

- When installing some drivers, Windows Vista may complain that the driver is not digitally signed. This confusing and rather harsh message simply informs you that the manufacturer of the driver you're installing hasn't added a digital signature to the driver software, which, in most cases, will pose no problem. Just click Continue Anyway to proceed. See the "Signature Verification Tool" section, later in this chapter, for more information on driver signing.

See also

"Add Printer," "Scanners and Cameras," and "Printers"

Add Printer

Add and configure a printer.

To open

Control Panel → [Hardware and Sound] → Add a printer

Description

When you connect a printer to your PC via a Universal Serial Bus (USB) connection, Windows Vista should automatically recognize it and install drivers for it, or prompt you to install drivers. But if you want to use a network printer, use a wireless printer (either WiFi or Bluetooth), or connect a printer to your PC via the printer port (also called a *parallel port*), you'll need to use the Add Printer dialog.

You'll be presented with two choices: to add either a local printer or a network printer. If you choose to add a local printer, you'll be asked which printer port you want it to use; after that point, the instructions are the same as those for the Add Hardware Wizard, so follow those.

If you install a network or wireless printer, Windows will search for the printer and then install it. If Windows can't locate the network printer, click "The printer that I want isn't listed." A dialog, such as the one shown in Figure 9-2, will appear. If you know the network location name or the IP address of the printer, enter it. Otherwise, click Browse, browse to the printer's network location, and install it that way.

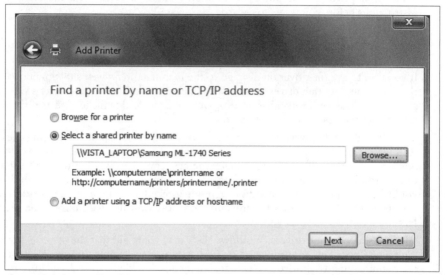

Figure 9-2. Manually adding a network printer when the wizard can't find one

Notes

- In order to use a network printer, you'll need to have its printer driver available to install on your PC. Windows may have the driver for the printer, but if not, you'll need the installation or driver disk, or the driver downloaded from the manufacturer's web site.

- Before you can add a network printer, you first need to share it. See "Sharing Resources and Files," in Chapter 7, for details.

- Unless you have reason to choose another port for your printer, choose LPT1: if you're connecting your printer via its parallel port.

- If you have a network printer that Windows refuses to connect to, try installing it as a local printer. When prompted to choose a port, select Create a new Port → Standard TCP/IP Port, and enter the IP address or hostname when prompted.

See also

"Printers" and "Add Hardware Wizard"

AutoPlay

Set options for how Windows handles the insertion of various types of media and content.

To open

Control Panel → [Hardware and Sound] → AutoPlay

Description

Whenever you insert a CD or DVD in your PC, Windows either takes an action or asks you what action it should take. AutoPlay (Figure 9-3) lets you set how Windows should handle many different types of media—and can even take different actions based on the media's content.

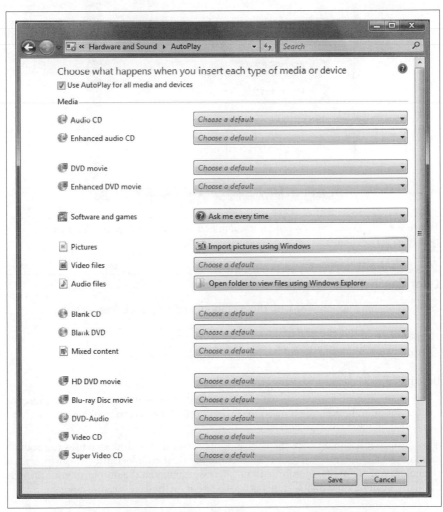

Figure 9-3. AutoPlay, which controls the actions Windows should take when you insert various types of media and content

Working with Hardware

Configuration is straightforward. For each type of media or content, select the action you want Windows to take when the media or content is inserted and then click Save.

If you don't choose an action for a particular type of media or content, you'll receive a message such as that shown in Figure 9-4 whenever you insert that kind of media. You can set AutoPlay options from this screen.

Figure 9-4. The message you receive if you don't choose AutoPlay options for a particular type of media or content

Color Management

Align colors on your monitor with those of input and output devices.

To open
Control Panel → [Hardware and Sound] → Color Management

Description
Color management allows you to align the colors of your monitor with those of various input and output devices so that what you see on-screen matches as closely as possible with what will be printed.

This mismatch has to do with the nature of processes that each device uses to produce colors. An LCD monitor uses different technology than an inkjet printer, obviously, so the colors you see on the monitor will not necessarily match the output of your printer. Similarly, scanners and digital cameras use different methods to capture colors.

To most of us, this is not particularly important, because what you see on-screen and what you print are close enough to one another. But professional designers and artists need more control than this approximation, and they can use Color Management for that purpose.

Color Management lets you create and choose profiles for your devices and then match them to each other. It's often used in concert with print production houses, so confer with yours to find out the best settings.

Computer Management

\windows\system32\compmgmt.exe

See "Microsoft Management Console," in Chapter 10.

Device Manager

\windows\system32\devmgmt.msc

Configure all hardware installed in or attached to a computer.

To open

Control Panel → [System and Maintenance] → Device Manager

Control Panel → [System and Maintenance] → System → Device Manager

Control Panel → [Hardware and Sound] → Device Manager

Command Prompt → `devmgmt.msc`

Description

Device Manager is the central interface for gathering information about and making changes to all the hardware installed in a system. Device Manager has an Explorer-style tree listing all of the various hardware categories, as shown in Figure 9-5; expand any category branch to display all installed devices that fit in that category. For example, expand the Network adapters branch to list all installed network cards in the system. Right-click any device and choose one of the following actions:

Update Driver
> If you have a newer driver than what is currently installed (find out by using Properties), select Update Driver to locate and install the new driver. This is the preferred way to update drivers in Windows Vista, though some devices may have proprietary installation programs and don't support their drivers being updated in this way.
>
> From the screen that appears, you can have Windows search your computer and the Internet for an updated driver, or you can manually point Windows to a drive or location on your CD where you have the updated driver.

Disable
> Select Disable to effectively turn off this device, usually releasing hardware resources it normally consumes. This can be very handy when attempting to resolve hardware conflicts; if you removed the device using Uninstall, discussed next, Windows Vista would simply reinstall the device the next time Windows starts. Disabling the hardware instead turns off the device but keeps the drivers intact; you can then enable it whenever you want.

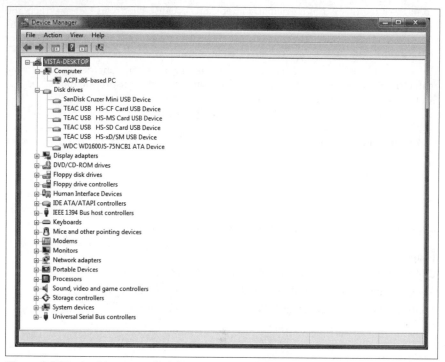

Figure 9-5. Device Manager, which lets you view and change the settings for nearly any hardware device attached to your system

Uninstall

Uninstall is more useful than it might seem on the surface. When you uninstall a device from Device Manager, it completely removes the driver from the system and erases all the corresponding configuration settings for that device. In addition to using Uninstall when you're physically removing a device from your system, it's also very handy when you're experiencing a problem with the device. When you remove a device from Device Manager and restart your computer, Windows will redetect the device and install it as though it were plugged in for the first time; this can be a very useful tool for repairing corrupt installations and fixing all sorts of problems with devices and their drivers.

 Uninstall is not the way to force Windows to stop recognizing the uninstalled device, because Windows will just reload the driver the next time it starts. Instead, use Disable for this purpose.

Scan for hardware changes

This option will force Windows to rescan the device, checking to see whether it has been removed, turned on, turned off, or reconfigured in some way.

Highlight a category in the Device Manager tree and select "Scan for hardware changes" to not only scan for changes in the installed hardware, but also force Windows to look for new devices in this category. Typically, you'd use the Add

Hardware Wizard to install new devices. However, this procedure is useful for reattaching devices that have already been installed, such as USB devices or removable hard disks that are attached and reattached repeatedly. Likewise, highlight the root (the entry at the top of the tree, named for your computer) and select "Scan for hardware changes" to scan all categories for newly attached, recently changed, or recently disconnected devices.

Properties

The Properties sheet for any device contains a great deal of information about the device's driver, the status of the device, and several troubleshooting features (including those mentioned previously). Information and settings are divided into the following tabbed pages, some of which may or may not be present, depending on the device (see Figure 9-6).

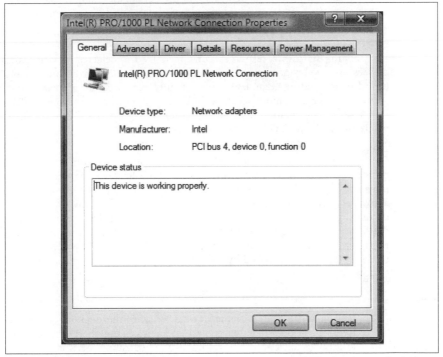

Figure 9-6. The Properties sheet for a device on your system, which also shows whether Windows thinks the device is working

The General tab
Shows the name, type, manufacturer, and physical location of the device (if applicable). The Device status box shows relevant messages stating whether the driver is installed properly or whether the device is functioning.

The Advanced tab
Contains settings specific to the device. For example, the Advanced tab for network adapters contains several settings that select how to handle speed and flow control features, and many other options.

The Driver tab

Displays several pieces of information about the currently installed driver, such as the provider (which corresponds to the distributor, not the manufacturer, of the software), the driver date and version, and whether the driver has a digital signature (used to verify the integrity of the driver, available only on drivers designed especially for Windows Vista). Click Driver Details to see the individual files that make up the driver, or click Roll Back Driver to uninstall the current driver and replace it with the previously used driver (available only if the driver has been updated since Windows was installed). The Update Driver and Uninstall buttons have the same effect as the actions of the same name, described earlier.

The Details tab

Lists a great many technical details about the device, including not only basic information such as the manufacturer and a description of the device, but also other details useful primarily to developers.

The Resources tab

Lists all the hardware resources consumed by the selected device. Most devices use one or more of the following: a range of memory (expressed as a hexadecimal address), an I/O range (again, expressed as a hexadecimal address), a direct memory access (DMA) line, or an interrupt request (IRQ) line. Use the information on this page to help diagnose hardware conflicts, where two or more devices try to use the same address or IRQ.

The Power Management tab

Controls how Windows uses power-saving features in concert with the device. It controls whether Windows can turn off the device to save power in power-saving modes, and similar actions. It also gives you the option to allow the device to bring Windows out of power-saving modes, if the device needs to perform an action. Be careful when choosing this option, because the device may wake the computer at times when you don't want it awakened, or it may use up too much power. Whenever possible, use the configuration utility supplied by the vendor to configure power management options.

Notes

- Open the View menu to rearrange the devices by type (the default) or connection. (Group all PCI devices together and all USB devices together, for example.) You can also arrange devices by the resources they consume. This is useful for resolving conflicts. See the earlier discussion of the Resources tab, under "Properties," for more information.

- You use the "Show hidden devices" entry in the View menu to display all currently installed drivers, including those for some of the more obscure "non-PnP drivers." It is also useful for uninstalling drivers from devices you no longer use but that Windows still believes are on your system. Show the hidden devices, and then uninstall the drivers.

When you remove a drive, card, or other piece of hardware from your computer, Windows does not automatically remove the corresponding drivers, but deactivates them. To remove the drivers for a device you don't plan to reinstall later on, you should locate the device in Device Manager, right-click, and select Uninstall before you physically disconnect the device.

- Device Manager is a snap-in used with the Microsoft Management Console, discussed in Chapter 10.
- Although you can use Device Manager to configure and remove installed devices, and even add devices by using "Scan for hardware changes," the preferred way to add new hardware is to use the installation software supplied by the vendor, or the Add Hardware Wizard if needed.
- All branches in Device Manager are collapsed by default; to expand the branches, highlight the root entry and press the asterisk (*) key on the numeric keypad.

DirectX Management Tool

See Chapter 11.

Disk and Volume Properties

View and change the properties of disks and volumes, including removable disks.

To open

Right-click a drive → Properties

Click a drive → Organize → Properties

Description

The exact number of tabs on the Disk Properties page varies according to the type of drive or volume and its characteristics. For example, a hard drive may have seven tabs: General, Tools, Hardware, Sharing, Security, Previous Versions, and Customize. A USB flash drive, on the other hand, may have six: General, Tools, Hardware, Sharing, ReadyBoost, and Customize. And a DVD-RW drive may have five: General, Hardware, Sharing, Customize, and Recording.

There is a difference between a physical disk and a volume, although Windows Vista calls them both disks. The physical disk is the hardware itself, and a volume is a separate section of the hard disk. So a single disk may have multiple volumes, or it may have only a single volume.

Following are the tabs you'll typically find on a variety of drives and volumes:

General

This tab (Figure 9-7) displays basic information about the drive, including its type, filesystem (if applicable), capacity, free space and used space, and so on. If it's a drive used for storage, it will also include tools for disk cleanup, tools for using compression to save space, and an option for whether the disk should be indexed. You can set the label of the drive or volume by typing it into the box at the top of the screen.

Figure 9-7. The General tab, which shows you basic information about the disk

Tools

This tab includes a variety of maintenance tools, including tools to defragment the drive, back up the drive, and check the drive for errors.

Hardware

This tab (Figure 9-8) lists each physical disk drive on your system, including type, manufacturer name, and so on, and shows whether it is working properly. Highlight any drive and click the Properties button, and the Device Properties dialog box appears with tabs that:

- Include information about the drive
- List the volumes on the drive
- Provide information about the device's drivers
- Let you update, roll back, disable, or uninstall the driver
- Let you set policies for removable storage devices, such as whether they should be optimized for quick removal or for high performance
- Offer a variety of highly technical information about the drive's specifications and capabilities

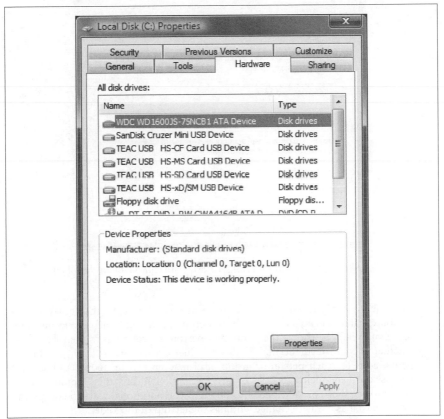

Figure 9-8. The Hardware tab, which lists all of the physical disk drives on your system

Sharing

This tab (Figure 9-9) lets you set sharing options for the drive. Click Share to share the folder or change sharing options if the folder is already shared. Click Advanced Sharing if you want to give it a *share name* in addition to its existing folder name (do this if you want to make it easier for someone to find the folder). The Advanced Sharing button also lets you create custom permissions for the share.

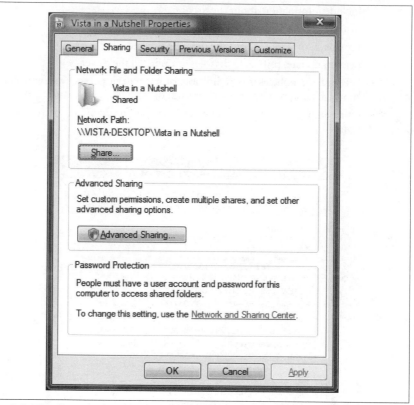

Figure 9-9. The Sharing tab, where you can see basic information about the folder

Security

This tab shows you who has access to read and modify the folder and its attributes, and it lets you change those permissions. Click each group and user-name and you'll be shown the rights that person or group has to the folder file—whether she can read the file, modify the file, and so on. You can modify the permissions for each person or group, add new groups or people and set their permissions, and delete people or groups, which means they would have no access to the file. The Advanced button gives you additional ways to edit permissions, as well as a way to change who has ownership of the folder.

The various permission options and their meanings are quite complex, and beyond the scope of this book. However, if you want more details about all the available options, go to the Microsoft Knowledge Base article at *http://support.microsoft.com/kb/308419/en-us*.

Previous Versions

This tab lets you view, save, or restore a previous version of a drive, if such a version is available. Two types of previous versions may be available: those from a backup, and those from what Windows Vista calls shadow copies. A shadow copy of a folder is a copy of a file made when Windows creates a restore point. (See "System Protection and System Restore," in Chapter 11, for details.)

Customize

This tab lets you customize how the root folder of the drive looks and acts. You can choose the kind of folder it is (All Items, Documents, Pictures and Videos, Music Details, or Music Icons). Based on what type of folder it is, the documents in it will be displayed differently, and different features will be available. For example, if a folder is a Pictures and Videos folder, the details it will display about each file include the Date Taken, Tags, and Size and Rating, and the folder toolbar will include a Slide Show button so that you can display a full screen show of the files in the folder. If, instead, the folder is a Documents folder, the details it will display are the Date Modified, Type, Size, and Tags. No Slide Show button will appear on the toolbar.

The tab also lets you choose a file that will be displayed on the root folder's icon in Windows Explorer, and it lets you choose an icon different from the default.

ReadyBoost

This tab (Figure 9-10) lets you configure a flash drive (USB, SD, MMC, etc.) to use ReadyBoost as a way to improve Windows Vista performance. You can select how much of the drive to use for ReadyBoost and how much for storage. For details, see "ReadyBoost," in Chapter 11.

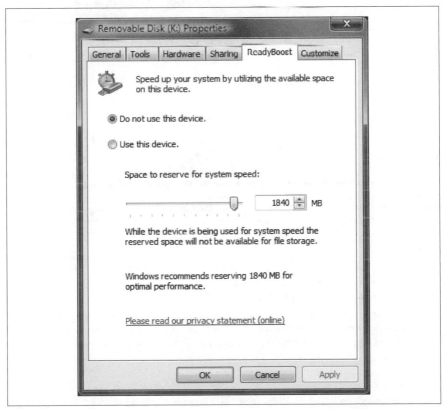

Figure 9-10. The ReadyBoost tab, which lets you configure ReadyBoost on a flash drive

Recording

This tab (Figure 9-11) lets you select the default recorder, the drive to use to store temporary files necessary for burning discs, and settings related to burning discs, such as whether to eject the disk after burning.

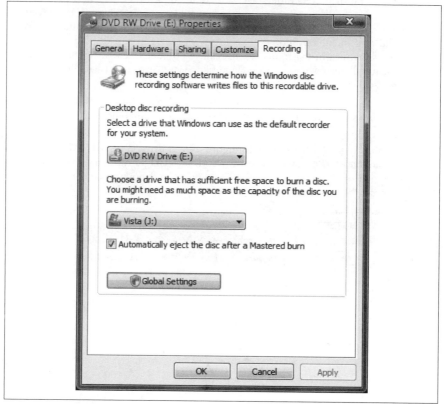

Figure 9-11. The Recording tab, which controls burning options, including which drive should be the default one for recording

Notes

- Not all flash drives meet the performance requirements needed to use Ready-Boost, so Windows Vista tests the drive when you insert it. If it doesn't meet the requirements, a screen appears, telling you that it can't be used for ReadyBoost.
- To restore a previous version of a drive without using the Drive Properties screen, right-click the drive in Windows Explorer and select "Restore previous versions." You'll receive a warning before you overwrite the existing drive with the previous one.

See also

"File Properties" and "Folder Properties," in Chapter 4, "ReadyBoost," in Chapter 11, and "Sharing Resources and Files," in Chapter 7

Display Settings

Change the settings of your display adapter and monitor.

To open

Control Panel → [Appearance and Personalization] → Adjust screen resolution

Control Panel → [Appearance and Personalization] → Personalization → Display Settings

Right-click on an empty portion of your Desktop → Personalize → Display Settings

Command Prompt → `desk.cpl`

Description

This dialog (Figure 9-12) lets you choose the resolution and color depth of your screen, change your display hardware settings, and customize how you use two monitors on the same system. Two limitations of your video card may affect the settings here. First, the amount of memory on your video card dictates the maximum color depth and resolution you can use. Second, as you adjust your color depth, Windows may automatically adjust other settings depending on your card's capabilities. If you increase your color depth, your resolution might automatically decrease; likewise, if you raise the resolution, your color depth might go down.

If you have more than one monitor, using either two separate video cards or a single video card that supports two monitors, all configured screens will be shown in the preview area. Click any screen icon to activate it; the settings below apply only to the selected monitor. You can even drag and drop monitor icons to rearrange them so that, for example, a different monitor assumes the role of the upper left. If you're not sure which monitor is #1 and which is #2, click Identify Monitors.

The Advanced button allows you to view the hardware properties for your video adapter(s) and monitor(s). You'll really never need to adjust these settings unless you're updating a driver for your monitor or display adapter, configuring color profiles (for matching the color output of your printer with your scanner and monitor), or adjusting your monitor's refresh rate.

It's worth taking a few minutes to discuss the refresh rate. Although the maximum refresh rate does not depend on the amount of memory your card has, you may have to lower your resolution to achieve the desired rate. Windows should automatically adjust your refresh rate to the highest setting your card supports, but this does not always happen. If you notice that your display appears to be flickering, especially under fluorescent lights, you'll need to raise your refresh rate either by adjusting the refresh rate setting directly or by lowering your resolution or color depth. (Note that this does not apply to flat-panel or laptop displays, which never flicker.) Consequently, if you hear a slight whine from your monitor, it means your refresh rate is too high. The minimum refresh rate you should tolerate is 72 Hz. People with corrective lenses seem to be more sensitive and might require a higher setting to be comfortable. Most cards available today support refresh rates of 85 Hz and higher, so this is usually not a problem. If your display driver supports it, you can adjust your refresh rate with the Refresh Rate setting by clicking the Advanced button, clicking the Monitor tab, and changing the rate in the "Screen refresh rate" drop-down box.

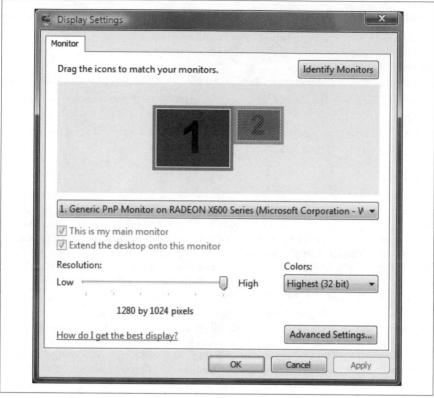

Figure 9-12. Choosing your screen resolution, color depth, and multiple-monitor setup with the Display Settings dialog

---

Driver Verifier Manager

\windows\system32\verifier.exe

A tool for monitoring Windows kernel-mode drivers and graphics drivers.

To open

Command Prompt → **verifier**

Description

Driver Verifier Manager is included with Windows Vista primarily for hardware manufacturers to test their drivers to ensure that they are not making illegal function calls or causing system corruption.

Notes

For more information on using the Driver Verifier Manager, see *http://www.microsoft.com/whdc/DevTools/tools/vistaverifier.mspx*.

DriverQuery

\windows\system32\driverquery.exe

Display a list of the installed device drivers and their properties.

To open

Command Prompt → **driverquery**

Usage

```
driverquery [/fo] [/nh] [/si] [/v] [/s [/u [/p]]]
```

Description

Although Device Manager displays a hierarchical view of all of the devices attached to the system, only Driver Query provides a comprehensive list for every installed driver, either on a local machine or on any remote computer on the network.

Run Driver Query without any options to print out the basic list, or use one of the following options:

/fo *format*
> Specify the format of the display: type **/fo table** (the default) for a formatted table, **/fo list** for a plain-text list, or **/fo csv** for a comma-separated report, suitable for importing into a spreadsheet or database.

/nh
> If using the /fo table or /fo csv format (as just discussed), the /nh option turns off the column headers.

/v
> Display additional details about drivers other than signed drivers.

/si
> Display additional details about signed drivers.

/s *system*
> Connect to a remote system, where *system* is the name of the computer.

/u *user*
> Specify a user account (include an optional domain before the username) under which the command should execute.

/p *password*
> Specify the password for the user account specified with the /u parameter; prompts for the password if omitted.

Game Controllers

\windows\system32\joy.cpl

Configure any joysticks, steering wheels, and game pads attached to your system.

To open

Control Panel → [Hardware and Sound] → Game Controllers

Command Prompt → **control joy.cpl**

Description

Before you can use a joystick or other game controller with Windows-based games, you must install its driver here. If your game controller doesn't appear in the list, run the Add Hardware Wizard.

Notes

- Not all game controllers have settings that you can change, so the Properties button may be grayed out.

Keyboard Properties

Change the keyboard repeat rate and text cursor blink rate.

To open

Control Panel → [Hardware and Sound] → Keyboard

Command Prompt → `control main.cpl Keyboard`

Command Prompt → `control keyboard`

Description

The Keyboard Properties dialog controls the way characters are repeated when keys are held down, as well as how quickly the text cursor (insertion point) blinks. Tip: move the "Repeat rate" slider all the way to the right (toward Fast), and your computer may actually seem faster (see Figure 9-13).

The Hardware tab simply provides access to the Properties sheet for your keyboard (the same one you'll get in Device Manager, discussed earlier in this chapter).

Notes

- Some keyboards, especially those with additional function buttons (such as web links and CD player controls), come with their own software. Some of this software includes hardware drivers and is absolutely necessary for operation, and other software is purely optional, adding only trivial features. Given the potential compatibility problems with Windows Vista and older hardware, it's best to install such software only if it's necessary, if it provides features you can't live without, or if the hardware is recent enough that the vendor makes Vista-compatible drivers available.

See also

"Control Panel," in Chapter 3

Mouse Properties   \windows\system32\main.cpl

Change settings that affect the behavior of your pointing device and the appearance of the mouse cursor.

To open

Control Panel → [Hardware and Sound] → Mouse

Command Prompt → `control main.cpl`

Command Prompt → `control mouse`

Figure 9-13. Making a computer seem faster by moving the Repeat rate slider all the way to the right in Character repeat

Description

The Mouse Properties dialog controls the buttons and motion of your pointing device and the appearance of the various mouse cursors, such as the arrow and hourglass. Settings are distributed into the following sections:

Buttons

The three settings on this page allow you to switch the left and right mouse buttons (useful for southpaws or those with unusual pointing devices), change the speed at which items respond to double-clicks, and control the ClickLock feature (which enables dragging without having to hold down any buttons).

Pointers

The Pointers tab (Figure 9-14) lets you choose how your mouse pointer looks. This affects not only the standard arrow cursor, but also the hourglass, the arrow/hourglass combination, all of the resize arrows, and even the hand cursor used in Internet Explorer. Cursors that ship with Windows are stored in the *Windows*\ *Cursors* folder and additional cursors are available on the Internet from such web sites as *http://www.anicursor.com*. You can also get a cursor editor, allowing you to create your own static and animated mouse pointers (try AX-Cursors at *http:// www.axialis.com/axcursors*, or Microangelo at *http://www.microangelo.us*).

Figure 9-14. Choosing custom mouse pointers

 A free program called Comet Cursor promises to let you customize your cursor. However, many people consider it spyware, and once you install it, it may be difficult to remove, even with antispyware software such as Windows Defender.

Pointer Options

These settings adjust how the mouse pointer responds to the physical motion of your pointing device. A fast pointer speed makes the cursor more sensitive. The "Enhance pointer precision" option enables minor mouse acceleration and deceleration, which moves the pointer more slowly when you move only a short distance.

 If you use a laptop, it's easy to lose track of your pointer, and it may be difficult to find at times. Two Pointer Options settings can help solve the problem. With the "Display pointer trails" option, your pointer will leave a series of visual "trails" as it moves across the screen, making it easier to see. And the "Show location of pointer when I press the CTRL key" option is particularly helpful for those times when the pointer appears to have vanished; if you choose this option, a bull's-eye appears around the pointer when you press Ctrl.

Wheel

The mouse wheel is intended to aid scrolling. Just roll the wheel to scroll up or down in a listbox, document, or web page instead of controlling the scroll bar directly with the mouse pointer. The options here also let you control wheels that tilt. If your pointing device doesn't have a wheel, these settings are ignored.

Hardware

Finally, the Hardware tab simply lists the pointing devices attached to the system. Note that the Properties page is the same one you'll get in Device Manager (discussed earlier in this chapter).

Notes

- Many pointing devices come with their own software. Some of this software includes hardware drivers and is absolutely necessary for operation, and other software is purely optional, adding only trivial features. Given the potential compatibility problems with Windows Vista and older hardware, it's best to install such software only if it's necessary, if it provides features you can't live without, or if the hardware is recent enough that the vendor makes Vista-compatible drivers available.

- Laptops include built-in touchpads or other devices that serve the function of mice. Many include their own software for adjusting how they work, which may either run separately from the Mouse Properties dialog or add an additional tab or tabs to the Mouse Properties dialog.

See also

"Keyboard Properties"

Pen and Input Devices

See Chapter 7.

Phone and Modem Options

See Chapter 7.

Power Options

See Chapter 7.

Printers

Manage printers.

To open

Control Panel → [Hardware and Sound] → Printers

Description

Printers (Figure 9-15) is actually a specialized Windows Explorer folder that offers a variety of ways to manage your printers and printing. The folder lists all of your printers and includes a toolbar for managing them, including adding a printer, opening the print queue, choosing printing preferences, pausing a printer, renaming and deleting a printer, sharing a printer, and so on.

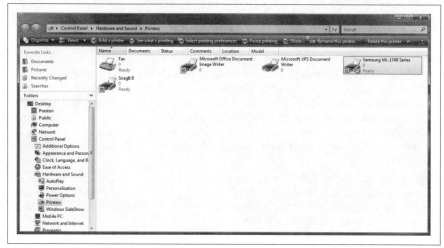

Figure 9-15. The Printer folder, which lets you manage all your printers

Many of the same options are also available when you right-click a printer. To set a printer as the default, right-click it and choose Set as Default Printer.

 Printers need not be actual physical printers connected to your PC; they can also be virtual. For example, the Microsoft XPS Document Writer is listed as a printer, but it's used to create XPS documents. (For details, see "XPS Document Viewer," later in this chapter.) Your computer's fax capabilities appear as a virtual printer as well. To use a virtual printer, select the virtual printer when you print from within a program, such as Microsoft Word.

For configuring a printer and setting its options, your best bet is to right-click it and choose Properties. The Properties dialog has these tabs available:

General
  This tab (Figure 9-16) displays the printer name, location, and details such as its rated print speed, maximum resolution, and other specifications.

Sharing
  This lets you turn sharing on and off, and set whether the print jobs should be rendered on your computer or on the computer connecting to your printer.

Ports
  This lets you choose which ports the printer should use.

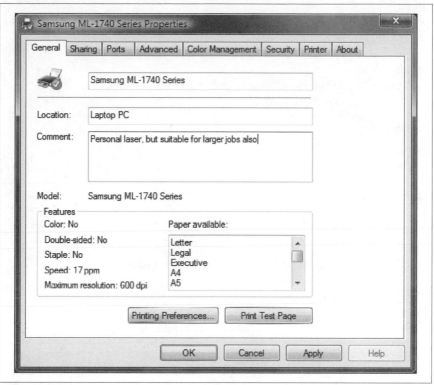

Figure 9-16. The General tab, which shows detailed information about the printer's specifications

Advanced
> This sets many different options, including whether the printer should wait to print until the final page of the job is spooled or start printing immediately, and whether to set a separator page that will print between print jobs.

Color Management
> This lets you match the output of a printer to your screen colors. This is primarily for professional designers. See "Color Management," earlier in this chapter, for details.

Security
> This lets you set permissions for those who are allowed to use the printer, and how they can use it—for example, can they manage the printer as well as print to it?

Printer
> This lets you set any special options associated with the printer, such as using power-saving features.

About
> This provides basic information about the manufacturer and driver.

Notes

- The default printer will have a small green checkbox on its icon.
- Any shared printer will have a small sharing symbol on its icon.

See also

"Add Printer," "Add Hardware Wizard," and "Color Management"

ReadyBoost

See Chapter 11.

Scanners and Cameras

Displays and configures scanners and digital cameras.

To open

Control Panel → [Hardware and Sound] → Scanners and Cameras

Description

The Scanners and Cameras window (see Figure 9-17) lists any digital cameras or scanners attached to the system.

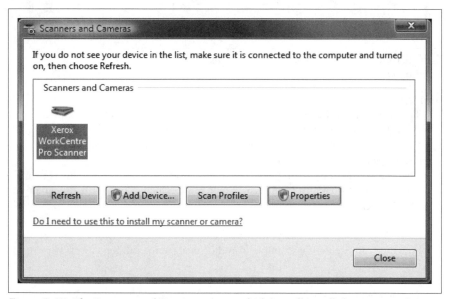

Figure 9-17. The Scanners and Cameras screen, which lists all installed scanners and printers and lets you configure them

If you have a scanner or digital camera attached to your system and it's not showing up, click Refresh. If it still doesn't show up, click Add Device, and the Scanner and Camera Installation Wizard appears. It is, in fact, the same wizard as the Add Hardware Wizard, so just follow those instructions.

When you add a USB scanner or digital camera to your PC, Windows Vista should recognize it and install the driver for it, or it should walk you through the process of installing the driver. You should also consider first running the installation routine that comes with the scanner or camera.

You can set up separate scan profiles for your scanners to set things such as the default file format and resolution for your scanned files. Click Scan Profiles to view, edit, or delete your existing profiles, or to add new ones.

The Scanner and Cameras screen also lets you view the properties of any of your installed devices and change the way the device works—for example, setting which program should work, by default, with your scanner, or changing a network scanner's IP address. The exact tabs and properties available will vary from device to device.

Importing pictures from cameras

Most cameras come with software for importing pictures into Windows. But the truth is, you don't need that software because Windows Vista gives you multiple ways to view and import pictures.

Windows will recognize the memory card in the camera as a removable disk when you plug in the camera (Figure 9-18). You have these options for viewing or copying the pictures.

Figure 9-18. Options for importing or viewing pictures from a digital camera

Working with Hardware

View Pictures using Windows Media Center

This opens Windows Media Center and lets you view or play the pictures. For details, see "Windows Media Center," in Chapter 12.

 Windows Media Center is not available in the Home Basic, Business, or Enterprise editions.

Import Pictures using Windows

This launches a wizard (Figure 9-19) that imports your pictures into a new folder it creates in *\Users\username\Pictures*. The new folder has the current date, so the whole path would be *\Users\username\Pictures\2007-11-21* if you imported the pictures on November 21, 2007. As you import the pictures, you can tag them so that they'll carry whatever tags you apply to them.

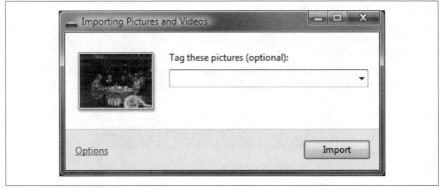

Figure 9-19. Importing pictures from a digital camera

View Pictures using Windows

This opens the pictures in the Windows Photo Gallery, where you can handle them as you can any other photos. For details, see "Windows Photo Gallery," in Chapter 12.

Open Folder to View Files using Windows Explorer

This opens Windows Explorer to the drive of the camera, where you can view and manage the files using Windows Explorer's normal tools.

Scanning pictures using Windows Fax and Scan

It's best to use scanning software that came with your printer in order to do scans. But if you prefer, you can use Windows Fax and Scan to scan pictures as well. (For details, see "Windows Fax and Scan," in Chapter 10.)

Run Windows Fax and Scan by selecting Control Panel → [Hardware and Sound] → Scan a Document or Picture, or by typing **wfs** at a command prompt. When Windows Fax and Scan launches, click New Scan and follow the instructions.

See also

"Windows Fax and Scan," in Chapter 10, and "Windows Media Center" and "Windows Photo Gallery," in Chapter 12

Signature Verification Tool

\windows\system32\sigverif.exe

Verify digital signatures in device drivers.

To open

Command Prompt → **sigverif**

Description

Microsoft digitally signs device drivers shipped with Windows so that you can verify that they have not been modified since testing. Drivers developed by third-party manufacturers are submitted to Microsoft for testing and, once those drivers pass the hardware standards testing, they are signed as well. The Signature Verification Tool (*sigverif.exe*) lets you manually verify that your installed drivers have not been modified in any way since testing.

Click Start to scan your system for unsigned drivers; if any are found, you'll be notified. Click Advanced to search files other than drivers and to enable logging.

Notes

- Windows automatically checks every driver installed through traditional channels (such as the Add Hardware Wizard) for a digital signature. If one is found, it is displayed; if no such signature is found, a warning message is shown instead.

Sound Recorder

\windows\system32\SoundRecorder.exe

Record and play sound files.

To open

Start → All Programs → Accessories → Sound Recorder

Command Prompt → **Soundrecorder**

Description

You use the Sound Recorder (Figure 9-20) to record simple sound clips, either in Windows Media Audio (*.wma*) or Waveform audio (*.wav*) format, depending on your version of Windows Vista. Windows Vista Basic and Windows Vista record sound files as *.wav* files, and all other versions record sound files as *.wma* files.

Figure 9-20. Using Sound Recorder to create short audio clips

Unlike the Sound Recorder in Windows XP, the Windows Vista version only records sounds and cannot play them back or edit them. (For playing them back, use Windows Media Player.) There are virtually no controls. Click Start Recording to begin recording sound; click Stop Recording to stop and save the sound, or click Resume Recording after you've stopped to continue recording where you left off.

Notes

- *.wav* files are extremely large and are rarely used in sound and multimedia applications. A typical five-minute *.wav* file recorded by the Sound Recorder will take up approximately 51 MB, and a five-minute *.wma* file will be approximately 3.5 MB.

- The Sound Recorder records both *.wma* and *.wav* files at 96 kilobits per second, at a 44.1 kHz sample rate.

See also

"Windows Media Player," in Chapter 12

Sound

\windows\system32\mmsys.cpl

Configure the sounds and sound devices used in Windows.

To open

Control Panel → [Hardware and Sound] → Sound

Command Prompt → `mmsys.cpl`

Description

The Sound dialog (Figure 9-21) contains these tabs:

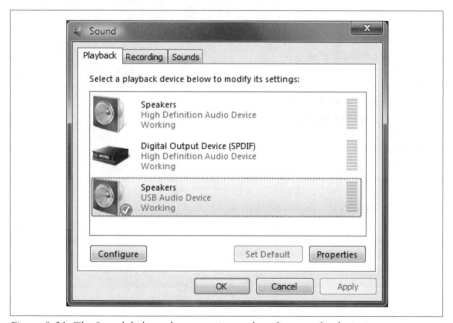

Figure 9-21. The Sound dialog, where you view and configure audio devices

Playback

Lists all the audio playback devices for your PC, including speakers, USB speakers, or any other audio hardware. A green checkmark will appear next to the one that is the default for the system. To select any other as the default, highlight it and click Set Default.

The Configure button lets you view and choose any special configurations for the device, and it includes a Test button so that you can test each sound device—for example, if the device is a pair of stereo speakers, you can test each one independently.

The Properties button leads to a Properties dialog with multiple tabs, the exact nature of which will vary according to the device. But generally you'll be able to set audio levels, use any special enhancements such as virtual sound and bass boost, and set the default audio playback quality.

Recording

Lists all the recording devices such as microphones attached to your PC. The Properties button, like the one for the Playback tab, offers a variety of advanced configuration options, such as setting the audio level and quality. The Configure button doesn't lead you to a configuration screen, as you would expect. Instead, it links to the Speech Recognition dialog, which allows you to set speech recognition options.

Sounds

This tab allows you to associate short clips of sounds with various system events and messages. Select an event from the list and then choose a sound (*.wav*) file to associate with it. When you're done, save your choices into a Sound scheme for easy retrieval later (see Figure 9-22).

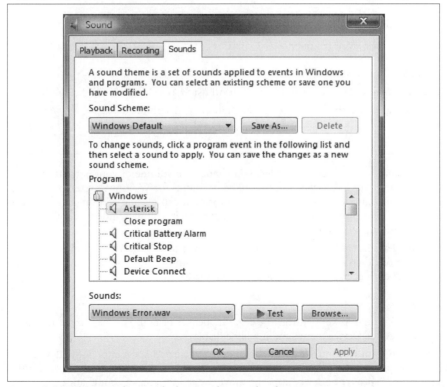

Figure 9-22. Changing the sounds that Windows makes for system events

Notes

- To get to any of the individual tabs on this dialog, right-click the speaker icon in the notification area, select Sounds, and then choose the tab.

See also

"Volume Mixer"

System Information

See Chapter 11.

System Properties

See Chapter 11.

Tablet PC Settings

See Chapter 7.

Volume Mixer

Control the volume of sound devices.

To open

Control Panel → [Hardware and Sound] → Adjust System Volume

Tray → Right-click the speaker icon and choose Open Volume Mixer

Tray → Left-click the speaker icon and choose Mixer

Description

The Volume Mixer (Figure 9-23) lets you change the volume of your current speakers or other audio device, as well as the volume of sounds for Windows system events and for individual applications that use sounds for notifications and warnings. If you have multiple applications running, you can change their volumes independently of one another, through separate sliders.

For the device or application for which you want to change the volume, move the slider up or down to increase or decrease the volume. Click the Mute button at the bottom of each to mute it; click it again to unmute.

Notes

- The Volume Mixer controls the current speaker or audio device; to see its name, choose the Device menu, and it will be displayed.

- If you want to control the volume of only the current speaker or audio device and not system or application volumes, click the speaker icon, and a control for the current speaker or device appears; move the slider to make your change.

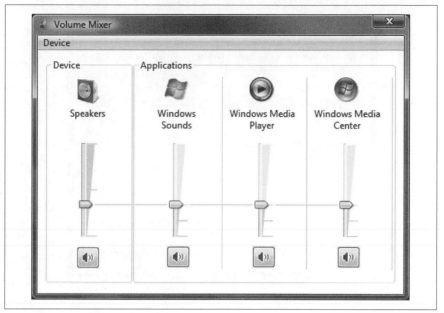

Figure 9 23. Configuring the volume

See also

"Sound"

Windows Update Driver Settings

Control how Windows finds new drivers.

To open

Right-click Computer on Start menu → Properties → Advanced System Settings → Hardware → Windows Update Driver Settings

Control Panel → [System and Maintenance] → System, then click Change Settings → Hardware → Windows Update Driver Settings

Command Prompt → **sysdm.cpl** → Hardware → Windows Update Driver Settings

Description

When you connect a new device to your PC, Windows automatically finds and installs the driver. The Windows Update Driver Settings dialog (Figure 9-24) lets you change that default behavior. You can have Windows ask each time before checking for drivers, or not check for drivers at all.

See also

"System Properties," in Chapter 11

Figure 9-24. Changing the default behavior for updating drivers

XPS Document Viewer

View documents in the new .xps format.

To open
Double-click any file in the .xps format.

Description
The new XML Paper Specification (XPS), introduced with Windows Vista, is Microsoft's answer to Adobe's popular Portable Document Format .pdf format. It displays a document with all of its layout, fonts, and graphics intact. Any Windows application can create a .xps file by printing as it would normally, except choosing the Microsoft XPS Document Writer as the printer and then saving the results on disk to an .xps file. XPS documents can be read but not edited.

Windows Vista's built-in XPS Document Viewer (Figure 9-25) runs as a specialized instance of Internet Explorer.

The XPS Document Viewer has a special toolbar across the top that lets you save a copy of the document under another name, digitally sign the document so that recipients know that it came from you, and set permissions and a password that control who can view the document.

The upper-righthand portion of the viewer has a Search box. Click the down arrow to the right of the box for special searching options, such as matching case, matching the whole word, matching diacritic marks, and so on.

The bottom of the view has controls for navigation and for the display of pages—for example, displaying multiple pages, setting page-width viewing, and other options.

Figure 9-25. The XPS Document Viewer, which runs inside Internet Explorer

Notes

- The XPS Document Viewer is built into Windows Vista but not other versions of Windows. Those with other Windows versions can download a version of the XPS Document Viewer from *http://www.microsoft.com/whdc/xps/viewxps.mspx*.

- You can copy and paste text from an *.xps* document just as you can from any other document.

10

Managing Programs, Users, and Your Computer

An operating system by itself is a lonely thing—what's the point of it, after all, unless you run programs on top of it to actually do things such as create and edit documents, perform calculations, and yes, even play games?

This chapter details the applications built into Windows Vista, including Notepad, WordPad, Windows Fax and Scan, and many others. It covers only applications that do not fit into specialized categories, which instead are covered elsewhere in the book. For example, Internet Explorer is covered in great detail in Chapter 5, Windows Mail gets its own chapter in Chapter 6, Windows Defender is covered in Chapter 8, Windows Media Player in Chapter 12, and so on.

The chapter covers not just the applications themselves, but how to manage them as well. So you'll find out how to uninstall them, set file association defaults, make older applications run with Windows Vista using the Program Compatibility Wizard, and so on.

Also included in this chapter are details about how to set up and manage user accounts. User accounts should be used not only when multiple people use the same PC, but even when only one person uses Windows Vista, as a way to keep the computer and its files safe.

To help you find what you want fast, this chapter is divided into three sections: "User Accounts and Computer Management"; "Applications and Utilities"; and "Games." Here is an alphabetical reference of entries in this chapter:

Cabinet (CAB) Maker	Fax Cover Page Editor	InkBall
Calculator	FreeCell	Local Security Policy
Character Map	Games Explorer	Logoff
Chess Titans	Group Policy Object Editor	Mahjong Titans
Component Services	Group Policy Refresh Utility	Microsoft Magnifier
Computer Management	Hearts	Microsoft Management Console
Default Programs Control Panel	IExpress	Minesweeper

Narrator	Purble Place	User Accounts
Notepad	Run As	User Accounts and Family Safety Control Panel
ODBC Data Source Administrator	Rundll32	Windows CardSpace
On-Screen Keyboard	Solitaire	Windows Fax and Scan
Private Character Editor	Spider Solitaire	Windows Speech Recognition
Program Compatibility Wizard	Uninstall or Change a Program	WordPad

User Accounts and Computer Management

Component Services
\windows\system32\dcomcnfg.exe

See "Microsoft Management Console," later in this chapter.

Computer Management
\windows\system32\compmgmt.exe

See "Microsoft Management Console," later in this chapter.

Group Policy Object Editor
\windows\system32\gpedit.msc

Refresh group policies and settings.

To open

Command Prompt → **gpedit.msc** (not available in Home versions)

Description

The Group Policy Object Editor (see Figure 10-1) offers tools that go far beyond anything offered in the Control Panel—or anywhere else in Windows, for that matter—affecting settings that most users have never even heard of. It gives a system administrator the ability to create a variety of policies for individual machines and users, quickly rolling them out across a network and relying on Windows Vista for enforcement. However, although it was primarily designed for system managers on networks, it can be very useful for single machines as well, not only for creating policies for every user of the single computer, but also for offering access to settings and controls not otherwise accessible.

Unlike the Registry, which presents its arcane settings in a mountain of folders and subfolders, the Group Policy Object Editor's options are shown in a handful of folders in (sometimes) plain English, such as "Hide/Add New Programs Page" and "Turn off Windows Sidebar." (And there are obscure ones as well, such as "User Group Policy loopback processing mode.") Although the presentation is different, most settings here are implemented as changes to values and keys in your Registry.

Before applying any option that you don't recognize, make sure you understand exactly what it will do to your system. Double-click the entry in the right window to summon its full Properties dialog box, which is often accompanied by an Explain tab with details. For another good source, select Help → Help Topics from the Group Policy Object Editor's menu bar. Failing that, go to Microsoft's Knowledgebase at *http://support.microsoft.com* and search for "Group Policy Object Editor" for a list of articles.

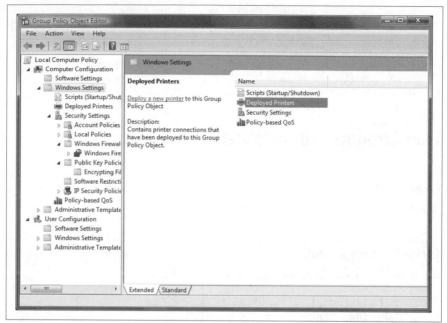

Figure 10-1. The Group Policy Object Editor, which gives you complete administrator access to Windows Vista's deepest settings

 Be very careful when using this tool. It makes it possible to restrict or reconfigure almost every security setting on your computer, which means that it's very easy to break something. And there's no Undo feature.

There are two major folders in the Group Policy Object Editor: Computer Configuration and User Configuration. Computer Configuration lets you set policies computerwide (or network-wide), and User Configuration lets you set them for individual users. To a certain extent, the folders mirror one another, with the same subfolders and individual settings in each. But that's not always the case, because some settings are available only in Computer Configuration and others only in User Configuration.

Changing a setting is straightforward. Double-click it and select Enabled or Disabled, as you can see in Figure 10-2.

Here's a handful of the more entertaining and useful settings you can play with in the Group Policy Object Editor:

Pretty-Up Internet Explorer
 Several settings in this subfolder let you do things you most likely never thought possible: change the Internet Explorer title bar, change the Internet Explorer logo, and change the background of the Internet Explorer toolbar. Go to *User Configuration\Windows Settings\Internet Explorer Maintenance\Browser User Interface* and double-click the Browser Title entry to change the Internet Explorer title bar; the Custom Logo and Animated Bitmaps entry to change the Internet Explorer logo and logo animation; and Browser Toolbar Customization to change the

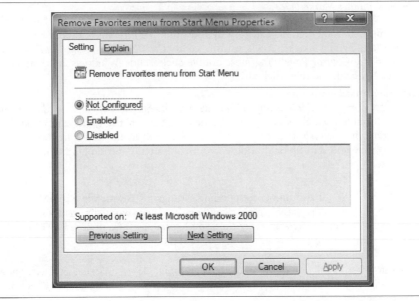

Figure 10-2. Changing settings using the Group Policy Object Editor

background of the Internet Explorer toolbar. Note that for changing the logo and toolbar background, you'll have to create or find suitable graphics.

Choose Places for your Places Bar

Go to *User Configuration\Administrative Templates\Windows Components\ Windows Explorer\Common Open File Dialog* and double-click the Items Displayed in Places Bar option. Click Enabled, and then type the full pathnames of up to five folders on your hard disk. Click OK, and these folders will appear in the Favorite Links area on the left side of most File → Open and File → Save dialog boxes.

There aren't any Browse buttons in this dialog, but you can specify folder paths without typing by opening Windows Explorer, navigating to the folders you want, highlighting the text in the Address Bar, copying it, and pasting the text into the Group Policy Object Editor's dialog box. Alternatively, you can use the Places Bar in Microsoft Office file dialogs to customize your Places Bar. Doing that, of course, will affect only Office applications.

Bring Back the Run Command

Were you a big fan of Windows XP's Run command on the Start menu, and sorry to see it bite the dust in Vista? No problem—you can bring it back. Go to *User Configuration\Administrative Templates\Start Menu and Taskbar*, and then double-click the "Add the Run Command to the Start menu" entry on the right. Click Enabled and then OK, and the Run command will now show up on the Start menu. You can also press the Windows Key-R combination to launch the Run box, or simply type many commands directly into the Start menu Search box.

Hide the Windows Marketplace

The Windows Marketplace shows up on several spots on the Control Panel—for example, in the Programs category. If you think it's little more than a marketing ploy and would like to see it vanish, go to *User Configuration\Administrative Templates\Control Panel\Programs*, double-click "Hide Windows Marketplace," click Enabled, and then click OK.

Startup and Shutdown Scripts

Go to *Computer Configuration\Windows Settings\Scripts (Startup/Shutdown)* and then double-click the Startup or Shutdown entry on the right. Click the Add button, choose a *.vbs* (VBScript) file on your hard disk, and that script will be run every time you start up or shut down your computer, depending on which you've chosen.

 You'll also find corresponding settings in *User Configuration\Windows Settings\Scripts (Logon/Logoff)*. These work similarly, except they're activated every time you log on or off (as opposed to when you turn on your computer or shut it down).

Go to *User Configuration\Administrative Templates\System\Scripts* and *Computer Configuration\Administrative Templates\System\Scripts* for settings that affect how these scripts work.

Turn Off CD/DVD Autoplay

Go to *Computer Configuration\Administrative Templates\Windows Components\ AutoPlay Policies* and double-click the Turn off Autoplay option on the right. If you enable this option, Windows will no longer play CDs and DVDs automatically when you insert them.

Improve Security Logging

Go to *Computer Configuration\Windows Settings\Security Settings\Local Policies\ Audit Policy* and enable any of the settings here to log the corresponding events. For example, set both the "Audit account logon events" and "Audit logon events" settings to Success, and any failed attempt to log on to your system will be logged. To view these logs, open the Event Viewer (*eventvwr.msc*). See "Event Viewer," in Chapter 11, for details.

 Each setting in this branch has two options, Success and Failure, and this can be somewhat confusing. Choose Success to log instances in which the security policy has been successful, such as when your computer successfully keeps out an intruder. Conversely, select Failure to log instances when security has been compromised.

Disable User Tracking

Go to *User Configuration\Administrative Templates\Start Menu and Taskbar*, double-click the "Turn off user tracking" entry to the right, and click Enabled. This will stop Windows from recording every program you run, every document you open, and every folder path you view, thus hobbling such features as "personalized" menus and the Recent Documents menu.

Notes

- The Group Policy Object Editor is not actually a standalone tool. Instead, it's a snap-in to the more comprehensive Microsoft Management Console. To run it from there instead of as a standalone tool, first run the Microsoft Management Console (see "Microsoft Management Console," later in this chapter, for details), then choose File → Add/Remove Snap-In, and select Group Policy Object Editor.

Group Policy Refresh Utility

\windows\system32\gpupdate.exe

Refresh group policies and settings.

To open

Command Prompt → **gpupdate** (not available in the Home editions)

Usage

```
gpupdate [/target] [/force] [/wait] [/logoff] [/boot] [/sync]
```

Description

Type **gpupdate** at the command prompt to refresh Group Policy settings. The Group Policy Refresh Utility accepts the following options:

/target:computer *or* /target:user
Refresh only user or only computer policy settings; by default, both are refreshed.

/force
Reapply all policy settings; by default, only policy settings that have changed since the last refresh are applied.

/wait:*value*
Wait a specified number of seconds for policy processing to finish before being returned to the command prompt. The default is 600 seconds; specify 0 (zero) to not wait at all or 1 (one) to wait indefinitely.

/logoff
Log off the current user after the Group Policy settings have been refreshed.

/boot
Restart Windows after the Group Policy settings have been refreshed.

/sync
Cause the next foreground policy application (occurring at computer startup and user logon) to be done synchronously. If /sync is specified, /force and /wait parameters will be ignored.

Local Security Policy

\windows\system32\secpol.msc

See "Microsoft Management Console," later in this chapter.

Logoff

\windows\system32\logoff.exe

Log off the current user (or another user).

To open

Command Prompt → **logoff**

Usage

```
logoff [session | id] [/server:name] [/v]
```

Description

Among other things, Logoff is the quickest way to log off the current user, rather than clicking the Start Menu, then clicking the right arrow on its right edge, then selecting Log Off. In fact, you can create a shortcut to Logoff on your Desktop and simply double-click it to end the current session.

You also can use Logoff to end the session of a remotely connected user, either through Terminal Services or through the Telnet daemon. For example, if someone has connected to a Windows Vista computer using Telnet, you can disconnect her, either from another Telnet session or from the command prompt, by using Logoff and the following options:

session

    The name of the session to end; use either session or id to end a session, but not both.

id

    The ID of the session to end; use either session or id to end a session, but not both.

/server:name

    Specifies the terminal server containing the session to end; the default is the current server.

/v

    Displays additional information about the actions being performed.

Microsoft Management Console

\windows\system32\mmc.exe

A single interface for dozens of administrative tools in Windows Vista.

To open

Start → All Programs → Administrative Tools → Computer Management

Command Prompt → **mmc**

Usage

```
mmc filename [/a] [/64] [/32]
```

Description

The Microsoft Management Console (MMC) is a host for most of the administrative tools that come with Windows Vista (see Figure 10-3). Each tool that works with the MMC is called a snap-in; several snap-ins can be shown in the MMC at any given time, and they appear as entries in the Explorer-style tree in the left pane.

You can save a collection of one or more snap-ins into a Console (.*msc*) file, which is a small file that simply lists snap-ins to display in the Console window. Double-click any .*msc* file to open it in the MMC. Windows Vista ships with more than two dozen predefined Console files, and you can modify them (or even create your own) by

---

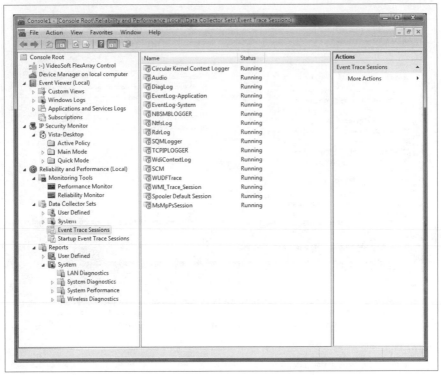

Figure 10-3. The Microsoft Management Console, which houses many important troubleshooting and system-maintenance tools

adding or removing snap-ins or creating custom Taskpad Views—pages with lists of shortcuts to programs or other snap-ins.

To add a snap-in to the current Console file (select File → New to start a new Console), go to File → Add/Remove Snap-in and click Add (see Figure 10-4). Then, choose one of the available snap-ins (note that not all snap-ins described here are available in all versions of Windows Vista), and click Add to add it to the list in the previous window. A wizard or other dialog may appear when certain items are added, and is used to configure this instance of the snap-in being added; any preferences set here are saved into the Console file. You can continue to add additional items as needed; when you're done, click Close. Note that it's possible to add the same snap-in more than once, so you may want to position the windows side by side so that you can see what has been installed.

Following are all of the most important snap-ins included with Windows Vista; most of them are documented further in the MMC online help. Note that all Console (*.msc*) files mentioned are in the *windows**system32* folder unless otherwise noted.

ActiveX Control

Use this snap-in to add an ActiveX control to your Console file. Although Windows Vista ships with a number of ActiveX controls, most of them aren't appropriate for the MMC. More advanced users may want to use this feature to install custom snap-ins they have written themselves or obtained from a third party. Most users are likely to find the System Monitor Control to be the only useful ActiveX snap-in included with Windows Vista.

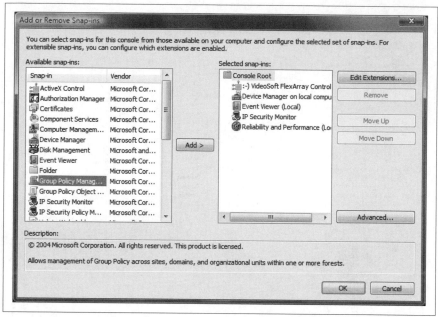

Figure 10-4. Adding tools to the current view by installing snap-ins

Certificates

Installed by default in *certmgr.msc*.

Use this snap-in to browse all the security certificates used by Internet Explorer.

Component Services

Installed by default in *comexp.msc*.

Use this snap-in to manage installed component object model (COM) components.

Computer Management

Installed by default in *compmgmt.msc*.

Computer Management doesn't have any functionality by itself; rather, it is a collection of the following 13 snap-ins: Event Viewer, Shared Folders, Local Users and Groups, Performance Logs and Alerts, Device Manager, Removable Storage, Disk Defragmenter, Disk Management, Services, WMI Control, Indexing Service, Message Queuing, and Internet Information Services.

Device Manager

Installed by default in *devmgmt.msc* and *compmgmt.msc*. See "Device Manager," in Chapter 9.

Disk Defragmenter

Installed by default in *compmgmt.msc*. See "Disk Defragmenter," in Chapter 11.

Disk Management

Installed by default in *diskmgmt.msc* and *compmgmt.msc*.

The Disk Management snap-in lists all the installed drives, including hard disks, CD and DVD drives, and other removable storage devices (floppies are not included). Right-click on any drive (except the one on which Windows is installed) to change its drive letter. Go to View → Top and View → Bottom to configure the view for the top and bottoms panes; you can choose whether drives are viewed as disks (physical devices), volumes (local drives, including partitions), or disks using a graphical view. Disk Management also has the capability to create, resize, and delete partitions (see also "DiskPart," in Chapter 11), but it cannot make any modifications that affect the volume on which Windows is installed.

Among the features of the Disk Management console is the ability to change drive letters of your CD or DVD drive, removable cartridge drive, and even hard-disk partitions. Just right-click a volume in the upper pane (for hard-disk partitions) or one of the large buttons on the left side of the lower pane (for CD drives and the like) and select Change Drive Letter and Paths. Then, click Change to choose a new drive letter. If there's a drive letter conflict, you may have to click Remove first, resolve the conflict, and then return to the Change Drive Letter and Paths dialog and click Add to choose a drive letter.

Event Viewer

Installed by default in *eventvwr.msc* and *compmgmt.msc*.

Use this snap-in to view a wide variety of system event logs, including the application log, security log, system log, setup log, applications and services logs, and others. The application log lists every application crash, status reports and warnings generated by services (see "Services," later in this list), and other events logged by some applications. The security log records events such as valid and invalid logon attempts, as well as events related to the use of shared resources. The system log contains events logged by Windows Vista system components, such as driver failures and system startup errors. Individual programs may have their own logs as well.

The setup log records setup events in computers configured as domain controllers, and it includes two additional logs: Directory service and File Replication service. A computer running Windows configured as a Domain Name System (DNS) server records events in an additional log, DNS server.

Event Viewer logs contain five types of events: Errors (driver and service failures), Warnings (indications of possible future problems), Information Entries (the successful operation of an application, driver, or service), and Success Audits and Failure Audits (audited security access attempts that succeed and fail, respectively).

Folder

A folder is used to organize snap-ins in the tree display. To use a folder, first add it using the procedure explained earlier in this section. Then, close the Add Standalone Snap-in dialog, select the new folder from the "Snap-ins added to" list, and click Add again; this time, added items will appear in the new folder. Unfortunately, you can't drag and drop items from one folder to another, so the only way to move an item is to remove it from one folder and then add it to another. You can rename folders only from the main MMC window.

Group Policy Object Editor

Installed by default in *gpedit.msc*.

This snap-in is a collection of policy settings controlling startup and shutdown scripts, security settings for Internet Explorer, and user account policies. See "Group Policy Object Editor," earlier in this chapter, for more information.

Group Policy

    Installed by default in *gpmc.msc*.

    This snap-in is the equivalent of Group Policy Object Editor but for computers with domain user accounts.

IP Security Monitor

    Use this snap-in to monitor the IP Security status; see "IP Security Policy Management" next, for more information.

IP Security Policy Management

    Manage Internet Protocol Security (IPsec) policies for secure communication with other computers. You can think of IPsec as a kind of Virtual Private Network (VPN) infrastructure, allowing and disallowing certain communications over an Internet connection.

Internet Information Services (IIS) Manager

    Installed by default in *compmgmt.msc* (only if you first enable IIS; see the following note).

    IIS is the web/FTP/SMTP server available in Windows Vista, and the IIS Manager snap-in allows you to administer the various functions associated with the server service. For example, you can configure how CGI scripts are run on the server.

    By default, IIS is not available in Windows Vista. You'll first have to turn it on by going to Control Panel → Programs → Turn Windows features on or off and selecting Internet Information Services. You'll have to enable individual features one at a time. Click the + button next to Internet Information Services and then select which to turn on and off. Make sure you enable IIS Management Console under Web Management Tools.

Link to Web Address

    The Link to Web Address snap-in allows you to insert, not surprisingly, the web site as an entry in the tree. For example, you may want to include a link to a software downloads site, an HTTP-based administration page for a web site, or another troubleshooting web site.

Local Computer Policy

    See "Group Policy" (also known as Local Computer Policy), earlier in this list.

Local Security Policy

    Installed by default in *secpol.msc*.

    This plug-in lets you set a variety of security policies relating to user accounts, passwords, encryption, IP security, use of the Windows Firewall, and other similar matters.

Local Users and Groups

    Installed by default in *lusrmgr.msc* and *compmgmt.msc*.

    This plug-in provides more advanced settings, using a simpler and more direct interface, than Control Panel → User Accounts. Here, you can set preferences relating to the expiration of passwords, the assignment of certain users to groups, logon scripts, the location of a user's home folder, and other advanced options.

NAP Client Configuration

    Installed by default in *napclcfg.msc*.

This plug-in configures and manages rules and settings for Windows Vista's Network Access Protection (NAP) client. NAP, new in Windows Vista, allows IT administrators to create security specifications that all PCs trying to connect to a network must meet before they are allowed to connect. This ensures that a PC infected by a worm, virus, or other malware can't connect to a network and then infect other PCs. For example, you can create rules that won't allow PCs to connect unless antivirus software is installed and the virus definitions are up-to-date.

Print Management

Installed by default in *printmanagement.msc*.

This snap-in controls installed printers in Windows Vista, including managing drivers, printer sharing, port use, and so on. It also lets you view and manage current jobs in the print queue for any printer.

Reliability and Performance Monitor

Installed by default in *perfmon.msc* and *compmgmt.msc*.

Reliability and Performance Monitor (see Chapter 11 for more information) displays information about the performance and reliability of your PC, both currently and over time. It allows you to collect performance data automatically from certain applications and then create logs that can be exported and analyzed. See the online Help for more information on setting up performance data.

Resultant Set of Policy

Installed by default in *rsop.msc*.

This snap-in allows you to view and change the policy settings for a particular user. See "Group Policy" (also known as Local Computer Policy), earlier in this section, for more information.

Security Configuration and Analysis

You use this snap-in to view and manage security databases for computers using Security Templates (discussed next). It is especially helpful for tracking changes to security.

Security Templates

Installed by default in *secpol.msc*.

You use Security Templates to create a security policy for computers. They are used mostly by administrators for Windows-based servers. See the online Help for detailed information.

Services

Installed by default in *services.msc* and *compmgmt.msc*.

A service is a program that runs invisibly in the background, usually started when Windows starts. You can set up any program to run automatically when Windows starts by placing a shortcut in your Startup folder, but such a program would be run only when you log in. A service is run when Windows starts and is already running when the login prompt is shown. Windows XP comes with nearly 80 preinstalled services, some of which are active by default (called *Started* in the Services window), and some of which are not.

Double-click any service in the list to view its properties, such as its status (Started or Stopped), whether it's started automatically, under which user accounts it is enabled, what actions to take if the service encounters a problem, and which other components the service depends on (if any). Common services include the plug-and-play manager, the task scheduler, the print spooler, automatic updates, the autoconfiguration services for wired and wireless networks, a web server, and many other programs responsible for keeping Windows Vista running. You can start or stop any service by right-clicking on it and selecting Start or Stop, respectively. Stopping unnecessary services will not only increase system performance, but it will also close potential security "backdoors" that could be used to break into a computer. Naturally, you should use caution when disabling any enabled service, but most home users won't need the World Wide Web Publishing service to be running all the time.

See Appendix E for a list of the default services in Windows Vista, their corresponding filenames, and their descriptions.

Shared Folders
  Installed by default in *fsmgmt.msc* and *compmgmt.msc*.

As described in Chapter 4, any folder or drive can be shared, allowing access to it from another computer on the network. The Shared Folders snap-in lists all of the shared resources in one place, as well as any open connections to those resources from other computers. Rather than "sharing and forgetting," this tool allows you to keep a more active watch on how shared resources are being used.

One thing to note is the existence of administrative shares, those items listed in the Shares portion of the Shared Folders snap-in, denoted by a dollar sign ($) at the end of the share name. Administrator shares cannot be disabled, and if you've permitted others to share these folders, they can even be a security risk, in which someone else with your username and password can access any file or folder on your computer without ever sitting in front of it. Suffice it to say, if you're on a network or even an Internet connection, you should investigate the security settings in your computer and try to close as many backdoors as you can without disabling functions that you still need. If you're concerned about security, you may want to use Windows Vista's built-in firewall (see Chapter 8) or invest in third-party firewall software such as Norton Personal Firewall (*http://www. symantec.com*), each of which actively helps prevent unauthorized access to your computer.

Task Scheduler
  Installed by default in *taskschd.msc*.

This plug-in offers the same functionality as the Task Scheduler built into Windows Vista, allowing you to automate the running of tasks. See "Task Scheduler," in Chapter 11, for more details.

Trusted Platform Module (TPM) Management
  Installed by default in *tpm.msc*.

This plug-in works only on computers whose hardware meets the TPM requirements. TPM allows PCs to use Windows Vista's BitLocker Drive Encryption to encrypt entire hard drives for security purposes.

WMI Control
  Installed by default in *wmimgmt.msc* and *compmgmt.msc*.

Windows Management Instrumentation (WMI) is a set of standards for accessing and sharing management information over an enterprise network. WMI will be of little use to most users; for more information, see the online Help.

One of the most interesting features of the MMC is its capability to access most of these tools remotely. For example, you can use it to run Device Manager on a machine other than the one you're using. Naturally, this would be most useful to an administrator, who can now configure and maintain a whole group of computers from a single machine. However, as home networks become more common, ordinary users are being turned into administrators. For instance, if you were responsible for setting up a network between the two or three computers used by the members of your family, you'd be able to run Disk Defragmenter on all the machines without having to jump around between them.

Connecting to another computer with MMC depends on the particular snap-in you're using. Most snap-ins that support remote administration will prompt you when you first add them, asking whether the snap-in should be used with the current computer or with another on the network. In the case of Computer Management (*compmgmt.msc*), just right-click on the Computer Management root entry of the tree, select "Connect to another computer," and type the name of the computer in the box that appears. When connected to another computer, the root entry will be named Computer Management (*computername*).

The MMC also has a few command-line options:

/a   Some Console (*.msc*) files have been configured so that the snap-in tree normally shown is not only hidden, but also inaccessible. Furthermore, you may not have access to the standard MMC menus, meaning that you will not be able to add or remove snap-ins as desired. The /a option opens the MMC in "author" mode, allowing you to treat any saved Console file as though you created it, giving you power to modify the Console by adding or removing snap-ins.

/s   The /s parameter is included with some shortcuts to *.msc* files in the Start menu, but it does not appear to have any effect.

/32 or /64
      Run the MMC in 32-bit or 64-bit mode, respectively; these options are available only on 64-bit systems.

Notes

- Eventually, you'll probably want to create your own Console file with the snap-ins you use most. Although the MMC can create a new Console file from scratch, it may be easier to modify one of the supplied *.msc* files and then save it with a new name. To modify a saved Console file, start the MMC with the /a switch, as described earlier.

- Programmers who want to learn how to create custom snap-ins can find more information at *http://msdn.microsoft.com*.

Run As   *\windows\system32\runas.exe*

Run a program under a different user's account.

To open
Command Prompt → **runas *program***

Usage
```
runas [/noprofile] [/env] [/netonly] /user:username program
runas [/noprofile] [/env] [/netonly] /smartcard
 [/user:username] program
```

Description

Windows Vista is a multiuser environment. When you open an application, Windows runs that program in a "user context," which means that the settings and capabilities imposed upon an application are those associated with your user account. Use Run As to instruct Windows to open an application in another user's context. This is especially useful when running services or other background applications, where you can't always assume which user will be logged on at any time but you want to make sure the settings and permissions are correct.

Run As takes the following parameters:

program

> The full path, filename, and optional command-line parameters for the *.exe* file to run.

`/user:`*username*

> The username under which to run *program*; *username* should be of the form *user@domain* or *domain\user*.

`/noprofile`

> Specifies that the user's profile should not be loaded. This causes the application to load more quickly, but it can cause applications that rely on settings stored in the HKEY_CURRENT_USER Registry key to malfunction.

`/env`

> Uses the current environment instead of *username*'s.

`/netonly`

> Specifies that the credentials specified are for remote access only.

`/savecred`

> Uses credentials previously saved by the user. This option is not available on the Home editions and will be ignored.

`/smartcard`

> Specifies that the credentials are to be supplied from a smart card.

Notes

- Scheduled Tasks, discussed in Chapter 11, also lets you run programs under different user accounts.

User Accounts and Family Safety Control Panel

Add or remove user accounts and change the privileges of existing users.

To open

Control Panel → [User Accounts and Family Safety]

Description

The User Accounts and Family Safety Control Panel (Figure 10-5) gives you quick access to most common tasks related to user accounts, including changing your account picture, changing your password, and adding or removing accounts. It also includes links to Parental Controls (see "Parental Controls," in Chapter 8) and Windows CardSpace, formerly known as InfoCard, which is used to log on to web sites (see "Windows CardSpace," later in this chapter).

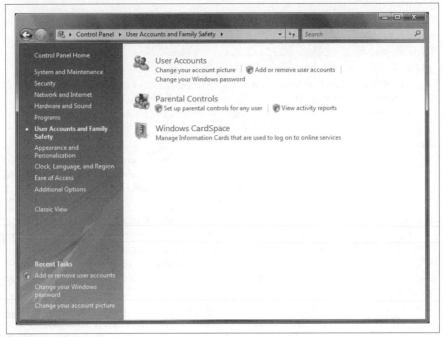

Figure 10-5. The User Accounts and Family Safety Control Panel, which gives you quick access to the most common tasks related to user accounts

In the User Accounts portion of the screen, most links take you directly to the User Accounts Control Panel subcategory (covered in the next entry in this chapter), with the exception of "Add or remove user accounts," which takes you directly to the applicable screen.

User Accounts

Add, remove, and customize user accounts and change the privileges of existing users.

To open
Control Panel → [User Accounts and Family Safety] → User Accounts

Command Prompt → **control userpasswords**

Description
Windows Vista fully supports multiple users, each with his own Start menu, Desktop, color and display theme preferences, application settings, folder for documents, music, downloads, pictures, saved games, and a variety of other odds and ends. Each user has a password and a home directory (located in *\Users\username*), under which his personal files and folders are stored by default. The user, of course, can create folders outside of that home directory if he wants.

Windows Vista lets you create separate accounts not only as a way to let multiple people share the same PC, but also for security reasons. It has several different kinds of user accounts, each with its own level of privileges for performing tasks such as installing and uninstalling software, changing system settings, and so on, and Windows Vista uses these differences in privileges for security purposes with its User Account Control (UAC) feature. More on that a little later, though.

There are two basic kinds of user accounts in Windows Vista:

Administrator
> An administrator has control over the entire system and can run programs, install or remove hardware and software, change system settings, and create, remove, and modify other user accounts. There doesn't have to be just one administrator; there can be multiple administrators on a single PC.

Standard user
> A standard user is more limited in what he can do on the computer than an administrator and may not be able to change various system settings, install and uninstall hardware and software, access certain files and folders, and so on. There can be multiple standard users on a single PC.

In addition, there is a built-in Guest account; users with this account have even fewer privileges than standard users and cannot make any changes to the system, install or uninstall software, or read or modify password-protected files and folders. There is only one Guest account, and it is supposed to be used to give someone access to your PC on a temporary basis. By default, the Guest account is turned off, although as you'll see, it can easily be turned on.

How does the use of different types of user accounts help security? Microsoft suggests that people not use an administrator account unless they need to make system changes. In that way, access to the system is limited—an administrator has access to many features and areas of the PC that a standard user doesn't have, so when that standard account is being used, dangerous changes can't be made. But even if you are a standard user, the UAC feature can let you run commands as an administrator, but you'll need to know the administrator password to do this.

There's a lot more to UAC than this, though. For details, see "User Account Control," in Chapter 8.

In addition to normal administrator accounts, there is a kind of super Administrator account that, by default, is hidden and turned off and has even more privileges than the administrator accounts you create. A PC can have only one of these super Administrator accounts. This super Administrator has UAC turned off and pretty much has the run of the entire PC. By contrast, administrator accounts that you create are subject to UAC. With some dedicated tweaking, you can turn on the hidden super Administrator account, but you need to be careful when doing so, because if you make a mistake, you can end up locking yourself out of your system. For details on how to turn it on, see Scot Finnie's excellent article in *Computerworld*, "How to access the true Administrator account in Windows Vista," located at *http://www.computerworld.com/action/ article.do?command=viewArticleBasic&articleId=9001970*.

The User Accounts Control Panel subcategory (Figure 10-6) lets you create, edit, and manage accounts on your PC. The main pane, which takes up most of the screen, lets you make changes to your account, manage another account, and turn UAC off (or on). Listed on the lefthand side are other tasks you can accomplish.

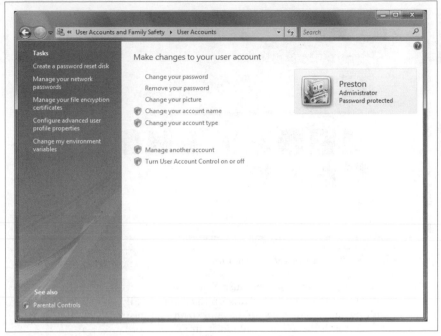

Figure 10-6. Editing your account in the User Accounts window

Here are all of your options for the main pane:

Change your password
> This brings you to a screen that asks for your old password, asks you to type in a new password, and then lets you type in a hint for the password in case you forget it. If a user account has no password defined, you'll see "Create a password" here instead of the standard "Change your password." Administrators can change any account, but standard users can make changes only to their own accounts.

Remove password
> Click here, and your password won't be immediately removed. Instead, you'll be prompted again, just to make sure you really want to remove it. As a general rule for security purposes, it's not a good idea to remove a password from an account.

Change your picture
> A picture is associated with every user account. It's the picture you see on top of the Start menu, and it appears in other places as well. You'll be able to choose from 13 different built-in pictures (Figure 10-7) for your account, including the inevitable kitten, puppy, and flower, when you choose this option. But you're not limited to just those pictures. Click Browse for more pictures at the bottom of the screen that appears, and use any picture on your hard disk in a variety of graphics formats, including *.bmp*, *.gif*, *.jpg*, *.png*, *.dib*, and *.rle*.

Change your account name
> As the name says, this changes your account name.

Change your account type
> This changes the account from an administrator to a standard user, and vice versa. If you have only one administrator account on the PC, you won't be able to

Figure 10-7. Choosing a new picture for your user account

change it to a standard user, because Windows Vista requires that there be at least one active administrator account on the computer. If you're a standard user, you won't be able to change your account to an administrator; to do so requires an administrator or the use of an administrator's password.

Manage another account

This lets administrators manage other accounts on the PC, including changing the account name, password, picture, and type; setting up Parental Controls; and deleting the account. It also lets you create new accounts. You'll be shown a screen of all users on the PC (see Figure 10-8); click an account to be brought to a screen to let you manage it.

Figure 10-8. Managing another account

Turn User Account Control on or off

> This lets you turn UAC off or turn it back on. Although UAC can be annoying, it's not a good idea to turn it off because it offers your PC an extra layer of security.

Here are all of your options for the Tasks pane:

Create a password reset disk

> What if you've created an account with a password, and then forgotten your password? How to get back into that account? Create a password reset disk. The disk will let you create a new password for the account so you can log back in. A wizard helps you create the disk, which can be a floppy disk (remember those?), CD, DVD, Universal Serial Bus (USB) flash drive, or other type of removable media.

Manage your network passwords

> Many web sites and services require that you log on with a username and password. This option lets you create logon credentials for each account so you can log on automatically.

Manage your file encryption certificates

> This lets you create and back up file encryption certificates and keys, and update previously encrypted files to use a different certificate and key. It also lets you set up the Encrypting File System to use a smart card for authentication. For details about the Encrypting File System and encryption in general, see Chapter 8.

Configure advanced user profile properties

> A user profile stores settings related to user accounts, such as desktop setup and items. If you're connected to a domain via Active Directory, you have a *roaming profile* that will let you use that same user account—with all its settings—on other computers on the network. "Configure advanced user profile properties" lets you control whether your account should use your local profile or a roaming profile.

Change my environment variables

> Environment variables control a variety of settings in Windows, such as the Windows drive and directory, where temporary files should be stored, the path along which the operating system should look for executable files, and so on. This option lets you edit and create environment variables.

Notes

- There are several ways to create a new account. The fastest is to click "Add or remove user accounts" just underneath User Accounts and Family Safety in the Control Panel. Usernames can be anything, as long as they're not the same as preexisting usernames.

- You can find more user account options in the Local Users and Groups console (*lusrmgr.msc*; see "Microsoft Management Console," earlier in this chapter).

- To quickly switch among different user accounts, click the right arrow at the bottom right of the Start menu and select Switch User.

See also

"Control Panel," in Chapter 3, and "User Account Control" and "Encrypting File System (EFS)," in Chapter 8

Applications and Utilities

Cabinet (CAB) Maker

\windows\system32\makecab.exe; diantz.exe

Cabinet file (*.cab*) compression utility.

To open

Command Prompt → **makecab**

Usage

```
makecab [/v[n]] [/d var=value] [/l dir] source [destination]
makecab [/v[n]] [/d var=value] /f directive_file
```

Description

A cabinet file is a compressed archive commonly used to package application installation files. Cabinets are similar to *.zip* files, although they have added features such as a rudimentary script system intended to install and register application components.

There are two ways to use the Cabinet Maker. First, you can compress one or more files directly, like this:

```
makecab \windows\greenstone.bmp greenstone.cab
```

The preceding code compresses the file *greenstone.bmp* into the *greenstone.cab* archive. The new cabinet file, *greenstone.cab*, is created automatically in the current directory; if it already exists, it is replaced with the new archive. Unfortunately, wildcards (*.*) aren't allowed in the source, so you can specify only one file at a time. This is where the second usage of the Cabinet Maker comes in: instead of specifying options and files directly, a single plain-text file, called a directive file (*.ddf*), is used. The simplest directive file lists all the files to include. A line beginning with a semicolon is treated as a comment.

Assuming the lines:

```
;Example directive file
c:\windows\greenstone.bmp
c:\windows\rhododendron.bmp
```

are saved into a file called *test.ddf*, the makecab command would then look like this:

```
makecab /f test.ddf
```

You can specify multiple directive files in the same command, listed one after another.

Notes

- Diamond Cabinet Builder (*diantz.exe*) is identical to *makecab.exe*; it's included only for legacy support.
- There are two ways to open Cabinet files and extract their contents. The easiest way is to double-click on any *.cab* file in Explorer to display a folder view of the contents. You can then drag files out of the *.cab* file (you cannot add items here, however). The other way is to use the File Expansion Utility (*expand.exe*).

- You also can use WinZip (*http://www.winzip.com*) to open *.cab* files, but it's not compatible with all variants of the *.cab* format, and thus it won't open every *.cab* file you encounter.

- More complicated directive files, including the use of *.inf* installation routines, are possible with the Cabinet Maker. See *http://msdn.microsoft.com* for details, including the use of the /v and /d parameters.

See also

"File Expansion Utility," in Chapter 4, and "IExpress," in this chapter

Calculator

\windows\system32\calc.exe

Numerical scientific and nonscientific calculator.

To open

Start → All Programs → Accessories → Calculator

Command Prompt → **calc**

Description

By default, the Calculator starts in Standard mode, containing only the numeric keypad and some basic functions (add, subtract, invert, square root, etc.). Select Scientific from the View menu to use the calculator in Scientific mode, useful for more advanced functions, such as logarithmic, logical, trigonometric, and base functions (see Figure 10-9). Each time you subsequently open the Calculator, it will appear in the previously used mode.

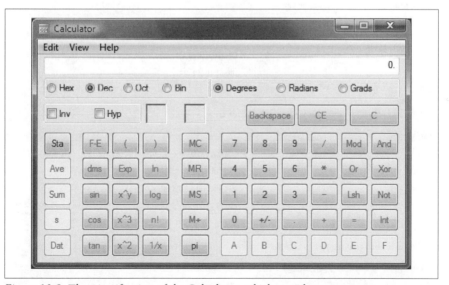

Figure 10-9. The scientific view of the Calculator, which provides access to many more functions than the standard view

Entering data and performing calculations

You can enter data by clicking the buttons or by pressing keys on the keyboard. All keys have keyboard equivalents (see Table 10-1); key mappings that are not quite obvious (such as Log) are documented in Table 10-7. Note that many of the functions in Table 10-1 are available only in Scientific Mode.

Table 10-1. Calculations and keyboard equivalents

Calc button	Keyboard key	Action
C	Esc	Clears all calculations.
CE	Delete	Clears the last entry.
Back	Backspace	Clears the last digit.
MR	Ctrl-R	Displays the number stored in memory.
MS	Ctrl-M	Stores the current value in memory.
M+	Ctrl-P	Adds the current value to the number stored in memory.
MC	Ctrl-L	Clears the memory.
+/-	F9	Changes the sign (negative).

When in Hex mode, you can enter hexadecimal values A–F from the keyboard or by using the A–F buttons on the Calculator. Table 10-2 shows number systems and keyboard equivalents. Table 10-3 and Table 10-4 show binary-mode keyboard equivalents and bitwise (logic) functions and keyboard equivalents, respectively.

Table 10-2. Number systems and keyboard equivalents

Calc button	Keyboard key	Action
Hex	F5	Hexadecimal (base 16)
Dec	F6	Decimal (base 10)
Oct	F7	Octal (base 8)
Bin	F8	Binary (base 2)

Table 10-3. Binary-mode keyboard equivalents

Calc button	Keyboard key	Action
Qword	F12	64-bit value
Dword	F2	32-bit value
Word	F3	16-bit value (low order bit)
Byte	F4	8-bit value (low order bit)

Table 10-4. Bitwise (logic) functions and keyboard equivalents

Calc button	Keyboard key	Action
Mod	%	Modulus
And	&	Bitwise AND
Or	|	Bitwise OR
Xor	^	Bitwise exclusive OR

Table 10-4. Bitwise (logic) functions and keyboard equivalents (continued)

Calc button	Keyboard key	Action
Lsh	<	Left-shift (right-shift via Inv + Lsh or >)
Not	~	Bitwise inverse
Int	;	Integer (remove the decimal portion)

When in Decimal mode, the Deg, Rad, and Grad radio buttons switch among degrees, radians, and gradients (see Table 10-5).

Table 10-5. Decimal-mode keyboard equivalents

Calc button	Keyboard key	Action
Deg	F2	Calculates trigonometric functions in degrees.
Rad	F3	Calculates trigonometric functions in radians.
Grad	F4	Calculates trigonometric functions in grads.

Statistical functions

To perform a statistical calculation, start by entering the first data, then click Sta to open the Statistics Box, click Dat to display the data in the Statistics Box, and then continue entering the data, clicking Dat after each entry. When you've finished entering all the numbers, click the statistical button you want to use (Ave, Sum, or S). The buttons available in the Statistics Box are listed in Table 10-6.

Table 10-6. Statistics Box buttons

Calc button	Action
RET	Returns the focus to the calculator.
LOAD	Displays the selected number in the Statistics Box in the Calculator display area.
CD	Clears the selected number (data).
CAD	Clears all numbers (data) in the Statistics Box.

Scientific calculations

Scientific calculation buttons and keyboard equivalents are shown in Table 10-7.

Table 10-7. Scientific calculation buttons and keyboard equivalents

Calc button	Keyboard key	Action
Inv	i	Sets the inverse function for sin, cos, tan, Pl, xy, x2, x3, Ln, log, sum, and s.
Hyp	h	Sets the hyperbolic function for sin, cos, and tan.
F-E	v	Turns scientific notation on and off. You can use this only with decimal numbers. Numbers larger than 10^{15} are always displayed with exponents.
( )	( )	Starts and ends a new level of parentheses. The maximum number of nested parentheses is 25. The current number of levels appears in the box above the) button.
dms	m	If the displayed number is in degrees, convert to degree-minute-second format. Use Inv + dms to reverse the operation.
Exp	x	The next digit(s) entered constitute the exponent. The exponent cannot be larger than 9999. Decimal only.

Calc button	Keyboard key	Action
Ln	n	Natural (base e) logarithm. Inv + Ln calculates e raised to the nth power, where n is the current number.
sin	s	Sine of the displayed number. Inv + sin gives arc sine. Hyp + sin gives hyperbolic sine. Inv + Hyp + sin gives arc hyperbolic sine.
x^y	y	x to the yth power. Inv + x^y calculates the yth root of x.
Log	l	The common (base 10) logarithm. Inv + log yields 10 to the xth power, where x is the displayed number.
Cos	o	Cosine of the displayed number. Inv + cosin gives arc cosine. Hyp + cosin gives hyperbolic cosine. Inv + Hyp + cosin gives arc hyperbolic cosine.
x^3	#	Cubes the displayed number. Inv + x^3 gives the cube root.
n!	!	Factorial of the displayed number.
tan	t	Tangent of the displayed number. Inv + tan gives arc tan. Hyp + tan gives hyperbolic tan. Inv + Hyp + tan gives arc hyperbolic tan.
x^2	@	Squares the displayed number. Inv + x^2 gives the square root.
1/x	r	Reciprocal of displayed number.
Pi	p	The value of *pi* (3.1415…). Inv + Pi gives 2 pi.

Notes

- If you convert a fractional decimal number to another number system, only the integer part will be used.
- Those serious about calculators will probably notice that there is no Reverse Polish Notation (RPN) mode. Fortunately, there are literally dozens of freely available alternatives on the Web (try AepCalc from *http://www.aepryus.com*).

Character Map
\windows\system32\charmap.exe

Display all the characters and symbols in a particular font. This provides access to symbols not easily accessible with the keyboard.

To open

Start → All Programs → Accessories → System Tools → Character Map

Command Prompt → **charmap**

Description

Character Map displays a visual map of all the characters in any font, making it easy to paste them into other documents (see Figure 10-10).

To use Character Map:

1. Select a font from the Font drop-down list. If you're inserting a character into an existing document, you should select the same font that is used in the document.
2. Find the character you want to use; click once on any cell to magnify its character. If you can't find the desired character, remember to scroll down. If the selected font doesn't have the character you want, try another font.

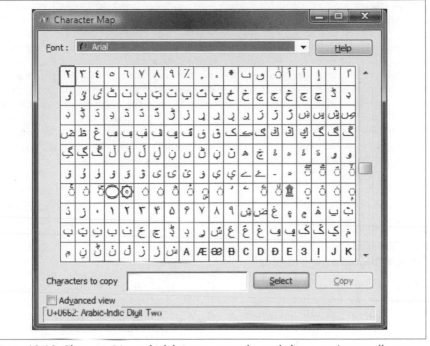

Figure 10-10. Character Map, which lets you access the symbols you can't normally type from the keyboard

3. Double-click the character you want (or click once and then click the Select button) to place the character in the "Characters to copy" box. You can place as many successive characters as you want in this box.

4. Click Copy to copy the character(s) to the Windows Clipboard.

5. Switch to your other application, click where you want the character(s) to appear, and paste (using either the Edit menu or Ctrl-V).

6. If the font in the target application isn't the same as the one you've selected in Character Map, you'll need to highlight the newly inserted character(s) and then change it to the same font you used in Character Map. If the character in your document doesn't look as it did in Character Map, it's because the wrong font is being used.

Notes

- Effective use of Character Map relies on correct font selection, especially when you're pasting characters into applications that don't support multiple fonts. For example, the default font used in Notepad is Lucida Console (which you can change by going to Notepad → Format → Font).

- Character Map is helpful not only for selecting extended characters in standard fonts, but also for accessing dingbats, such as those found in the Webdings, Wingdings, Symbol, and Marlett fonts.

- Character Map is useful for finding out what key combination will produce a nonstandard character in any given font. This can eliminate the need to repeatedly go back to Character Map to retrieve the same character. Select a character in any cell and see the corresponding character code in the status bar. For example, the Yin-Yang symbol in Wingdings is character code 0x5B. Now, this is a hexadecimal code, so you'll need to use the Calculator to convert it to a decimal number. In the Calculator's Scientific mode, click Hex, type the code (not including the 0x prefix—5B in this case), and then click Dec to view the decimal equivalent (91 in this case). To then insert the character into an application using the keyboard, hold down the Alt key and type the code using the numeric keypad (the numbers above the letters won't work). In the case of the Yin-Yang, press Alt and type **91**. Appendix C lists some of the most useful character codes.

See also

"Fonts Folder," in Chapter 3, and "Calculator" and "Private Character Editor," in this chapter

Default Programs Control Panel

Change a variety of program-related settings, including specifying the default programs to use for various file types and protocols, changing AutoPlay settings, and controlling access to certain programs.

To open

Start → Default programs

Description

By default, certain programs are associated with certain file types and protocols and will automatically launch when those files and protocols are opened. For example, by default Internet Explorer opens all *.html* files and Windows Contacts opens all *.vcf* files—vCard files that contain contact information. So whenever you double-click to open either of those file types—in Windows Explorer, in Windows Mail, or anywhere else—the default program will launch and open the file.

The Default Programs Control Panel (Figure 10-11) lets you make changes to those defaults, and lets you change a variety of other settings as well, such as whether CDs, DVDs, and other media should auto-play when inserted.

The Default Programs Control Panel lets you make these changes:

Set your default programs

Many programs can handle a wide variety of file types, but when they are installed, they are not necessarily the default programs for all those file types. Choosing this option lets you change the default associations on a program-by-program basis. When you click it, the screen shown in Figure 10-12 appears. As you can see, only programs that ship as part of Windows Vista are included; you can't use this option to make changes for other programs. (Notable exceptions include third-party email and web programs such as Mozilla Thunderbird and Firefox.)

Select the program whose defaults you want to check. If the program is not set to open by default all the file types it can handle, you'll be told the total number of file types it can handle, as well as the total number it is set by default to open. To

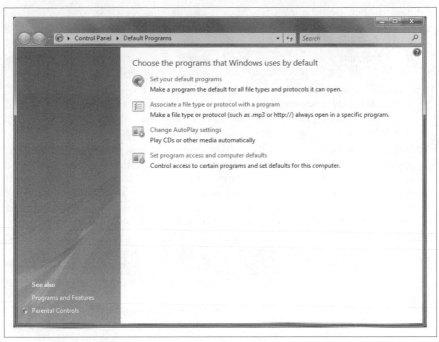

Figure 10-11. The Default Programs Control Panel, where you can change a variety of program and Windows defaults

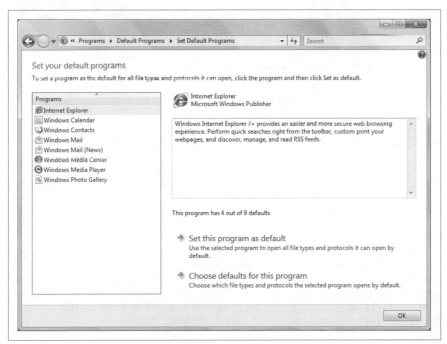

Figure 10-12. Configuring the default programs for the file types and protocols handled by core Windows Vista applications

have it open by default all file types it can handle, click "Set this program as default." To choose some file types but not others, click "Choose defaults for this program" and select from the list.

If the program is already set to open by default any file type it can handle, when you highlight the file it will read "This program has all its defaults."

Associate a file type or protocol with a program
Select this to choose, on a file type-by-file type basis, which programs should open various file types. For example, if you want *.mp3* files to be opened by the WinAmp freeware program, you would do that in this screen.

When you make this choice, the Set Associations screen, shown in Figure 10-13, appears. For each file extension, you're shown a description of what the file type is, as well as which program will open it by default. To change which program opens the file by default, click "Change program." You'll be shown the recommended default program, as well as other installed programs that can handle the file. If you want to choose a program not on either list, click Browse to locate it.

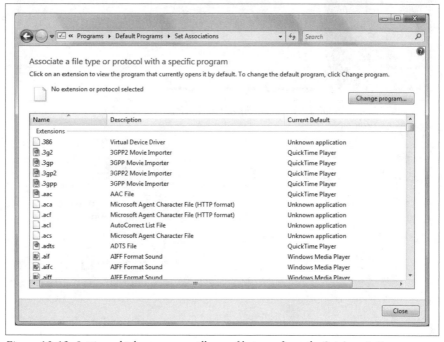

Figure 10-13. Setting which programs will open file types from the Set Associations screen

Change AutoPlay settings
This lets you choose what action Windows Vista should take when you insert a CD or DVD into a drive—use AutoPlay to play the media, or let you decide which action to take. It also lets you choose which program should play the media. As you can see in Figure 10-14, you can make choices for a wide variety of media and content, ranging from Blu-ray Disc movies, to mixed content on a CD or DVD, to HD DVD movies, and more.

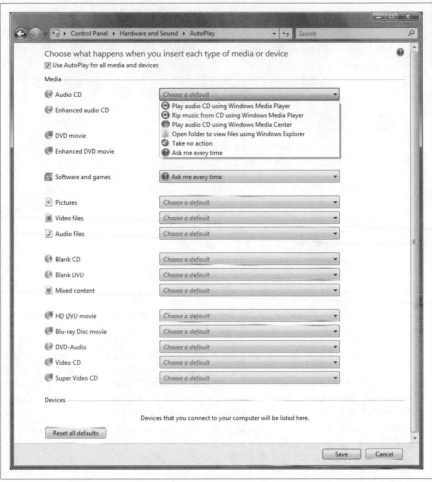

Figure 10-14. Choosing how Windows Vista decides what actions to take when a CD or DVD is inserted into a drive

Set program access and computer defaults

Several years back, Microsoft fell afoul of the U.S. Justice Department, which claimed that the company was illegally using its Windows monopoly power to promote its own software, such as Internet Explorer, over rivals such as Netscape Navigator. As part of that suit's settlement, Microsoft had to allow PC makers to ship Windows with whatever default programs they wanted for web browsing, media playing, and so on. Microsoft also had to allow consumers to easily change those defaults.

Why am I telling you all this? Because that's the reason for this feature's existence. Click the link, and you'll come to the page shown in Figure 10-15, which lets you choose an overall configuration of select programs for your PC, for web browsing, email, media playing, instant messaging, and using Java.

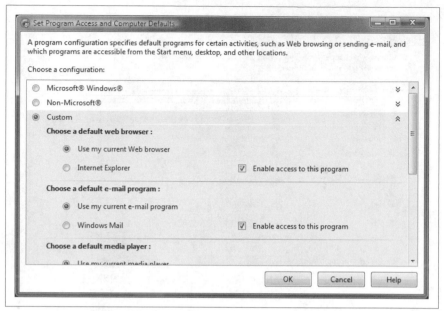

Figure 10-15. Choosing default programs for web browsing, email, media playing, instant messaging, and using Java

Choose Microsoft Windows, and you'll use all of Windows Vista and Microsoft programs. Choose Non-Microsoft, and not only will your system use non-Microsoft programs for all those purposes, but you'll also disable access to the Microsoft programs. Choose Custom to select a mix of Microsoft and non-Microsoft programs, and to enable or disable access to them.

If Windows Vista came preinstalled on a PC you bought, you may see another option here, Computer Manufacturer, which will restore your settings to those chosen by the manufacturer from which you bought your PC.

Notes

* Windows Vista offers you far less control over file associations than did Windows XP. In Windows XP, you could set multiple associations for files, as well as customize precisely what actions a program should take when it opens a file. You could, for example, set one program to play a file type by default, but a different program to edit the file by default. None of that is possible in Windows Vista, though.

* The choices you make in the Default Programs Control Panel are applied to all users of the PC; you cannot choose different settings for different users.

See also

"Windows Media Player," in Chapter 12

Fax Cover Page Editor

\windows\system32\fxscover.exe

Create and modify cover pages for use with Windows Fax and Scan.

To open
Windows Fax and Scan → Tools → Cover Pages → New

Command Prompt → **fxscover**

Description
The Fax Cover Page Editor (Figure 10-16) works like an ordinary drawing/layout program, in that you can indiscriminately place text, shapes, and images on a blank page. Pages created with the Cover Page Editor are used automatically when sending faxes with Windows Fax and Scan.

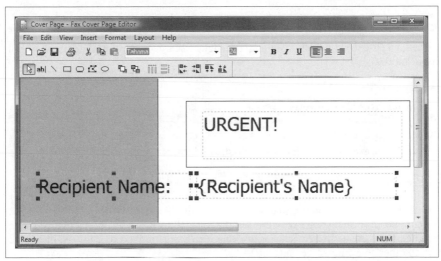

Figure 10-16. The Fax Cover Page Editor, which, among other things, enables you to support fields to import data such as recipient names

What makes the Cover Page Editor different from other drawing/layout programs to which you might be accustomed is its support for fields. Naturally, it wouldn't do you much good to create a custom cover page for only a single recipient; rather, it is desirable to create a single cover page (or a series of cover pages) that you can use with any number of recipients. Use the Insert menu to place text fields on the page; fields are divided into the following three categories (menus):

Recipient
> Place the name or phone number fields on your cover page, and Windows Fax and Scan will insert those details of the recipient on each fax that is sent out.

Sender
> The information in the Sender menu does not change from fax to fax; rather, you set it in the Windows Fax and Scan application (discussed later in this chapter) by going to Windows Fax and Scan → Tools → Sender Information. Note that it's generally preferred to use fields rather than static text, even if the information contained therein is the same for all faxes—it not only makes it easier to change later on, but it also means that your cover pages can be used easily by others.

Message
> Like items in the Recipient menu, Message details the message change from fax to fax, such as the subject, time, date, and number of pages.

When you've created or modified the cover pages desired, you must save them into a Cover Page (*.cov*) file, stored, by default, in *\Users\username\Documents\Fax\Personal Coverpages*. Then, when sending a fax, simply specify the desired Cover Page file, and it will be used as the first page in your outgoing fax.

You may want to preview outgoing faxes immediately after creating or modifying a cover page to make sure information is inserted into the fields properly.

See also
"Windows Fax and Scan"

IExpress
\windows\system32\iexpress.exe

Create a self-extracting/self-installing package, used to distribute files and install applications.

To open
Command Prompt → **iexpress**

Usage
```
iexpress.exe [/n [/q] [/m]] file [/o:overide file,section]
```

Description
A self-extracting/self-installing package is actually an application, commonly known as an installer or setup program, that is used to install one or more files onto a Windows system and, optionally, to execute a setup script. IExpress is an interactive program that helps you create these packages, making it easy to, among other things, distribute files to other computers (see Figure 10-17).

Say you want to put together a collection of documents that can be sent to another user, either via email or by using a floppy disk or CD. Rather than simply sending the files separately or compressing them into a *.zip* file, both of which would require additional instructions (not to mention a reasonably knowledgeable and patient recipient), you can make a full-featured, professional-looking installer with IExpress.

When you start IExpress, the IExpress Wizard guides you through the steps for creating a self-extracting package. The first step prompts for a Self Extraction Directive (*.sed*) file, a file that contains all the options and files to include. If you don't have one, select "Create new Self Extraction Directive file" and click Next.

The next page, "Package purpose," asks what you want the installer to do with the files on the target computer when the recipient opens the package. If you select the first option, "Extract files and run an installation command," the files will be copied to a temporary folder and a separate installer program that you provide will be launched. If you don't have a separate installation program, choose "Extract files only" and click Next. The last option, "Create compressed files only," is used by application developers to assist in the distribution of application components and is of little use to most users.

The subsequent steps allow you to specify a package title, type welcome and "finished" messages, and even include a license agreement. When you reach the "Packaged files" page, use the Add button to select one or more files to be included in the package; you can choose as many files as you like, and they can be any format. In fact, IExpress will compress the files so that they take up less space (like *.zip* files).

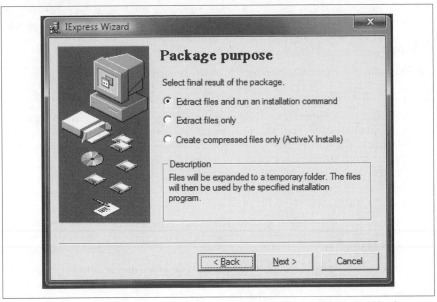

*Figure 10-17. The IExpress Wizard, which lets you package up a collection of files for easy
distribution*

Then, IExpress will ask you to specify a package name, which is the path- and filename of the package (*.exe*) to be created. IExpress will also optionally save your
choices into a Self Extraction Directive (*.sed*) file, making it easy to re-create this
package without having to answer all the aforementioned prompts again.

When the process is complete, you'll end up with a new *.exe* file that you can run on
any Windows system. This package can now be emailed, FTP'd, distributed on a CD
or floppy, or even posted on a web site; the recipient won't need any special tools or
elaborate instructions to extract the files from the package.

IExpress also has an automated, noninteractive mode for advanced users who want to
skip the somewhat cumbersome wizard interface and instead create a package using
the following command-line parameters:

file
> The full path and filename of a Self Extraction Directive (*.sed*) file. If you don't
> have a *.sed* file, you'll have to use the wizard interface to create one.

/n
> Build package now (*file* must be specified). If you omit /n, IExpress will open in
> the interactive wizard interface.

/q
> Quiet mode (no prompts); used only with /n.

/m
> Use minimized windows; used only with /n.

/o
> Specify override *.sed* file and section.

/d
> Override directory for *.exe* stub.

If you've already created a .sed file (say, c:\stuff\thing.sed) and you want to generate the corresponding package without walking through the wizard or being bothered with any prompts, type the following at a command prompt:

```
iexpress /n /q c:\stuff\thing.sed
```

The filename of the resulting package will be as specified in the .sed file.

Notes

- Self Extraction Directive (.sed) files are just plain-text files, similar in format to Configuration Files (.ini), and you can edit them with a plain text editor, such as Notepad. The easiest way to get started with .sed files is to use the IExpress Wizard to create one and then edit (if necessary) to suit your needs.

See also

"Cabinet (CAB) Maker"

Microsoft Magnifier   \windows\system32\magnify.exe

Show an enlarged version of the area of the screen near the mouse cursor.

To open

Start → All Programs → Accessories → Ease of Access → Magnifier

Command Prompt → **magnify**

Description

The Microsoft Magnifier is used to assist those with visual impairments by magnifying a portion of the screen. When you start Magnifier, the top 15 percent of the screen turns into an automatic magnifying glass, which follows the mouse cursor around the screen. If you have trouble seeing something on the screen, just float the cursor over it to magnify it (see Figure 10-18).

You can resize or move the Magnifier with the mouse. Furthermore, when the Magnifier is first opened, the "Magnifier settings" window appears, allowing you to change the magnification level and choose whether the Magnifier follows the mouse cursor, keyboard focus, or text cursor. To hide the settings window, just minimize it; if you close it, the Magnifier will close.

Notes

- The Magnifier can also be very handy for application developers and web site authors, who may need to see pixel detail in their work.

See also

"Narrator" and "On-Screen Keyboard"

Narrator   \windows\system32\narrator.exe

A text-to-speech program intended for visually impaired users.

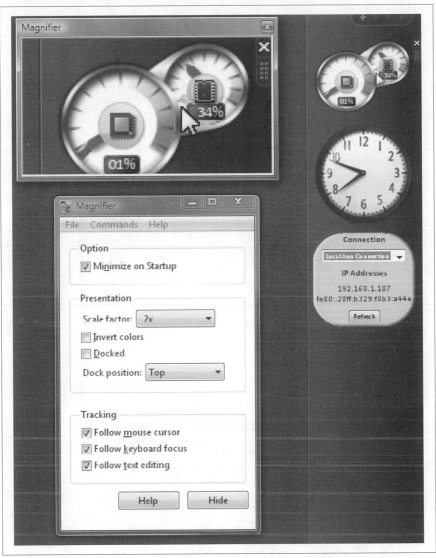

Figure 10-18. The Magnifier tool, which can follow your mouse cursor, enlarging any portion of the screen you point to

To open

Start → All Programs → Accessories → Ease of Access → Narrator

Command Prompt → **narrator**

Description

The Narrator assists those with visual impairments by using a voice synthesizer and the sound hardware on the user's computer to read aloud text and the titles of screen elements (see Figure 10-19). You can configure the Narrator with these options:

Echo User's Keystrokes
> The Narrator will speak each letter, number, and keyboard action as its corresponding key is pressed on the keyboard.

Announce System Messages
> The Narrator will speak any Windows Vista system messages as they appear on the screen, as well as the titles of Windows when they are activated and the captions of many types of screen elements.

Announce Scroll Notifications
> The Narrator will tell you when the screen scrolls.

Start Narrator Minimized
> This will start Narrator minimized to the toolbar.

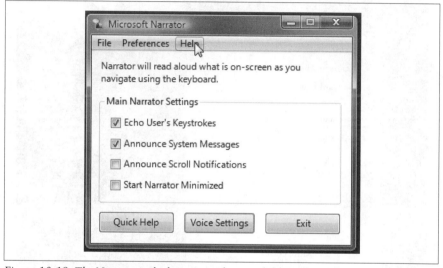

Figure 10-19. The Narrator, which uses speech to read the captions of various screen elements over your speakers

In addition to these functions, you can use the following keyboard shortcuts to read additional items:

- To read an entire window, click the window and then press Ctrl-Shift-Space bar.
- To read the caption of the control with the focus, or to read the contents of a text field, press Ctrl-Shift-Enter.
- To get a more detailed description of an item, press Ctrl-Shift-Insert.
- To read the title bar of a window, press Alt-Home.
- To read the status bar of a window, press Alt-End.
- To silence the speech, press the Ctrl key by itself.

Notes

- A far more impressive, related technology is that used in speech recognition software, in which the computer will take dictation, translating anything spoken into a microphone into text on the screen. Although initially developed for physically challenged users, speech recognition has become very popular among all types of users, partly because of the novelty, partly because of the speed (some can type up to 160 words per minute), and partly to help reduce repetitive stress injuries. Windows Vista also comes with a new voice recognition feature, although it's not nearly as sophisticated as NaturallySpeaking (*http://www.dragonsys.com*) or IBM's ViaVoice (*http://www.ibm.com/speech*).

See also

"Microsoft Magnifier," "On-Screen Keyboard," and "Windows Speech Recognition"

Notepad

\windows\notepad.exe

A rudimentary plain-text editor.

To open

Start → All Programs → Accessories → Notepad

Command Prompt → **notepad**

Usage

```
notepad [/p] [filename]
```

Description

Notepad is one of the simplest yet most useful tools included with Windows Vista. Those familiar with word processors may find Notepad to be laughably limited at first glance, as it has no support for even the simplest formatting. However, the fact that it supports only text in the documents that it creates is an absolute necessity for many of the tasks for which it is used on a daily basis (see Figure 10-20).

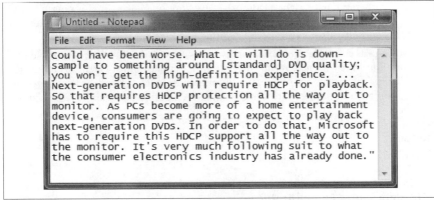

Figure 10-20. Notepad, for editing text files without the bother of a word processor

Among the file types Notepad can edit are *.txt* files (plain-text files), *.reg* files (see "Exporting and Importing Registry Data with Patches," in Chapter 13), *.bat* files (see "Batch Files," in Chapter 14), *.ini* files (configuration files), *.html* files (web pages), Unicode, and any other ASCII text-based file type.

Notepad has gained a bit more popularity recently, with the rise of blogging. When you copy and paste text from a word processor, such as Microsoft Word, into some blogging tools, the copied text brings along with it stray bits of code and invisible HTML. This causes problems with the blog. Notepad, on the other hand, handles only text, so it doesn't cause the same problems.

Notepad is the default application for *.txt* and *.log* files and is set up as the Edit context menu action for *.bat*, *.inf*, and *.reg* files, among others. Furthermore, via the /p command-line parameter, Notepad is used to print most text-based file types via the Print context menu action.

Notes

- In some previous versions of Windows, Notepad had a limit as to the size of the documents it could open. The Windows Vista version of Notepad has no such limit, and you can use it to open a file of any size.

- Notepad has no intrinsic formatting of its own, so any file that is opened in Notepad is displayed exactly as it is stored on the hard disk, with the proviso that only visible characters will be shown. This means that you can open any file, text-based or otherwise, in Notepad; if you try to open a binary file, however, you'll see mostly gibberish. There are times, though, when this can be useful; if you suspect that an image file or a movie file has the wrong extension, you can open it in Notepad to verify its contents. (Naturally, some experience is required to correctly identify different types of files.)

- The Word Wrap feature (Edit → Word Wrap) will break apart long lines of text so that they are visible in the Notepad window without horizontal scrolling. However, no permanent changes will be made to the file, so you can use the Word Wrap feature without fear of damaging the integrity of the document.

- If you type the text **.LOG** (in uppercase and including the period) as the first line in a text file, Notepad will automatically place the time and date at the end of the file (with the cursor right below it) every time you open it, forming a simple logfile. Furthermore, you can use the F5 key to manually place a date/timestamp at the current cursor location while editing any file.

- Notepad is a simple program, but by no means is it a full-featured text editor. UltraEdit (*http://www.ultraedit.com*) is a much more sophisticated text editor that you also can use as a hex (binary) editor. NoteTab Pro (*http://www.notetab.com*) is also far more sophisticated, and it includes a very easy-to-use HTML editor as well.

See also

"WordPad"

ODBC Data Source Administrator
\windows\system32\odbcad32.exe

Add, remove, or configure sources of database management system data.

To open

Control Panel → [System and Maintenance] → Administrative Tools → Data Sources (ODBC)

Command Prompt → **odbcad32**

Description

Open Database Connectivity (ODBC) is a system that connects ODBC-enabled applications to the database management systems that provide the data. You use the ODBC Data Source Administrator to configure your applications so that they can get data from a variety of database management systems. For example, if you're using an application that accesses data in an SQL database, the ODBC Data Source Administrator lets you connect that application to a different data source, such as a Microsoft Excel spreadsheet or a Paradox database.

In the ODBC Data Source Administrator, the different sources of data are called *data providers*. To add a new provider, click Add under the User DSN, the System DSN, or the File DSN tab. A list of the available drivers is listed under the Drivers tab; you can install new drivers separately. The Tracing tab allows you to log the communication between applications and the ODBC data sources they use. You use the Connection Pooling tab to improve performance with ODBC servers. Finally, you use the About tab to check the versions of the installed ODBC components.

On-Screen Keyboard

\windows\system32\osk.exe

A full, on-screen keyboard controlled by the pointing device.

To open

Start → Programs ▸ Accessories ▸ Accessibility → On-Screen Keyboard

Command Prompt → **osk**

Description

Among the tools provided with Windows XP to assist users with physical disabilities is the On-Screen Keyboard. Intended to be used by those who are unable to comfortably use a keyboard, the On-Screen Keyboard allows any key normally available on the keyboard to be pressed with a click of the mouse, or whatever pointing device is currently being used (see Figure 10-21).

Figure 10-21. The On-Screen Keyboard, which lets you type by pointing and clicking

What makes the On-Screen Keyboard especially appropriate as a primary input device is that you can click keys when another application has the focus. For example, open the On-Screen Keyboard and then open your word processor; the keyboard will float above the word processor, allowing you to click any key to "type" it into your document.

Configuring the On-Screen Keyboard is straightforward. Use the Keyboard menu to change the layout of the keys, or Settings → Font to change the font of the key labels. Go to Settings → Typing Mode to choose how keys are pressed; by default, each key must be clicked, but you can set it up so that you can hover over keys to select them, or even use a joystick to control the keyboard.

Notes

- Also included with Windows Vista is the Character Map (discussed earlier in this chapter), which allows access to symbols and other characters not normally available on a standard keyboard. However, only the On-Screen Keyboard is designed to be a primary input device.

See also

"Microsoft Magnifier," "Narrator," and "Character Map"

Private Character Editor

\windows\system32\eudcedit.exe

Create special characters, such as logos or symbols, that can be inserted into ordinary documents.

To open

Command Prompt → `eudcedit`

Description

The Private Character Editor is like a small-image editor, except that the images created with it are used like symbol fonts, making it easy to insert any custom logo or symbol into your documents.

When you first start the Private Character Editor, you'll be presented with a rather confusing Select Code window. You use this to associate the new (or existing) character you'll be editing with a particular slot, and it is somewhat akin to the main Character Map window. Select any slot and click OK to proceed.

The main window contains the character editor and a simple set of drawing tools (such as those found in Paint). Each character is a 50×50 black-and-white bitmap. Draw in black with any of the available tools and the left mouse button; draw in white with the right mouse button. You can copy and paste bitmap selections between the Private Character Editor and other image editing programs, such as Paint.

When you're done, save your work into the slot you chose in the first screen by going to Edit → Save Character (Ctrl-S). Or, save it into a different slot by going to Edit → Save Character As. At any time, you can choose a different slot to edit with Edit → Select Code, or with View → Next Code (Ctrl-N) and View → Prev Code (Ctrl-P). As you choose slots in which to place your new characters, you can use another font as a reference to decide which are the most convenient slots to use. Select Window → Reference to view the orientation of an existing font on your computer.

To use your new character in another application, open Character Map (*charmap.exe*) and choose All Fonts (Private Characters) from the top of the list. If this entry is not present, you didn't save your work. See "Character Map," earlier in this chapter, for more information on pasting characters into other applications.

See also

"Character Map"

Program Compatibility Wizard

Configure older programs to help them run under Windows Vista.

To open

Control Panel → Programs → Use an older program with this version of Windows

Description

Old programs, especially old DOS-based programs and games, may have problems running under Windows Vista. The Program Compatibility Wizard helps you troubleshoot problems with those programs, and help them run under Windows Vista.

Run the wizard, then choose the program from a list of programs, browse for it on your hard disk, or choose a program in your CD or DVD drive. After you select it, you can choose one of five compatibility modes—Windows 95, Windows NT 4.0 (Service Pack 5), Windows 98/Me, Windows 2000, or Windows XP (Service Pack 2). Choose the version of Windows under which the program was developed or worked previously. When you do that, the Program Compatibility Wizard will apply settings so that whenever the program runs, it will in essence think it's running under the older operating system, and all should be right in its world. So, for example, it may run at 256 colors and in 640×480 resolution.

What if that doesn't work, or if you don't know under what version of Windows it previously ran? Choose "Do not apply a compatibility mode" instead. You'll be walked through a series of screens letting you manually choose settings (Figure 10-22), such as under what screen resolution and color depth to run the program, whether to run the program as an administrator, and so on. When you're done, if the program still doesn't work, go back in and change the settings until you find a set that works.

Notes

- You shouldn't use the Program Compatibility Wizard with older virus detection, backup, or system programs, because using those older programs on Windows Vista can potentially cause serious system problems.

- If you're experiencing problems with the program's menus, buttons, or title bar, check the box next to "Disable visual themes" when you're choosing your settings manually. Select "Disable desktop composition" if you're experiencing problems with the display.

Rundll32

\windows\system32\rundll32.exe

Run a single routine in a DLL file from the command line.

To open

Command Prompt → **rundll32**

Usage

```
rundll32 filename,function_name [function_arguments...]
```

Description

Rundll32 provides "string invocation," which lets you execute a command buried in a Dynamic Link Library (DLL) file.

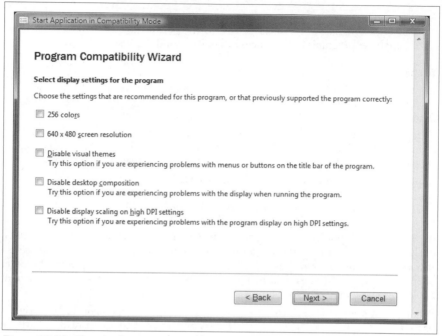

Figure 10-22. Choosing how to run an older program to get it to work in Windows Vista

Rundll32 accepts the following options:

filename
> The filename of a DLL (*.dll*) file.

function_name
> The case-sensitive name of a function in the DLL file.

function_arguments
> Any parameters used by *function_name*; refer to the function's documentation for details. Note that any string parameters are case-sensitive.

Examples

The following example switches the functions of the mouse buttons so that the right operates as the left, and vice versa. Note, though, that it doesn't work as a toggle, so you can't use the command again to switch the functions back.

```
RUNDLL32.EXE USER32.DLL,SwapMouseButton
```

This batch file allows you to display an Open As dialog box for unknown file type *.xyz* without actually having a file of type *.xyz* handy (see Chapter 14 for more information about batch files):

```
echo blah blah blah > foobar.%1
rundll32 shell32.dll,OpenAs_RunDLL foobar.%1
```

Then type the following at a command line:

```
C:\>openas xyz
```

Notes

- Rundll32 provides dynamic linking to functions exported from 32-bit DLLs. Rundll, the 16-bit equivalent found in versions of Windows before Windows XP, is not included in Windows Vista.

Uninstall or Change a Program

\windows\system32\appwiz.cpl

Uninstall programs, or add or remove extra program features.

To open

Control Panel → Programs → Programs and Features

Command Prompt → `appwiz.cpl`

Description

This Control Panel applet (Figure 10-23) lets you uninstall any program on your PC, as well as change the program by adding new features, or repair the program if for some reason it has been damaged.

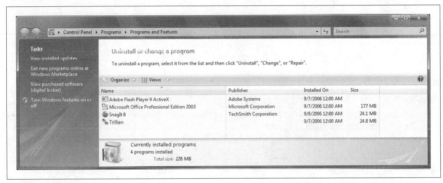

Figure 10-23. The Control Panel applet where you can uninstall programs

To uninstall a program, double-click it and follow the prompts that appear. (You can also right-click it and choose Uninstall.) To add new features or remove features from the program, right-click it and select Change. In many instances, you'll need the CD or DVD from which you installed the program in order to add—and sometimes remove—features. You'll be prompted for the CD or DVD. Right-click and choose Repair to fix a damaged program—and again, you'll usually need the CD or DVD installation disk in order to do that.

The Uninstall or Change a Program applet also lets you turn Windows features and programs on and off—features and programs such as games, Windows Media Player, and so on. Click "Turn Windows features on or off," and the screen shown in Figure 10-24 appears. Turn a feature on by checking the box next to it; turn it off by unchecking the box. Note that turning off a Windows feature doesn't actually delete the files from your hard disk; it only turns off access to them. In this way, when Windows Update runs, you know that every possible program you could run is safe (otherwise, if you had to install the program anew from Windows DVD, you could install older, buggy versions).

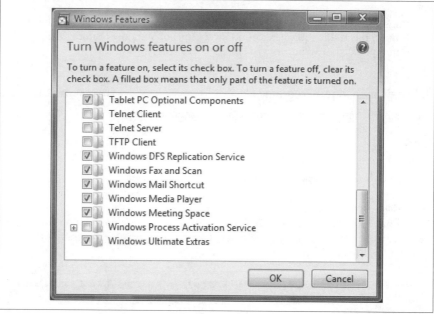

Figure 10-24. Turning Windows programs and features on and off

Notes

- Remove or disable add-ins to Internet Explorer and/or ActiveX controls using Internet Explorer. In Internet Explorer, choose Tools → Manage Add-ons → Enable or Disable Add-ons.

Windows CardSpace

Send and receive faxes, including scanning documents to be faxed.

To open

Control Panel → [User Accounts and Family Safety] → Windows CardSpace

Description

Windows CardSpace, formerly known as InfoCard, stores "cards" that identify you to web sites, services, and applications, and let you log on to them automatically. When you visit a CardSpace-enabled web site or run a CardSpace-enabled application and the application or site needs to get information from you, Windows CardSpace automatically runs, displays all the cards you've created, and lets you select the appropriate one. The information is then sent to the site or application.

Windows CardSpace is self-explanatory; click Add Card to create a new card, Delete Card to delete an existing card, and so on.

Notes

- As of this writing, Windows CardSpace is not particularly popular, and very few web sites and applications use it, just as very few used its predecessor, InfoCard. So you may not want to spend much time using this Windows Vista feature.

- For security purposes, when you create or manage your cards, your screen turns into Windows Vista's Secure Desktop, in which the background of the screen is dark and only the Windows CardSpace area is live. When the Secure Desktop is running, only trusted processes are allowed to run, making for increased security.

Windows Fax and Scan   *\windows\system32\WFS.exe*

Send and receive faxes, including scanning documents to be faxed.

To open
Start → Windows Fax and Scan

Command Prompt → **wfs**

Description
Windows Fax and Scan lets you send, receive, and manage all incoming and outgoing faxes (see Figure 10-25). It is set up like Outlook Express, with folders shown in a hierarchical tree in the left pane and the contents of the currently selected folder shown in the right pane.

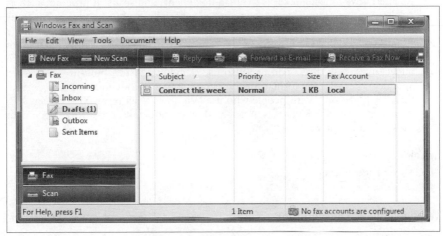

Figure 10-25. Windows Fax and Scan, which lets you view and manage all incoming and outgoing faxes

Windows Fax and Scan lets you create documents to fax with its message editor, which looks much like the editor included with Windows Mail. You can use different fonts and font attributes, embed graphics, and so on, and then fax the document.

If you have a document on paper that you need faxed, you can use the scan features to scan the document and then fax it. Switch between the fax and scanning features by clicking either Fax or Scan at the bottom of the screen.

Windows Fax and Scan works much like an email program. For example, if you receive a fax and want to respond to it, click Reply, and you'll be able to send a fax back to the sender, using the built-in editor to create it. You can even take a fax you've gotten, attach it to an email, and send it. (Click Forward as E-Mail.) Of course, it prints faxes as well.

If you're attached to a network that has a network fax, you can use that instead of a fax connected to your PC.

If you create documents using Word, Excel, or other applications that you want to fax, you can instead fax the documents straight from the application. Applications consider the fax as little more than a remote printer connected to a phone line. Print as you normally would, except choose Fax instead of your normal printer. After your application has sent the document to the fax printer driver, a new wizard appears and asks you for the recipient name and phone number, as well as any queuing options (useful if you want to postpone sending the fax until off-peak hours).

To receive faxes, start Windows Fax and Scan and click Receive a Fax Now.

Notes

- Not surprisingly, if you don't have a modem, you won't be able to send or receive faxes; you can't send them from Windows Fax and Scan via the Internet.

- If you want to receive faxes but don't have a modem, or if you just don't want to leave Windows Fax and Scan running all the time, Internet-based fax services (such as *http://www.efax.com*), some of which are completely free, send incoming faxes to you as email attachments.

- An alternative to using faxes is to email documents and scans. A program such as Adobe Acrobat (*http://www.adobe.com*) is especially useful for preserving fonts and formatting in computer-generated documents, and it can even accommodate scanned pages, making it easy for the recipient to view or even print them. Not only will this result in higher-quality documents and lower phone bills, but it also might save a few trees. You can also use Windows Vista's built-in XML Paper Specification (XPS) file format for the same purpose, although the document can then be shared only with people who use Windows Vista or an XPS viewer. XPS isn't in as widespread use as Acrobat. For more details, see "XPS Document Viewer," in Chapter 9.

See also

"Fax Cover Page Editor"

Windows Speech Recognition
\windows\Speech\Common\sapisvr.exe

To open

Start → All Programs → Ease of Access → Windows Speech Recognition

Command Prompt → **sapisvr.exe -SpeechUX**

Description

Windows Speech Recognition lets you dictate to Windows, which will recognize your speech and input it into an application. In addition, you can use spoken commands to perform tasks, such as opening files, saving files, switching between applications, and so on.

You'll need a microphone for speech recognition to work. The first time you start the application, a wizard runs, letting you configure your hardware. In addition, a tutorial will run, teaching you how to use the program.

WordPad

\Program Files\Windows NT\Accessories\wordpad.exe

A simple word processor.

To open

Start → All Programs → Accessories → WordPad

Command Prompt → **wordpad**

Description

Although WordPad lacks many of the features that come with full-blown word processors such as WordPerfect and Microsoft Word, it has enough features to let you create and edit rich-text documents. WordPad is the default editor for *.rtf*, *.doc*, and *.wri* files (unless Microsoft Word is installed). You also can use WordPad to edit plain-text files (*.txt*), although Notepad (discussed earlier in this chapter) is the default and is more appropriate for this task (see Figure 10-26).

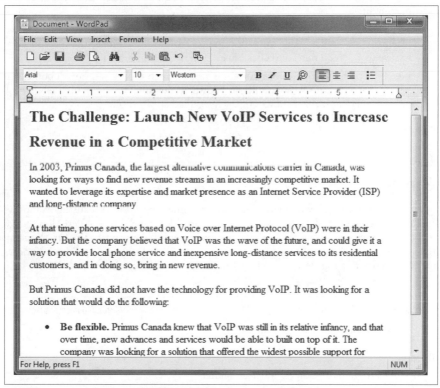

Figure 10-26. WordPad, the rudimentary word processor that comes with Windows XP

Depending on the type of file opened, WordPad may or may not display its formatting toolbar and ruler. When you use File → New, WordPad prompts you to choose a document type, including Rich Text Document (formatted text, such as word processor documents), Text Document (plain ASCII text), and Unicode Text Document (plain text using the Unicode character set). Once a file is open, however, you can turn on or off the formatting bar and ruler and even apply formatting to plain-text documents. If you try to save a text document with formatting, though, WordPad will warn you that your formatting will be lost (because text files don't support formatting).

WordPad has several advantages over the simpler Notepad application. Among other things, WordPad lets you choose from a wide selection of fonts and font sizes, use colors in your documents, set tab stops, use rulers, and even insert objects (e.g., images, some clips, etc.). Although not a full-featured word processor, WordPad does enough to create simple formatted documents that can then be printed, emailed, or faxed.

Notes

- You can open Microsoft Word documents with WordPad, but you might lose some formatting if you save the file (which will prompt WordPad to warn you).

- When dragging a file onto WordPad, be sure to drop the file icon onto the WordPad title bar if you want to view it or edit it, or drop it onto the middle of the document if you want to embed the icon as an object into the currently open document.

- To prevent WordPad from overwriting your file extensions and adding its own when you save a file, place quotation marks around the name of the file you want to save (e.g., "*read.me*") and click Save. Otherwise, you'll get *read.me.doc*.

- Like Notepad, WordPad does not allow you to open more than one document at a time. If you want to view multiple WordPad documents simultaneously, you'll need to open multiple instances of the WordPad application.

See also
"Notepad"

Games

Windows Vista comes with plenty of built-in games, but if you're using Windows Vista Business, you may wonder why everyone else gets all the fun—there don't seem to be any games for you to play. Worry not; you won't be left out of the fun. You can turn on access to the games by going to Control Panel → Programs → Turn Windows features on or off, and selecting Games. Just don't let your boss know you did it.

Chess Titans   *\Program Files\Microsoft Games\chess\chess.exe*

Play chess against your computer.

To open
Start → All Programs → Games → Chess Titans

Description
Chess Titans (Figure 10-27) lets you play chess against your computer or against a human opponent, although you don't play a human online—instead, you each take turns at the keyboard. When you play against the computer, you can choose from beginner, intermediate, and advanced levels.

Figure 10-27. Chess Titans

Choose Game → Options to change whether you play as white or black, to change the level of difficulty, to change the graphics quality, and to choose many other options, such as whether to play animations and sounds, and what view to use.

To change the view of the game, hold down the right button and drag with your mouse. To choose a different-looking chess set or to change the board background, choose Game → Change Appearance or press F7.

Notes

- Make a move, only to have the computer wipe you out? Press Ctrl-Z, and you'll undo your last move.

FreeCell
\Program Files\Microsoft Games\FreeCell\FreeCell.exe

A solitaire card game, considered by many users to be more addictive than traditional Solitaire (Klondike).

To open

Start → All Programs → Games → FreeCell

Description

FreeCell is a solitaire card game (see Figure 10-28), but you play it differently than the traditional Klondike game (see "Solitaire," later in this chapter). The object of the game is to move all the cards to the home cells.

As with Klondike, you arrange your cards by placing them in descending value and alternating color (you can place the Four of Clubs on the Five of Hearts or the Five of

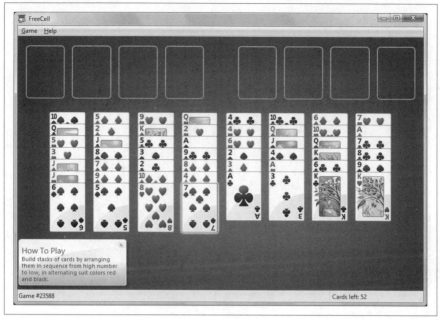

Figure 10-28. FreeCell

Diamonds). Click a card to highlight it and click another card to move the highlighted card. You can move multiple cards, but only those that are arranged accordingly. You also can move cards to one of the four "free cells," temporary storage slots that fill up fast.

FreeCell is somewhat like a cross between Klondike and the Towers of Hanoi puzzle.

Notes

- In FreeCell, cards are not dealt randomly. Rather, there are 32,000 distinct, numbered games, each representing a different predetermined deal of the cards. According to the help, "It is believed (although not proven) that every game is winnable." In fact, it has been proven that game #11,982 is indeed not winnable. Don't believe me? Press F3 and then select 11982.

See also

"Solitaire" and "Spider Solitaire"

Games Explorer

A specialized Windows Explorer folder that serves as the central location for all your games.

To open

Start → All Programs → Games → Games Explorer

Description

Games Explorer (see Figure 10-29) is a specialized Windows Explorer folder that lists all of your games and gives you a variety of other features and tools related to them. It shows a list of every game; click on one and in the preview pane you'll see various ratings related to it. Games Explorer will list the performance ratings recommended and required for that game, and your current system's performance ratings, so that you'll know whether your hardware can properly handle it. (For details about performance ratings, see "Performance Information and Tools," in Chapter 11.) It also lists the Entertainment Software Rating Board (ESRB) suitability rating for the game.

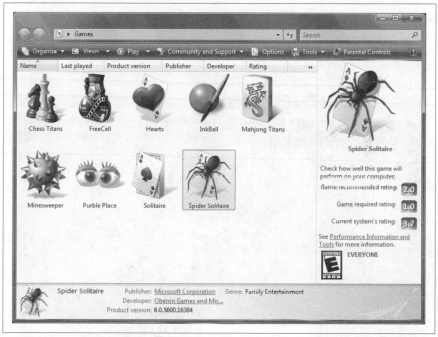

Figure 10-29. Games Explorer, the central location for all your games

Click the Play button and you'll get a list of all of your saved games for every game. The Community and Support button leads you to relevant (and not-so-relevant) web sites. The Options button lets you control whether to download information about your installed games and whether to list your most recently played games, and will clear out the list of your most recently closed games, if you so choose.

Notes

- New games generally will show up in Games Explorer automatically, but some older ones might not. If a game doesn't appear, open Games Explorer and drag the game's executable file into the folder. Games Explorer might not recognize the game; if that's the case, it will ask you for information about it.

- For extra features, display the menu bar in the folder by choosing Organize → Layout → Menu Bar. Among the extra features you can access is the ability to hide a game from view. You can also hide a game without relying on the menu bar. Right-click a game and choose Hide.

See also

"Performance Information and Tools," in Chapter 11

Hearts

\Program Files\Microsoft Games\Hearts\Hearts.exe

A card game played with three opponents.

To open

Start → All Programs → Games → Hearts

Description

Hearts is a trick-based game, like Spades, but the object is to have the lowest score at the end of each hand. The online help tells you how to play the game and provides strategy and tips (see Figure 10-30).

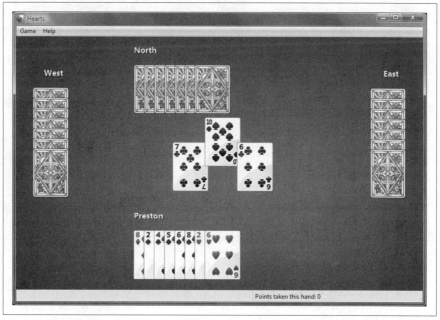

Figure 10-30. Hearts, which lets you play the classic card game against artificial opponents or other people on your network

Notes

- Normally, the object of Hearts is to stick your opponents with as many points (hearts) as possible. However, if one player takes all the points in a hand, it's called "shooting the moon": that player gets 0 points and everyone else gets 26 points.

InkBall

\Program Files\Microsoft Games\inkball\InkBall.exe

Guide the colored balls into holes of the same color.

To open

Start → All Programs → Games → InkBall

Description

This simple game (Figure 10-31) is best suited for Tablet PCs, although it also works fine on regular PCs. You guide colored balls into holes of the same color by drawing barriers with the mouse or tablet. Similarly, you need to keep balls from going into a hole of a different color. When you draw a line, the ball bounces off it; as soon as the ball bounces away, the line disappears. You can draw multiple lines as well. You lose when a ball falls into a hole of a different color or the timer runs out.

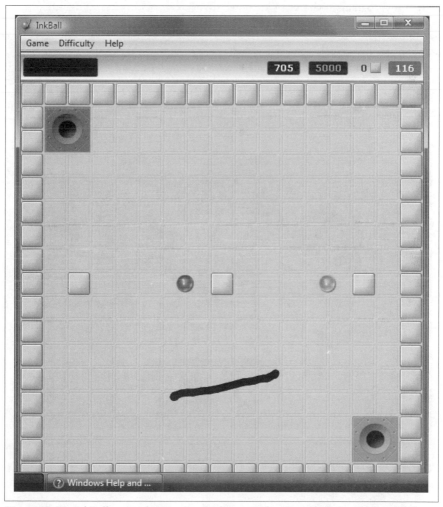

Figure 10-31. InkBall, a simple game in which you guide colored balls into holes of the same color by drawing barriers with the mouse or tablet

There are five levels of difficulty; at upper levels there are barriers, multiple balls of multiple colors that spin at odd angles, and other conundrums.

Notes

- Gray balls are allowed to enter any colored hole, and gray holes accept a ball of any color. No points are awarded when a gray ball enters a hole, and the game does not end when a colored ball enters a gray hole.
- An ink stroke can affect only one ball.

Mahjong Titans
\Program Files\Microsoft Games\Mahjong\Mahjong.exe

Clear all the tiles by eliminating matching ones.

To open

Start → All Programs → Games → Mahjong Titans

Description

Mahjong, as played on the computer, isn't the same thing as the classic Chinese game, as I can attest from personal experience because my decidedly non-Asian mother played countless rounds of the game against her friends throughout my youth. On the PC, there is no betting or clicking of tiles. Instead, Mahjong Titans (Figure 10-32) is a much simpler game. You click on matching tiles to remove them, and if you clear all the tiles you win. You play against the clock.

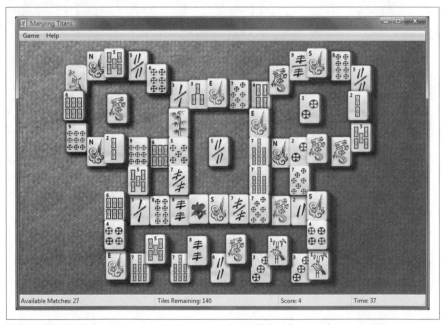

Figure 10-32. Mahjong, a game in which you clear all the tiles to achieve victory

---

You choose from multiple boards with varying levels of difficulty, and you can also choose different tile backgrounds, specify whether to use animation, and so on, by selecting Game → Options.

Minesweeper
\Program Files\Microsoft Games\Minesweeper\Minesweeper.exe

A quick game relying on the process of elimination.

To open
Start → All Programs → Games → Minesweeper

Description
The object of Minesweeper is to uncover "safe" areas on a playing field without hitting any landmines. Start by clicking a square with the left mouse button to uncover it; if it's a mine, the game is over. Otherwise, you'll either see a number corresponding to the number of mines immediately adjacent to the clicked square, or the square will be blank, meaning that there are no adjacent mines. If you click a square with no adjacent mines, all the connecting squares are automatically uncovered until a numbered square is reached. Use the numbers as hints to where the mines are located; use the process of elimination to uncover all the squares that aren't mines. Use the right mouse button to mark and unmark uncertain squares, which has the added benefit of preventing them from being clicked accidentally (see Figure 10-33).

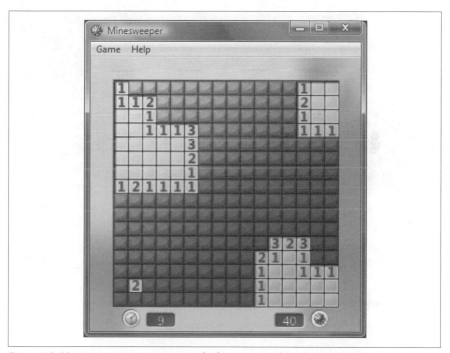

Figure 10-33. Minesweeper, a game in which you try to clear the minefield

Notes

- The beginner game uses a 9×9 grid with 10 mines; intermediate uses a 16×16 grid with 40 mines; and advanced uses a 30×16 grid with 99 mines. You can also create custom games, such as an easy 30×30 grid with only 10 mines or a difficult 8×8 grid with 60 mines.

- If a number appears on a square, it specifies how many mines are in the eight squares that surround it.

Purble Place

\Program Files\Microsoft Games\Purble Place\PurblePlace.exe

Three simple games for children.

To open

Start → All Programs → Games → Purble Place

Description

These three simple games for very young children focus on matching and memory skills. One is a concentration-type game in which children click on tiles to reveal pictures beneath and match tiles to remove them from the board. In another (Figure 10-34), children have to match shapes and colors to those on a cake in order to make a cake and ship it. In the third, children design a simple face.

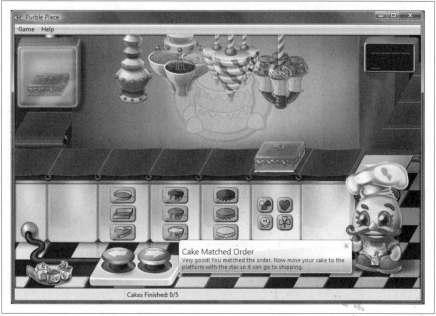

Figure 10-34. One of three simple children's games that make up Purble Place

Solitaire

The traditional Klondike solitaire card game.

To open

Start → All Programs → Games → Solitaire

Description

Solitaire, the simple card game included with every version of Windows since Windows 3.0, is a single-player game that follows the traditional Klondike rules (see Figure 10-35). The object of the game is to organize all the cards by suit and place them in order (starting with the Ace) in the four stacks at the top of the window. You move cards by placing them on the seven piles in sequential descending order, alternating color. For example, place a black four on a red five, or a red Jack on a black Queen. The game is over when all the cards have been moved to the top stacks.

Figure 10-35. The original Solitaire (Klondike) game, a great way to waste time at work

You can choose a new look for the deck by going to Game → Change Appearance or pressing F7. Go to Game → Options to choose whether one or three cards are drawn from the deck at a time, which type of scoring to use, whether the game is timed, whether to display animations, and more.

If you start a game drawing three cards at a time, trying to switch to Game → Options → Draw One will start a new game, or let you finish the game but still drawing three cards. The single-card draw will apply for the next game. Press Ctrl-Alt-Shift while you draw to draw a single card in a Draw Three game.

Notes

- Solitaire is a teaching tool for those just learning to use a mouse. It's a great way to learn clicking, double-clicking, and dragging, and best of all, the student often becomes addicted to the lesson!

- When Windows 3.0 was first released in the late 1980s, the most flattering thing that some critics had to say about Microsoft's latest and greatest operating system was that it was a "great solitaire game."

See also

"FreeCell" and "Spider Solitaire"

Spider Solitaire

\Program Files\Microsoft Games\SpiderSolitaire\SpiderSolitaire.exe

A variation on the Solitaire card game, using eight piles.

To open

Start → All Programs → Games → Spider Solitaire

Description

Spider Solitaire (see Figure 10-36) is a simple card game, similar to Solitaire (discussed in the preceding section). The object is to arrange the cards sequentially and by suit. You move cards by placing them on the eight piles in descending order, following suit. For example, place the Jack of Spades on the Queen of Spades, or the Two of Hearts on the Three of Hearts. When you complete an entire suit, King to Ace, it is removed from the board. The game ends when all cards have been removed.

Figure 10-36. Spider Solitaire, not nearly as addictive as Klondike or FreeCell, but if you like arachnids…

The game is always played with 52 cards, but easier skill levels (chosen at the beginning of the game) reduce the number of suits; for example, the easiest skill level uses all spades. Go to Game → Options to choose your preferences, such as whether your game is saved when you exit.

See also

"Solitaire" and "FreeCell"

11

Performance and Troubleshooting

Windows Vista offers an array of tools for tracking, improving, and tweaking your system's performance, as well as for troubleshooting problems. These tools are greatly improved over previous versions of Windows, and they include automated fixes so that Windows Vista watches behind the scenes for problems and then recommends fixes for them, such as automatically downloading any necessary patches.

This chapter outlines all of Windows Vista's troubleshooting tools. It's divided into two sections: "Performance, Maintenance, and Troubleshooting" and "Startup." As with the rest of the book, the tools and features are alphabetized within each section to make them easier to find.

Note that other chapters include some troubleshooting tools as well. For example, to get help for network problems, turn to Chapter 7.

Here is an alphabetical reference of entries in this chapter:

Administrative Tools	DiskPart	Query Process
Advanced Boot Options	Dr. Watson	ReadyBoost
Backup and Restore Center	Event Viewer	Reliability and Performance Monitor
Boot Configuration Data Store Editor	FAT to NTFS Conversion Utility	Remote Assistance
Chkdsk	Format	Scheduled Tasks Console
Chkntfs	Help and Support	Services
Component Services	Memory Diagnostics Tool	Startup and Recovery
Computer	Performance Information and Tools	Startup Repair
Computer Management	Performance Log Manager	System Configuration Editor
DirectX Management Tool	Performance Options	System Configuration Utility
Disk Cleanup	Prefetch	System Control Panel
Disk Defragmenter	Problem Reports and Solutions	System Information

System Properties	Taskkill	Windows Easy Transfer
System Protection and System Restore	Tasklist	Windows File Checker
Task Manager	Welcome Center	Windows Script Host
Task Scheduler		

Performance, Maintenance, and Troubleshooting

Administrative Tools

Provides a simple way to run a variety of troubleshooting and performance tools.

To open

Control Panel → [System and Maintenance] → Administrative Tools

Description

This Control Panel applet opens a Windows Explorer window that includes shortcuts to a variety of performance and troubleshooting tools, such as the Reliability and Performance Monitor and other Microsoft Management Console applications.

See also

"Microsoft Management Console," in Chapter 10

Backup and Restore Center

Back up (copy) files from your hard drive to a CD drive, DVD drive, removable storage device, or another PC or drive on a network for the purpose of safeguarding or archiving your data, or for saving your computer configuration so that you can restore it in the event of a crash.

To open

Control Panel → Back up your computer

Control Panel → System and Maintenance → Backup and Restore Center

Description

The Backup and Restore Center (Figure 11-1), new in Windows Vista, offers tools for backing up data as well as creating a restore "image" of your computer, which can be used to re-create the state of your PC—including the operating system, applications, and settings—in the event of a hardware failure. It fixes a variety of shortcomings in the backup program built into Windows XP, such as not being able to back up across a network. On the other hand, it's less flexible than the XP backup program because it doesn't allow you to customize it to a great extent. You can't, for example, choose specific folders, or files from specific folders, to be backed up. Instead, you have to back up all files of a particular file type, such as documents.

Click "Back up files" to back up data, or "Back up computer" to back up an image of your PC, called a Windows Complete PC Backup and Restore image. (Note that the

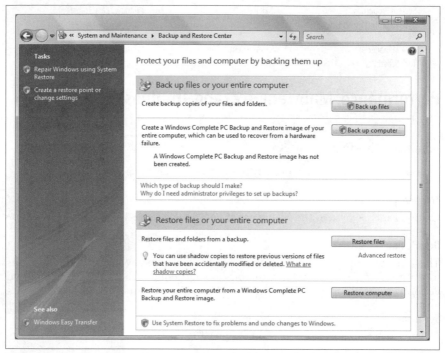

Figure 11-1. The Backup and Restore Center, which lets you back up data, as well as create an image of your PC that can be used in the event of a system failure

Complete PC Backup and Restore feature is not available with Windows Vista Home Basic or Windows Vista Home Premium.)

A wizard appears that walks you through the backup process. You'll choose where to save the backup, such as to a network drive or PC.

You choose the backup location, as well as the location of the files or image being backed up and the types of files to back up. You also choose a backup schedule (Figure 11-2) so that backups can be performed automatically.

 If you back up to a drive on a PC attached to the network, you'll need to have a user account on that PC, and you'll need to enter your username and password for that account. Make sure when entering the username that you include the computer name as well, such as *MainPC\joeuser*.

When you do all this, you create what's called a *backup set*—a collection of selected files to be backed up. The set and all the settings you've chosen, are collectively known as a backup "job."

After your first backup, you can change the backup settings—for example, the backup location, the files to be backed up, and the backup schedule—by clicking Change Settings in the Backup and Restore Center.

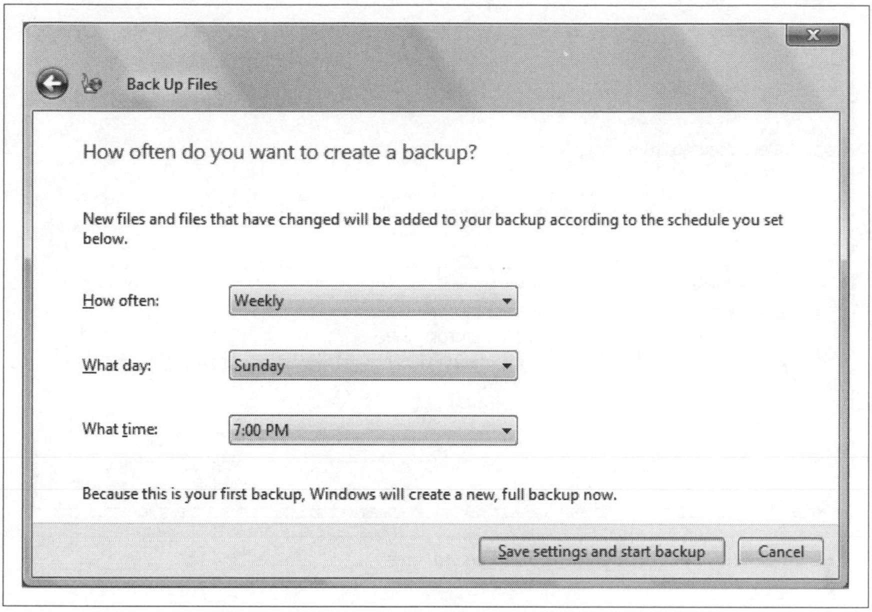

Figure 11-2. Scheduling a backup

To restore files from a backup that you've made, select Restore Files (or Restore Computer, if you've chosen to make a Complete PC backup). A wizard appears, letting you restore files. You can restore not only from the most recent backup, but also from previous backups so that you can restore previous versions of your files, not just the most recent versions. Or you can restore files that you have deleted since an earlier backup (see Figure 11-3). In addition, you can restore individual files and folders rather than the entire backup. Browse to the files or folders you want to restore, and select them.

You can also restore backup files from a different computer. For example, if a backup has been made from another computer to the computer that you are currently using, you can restore files from that backup. To do so, select Advanced Restore from the Backup and Restore Center, choose "Files on a backup made from a different computer," browse to the location, and restore the files as you would normally.

Notes

- When files are backed up, they are stored in compressed *.zip* files inside normal files. So you can restore them without having to actually use the Windows Backup and Restore Center. Browse to the location of the backup file and look for backup files. The folder will be named something like *Backup Set 2006-09-05 125516* or *Backup Files 2006-09-05 125516*. Open the folder and any other folders beneath it until you come to compressed files named *Backup Files 1.zip*, *Backup Files 2.zip*, and so on. Double-click the files, and you'll open the compressed folder. You can now extract and use the files.

- You can use Windows Backup and Restore to recover shadow copies of files.

See also

"System Protection and System Restore"

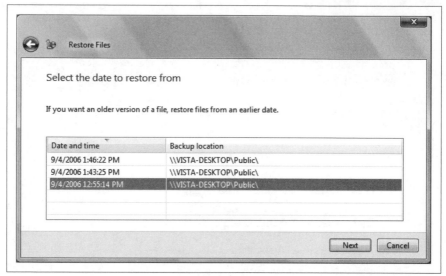

Figure 11-3. Restoring files from a previous backup

Chkdsk

Check the disk for errors and fix any that are found.

To open

Command Prompt → **chkdsk** (requires an Administrator command prompt)

Usage

```
chkdsk [drive[filename]] [/f] [/r] [/x] [/i] [/c] [/v]
```

Description

Chkdsk scans the disk surface, checks the integrity of files and folders, and looks for lost clusters (among other things), correcting any problems that it finds and sometimes even freeing disk space consumed by unusable fragments of data.

If you run Chkdsk with no command-line parameters, it will check the current drive for errors. Or you can specify a drive letter to check a specific drive, like this:

```
chkdsk e:
```

However, running Chkdsk this way will only report problems—it won't correct them. The report you'll get looks something like this:

```
The type of the file system is NTFS.

WARNING!  F parameter not specified.
Running CHKDSK in read-only mode.

CHKDSK is verifying files (stage 1 of 3)...
  36480 file records processed.
```

```
File verification completed.
  33 large file records processed.
  0 bad file records processed.
  0 EA records processed.
  44 reparse records processed.
CHKDSK is verifying indexes (stage 2 of 3)...
  144121 index entries processed.
Index verification completed.
  5 unindexed files processed.
CHKDSK is verifying security descriptors (stage 3 of 3)...
  36480 security descriptors processed.
Security descriptor verification completed.
  6991 data files processed.
CHKDSK is verifying Usn Journal...
  3478288 USN bytes processed.
Usn Journal verification completed.
Windows has checked the file system and found no problems.

  16774143 KB total disk space.
   7062360 KB in 29402 files.
     18156 KB in 6992 indexes.
         0 KB in bad sectors.
    106959 KB in use by the system.
     65536 KB occupied by the log file.
   9586668 KB available on disk.

      4096 bytes in each allocation unit.
   4193535 total allocation units on disk.
   2396667 allocation units available on disk.
```

The report starts with a warning about the /f parameter (discussed in the following list), followed by descriptions of the stages of the scan. Without the /f parameter, Chkdsk will note errors but not fix them. Next comes the summary of the total disk space, used space, and other statistics, which are fairly self-explanatory.

To use Chkdsk effectively, you'll need to use the following optional parameters:

/f   Fixes any errors found. If /f is omitted, errors are merely reported and no changes to the disk are made. If you are running Chkdsk on your boot disk, the check won't be performed until you reboot.

/r   Locates bad sectors and recovers readable information. Using the /r parameter implies /f (see preceding entry). Think of the /r parameter as a beefed-up version of /f. Keep in mind that bad sectors represent physical errors on the disk surface, and safe recovery of the data residing in those areas is not guaranteed. Use the /r option only if you have reason to believe you have one or more bad sectors, either because Chkdsk is reporting this problem or because you encountered another symptom, such as your computer crashing or freezing every time you attempt to access a certain file.

/x   Forces the volume to dismount before the scan is performed. Using the /x parameter implies /f (discussed earlier). This effectively disconnects the drive from Explorer and all other programs, closing any open files stored on the drive before any changes are made. You may want to use this option when checking or repairing a shared drive used frequently by the several users on a network; otherwise, access to the drive might interrupt Chkdsk, or even corrupt data further.

/i   Performs a less vigorous check of index entries. You can use the /i option only on NTFS disks, as index entries exist only on NTFS volumes. You'll probably never need this option, although you may choose to use it to reduce the amount of time required to check the disk.

/c   Skips checking of cycles within the folder structure. Like /i, you can use the /c option only on NTFS disks. Likewise, you'll probably never need this option either, although you may choose to use it to reduce the amount of time required to check the disk.

/v   Use of the /v parameter abandons Chkdsk's primary purpose and instead simply displays a list of every file on the entire hard disk (in no particular order). The /v parameter exhibits this behavior only on a disk with a FAT or FAT32 filesystem; on NTFS, it displays additional information about the volume's state.

Notes

- To get to the Administrator command needed to run Chkdsk, locate Command Prompt in the Start menu, right-click on it, and choose Run as Administrator.

- You also can use Chkdsk to check a single file or a specific group of files for fragmentation (see "Disk Defragmenter," later in this chapter), but only on FAT or FAT32 disks. To do this, specify the full path- and filename (or use wildcards, such as *.*, to specify multiple files) instead of the drive letter on the command line.

- In Windows 9x/Me, regular usage of Scandisk was recommended, but that's not necessarily the case with Chkdsk and Windows Vista. Whenever Windows isn't properly shut down, or when it detects a potential problem during startup, Chkdsk is run automatically during the boot process. Additionally, given the added stability of Windows Vista, you may never need to run Chkdsk manually unless you suspect a problem.

- When Chkdsk is launched during Windows startup, it is preceded by a message and a 10-second delay, giving you the option of skipping the scan. While Chkdsk is running, either during Windows startup or at any other time, you can interrupt it by pressing Ctrl-C.

- During normal use of Chkdsk, you'll see references to various terms describing problems on your hard disk. Among the more popular players are *lost clusters* (pieces of data no longer associated with any file), *bad sectors* (actual flaws in the disk surface), *cross-linked files* (two files claiming ownership of the same chunk of data), invalid file dates and filenames, and a few other, more obscure errors.

- On a FAT or FAT32 disk, the /v parameter is a funny option, especially considering that it has very little to do, at least in terms of results, with the other functions of this program. However, when used in conjunction with pipe operators (see Chapter 14), this feature can generate filtered reports of the contents of a drive.

- If you want to schedule Chkdsk at regular intervals to help ensure a healthy disk, you can configure the Task Scheduler (discussed later in this chapter) to run Chkdsk, say, every Friday at 3:30.

See also

"Chkntfs"

Chkntfs

Display or change the checking of a disk (using Chkdsk) at Windows startup.

To open

Command Prompt → **chkntfs**

Usage

```
chkntfs [drive | /d | /t:time | /x drive | /c drive]
```

Description

Chkdsk, described in the preceding section, is run automatically during Windows startup, either if the previous session was not ended gracefully (the computer was turned off without shutting down) or if errors are detected. Chkntfs is used to modify this behavior for one or all of your drives.

If you run Chkntfs with only a drive letter (e.g., chkntfs c:), you get a somewhat cryptic report, like this:

```
The type of the file system is NTFS.
C: is not dirty.
```

The identification of the filesystem type on the first line is fairly self-evident. The "not dirty" report implies that the drive was properly "cleaned up" the last time the system shut down. In other words, the system shut down properly. If the system isn't shut down properly, any drives in use (drives containing one or more files that were open when the computer lost power, for example) are marked "dirty," and those drives are scanned the next time Windows starts. To change this behavior, use one of the following options. Note that all options, including the specification of the drive letter, are exclusive; you can use only one at a time.

/d

Type **chkntfs /d** to restore the default behavior of the entire machine; all drives are automatically checked at boot time, and any drives found to be "dirty" are checked with Chkdsk.

/t:time

Used to change the countdown before this scan is started, during which time the user can press the Space bar to skip the scan. Time is simply any number, in seconds; chkntfs /t:5 configures Windows to wait five seconds before running Chkdsk.

/x drive

Excludes a particular drive from those checked at startup. For example, type **chkntfs /x e:** to exclude drive E: from the auto-check.

/c drive

Includes a particular drive in those checked at startup; /c is the opposite of /x. For example, type **chkntfs /c e:** to instruct Windows to check drive E: during startup, and if it is found "dirty," to run chkdsk e: /f.

See also

"Chkdsk"

Component Services

\windows\system32\dcomcnfg.exe

See "Microsoft Management Console," in Chapter 10.

Computer

Shows an overview of all your system's drives.

To open

Start → Computer

Start → All Programs → Accessories → System Tools → Computer

Description

Gives a quick overview of all of your computer's drives and folders in Windows Explorer (see Figure 11-4).

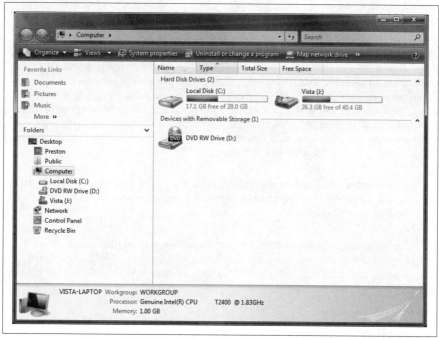

Figure 11-4. Computer, which provides a quick view of all of the drives attached to your PC

Computer Management

\windows\system32\compmgmt.msc

Perform computer management tasks and run tools such as the Task Scheduler.

To open

Run as a plug-in for the Microsoft Management Console

Command Prompt → compmgmt

Description

This plug-in to the Microsoft Management Console lets you perform a variety of computer management tasks, including monitoring performance and reliability. It also provides a way to run tools such as the Task Scheduler.

For more details, see "Microsoft Management Console," in Chapter 10.

See also

"Reliability and Performance Monitor"

DirectX Management Tool   \windows\system32\dxdiag.exe

Test, diagnose, and tweak DirectX drivers.

To open

Command Prompt → **dxdiag**

Description

DirectX is the system that allows applications—usually games—to directly access graphics, audio, and input devices to maximize performance. Unless you're experiencing a problem with DirectX or a program that uses DirectX, you should never need to use the DirectX Management Tool. If you do indeed encounter a problem, such as poor performance, an apparent glitch in a game, an error message, or some other compatibility issue, follow these steps to diagnose and treat it:

1. DirectX relies on hardware drivers, so the first thing you should do whenever you encounter problems with it is to make sure you have the latest drivers for your display adapter, sound card, and game controller (if applicable).

2. Next, go to *http://www.microsoft.com/directx* and see if there's a more recent version of DirectX than the one installed on your system. To determine the currently installed version, open the DirectX Management Tool and read the DirectX Version on the bottom of the System tab.

3. If you're experiencing problems with only a certain application or game, check with the manufacturer of that software to see if there's an update or compatibility issue with your specific hardware. Often, manufacturers will post workarounds, patches, or other fixes on their web sites.

4. If you want to start exploring troubleshooting options, run the DirectX Management Tool and then choose the appropriate tab (e.g., display, sound, etc.) and see the test results, as shown in Figure 11-5.

Disk Cleanup   \windows\system32\cleanmgr.exe

Reclaim disk space by removing unwanted files from your hard drive.

To open

Start → All Programs → Accessories → System Tools → Disk Cleanup

Control Panel → [System and Maintenance] → Free up disk space

Command Prompt → **cleanmgr**

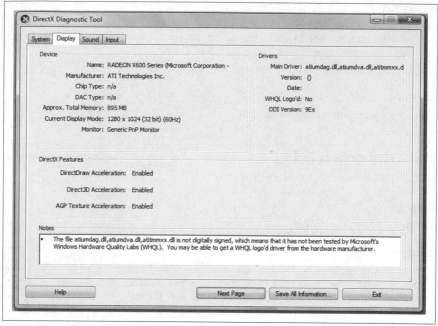

Figure 11-5. The DirectX Management Tool, which can help track down the cause of problems with DirectX

Description

Disk Cleanup summarizes the disk space used by several predefined types of files, such as Temporary Internet Files and items in the Recycle Bin (see Figure 11-6). If you have more than one hard drive, Disk Cleanup prompts you to choose one. It also asks whether you want to clean up only your files, or files from all users on the computer (you'll need Administrator rights to do the latter).

When you run it, after asking which drive you want to clean up, Disk Cleanup calculates how much space can be saved by doing a cleanup. Then, it presents a list of file categories from which desired items can be checked to have the corresponding files deleted. The approximate space to be reclaimed by any category is shown to the right. Here are descriptions of the various categories:

Downloaded Program Files

This folder contains mostly ActiveX and Java applets downloaded from the Internet. If you clean out this folder, these components will simply be downloaded again when you revisit the sites that use them.

Temporary Internet Files

Temporary Internet Files, commonly known as the browser cache, are web pages and images from recently visited web sites, stored in your hard disk for the sole purpose of improving performance when browsing the Web. Deleting the files will have no adverse effects other than requiring that they be downloaded again the next time the corresponding web sites are visited.

You can set the maximum size of this folder. Choose Control Panel → [Network and Internet] → Internet Options, and from the dialog box that appears, click the

Figure 11-6. The Disk Cleanup dialog, which shows several locations of files that can probably be safely deleted

General tab, then click Settings in the Browsing History area. Select the amount of space in the Disk Space area.

Offline Webpages

If you store web pages on your PC so that you can view them when you're not connected to the Internet, they take up disk space. If you no longer need to view those pages, you can delete them here to free up disk space.

Hibernation File Cleaner

The Hibernation file contains information about your computer that is used to restore your computer from a state of hibernation. If you don't use hibernation, you can safely delete this file. If you do use hibernation, deleting it will disable hibernation.

Recycle Bin

By default, files that are deleted aren't really deleted; they are simply moved to the Recycle Bin for deletion at a later time. You can empty the Recycle Bin at any time by right-clicking the Recycle Bin icon on your Desktop and selecting Empty Recycle Bin. Right-click the Recycle Bin and select Properties to change the maximum amount of disk space allocated to the storage of deleted files (or to disable the Recycle Bin and have files permanently erased immediately).

Temporary Files

Many applications open files to store temporary data but aren't especially meticulous about deleting those files when they're no longer needed. Application crashes and power outages are other reasons why temporary files might be left behind. The disk space consumed by temporary files, especially after several weeks without maintenance, can be several megabytes.

Thumbnails

Windows keeps copies of all of your pictures, videos, and documents so that they can be displayed as thumbnails—for example, when browsing in Internet Explorer. If you delete thumbnails, they will be re-created when they are needed, but it will slow down browsing.

System Archived Windows Error Reporting

These files are used for troubleshooting and error reporting. If you delete them, you will lose that information.

Temporary Offline Files, Offline Files

Temporary offline files are local copies of recently used documents normally stored on remote computers and marked "Offline." If you take advantage of the Offline Files feature in Windows Vista, you may want to examine the files in these folders before you indiscriminately delete them with this utility.

Notes

- You may find other files in addition to what's listed. Some programs store installation files, and if Disk Cleanup is aware of them, it will list them here. For example, Microsoft Office setup files are listed here if they have been stored on your PC.

Disk Defragmenter

\windows\system32\dfrgui.exe

Reorganize the files on a disk to optimize disk performance and reliability.

To open

Control Panel → [System and Maintenance] → Defragment your hard drive

Command Prompt → `dfrgui`

Description

As you create files on your hard disk, they become defragmented so that a single file is stored in several different noncontiguous locations. As more files become fragmented, the reliability and performance of the hard drive diminish. Disk Defragmenter reorganizes the files and folders on a drive so that the files are stored contiguously, and the free space is contiguous as well.

Running the Disk Defragmenter (Figure 11-7) is one of the simplest tasks you'll ever perform in Windows Vista. Click Defragment Now, and it goes to work rearranging the files and folders on your disk for optimal performance. If you don't need to defragment, you'll see the message "You do not need to defragment at this time." You'll get this message if the percentage of defragmented files on your hard disk is lower than about three percent.

Click Defragment Now to begin the defragmentation. Unlike with previous versions of Windows, when you defragment your hard disk, you get no visual feedback that the job is being performed. And you get no time estimate; you're told only that it will take

---

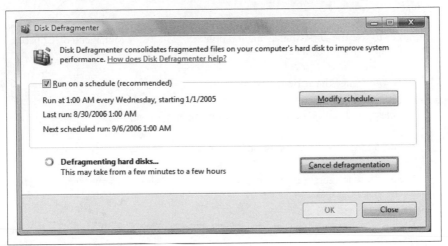

Figure 11-7. Disk Defragmenter, which reorganizes the data on your hard disk for quicker, more reliable operations and offers advice on whether your disk needs to be defragmented

anywhere from a few minutes to a few hours. The time it takes will depend on the speed of your drive and processor, the level of fragmentation, and the amount of data to move.

Notes

- You can automatically schedule the Disk Defragmenter to run at specified times. Check the box next to "Run on a schedule," click Modify Schedule, fill out the form that appears, and click OK.

See also

"Chkdsk," earlier in this chapter, and "Microsoft Management Console," in Chapter 10

DiskPart

\windows\system32\diskpart.exe

Prepare and partition a hard disk.

To open

Command Prompt → **diskpart**

Description

DiskPart is a full-featured program used to prepare hard disks and, optionally, divide them into two or more partitions. It's a command-line program and has no interface to speak of. When you start DiskPart, you'll see a simple prompt: DISKPART>. Type **help** and press Enter to view a list of all the available commands:

active
>   Activates the current basic partition so that it can be used as a boot disk; using it is not necessary if there's only one partition in the volume.

add
>   Adds a mirror to a simple volume.

`assign`

> Assigns a drive letter or mount point to the selected volume. Note that it may be easier to use the Disk Management Tool; see "Microsoft Management Console," in Chapter 10, for details.

`attributes`

> Lets you change the attributes of the volume.

`automount`

> Enables and disables the automatic mounting of basic volumes.

`break`

> Breaks a mirror set (undoes the `add` command).

`clean`

> Clears the configuration information, or all information, off the disk; this effectively erases the disk.

`convert`

> Converts between different disk formats; most users will never need this command.

`create`

> Creates a volume or partition; this is the first step in preparing a hard disk.

`delete`

> Deletes an object (undoes the `create` command).

`detail`

> Displays details about a disk, partition, or volume. Note that you'll need to use `select` first.

`exit`

> Exits DiskPart (Ctrl-C also works).

`extend`

> Extends a volume.

`filesystems`

> Displays the current and supported filesystems on the volume.

`format`

> Formats the volume or partition.

`GPT`

> Assigns attributes to the selected GUID Partition Table (GPT) partition. GPT offers a more flexible mechanism for disk partitioning than does the older Master Boot Record (MBR) partitioning scheme.

`import`

> Imports a disk group.

`inactive`

> Marks the selected basic partition as inactive.

`list`

> Prints out a list of objects; similar to `detail`.

`online`

> Changes the status of the disk from offline to online.

`REM`

> Used to add remarks in scripts.

remove

Removes a drive letter or mount point assignment (undoes the `assign` command). Note that it may be easier to use the Disk Management Tool; see "Microsoft Management Console," in Chapter 10, for details.

repair

Repairs a RAID-5 volume.

rescan

Rescans the computer, looking for disks and volumes.

retain

Places a retainer partition under a simple volume. If you delete a partition at the end of a disk, you will change a dynamic volume to a basic volume. If you place a retainer partition on a dynamic volume, it will keep the volume as dynamic.

select

Chooses a disk, partition, or volume to view or modify. Even if you have only one disk or partition, you'll still need to select the object before carrying out any other commands. Use `list` to obtain object numbers for use with `select`, and then use `detail` to get more information.

setid

Changes the partition type.

shrink

Shrinks the size of the volume.

Each of these commands (with the exception of exit) has one or more subcommands. For example, if you simply type **detail** at the prompt, you'll get a list of the subcommands for use with the `list` command: disk, partition, and volume. So, to display a list of all the disk volumes on the system, you would type:

```
list volume
```

and you'll get a report that looks look something like this:

```
Volume ###  Ltr  Label   Fs     Type         Size    Status     Info
----------  ---  ------  -----  ----------   -------  ---------  ------
Volume 0    C            NTFS   Partition    16 GB   Healthy    System
Volume 1    D                   DVD-ROM       0 B    No Media
```

From the report, it is clear that drive *C:* is Volume 0; the next step is to select the volume, like this:

```
select volume 0
```

Subsequent commands will then apply to the currently selected volume.

Notes

- Disk partitioning is tricky business and unless you're preparing a new drive, you'll probably never need to use DiskPart. If you need to repartition a drive that you're currently using, DiskPart is not the way to go, as it will erase any drive you attempt to repartition. A better choice is to use PartitionMagic by Symantec (*http://www.symantec.com*), which allows you to add, remove, and resize partitions without destroying the data they contain. Note that the Disk Management Tool of the Microsoft Management Console allows you to perform some elementary volume resizing as well.

See also

"Microsoft Management Console," in Chapter 10

Dr. Watson

\windows\system32\drwatson.exe; drwtsn32.exe

Records system error information when a system error occurs. It has been replaced by Vista's new error reporting mechanism and is used for compatibility with older applications and tools.

To open

Command Prompt → **drwatson**

Description

Dr. Watson is a diagnostic tool that records information on the internal state of Windows when a system error occurs. It collects information such as system details, running applications, startup applications, kernel drivers, and user drivers. Although the reports that Dr. Watson produces are of little use to most users, they contain diagnostic information that may be helpful to developers and Microsoft support technicians for diagnosis of the problem.

If activated, Dr. Watson waits invisibly in the background until a system error occurs, at which time a dialog box appears, asking for comments on the activities prior to the error. The comments you type will be added to a file as long as you select File → Save or File → Save As from the dialog. The two available formats include Dr. Watson logfiles (*.wlg*) and plain-text files (*.txt*). The default is a *.wlg* file, and it is recommended if you want to subsequently use the Dr. Watson application to view a GUI version of the information.

If Dr. Watson detects a fault that might not be fatal, you'll have the opportunity to ignore the fault or close the application. If you choose to ignore the fault, Windows continues without performing the faulting instruction. You might be able to save your work in a new file at this point, but you should then restart Windows.

When you run Dr Watson, it also issues a report indicating whether it has found any current problems with your system, and then runs in the background.

See also

"System Properties" (specifically, the topic of error reporting in the Advanced tab)

Event Viewer

\windows\system32\eventvwr.msc

Read system logs and view other system events.

To open

Run as a plug-in for the Microsoft Management Console.

Command Prompt → **eventvwr**

Description

A plug-in to the Microsoft Management Console, the Event Viewer (Figure 11-8) provides an easy way to read system logs and view other system events.

For more details, see "Microsoft Management Console," in Chapter 10.

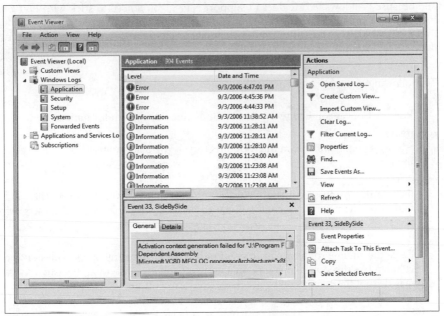

Figure 11-8. The Event Viewer, which provides a way to read a variety of performance and troubleshooting logs

FAT to NTFS Conversion Utility

\windows\system32\convert.exe

Convert a drive using the File Allocation Table (FAT) filesystem to the more robust NT File System (NTFS).

To open

Command Prompt → **convert**

Usage

```
convert volume /fs:ntfs [/v] [/cvtarea:fn] [/nosecurity] [/x]
```

Description

The filesystem is the invisible mechanism on any drive that is responsible for keeping track of all the data stored on the drive. Think of the filesystem as a massive table of contents, matching up each filename with its corresponding data stored somewhere on the disk surface. The FAT filesystem first appeared in DOS and has been the basis for each successive version of Windows, including Windows 95, Windows 98, and Windows Me. A slightly improved version of FAT, called FAT32, was introduced in Windows 95 OSR2 and included support for larger drives and smaller cluster sizes.

Meanwhile, the Windows NT/2000 line of operating systems also supported the newer and more robust NTFS filesystem. Among other things, NTFS provides much more sophisticated security than FAT or FAT32 does, as well as encryption and compression. However, NTFS and FAT/FAT32 are not compatible with each other, and because Windows 9*x*/Me doesn't support NTFS, you'll need to stick with FAT or FAT32 if you intend to have a dual-boot system. This tool is used to convert a FAT or FAT32 drive to an NTFS drive without damaging the data stored on it. To convert drive C:, for example, type the following:

```
convert c: /fs:ntfs
```

The following options are also available:

/v

Run the Conversion Utility in verbose mode (provide more information).

/cvtarea:*filename*

Specify a contiguous file in the root directory as the placeholder for NTFS system files.

/nosecurity

Include this parameter if you want the initial security privileges for all files and folders on the newly converted volume to be set so that the files and folders are accessible by everyone.

/x

Force the volume to dismount first—if necessary, closing any opened files on the volume. Use this option if you're on a network and are concerned that other users may disrupt the conversion by accessing your drive during the process.

Notes

- To determine the filesystem currently used on any drive, right-click the drive icon in My Computer or Explorer and select Properties.

See also

"Chkntfs" and "DiskPart"

Format

\windows\system32\format.com

Prepare floppy diskettes, hard disks, and some removable media for use.

To open

Command Prompt → **format.com**

Usage

```
format volume [/q] [/c] [/x] [/v:label] [/fs:file-system] [/a:size]
```

Description

Before you can store data on a floppy disk, hard disk, or many removable media disks (such as ZIP disks), you must format the disk. This process creates various low-level data structures on the disk, such as the filesystem (FAT, FAT32, NTFS, etc.). It also tests the disk surface for errors and stores bad sectors in a table that will keep them from being used. If there's any data on the disk, it will be erased.

The options for Format are:

volume

> The drive letter, followed by a colon, containing the media to be formatted. For example, to format the floppy in drive *A:*, type:
>
> > format a:
>
> If the specified drive is a hard disk, you'll be prompted to verify that you actually want to erase the disk.

/q

> Performs a "quick" format, a process that wipes out only the file table, resulting in an empty disk. This option does not check for bad sectors, nor does it rewrite the filesystem. Also, it does not write over data on the disk, meaning that files could potentially be recovered or "undeleted." The advantage of the /q option is that you can erase a disk in a few seconds.

/c

> Files created on the new volume are compressed by default (NTFS volumes only).

/x

> Forces the volume to dismount first, if necessary. All opened handles to the volume would no longer be valid. This effectively disconnects the drive from Explorer and all other programs, closing any open files stored on the drive, before any changes are made.

/v:label

> Specifies the volume label, an arbitrary title you assign to any disk. It can be up to 11 characters and can include spaces. The volume label will show up next to the drive icons in Explorer (hard disks only) and at the top of dir listings (see Chapter 14). See "Label," in Chapter 4, for more information. If the /v option is omitted or the label isn't specified, a prompt for a volume label is displayed after the formatting is completed. If a label is specified with /v and more than one disk is formatted in a session, all disks will be given the same volume label.

/f:size

> Specifies the size of the floppy disk to format (such as 160, 180, 320, 360, 720, 1.2, 1.44, 2.88). The format size (specified with the /f option) must be equal to or less than the capacity of the disk drive containing the disk to be formatted. For example, a 2.88 MB capacity drive will format a 1.44 MB disk, but a 1.44 MB drive will not format a 2.88 MB disk.

/fs:filesystem

> Specifies the type of the filesystem; can be fat, fat32, or ntfs.

/a:size

> Overrides the default allocation unit size, which, when multiplied by the number of clusters, equals the final capacity of the disk. Allowed values for *size* depend on the filesystem:
>
> - NTFS supports 512, 1,024, 2,048, 4,096, 8,192, 16K, 32K, and 64K.
> - FAT and FAT32 support 512, 1,024, 2,048, 4,096, 8,192, 16K, 32K, and 64K (and 128K and 256K for sector size greater than 512 bytes).

- Note that the FAT and FAT32 filesystems impose the following restrictions on the number of clusters on a volume: for FAT, the number of clusters must be less than or equal to 65,526; for FAT32, the number of clusters must be between 65,526 and 4,177,918.
- NTFS compression is not supported for allocation unit sizes greater than 4,096.

Notes

- The /f, /t, and /n parameters are also available for use with Format but are essentially obsolete. Type **format /?** for more information.
- If formatting an ordinary 3.5-inch floppy diskette, the disk will always be formatted to a capacity of 1.44 MB. The DMF diskette format, which squeezes about 1.7 MB on a standard floppy, is not directly supported by Format. If formatting a preformatted DMF diskette, use the /q parameter to preserve the format and erase only the files. To create new DMF diskettes, you'll need the WinImage utility (version 2.2 or later), which you can download from *http://www.annoyances.org*.
- The easiest way to format a disk is to right-click on the drive icon in Explorer or My Computer and select Format. However, using Format from the command line is more flexible and, in some cases, faster.

See also

"FAT to NTFS Conversion Utility," earlier in this chapter, and "Label," in Chapter 4

Help and Support

The primary online documentation for Windows Vista.

To open

Start → Help and Support

Description

Think of Help and Support (see Figure 11-9) as a Windows help file on steroids. It provides documentation for many of the components included in Windows Vista, a collection of tips and tricks, troubleshooting information, and walkthroughs for such tasks as keeping your computer up-to-date and adding hardware and software. It's more than just a plain-text file, though, because it also includes direct links to the tools you need to accomplish tasks. So in the entry on connecting to a network, for example, a link opens the Connect to a Network screen.

Help and Support works particularly well when you're connected to the Internet, because it integrates with Microsoft help and other tools. After you do a search, click "Ask someone or expand your search" at the bottom, and a new screen launches with links to posting a question or searching for an answer in Microsoft newsgroups, launching Remote Assistance to get online help, and most useful of all, accessing Microsoft Knowledge Base, an immense database of troubleshooting information, frequently asked questions, bug reports, compatibility lists, and other technical support issues. In addition, you can click the link to Windows Online Help to visit the Windows Vista online help site.

Figure 11-9. The Help and Support Center, which includes links to tools, as well as information on how to accomplish Windows tasks

Notes

- If you need help with a specific Windows component, such as WordPad or Explorer, use that application's Help menu, rather than the more general Help and Support.

See also

"Remote Assistance"

Memory Diagnostics Tool

\windows\System32\MdSched.exe

Check a PC's memory for problems.

To open

Command Prompt → `mdsched`

Description

This tool checks your PC's memory for any errors and reports on the results. You should save all your files and close all your programs before running the program, because it restarts your computer in order to run the tests. After the restart, it runs tests before your system boots. (They take several minutes to run, so be patient.) After the tests run, you boot into Windows, and after you log in, a report will be displayed telling you whether any errors have been found.

Notes

- You can specify which memory tests to run and set other options, such as how many times you want to repeat the tests. When the Memory Diagnostics Tool starts, press F1, make your selections, and then press F10 to start the test.

- You can also run this tool from the boot menu. Press F1 when you restart your PC to display the boot menu, and then run the tool from there.

Performance Information and Tools

Rate your computer's capability to run Windows Vista.

To open

Control Panel → System and Maintenance → Performance Information and Tools

Description

This screen (Figure 11-10) rates your PC according to how well it runs Windows, using what it calls a Windows Experience Index. It rates the processor, RAM, graphics subsystem, gaming graphics subsystem, and primary hard disk on a scale of one to five. The higher the number, the better the performance. The lowest rating of any of those is called the system's Base Score.

The rating system is designed to be used in concert with software being rated by the same system. So, for example, you would check your hardware rating before buying a piece of software to know it was capable of running it.

As of this writing, no software actually uses the rating system, so it's hard to know how useful this system will be.

Performance Log Manager

\windows\system32\logman.exe

Manage the Performance Logs and Alerts service for creating and managing Event Trace Session logs and Performance logs.

To open

Command Prompt → `logman`

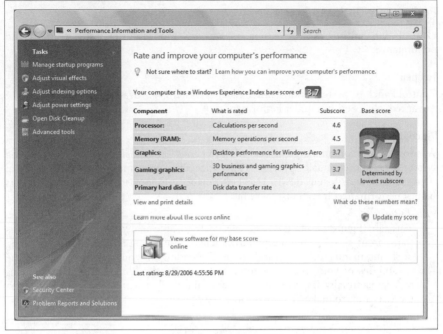

Figure 11-10. Rating how well a PC can run Windows Vista

Usage

```
logman command collection_name [options]
```

Description

The Performance Log Manager is a command-line utility used to manage Performance Logs and Event Trace Session logs. Commands can be any of the following (type **logman command /?** for help with each one):

create
: Creates a new collection.

start
: Starts an existing collection and sets the beginning time to manual.

stop
: Stops an existing collection and sets the end time to manual.

delete
: Deletes an existing collection.

query
: Queries collection properties. If *collection_name* is omitted, all collections are listed.

update
: Updates the properties of an existing collection.

Notes

- The Performance Log Manager is largely replaced by the Reliability and Performance Monitor. See details later in this chapter.

Performance Options

Controls the balance between using advanced Windows Vista visual features and performance.

To open

Control Panel → [System and Maintenance] → System → Advanced System Settings → Advanced, click Settings under Performance

Description

Windows Vista contains a great deal of "eye candy" that makes using the operating system a far more visually pleasing experience. But on some systems, these visual effects can slow a system down. Use Performance Options to balance visual effects against performance. It contains these tabs:

Visual Effects

This tab (Figure 11-11) lets you selectively disable many visual effects, such as transparent glass, animating windows when minimizing and maximizing, fading or sliding menus into view, and so on. Depending on your system, especially the capabilities of your display adapter (video card), disabling some of these items may substantially improve system performance. It's worth experimenting with these settings to make Windows more responsive.

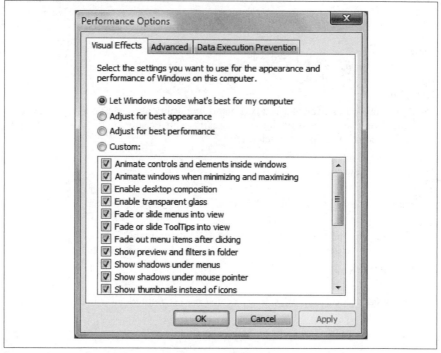

Figure 11-11. Balancing system effects against performance in the Performance Options dialog box, accessible from the Advanced tab

If you don't want to experiment with turning effects on and off individually, choose one of the settings at the top of the tab to let Windows choose what's best for your computer, or have Windows automatically adjust for best appearance or best performance.

Advanced

The "Processor scheduling" section lets you decide whether to adjust for best performance or for programs or services. In most cases, you'll want both of the "Processor scheduling" usage options set to Programs. However, if your computer is used as a web server, for example, you may experience better performance if you change this setting.

Click Change in the Virtual Memory section to adjust how Windows uses virtual memory, commonly known as your *swap file*. When Windows has used up all of your physical memory (RAM) with programs and data, it stores some of that data on your hard disk to make room for other running programs. Because your hard disk is much slower than your RAM, this process (known as *paging* or *swapping*) can significantly impair system performance, which is why adding more memory to your system (up to a point) will make it faster. In most cases, you'll want to leave these settings alone, but if you're running out of disk space, you may want to limit how much of it is used as virtual memory.

Data Execution Prevention

This controls the use of Data Execution Prevention (DEP), a security feature that helps prevent damage from viruses, malware, and other threats by monitoring programs to make sure they use system memory safely. By default, DEP is turned on for essential Windows programs and services. But if you think that a program isn't running properly under DEP, you can turn it off for individual programs.

Notes

- If a program is having trouble running because of DEP, check with the publisher to see whether there is a DEP-compatible version of the program or an update from the software publisher before you change any DEP settings.

See also

"System Properties"

Prefetch

Speeds up the performance of your PC by prefetching commonly used files.

Description

As a way to speed up the startup process, Windows tracks how your computer starts and which programs you frequently open. This information is automatically saved in the prefetch folder, located in *\Windows\prefetch*. Whenever you start your PC, Windows uses the files in the folder to speed up startup and application and file launches.

You can delete the files in *\Windows\prefetch* if you're an administrator; use Windows Explorer to delete them as you would any other files. But if you do, startup and applications will most likely load more slowly the next time you start Windows.

Notes

- Windows Vista's new ReadyBoost feature speeds up Windows even more than prefetch. It requires a flash Universal Serial Bus (USB) drive. For details, see "ReadyBoost," later in this chapter.

Problem Reports and Solutions

Automatically solve problems with your computer and Windows Vista.

To open

Control Panel → [System and Maintenance] → Problem Reports and Solutions

Description

One of the best new troubleshooting features in Windows Vista is its capability to automatically detect problems with your computer and offer automated fixes for them. The Control Panel's Problem Reports and Solutions applet, shown in Figure 11-12, is the place to go to find and launch these solutions.

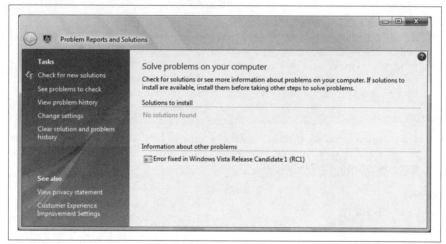

Figure 11-12. Problem Reports and Solutions, command central for checking and fixing computer problems

The applet displays any solutions to install, as well as information about problems that do not yet have solutions, are not serious enough to require solutions, or will have solutions. Click any to launch a wizard that walks you through the steps to fix the problem.

In addition, the Problem Reports and Solutions applet lets you perform the following tasks by clicking the appropriate links on the lefthand side of the screen:

Check for new solutions

    Checks for additional solutions to any problems you may be having.

 During the process of finding fixes for your PC, Windows Vista sends details about the problem to Microsoft, which not only uses it to find a solution to the problem, but also puts the information in a database to help create patches to make Windows Vista more stable.

See problems to check

    Lists all the errors and problems that Windows has detected (see Figure 11-13) but that have not yet been fixed or checked. These are not necessarily ongoing problems; they may include a one-time instance of an application not responding, for example. Check the boxes next to any that you want to find solutions for, then have Windows Vista see if there are solutions. If it finds any, you can launch a wizard to fix the problem.

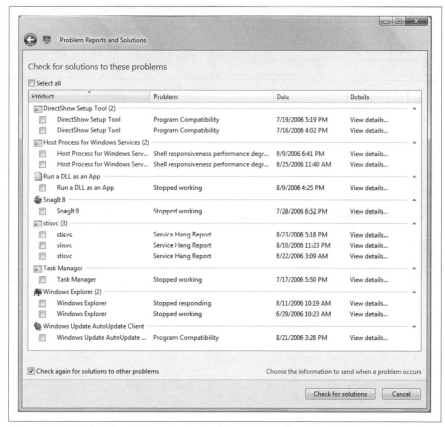

Figure 11-13. A list of problems encountered by this Windows Vista PC

View problem history

Displays a list of problems that Windows has detected and fixed, or that Windows has been unable to fix but has sent an error report to Microsoft about. This list won't include current problems. The screen lists the product, program, or service involved, what the problem was, the occurrence date, and the status of the problem. Double-click any problem for more details, as shown in Figure 11-14. Click Copy to Clipboard if you want to send the details to tech support for additional help.

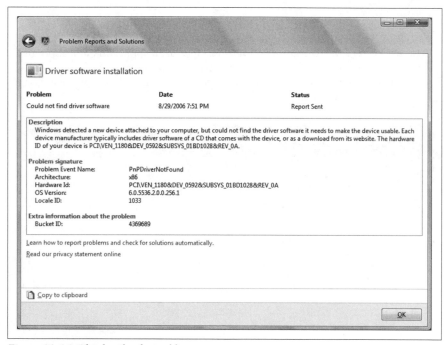

Figure 11-14. The details of a problem report

Change settings

This lets you change how solutions are checked for and solved. The default is to check for solutions, but you can change that so that instead, Windows Vista will prompt you to check for a solution when an error occurs.

Some settings related to automatic problem checking are set by the administrator account, rather than a standard user account. To change them, log in as an administrator, and then on this screen click Advanced Settings. The screen shown in Figure 11-15 appears. From here, you can turn problem reporting on or off, block information from being sent about specific programs, and change these settings globally or on an account-by-account basis.

Clear solutions and problem history

This clears the list of your problems. Note that this list includes problems that have yet to be solved, and if you clear them, you may not be able to find their solutions.

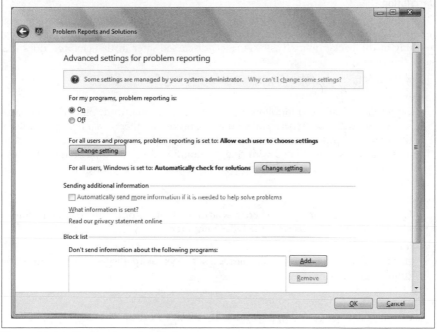

Figure 11-15. Configuring advanced options

Notes

- To help diagnose and fix problems, data about errors is sent to Microsoft over the Internet. The information may include the application or hardware in which the error occurred, the type of problem, the system- or report-generated files related to the problem, basic software and hardware information about your system, and your Internet Protocol (IP) address. It's possible that personal information could be sent as well—for example, if that information is found in a snapshot of memory that needs to be sent to Microsoft for troubleshooting. Microsoft claims that this information is not used to identify you and is kept private. When a problem is found, you are alerted and asked whether to send the information, so if you are worried that your privacy may be impinged upon, do not send the information.

- If you're part of a corporate network, even a local administrator may not be able to change settings because they are managed by system administrators using Group Policy. For details, see "Group Policy Object Editor," in Chapter 10.

Query Process

\windows\system32\qprocess.exe

Display a list of running processes.

To open

Command Prompt → **qprocess**

Usage

```
qprocess [target] [/server:computer] [/system]
```

Description

Query Process is a simple, command-line utility used to display a list of the running processes. A process is essentially any program running in the foreground or running invisibly in the background. Task Manager, discussed later in this chapter, does the same thing but is much easier to use.

Query Process takes the following parameters:

target

> target can be any of the following: specify a username to display the processes started by that user; specify a session name or number (via /id:*sessionid*) to display all the processes started in that session; specify a program name to display all the processes associated with that program; and specify an asterisk (*) to list all processes. Finally, omit target to display all the processes started by the current user.

/server:*computer*

> Query a remote computer, where *computer* is the network name of the machine. Omit to display processes for the local computer.

/system

> Include system processes. Type **qprocess * /system** to display all the currently running processes.

See also

"Task Manager," "Taskkill," and "Tasklist"

ReadyBoost

Speeds up computer performance by storing commonly used files in a flash device.

Description

ReadyBoost, new to Windows Vista, uses a flash memory device (USB stick, SD card, etc.) to prefetch and store commonly used files, and essentially treats the device as a way to augment RAM. It's an inexpensive and easy way to speed up Windows Vista performance.

ReadyBoost speeds up Windows Vista performance in several ways. It increases the size of the prefetch cache, and it frees up RAM that would otherwise be used by prefetch. Depending on your system configuration, you may see a dramatic speed improvement.

To use ReadyBoost, connect a flash drive to your PC. Windows Vista will recognize the device, and then it will ask whether to use it to speed up your PC with ReadyBoost (Figure 11-16) or use it as a normal drive. Select "Speed up my system" and Ready-Boost goes into action, without further intervention required on your part.

Not all flash drives meet the performance requirements needed to use ReadyBoost, so Windows Vista tests the drive when you first insert it. If it doesn't meet the requirements, a screen appears, telling you that it doesn't.

If the device meets the requirements, a configuration screen appears (Figure 11-17), allowing you to set the amount of space on the device that you want to devote to ReadyBoost. It's a good idea to accept at least the minimum, and to possibly add more as well.

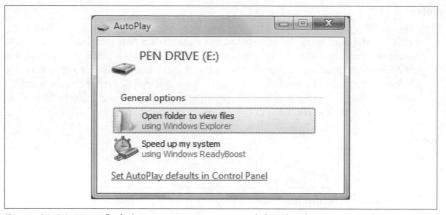

Figure 11-16. *Pop a flash drive into your system, and this alert lets you use it for ReadyBoost*

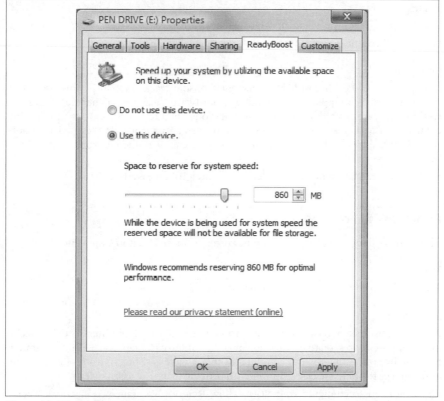

Figure 11-17. *Configuring ReadyBoost*

Notes

- To use ReadyBoost, a USB flash drive must be at least USB 2.0. Flash drives used with ReadyBoost must be able to access data at 3.5 MB per second for 4 KB random reads uniformly across the entire device, and at 2.5 MB per second for 512 KB random writes uniformly across the device. It also has to have at least 64 MB of free space. Microsoft is working to have a ReadyBoost label for manufacturers so that the packaging and advertising of the devices will make it clear that they work with ReadyBoost.

See also

"Prefetch"

Reliability and Performance Monitor

\windows\system32\perfmon.msc
or *\windows\system32\perfmon.exe*

Track and review system performance.

To open

Run as a plug-in for the Microsoft Management Console.

Command Prompt → `perfmon`

Description

This plug-in to the Microsoft Management Console tracks system performance and shows a history of application, Windows, hardware, and miscellaneous failures, as well as software installations and uninstallations (Figure 11-18). Go to any day for details for the failures, installations, and uninstallations for that day. The graph displays the overall reliability over time, so you can see whether your computer is becoming less reliable as it ages.

See "Microsoft Management Console," in Chapter 10, for details.

Remote Assistance

Allow others to connect to your computer using Remote Desktop Connection.

To open

Start → Help and Support → Remote Assistance

Description

Remote Assistance allows another user to connect to your computer so that a technical support representative, a friend, or a coworker can help you with a computer problem by connecting to your computer as though she is sitting in front of it. You can also connect to someone else's computer to provide technical assistance.

First you need to configure your PC to allow Remote Assistance connections. Select Control Panel → [System and Maintenance] → Allow Remote Access. Then under Remote Assistance, select "Allow Remote Assistance connections to this computer."

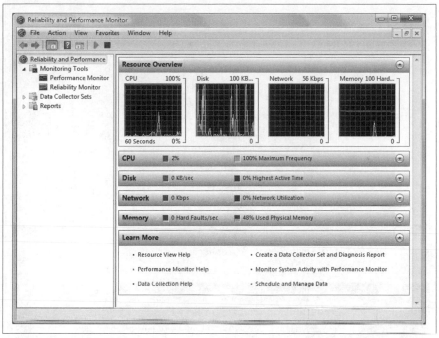

Figure 11-18. The Reliability Monitor in the Microsoft Management Console, which tracks system reliability over time and lets you quickly see the details of failures on any given day

Once that is done, you need to invite another user to connect. Select Start → Help and Support → Remote Assistance, and select "Invite someone you trust to help you" if you want to get help, or "Offer to help someone" if you want to offer help. You'll send an invitation via email—and you can choose either to use your default email program, or to save the necessary information to a file so that you can send it as an attachment via a web-based email program. You'll need to provide the remote user with a password, which you can do by telephone for maximum security, or via instant messaging or email, which is much less secure.

 If you choose to send the invitation as a file, you can also copy the file to a disk, removable drive, or network folder, and have it accessed that way.

After you send the invitation, a screen appears, telling you that you're waiting for an incoming connection. When the remote person makes a connection, you're asked if you want to accept it. Click Yes, and the connection is made. From this point on, the remote user sees everything on your screen. You can also chat with each other and send files back and forth to help with troubleshooting. You can also pause the connection by clicking Pause, or end the connection by clicking Disconnect.

Figure 11-19 shows what Remote Assistance looks like on the PC that is getting assistance; Figure 11-20 shows what it looks like on the PC providing assistance, with the Remote Assistance connection inside a window.

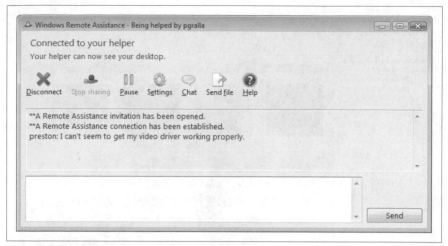

Figure 11-19. Getting help with Remote Assistance

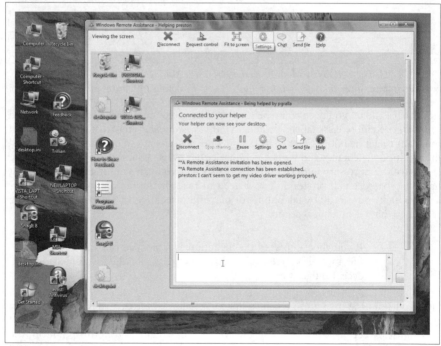

Figure 11-20. Providing help with Remote Assistance

Notes

- When you send an invitation via email, the recipient receives a link to *http://windows.microsoft.com/RemoteAssistance/RA.asp*, as well as a file attachment (*rcBuddy.MsRcIncident*) with your connection information. The information stored in the file attachment is not easily readable; the recipient simply opens the attachment to initiate a connection.

See also

"Remote Desktop Connection," in Chapter 7

System Information

\windows\system32\msinfo32.exe

Collect and display information about your computer.

To open

Start → All Programs → Accessories → System Tools → System Information

Command Prompt → **msinfo32**

Description

Microsoft System Information is a reporting tool used to view information about hardware, system resources used by that hardware, software drivers, and Internet Explorer settings (see Figure 11-21). Information is arranged in a familiar Explorer-like tree. Expand or collapse branches with the little plus (+) and minus (–) signs, and click any category to view the corresponding information in the righthand pane.

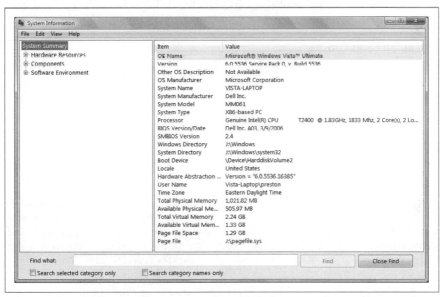

Figure 11-21. The System Information window, which shows an exhaustive amount of information about your system

The Components view of your hardware is similar to Device Manager, except that Device Manager also allows modification and removal of the devices. Likewise, the Hardware Resources view can also be duplicated in Device Manager with View → Resources by type. One advantage Microsoft System Information has over Device Manager is its capability to show a history of changes, using View → System History.

The information displayed in the Software Environment category is also available in bits and pieces through other utilities (such as Driver Query, discussed in Chapter 9), but only here is it presented all in one place.

Notes

- Rather than wading through all of the categories, jump right to the item you want by using the "Find what" field at the bottom of the window.
- As with Device Manager, you can also connect to another computer and view information about that system. Go to View → Remote Computer and enter the name of the remote machine.
- You can also use System Information to view reports and logs generated by other utilities, such as Dr. Watson (.wlg files), Windows Report Tool (.cab files), and even .txt files.
- You can print a report with System Information, but you can print only the entire system information collection, which usually comes out to more than 75 pages. If you want to print only sections of the system information, copy it to Notepad and print it from there.
- If information appears to be incorrect, out-of-date, or missing altogether, try View → Refresh or press F5.

See also

"Microsoft Management Console," in Chapter 10

Scheduled Tasks Console
\windows\system32\schtasks.exe

Control the Task Scheduler from the command line.

To open

Command Prompt → **schtasks**

Usage

    schtasks /command_name [arguments]

Description

The Scheduled Tasks Console is the command-line equivalent of the Task Scheduler, discussed later in this chapter. Although it doesn't do anything not already possible with the Task Scheduler window, it can be convenient for automating the creation and management of tasks. The Scheduled Tasks Console accepts one of six options. To find out more about any of the commands, type **schtasks /command_name /?**:

/create [/s system [/u user [/p password]]] /ru user [/rp password]] /sc schedule [/mo modifier] [/d day] [/i idletime] /tn taskname /tr taskrun [/st starttime] [/m months] [/sd startdate] [/ed enddate]
>Creates a new scheduled task on the local computer or a remote system

/delete [/s system [/u user [/p password]]] /tn taskname [/f]
>Deletes one or more scheduled tasks

/query [/s system [/u user [/p password]]] [/fo format] [/nh] [/v]
>Displays all scheduled tasks on the local computer or a remote system

/change [/s system [/u username [/p password]]] [/ru runasuser] [/rp runaspassword] [/tr taskrun] /tn taskname
>Changes some of the properties of an existing task, such as the program to run or the username and password

---

/run [/s *system* [/u *user* [/p *password*]]] /tn *taskname*
  Runs a scheduled task immediately

/end [/s *system* [/u *user* [/p *password*]]] /tn *taskname*
  Stops a currently running scheduled task

See also
"Task Scheduler"

Services   *\windows\system32\services.msc*

Manage system services.

To open
Run as a plug-in for the Microsoft Management Console.

Command Prompt → **services**

Description
This plug-in to the Microsoft Management Console displays system services and lets
you start and stop services, control whether they run at startup, and customize how
they run. It's pictured in Figure 11-22.

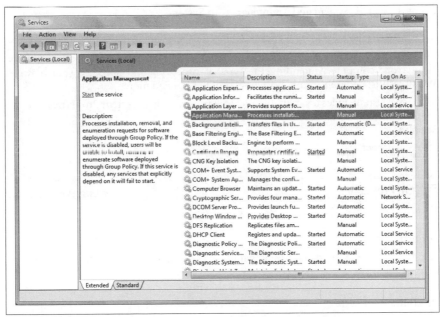

Figure 11-22. Customizing how services run, using the Services console

See "Microsoft Management Console," in Chapter 10, for more details.

System Configuration Editor

\windows\system32\sysedit.exe

Obsolete; quick editor for *system.ini*, *win.ini*, *config.sys*, and *autoexec.bat*.

To open

Command Prompt → `sysedit`

Description

The System Configuration Editor is essentially a special version of Notepad that provides convenient access to a few configuration files used in previous versions of Windows. When you start it, the four following files are opened: *system.ini*, *win.ini*, *config.sys*, and *autoexec.bat*. Because none of these files is actively used in Windows Vista (except for legacy application support), this tool has very little use. It's included for legacy purposes only, and you should not use it unless such changes are specifically required for old applications you may be running.

System Control Panel

Get basic information about your computer.

To open

Control Panel → [System and Maintenance] → System

Description

The System Control Panel (Figure 11-23) shows you at a glance basic information about your computer, including the type of processor and speed, installed RAM, Windows Vista edition, computer name, product ID, and more.

The panel also includes a variety of links to settings, such as System Properties.

See also

"System Properties"

System Properties

\windows\system32\sysdm.cpl

View and modify many general Windows settings.

To open

Control Panel → [System and Maintenance] → System, then click Change settings

Command Prompt → `control sysdm.cpl`

Description

The System Properties window contains settings that affect hardware, system performance, networking, and other Windows features. The tabs in this dialog are as follows:

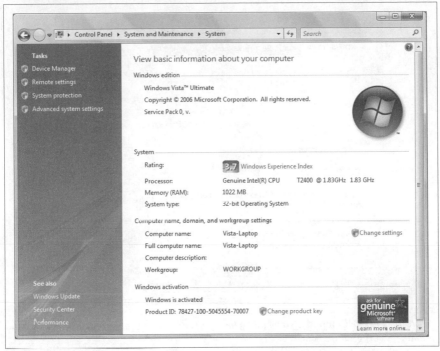

Figure 11-23. The System Control Panel, where you can get a quick overview of your Windows version, amount of installed memory, and other information

Computer Name

These settings affect how your computer is identified on your network, such as the computer's name and whether you're connected to a domain or workgroup. The Computer description field is for entering a comment only; it has no effect on any networking settings. To join a domain or workgroup, click Network ID; to change your computer name or its domain or workgroup, click Change (see Figure 11-24).

Hardware

This gives you access to the Device Manager that lists all the hardware on your system (see Chapter 9 for details). The Windows Update Driver Settings button controls whether to have Windows automatically check for new and updated hardware drivers.

Advanced

In this tab, you'll find important Windows settings covering a wide variety of areas, including how to handle visual effects, how to handle logons and user accounts, and startup and recovery options. The "Performance settings" button leads to the Performance Options dialog box, which lets you selectively disable and change several enhanced display features, such as transparent glass, animated windows when minimizing and maximizing, facing or sliding menus into view, and so on. For more details, see "Performance Options," earlier in this chapter.

Figure 11-24. The Computer Name tab, where you can rename your computer or join a domain or workgroup

System Protection

> This tab offers tools to control the System Restore feature for the drives in your computer. See "System Protection and System Restore," later in this chapter, for details.

Remote

> These settings control the Remote Desktop (see Chapter 7) and Remote Assistance features (discussed earlier in this chapter). Unless you specifically want others to be able to connect to your computer using Remote Desktop or Remote Assistance, it's strongly recommended that you disable both options on this page. If you are running one of the Home editions of Windows Vista, you will not see the Remote Desktop option here.

See also

"System Control Panel"

System Protection and System Restore

\windows\system32\restore\rstrui.exe
(System Restore only)

Roll back your computer's configuration to an earlier state, with the intention of undoing potentially harmful changes.

To open

Start → All Programs → Accessories → System Tools → System Restore

Control Panel → [System and Maintenance] → System → System Protection

Command Prompt → `rstrui`

Description

System Protection (also confusingly called System Restore) is a feature that runs invisibly in the background, continuously backing up important system files and Registry settings. The idea is that at some point, you may want to roll back your computer's configuration to a time before things started going wrong (see Figure 11-25). By default, System Restore is turned on, using at least 300 MB of your computer's hard-disk space.

System Restore is particularly useful for restoring the state of your computer if you ever install an application that wreaks havoc on your system. Theoretically, every time you install a new application or drive, a new restore point is created, which is then used to restore the state of your PC to what it was before the installation. But a restore point may not always be created, so if you're about to install a new application that you fear may not be well behaved, it's a good idea to manually create a restore point. (I'll discuss how to do that later in this section.) System Restore automatically creates a Restore Point once a day as well as whenever a significant system event occurs, such as installing a driver or a new program.

Oddly enough, Windows calls the feature both System Protection and System Restore. System Protection actually refers to the overall configuration screen for System Restore (see Figure 11-25), and System Restore is the actual application that creates restore points and performs system restorations.

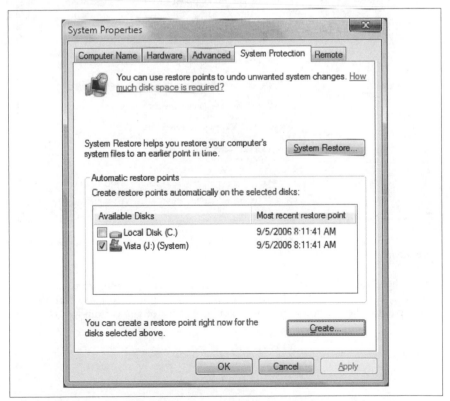

Figure 11-25. The System Protection screen, which lets you configure and access System Restore

System Protection lets you turn System Restore on and off for specific volumes. Check the box next to any volumes for which you want to turn on System Restore. Note that if you have a volume that contains only data and no system settings, you should still use System Restore on it because it creates shadow copies that you can use to restore old versions of your files.

To manually create a restore point, click Create.

Start the System Restore application if you want to restore an earlier configuration or create a restore point. Restore points are packages containing files and settings, created at regular intervals. To roll back your computer's configuration to an earlier time, click System Restore, or bypass the System Restore screen altogether and go straight to System Restore by typing **rstrui** at a command prompt (see Figure 11-26).

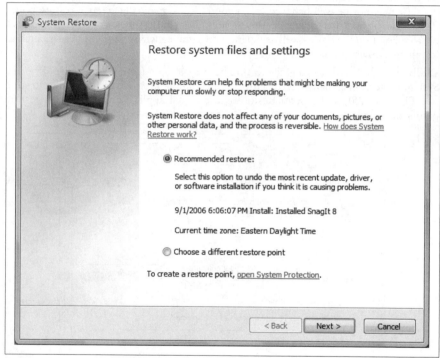

Figure 11-26. Launching System Restore to restore your computer to a time when it was more stable

Follow the wizard's instructions. It will recommend a restore point to use, but it's a good idea to instead select "Choose a different restore point" to make sure that the restore point is the one you want to use. You'll see a list of points from which you can choose.

See also
"Backup and Restore Center"

Taskkill

End one or more running processes, either on a local or a remote system.

To open

Command Prompt → **taskkill**

Usage

```
taskkill [/s system [/u username [/p [password]]]]
{ [/fi filter] [/pid pid | /im image] } [/f] [/t]
```

Description

You use Taskkill to end one or more running processes from the command line. Task-kill works together with Tasklist, discussed in the next section, to provide command-line equivalents to the functionality provided by the Processes tab in the Task Manager. For more information on processes, see "Task Manager," later in this chapter.

Taskkill takes the following command-line parameters:

/s *system*
> Specifies the remote system to which to connect.

/u [*domain*]*user*
> Specifies the user context under which the command should execute.

/p [*password*]
> Specifies the password for the user specified by \u; prompts for input if omitted.

/f
> Specifies to forcefully terminate process(es).

/fi *filter*
> Displays a set of tasks that match given criteria specified by the filter. Use Tasklist for more display options.

/pid *process_id*
> Specifies the process ID of the process to be terminated. To obtain the process IDs, use Tasklist.

/im *image_name*
> Specifies the image name of the process to be terminated; specify * to terminate all image names.

/t
> Terminates the specified process and process tree, which includes any child processes that were started by it.

See also

"Tasklist" and "Task Manager"

Tasklist

Display a list of running applications and processes running on either a local or a remote system.

To open

Command Prompt → **tasklist**

Usage

```
tasklist [/s system [/u username [/p [password]]]]
    [/m [module] | /svc | /v] [/fi filter] [/fo format] [/nh]
```

Description

You use Tasklist to list running processes from the command line. Tasklist works together with Taskkill, discussed in the preceding section, to provide command-line equivalents to the functionality provided by the Processes tab in the Task Manager. For more information on processes, see "Task Manager," later in this chapter.

Tasklist takes the following command-line parameters:

/s system
> Specifies the remote system to which to connect.

/u [domain\]user
> Specifies the user context under which the command should execute.

/p [password]
> Specifies the password for the user specified by \u; prompts for input if omitted.

/m [module]
> Lists all tasks that have Dynamic Link Library (DLL) modules loaded that match the pattern, *module*. If *module* is not specified, /m displays all modules loaded by each task.

/v
> Verbose mode; display all available information.

/fi filter
> Displays a set of tasks that match given criteria specified by the filter. Use Tasklist for more display options.

/fo format
> Specifies the format of the display: type **/fo table** (the default) for a formatted table, **/fo list** for a plain-text list, or **/fo csv** for a comma-separated report, suitable for importing into a spreadsheet or database.

/nh
> If using the /fo table or /fo csv format, the /nh option turns off the column headers.

See also

"Taskkill," "Task Manager," and "Query Process"

Task Manager

\windows\system32\taskmgr.exe

Display currently running programs, background processes, and some performance statistics.

To open

Ctrl-Alt-Delete → Start Task Manager

Right-click on empty portion of the Taskbar → Task Manager

Command Prompt → **taskmgr**

Keyboard shortcut: Ctrl-Shift-Esc

Description

The Task Manager is an extremely useful tool, but you won't find it on the Start menu. In its simplest form, it displays all running applications, allowing you to close any that have crashed or stopped responding. The main window is divided into the following six tabs:

Applications

Shows all foreground applications as well as the status of each one (see Figure 11-27). The Status can be "Running" or "Not responding." You can switch to any running application by double-clicking it, which makes it similar to the Taskbar in this respect. Click New Task or go to File → New Task (Run) to start a new program by typing a filename or command.

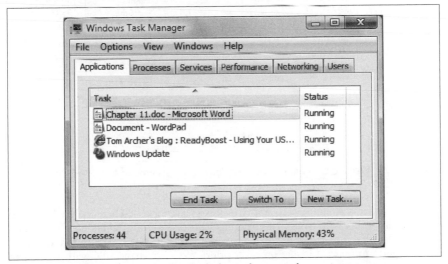

Figure 11-27. The Applications tab, which shows the currently running programs

Select any item and click End Task to close the program. Although it is preferred to use an application's own exit routine, this function is useful for programs that have crashed or have stopped responding.

Processes

A process is any program running on your computer, including foreground applications shown in the Applications tab and any background applications that might be running (see Figure 11-28). Like the End Task button in the Applications tab, the End Process button is used to close unresponsive programs. Additionally, however, it allows you to close background applications that otherwise have no window or other means of exiting gracefully.

Right-click on any running task to display a list of options, including End Process (discussed earlier), End Process Tree (similar to End Process, but ends all "child" processes as well), Set Priority, and Set Affinity, among others. The Set Priority menu allows you to increase or decrease the priority of a program; higher-priority processes may run better and are less likely to be interrupted or slowed down by

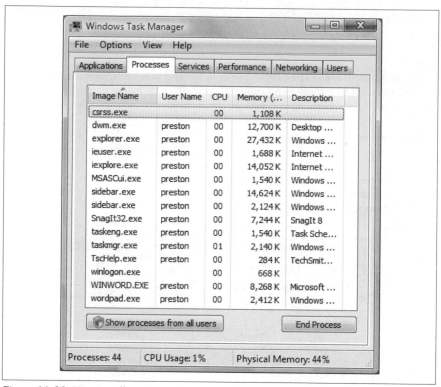

Figure 11-28. Viewing all running programs (including background tasks) with the Processes tab

other processes, and lower-priority processes are more likely to yield CPU cycles to other processes. Note that changing a process's priority may have unpredictable results. It should be used only if that process or application explicitly supports running at higher or lower priorities. If you have a PC with more than one processor, use Set Affinity to determine which processor(s) the process is allowed to use.

Services

A service is a program or process that runs in the background in Windows and provides support to other programs. For example, the Windows Image Acquisition (WIA) service helps scanners and cameras obtain graphics via Windows. The Services tab (Figure 11-29) displays all services; the status can be Stopped or Running. Right-click any service and choose Start Service to start it, or Stop Service to stop it.

Performance

The Performance tab shows several graphs, all updated in real time, used to monitor the performance of the system. You can change the refresh rate of the graphs by going to View → Update Speed.

The CPU Usage is expressed as a percentage, in which an average idling computer will take about 3 to 7 percent of a processor's clock cycles and a computer

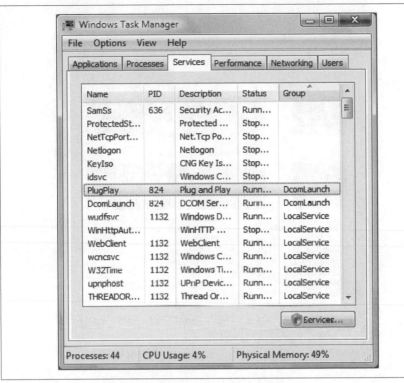

Figure 11 29. Viewing all running services with the Services tab

running a graphics-intensive game might take 80 to 90 percent. Don't be alarmed if your CPU Usage appears to be unusually high, but if such usage has no reasonable explanation, you may want to investigate running processes for crashed programs or even tasks that may have been started by unauthorized intruders. CPU Usage History provides a running history of the last few minutes of CPU Usage readings; it can be very interesting to see what happens to the CPU Usage History when you start a particular program or just move the mouse around the screen. If you have a multiprocessor system, you'll see a separate graph for each processor, which can be very useful to see how your processors are being utilized (see Figure 11-30).

Page File Usage and Page File Usage History work the same as CPU Usage, except that they report on the performance of the virtual memory. Virtual memory is the portion of your hard disk used to store data when Windows has used up all of your installed RAM. To change virtual memory settings, go to Control Panel → [System and Maintenance] → System → Change Settings → Advanced tab, click Settings in the Performance section, choose the Advanced tab, and click Change.

Also shown in the Performance tab are several performance-related statistics, such as the amount of total and available memory, or even the number of active handles (unique identifiers of resources, such as menu items, windows, Registry keys, or anything else Windows has to keep track of).

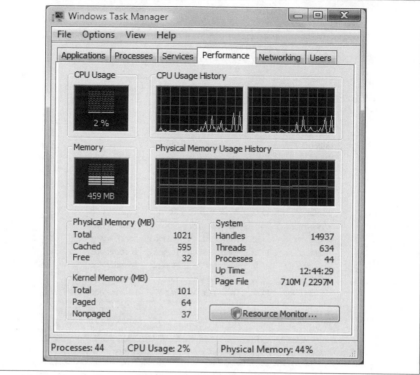

Figure 11-30. The Performance tab, which shows a time-based graph of the load on your processor and virtual memory

Networking

Similar to the Performance tab, the Networking tab shows real-time graphs depicting the performance of your network connections. You'll see a graph for each network connection currently in use. See Chapter 7 for more information.

Users

This tab lists the current users of the PC and lets you disconnect them or log them off.

You can use the Options and View menus to set several preferences; note that the options available in these menus change depending on the currently selected tab. For example, if you want to leave the Task Manager open all the time, you may want to turn off the Always On Top option so that you can see other running applications.

At the bottom of many of the tabs are buttons that perform additional tasks, launch a related utility, or launch a related Microsoft Management Console plug-in. For example, click Resource Monitor at the bottom of the Performance tab to launch the Resource Monitor, which provides more details about the current PC's performance and resource use.

See also

"Query Process," "Taskkill," "Tasklist," and "Reliability and Performance Monitor"

Task Scheduler

Run a program or script at a specified time.

To open

Control Panel → [System and Maintenance] → Schedule tasks

Command Prompt → **taskschd**

Description

The Task Scheduler allows you to schedule any program or WSH script to run at a specified time or interval (see Figure 11-31).

Figure 11-31. The Task Scheduler, which lets you run programs at predetermined times or intervals

To create a new scheduled task, click Create Basic Task to open the Task Scheduler Wizard (Figure 11-32). You'll be prompted to do the following:

1. Type in a name for the task and its description.

2. Select a trigger (for example, at a specific day, when your computer starts, when you log on, when a specific event occurs, and so on). The trigger can also be a specific time of the day and day of the week.

3. Select an action that the Task Scheduler should take (for example, run a program, send an email, or display a message).

Click Finish, and you're done. The task will now run at the scheduled time.

What if you want to delete or edit the task? At first, there seems to be no clear way to do that. The task you just created may not show up in the Task Activity and Status

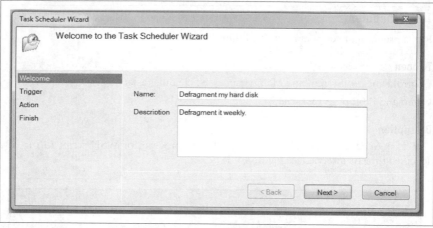

Figure 11-32. Starting the Task Scheduler Wizard

area. It will appear in the Active Tasks area, but only the name shows up—double-click it, or highlight it and press the Delete key, and nothing happens.

To edit or delete the task, click Task Scheduler Library in the lefthand pane. Your task now shows up. To delete it, highlight it and select Delete from the rightmost pane. To edit it, double-click it.

Editing the task doesn't launch a wizard but instead brings up a multitabbed screen (shown in Figure 11-33). This screen gives you far more control over how the task runs.

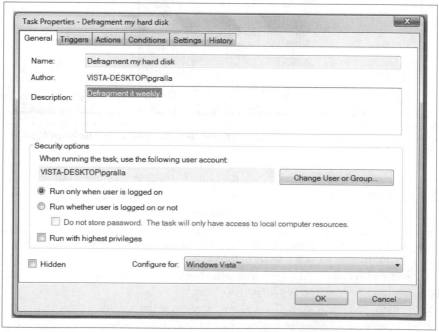

Figure 11-33. Editing a task, which gives you far more control over how the task will run

Here is a brief rundown of each tab, and what each controls:

General
> Lets you select a user account that should run the task, as well as choose other options such as whether to run when the user is logged in, and whether to run with the highest privileges. (For details about privileges, see "User Account Control," in Chapter 8.)

Triggers
> Lets you pick an extremely wide variety of triggers—for example, when connecting to or disconnecting from a user session, when a workstation is locked or unlocked, and so on. It also allows you to delay tasks for a certain amount of time after a trigger, repeat tasks, stop tasks from running too long, set an expiration date, and more.

Actions
> Allows you to specify the command line, the full path- and filename of the application, or the script to run. You can also choose the default folder in which to run the program.

Conditions
> Lets you determine the conditions under which the task will run—for example, when the computer is idle for a certain amount of time, when the computer is on AC power or when it switches to battery power, and so on.

Settings
> Lets you set more preferences, including what actions to take if the task fails (whether to restart it, and how often to try, for example), under what circumstances to have the task automatically deleted, and more.

History
> Displays a history of the running of the task.

If you want the kind of control over your tasks that these tabs afford, you can bypass the wizard entirely. Click Create Task, instead of Create Basic Task, and you'll be presented with the multitabbed screen that you can fill out, instead of filling out a wizard.

The Task Scheduler also lets you look at all the tasks scheduled to be run on your PC and at those that have completed, using the Task Activity and Status as well as the Active Tasks areas.

Notes

* The Scheduled Tasks Console allows you to create new tasks from the command line.

See also

"Scheduled Tasks Console" and "Windows Script Host"

Windows Easy Transfer

Transfers file, folders, and settings among PCs.

To open

Control Panel → [System and Maintenance] → Welcome Center → Transfer Files and Settings

---

Description

Windows Easy Transfer can transfer files, programs, and settings from a PC running Windows 2000, Windows XP, or Windows Vista to a PC running Windows Vista.

 If you upgrade from a PC running Windows XP to Windows Vista, your files, settings, and programs will be transferred automatically.

You can use Windows Easy Transfer to transfer files and program settings from a computer running Windows 2000, Windows XP, or Windows Vista to another computer running Windows Vista. Start Windows Easy Transfer on the computer running Windows Vista, and then follow the instructions.

To transfer files, you need to connect the two PCs via a direct USB cable or via a network, or copy the files to a CD, DVD, or USB flash drive and then copy from there to the new PC.

You'll be able to copy only selected files and folders (Documents, Pictures, and Shared Documents folders). You can copy email settings from Windows Mail, Outlook, Outlook Express, and other email programs. Windows Easy Transfer also transfers a variety of program settings, but it doesn't actually copy the programs themselves; for those you'll have to go through a normal installation procedure. You'll also copy user accounts and settings including color schemes, desktop backgrounds, and so on, as well as Internet connection settings, favorites, and cookies.

Performing the transfer is straightforward. A wizard appears, letting you select which files, folders, and settings to transfer; just follow the directions.

Notes

- If you're transferring program settings to a new PC, you need to first install the program on the new PC before you use Windows Easy Transfer, or else the settings won't transfer.

Windows File Checker   *\windows\system32\sfc.exe*

Verify the existence and integrity of some Windows files.

To open

Command Prompt → **sfc** (requires an Administrator command prompt)

Usage

```
sfc [/scannow] [/verifyonly] [/scanfile=filename] [/verifyfile=filename]
[/offwindir=offline windows directory /offbootdir=offline boot directory
Description
```

Description

Windows File Checker scans your system for corrupt, changed, or missing files, as long as those files are specified in a predetermined list of important system files. By default, Windows File Checker automatically scans your system every time Windows is started. Use the Windows File Checker utility to perform a manual scan or change the automatic settings. The Windows File Checker takes the following options:

`/scannow`
Performs an immediate scan of all protected system files.

`/verifyonly`
Scans the integrity of all protected system files. No repair operation is performed.

`/scanfile`
Scans the integrity of the file and repairs the file if problems are identified. You must specify the full path of the file.

`/verifyfile`
Verifies the integrity of the file but does not perform a repair operation. You must specify the full path of the file.

`/offwindir`
When performing an offline repair, specifies the location of the offline Windows directory.

`/offbootdir`
When performing an offline repair, specifies the location of the offline boot directory.

Windows Script Host

\windows\system32\wscript.exe; cscript.exe

Runs WSH scripts.

To open
Command Prompt → **wscript**

Command Prompt → **cscript**

Usage
```
wscript filename [options] [arguments]
cscript filename [options] [arguments]
```

Description
The Windows Script Host runs WSH script files you create and edit. Of the two executables, *wscript.exe* is used to run.

Both executables take the following options (note the use of double slashes to distinguish them from ordinary arguments passed onto the script):

`//b`
Batch mode; suppresses script errors and prompts from displaying.

`//d`
Enables active debugging.

`//e:engine`
Uses *engine* for executing the script; the default depends on the filename extension of the script file.

`//h:cscript`
Changes the default script host to *cscript.exe*, the command-prompt-based host.

`//h:wscript`
Changes the default script host to *wscript.exe*, the Windows-based host (the default).

```
//job:xxxx
```
Executes a WSF job.
```
//nologo
```
Prevents the display of the banner logo at execution time.
```
//s
```
Saves current command-line options as the default for this user.
```
//t:nn
```
Timeout in seconds; the maximum time a script is permitted to run.
```
//x
```
Executes the script in the debugger.
```
//u
```
Uses Unicode for redirected I/O from the console.

Welcome Center

Offers access to basic settings and services for getting started with Windows Vista.

To open

Control Panel → [System and Maintenance] → Welcome Center

Description

The Welcome Center (Figure 11-34) appears not only the first time you start Windows, but every time thereafter as well. It includes links to common tasks you'd want to perform when you start up, including transferring files and settings from another computer, adding new users, creating an Internet connection, and seeing system details.

To see more items and tasks you can perform, click the "Get started with Windows" link.

To turn off the Welcome Center so that it doesn't launch every time you start up Windows, uncheck the box next to Run at Startup.

Startup

Advanced Boot Options

Starts Windows in advanced troubleshooting modes to fix computer problems.

To open

Reboot Windows and press F8 before Windows starts.

Description

This text menu, which you can invoke before Windows starts, lets you troubleshoot Windows problems. You can use it to restart Windows in Safe Mode, where only the Windows essentials are started. If Windows starts properly in this mode, you will know the default settings and minimum device drivers are not causing problems, and you can then proceed to further troubleshooting. The menu has these options:

Figure 11-34. The Welcome Center, which includes links to common tasks you might want to perform when you start up Windows Vista

Safe Mode
> Starts Windows with the minimal drivers and services.

Safe Mode with networking
> Starts Windows in Safe Mode, including network drivers and services.

Safe Mode with Command Prompt
> Starts Windows in Safe Mode with a command prompt instead of the Windows interface.

Enable Boot Logging
> Creates a text file, *ntbtlog.txt*, that lists the drivers that load during startup, which can be helpful for advanced troubleshooting.

Enable low-resolution video (640×480)
> Starts Windows using low resolution and refresh-rate settings. Use this to start Windows if there is a problem with your display settings. After you start in this mode, you can change your display settings in Windows itself.

Last Known Good Configuration
> Starts Windows with the last Registry and driver configuration that worked properly.

Directory Services Restore Mode
> Used by IT staff and administrators, this mode starts Windows domain controllers running Active Directory so that a directory service can be restored.

Debugging Mode
> Starts Windows in advanced troubleshooting mode.

Disable automatic restart on system failure
> Stops Windows from automatically restarting if an error causes it to fail. Use this only if Windows is stuck in a loop where it fails, attempts to restart, and then fails repeatedly.

Disable Driver Signature Enforcement
> Allows drivers that contain improper signatures to be loaded.

Start Windows Normally
> Starts Windows as it would normally.

Boot Configuration Data Store Editor

\windows\System32\bcdedit.exe

Configure the way Windows Vista boots.

To open

Command Prompt → **bcdedit**

Description

In Windows versions before Windows Vista, the way a PC booted was controlled by the system file *boot.ini*, which contained startup configuration information. *boot.ini* was a plain-text file and could be edited using a text editor or tools built into Windows, such as the System Configuration Utility. It was used for booting multiple operating systems on the same PC, or to customize how Windows started.

That's changed in Windows Vista. Instead of the *boot.ini* file, the Boot Configuration Data (BCD) file controls system startup. Microsoft made the change because it says the file is more versatile than *boot.ini* and can be used by hardware that starts up without a basic input/output system (BIOS) to start.

That may be true, but the change also makes it more difficult to customize Windows startup. Once you learned the basics of *boot.ini*, you could relatively easily configure startup to your liking. BCD, by contrast, is exceedingly difficult to understand, and quite confusing; even power users will usually be stymied by it.

There are three ways to edit BCD: using the System Configuration Utility, using the System startup screen in Startup and Recovery, and using the command-line tool Boot Configuration Data Store Editor. (See "System Configuration Utility" and "Startup and Recovery," later in this chapter, for more details.)

The Boot Configuration Data Store Editor includes many features and options, and a full explication of it is beyond the scope of this book. But here are the primary commands.

Commands that operate on a store:

/createstore
> Creates a new, empty boot configuration data store

/export
> Exports the contents of the system store to a file, which can be used to restore the state of the system store

/import
> Restores the state of the system store using a backup file created with /export

---

Commands that operate on entries in a store (you'll have to use these commands along with identifiers, which identify entries in the store; for details and help, use the /bcdedit /? ID command):

/copy

Makes copies of entries in the store

/create

Creates new entries in the store

/delete

Deletes entries from the store

Commands that operate on entry options (run bcdedit /? TYPES for a list of data types used by these commands):

/deletevalue

Deletes entry options from the store

/set

Sets entry option values in the store

Commands that control the boot manager (note: you'll need the identifier to use these commands, as well as a list of additional switches; for details, type **bcdedit /bootsequence /?**, **bcdedit /default /?**, and so on):

/bootsequence

Sets the one-time boot sequence for the boot manager

/default

Sets the default entry that the boot manager will use

/displayorder

Sets the order in which the boot manager displays the multiboot menu

/timeout

Sets the boot manager time-out value

/toolsdisplayorder

Sets the order in which the boot manager displays the tools menu

Notes

- If you have a multiboot configuration for multiple versions of Windows, you can change which Windows operating system opens by default, and other settings, by using the Startup and Recovery dialog box.

- A third-party utility, VistaBootPRO, lets you customize and control how Windows Vista starts up, without having to use *Bcdedit.exe*. Get it from *http://www.pro-networks.org/vistabootpro*.

See also

"Advanced Boot Options" and "Startup and Recovery"

Startup and Recovery

Control system startup, including configuring multiboot options for running multiple operating systems, and logging system failures.

To open

Control Panel → [System and Maintenance] → System → Advanced system settings → Advanced tab, click Settings in Startup and Recovery

Description

The BCD file controls system startup and how multiboot systems work. The easiest way to configure multiboot systems is to use the Startup and Recovery tab (Figure 11-35) of the System Properties dialog box.

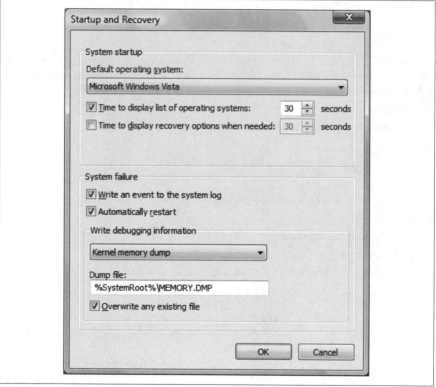

Figure 11-35. The Startup and Recovery tab, where you can configure options for multiboot systems

If you have a multiboot system, when your PC starts up a menu appears with all the operating systems that can boot. By default, the menu displays for 30 seconds, during which you can select any operating system to boot. After that time your PC will boot into the default operating system.

Choose the default operating system from the drop-down list in the Startup and Recovery tab. You can also select how long to display the menu, along with similar options. The screen also allows you to determine what Windows should do in the event of a system failure on startup (write the event to a system log, automatically restart, etc.).

See also

"Advanced Boot Options" and "System Configuration Utility"

Startup Repair

Fixes problems that can stop Windows from starting properly, such as missing or damaged files.

To open

Insert the Windows installation disk into your PC, restart the computer, and click "View system recovery options." After typing in a username and password of an account on the computer, click Startup Repair.

Description

If you can't start Windows properly, this utility scans your system and automatically tries to fix the problem. In some instances, a computer manufacturer will install Startup Repair on your hard disk. If so, you can run it not only from the Windows installation disk, but also from the Windows Advanced Startup Options menu (Control Panel → [System and Maintenance] → System → Advanced system settings → Advanced tab, click Settings in Startup and Recovery).

System Configuration Utility   \windows\System32\msconfig.exe

Selectively enable or disable several startup options and get access to specialized tools to optimize performance, customize Windows Vista, and perform diagnostic/troubleshooting tasks.

To open

Command Prompt → `msconfig`

Description

The System Configuration Utility (see Figure 11-36) allows you to selectively enable or disable various settings that affect system startup, including the ability to stop specific programs and services from starting. In many instances, there is no other way to stop the programs or services from starting, so this utility is particularly useful. It can also help track down the causes of startup errors; use the utility to selectively disable programs or services from starting until you isolate the cause of the problems.

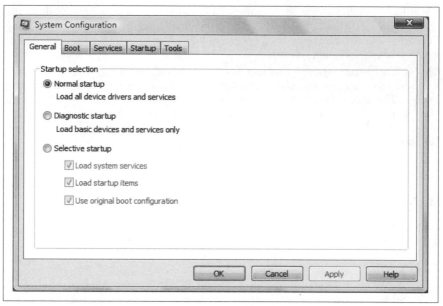

Figure 11-36. The System Configuration Utility, which helps you troubleshoot startup problems, stops programs and services from loading at startup, and offers diagnostic and customization tools

In addition, this utility gives you fast access to a variety of configuration tools—for example, it allows you to disable (and then enable) User Account Control (UAC). The System Configuration Utility has the following tabs:

General

Lets you diagnose and troubleshoot startup problems by performing several different kinds of diagnostic startups. Normal startup loads all programs and services when you start up Windows. Diagnostic startup loads only basic programs and services, so you can see whether those basic Windows files are the cause of a startup problem. If they are not the cause of the problem, you know that another program or service is causing the problem. In that event, use Selective startup, which will let you turn on and off only system services, only startup services, or both. The Services and Startup tabs, detailed shortly, let you turn on and off individual programs and services at startup.

Boot

Lets you control how Windows boots by modifying the BCD store. (See "Boot Configuration Data Store Editor," earlier in this chapter, for details about the BCD store.) It lets you set a variety of options, including whether to use the Safe Boot option, which is a troubleshooting mode that starts your computer in a limited state, with only the basic files and drivers necessary to run Windows. You can customize how Safe Boot starts by booting directly into a Command Prompt (no GUI boot option), starting with or without network drivers, and so on. The "Advanced options" button lets you select from a variety of other options, such as how many processors your PC should use if you have a multiprocessor or multi-core PC, whether to debug when you reboot, and so on.

Services
> Displays system services that run on startup. To disable any from running the next time Windows Vista starts up, check the box next to it and click OK. You can also view and control system services using the Services snap-in (*services.msc*) of the Microsoft Management Console, discussed in Chapter 10.

Startup
> Shows some of the programs that are configured to run automatically when Windows starts. Although most startup programs are configured by placing Windows Shortcuts in the Startup folder in the Start menu, the Start tab shows those along with the seemingly hidden entries specified in the Registry (see Chapter 13) at `HKEY_LOCAL_MACHINE\SOFTWARE\Microsoft\Windows\CurrentVersion\Run`.

Tools
> Gives you quick access to a variety of troubleshooting and maintenance tools, such as System Restore, the Registry Editor, the Task Manager, and others. Click the one you want to run and choose Launch. A useful feature is that each entry shows the path- and filename to the tool, or the Registry key.

Notes

- Some security-related services cannot be disabled.
- The Tools tab offers a way to turn off (and on) UAC, which can also be turned on and off from the User Accounts Control Panel.

See also

"Boot Configuration Data Store Editor," "Advanced Boot Options," and "Startup and Recovery"

12

Graphics and Multimedia

Windows Vista offers considerable multimedia capabilities; it is a substantial upgrade over Windows XP. Windows Movie Maker, for example, is a far more powerful and sophisticated program than the version that shipped with Windows XP, and Windows Media Player 11 is a significant upgrade as well. In addition, Windows Vista has new graphics applications, such as the Windows Photo Gallery and the Snipping Tool.

This chapter covers Windows graphics and multimedia tools; for information about installing related hardware, see Chapter 9.

Here is an alphabetical reference of entries in this chapter:

Fax Cover Page Editor	Snipping Tool	Windows Media Player
Microsoft Magnifier	Windows DVD Maker	Windows Movie Maker
Paint	Windows Fax and Scan	Windows Photo Gallery
Private Character Editor	Windows Media Center	

Fax Cover Page Editor

See Chapter 10.

Microsoft Magnifier

See Chapter 10.

Paint   \windows\system32\mspaint.exe

A rudimentary image editor, used to create and modify *.bmp*, *.jpg*, *.gif*, *.tif*, *.ico*, and *.png* image files.

To open

Start → All Programs → Accessories → Paint

Command Prompt → `mspaint`

Description

Paint is a basic image editor (often called a "paint program") capable of creating and modifying most Windows Bitmap (*.bmp*), Joint Photographic Experts Group (*.jpg*), Compuserve Graphics Interchange Format (*.gif*), Tagged Image File Format (*.tif*), and Portable Network Graphics (*.png*) image files. It can open icon (*.ico*) files but cannot save graphics in the *.ico* format. In essence, Paint is to image files as Notepad is to text files (see Figure 12-1).

Figure 12-1. The Paint utility, which provides a few rudimentary tools for working with image files

The first time you start Paint, you'll get a blank (white) image that is 512×320 pixels. Depending on the size of the Paint window, you may see the entire canvas, surrounded by a gray border.

 To change the size of the image, go to Image → Attributes and enter the new dimensions in the Width and Height fields. The default units are pixels, but if you choose inches or centimeters, the size of the image will be calculated using the resolution displayed at the top of the window.

At the top of the Paint window, you'll see a color palette; the leftmost box shows the currently selected foreground and background colors. Choose a new foreground color by left-clicking on any color in the palette; choose a new background color by right-clicking. The roles of the foreground and background colors depend on the currently selected tool (discussed shortly). For example, if you draw a filled-in ellipse (click the ellipse tool, select the second variation from the menu that appears, then left-click and drag to draw the ellipse), the foreground color will appear as the border and the background color will be used to fill the ellipse. You can mix your own colors by going to Colors → Edit Colors.

To the left of the document area is a simple toolbox. Each tool has a different function used to manipulate the image in some way. The first two tools are used to select portions of the image: the irregularly shaped dotted line selects an irregular shape and the rectangle selects a rectangle. The eraser tool works like a paintbrush, except that it paints with the background color. The paint bucket is used to fill a bounded area with a solid color. The eyedropper is used to set the foreground or background color from a selected color in the image (left-click on a color to set the foreground color, right-click to set the background color). The magnifying glass zooms in and out; left-click to zoom in and right-click to zoom out.

The pencil icon draws single-pixel-width lines, and the paintbrush draws with a variety of brush sizes, chosen in the brush palette beneath the toolbox; the left mouse button draws with the foreground color, and the right mouse button draws with the background color. The spray can draws by splattering random dots. The A tool is used to add text to an image, although once text has been applied, it becomes part of the image and can't be changed. The line tool is used to draw a straight line between two points; with the squiggly line tool, you'll need to first draw a straight line and then distort the line with a third click. The last four tools are shapes; choose the shape, and then choose whether it will be filled or have a border by using the brush palette below.

In addition to these basic tools, there are some other goodies. Go to File → Set as Background (Tiled, Centered, or Stretched) to set the current image as the Windows Desktop wallpaper. Use View → View Bitmap to temporarily fill the screen with the image (note that this works on all file types, not just bitmaps); click or press any key to go back. Entries in the Image menu let you perform some extra functions, such as flipping, rotating, and resizing the image.

Notes
- If you're creating an image file to be used on a web page, you must save that file using the *.jpg*, *.png*, or *.gif* format, a selection that is made in the File → Save As box. Note that it is not enough to simply rename a file to a different format in Explorer; you must open it in Paint and save it as the new format.
- If you paste an image into Paint that is larger than the bitmap you currently have open, you are prompted and can choose to have the bitmap enlarged.

See also
"Windows Photo Gallery"

Private Character Editor

See Chapter 10.

Snipping Tool

Capture, annotate, and save screen captures.

To open

Start → All Programs → Accessories → Snipping Tool

Command Prompt → **snippingtool**

Description

The Snipping Tool, new to Windows Vista, lets you capture any portion of your screen, annotate that screen capture, and then copy it to the Clipboard or save it as a *.mht*, *.png*, *.gif*, or *.jpeg* file. When you run the Snipping Tool a small screen appears (Figure 12-2). The rest of your screen dims, and your cursor turns into a big + sign. If you want to snip a rectangular area, use the cursor to define the area. You can instead capture a freeform area, the entire screen, or a screen or object such as the Taskbar. To do that, click New in the Snipping Tool and make your choice of screen captures.

Figure 12-2. The Snipping Tool, which lets you capture Windows screens

Next, the Snipping Tool displays your screen capture and lets you annotate it and/or save it to the Clipboard or to a file (see Figure 12-3). There's a highlighter, pen, and eraser for annotations. To save the clip to the Clipboard, click the Copy icon; to send it via email, click the Email icon.

You can also customize several Snipping Tool features by clicking the Options button when the Snipping Tool first pops up, or by choosing Tools → Options from the Annotation window. You can choose options such as whether to always copy the snip to the Clipboard automatically, whether you should be prompted to save the snip when you exit, whether to display the Snipping Tool icon in the Quick Launch Toolbar, and so on.

Notes

- The Alt-Print Screen and Ctrl-Print Screen combinations will capture your screen to the Clipboard. You can paste the contents of the Clipboard into a graphics application, such as Paint, in order to save the screen as a file.

- If you want a more powerful screen capture program than the Snipping Tool, try SnagIt, downloadable from *http://www.techsmith.com*.

See also

"Clipboard," in Chapter 3

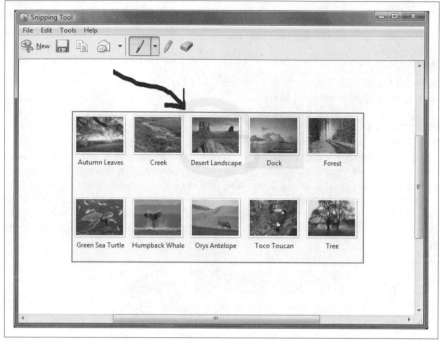

Figure 12-3. Annotating a screenshot with the Snipping Tool

Windows DVD Maker

\Program Files\Movie Maker\DVDMaker.exe

Create DVDs that you can watch on a TV.

To open

Start → All Programs → Windows DVD Maker

Command Prompt → **dvdmaker**

Description

Windows DVD Maker is a simple program for creating DVDs that you can play on a TV. It features a wizard-style interface and walks you through two screens to create a DVD:

Add pictures and video to the DVD

This screen (Figure 12-4) lets you add videos and pictures to your DVD by clicking the "Add items" button; remove them by highlighting them and clicking the "Remove items" button. You can rearrange the order of the items as well. The Options link lets you choose from a variety of settings for the DVD, and for creating the DVD:

Choose DVD playback settings

Choose whether the DVD should start with a DVD menu, play the video, and then end with a DVD menu, or play the video in a continuous loop.

DVD aspect ratio

Choose between 4:3 and 16:9.

Video format
> Choose between NTSC and Pal.

DVD burner speed
> Choose the speed at which you burn the DVD—fastest, medium, or slow. If you have trouble viewing DVDs you create, try a slower setting when you burn them.

Temporary file location
> Choose where to store the temporary files used for DVD burning. If you don't have enough space on your boot drive, you can specify another internal drive or an external USB or FireWire drive here.

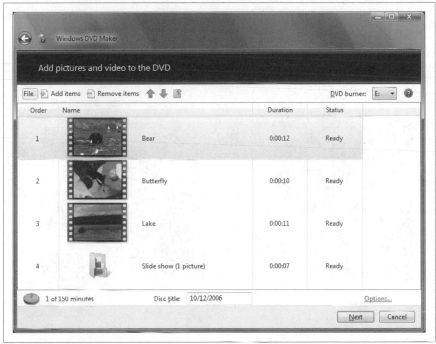

Figure 12-4. Windows DVD Maker, which lets you choose videos and pictures to burn onto a DVD that you can play on a TV

Ready to burn disk
> This screen (Figure 12-5) lets you customize and preview your DVD before burning it to disk. It has the following options:

> *Preview*
>> As the name implies, this lets you preview what the final DVD will look like.

> *Menu text*
>> This lets you change the text on the DVD menu. You can add a disc title, change the font, and choose different words for the Play, Scenes, and Notes buttons.

Customize menu

Use this option to choose pictures or videos for the foreground and background of the menu page, play an audio file while the menu is displayed, choose a button style, and change the font for the menu. You can save your settings as a new style and then use that style whenever you want.

Slide show

This lets you create a slide show out of the videos and pictures on the DVD by playing the first few seconds of each, with music. You can customize most things about the slide show, including the length of each clip, the music that plays, effects to use between clips, the order of the clips, and so on.

Figure 12-5. Finalizing the DVD before burning it to disc

The righthand side of the screen lets you choose a menu style. The Burn button, as you might imagine, burns your content to the DVD.

Notes

- You can launch Windows DVD Maker directly from Windows Movie Maker so that you can easily burn DVDs of the movies you create in Windows Movie Maker. See "Windows Movie Maker," later in this chapter, for details.

- To use Windows DVD Maker, you have the proper video card. It must support DirectX 9 with video drivers for Windows Vista.

See also

"Windows Movie Maker"

Windows Fax and Scan

See Chapter 10.

Windows Media Center

C:\Windows\ehome\ehshell.exe

Play and record media of all types, including TV.

To open

Start → All Programs → Windows Media Center

Command Prompt → **ehshell** (only when you're in *C:\Windows\ehome*)

Description

The Windows Media Center, previously available only in a special edition of Windows XP, ships with every copy of Windows Vista Home Premium and Windows Vista Ultimate. It uses an interface unlike any other program built into Windows (Figure 12-6), and it dispenses with menus, toolbars, and the usual screen elements you've grown used to in Windows; you instead navigate and choose features by using your mouse or arrow keys, or if you have one, a remote control. In fact, it looks more like it's been designed to be used with a remote control, rather than the keyboard.

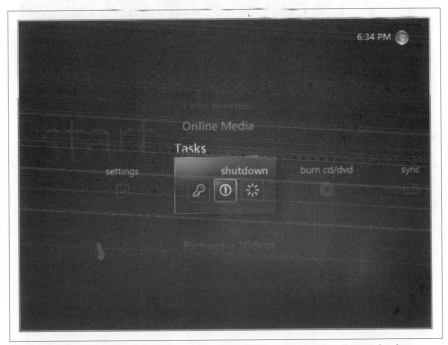

Figure 12-6. The Windows Media Center, which features an interface designed to be navigated from a remote control as much as from the keyboard

Microsoft has been trying to make the Windows Media Center the center of home entertainment systems, and it has been designed to connect to TVs. Because it is supposed to have its place in the living room and has been designed to be accessed via remote control, it's simple and intuitive to use, so there's no need to delve into its general use in any great detail here.

The Windows Media Center interface is self-explanatory. Scroll to the kind of media you want to watch or record (Pictures & Videos, Music, TV & Movies, and so on) and select Program Library, or Recorded TV, to view a library of all the media in that category, as you can see in Figure 12-7. Then select it to view it. The Windows Media Center uses the familiar VCR-like controls along the bottom of the screen (e.g., Play, Stop, etc.) to control your playing. You can also watch TV and play DVDs.

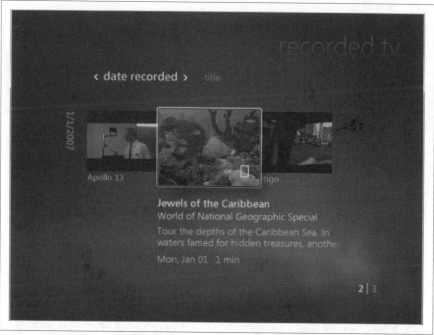

Figure 12-7. Viewing a library of all the media in the Recorded TV selection

To watch TV, you need to have a TV tuner card in your PC (or an external tuner) that can either play on-air signals or connect to your cable TV. After you install the card, run the Windows Media Center and choose Set Up TV from TV & Movies.

The Tasks choice lets you change settings and perform tasks that otherwise might not be obvious. Scroll to Tasks, and then select Settings (Figure 12-8). From here, you can choose settings for the way the Windows Media Center plays media, functions, and interacts with Windows Vista and hardware. Again, the settings are quite straightforward and need no further explanation.

Notes

- The Windows Media Center and Windows Media Player perform many of the same functions and play all kinds of media. Windows Media Player, though, cannot play or record TV shows. And the Windows Media Center is not as well

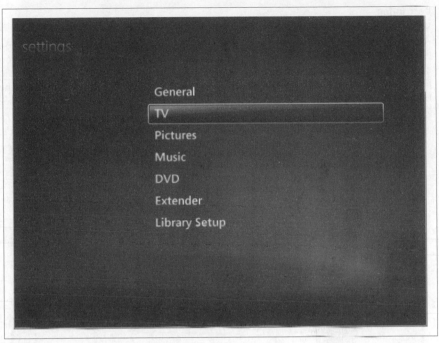

Figure 12-8. The Windows Media Center's Settings menu

suited as Windows Media Player to managing media libraries, although it is well suited to playing media.

- To connect your PC to many external devices and control them using the Windows Media Center, you can use a *Windows Media Center Extender*, a separate device that connects to your cable system and to your home network. You can also get a Media Center Extender for Xbox that connects your Xbox to your PC. For details, visit *http://www.microsoft.com/windowsxp/mediacenter/extender/default.mspx*.

See also
"Windows Media Player"

Windows Media Player

C:\Program Files\Windows Media Player\wmplayer.exe

Play back a wide variety of video and audio media files, such as *.mpg* movies, *.mp3* songs, *.wma* Windows media songs, audio CD tracks, *.dvr-ms* recorded TV shows, media files, and other streaming media.

To open
Start → All Programs → Windows Media Player

Double-click on any associated media file

Command Prompt → **wmplayer** (note: you have to be in *C:\Program Files\Windows Media Player* to run it from the command prompt)

Description

Windows Media Player is the default application used to open and play most of the types of video and audio media supported by Windows Vista (see Figure 12-9). You can open Windows Media Player from the Start menu, as well as by double-clicking on a supported media file or clicking on a link in a web page to open that video or audio clip and play it. The program isn't configured or enabled until you launch it for the first time, at which point a simple configuration screen will appear. (For details, see "Privacy issues," later in this entry).

Figure 12-9. Windows Media Player, which is used to play video and audio clips

Basic operation of Windows Media Player is fairly straightforward, with the standard VCR-like controls along the bottom of the screen (e.g., Play, Stop, etc.), the current view of your media or operations in the large, middle part of the screen, and navigation on the left part of the screen. This basic view, however, changes according to your current activity.

Windows Media Player has become increasingly sophisticated with each version, and the current version—version 11—has become a kind of multimedia powerhouse, allowing you to view media of many different types; record TV shows and DVDs; "rip" music from CDs to play on your PC; burn audio CDs or data CDs or DVDs; sync with portable music players, Pocket PCs, and Smartphones or Microsoft's own Plays4Sure devices; and buy music and videos online through Microsoft's URGE store and other online media stores.

 Windows Media Player doesn't display the traditional menu, with File, View, Play, Tools, and so on. To make that menu appear, press the Alt key; to make it disappear, press the Alt key again. You can also make the traditional menu stay permanent by right-clicking on an empty portion of the toolbar and choosing Show Classic Menus.

Across the top of the screen is a toolbar that gives you access to all of Windows Media Player's features. To perform a function, click the main part of any button; to select options for that button, click the bottom part of the button and a down arrow will appear, revealing a drop-down menu. Here's what you can do with each toolbar option:

Now Playing
This lets you choose options related to your current selection, and how it plays and displays media. The most important options relate to enhancements, visualizations, and plug-ins:

Enhancements
This includes adding SRS WOW effects, which let you optimize bass, stereo, and other audio effects; using a graphics equalizer to choose how to enhance and mix your music; changing your video color settings, including changing the hue, brightness, saturation, and contrast; and other similar options.

Visualizations
These are graphics displays (see Figure 12-10) that react to the music you're playing; you can choose from dozens of different visualizations.

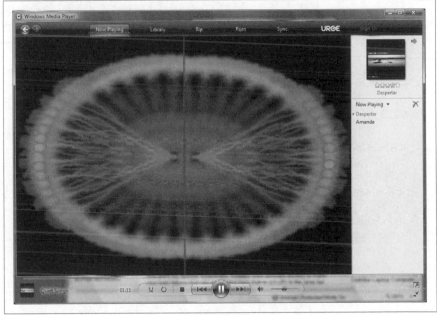

Figure 12-10. One of the many visualizations you can use with Windows Media Player

Plug-ins
These are add-ins that work in concert with Windows Media Player—for example, to add surround sound to Windows Media Player. You can configure existing plug-ins or click a link to go to a web site where you can download more plug-ins.

Library
This lets you switch among various libraries—for example, among all of your recorded music, recorded TV shows, videos, and pictures. It also lets you create playlists and add new media to any of your libraries.

Rip

This controls your options for when you "rip" music from a CD, that is, convert its audio CD tracks to digital files that you can play on Windows Media Player. Before you place a CD in your PC to rip music from it, set your options by clicking the bottom of the Rip button, where a down arrow will appear. When you select Format from the Rip menu, you can choose from the following audio types:

Windows Media Audio

This is the default type for ripping music. Microsoft claims that Windows Media Audio files are of a superior quality to MP3s ripped at the same bit rate.

Windows Media Audio Pro

The quality of sound produced by this file type is superior to that of Windows Media Audio. However, it is not supported by as many portable music devices as Windows Media Audio or MP3 files, and so it has not caught on to the same extent.

Windows Media Audio (variable bit rate)

Using this file type, you'll get smaller files when you record at the same bit rate as Windows Media Audio, but with the same general quality. When you use this standard, tracks will be recorded at lower bit rates than your chosen rate if recording them at that rate will not lead to a reduction in quality—for example, if you're listening to a less complex piece of music.

Windows Media Audio (lossless)

This file type produces files of higher sound quality than other Windows Media formats—*lossless* means that there is no loss of quality when you record music—but it produces files of much larger size.

MP3

This is the most common standard for recording and listening to music.

WAV (lossless)

This is a noncompressed digital format that is of a very high quality but produces files of an extremely large size.

Bit Rate, another choice on the Rip menu, lets you choose your recording bit rate. The available options will vary according to the audio type you've chosen. For example, if you select Windows Media Audio, you can choose bit rates between 48 Kbps and 192 Kbps, and if you select MP3, you can choose bit rates between 128 Kbps and 320 Kbps.

The Rip menu gives you several other options, including whether to start ripping music as soon as you place a CD in a drive, and whether to eject the CD after you're done ripping. With both of these settings enabled, you can stack up your CD collection next to your PC, and the only time you'll be distracted is when you need to insert a new disc.

Burn

This lets you choose the type of CD to burn—an Audio CD, or a data CD or DVD. You can also choose whether to automatically eject a disk after you're done burning. An especially important option on this menu is Apply Volume Leveling Across Tracks on Audio CD. If you're burning an audio CD with music on it from different sources, the volume at which the music has been recorded may vary, so on your recorded CD, some tracks may be too loud and others too soft. Volume leveling will make all of the tracks on the CD you burn the same general volume.

Click the Burn button to burn your CD.

Sync

This will let you synchronize with portable music players such as Play4Sure-compliant players, with Pocket PCs and Smartphones, and with Universal Serial Bus (USB) flash drives. If you have multiple devices, you can choose which one to sync, and you can control basic sync options for the device, such as whether to include files you've skipped in a previous sync.

When you sync a device, it will automatically sync all of your files. But if you want it to sync only some of your files, select the device from the Sync menu and then choose Set Up Sync. A screen such as that shown in Figure 12-11 appears. Select the playlists you want to sync, remove those you don't, and click Finish.

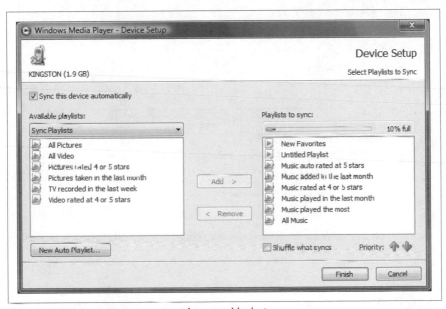

Figure 12-11. Customizing a sync with a portable device

At this point, you've set up a sync but not actually performed it. Click the Sync button to perform the sync.

URGE

This brings you to the URGE online music store, where you can buy and download music.

Sharing your media

If you have a network of two or more computers with Windows Vista on them and Windows Media Player enabled, you can set up the computers to share their media libraries so that you can play music from any other computer on the network with which you've enabled sharing. Windows Vista will automatically recognize any other Windows Vista PCs on your network, and a message will appear on the Taskbar telling you it's found another PC. Click it, and a notification screen appears; to share your libraries, click Allow.

You can also customize how your media is shared (Library → Media Sharing). Instead of Allow, click Sharing Settings, and the screen shown in Figure 12-12 appears. Check the box next to "Share my media to," highlight any PC you see, and click "Allow" to share libraries or "Deny" to deny library sharing.

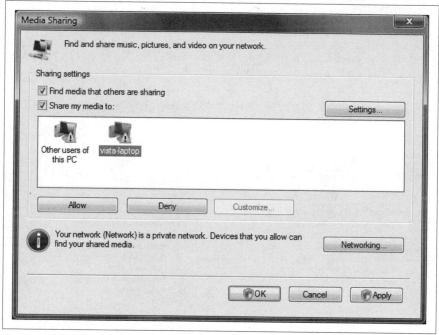

Figure 12-12. Selecting devices with which you want to share media libraries

You can also further customize how you'll share libraries with each PC. Click Settings (Figure 12-13), and you can choose which media types to share and even whether to share files above or below certain ratings.

Privacy issues

In the past, there has been some controversy over whether using Windows Media Player has any privacy implications. Because of that, Microsoft has built options into the program to let you decide how Windows Media Player contacts Internet servers.

The first time you start Windows Media Player, you'll get a choice of using the default settings (the Express option), or using custom settings, where you can customize your playback, privacy, and online store options (the Custom option). If you want to change your privacy options, select the Custom option. After you do that, the first screen you'll see is the Select Privacy Options screen, shown in Figure 12-14.

All of these settings have to do with how Windows Media Player interacts with various Internet services, and with Microsoft. Because these options send information back and forth between your PC and various servers and sites, and in some instances send information about your system to a server or site, some people worry about their privacy implications. Here are the settings you can change:

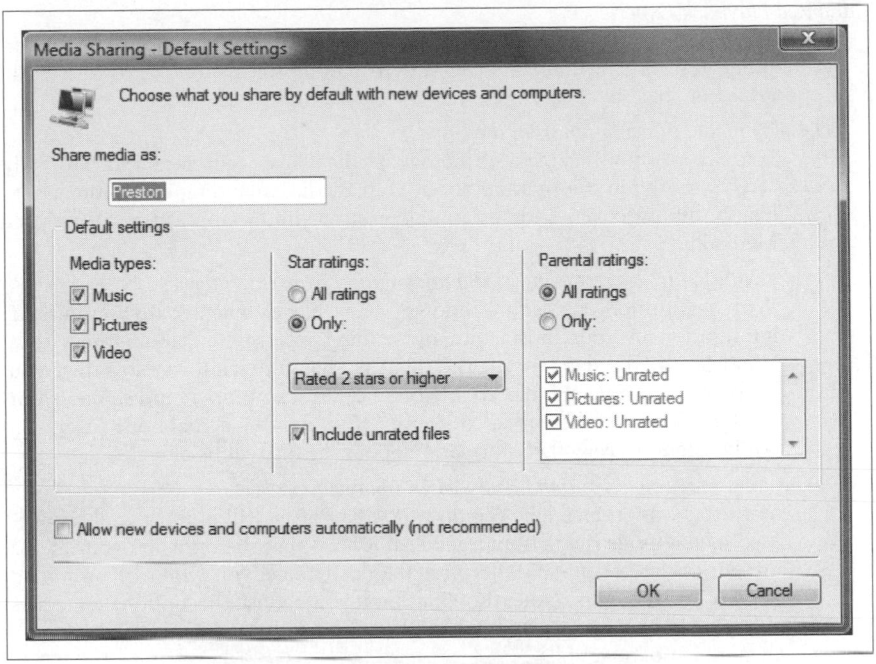

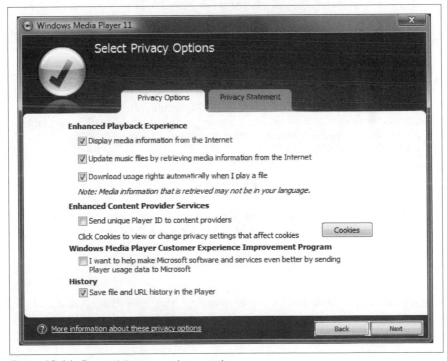

Figure 12-13. *Customizing how you share your media library*

Figure 12-14. *Customizing your privacy settings*

Enhanced Playback Experience

This section controls several settings related to how Windows Media Player communicates with media-related servers to handle the media on your PC. All options are enabled by default:

Display media information from the Internet

With this option enabled, Windows Media Player will communicate with servers to obtain information about your media, including song title, artist, length, album cover, and so on, and use that information inside Windows Media Player.

Update music files by retrieving media information from the Internet

With this option enabled, Windows Media Player will update any missing information in your music files by sending information about them to a Windows Media database. If the database has more information than you have—for example, if it has an artist name, a track number, and so on—your local music files will be updated from it. Note that the actual music itself will not be changed; only the information about the file will be altered.

Download usage rights automatically when I play a file

With this option enabled, Windows Media Player will automatically download media usage rights from a server if it finds that the rights on your media are out-of-date or missing. If you make this choice, you won't be prompted to look for the rights. Note, though, that if you choose this option, some files that you can normally play but that do not have these rights associated with them may no longer play.

Enhanced Content Provider Services

By default, this is not enabled because it has proved to be very controversial in the past. With this option enabled, Windows Media Player will report your music and movie use to Microsoft and will place a so-called "supercookie" on your hard disk that some privacy advocates claim can leave you open to privacy invasions, something that Microsoft disputes.

Windows Media Player Customer Experience Improvement Program

This option, not enabled by default, sends information about your hardware and your usage of Windows Media Player to Microsoft. Microsoft says it uses the information in order to improve the quality of Windows Media Player, and that all information is anonymous. Users worried about their privacy usually do not enable this option.

History

This option saves your file and URL history in Windows Media Player.

You can always change these options, even after the first time you've set up Windows Media Player. Click the down arrow at the bottom of any button on the toolbar and select More Options from the drop-down menu. Then click the Privacy tab, and you can make your changes.

The rest of the options in the custom setup control whether to download the URGE online music store, and other options.

Notes

- There are many options you can change for how Windows Media Player works. To select them, click the bottom of any button on the toolbar so that the down arrow and the drop-down menu appear, then choose Properties. Then click any tab to change the options—for example, click Burn to change burning options.

- If you encounter a video or audio file that Windows Media Player doesn't understand, you can usually add support for it by downloading the appropriate codec (compression/decompression driver). Right-click on the media file, select Properties, and choose the Details tab to view the name of the required codec (if available), or the file type. Then, use an Internet search engine (such as *http:// www.google.com*) to locate the codec installer. You can also try VLC, an open source media player that seems to be able to play any media type in existence. Find it at *http://www.videolan.org/vlc*.

- Use the Windows Update feature, discussed in Chapter 8, to install the latest drivers, codecs, and updates to Windows Media Player.

- You cannot use Windows Media Player with an iPod.

Windows Movie Maker   *\program files\movie maker\moviemk.exe*

Capture and edit video, and create video clips.

To open

Start → All Programs → Windows Movie Maker

Command Prompt → **moviemk** (you must be in the *movie maker* subdirectory to run this)

Description

Windows Movie Maker has been significantly beefed up from its Windows XP incarnation, and it is now a full-featured program for creating videos. The Windows XP and Windows Vista versions of it have become popular for creating videos uploaded to video-sharing sites such as YouTube (*http://www.youtube.com*).

The program can import video clips, graphics files, and sounds from a digital video camera, or from files on your hard disk or other PCs on your networks. With a digital video camera, you can create your own video clips from scratch. Windows Movie Maker (and most video editing software) can be quite complex, so I will include only an introduction here.

In Windows Movie Maker (Figure 12-15), on the lefthand side of the screen are the tasks you need to complete—in step-by-step order—to create a movie, beginning with importing various media, moving on to editing the movie, and finishing up with publishing it.

Here are the basics of each major step:

Import

You can import video from a digital video camera connected to your PC, via the USB or FireWire ports. You can also import video, pictures, or audio and music files from your PC, from PCs connected to your network, from storage devices attached to your PC, and from digital cameras connected to your PC. When you import any files, you'll see thumbnails of them in the central part of your screen. The currently highlighted video or clip appears on the large window on the right side of the screen, so you can display or view it.

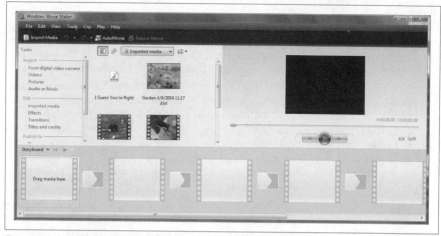

Figure 12-15. The beefed-up Windows Movie Maker, which lets you edit video clips and create movies

Once you've imported the videos and pictures, drag them to the storyboard at the bottom part of the screen (Figure 12-16) and drag each object into a frame.

Figure 12-16. Dragging a clip to the storyboard

If you want your movie to have a soundtrack, apart from the sounds within each individual video clip, drag a music file onto the storyboard. When you do this, a timeline appears (Figure 12-17), showing the music clip underneath and the frames above it. You can rearrange your clips and pictures by dragging them into different locations.

Figure 12-17. The timeline from which you can coordinate music with clips and pictures

Edit

Once you have your storyboard in place, you can edit the movie in these ways:

Effects

Adds effects to clips and pictures, such as rippling, blurring, aging, panning, pixelating, posterizing, and so on. Just drag the effect onto the clip or picture.

Transitions

Adds transitions (Figure 12-18) between clips and pictures, such as dissolves, cross-cuts, fading in and out, fanning, and so on.

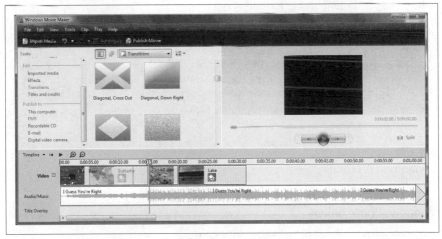

Figure 12-18. Adding transitions between clips, scenes, or pictures

Titles and credits

Adds titles and credits. You can add titles at the beginning, before clips, or on top of clips.

Use the controls at the bottom of the screen to play your movie and continue to add media, effects, transitions, and so on, until you have it the way you want. The actual video project consists of clips inserted into the storyboard. Using the magnify controls to the left of the timeline, you can zoom in for more precise work or zoom out to see more of the timeline at once.

To the left of the magnify controls is the storyboard/timeline link: click it to switch between the default Storyboard view (where each clip is the same size) and the more sophisticated Timeline view (where clips are sized relative to their duration). The Timeline view (the view with the numbers across the top) is much more intuitive and easier to use, as it shows a more accurate view of the project and allows more precise control when splitting.

The video preview, shown in the upper right, allows you to view the video project as it will appear when you're done. Click the Play button, or simply drag your mouse across the timeline to view any portion of the video project.

Publish To

Once you've gotten your movie the way you want it, click any of the links in this section to publish your movie to your computer, DVD, CD, and so on. If you publish to a DVD, it will launch Windows DVD Maker; if you publish to a recordable CD, it will burn it directly onto the CD.

There are other tools as well, notably the file menu across the top of the screen. A full description of those tools is beyond the scope of this book, but it will be worth your while to experiment with them.

You can also edit clips and graphics placed on the storyboard/timeline by right-clicking and making choices from the menu, including adding effects fading in and out, removing the graphic or clip, and so on.

Notes

- Windows Movie Maker supports a variety of video, graphics, and audio formats, allowing you to import media from a number of different sources into your projects. Suffice it to say, if there is a major (or not-so-major) format, Windows Movie Maker will be able to import it, with one very notable exception: QuickTime (*.mov*) files.
- When you delete items from Windows Movie Maker, it does not affect the original source files.

See also

"Windows DVD Maker"

Windows Photo Gallery   *\program files\Windows Photo Gallery\WindowsPhotoGallery.exe*

Organize, view, and edit pictures and video clips.

To open

Start → All Programs → Windows Photo Gallery

Command Prompt → `windowsphotogallery` (you must be in the *Windows Photo Gallery* subdirectory to run this)

Description

Windows Photo Gallery (Figure 12-19) is an organizational, viewing, and editing tool for handling digital pictures and video clips. It won't replace more powerful editing programs, but for most basic tasks such as viewing and organizing your clips, as well as for basic photo-editing tasks such as eliminating red eye, it's perfectly serviceable.

Figure 12-19. Windows Photo Gallery, for organizing pictures and video clips

When you load Windows Photo Gallery, you may notice that not all of your pictures and video clips are in it. That's because by default, it loads only pictures and videos from your Pictures folder (*\users\username\Pictures*). You can, however, add other folders, or even other individual pictures and clips, to it. To add folders, choose File → Add Folder to Gallery, or open Windows Explorer and drag a folder from Windows Explorer to Windows Photo Gallery. You can also add individual pictures and clips, or groups of them, by dragging them in.

The lefthand side of the screen lets you filter the pictures and videos you're viewing in a variety of different ways, including by tag, date, ratings, folder in which they're located, and so on.

Right-click any picture to display a menu that lets you accomplish a variety of tasks:

- Previewing the picture or clip in a kind of full-screen mode
- Opening the picture or clip in a graphics or video program or player
- Setting the file as your desktop background
- Adding tags
- Clearing the rating
- Rotating the picture
- Changing the time the picture was taken

- Copying, deleting, and renaming the picture or clip
- Viewing the file properties

To view a single picture or video, double-click it and it will be displayed as shown in Figure 12-20. The righthand side of the screen displays the file's details, such as size, resolution, date taken, rating, and tags. To add tags, click the Add Tags button.

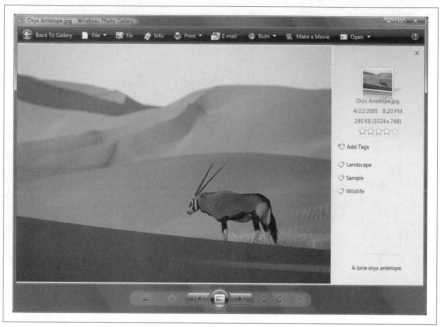

Figure 12-20. Viewing an individual picture in Windows Photo Gallery

Back on the main screen, to change the way Windows Photo Gallery displays pictures and clips, click the down arrow next to the thumbnail icon just beneath the toolbar. You have a variety of options, including tiling them, displaying them as thumbnails (the default) or as thumbnails with text, grouping or sorting them in many different ways (date taken, date modified, file size, and so on), and an odd kind of Table of Contents option that lists the filter you're currently using to summarize groups of files on the left side of the screen.

There's also a Search box that searches through filenames, properties, and tags.

The bottom of the screen sports CD-like controls. Press the large, central Play button to play a slideshow of the pictures and clips. When you do this, it takes over your PC and plays full-screen. You can pause the show, move forward or backward, and change a variety of playing options by clicking the Options button, where you can change the speed of the show, play or mute the music, and either shuffle or loop the pictures and videos. To stop the show and return to normal view, click Exit.

Also at the bottom of the Windows Photo Gallery screen, along with the Play, Forward, and Back buttons, are several other controls. The far-right magnifying glass icon lets you change the size of the displayed thumbnails; click it and move the slider to change the thumbnail size. There are also buttons for rotating and deleting any file you highlight.

The toolbar is a particularly important feature. Here is what each button does:

File

> This drops down a File menu and lets you do the normal tasks you would expect, such as copying, deleting, and renaming files. But it lets you do a lot more as well, including adding folders to the gallery and importing pictures from a camera or scanner. If you choose Share with Devices from this menu, you can share all the media in Windows Photo Gallery with other users on your network via file sharing, and find media from other PCs on the network. Oddly enough, there's also an option for changing your screensaver settings, even though Windows Photo Gallery has nothing to do with your screensaver.

> The Options choice lets you set global options for Windows Photo Gallery, including a variety of import settings for cameras, scanners, and CDs and DVDs, such as into which folder to import pictures and clips, and whether to prompt for tags when importing.

Fix

> This brings you to a new screen (Figure 12-21) that has a variety of basic photo-editing tools.

Figure 12-21. Windows Photo Gallery's photo-editing tools

You can use the following tools:

Auto Adjust

> Automatically adjusts both the contrast and the color.

Adjust Exposure

> Displays sliders that let you control the brightness and contrast individually.

Adjust Color

Displays sliders that let you control the color "temperature," tint, and saturation individually. The "temperature" control makes the picture appear either warmer (more reds) by moving its slider to the right, or cooler (more blues) by moving its slider to the left. The tint selection controls what is called a *color cast* in the pictures—the predominant color that makes the other colors in the picture appear to be inaccurate. The saturation slider makes the colors appear more or less vivid.

Crop Pictures

Gives you a variety of tools for cropping the picture. It includes a number of predetermined crop sizes, or lets you choose your own custom crop size.

Fix Red Eye

Fixes the dreaded, ghostly looking red center in the middle of people's eyes when a flash photograph is taken.

You can undo your changes by clicking the undo button at the bottom of the screen, and you can redo them by clicking the redo button.

Info

This displays a preview pane that gives you detailed information about the currently selected picture. If you want to add tags to the picture, in the preview pane click Add Tags, and type them in.

Print

From here you can either print or order photo prints to be made of the picture. If you choose to order photo prints, a wizard appears that first lets you choose which online photo site to use for ordering and then walks you through the process of uploading the picture to the site and ordering the print.

E-mail

This will attach the picture to an email, and it will shrink the size to make for a smaller attachment if you want. When you click the button, you'll first be presented with a screen (Figure 12-22) with suggested dimensions, and beneath that, the file size of the picture in kilobytes at those dimensions. Choose a different size from the drop-down list; when you do, the new file size in kilobytes will be displayed. After you choose the new size, a new email message will be created in your default email program, with the file attached to it.

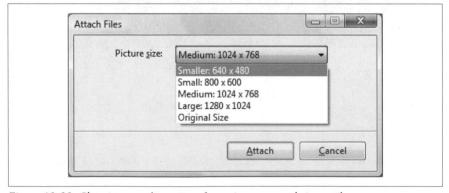

Figure 12-22. Choosing new dimensions for a picture to send via email

Burn

From here, you can choose to burn your pictures to disc, in either a video DVD or a data disc.

Make a Movie

This opens Windows Movie Maker, with your selected pictures or video clips imported into it. For details about making a movie, see "Windows Movie Maker," earlier in this chapter.

Open

This will open the selected picture or clip in any of the graphics- or video-editing programs on your PC.

Notes

- When you double-click on a graphics file, depending on what other graphics software is installed on your hard disk, the graphic may open inside Windows Photo Gallery or in another graphics program. If you have no other graphics program installed, graphics files will open in Windows Photo Gallery. But when you install another graphics program, that other program may change defaults so that files open in it instead. To change defaults for which files Windows Photo Gallery opens, and which other graphics programs open, select Start → Default Programs. For details about how to use the resulting screen, see "Default Programs Control Panel," in Chapter 10.

- Some applications that are not graphics programs but that include a graphics component may also change defaults so that graphics files open in them rather than in Windows Photo Gallery. For example, if you install Microsoft Office, *.tif* files will open in the Microsoft Office Document Imaging applet.

- If you've edited a file and decide that you want to undo all your changes, choose File → Revert to Original.

See also

"Paint" and "Windows Movie Maker"

13

The Registry

The Windows Registry is a database of settings used by Windows Vista and the individual applications that run on it. Knowing how to access and modify the Registry effectively is important for troubleshooting, customizing, and unlocking hidden features in Windows Vista.

An amazing amount of what you might assume to be "hardwired" into Windows—the locations of key directories, the titles of on-screen objects such as the Recycle Bin, and even the version number of Windows Vista reported in the Control Panel—is actually the product of data stored in the Registry. Change a setting in the Registry, and key parts of your system can be affected; for this reason, Microsoft passively discourages tampering by providing only minimal user documentation on the Registry Editor and no documentation at all on the structure of the Registry itself.

 Despite the enormous potential for harm, the Registry is fairly robust, and for every entry that you can wreak havoc by changing, there are hundreds that you can change with impunity. Nonetheless, you should back up the Registry files before making significant changes with the Registry Editor. See "Backing Up the Registry," later in this chapter, for details.

The Registry is normally consulted silently by the programs (such as Explorer) that comprise the Windows user interface, as well as by nearly all applications. Programs also commonly write varying amounts of data to the Registry when they are installed, when you make changes to configuration settings, or just when they are run. For example, a game such as FreeCell keeps statistics in the Registry on how many games you've won and lost. Every time you play the game, those statistics are updated. For that matter, every time you move an icon on your Desktop, its position is recorded in the Registry. All of your file type associations are stored in the Registry, as are all of the network, hardware, and software settings for

Windows and all of the particular configuration options for most of the software you've installed. The settings and data stored by each of your applications and by the various Windows components vary substantially, but more often than not, a given Registry setting will appear in plain English, making it relatively easy to decipher. There are also several advanced techniques that not only help to identify more obscure settings, but also allow you to use undocumented settings to uncover hidden functionality.

Microsoft provides the Registry Editor (*regedit.exe*), which is used to view and modify the contents of the Registry. Don't confuse the Registry with the Registry Editor; the Registry Editor merely reads and writes data in the Registry like any other Windows application. When you start the Registry Editor, you'll see a window similar to the one in Figure 13-1.

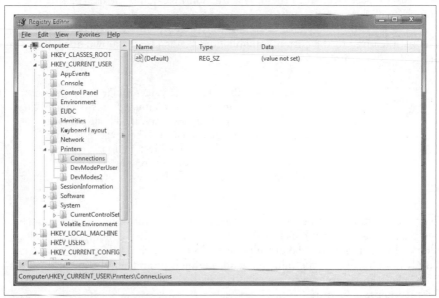

Figure 13-1. The Registry Editor, which uses a familiar interface to manipulate unfamiliar data

The organizational structure of the Registry is hierarchical, so Microsoft chose an interface familiar to anyone who has used Windows Explorer. As in Explorer, there are two panes: the folders (keys) are displayed in a cascading tree on the left, and the contents of the currently selected key appear on the right. Use the small right- and downward-facing triangle icons to expand and collapse the branches, respectively; cursor keys also work here.

Although the interface elements might appear familiar, the data that you manipulate with the Registry Editor is nothing like the files and folders you are used to dealing with in Explorer. Although you can certainly dive in and begin wading through the thousands of keys and values in the Registry, you're not likely to find anything of value until you arm yourself with a basic understanding of the way data is stored and organized in the Registry. And, of course, this is the focus of the next few sections.

What's in the Registry

Data in the Registry is stored in individual pieces called *values*. Every value has a name and is capable of holding one of several types of data. Values are grouped and organized in *keys*, which are represented by Folder icons in the Registry Editor. Keys can also contain other keys, thereby forming the basis for the hierarchy in the Registry. Like Explorer, the Registry Editor arranges the keys in a collapsible tree structure, allowing you to navigate through the branches to locate a particular key, and hence, all the values contained therein.

Often, in order to view or modify a certain key or value, you must follow a *Registry path*. A path is merely a series of key names, separated by backslashes (\), used to specify an absolute location in the Registry. For example, to navigate to HKEY_CURRENT_USER\Control Panel\Keyboard, simply expand the HKEY_CURRENT_USER branch by clicking on the right-facing triangle next to it, then expand the Control Panel branch, and finally click on the Keyboard key name to display its contents. The path leading to the currently highlighted key is always shown at the bottom of the Registry Editor window.

 It's easy to get confused about keys and values. In fact, value names sometimes appear at the end of a path, although this is mostly a holdover from the early days of the Registry. It's important to realize that only values can contain data, and keys are used only to organize values—just like files and folders in Explorer, respectively. Note that unlike folders in Explorer, keys never appear in the right pane of the Registry Editor window, even though they can contain other keys.

Every key contains a value named (Default). If the default value contains no data, you'll see (value not set), as in Figure 13-1. If a given key contains other values, they will be listed below the default value. To modify the data stored in a value, simply double-click on the value name, or highlight it and select Modify from the Edit menu. To rename a value, which is not the same as changing its data, highlight it and press F2 or right-click it and select Rename.

For example, if I wanted to change the default font used by Notepad, I could navigate to HKEY_LOCAL_MACHINE\SOFTWARE\Microsoft\Notepad\DefaultFonts, double-click on the ifFaceName value, and use the edit dialog box shown in Figure 13-2 to type the name of a different font to use.

The data stored in the ifFaceName value is a string of text, which means that ifFaceName is a *string value* (the most common type). There are six types of values in all, each having a common name and a symbolic name (shown in parentheses in the following list):

String values (REG_SZ)
> String values contain strings of characters, more commonly known as text. Most values discussed in this book are string values; they're the easiest to edit and are usually in plain English. In addition to standard strings, there are two far less common string variants, used for special purposes:

Figure 13-2. Editing a string value to change the default font for Notepad

Multistring values (REG_MULTI_SZ)
Contain several strings (usually representing a list of some sort), concatenated (glued) together and separated by null characters (ASCII code 00). The dialog used to modify these values is the same as for binary values. Note that the individual characters in REG_MULTI_SZ keys are also separated by null characters, so you'll actually see three null characters in a row between multiple strings.

Expandable string values (REG_EXPAND_SZ)
Contain special variables into which Windows substitutes information before delivering to the owning application. For example, an expanded string value intended to point to a sound file may contain %SystemRoot%\media\startup.wav. When Windows reads this value from the Registry, it substitutes the full Windows path for the variable, %SystemRoot%; the resulting data then becomes (depending on where Windows is installed) c:\windows\media\startup.wav. This way, the value data is correct regardless of the location of the Windows folder.

Binary values (REG_BINARY)
Similarly to string values, binary values hold strings of characters. The difference is the way the data is entered. Instead of a standard text box, binary data is entered with hexadecimal codes in an interface commonly known as a *hex editor*. Each individual character is specified by a two-digit number in base 16 (e.g., 6E is 110 in base 10), which allows characters not found on the keyboard to be entered. See Figure 13-3 for an example. Note that you can type hex codes on the left or normal ASCII characters on the right, depending on where you click with the mouse.

Note that hex values stored in binary Registry values are displayed in a somewhat unconventional format, in which the lowest-order digits appear first, followed by the next-higher pair of digits, and so on. In other words, the digits in a binary value are paired and their order reversed: the hex value 1B3 thus needs to be entered as B3 01. If you want to convert a binary value shown in the Registry Editor to decimal, you'll have to reverse this notation. For example, to find the decimal equivalent of 47 00 65 6e, set the Windows Calculator to hexadecimal mode and enter 6e650047, and then switch to decimal mode to display the decimal equivalent, 1,852,112,967.

Binary values are often not represented by plain English and, therefore, should be left unchanged unless you either understand the contents or are instructed to change them by a solution in this book.

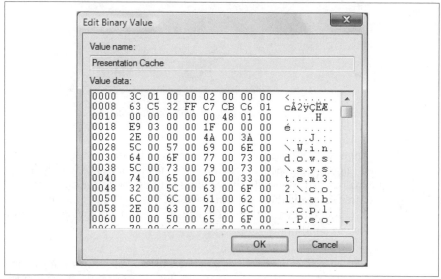

Figure 13-3. Binary values are entered differently from the common string values, but the contents are sometimes nearly as readable

DWORD values (REG_DWORD)

Essentially, a DWORD is a number. Often, the contents of a DWORD value are easily understood, such as 0 for no and 1 for yes, or 60 for the number of seconds in some timeout setting. A DWORD value is used only where numerical digits are allowed; string and binary types allow anything.

In some circumstances, the particular number entered into a DWORD value is actually made up of several components, called *bytes*. The REG_DWORD_BIGENDIAN type is a variant of the DWORD type, where the bytes are in a different order. Unless you're a programmer, you'll want to stay away from these types of DWORD values.

The DWORD format, like the binary type, is a hexadecimal number, but this time in a more conventional representation. The leading 0x is a standard programmer's notation for a hex value, and the number is properly read from left to right. The equivalent decimal value is shown in parentheses following the hex value. What's more, when you edit a DWORD value, the edit dialog box gives you a choice of entering the new value in decimal or hex notation.

Even if you're not a programmer, you can figure out hexadecimal values pretty easily with the Windows Calculator (*calc.exe*; see Chapter 10). Just enter the number you want to convert and click the Hex radio button to see the hexadecimal equivalent; 435 decimal is equal to 1B3 hex.

If you aren't sure about the meaning of a specific Registry value, don't be afraid to experiment. Experimenting might include editing a value with the Registry Editor, but it might be easier or safer to work from the other end: open the application whose data is stored there (e.g., a Control Panel applet), change a setting, and watch how the Registry data changes. In this way, you can derive the meaning of many binary-encoded values. Note that although the Registry data will often change immediately, you may need to press F5 (Refresh) to force the Registry Editor to display the newly affected data. It's a good idea, though, to make a backup copy of a Registry key before making any changes. See "Adding and Deleting Registry Keys and Values" and "Exporting and Importing Registry Data with Patches," later in this chapter, for details.

QWORD values (REG_QWORD)
    This is much like a DWORD value, with one difference: it is a 64-bit value, rather than a 32-bit value like DWORD.

In addition to editing values, you can create new ones. For example, to create a new DWORD value, highlight a key for which you want to create a new value, and then in the Registry Editor choose Edit → New → DWORD Value. This brings up a very important point: a Registry entry is superfluous unless a program actually reads it. You can enter new keys and values all you like, with the only consequence being that you've bloated your Registry. (Note that there are sometimes undocumented Registry values that are meaningful to a program but that are not normally present; adding them to the Registry can make useful changes; see *Windows Vista Annoyances* by David Karp [O'Reilly] for several examples.) The chief concern is in deleting or modifying existing entries; the odds of randomly creating a value that an application might be looking for are extremely small.

You can take advantage of this fact by occasionally leaving yourself notes in new Registry values. For example, before modifying a value, you might place a backup of its data in a new value in the same key. The application will ignore it, and it may come in handy to have a record of the original value!

A final note: any changes you make in the Registry Editor are saved automatically and immediately; there's no "undo" command in the Registry Editor, and the automatic Registry backups made by Windows are of little use when small changes are made. The saving grace is the use of Registry patches, discussed later in this chapter.

Adding and Deleting Registry Keys and Values

The Registry Editor, as mentioned earlier, is the primary tool for viewing, modifying, and deleting data in the Registry. And as you'll see later in this chapter, it also allows you to conveniently import and export data (via Registry patches), which you can think of as another form of data entry.

Basic data entry in the Registry Editor is fairly simple. In order to type data, you must first create a value to hold it. Depending on your goal, you may also need to create a new key in which to place the value.

To create a new key or value, use Edit → New. The key or value then appears within the currently selected key, with the name New Key or New Value #1, respectively. A new string value will have the null string as its value; a new binary value will show the following message in parentheses: "(zero length binary value)." A new DWORD value will show up as zero: 0x00000000 (0). You can then edit that value (see later in this chapter) to change it. New keys aren't created empty, either. They all contain the (Default) value described in the preceding section.

To delete a key or value, select it and click Edit → Delete, or simply press the Delete key. But be warned, there's no undelete, so you might want to first write out the branch containing the key you're about to delete as a *.reg* file (see "Backing Up the Registry" and "Exporting and Importing Registry Data with Patches," later in this chapter). Or, you can use Edit → Rename to rename the value or key. Because applications access values and keys by their names, renaming has the effect of disabling or "hiding" the item from the application that uses it, while preserving its data.

To edit a value, double-click on its icon or name, or highlight it and use Edit → Modify. You will see an edit box appropriate to the value type. When editing a string value, the Registry Editor provides a standard text box, in which you can type text as well as copy and paste (by right-clicking on the text, or by using Ctrl-C, Ctrl-X, and Ctrl-V). Binary values have a more complicated and less familiar edit dialog, which allows data entry via hex codes on the left, or plain text on the right. Finally, DWORD values have a simpler edit interface, providing only for entry of a single number (in either hex or decimal format). Cut, Copy, and Paste work in DWORD and Binary dialogs as well. See the preceding section, "What's in the Registry," for more details on the different types of values.

Unfortunately, automation in the Registry Editor is virtually nonexistent. For example, you can't copy and paste whole keys or values like you might expect (given the familiar Explorer-like interface), but you can copy key and value *names* to the Clipboard by pretending you're going to rename them, and then pressing Ctrl-C to copy. Another useful tool is the Copy Key Name command on the Edit menu, which copies the full path to the selected key to the Clipboard (very handy for writing this book, for example). It doesn't copy the contents of the key, nor does it include the selected value, however.

If you want to duplicate an existing value, double-click it and select all of the data in the Edit window (see Figure 13-4).

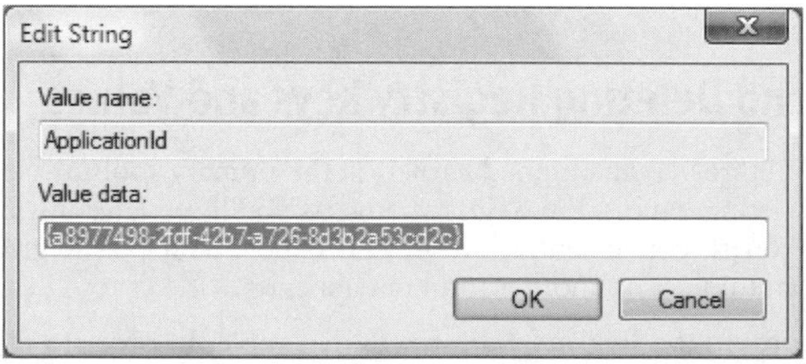

Figure 13-4. Copying an existing Registry value

Ctrl-C will copy the data to the Clipboard. Then create a new value, being sure to match the type (string, binary, or DWORD) of the original value. Type the desired value name, double-click the new value to edit it, and then use Ctrl-V to paste the copied data into the edit window.

Duplicating values can be handy not only when using an existing value as a template for a new value, but also whenever you're going to make changes to an existing value. You can make little "inline backups" by creating a new value (*whatever.bak,* for instance) and pasting in the old value data before you change it. This might seem a little tedious, but it can prevent future headaches if you're about to change a complex value whose format you aren't completely sure you understand, or even if you anticipate having to roll back a value to its previous state for some reason.

Unfortunately, there's no easy way to copy a key and all of its contents in the Registry Editor. If you want to copy an entire key and all its values, you'll have to do it one value at a time. It's usually much easier to export the key, edit the resulting file with a text editor, and then import the edited file. (See "Exporting and Importing Registry Data with Patches," later in this chapter.)

In addition to the Edit menu, you may find the Registry Editor's context menus convenient. Right-clicking on a key in the left pane gives a context menu with Expand or Collapse, New, Find, Delete, Rename, and Copy Key Name. (Expand displays a key's subkeys. It will be grayed out if there are no subkeys to display, and it will be replaced with Collapse if said subkeys are already showing.) Right-clicking with a value selected in the right pane gives a context menu with Modify, Delete, and Rename. Right-clicking in the right pane with no value selected gives a context menu with New (to create a new value). Press Shift-F10 to open a context menu without having to use the mouse.

Registry Protection in Windows Vista

Many of the changes made in Windows Vista have to do with safety and security, and with ensuring that the operating system doesn't accidentally become damaged. Toward that end, in Windows Vista, only accounts with administrator privileges can make changes to the Registry. This affects not just editing the Registry directly, but also taking an action that will change the Registry, such as installing software.

So, what happens when a standard user wants to edit the Registry or make a change that affects the Registry? Windows Vista handles that in several ways:

- When a standard user tries to run the Registry Editor, User Account Control (UAC) springs into action, asking for an administrator password. If one is provided, the Registry Editor can be used and changes made. If none is provided, the Registry Editor will not be allowed to run, and no changes will be made.

- When a standard user installs software, UAC will ask for an administrator password. If the user provides one, the software will make the appropriate changes to the *%SystemRoot%* and *%ProgramFiles%* folders and to the Registry.

- If a legacy application fails to work correctly with UAC, Vista will use a new feature called *file and Registry virtualization*. This will create virtual *%System-Root%* and *%ProgramFiles%* folders, and a virtual HKEY_LOCAL_MACHINE Registry entry. These virtual folders and entry are stored with the user's files. So the Registry itself—as well as the *%SystemRoot%* and *%ProgramFiles%* folders—are not altered in any way, so system files and the Registry are protected.

Organization of the Registry

The Registry is enormous and complex; a full Registry might easily contain 15,000 keys and 35,000 values. Entire books have been written about it, and I can't do it justice here. The purpose of this section is to arm you with a basic understanding of how the Registry is organized, not to document individual values in detail or suggest changes you might want to make with the Registry Editor.

The top level of the Registry is organized into five main *root* branches. By convention, the built-in top-level keys are always shown in all caps, even though the keys in the Registry are not case-sensitive. (For example, HKEY_CURRENT_USER\SOFTWARE\MICROSOFT\Windows is identical to HKEY_CURRENT_USER\Software\Microsoft\Windows.) Their purposes and contents are listed in the following summaries. Note that the root keys are sometimes abbreviated for convenience in documentation (although never in practice); these abbreviations are shown in parentheses. Subsequent sections discuss the contents of the root keys in more detail.

HKEY_CLASSES_ROOT (HKCR)
> Contains file types, filename extensions, URL protocol prefixes, and registered classes. You can think of the information in this branch as the "glue" that binds Windows with the applications and documents that run on it. It is critical to drag-and-drop operations, context menus, double-clicking, and many other familiar user interface semantics. The actions defined here tell Windows how to react to every file type available on the system.
>
> This entire branch is a mirror (or symbolic link) of HKEY_LOCAL_MACHINE\SOFTWARE\Classes, provided as a root key purely for convenience.

HKEY_CURRENT_USER (HKCU)
> Contains user-specific settings for the currently logged-in user. This entire branch is a mirror (or symbolic link) of one of the subkeys of HKEY_USERS (discussed shortly). This allows Windows and all applications to access and store information for the current user without having to determine which user is currently logged in.
>
> An application that keeps information on a per-user basis should store its data in HKEY_CURRENT_USER\Software and put information that applies to all users of the application in HKEY_LOCAL_MACHINE\SOFTWARE. However, what Windows applications consider user-specific and what applies for all users on the machine is somewhat arbitrary. Like many aspects of Windows, the Registry provides a mechanism for applications to store configuration data, but it does little to enforce any policies about how and where that data will actually be stored.

HKEY_LOCAL_MACHINE (HKLM)

Contains information about hardware and software on the machine that is not specific to the current user.

HKEY_USERS (HKU)

Stores underlying user data from which HKEY_CURRENT_USER is drawn. Although several keys will often appear here, only one of them will ever be the active branch. See the discussion of HKEY_USERS, later in this chapter, for details.

HKEY_CURRENT_CONFIG (HKCC)

Contains hardware configuration settings for the currently loaded hardware profile. This branch works similarly to HKEY_CURRENT_USER in that it is merely a mirror (or symbolic link) of another key. In this case, the source is HKEY_LOCAL_MACHINE\SYSTEM\CurrentControlSet\Hardware Profiles*XXXX*, in which *XXXX* is a key representing the numeric value of the hardware profile currently in use. On a system with only a single hardware profile, its value will most likely be 0001.

HKEY_CLASSES_ROOT (HKCR)

At first glance, Windows Vista seems very object-oriented. Files, folders, and devices are represented by icons that respond differently to various actions such as single-, double-, right-, and left-clicks. But in a true object-oriented system, the object itself contains the knowledge of how to respond to events such as mouse clicks.

By contrast, Windows Vista performs much like the Wizard of Oz, not with true object-oriented magic, but with complex machinery hidden behind a screen. The knowledge of how the Explorer should treat each object is stored in the Registry in a complex chain of interrelated keys.

Much of the system's behavior depends on filename extensions. A filename extension, the string of letters that appear after the last dot in a filename, is the primary mechanism Windows uses to determine a file's type. Therefore it's essential that each filename extension accurately reflect the file type. For example, a file named *stuff.txt* will be treated by Windows as a text file. If you were to rename the file to *stuff.old*, it would still be a text file, but Windows would treat it differently: it would have a different icon in Explorer, a different description in Explorer's Details view, and a different action when double-clicked. This illustrates how fragile and fallible Windows' file types system is, how some applications can so easily register themselves as the default for any given file type, and how stupid it is that filename extensions are hidden in Explorer by default.

When you open HKEY_CLASSES_ROOT, the first thing you'll see is a very long list of file extensions known to the system, from something such as *.ai* (Adobe Illustrator Document) to *.zip* (ZIP archive). What follows is a list of *document type keys*, which typically contain the actual file type information. These two sets of keys make up the file types in Windows Vista.

Here's how it works: a file extension key (one that has a dot at the beginning of its name) has its default value set to the name of a document type key (and thus "points" to that key). For example, HKEY_CLASSES_ROOT\.txt, which corresponds to all files with the *.txt* extension, has its default value set to txtfile. Lower down, the HKEY_CLASSES_ROOT\txtfile key contains several keys that describe files of this type and instruct Windows what to do when you right-click on a *.txt* file and select options such as open and print.

You may notice that the HKEY_CLASSES_ROOT\.log key also has its default value set to txtfile; in this way, many extension keys can point to a single file type key, and hence, a single file type can encompass several different filename extensions.

Applications frequently add new file types to the Registry, registering themselves with certain filename extensions. In the case of the txtfile file type, Notepad is registered as the default application when Windows Vista is first installed; thus, when you double-click on a *.txt* or *.log* file, the file is opened in Notepad.

A common conflict occurs when two or more applications find themselves fighting to be the default application. For example, should a file with the *.htm* extension be opened by Firefox or Microsoft Internet Explorer? If you use Internet Explorer, the value name (Default) will have the value data htmlfile. If you then install Firefox, the .htm key will have the value name (Default) with the data FirefoxHTML. If you then look at either of those two class definition keys (FirefoxHTML or htmlfile), you'll see a different chain of subkeys. Although both Firefox and Internet Explorer know how to handle HTML files, they use a different set of internal instructions for figuring out how to display or edit the files, which icon to display for the file, and so on.

The detailed subkeys and values that appear under the class definition and document type keys start to get really confusing. (See *Windows Vista Annoyances* for an in-depth examination of file types.)

Because each program may record and retrieve different keys, it's very hard to generalize about them. The best I can do is mention some of the kinds of keys you might see associated with a particular file extension subkey or class definition subkey. Here are some of the most common keys and values you may find in HKEY_CLASSES_ROOT:

CLSID

Class identifier for an ActiveX component, a unique, 16-byte number in the following format {aaaaaaaa-bbbb-cccc-dddd-ffffffffffff}, in which each letter represents a hexadecimal digit. (That's a sequence of 8, 4, 4, 4, and 12 hex digits, with a hyphen between each group of digits and the whole thing enclosed in curly braces.)

CLSID appears both as a subkey of many file type definition keys and as a class definition key in its own right. That is, the key HKCR\htmlfile might have a subkey CLSID with the data value {25336920-03F9-11cf-8FD0-00AA00686F13}, but there's also a key called HKCR\CLSID with the subkey {25336920-03F9-11cf-8FD0-00AA00686F13}, which in turn has the data value HTML Document. The first entry is simply a pointer to the second, which contains the actual class data. You must always be on the lookout for this kind of indirection.

CLSID keys don't necessarily correspond to filename extensions or file types. The HKEY_CLASSES_ROOT\CLSID branch, for example, contains a huge list of class ID keys, which each represent a different component. Most of the components are of little interest to mere mortals, but some correspond to visual elements in Windows Vista.

Content Type

The data in this value is the Multipurpose Internet Mail Extension (MIME) descriptor for the corresponding file type. This key will typically appear in the file type key for Internet-related file types such as GIF and JPEG. It's used by email programs that support attachments and web browsers, such as Firefox and Internet Explorer, to help them identify downloaded files.

DefaultIcon

The location (usually a pathname and an optional "icon index" within the file) of the file containing the default icon to use for a file type or CLSID. Note that there may be more than one default icon for a given file type. A good example is the Recycle Bin, which shows a different icon when it is empty and when it is full. In cases such as this, the program knows to copy its icon for the appropriate state to the DefaultIcon (Default) value. In other cases, though, a DefaultIcon may be specified in more than one place (e.g., under a document type key and under an associated CLSID key).

Shell

Contains subkeys that define actions (open, edit, print, play, and so forth) appropriate to the object. These actions appear on the context menu for the associated file type, among other things.

A common structure that uses the Shell key is Shell\Open\Command, where the default value in the Command key is the executable filename for a registered application. The command line often ends with "%1" (including the quotes), which represents a command-line parameter passed to the application (familiar to those who use batch files). For example, when you double-click on a .txt file (say, c:\stuff\junk.txt), Windows replaces "%1" in the command line with the name of the file, resulting in the following command being run: notepad c:\stuff\junk.txt. If you were to select Run from the Start menu, and type that command, Notepad would appear and open the file. Note that the quotes around the %1 accommodate any spaces in the filename; otherwise, Windows would interpret a single filename with a space as two distinct filenames, and you'd get an error.

You might also find the key, Shell\Open\ddeexec, which contains information necessary for a Dynamic Data Exchange (DDE) conversation. DDE is the mechanism with which Windows communicates with applications that are already open. For example, Windows might send a DDE message to an application to tell it to print a file after opening it. Microsoft insists that DDE is obsolete, but you'd never know it from the important role DDE plays in Windows file types.

You'll see the same split between command-line options and DDE using the Explorer interface to file associations, via Start → Default Programs → Associate a file type or protocol with a program. Some actions will list a command line; others will use DDE. If you're not a programmer with access to the DDE documentation for a particular application, you may find this difficult to follow at times.

You may find that a particular Shell branch doesn't contain all the actions for a particular file type. This is because these items may be specified in three other places. First, the ShellEx key contains more advanced actions. Second, the HKEY_CLASSES_ROOT* key contains additional actions that apply to all file types. Third, some actions available to all files, such as the Delete and Properties actions, can't be removed and therefore don't appear in this key.

ShellEx

This is short for *Shell Extensions*. These keys contain entries that supplement a file's context menu (via the ContextMenuHandlers subkey), a file's Properties sheet (via the PropertySheetHandlers subkey), and a file's drag-and-drop behavior (via the CopyHookHandlers subkey). These extra features are too complex to be simple Shell\Command structures; instead, these keys simply point to registered CLSIDs (described earlier) and special programs that perform advanced features. For example, if you install the WinZip utility (*http://www.winzip.com*), all ZIP files will have extra items in their context menus (click with the right mouse button) and their drag-and-drop menus (drag with the right mouse button) that handle certain ZIP operations. Also, movie files (*.avi*, *.asf*, and *.mpg*) and Word documents (*.doc*) all have an extra Summary tab in their Properties sheets that displays additional information about the contents of the file.

ShellNew

Defines whether the file type will appear on Explorer's New menu. If the ShellNew key is present inside a file type or file extension key, the file type will appear in the list when you select New from Explorer's File menu. In most cases, this key will be empty, if it exists at all. (Contrast the enormous number of file types defined in the Registry with the much smaller number that appear on the New menu.)

Command

Contains a command line to create the new file, used only for Briefcases and Windows Shortcuts (the *.bfc* and *.lnk* extensions, respectively), as well as any other file type that can't be created merely by copying a template (see next).

Filename

Contains the name of a file "template" to copy to the new location. Its value data may contain a complete pathname, but if it's just a filename (e.g., *netscape.html*, *winword.doc*, or *winword8.doc*), it will be found in the directory *Windows\ShellNew*. If the Filename value is not present, Windows will create an empty, zero-byte file.

Nullfile

If present, instructs Windows not to create the file at all but instead to launch a program that will create the file when first saved. Some file types (such as *.bmp* files, which may contain data in any one of a number of related formats, as specified by binary header data within the file itself) are described by the NullFile value. NullFile has the empty string ("") as its value data.

Data

Contains binary data that needs to be written to the new file. This might, for example, be some kind of binary header data.

Before leaving HKEY_CLASSES_ROOT, two other keys are worthy of note:

HKCR*

Contains information that will be applied to all files, regardless of their extension. Be sure to check out the ShellEx entries here.

HKCR\Unknown

Describes, via its Shell\OpenAs\Command subkey, what will happen to a file whose type is unknown, either because the file has no extension or because the particular extension has not yet been registered with Windows. By default, if you double-click on a file Windows categorizes as unknown, a dialog appears allowing you to choose the correct program to use, thereby automatically creating new file type keys in the Registry.

HKEY_CURRENT_USER (HKCU)

The Registry separates settings specific to individual users from global Windows settings applicable to all users. In the FreeCell example earlier in this chapter, each user of the machine can have his own separate won/lost statistics because the program keeps these statistics in the HKEY_CURRENT_USER branch of the Registry. If it instead used HKEY_LOCAL_MACHINE, all users would share the same statistics.

This entire branch has the same structure as HKEY_USERS\.DEFAULT (discussed shortly) and is a mirror of the HKEY_USERS entry corresponding to the current user, and its contents always correspond to those of the currently logged-in user.

By default, there are 13 top-level subkeys in HKCU: AppEvents, Console, Control Panel, Environment, EUDC, Identities, Keyboard Layout, Network, Printers, SessionInformation, Software, System, and Volatile Environment. Here are descriptions of some of the most important subkeys:

HKCU\AppEvents

The associations between events and system sounds are kept here. There are two branches: EventLabels and Schemes. EventLabels contains the labels that will be used for the sounds; Schemes contains the pointers to the actual sounds.

Schemes has two main subkeys: Apps and Names.

Applications that use sounds can create their own subkey under Schemes\ Apps, or they can add sounds into the default list, which is kept in the subkey Apps\.Default. If they add their own subkey, the sounds will show up in a separate section of the sounds list in Control Panel → Sounds. So you might see a subkey such as Mplayer or Office, because these applications add some of their own sound events in addition to the default sounds. Note that unless Windows or an application is specifically designed to look for an event listed here, any new events you might add will have no effect.

Schemes\Names is where Windows stores the settings for each sound scheme. When you change the sound scheme using the drop-down Scheme list on Control Panel → Sounds, the appropriate scheme is copied into .Default.

HKCU\Console

This stores data for the console, which is what hosts all command-line applications, including the Command Prompt. So, for example, it contains data about the font size, screen colors, buffer size, and so on, used by the *cmd.exe* command prompt. To see the kinds of information stored here, open the Command Prompt, right-click on the window's title, and select Properties. You'll see tabs for all of the different options for the Command Prompt; each option has a corresponding value in HKCU\Console. For example, FontSize corresponds to the choice you make for font size on the Font tab.

HKCU\ControlPanel

Data from several of the Control Panel applets is stored here, particularly Accessibility and some of the Display settings. The names don't match up cleanly to the names used in the Control Panel, but you can usually figure out what's what by going back and forth between the Registry Editor and the target Control Panel applet. For example, HKCU\ControlPanel\Accessibility maps to Control Panel → [Appearance and Personalization] → Ease of Access Center, but HKCU\ControlPanel\Cursors maps to Control Panel → Mouse → Pointers.

As is typical in the convoluted world of the Registry, some entries point somewhere else entirely. For example, HKCU\ControlPanel\International controls a wide variety of settings related the specific international version of Windows you're using—for instance, a Locale value, such as 00000409, which is the standard code for what the Control Panel calls "English (United States)." There are many other similar settings here, such as for your local currency (sCurrency), and so on. It also controls your date and time format, and similar settings. If you use the Registry Editor's Find function to trace this value, you'll eventually find the scattered locations of many of the individual values that Control Panel → [Clock, Language, and Region] → Regional and Language Options brings together in one place.

 This example illustrates a key point: there's usually little reason to poke around in the Registry for values that have a convenient user interface in the application. The exception is where the interface has limited which values can be entered—making the Registry a tool you can use for greater control (at the expense of the convenience of a user interface)—as well as where there is simply no interface for some of the more obscure settings.

HKCU\Environment

The *environment* is a small chunk of memory devoted to storing a few system-wide settings, primarily for use with command-line applications, but still used by Windows Vista. In Windows 9x and Windows Me, information was added to the environment via the *AUTOEXEC.BAT* file (now obsolete). Environment variables in Windows Vista are set via Control Panel → [User Accounts and Family Safety] → User Accounts → Change my environment variables. The upper section of this dialog box (user variables for *username*) is where user-specific variables are entered, and they are thus stored in the HKCU\Environment Registry key. The lower box (system variables) is for system-wide, user-independent variables and is stored in HKLM\SYSTEM\ CurrentControlSet\Control\SessionManager\Environment. Note also that the HKCU\Volatile Environment key, which contains temporary environment variables, resets each time Windows is started.

HKCU\keyboard layout

This key is used only if you have installed more than one keyboard layout via Control Panel → [Clock, Language and Region] → Keyboards and Languages. A Preload subkey lists a separate subkey for each installed language, with subkey 1 specifying the default language.

HKCU\Software

Probably the most useful key in HKEY_CURRENT_USER, this key contains subkeys for each vendor whose software is loaded onto the machine and, within each vendor's area, subkeys for each product. The keys stored here are supposed to contain only user-specific settings for each software application. Other settings, which are common to all users of software on the machine, are stored in HKLM\SOFTWARE.

The structure of this branch (and particularly of the Microsoft\Windows\ CurrentVersion branch under both) is described later in this chapter, in "HKCU\Software and HKLM\SOFTWARE."

HKEY_LOCAL_MACHINE (HKLM)

HKLM contains hardware settings and global software settings that apply to all users. It has five top-level subkeys: HARDWARE, SAM, SECURITY, SOFTWARE, and SYSTEM. Each of these keys is stored in a separate hive file (see "Hives," later in this chapter):

HKLM\HARDWARE

The data stored in this branch is used by Windows Vista to load drivers and initialize resources for the various hardware components of your computer. All of the settings here are more easily accessible through the Device Manager (Control Panel → [System and Maintenance] → System → Device Manager); there's little need to edit them directly. However, you may find it interesting to snoop around in this branch and see the various pieces of information that are stored for your CD Writer, your scanner, your hard disk, and your processor. The HKLM\HARDWARE\DESCRIPTION\System\CentralProcessor\0 key tells me that my CPU's vendor identifier is "GenuineIntel," for example.

HKLM\SAM

This key stores data for the Security Accounts Manager (SAM), used only if your Windows Vista system is providing domain services. You'll find little reason to ever mess with the settings in this branch, and as most of the data is in binary format, you'll have a hard time deciphering it anyway. The information stored in this key is managed primarily through User Manager for Domains (on Windows Server). You can access all of the settings here through the Local Security Policy Editor (secpol.msc).

HKLM\SOFTWARE

> Probably the most useful key in HKEY_LOCAL_MACHINE, this key contains subkeys for each vendor whose software is loaded onto the machine and, within each vendor's area, subkeys for each product. The keys stored here are supposed to contain global system settings for each application, common to all users on the machine. Other settings, specific to each user, are stored in HKCU\SOFTWARE.
>
> The structure of this branch (and particularly of the Microsoft\Windows\CurrentVersion branch under both) is described later in this chapter, in "HKCU\Software and HKLM\SOFTWARE."

HKLM\SYSTEM

> The settings in this branch primarily handle multiple hardware profiles. Windows uses this data together with HKLM\HARDWARE to handle drivers and Plug and Play management for all hardware on the system.

HKCU\Software and HKLM\SOFTWARE

As noted earlier, both HKEY_CURRENT_USER\Software and HKEY_LOCAL_MACHINE\SOFTWARE are structured similarly. Each area has a branch for each manufacturer that has software installed on the system, and most vendors will have keys that appear in both areas. In each manufacturer key, there will be one or more subkeys, corresponding to each of that manufacturer's applications that are installed. For example, under the Adobe key, you might see an entry for Photoshop and one for Illustrator, assuming both of those applications are installed on your system.

In theory, the HKCU branch should include information that is configurable on a per-user basis (which is the case, for instance, with a software package with a per-user license or per-user customization). The HKLM branch should include software that is standard for all users. In practice, though, it doesn't seem to be as consistent as that. Some data might seem to be placed in the wrong branch, and other data might be placed in both branches. Fortunately, this doesn't pose much of a problem in practice, partly because the vast majority of systems will have only a single user account, but more important, because the only practical rule as to the location and organization of data in the Registry is that it is consistent with the application that uses it. For example, because WordPerfect knows where to look for its own settings, it doesn't really matter that they aren't in a place the casual user would expect. Basically, if you're looking for something, look in both branches (HKLM and HKCU).

Because this is a book about Windows Vista and not about the third-party applications that might be installed in it, the primary focus of this discussion is on the Microsoft\Windows\CurrentVersion branch, located in both HKCU and HKLM. There is a ton of information in these two areas, and the following keys represent the more useful and intelligible data:

..\Microsoft\Windows\CurrentVersion

> This key contains seven values describing some basic Windows settings, such as the folder location for Program Files, and the default folder location for your media. There are also many keys underneath here. Note the use of REG_EXPAND_SZ values, described earlier in this chapter.

`..\Microsoft\Windows\CurrentVersion\App Paths` (HKLM *only*)

This branch lists a path for many application executables (Microsoft and otherwise) that are installed in nonstandard locations (i.e., not in \, *Windows*, or *Windows\Command*). It is the reason why you can successfully type a command name such as excel or winword at the Run prompt, but not at the command prompt, unless you add *Program Files\Microsoft Office\Office* to your search path. They have listed their paths individually under this key.

 If you have an application that installs a shortcut on the Start menu but doesn't let you type its name at the Run prompt, add a key for it in the App Paths key (using an existing entry as a template). For example, you can add a PHOTOSHOP.EXE key, with the values:

> (Default) "C:\Program Files\Adobe Photoshop\Photoshop.exe"
>
> Path "C:\Program Files\Adobe Photoshop"

The result is something like the Path environment variable, except that the target is a specific executable rather than an entire folder.

`..\Microsoft\Windows\CurrentVersion\Explorer\ShellFolders`
`..\Microsoft\Windows\CurrentVersion\Explorer\User Shell Folders`

Specifies the locations of many of the standard Windows system folders, including Desktop, Programs, Send To, Start Menu, Startup, and Templates.

This branch really brings home the extent of the mutability of Windows. Even the directory names that Explorer relies on, such as *Users\username\ Desktop*, are not hard-wired. So Explorer doesn't know anything about *c:\ Users\username\Desktop*. All it knows is that it can get the name of the folder it's supposed to use as the Desktop from the Registry. Most of these values probably shouldn't be changed.

The ShellFolders and User Shell Folders keys each exist in the HKCU and HKLM branches. If you're looking for a particular setting, make sure you look in all four keys; whenever a key seems to be duplicated in more than one place, it's good practice to make changes in both places. Note also that the REG_EXPAND_ SZ data type (explained earlier in this chapter) is used for some of the values.

`..\Microsoft\Windows\CurrentVersion\Explorer\Desktop\NameSpace` (HKLM *only*)

Contains keys named with the CLSID of system icons that appear on the Desktop, such as the Recycle Bin, My Documents, and My Network Places. Because these are simply pointers to objects defined elsewhere in the Registry (such as Windows Shortcuts), they can be safely deleted (one method of removing the respective icons from your Desktop).

`..\Microsoft\Windows\CurrentVersion\Explorer\FindExtensions` (HKLM *only*)

Contains keys corresponding to the various entries in the Start menu's Search menu and in the Explorer Search Bar. Although you can't indiscriminately add items here (unless you're a programmer), you can remove unwanted entries.

`..\Microsoft\Windows\CurrentVersion\Explorer\MyComputer`

Contains several keys that relate to the Computer window. The NameSpace subkey, for example, contains keys pointing to CLSIDs of various optional components that might appear in your Computer window. To identify any unlabeled CLSID that shows up here or anywhere else, copy the entire CLSID string to the Clipboard and paste it into the Registry Editor's Search box.

..\Microsoft\Windows\CurrentVersion\Explorer\StartMenu *(HKLM only)*

Contains several keys that relate to the seemingly hardcoded entries that appear in the Start Menu → My Computer window. The NameSpace subkey, for example, contains keys pointing to CLSIDs of various optional components that might appear in your My Computer window. To identify any unlabeled CLSID that shows up here or anywhere else, copy the entire CLSID string to the Clipboard and paste it into the Registry Editor's Search box.

..\Microsoft\Windows\CurrentVersion\Internet Settings

Contains a whole slew of settings for Internet Explorer and the Internet Options dialog in the Control Panel. You'll find settings in this key for just about everything, from Passport settings to the filename of the bitmap used for the background of Internet Explorer's toolbar.

..\Microsoft\Windows\CurrentVersion\Run *(HKLM only)*
..\Microsoft\Windows\CurrentVersion\RunOnce

In these keys, you'll find a list of programs that Windows loads at startup. Note that these aren't the same as those found in the Startup folder in your Start menu, but they work similarly. The format is simple enough: the data in each value contains the full path- and filename of a program to be launched, and the name of the value is merely a reminder as to the purpose of the entry. You can safely add any program you like, or remove entries you'd like to stop loading automatically. Note that values placed in either of the RunOnce keys (HKCU or HKLM) will only be run the next time Windows starts, and will be deleted immediately thereafter. There are several advantages of these keys over the Startup folder. For example, they're more concealed and therefore more tamper-resistant.

 Another way to look for programs that run on startup—and to disable them if you want—is to use the System Configuration Utility (*msconfig.exe*). For details, see Chapter 11.

In addition to the preceding specific keys, a few paradigms show up again and again, such as the following:

../MRUList

MRU stands for Most Recently Used. Anytime Windows shows you a "history" of the last few things you've typed into a field or otherwise launched, those items are stored in a key in the Registry. A quick search for MRUList in the Registry Editor will yield dozens of instances.

Knowing the location and use of a particular MRU list has several advantages. For example, you can write a script to clear a given list to erase your "footprints," so to speak. Or, perhaps you could create a Registry patch that would preload a drop-down list with a set of long names you wanted to search for or open repeatedly.

MRUList values contain a series of letters; for each letter, you'll find a value in the same key that is a lookup table into the MRUList. For example, you might find an MRUList whose value is bdca. Right next to it, you'd find four values (a, b, c, and d) with the corresponding filenames or search terms (the MRUList specifies the order in which they appear). For example, in HKEY_CURRENT_USER\Software\Microsoft\Windows\CurrentVersion\Explorer\FileExts\.jpg\OpenWithList, a might correspond to *mspaint.exe*, b to *PhotoViewer.dll*, and so on.

../Namespace
Keys named Namespace usually contain values or subkeys that point to CLSIDs (16-byte identifiers to registered program components), which, in effect, instructs Windows to load those components. For example, if a CLSID for the Recycle Bin is listed under the Desktop\Namespace key, it corresponds to the Recycle Bin object appearing on the Desktop. Sometimes, removing these entries will have the effect of removing the corresponding objects, but not always. I recommend experimentation with some degree of caution.

HKEY_USERS (HKU)

Despite its name, this branch does not contain the Registry entries for all users configured on the system. This is because user information is loaded when a user logs in, and only one user can be logged in at any given time. Rather, it contains only information for the currently logged-in user as well as a template for new user profiles.

This branch contains several keys, although only one of them is mirrored as HKEY_CURRENT_USER (discussed earlier). Usually, it's the one that looks like S-*x-x-xx-xxxxxxxxx-xxxxxxxxxx-xxxx*, where the long string of *x*s is the Windows serial number. If it's not clear which key is the active one, just create a new key or value in one of the branches called test. Then, move up to HKEY_CURRENT_USER and press F5 to refresh the view. If the test entry you just added shows up here as well, you've found the active key; if not, delete test and try again in a different key.

You use the .DEFAULT key as a template for creating new users, and unless you want to affect new user settings, you should leave this key alone. In fact, there's little reason to ever play with the HKEY_USERS branch, as all applicable settings for the active user are more easily accessible through HKEY_CURRENT_USER.

This design prevents one user from easily viewing or changing another user's settings.

HKEY_CURRENT_CONFIG (HKCC)

As noted earlier, HKCC is mirrored from the HKEY_LOCAL_MACHINE\SYSTEM\CurrentControlSet\Hardware Profiles*XXXX*, in which *XXXX* is a key representing the numeric value of the hardware profile currently in use. On a system with only a single hardware profile, its value will most likely be 0001. This branch contains hardware configuration settings for the currently loaded hardware profile.

Hives

You can think of HKEY_USERS and HKEY_LOCAL_MACHINE as the only true root keys, because the Registry's three other root keys are simply symbolic links, or mirrors, of different portions of these two. This means that these two branches are the only ones that actually need to be stored on your hard disk, and this is where *hives* come into play.

For every branch in HKEY_LOCAL_MACHINE, a corresponding hive file is stored in your *\Windows\System32\config* folder. For example, HKEY_LOCAL_MACHINE\Software is stored in a file called *software* (no filename extension). Because new branches can be added to HKEY_LOCAL_MACHINE, new hives can be generated at any time. Most systems will have the following hives: *sam*, *security*, *software*, *components*, and *system*.

Not all Registry data is stored on your hard disk, however. Some keys are dynamic, in that they are held only in memory and are forgotten when you shut down. An example of a dynamic branch is HKEY_LOCAL_MACHINE\HARDWARE, which is built up each time Windows is started (an artifact of Plug and Play). Only nondynamic branches are stored in hives, so you won't see a hive called *hardware*.

The branches in HKEY_USERS, one for each configured user, are similarly stored in hives. The hive file for each user is called *ntuser.dat*, and it is located in *\Users\username*.

Knowing which files comprise the Registry is important only for backup and emergency recovery procedures (see "Backing Up the Registry," next) and for troubleshooting (and so that you don't accidentally delete them). The storage mechanism is quite transparent to the Registry Editor and the applications that use the Registry; there's no reason to ever edit the hive files directly. If you want to migrate a key or a collection of keys from one computer to another, don't even think about trying to copy the hive files. Instead, use Registry patches, discussed later in this chapter.

Backing Up the Registry

Given that the Registry is an essential component of Windows, and a damaged Registry can make Windows totally inaccessible, a good backup of the Registry is one of the most important safeguards you can employ.

Windows Vista does not come with a distinct mechanism that automatically backs up the Registry, which means you'll have to implement one of your own to fully safeguard your Windows environment.

 When System Restore creates a restore point, it captures a snapshot of your Registry, so if you use a restore point, you'll be able to return to the state of your Registry at a specific point in time. But it's an all-or-nothing proposition; you can't pick and choose individual Registry settings to restore.

The Registry is stored in certain files (see the preceding section, "Hives") on your hard disk, so you can create a backup by simply copying the appropriate files to another location.

 The CompletePC Backup and Restore feature of Windows Vista (Control Panel → [System and Maintenance] → Back up your computer) creates an image of your PC's current state, including the Registry. So performing that backup is a good idea as well as backing up the Registry itself. (For details, see Chapter 11.)

When you start Windows, the information in the Registry is loaded into memory. While Windows is running, some changes may not be physically written to the Registry files until you shut down your computer; others, such as those made by the Registry Editor, are usually written immediately. For this reason, if you've made any substantial changes to the contents of the Registry, you may want to restart Windows *before* backing up the Registry to ensure that the files on the disk reflect the most recent changes.

The other consequence of using the Registry files is that you may not be able to simply use Explorer to copy them while Windows is running, and you certainly won't be able to overwrite them. The workaround is to attempt these measures when Windows isn't running, which means using a Vista boot disk.

Although it's very useful to make backups of the Registry on your hard disk, it certainly can't prepare your computer for an actual disaster. If your hard disk crashes or becomes infected with a virus, or if your computer is stolen or dropped out of an eight-story building, those Registry backups on your hard disk won't do you much good. The most effective Registry backup is simply a matter of making a copy of all hives on your hard disk and keeping that copy somewhere other than inside your computer.

If you back up your entire system regularly, such as to a CD, DVD, hard drive, or other backup device, you should ensure that the backup software you use specifically supports safeguarding the Registry. The Registry will fit easily on a removable drive (CD, DVD, flash drive, etc.). In addition, most modern backup software includes a feature to back up the Registry, as does the Backup and Restore tool in Windows Vista.

One useful shortcut is a *local backup*. If you plan on modifying a specific value or key, it's wise to back up just that key, because restoring it in the event of a problem is much less of a hassle than attempting to restore the entire Registry. See the following section for details.

Exporting and Importing Registry Data with Patches

Hives have an arcane format, making direct editing all but futile. Fortunately, the Registry Editor conveniently supports the import and export of any number of keys and values with *Registry patches*. Patches (*.reg* files) are ordinary text files that can contain anything from a single key to a dump of the entire Registry.

You can create Registry patches with the Registry Editor or a standard text editor, such as Notepad. You can also use Notepad to view and modify patches, and then use the Registry Editor to reimport the patch.

Patches have many practical uses, including creating local backups of portions of the Registry as a preventive measure before editing keys (see the preceding section). You can create a Registry key on one computer and apply it on another, which is useful for migrating a single setting or a whole group of settings to any number of Windows systems. Patches can allow easier editing than with the Registry Editor, and they certainly afford quicker and more flexible searches.

To create a Registry patch, highlight the key you want to export and select File → Export. Once you've chosen a filename, the selected key, any subkeys, and all their values and respective data will be saved in a single file with the *.reg* extension. In most cases, you wouldn't want to select My Computer to export the entire Registry, because HKLM is enormous and you wouldn't want to reimport it in any case.

> Before making any changes to a Registry key, do a quick backup by exporting the key. Depending on what changes you've made, the Registry might not be identical after reimporting the key, but at least you'll have a record of what the key looked like before the changes.

Importing *.reg* files isn't quite as simple as creating them, partly because of the concept of merging and partly because of the potential for harm. It's important to note that the contents of a Registry patch are merged with existing keys; they don't simply overwrite them. So, if a given key contains four keys (apple, pear, banana, and peach), and you apply a Registry patch (pointing to the same key) that contains four keys (apple, pear, banana, and pomegranate), the resulting key will have five keys (apple, pear, banana, peach, and pomegranate). The existing values and keys will indeed be overwritten with those in the patch, but any additional values and keys in the Registry will remain intact.

Stop! Do Not Double-Click on This File!

The default action for double-clicking on a *.reg* file is not to edit the file, as you might expect, but to merge it into the Registry. The Registry Editor does warn you before committing a patch, and then informs you that the patch was successful. So before you double-click any *.reg* file, make sure that you want to apply the patch, not edit the file.

The format of *.reg* files is similar to that of *.ini* files, rather than anything resembling the way data is displayed in the Registry Editor. A section begins with the full path of a key in square brackets, like this: [section name]. This is followed by any number of values, each of the format name="data" (the default value appears as @="value"). Then, the next key (if any) is listed, followed by all the values *it* contains. The order of the keys, as well as the order of the values in each key, is irrelevant. However, if you were to move a key from one section to another, it would, in effect, be moving the value from one key to another.

The quotes around value data are used only for string values; binary and REG_ EXPAND_SZ values are prefixed with the keyword hex: and appear without quotes. Similarly, DWORD values are preceded by dword: and appear without quotes. Any backslashes in value data (found most often in folder and Registry paths) are doubled to distinguish them from the backslashes in key names.

Lastly, the first line in every Registry patch created in Windows Vista will be Windows Registry Editor Version 5.00, followed by a blank line. (The same holds true for Windows XP and Windows 2000.) Patches created in Windows 95, 98, and Me will instead begin with Registry Editor4, also followed by a blank line. There doesn't appear to be any difference in the treatment of these two types of patches by the Registry Editor.

Here is an excerpted Registry patch:

```
Windows Registry Editor Version 5.00

[HKEY_CURRENT_USER\Software\mozilla.org\Mozilla\0.9.2 (en)\Main]
"Program Folder Path"="C:\\Documents and Settings\\All Users\\
 Start Menu\\Programs\\Mozilla\\"
"Install Directory"="C:\\Program Files\\Mozilla\\"

[HKEY_CURRENT_USER\Software\Microsoft\Internet Explorer\Main]
"NoUpdateCheck"=dword:00000001
"Show_ChannelBand"="No"
"Display Inline Images"="yes"
"Show_ToolBar"="yes"
"Check_Associations"="no"
"SmoothScroll"=dword:00000001
"Play_Animations"="yes"
"Play_Background_Sounds"="yes"
"Display Inline Videos"="yes"
"Print_Background"="no"
```

You may notice that these two keys are in different manufacturer branches and wouldn't appear next to each other in the Registry. If you think about the way Registry patches are created, you'll realize that the one shown here couldn't have been created in a single step. Instead, two different Registry patches were created, and the contents of one were cut and pasted into the other using a plain-text editor. As long as you remove the redundant header, this is perfectly acceptable. In fact, it can be a very convenient way to implement several Registry changes in one step.

Extra-credit question: given the structure of file types discussed earlier in this chapter, how would you create a single Registry patch that contains all the necessary information to register a new file association on any computer? Could you use such a patch to restore your preferred file type settings if another application were to ever overwrite them?

Five Cool Things You Can Do in Your Registry

Armed with your new understanding of the Windows Vista Registry, you're no doubt ready to get in there and start exploring. Hopefully, this chapter has provided the "lay of the land" you need to get and keep your bearings in the otherwise confusing wilderness of the Registry. Although I don't have the kind of room in this book that it takes to make you an expert, I would like to send you on your way by pointing out some interesting landmarks—in other words, five cool changes you can make in your own Registry. (For more Registry hacks, see my upcoming book, *Windows Vista Hacks*, from O'Reilly.)

Open a Command Prompt from the Right-Click Menu

The command prompt is useful for a variety of down-and-dirty tasks, such as mass-deleting or renaming files. But if you find yourself frequently switching back and forth between Windows Explorer and the command prompt, there's help—you can easily open a command prompt using the right-click menu.

For example, let's say you want to open the command prompt at the folder that's your current location. Normally, that takes two steps: first open a command prompt, and then navigate to your current folder. However, there's a quicker way: add an option to the right-click context menu that will open a command prompt at your current folder. For example, if you were to right-click on the *C:\My Stuff* folder, you could then choose to open a command prompt at *C:\My Stuff*.

In the Registry Editor, go to HKEY_LOCAL_MACHINE/Software/Classes/Folder/Shell. Create a new key called Command Prompt. For the default value, enter whatever text you want to appear when you right-click on a folder—for example, **Open Command Prompt**. Create a new key beneath the Command Prompt key called Command. Set the default value to Cmd.exe /k pushd %L. That value will launch *Cmd.exe*, which is the Windows Vista command prompt. The /k switch puts the prompt into interactive mode—that is, it lets you issue commands from the command prompt; the command prompt isn't being used to issue only a single command and then exit. The pushd command stores the name of the current directory, and the %L uses the name of that stored directory to start the command prompt at it. Exit the Registry. The new menu option will show up immediately. Note that it won't appear when you right-click on a file—it shows up only when you right-click on a folder.

Change the Ribbons Screensaver

Inexplicably, Windows Vista screensavers such as the Ribbon screensaver don't allow you to change how they work—for example, to change the number or width of the ribbons. But you can change their options, using the Registry. Here's how to change the Ribbons screensaver to make it use a larger number of ribbons, and make each ribbon much thinner.

In the Registry Editor, go to:

```
HKEY_CURRENT_USER\Software\Microsoft\Windows\CurrentVersion\Screensavers\
Ribbons
```

Create a new DWORD called NumRibbons and give it the hexadecimal value of 00000100. Next, create a new DWORD called RibbonWidth and give it the hexadecimal value of 3c23d70a0. Exit the Registry. The Ribbons screensaver will now have the new settings. To restore the old settings, delete the DWORDs. (For more screensaver hacks, see my upcoming book, *Windows Vista Hacks*, from O'Reilly.)

Registry Editor Remembers Where You Were

Each time you open the Registry Editor, it automatically expands the branch you had open the last time the Registry Editor was used, but no others. So, if you find yourself repeatedly adjusting a particular setting and then closing the Registry Editor (such as when implementing the preceding tip), make sure the relevant key is highlighted just before the Registry Editor is closed, and that key will be opened next time as well.

Note also the Favorites menu, which works very much like the one in Internet Explorer, allowing you to bookmark frequently accessed Registry keys. Although it's useful, I find the existence of such a feature in a troubleshooting tool like the Registry Editor to be more than a little eerie.

Change the Registered Users and Company Names for Windows Vista

When Windows Vista is installed, a user and company name are entered. Unfortunately, there is no convenient way to change this information after installation. Surprise—you can do it in the Registry! Just go to:

```
HKEY_LOCAL_MACHINE\Software\Microsoft\Windows NT\CurrentVersion
```

The values you need are RegisteredOwner and RegisteredOrganization, both of which you can change to whatever you'd like. You may notice that the Registry key containing these values is in the Windows NT branch, rather than the more commonly used Windows branch. Don't worry, both branches are used in Windows Vista. The less-used Windows NT branch contains more advanced settings, mostly those that differentiate the Windows 9x and Windows NT lines of operating systems.

Some Handy Registry Navigation Shortcuts

The Registry has thousands of keys and values, which makes finding a single key or value rather laborious. Luckily, there are a few alternatives that will greatly simplify this task.

First, you can simply search the Registry. Start by highlighting the key at the top of the tree through which you want to search, which instructs the Registry Editor to begin searching at the beginning of that key. (To search the entire Registry, highlight "Computer.") Then, use Edit → Find, type in what you're searching for, make sure that all the "Look at" options are checked, and click Find Next.

Another shortcut is to use the keyboard. Like Explorer, when you press a letter or number key, the Registry Editor will jump to the first entry that starts with that character. Furthermore, if you press several keys in succession, all of them will be used to spell the target item. For example, to navigate to:

HKEY_CLASSES_ROOT\CLSID\{20D04FE0-3AEA-1069-A2D8-08002B30309D}

start by expanding the HKEY_CLASSES_ROOT key. Then, press C + L + S quickly in succession, and the Registry Editor will jump to the CLSID key. Next, expand that key by pressing the right-facing arrow, or by pressing the right arrow key, and press { + 2 + 0 (the first three characters of the key name, including the curly brace), and you'll be in the neighborhood of the target key in seconds.

14

The Command Prompt

The point-and-click graphical user interface (GUI) revolutionized the way we use computers, eliminating the need to remember cryptic commands and type them at the unfriendly *C:>* prompt. But there are still times when the Command Prompt interface is the quickest and fastest way to perform some tasks—and, in fact, times when it is the *only* way.

Although it's not readily apparent, the Command Prompt is still an integral part of Windows Vista. Some of the programs that come with Windows don't have corresponding shortcuts in the Start menu or Control Panel and must be started with some form of the Command Prompt. And most other applications, such as Notepad and Windows Explorer, have *command-line parameters*, special options that you can specify only if the program is started from the Command Prompt. And then there are programs, such as Telnet, that are still entirely command-line-based.

Understanding the Command Prompt in all of its forms not only is helpful in getting a better idea of how Windows works, but also can open up new ways of accomplishing tasks that would otherwise require repetitive pointing and clicking. Disk Operating System (DOS) was the command-line-only operating system run by early PCs, and Windows was merely an application that ran on top of DOS. Windows NT, the predecessor to Windows XP, was Microsoft's first version of Windows that did not rely on DOS. However, in Windows Vista, as well as in Windows NT, 2000, and XP, the Command Prompt is still made available as a standalone application.

Later in this chapter, you'll find complete documentation on batch files, which you can use to automate repetitive tasks by incorporating a list of commands into a single script that you can type like a command at the Command Prompt, or even double-click in Explorer.

Using the Command Line

The premise of the Command Prompt is simple enough: commands are typed, one at a time, at a blinking cursor. The commands are then issued when you press the Enter key. After the command has completed, a new prompt is shown, allowing you to type additional commands.

To run the Command Prompt, type:

```
cmd
```

at Start Search or in the Address Bar of Windows Explorer.

Some commands are fairly rudimentary, requiring only that you type their names. Other commands are more involved and can require several options (sometimes called arguments or command-line parameters). For example, you use the del command (discussed later in this chapter) to delete one or more files; it requires that you specify the name of the file after the command, like this:

```
del /p myfile.txt
```

Here, *myfile.txt* is the filename to be deleted and /p is an extra option used to modify the behavior of del (it requires confirmation before it will delete each file). The fact that this usage is not limited to internal command prompt commands (such as del) is what makes the command line (but not necessarily the Command Prompt application) such an important part of Windows Vista's design. For example:

```
notepad myfile.txt
```

is what Windows executes behind the scenes, by default, when you double-click the *myfile.txt* icon in Explorer. Notepad (discussed in Chapter 10) is effectively a "command" here. If you type the filename of any existing file at the Command Prompt, it instructs Windows to launch that file. This works for applications, Windows Shortcuts, batch files, documents, or any other type of file; the only requirement is that the file be located in the current working directory (see "cd or chdir," later in this chapter) or in a folder specified in the path (also discussed later in this chapter).

Specifying a filename as an argument when launching Notepad (such as *myfile.txt* in the preceding example) from the Command Prompt instructs Notepad to open that file. Throughout this book, you'll see references to a component's command-line syntax that documents these otherwise hidden features. Because every program and command has its own set of command-line options, it's best to get a feel for the way they work in general rather than trying to commit them all to memory.

If you've executed a command that takes a long time to complete, such as one that displays a great deal of information on the screen, you can usually interrupt it by pressing Ctrl-C.

Open the control menu of any open Command Prompt window (click the little icon in the top left of the window or press Alt-Space bar) and select Properties to customize the look and feel of the Command Prompt window (see Figure 14-1).

An important option here is Layout → Screen Buffer Size → Height, which controls the number of lines kept in memory; this enables you to scroll up to view a history of your entire session. This is useful, for example, if you're looking at long directory listings. Note that this is not the same as Options → Buffer Size, which contains a "most frequently used" list of typed commands; use the up and down arrow keys at the prompt to cycle through them, or press F7 to have an old-school character-mode menu pop up with your entire command history.

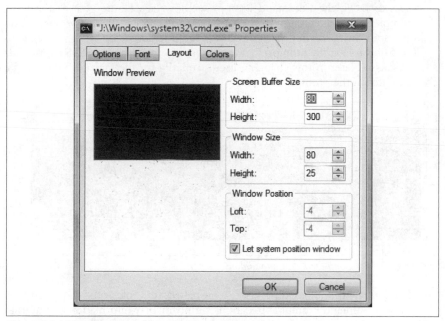

Figure 14-1. Setting options for the Command Prompt

Copy and paste operations are also possible at the Command Prompt, but not using the traditional keyboard shortcuts; Ctrl-X, Ctrl-C, and Ctrl-V won't work here. If QuickEdit is enabled (Properties → Options → QuickEdit mode), you can highlight text at any time with the mouse, copy it to the Clipboard by pressing Enter, and paste it by clicking anywhere in the window with the right mouse button. If QuickEdit is disabled (the default), right-clicking will display the Edit menu; select Mark to begin highlighting text and then go to Edit → Copy or simply press Enter to copy the text to the Clipboard.

Finally, the prompt itself is usually accompanied by a folder name representing the current working directory. Note that the term *directory* is synonymous with *folder* and is used throughout this chapter only because it is customary when discussing the Command Prompt.

See "Command Prompt," later in this chapter, for more information on the *cmd.exe* application and its command-line parameters. Of special interest is the /e parameter, which enables or disables "command extensions," which are additional features documented throughout this chapter.

Command Prompt Choices

Windows Vista provide three different components, all essentially different implementations of the command-line interface. These three components work similarly, but there are some important differences and limitations:

Command Prompt (cmd.exe)
> Commonly referred to as a *DOS box* because of its visual and functional likeness to DOS, the Command Prompt window (see Figure 14-2) is the most complete implementation of the Command Prompt in Windows Vista. You can start any program, GUI- or command-line-based, by typing its executable filename at the prompt. In addition, a variety of internal DOS commands (discussed later in this chapter), used primarily for file management, can be executed at the prompt.

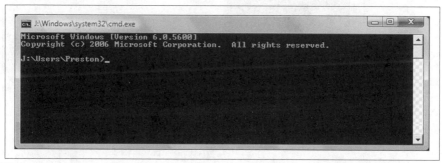

Figure 14-2. The Command Prompt window

If a command-line-based program is launched, it is run in the same window. Many Command Prompt applications simply display information and quit; in this case, you'd be returned to the prompt immediately after the program output.

An important distinction between the Command Prompt and the alternatives that follow is that the Command Prompt maintains context between commands. Each instance of the command interpreter runs in its own session, each with its own "environment." The environment includes such information as the current directory, the search path (the directories in which the command interpreter looks for the commands whose names you type), and the format of the prompt. Some commands, once issued, change the environment for subsequent commands. The most obvious example of this is when you type a sequence of commands, like this:

```
C:>cd \stuff
C:\Stuff>notepad myfile.txt
```

This command sequence couldn't be carried out at either the Start Search box or the Address Bar. Because they execute only one command at a time and then exit, the context is lost between each command. Concepts such as "change directory," therefore, have no meaning.

But the Command Prompt has limitations as well. Unlike the Address Bar or Start → Run, if you type a web address (URL) or the name of a folder at the

---

Command Prompt, you'll get a "not recognized" error. However, if you prefix the URL with **start**, as in **start www.oreilly.com**, you'll be able to launch the URL.

Note that Windows Vista also includes *command.com*, the Command Prompt application found in Windows 9*x*/Me. Although visually and functionally similar to *cmd.exe*, it's included for legacy support only. *cmd.exe* is more sophisticated and has native support for long filenames. *command.com*, on the other hand, runs under a virtualized 16-bit environment using *ntvdm*, the NT Virtual DOS Machine. And it does, through some kind of Windows sleight of hand, support long filenames. However, there are some things it can't handle as well as *cmd.exe*. For example, *cmd.exe* has no problem working with filenames that have spaces in them, but *command.com* needs you to use the 8+3 name:

```
C:\Temp>mkdir "Zip Files"

C:\Temp>command
Microsoft(R) Windows DOS
(C)Copyright Microsoft Corp 1990-2001.

C:\TEMP>cd "Zip Files"
Parameter format not correct - "Zip

C:\TEMP>dir /x
 Volume in drive C has no label.
 Volume Serial Number is A08C-22D0

 Directory of C:\Temp

10/24/2006  06:36 PM    <DIR>                           .
10/24/2006  06:36 PM    <DIR>                           ..
10/24/2006  06:36 PM    <DIR>          ZIPFIL~1     Zip Files
               0 File(s)              0 bytes
               3 Dir(s)   19,739,947,008 bytes free

C:\TEMP>cd ZIPFIL~1

C:\TEMP\ZIPFIL~1>
```

Start → Run

You can run any program by typing its executable filename here, as shown in Figure 14-3, just like in a Command Prompt window. However, in the case of command-line-based programs, the context is lost every time a new program is launched. Internal Command Prompt commands, such as CD and DIR, discussed later in this chapter, are not recognized here or in the Address Bar.

 The Start → Run box isn't visible by default in Windows Vista, but there is a way to turn it on. Right-click the Taskbar and choose Properties → Start Menu. Then click Customize next to the Start Menu entry, check the box next to the Run command, click OK, and then OK again. Windows XP's old Run box will now be available from the Start menu. You can also launch the Start → Run box by pressing Windows Key-R.

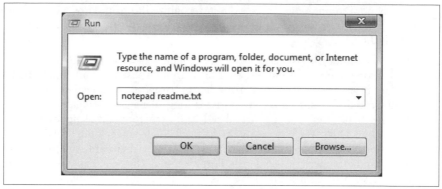

Figure 14-3. The Start → Run dialog

Unlike the Command Prompt, you can type a web address (URL) here to open it in the default web browser, or any folder name to open it in an Explorer folder window. If you're using the Command Prompt, though, you can preface a URL or folder name with **start** and you'll be able to launch the URL or open the folder.

Start → Run is commonly used to start programs, which is an alternative to wading through Start → Programs or opening a new Command Prompt window. However, if you've enabled the Address Bar, there's little need for Start → Run, because the toolbar is so much more convenient.

 You can also type commands into Start → Search, but doing so has similar drawbacks to the Start → Run box—and other drawbacks as well. It will perform a search rather than directly issuing a command, so you may launch a file accidentally rather than issue a command if Search finds a file that matches the command you type in.

Address Bar

The Address Bar, shown in Figure 14-4, is nearly the functional equivalent to Start → Run, with a few exceptions. There are actually two different Address Bars: the one attached to the Taskbar, and the one that's part of Windows Explorer.

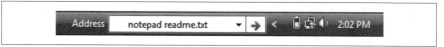

Figure 14-4. The Address Bar on the Taskbar

You can enable the Taskbar Address Bar by right-clicking on an empty area of the Taskbar and selecting Toolbars → Address. This implementation is functionally identical to Start → Run.

The Address Bar in Windows Explorer is automatically enabled. The launching of programs is handled the same way as with the Taskbar Address Bar and with Start → Run.

Internet Explorer also includes an Address Bar, although its purpose is to visit web sites rather than issue commands. However, you also can use it to launch Windows Explorer to a specific folder. For example, type **C:\My Files** into the Address Bar, and Windows Explorer will open to the *C:\My Files* folder.

You can also type web addresses, such as *http://www.windowsdevcenter.com*, into the Taskbar Address Bar, into Start → Run, and into Start → Start Search, and the site will be opened in your default browser.

The main difference between the Address Bar and the Start → Run prompt is in the assumptions that are made about ambiguous names and addresses. For example, if you type **Notepad** or **http://www.annoyances.org** into either place, Windows would launch a program or web site, respectively. If you type something that Windows won't recognize, though, such as **BigBadaBoom**, what happens next depends on where you typed the text. If you typed the text into an Address Bar, Windows Vista would open a web browser to the location *http://BigBadaBoom* and then complain that the web site doesn't exist. If you typed the same text at the Start → Run prompt, you'd get an error message explaining that "Windows cannot find BigBadaBoom."

Wildcards, Pipes, and Redirection

In addition to the various command-line parameters used by each of the commands documented in this chapter (and the components documented in other places in this book), certain symbols used on the command line have special meaning. Table 14-1 shows these special symbols and what they do. You must use them in conjunction with other commands (they don't stand alone), and you can use them in the Command Prompt window, in Start → Run, and in an Address Bar.

Table 14-1. Special symbols on the command line

Symbol	Description
*	Multiple-character wildcard, used to specify a group of files.
?	Single-character wildcard, used to specify multiple files with more precision than *.
.	One dot represents the current directory; see "cd or chdir," later in this chapter.
..	Two dots represent the parent directory; see "cd or chdir," later in this chapter.
\	Separates directory names, drive letters, and filenames. By itself, \ represents the root directory of the current drive.
\\	Indicates a network location, such as \\Joe-PC for a PC connected to your current network.
>	Redirects a command's text output into a file instead of the Console window; if that file exists, it will be overwritten.
>>	Appends a command's text output to the end of a file instead of the Console window.
<	Directs the contents of a text file to a command's input; use with filter programs (such as sort) or in place of keyboard entry to automate interactive command-line applications.
|	Redirects the output of a program or command to a second program or command (this is called a *pipe*).

For information about special operators for chaining commands and redirection, see *http://www.microsoft.com/resources/documentation/ windows/xp/all/proddocs/en-us/ntcmds_shelloverview.mspx* and *http:// www.microsoft.com/resources/documentation/windows/xp/all/proddocs/ en-us/redirection.mspx.*

Examples

The following examples demonstrate some uses of wildcards, pipes, and redirection:

.
>Specify all files with all extensions.

professor*.*
>Specify all files (with filenames that begin with *professor*) with any extension.

chap??.doc
>Specify all files named *chap* followed by any two characters and with the *doc* extension (e.g., *chap01.doc*, but not *chap1.doc* or *chap.doc*).

dir ..
>List all the files in the current directory's parent.

dir > c:\nutshell\mylist.txt
>List all files in the current directory and store this listing into a file called *mylist.txt* rather than displaying it in the Command Prompt window. If the file already exists, it will be overwritten.

>In addition to directing output to a file, you can direct to a device, such as NUL (an electronic void). This is useful if you want a command to run without sending output to the screen. Other special device names include CON (the console input/output stream), LPT*x* (the parallel printer port, where *x* is from 1 to the number of ports you have), and COM*x* (serial ports, including Bluetooth and USB/serial ports, where *x* corresponds to the numbers shown in Device Manager).

dir c:\windows >> c:\nutshell\mylist.txt
>Add the directory listing of the files in the *c:\Windows* directory to the end of the file *windows.txt.*

>If the specified file doesn't exist, one is created. If one does exist, the output from the command is added to it, unlike with the > key, where the original contents are overwritten.

echo y | del *.*
>Normally, the DEL command has no prompt. However, if you try to delete all the files in a directory, del will prompt you for confirmation. To automate this command, the output of the ECHO command (here, just a "y" plus a carriage return) is "piped" into the input (commonly known as STDIN, or standard input) of the DEL command.

```
del *.* < y.txt
```
Assuming *y.txt* contains only a letter *y* followed by a carriage return, this command has the same effect as the preceding example.

```
sort /+12 < c:\nutshell\mylist.txt
```
To sort the lines in a text file (*c:\nutshell\mylist.txt*) on the 12th character, the SORT command is fed input from the file. The output is sent to the screen, not reordered in the file.

Keep in mind that not all commands handle wildcards in exactly the same way. For example, dir * and dir *.* list the same thing.

Most of the following commands are not standalone applications, but rather internal functions of the Command Prompt (*cmd.exe*) application. This restricts their use only to the Command Prompt application. (They won't be recognized by the Address Bar or by Start → Run.) Some items that are standalone programs but are normally used only in the Command Prompt window, such as *xcopy.exe* and *move.exe*, are listed here rather than in Chapter 4.

Note that before listing each individual command, I'm first offering more details on how to use the Command Prompt. Here is an alphabetical reference of entries in this chapter:

Attrib	find	rem
call	for	ren or rename
cd or chdir	goto	robocopy
Choice	if	set
clip	md or mkdir	shift
cls	mklink	sort
Command Prompt	more	time
copy	move	timeout
date	Path	type
del or erase	pause	ver
dir	prompt	where
echo	query	whoami
errorlevel	quser	xcopy
exit	rd or rmdir	

Command Prompt

\windows\system32\cmd.exe

The Windows Vista command-line interface, commonly referred to as a DOS box or Command Prompt.

To open

Start → All Programs → Accessories → Command Prompt

Command Prompt → **cmd**

Usage

```
cmd [/q][/d] [/a|/u] [/e:on|off][/f:on|off][/v:on|off] /t:fg
  [[/s][/c|/k] string]
```

Description

As explained earlier in this chapter, the Command Prompt (see Figure 14-5) is a simple application in which you type commands rather than pointing and clicking. Although the Command Prompt is sparse and may be somewhat intimidating to new users, it carries out several very important functions in Windows Vista, including access to otherwise inaccessible programs and utilities and even some advanced file management functions.

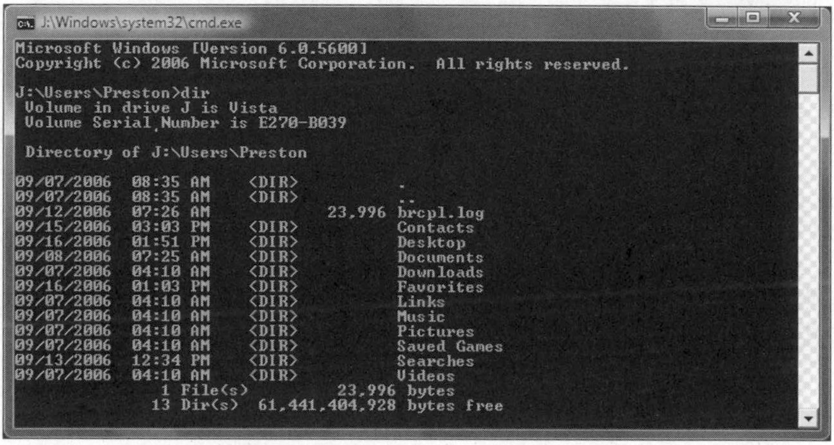

Figure 14-5. Using the DIR command to view the contents of the current directory in the Command Prompt

Cmd accepts the following parameters:

string

> When used with /c or /k, specifies a command to be carried out when the Command Prompt window is first opened. You can specify multiple commands here if you separate them with &&, and *string*, as a whole, is surrounded by quotation marks. *String* must be the last parameter on the command line.

/c

> Carries out the command specified by *string* and then stops.

/k

> Carries out the command specified by *string* and continues.

/s

> Strips any quotation marks in *string*. Type **cmd /?** for details.

/q

> Turns the echo off; see "echo," later in this chapter.

/d

> Disables execution of AutoRun commands. Without /d, any programs or commands listed in the Registry keys, HKEY_LOCAL_MACHINE\Software\Microsoft\ Command Processor\AutoRun and HKEY_CURRENT_USER\Software\Microsoft\Command Processor\AutoRun, are executed every time a Command Prompt window is opened.

/a

Formats all Command Prompt output so that it is American National Standards Institute (ANSI)-compliant.

/u

Formats all Command Prompt output so that it is Unicode-compliant.

/e:on|off

Enables or disables command extensions (the default is on). Turn off command extensions to disable certain advanced features of the commands discussed in this chapter.

/f:on|off

Enables or disables file and directory name completion (the default is off). Type **cmd /?** for details.

/v:on|off

Enables or disables delayed environment variable expansion (the default is off). Type **cmd /?** for details.

/t:fg

Sets the foreground and background colors (*f* and *g*, respectively) of the Command Prompt window. The single-digit values for *f* and *g* are as follows: 0 = Black, 1 = Blue, 2 = Green, 3 = Aqua, 4 = Red, 5 = Purple, 6 = Yellow, 7 = White, 8 = Gray, 9 = Light blue, A = Light green, B = Light aqua, C = Light red, D = Light purple, E = Light yellow, and F = Bright white.

Notes

- Also included with Windows Vista is *command.com*, the command prompt used in Windows 9*x*/Me. It's used similarly to *cmd.exe* but has limited support of long filenames and other Windows Vista features. *Command.com* is included for legacy purposes only and should be avoided; *cmd.exe* is the preferred command prompt in Windows Vista.

- If you need to play an old DOS game, take a look at DOSBox (*http://dosbox. sourceforge.net*), which not only emulates DOS well, but also supports sound in older games.

The Command Prompt

Attrib   *\windows\system32\attrib.exe*

Change or view the attributes of one or more files or folders.

To open

Command Prompt → **attrib**

Usage

```
attrib [+r|-r] [+a|-a] [+s|-s] [+h|-h] [filename] [/s [/d]]
```

Description

Attrib allows you to change the file and folder attributes from the command line—settings otherwise available only in the Properties window of a file or folder. You can think of the attributes as switches, independently turned on or off for any file or group of files. The individual attributes are as follows:

R *(read-only)*

Turn on the read-only attribute of a file or folder to protect it from accidental deletion or modification. If you attempt to delete a read-only file, Windows will prompt you before allowing you to delete it. Different applications handle read-only files in different ways; usually you will not be allowed to save your changes to the same filename.

A *(archive)*

The archive attribute has no effect on how a file is used, but it is automatically turned on when a file is modified or created. It is used primarily by backup software to determine which files have changed since a backup was last performed; most backup programs turn off the archive attribute on each file that is backed up.

S *(system)*

Files with the system attribute are typically used to boot the computer. There's little reason to modify a file with the system attribute, or to ever turn on or off the system attribute for any file. If you turn off the system attribute of an important file, it may stop the file from working. See "Notes," later in this section, for information on displaying or hiding system files.

H *(hidden)*

To hide any file or folder from plain view in Explorer or on the Desktop, turn on its hidden attribute. See "Notes," later in this section, for more information.

Examples

To hide a file in Explorer, right-click on it, select Properties, and turn on the hidden option. To hide the same file using the command line, type:

```
attrib +h filename
```

where *filename* is the full path- and filename of the file to change. To specify multiple files, include a wildcard, such as *.* (for all files) or *.txt (for all files with the *.txt* filename extension). Note the use of the plus sign (+) to turn on an attribute; use the minus sign (–) to turn it off. For example, to turn off the hidden attribute and simultaneously turn on the archive attribute, type:

```
attrib -h +a filename
```

To display the attributes of a file or a group of files in Explorer, select Details from the View menu. Then, select Choose Details from the View menu and turn on the Attributes option. To display the attributes of a file or a group of files on the command line, type:

```
attrib filename
```

where *filename* is the full path- and filename(s) of the files you want to view. Omit *filename* to display the attributes of all the files in the current folder. If *filename* is not used, or if it contains wildcards (in other words, if the command is intended to act on more than one file), you can use the /s option to further include the contents of all subfolders of the current folder. The /d option instructs Attrib to act upon folders as well as files, but it has meaning only if you use it in conjunction with the /s parameter.

Notes

- By default, files with the system or hidden attributes are not shown in Explorer. To display system and hidden files, go to Explorer → Organize → Folder and Search Options → View and select "Show hidden files and folders."
- Attrib does not let you change the Advanced attributes, such as those concerned with indexing, compression, or encryption.

cd or chdir

Display the name of, or change, the current working directory (folder).

Usage

```
cd [/d] [directory]
chdir [/d] [directory]
```

Description

With no arguments, cd displays the full pathname of the current directory. Given the pathname of an existing directory, it changes the current directory to the specified directory.

If *directory* is on a different drive (for example, if the current directory is *c:\dream* and you type **cd d:\nightmare**), the current working directory on that drive is changed, but the current working drive is not. To change the current drive, use the /d parameter, or simply type the letter followed by a colon, by itself, at the prompt (see the following examples).

Pathnames can be absolute (including the full path starting with the root) or relative to the current directory. A path can be optionally prefixed with a drive letter. The special path .. refers to the parent of the current directory.

Examples

If the current drive is *C:*, make *c:\temp\wild* the current directory:

```
C:\>cd \temp\wild
C:\temp\wild>
```

Note how the current working directory is displayed in the prompt. If the current directory is *c:\temp*, all that is necessary is:

```
C:\temp>cd wild
C:\temp\wild>
```

Change to the parent directory:

```
C:\more\docs\misc>cd ..
C:\more\docs>
```

Change to the root directory of the current drive:

```
C:\Windows\Desktop\>cd \
C:\>
```

Change to another drive:

```
C:\>cd /d d:\
D:\>
```

or simply:

```
C:\>d:
D:\>
```

Notes

- The chdir and cd commands are functionally identical.
- The "current working directory" has meaning only in the current command prompt session and any other command prompts or applications launched from that window. If you open a new command prompt window, it will start over with

its default (usually your home directory, but you can set it in the properties of the Windows Shortcut).

- The current directory is shown in the prompt; see "prompt," later in this chapter, for information on changing the information displayed.

---

clip

Redirects the output of command-line tools to the Windows Clipboard, where the text can then be pasted into another program.

Usage

```
[Command] | clip
clip < [filename.txt]
```

Description

clip is extremely useful for when you want to capture output from a command on the command line so that you can paste it into an application. A simple use would be to print out the listing of a directory: use the dir command along with clip and then paste the output from the Clipboard into a text editor, where you can print it. Note that when you use the command, the output is suppressed in the command box. So, for example, when you type **dir | clip**, the directory listing will not be displayed but will be placed into the Clipboard. You can also use clip to copy the entire text from a text file to the Clipboard. You can't, however, use it to copy the contents of other kinds, such as *.doc* files.

Examples

Copy information about currently logged-on users to the Clipboard:

```
quser | clip
```

Copy the text of the file *newinfo.txt* to the Clipboard. Note that the file has to be in your current directory:

```
clip < newinfo.txt
```

Notes

- clip is new to Windows Vista.

---

cls

Clear the Command Prompt window and buffer, leaving only the Command Prompt and cursor.

Description

Type **cls** at the prompt to clear the screen and the screen buffer (see "Using the Command Line," earlier in this chapter), which is useful for privacy concerns or simply reducing clutter.

The difference between using cls and simply closing the current Command Prompt window and opening a new one is that your working environment (such as the current directory) is preserved with cls.

---

cls is also useful in complex batch files—for clearing the screen after one set of inter-actions or command output. The name cls (Clear Screen) refers to the old days when DOS owned the whole screen.

copy

Copy one or more files to another location.

Usage

```
copy source destination
copy [/a | /b] source [/a | /b] [+ source [/a | /b]
[+ ...]] [destination [/a | /b]] [/v] [/y | /-y]
[/d] [/z] [/n] [/l]
```

Description

copy makes a complete copy of an existing file. If another file by the same name exists at *destination*, you will be asked whether you want to overwrite it.

Omit the destination to copy the specified files to the current working directory. If the file (or files) to be copied is in a different directory or on a different disk, you can omit the destination filename. The resulting copy or copies will have the same name as the original.

You can use the special device name con (or con:) in place of either the source (or destination) filename to copy from the keyboard to a file (or from a file to the screen).

copy accepts the following parameters and options:

/a   Specifies that the file to copy is in ASCII format.

/b   Specifies that the file to copy is a binary file.

/v   Verifies that new files are written successfully by comparing them with the originals.

/y   Suppresses prompting to confirm that you want to overwrite an existing destination file.

/-y   Enables prompting to confirm that you want to overwrite an existing destination file with the same name (default).

/d   Allows the new file to be created as a decrypted file (NTFS volumes only).

/l   When copying a symbolic link (see "mklink," later in this chapter), copies the file as a link rather than making a couple of the source file (the default behavior).

/n   Copies the file using the short filename that Vista generated for compatibility with DOS, old versions of Windows, and devices that can't support long filenames on their flash memory.

/z   Copies networked files in restartable mode. If the network connection is lost during copying (if the server goes offline and severs the connection, for example), /z will resume the copying after the connection is reestablished.

Examples

Copy the file *temp.txt* from *C:* to *d:\files* (all three examples do the same thing):

```
C:\>copy c:\temp.txt d:\files\temp.txt
C:\>copy c:\temp.txt d:\files
C:\>copy temp.txt d:\files
```

The third sample in the preceding code works here because the source file is located in the current directory. Here's another way to do it:

```
C:\>d:
D:\>cd \files
D:\files>copy c:\temp.txt
```

Copy all the files from the directory *d:\Cdsample\Images* to the current directory, giving the copies the same names as the originals:

```
C:\>copy d:\cdsample\images\*.*
C:\>copy d:\cdsample\images\*.* .
```

Copy the file *words.txt* in the current directory to *d:\files*, renaming it *morewords.txt*:

```
C:\>copy words.txt d:\files\morewords.txt
```

Copy all of the files in the current directory to *d:\files* (all three examples do the same thing):

```
C:\>copy *.* d:\files
C:\>copy .\*.* d:\files
C:\>copy . d:\files
```

Notes

- The copy command is easier to use, but xcopy (discussed later in this chapter) is more powerful and flexible.

- It is also possible to use the copy command to concatenate (combine) files. To concatenate files, specify a single file for the destination but multiple files for the source (using wildcards or *file1+file2+file3* format):

  ```
  copy mon.txt+tue.txt+wed.txt report.txt
  ```

- You can specify a relative or absolute path (including disk names and/or Universal Naming Convention [UNC] paths), or use a simple filename. When concatenating, if no destination is specified, the combined files are saved under the name of the first specified file.

- When attempting to concatenate files, copy expects ASCII files by default, so in order to concatenate binary files, you need to use the /b option. The reason for this is that binary files typically contain one or more bytes outside the normal ASCII printable range (i.e., 32 through 127).

- You also can use the con device (console) in conjunction with copy. To create a new text file by typing its contents directly, first enter:

  ```
  C:\>copy con mystuff.txt
  ```

- Then type the text to be saved into the file. When you're done, type Ctrl-Z and press Enter. All text typed from the keyboard in this example is then saved as *mystuff.txt*.

- Here's how to copy the contents of the file *mystuff.txt* to the screen (see also "type," later in this chapter):

  ```
  C:\>copy mystuff.txt con
  ```

- Binary file copying is assumed for normal copying, but you should use the /b option when appending one binary file to another, as in:

  ```
  C:\>copy file1+file2 newfile /b
  ```

- By default, when concatenating, both the source and destination files are assumed to be ASCII format, because binary files can seldom be usefully concatenated due to internal formatting.
- You can substitute a device (e.g., COM1) for either the source or the destination. The data is copied in ASCII by default.
- copy doesn't copy files that are 0 bytes long; use xcopy to copy these files.
- copy, move, and xcopy will prompt you before overwriting an existing file, unless you specify a command-line parameter instructing them to do otherwise. To change the default, set the copycmd environment variable to /y. To restore the default behavior, set copycmd to /-y. See "set," later in this chapter, for details.

date

Display or set the system date.

Usage

```
date [/t | date]
```

Description

date is essentially a holdover from the very early days of DOS when the user was required to enter the system date and time every time the computer was started. Now it's essentially included as a way to set the date from the command line; the preferred method is to use Control Panel → [Clock, Language and Region] → Date and Time.

If you type **date** on the command line without an option, the current date setting is displayed and you are prompted for a new one. Press Enter to keep the same date.

date accepts the following options:

date

Specifies the date. Use the *mm-dd-* [*yy*] *yy* format. Values for *yy* can be from 80 through 99; values for *yyyy* can be from 1980 through 8907. Separate month, day, and year with periods, hyphens, or slashes.

/t

Displays the current date without prompting for a new one. You can use this if you need to append a timestamp to the end of a file, as in date /t >> logfile.txt.

Notes

- The date format depends on settings in Control Panel → [Clock, Language, and Region] → Regional and Language Options.
- Windows records the current date for each file you create or change. This date is listed next to the filename in the dir directory listing.
- You can change the date display format for most applications in Control Panel → [Clock, Language, and Region] → Change the date, time, or number format → Customize this format, but this doesn't affect the output of the DOS date command.

See also

"time"

del or erase

Delete one or more files.

Usage

```
del [/p] [/f] [/s] [/q] [/a:attributes] filename
erase [/p] [/f] [/s] [/q] [/a:attributes] filename
```

Description

You use the del command to delete one or more files from the command line without sending them to the Recycle Bin.

The del options are:

filename
> Specifies the file(s) to delete. If you do not specify the drive or path, the file is assumed to be in the current directory. You can use standard * and ? wildcards to specify the files to delete.

/p
> Prompts for confirmation before deleting each file.

/f
> Forces deletion of read-only files.

/s
> Deletes specified files in all subdirectories (when using wildcards).

/q
> Quiet mode; do not prompt if *filename* is *.*.

/a:attributes
> Selects files to delete based on attributes (read-only, hidden, system, or archive). See "Attrib," earlier in this chapter, for more information on attributes.

Examples

Delete the file *myfile.txt* in the current directory:

```
C:\>del myfile.txt
```

Delete the file *myfile.txt* in the *c:\files* directory:

```
C:\>del c:\files\myfile.txt
```

Delete all files with the pattern *myfile.** (e.g., *myfile.doc*, *myfile.txt*, etc.) in the current directory, but prompt for each deletion:

```
C:\>del c:\files\myfile.* /p
```

Notes

- The del and erase commands are functionally identical.
- Using the del command to delete a file does not move it to the Recycle Bin. In other words, you can't get a file back once you use the del command, unless you have a special "unerase" disk recovery utility.

dir

Display a list of files and subdirectories in a directory (folder).

Usage

```
dir [filename] [/b] [/c] [/d] [/l] [/n] [/p] [/q] [/s] [/w] [/x]
    [/4] [/a:attributes] [/o:sortorder] [/t:timefield]
```

Description

Without any options, dir displays the disk's volume label and serial number, a list of all files and subdirectories (except hidden and system files) in the current directory, file/directory size, date/time of last modification, the long filename, the total number of files listed, their cumulative size, and the free space (in bytes) remaining on the disk.

If you specify one or more file or directory names (optionally including drive and path, or the full UNC path to a shared directory), information for only those files or directories will be listed.

You can use wildcards (* and ?) to display a subset of files and subdirectories in a given location.

dir accepts the following options:

/a:*attributes*

Displays only files with/without specified attributes (using - as a prefix specifies "not," and a colon between the option and attribute is optional). See "Attrib," earlier in this chapter, for more information on attributes.

/b

Use bare format (no heading information or summary). Use with /s to list all files in the current directory and subdirectories.

/c

Displays the thousand separator in file sizes. This is the default; use /-c to disable display of the separator.

/d

Same as /w, except files are sorted vertically.

/l

Use lowercase.

/n

Lists files in a Unix-like display, where filenames are shown on the right. This is the default view.

/o:*sortorder*

Lists files in sorted order (using - as a prefix reverses the order, and a colon between the option and attribute is optional):

d   By date and time (earliest first)

e   By extension (sorted alphabetically)

g   Group directories first

n   By name (sorted alphabetically)

s   By size (smallest first)

/p

Pauses after each screenful of information; press any key to continue.

/q

Displays the owner of each file.

/s

Includes all files in all subdirectories, in addition to those in the current directory.

/t:*timefield*

Controls which time is used when sorting:

c   Created

a   Last accessed

w   Last modified (written)

/w

Wide list format. File- and directory names are listed in columns and sorted horizontally. The actual number of columns varies based on the length of the longest filename and the screen width. Use /d instead to sort vertically.

/x

Include the "short" 8.3 versions of long filenames. For example, *Sam's File.txt* has an alternate filename, *samsfi~1.txt*, to maintain compatibility with older applications.

/4

Display the listed years as four digits. By default, two-digit years are displayed.

Examples

Display all files in the current directory:

    C:\>**dir**

Display all files in the current directory that end with the *.txt* extension:

    C:\>**dir *.txt**

Display all files, listing years in four digits and pausing for each screenful:

    C:\>**dir /4 /p**

Display all files, sorted by date and time, latest first:

    C:\>**dir /o-d**

Display only directories:

    C:\>**dir /ad**

List all files on disk, sorted by size, and store output in the file *allfiles.txt*:

    C:\>**dir \ /s /os > allfiles.txt**

List the contents of the shared folder *cdrom* on machine *bubba*:

    C:\>**dir \\bubba\cdrom**

Notes

- To change the default sort order, set the dircmd environment variable to the same value you'd use with the /o parameter. See "set," later in this chapter, for details.
- When using a redirection symbol (>) to send dir output to a file or a pipe (|) or to send dir output to another command, you may want to use /b to eliminate heading and summary information.

dir *filename* /b /s acts as a kind of "find" command, which looks in all subdirectories of the current directory. For example:

```
C:\>dir readme.txt /b /s
C:\Windows\readme.txt
C:\Stuff\Misc\FAQ\readme.txt
```

- One of Windows Explorer's weaknesses is that there's no way to print a directory listing or save a directory listing into a file. However, the dir command with some clever redirects will do the job.

- To print out a sorted directory listing of all files in the Windows directory:

```
C:\> dir c:\windows /oa > filename
C:\> notepad /p filename
```

- To create a file containing the directory listing of the same directory:

```
C:\>dir c:\windows /oa > c:\myfiles\windows.txt
```

- Files and folders that are hidden (see "Attrib," earlier in this chapter) will not show up in dir listings by default. However, if you know the name of a hidden directory, nothing is stopping you from displaying a listing of the contents in that directory. You can also use dir /a.

echo

Display a string of text; turn command echoing on or off.

Usage

```
echo [on | off | message]
```

Description

echo is typically used with other commands or in a batch file to display text on the screen. It's also used to control command echoing from batch files.

You can use the following options with echo:

on | off
> By default, each command in a batch file is echoed to the screen as it is executed; echo on and echo off toggle this feature. To turn echoing off without displaying the echo off command, use @echo off. The @ symbol in front of any command in a batch file prevents the line from being displayed.

message
> Types the message you'd like displayed to the console (screen).

Examples

To display an ordinary message, use the following:

```
echo Hello World!
```

To display a blank line, use one of the following (both are equivalent):

```
echo.
echo,
```

(Note the absence of the space between the echo command and the punctuation; you can also use a colon, semicolon, square brackets, backslash, or forward slash.)

One handy use of echo is to answer y to a confirmation prompt such as the one del issues when asked to delete all the files in a directory. For example, if you wanted to clear out the contents of the \temp directory from a batch file, you could use the following command:

```
echo y | del c:\temp\*.*
```

or even:

```
echo y | if exists c:\temp\*.* del c:\temp\*.*
```

This construct works because the pipe character takes the output of the first command and inserts it as the input to the second.

You can use echo to announce the success or failure of a condition tested in a batch file:

```
if exist *.rpt echo The report has arrived.
```

It's a good idea to give users usage or error information in the event that they don't supply proper arguments to a batch file. You can do that as follows:

```
@echo off
if (%1) == ( ) goto usage
. . .
goto end
:usage
echo You must supply a filename.
:end
```

See also

"type"

---

exit

End the current Command Prompt session and close the window.

Usage

```
exit [/b] [exitcode]
```

Description

Typing **exit** has the same effect as closing the Command Prompt window with the [x] button.

exit accepts the following options:

/b

> If you use exit from within a batch file, it will close the current Command Prompt window. Specify /b to exit the batch file but leave *cmd.exe* running.

exitcode

> Specifies a numerical "exit code" number that is passed to the application or process that launched the Command Prompt or started the batch file. *exitcode* is typically used when one batch file runs another batch file and wishes to report to the "parent" batch file whether it was successful.

Notes

- If you start a new Command Prompt session by typing **cmd** in an open Command Prompt window, exit will end that session. However, because the "parent" session is still active, the window won't close until you type **exit** again.

---

find

Search in one or more files for text.

Usage

```
find [/v] [/c] [/n] [/i] [/offline] "string" [filename[ ...]]
```

Description

After searching the specified files, find displays any lines of text that contain the string you've specified for your search. find is useful for searching for specific words (strings) in files.

The find options are:

`"string"`
> The text to look for, enclosed in quotation marks.

filename
> The file(s) in which to search. Wildcards (*, ?) are supported, and you can specify multiple filenames as long as you separate them with commas. If *filename* is omitted, find searches text typed at the prompt or piped from another command via the pipe character (|), as described in "Wildcards, Pipes, and Redirection," earlier in this chapter.

`/c`

> Displays only the count of lines containing the string.

`/i`

> Ignores the case of characters when searching for the string.

`/n`

> Displays line numbers with the displayed lines.

`/v`

> Displays all lines not containing the specified string.

`/offline`
> Includes files with the offline attribute set (that otherwise would be skipped).

Examples

Search for *redflag* in *myemployees.txt*:

```
C:\>find "redflag" myemployees.txt
```

Count occurrences of the word *deceased* in *myemployees.txt*:

```
C:\>find /c "deceased" myemployees.txt
```

Search the current directory for the string "cls" in all *.bat* files and store the result in the file *cls.txt* (note that >> rather than > is necessary when redirecting the output of a for loop):

```
C:\>for %f in (*.bat) do find "cls" %f >> cls.txt
```

Notes

- You can search through multiple files by specifying each file to search on the command line, but unfortunately, wildcards (* and ?) are not accepted in the filename. To search for a string in a set of files, however, it's possible to use the find command within a for loop structure. If redirecting for to a file, use >> rather than > (see the earlier example).

- If a filename is not specified, find searches the text input from the "standard" source (usually the keyboard), a pipe, or a redirected file.

- If you have a Unix background, you might be tempted to try something like this:

  ```
  dir c:\ /s /b | find "chap"
  ```

  to search the contents of all files for the string "chap", but in fact, all you'd be doing is running find on the list of filenames, not on their contents. You can accomplish this with the new forfiles command:

  ```
  forfiles /p C:\ /s /c "cmd /c find \"chap\" @path"
  ```

- find won't recognize a string that has a carriage return embedded in it. For example, if "chapter" is at the end of one line and "05" on the next, find won't report a match on "chapter 05."

- A similar command, findstr, offers even more ways to find strings of text in files. For example, you can match patterns only if they're at the beginning or the end of a line, among other capabilities. For details, type **findstr /?** at a command prompt.

 forfiles is an extremely powerful command-line tool for finding files and then performing an action on those files, and it is useful in batch files. Think of it as a light version of the Unix find command. For details, type **forfiles /?** at a command prompt.

md or mkdir

Create a new directory (folder).

Usage

```
md [drive:]path
mkdir [drive:]path
```

Description

Windows Vista, like its predecessors, uses a hierarchical directory structure to organize its filesystem. On any physical disk, the filesystem begins with the root directory, signified by a lone backslash.

md and mkdir accept the following option:

[drive:]path
> Specifies the directory to create.

Examples

Create a subdirectory named *harry* in the current directory:

```
C:\tom\dick>md harry
```

Create a new directory called *newdir* under the *c:\olddir* directory:

```
C:\>md c:\olddir\newdir
```

If *c:\olddir* doesn't exist, it will be created as well.

Create two new directories, *c:\rolling* and *c:\stones*:

```
C:\>md rolling stones
```

Create a single new directory, *c:\rolling stones*:

```
C:\>md "rolling stones"
```

(Enclose directory names in quotation marks to accommodate spaces.)

Notes

- The md and mkdir commands are functionally identical.
- You can also create new folders in Windows Explorer by going to Organize → New Folder.
- You may indicate an absolute or relative path for the path parameter. When absolute, the new directory is created as specified from the root directory. When relative, the directory is created in relation to the current directory.

mklink

Create a link to another file or directory

Usage

```
mklink [/d] | [/h] | [/j]] link target
```

Description

mklink is used to create a Unix-style link to another file or directory; that link can be used just as if it were the original file or directory. When you create a *symbolic* link to a file, that file will show up in Windows Explorer as a shortcut, and if you use the command line to get a directory listing, it will be listed as a <SYMLINK> instead of as <DIR>, and you'll see the symbolic link followed by the real file. For example, if you create a symbolic link called *newone* to the file *test*, here's what you would see:

```
<SYMLINK>      newone [c:\test]
```

The mklink options are:

/d

> Creates a symbolic link (the default). Use /j for directories.

/h

> Creates a hard link instead of a symbolic link. You will not see SYMLINK in the *dir* listing, because a hard link is a first-class filename. Creating a hard link to an existing file adds another filename, and the file is not deleted until you delete the last hard link to it.

/j

> Creates a directory junction. You will see JUNCTION in the *dir* listing instead of SYMLINK.

link

> Specifies the new symbolic link name.

target

> Specifies the path (relative or absolute) that the new link refers to.

Notes

- mklink is new in Windows Vista. It has to be run from an administrator prompt (locate Command Prompt in the Start menu, right-click on it, and select Run as Administrator).

- The difference between symbolic and hard links is subtle. If you delete the target of a soft link, the soft link remains, but it is invalid until you re-create the target. If you delete the target of a hard link, the hard link is still valid because it's essentially an additional filename by which the file is referenced.

---

more \windows\system32\more.com

Display the contents of a file with the output of another command, but pause the display so that only one screen of text is shown at a time.

Usage

```
more /e [/c] [/p] [/s] [/tn] [+n] [filename]
more [/e [/c] [/p] [/s] [/tn] [+n]] < filename
{some other command} | more [/e [/c] [/p] [/s] [/tn] [+n]]
```

Description

more displays one screen of text at a time. more is often used as a filter with other commands that may send a lot of output to the screen (i.e., to read standard input from a pipe or redirected file). Press any key to see the next screenful of output. Press Ctrl-C to end the output before it is done.

more accepts the following options:

filename
Specifies the name of a file to display.

/c
Clears the screen before displaying the file.

/e
If the /e option is specified, the following additional extended commands are available at the -- More -- prompt:

P*n*   Displays next *n* lines

S*n*   Skips next *n* lines

Spacebar
Displays next page

Enter
Displays next line

F   Displays next file

Q   Quits

=   Shows line number

?   Shows help

/p
Expands form-feed characters.

/s
Squeezes multiple blank lines into a single line.

/tn
> Expands tabs characters to *n* spaces (default 8).

+n
> Starts display of the file at line *n*.

filename
> Specifies the name of a file to display.

Examples

Display the contents of *Windows\readme.txt* and pause for each screenful of text (both of the following examples have the same effect):

```
C:\>more c:\windows\readme.txt
C:\>type c:\windows\readme.txt | more
```

Keep the output of dir from scrolling off the screen before you can read it:

```
C:\>dir c:\windows | more
```

Notes

- Some commands (such as dir) have a /p option that "pages" the output (e.g., dir | more is the same as dir /p), but many do not.

See also

"type"

---

move

Move files and directories from one location to another.

Usage

```
move [/y | /-y] filename[,...] destination
```

Description

move works like copy, except that the source is deleted after the copy is complete. *filename* can be a single file, a group of files (separated by commas), or a single file specification with wildcards.

The move options are:

filename
> Specify the location and name(s) of the file or files you want to move. Wildcards (*, ?) are supported.

destination
> Specify the new location of the file. The destination parameter can consist of a drive, a directory name, or a combination of the two. When moving one file, *destination* may include a new name for the file. If you include the new filename but omit the drive or directory name, move effectively renames the file.

/y
> Suppress prompting to confirm creation of a directory or overwriting of the destination. This is the default when move is used in a batch file.

/-y
> Cause prompting to confirm creation of a directory or overwriting of the destination. This is the default when move is used from the command line.

Examples

Move *myfile.txt* from the current directory to *d:\files*:

```
C:\>move myfile.txt d:\files\
```

Same, but rename the file to *newfile.txt*:

```
C:\>move myfile.txt d:\files\newfile.txt
```

Change the name of the directory *d:\files* to *d:\myfiles*:

```
D:\>move d:\files myfiles
```

Notes

- copy, move, and xcopy will prompt you before overwriting an existing file, unless you specify a command-line parameter instructing them to do otherwise. To change the default, set the copycmd environment variable to /y. To restore the default behavior, set copycmd to /-y. See "set," later in this chapter, for details.

See also

"ren or rename"

---

path

Set or display the command search path.

Usage

```
path [path1][;path2][;path3][;...]
```

Description

When you type an executable filename at the Command Prompt (as opposed to a command built into the Command Prompt), Windows starts by looking in the current directory for a file that matches. If no matching file is found, Windows then looks in a series of other folders, which are known collectively as the path or the *command search path*.

The path statement is used to define additional directories to be included while searching for files. The path consists of a series of absolute directory pathnames, separated by semicolons. No spaces should follow each semicolon, and there should be no semicolon at the end of the statement. If no drive letter is specified, all pathnames are assumed to be on the current directory's drive.

Type **path** without any arguments to display the current command search path. The default path in Windows Vista is c:\windows\system32;c:\windows;c:\windows\system32\wbem.

When you type the name of a command, DOS looks first in the current directory and then in each successive directory specified in the path. Within each directory, it will look for executable files by their extension in the following order: *.com*, *.exe*, *.bat*, *.cmd*. Windows searches your path for certain other file types (i.e., *.dll* or *.ocx*) as well, although most cannot be executed from the command line (see "Notes" for more information).

Examples

Specify the directories *c:\Stuff* and *d:\Tools* in the path:

```
C:\>path c:\stuff;d:\tools
```

However, this will replace the path with these two folders. To add these folders to the existing path, type the following:

```
C:\>path %path%;c:\stuff;d:\tools
```

Notes

- The path is actually an environment variable and the path command is merely a shortcut for the following:

  ```
  set path=%path%;c:\stuff;d:\tools
  ```

- See "set," later in this chapter, for more information on environment variables and details on setting global environment variables that don't expire when the Command Prompt window is closed.

- Windows Vista recognizes long folder names in the path (e.g., *c:\Program Files*). If the folder name has a semicolon in it, you may still have to use the short names equivalent (e.g., *c:\PROGRA~1*).

- Type **path ;** to clear all search path settings and direct your current Command Prompt to search only in the current directory.

- The order of directories in the search path is quite important. For example, you might run Cygwin (*http://www.cygwin.com*), a free set of open source tools that brings Unix functionality to Windows systems. Cygwin normally stores its files in *\cygwin\bin*, but if you have the path set as follows:

  ```
  path=C:\cygwin\bin;C:\Windows\system32;C:\Windows;C:\Windows\system32\
  wbem
  ```

  you won't be able to run a Windows command such as find without typing its full pathname because the Cygwin find command will be found and executed first. To avoid this problem, put *C:\cygwin\bin* at the end of your PATH.

- Windows also searches the path for Windows shortcuts, but the usage might be nonintuitive. To launch a shortcut named Widget, for example, you'd have to type **widget.lnk** at the prompt.

- All of the supported file types are specified in the PATHEXT environment variable (see "set," later in this chapter). By default, Windows searches the path for the following extensions: *.com*, *.exe*, *.bat*, *.cmd*, *.vbs*, *.vbe*, *.js*, *.jse*, *.wsf*, and *.wsh*.

---

prompt

Change the appearance of the prompt.

Usage

```
prompt [text]
```

Description

Type **prompt** by itself (without *text*) to reset the prompt to its default setting.

The prompt options are:

text

>Specifies a new command prompt. *text* can contain normal characters and the following special codes:

$_ Carriage return and linefeed

$$ Dollar sign ($)

$a Ampersand (&)

$b Pipe (|)

$c Left parenthesis (()

$d Current date

$e Escape character (ASCII code 27), used to provide extended formatting

$f Right parenthesis ())

$g Greater-than sign (>), commonly known as the caret

$h Backspace (erases preceding character)

$1 Less-than sign (<)

$n Current drive

$p Current drive and path

$q Equals sign (=)

$s Space

$t Current time

$v Windows version number

Examples

Specify the current drive and directory followed by the greater-than sign (>), the default prompt in Windows Vista:

>`C:\>prompt $p$g`

Specify the drive and directory on one line and the date, followed by the greater-than sign (>), on another:

>`C:\>prompt $p$_$d$g`

Specify the drive only, followed by the greater-than sign (>), which was the default prompt on early versions of DOS:

>`C:\>prompt $n$g`

Notes

- The current prompt setting is actually stored in the environment, and the prompt command is merely a shortcut for the following:

  >`set prompt=$p$g`

- See "set," later in this chapter, for more information on environment variables and details on setting global environment variables that don't expire when the Command Prompt window is closed.

query

Find out information about sessions, processes, and users.

Usage

```
query process | session | termserver | user
```

Description

The query options are:

process
    Lists the currently running processes, including filenames, and associated usernames

session
    Lists the current sessions, including their IDs and associated usernames

termserver
    Lists the currently running terminal servers

user
    Lists information about logged-in users, including the time they logged on, their amount of idle time, their session name, and their session ID

---

quser

Displays information about users currently logged on to the system. (Not available in the Home edition.)

Usage

```
quser username sessionname sessionid
```

Description

quser displays information about currently logged-on users. It displays when the user logged on, whether the user is active, and the current time, the username, the session name, the session ID, and the amount of idle time for the user. (To find the session ID, use the query command. See the preceding section, "query.") You can use the following commands with quser:

username
    Identifies the username of the user for whom you want to display information

sessionname
    Displays the session name (for example, console) of the user for whom you want to display information

sessionid
    Displays the session ID (for example, 2) of the user for whom you want to display information

Examples

Display information about the user preston:

    quser preston

Display information about the user with the session name console:

    quser console

Notes

* quser is new to Windows Vista.

rd or rmdir

Remove (delete) a directory.

Usage

    rd [/s] [/q] path
    rmdir [/s] [/q] path

Description

Unlike in Windows Explorer, files and folders are deleted differently; if you try to use del to delete a directory, it will simply delete all the files in the directory, but the directory itself will remain. You use rd to delete empty directories and, optionally, to delete directories and all of their contents.

rd accepts the following options:

path

Specifies the directory to delete.

/s

Removes all files and subdirectories of the specified directory.

/q

Quiet mode; don't prompt when using /s.

Examples

Delete the empty subdirectory called *newdir* located in the *c:\olddir* directory:

    C:\>**rd c:\olddir\newdir**

Delete the directory *Online Services* and all of its contents within the current directory, *c:\Program Files*:

    C:\Program Files>**rd /s "online services"**

Note that you must use quotes with rd for folders with spaces in their names.

Notes

* The rd and rmdir commands are functionally identical.
* As a safety feature, attempting to delete a directory that is not empty without including the /s option will display the message "The directory is not empty."
* rd with the /s option takes the place of the deltree command found in earlier versions of Windows but no longer included in Windows Vista.

- If you try to delete the current directory, you'll get the following error: "The process cannot access the file because it is being used by another process." In this case, you'll have to change to a different directory first.

ren or rename

Rename a file or directory.

Usage

```
ren [filename1] [filename2]
rename [filename1] [filename2]
```

Description

Use ren to rename any file or directory. Unlike in Windows Explorer, though, ren is capable of renaming several files at once (via the wildcards * and ?).

The ren options are:

[filename1]
:   The name of the existing file or directory

[filename2]
:   The new name to assign to the file or directory

Examples

Rename *myfile.txt* to *file.txt*:

```
C:\>rename myfile.txt file.txt
```

Rename *chap 5.doc* to *sect 5.doc* (the following two methods are identical):

```
C:\>ren "chap 5.doc" "sect 5.doc"
C:\>ren chap?5.doc sect?5.doc
```

Each of these examples represents different ways to rename files with spaces in their names. In addition to the standard quotation marks, in certain circumstances you can use wildcards to avoid the space problem. Here, both *chap 5.doc* and *sect 5.doc* have spaces in the fifth character position, so you can use the single wildcard character (?).

Rename the files *chap1.doc*, *chap2.doc*, etc., to *revchap1.doc*, *revchap2.doc*, etc.:

```
C:\>ren chap*.doc revchap*.doc
```

ren can be a convenient way to rename the filename extensions of several files at once, as well:

```
C:\>ren *.txt *.rtf
C:\>ren *.htm *.html
C:\>ren *.mpeg *.mpg
```

Notes

- The ren and rename commands are functionally identical.
- You can't move files from one directory to another with ren; use move instead.
- The file's Last Modified date is not changed when you use ren.

See also

"move"

robocopy

A powerful, flexible tool for copying files.

Usage

```
robocopy source [drive:\path or \\server\share\path] destination [drive:\
path or \\server\share\path] [file [file]...] /a /m /s /e /mov /move /lev:n
/fat
```

Description

robocopy stands for *Robust Copy for Windows*, and the name is apt. It is far more powerful than the copy and xcopy commands, and in fact, a full explication of all of its commands and uses would take up half this chapter. For details about its full usage, type **robocopy /?** to get help.

You can use the command to copy files not only on a PC, but also between PCs and servers, and between servers as well. It can use wildcards for file selection.

The following are some of the primary commands that you can use with robocopy:

/a

Copy only files with the Archive attribute set.

/m

Copy only files with the Archive attribute and reset it.

/s

Copy subdirectories, but not empty ones.

/e

Copy subdirectories, including empty ones.

/mov

Move files (delete from source after copying).

/move

Move files and directories (delete from source after copying).

/lev:*n*

Copy on the top *n* levels of the source directory tree.

/fat

Create destination files using 8.3 FAT filenames only.

/mir

Mirrors a complete directory tree. You also can use it with other commands, such as /b for copying files in backup mode, to copy only files that have been changed.

Examples

Copy all *.xls* files from *C:\newbudget* to *F:\newbudget*, and use only 8.3 FAT filenames:

```
robocopy *.xls c:\newbudget f:\newbudget /fat
```

Notes

* robocopy is new to Windows Vista.

See also

"copy" and "xcopy"

---

set

Display, assign, or remove environment variables.

Usage
```
set [variable[=[string]]]
set /p variable=[promptstring]
set /a expression
```

Description

The *environment* is a small portion of memory devoted to the storage of a few values called environment variables. You use set to manipulate environment variables from the command line, but because the Command Prompt's environment is reset when its window is closed, the usefulness of set is fairly limited for interactive use, although you'll use it a lot in your own batch files.

To make more permanent changes to environment variables, go to Control Panel → [System and Maintenance] → System → Advanced system settings → Environment variables. The variables in the upper listing are for the current user and the variables in the lower listing apply to all users. Some environment variables, such as the Temp user variable, are assigned with respect to other variables, like this:

```
%USERPROFILE%\AppData\Local\Temp
```

where %USERPROFILE% (note the percent signs [%] on both sides) signifies the USERPROFILE variable, which represents the path of the current user's home directory. See "path," earlier in this chapter, for another example of this usage.

In addition to providing a simple means of interapplication communication, environment variables are also useful for storing data used repeatedly in a batch file (see "Batch Files," later in this chapter).

Type **set** without options to display all of the current environment variables. Type **set** with only a variable name (no equals sign or value) to display a list of all the variables whose prefix matches the name.

The set options are:

variable
> Specifies the variable name. When assigning a new variable, the case used is preserved. But when referencing, modifying, or deleting the variable, *variable* is case-insensitive. If *variable* is specified by itself, its value is displayed. If *variable* is specified by itself with an equals sign, the variable is assigned an empty value and deleted. *Variable* cannot contain the equals sign (=).

string
> Specifies a series of characters to assign to *variable*. As stated earlier, this can contain references to other variables when surrounded with preceding and trailing percent signs (%).

/p
> Specifies that *variable* will be assigned by text input from the user, rather than *string*. As stated earlier, this can contain references to other variables with preceding and trailing percent signs (%).

promptstring

> The text prompt to display when using the /p option.

/a

> Specifies that *expression* is a numerical expression to be evaluated. If used from the Command Prompt, set /a will display the final evaluated result of *expression*, even if you include an assignment operator (such as =) to assign a variable.

expression

> When used with the /a option, *expression* is a collection of symbols, numbers, and variables arranged so that it can be evaluated by set. The following symbols are recognized (in decreasing order of precedence):

> ( )   Parentheses for grouping

> ! ~ - Unary operators (not, bitwise not, negative)

> */ % Arithmetic operators (multiply, divide, modulus)

> +-   Arithmetic operators (add, subtract)

> << >>
>   Logical shift

> &   Bitwise "and"

> ^   Bitwise "exclusive or"

> | Bitwise "or"

> = *= /= %= += -= &= ^= |= <<= >>=
>   Assignment

> '   Expression separator

> If you use /a with any of the bitwise or modulus operators, you need to enclose *expression* in quotes. Any non-numeric strings in *expression* are treated as environment variable names, and their values are converted to numbers during evaluation (zero is used for undefined variables); the percent signs (%) are not used here.

Examples

Set the variable dummy to the string not much:

```
C:\>set dummy=not much
```

Set the dircmd variable, which instructs the dir command (discussed earlier in this chapter) to sort directory listings by size, with the largest first:

```
C:\>set dircmd=/s /o-s
```

Append the directory *c:\mystuff* to the path (see "path," earlier in this chapter); note how the path variable is used on the right side of the equals sign so that its original contents aren't lost:

```
C:\>set path=%path%;c:\mystuff
```

Set the prompt (see "prompt," earlier in this chapter) to show the current time, followed by a right-angle bracket:

```
C:\>set prompt=$t>
```

Display the contents of the variable named dummy (both of the following statements are equivalent):

```
C:\>set dummy
C:\>echo %dummy%
```

You can also reference environment variables with other commands:

```
C:\>set workdir=C:\stuff\tim's draft
C:\>cd %workdir%
```

Here, the environment variable is used to store a long pathname for quick navigation to a frequently used directory.

Display the values of all variables that begin with the letter *H*:

```
C:\>set h
```

Clear the value of an environment variable, dummy:

```
C:\>set dummy=
```

Prompt the user to enter text to be inserted into the dummy variable. This is typically used in batch files (note that you have to put quotes around it, otherwise the > will be interpreted as the redirection operator):

```
C:\>set /p dummy="Enter text here >"
```

Evaluate an arithmetic expression (the two following expressions are not the same):

```
C:\>set /a 7+(3*4)
C:\>set /a (7+3)*4
```

The results of these two expressions, 19 and 40, respectively, will be displayed. To assign the result to a variable, type the following:

```
C:\>set /a dummy=7+(3*4)
```

Even though you're assigning the result variable, the result will still be displayed (unless set is executed from a batch file). To suppress the output, type this:

```
C:\>set /a dummy=7+(3*4) > nul
```

In addition to any custom environment variables you may use, Windows Vista recognizes the following variables (many of which are predefined):

ALLUSERSPROFILE

> The location of the All Users folder, usually *c:\Users\All Users*.

APPDATA

> The location of the Application Data folder, usually *c:\Users\%USERNAME%\AppData\Roaming*.

COMMONPROGRAMFILES

> The location of the Common Files folder, usually *c:\Program Files\Common Files*.

COMPUTERNAME

> The network name of the computer, which you can set by going to Control Panel → [System and Maintenance] → See the name of this computer → Change settings.

COMSPEC

> The location of the Command Prompt application executable, *c:\Windows\system32\cmd.exe* by default.

COPYCMD

> Whether the copy, move, and xcopy commands should prompt for confirmation before overwriting a file. The default value is /-y. To stop the warning messages, set copycmd to /y.

DIRCMD

> Specifies the default options for the dir command. For example, setting dircmd to /p will cause dir to always pause after displaying a screenful of output.

ERRORLEVEL

The return code of the last command run. A zero value (0) indicates success; anything else indicates failure.

HOMEDRIVE

The drive letter of the drive containing the current user's home directory, usually *c:*, used with HOMEPATH.

HOMEPATH

Along with HOMEDRIVE, the path of the current user's home directory, which is usually *\Users\%USERNAME%*.

LOGONSERVER

The name of the computer as seen by other computers on your network, usually the same as COMPUTERNAME preceded by two backslashes.

NUMBER_OF_PROCESSORS

The number of processors currently installed. In a multiprocessor or multicore system, it can be two, four, or more.

OS

Used to identify the operating system to some applications; for Windows XP, OS is set to Windows_NT. You may be able to "fool" an older program that is programmed not to run on an NT system by changing this variable temporarily.

PATH

The sequence of directories in which the command interpreter will look for commands to be interpreted. See "path," earlier in this chapter.

PATHEXT

The filename extensions (file types) Windows will look for in the directories listed in the path (see "path," earlier in this chapter). The default is *.COM*, *.EXE*, *.BAT*, *.CMD*, *.VBS*, *.VBE*, *.JS*, *.JSE*, *.WSF*, *.WSH*, and *.MSC*.

PROCESSOR_ARCHITECTURE

The type of processor; set to x86 for 32-bit Windows running on Intel-compatible processors (such as the Core 2 Duo or Athlon X2).

PROCESSOR_REVISION

A series of values the processor manufacturer uses to identify the processor.

PROGRAMFILES

The location of the Program Files folder, usually *c:\Program Files*.

PROMPT

The format of the command-line prompt, usually PG. See "prompt," earlier in this chapter, for details.

SESSIONNAME

The name of the current Command Prompt session, usually Console.

SYSTEMDRIVE

The drive letter of the drive containing Windows, usually *C:*.

SYSTEMROOT

The location of the Windows directory (or more specifically, the name of the folder in which the *\Windows\System32* folder can be found), usually *c:\windows*.

TEMP, TMP

The location where many programs will store temporary files. TEMP and TMP are two different variables, but they should both have the same value, usually set to *c:\Users\%USERNAME%\AppData\Local\Temp* (short name used to maintain compatibility with older DOS programs).

USERDOMAIN

The name of the domain to which the computer belongs (set by going to Control Panel → System → Computer Name → Change). If no domain is specified, USERDOMAIN is the same as COMPUTERNAME.

USERNAME

The name of the current user.

USERPROFILE

The location of the current user's home directory, which should be the same as HOMEDRIVE plus HOMEPATH, usually *c:\Users\%USERNAME%*.

WINDIR

The location of the Windows directory, usually *c:\windows*.

Notes

- Among the standard environment variables listed earlier, some represent certain system folders (such as PROGRAMFILES). These variables reflect only the corresponding settings in the Registry (and elsewhere); changing them will affect only what is reported to applications that use these variables; it won't actually change where Windows looks for these folders.

---

sort

\windows\system32\sort.exe

Sort text or the contents of text files in alphanumeric order.

Usage

```
sort [/r] [/+n] [/m kilobytes] [/l locale] [/rec recordbytes]
 [/t [tempdir]] [/o outputfilename] [filename]
```

Description

The sort command sorts text on a line-by-line basis. Each line of the input is ordered alphanumerically and output to the screen (or optionally, stored in a file). By default, sorting starts with the character in the first column of each line, but you can change this with the /+n option. sort is often used in conjunction with either pipes or output redirection (both discussed earlier in this chapter). That is, you might want to sort the output of another command, and you will often want to redirect the output to a file so that it can be saved. sort takes the following options:

/r

Reverses the sort order; that is, it sorts *Z* to *A* and then 9 to 0.

/+n

Sorts the file according to characters in column *n*.

/m kilobytes

Specifies the amount of main memory to allocate for the sort operation, in kilobytes. The default is 90 percent of available memory if both the input and output are files, and 45 percent of memory otherwise. The minimum amount of memory sort will use is 160 KB; if the available (or specified) memory is insufficient, sort will split up the operation using temporary files.

/l locale

Overrides the system default locale (see Control Panel → Regional and Language Options). The "C" locale yields the fastest collating sequence, and in Windows Vista, it is the only choice.

/rec recordbytes
> Specifies the maximum number of characters on a line (in a record); the default is 4,096 and the maximum is 65,535.

/t tempdir
> Specifies the location of the directory used to store temporary files, in case the data does not fit in main memory (see the /m option). The default is to use the system temporary directory.

/o outputfilename
> Specifies a file where the output is to be stored. If not specified, the sorted data is displayed at the prompt. Using the /o option is faster than redirecting output (with the > symbol).

filename
> The name (and optionally, full path) of the file to sort.

Examples

Display an alphabetically sorted directory (similar to dir /o):

```
C:\>dir | sort
```

Sort the contents of a file, *data.txt*, and store the sorted version in *results.txt* (the following four examples are equivalent, although the first is the most efficient):

```
C:\>sort /o results.txt data.txt
C:\>sort data.txt > results.txt
C:\>sort /o results.txt < data.txt
C:\>type data.txt | sort > results.txt
```

Notes

- The input to sort should be plain text so that each line can be considered a record of data.

- Using the /+n parameter, the lines (records) of the input text may be broken into fields, each beginning a fixed number of characters from the start of the line, facilitating multiple fixed columns.

- Blank lines and leading spaces will be sorted. This can result in many blank lines at the top of the sorted output; you may need to scroll down in an editor to see nonblank lines.

- If you do a lot of command-line sorting, you may want to get a Windows version of the Unix sort utility (available as part of Cygwin; *http://www.cygwin.com*), which is much more powerful. The Unix sort command lets you define and sort on fields within the line, ignore upper- and lowercase distinctions, and eliminate duplicate lines, among other things.

---

time

Display or set the system time.

Usage

```
time [/t | time]
```

Description

Like date (discussed earlier in this chapter), time is essentially a holdover from the very early days of DOS when the user was required to enter the system date and time every time the computer was started. Now it's essentially included as a way to set the data from the command line; the preferred method is to use Control Panel → [Clock, Language, and Region] → Date and Time.

If you type **time** on the command line without an option, the current time setting is displayed, and you are prompted for a new one. Press Enter to keep the same date.

The time options are:

time

> Sets the system time without a prompt. The format of *time* is *hh*:*mm*:*ss* [A|P], where:

> *hh* Hours: valid values = 0–23.

> *mm* Minutes: valid values = 0–59.

> *ss* Seconds: valid values = 0–59.

> A|P A.M. or P.M. (for a 12-hour format). If a valid 12-hour format is entered without an A or P, A is the default.

/t Displays the current time without prompting for a new one.

Notes

- The time format depends on settings in Control Panel → [Clock, Language, and Region] → Date and Time.

- Windows records the current time for each file you create or change. This time is listed next to the filename in the dir directory listing.

- You can change the time display format for most applications in Control Panel → [Clock, Language, and Region] → Date and Time, but this doesn't affect the output of the time command.

- To have Windows automatically synchronize the clock with an Internet time server, go to Control Panel → [Clock, Language, and Region] → Date and Time → Internet Time tab.

See also

"date"

---

type

Display the contents of a text file.

Usage

    type *filename*

Description

The type command is useful if you need to quickly view the contents of any text file (especially short files). type is also useful for concatenating text files, using the >> operator.

Notes

- If the file is exceptionally long, you can press Ctrl-C to interrupt the display before it's finished.

See also

"more" and "echo"

---

ver

Displays Windows version information.

Usage

```
ver
```

Description

ver shows the version of Windows you're using. You can also find the Windows version at Control Panel → [System and Maintenance] → System tab, but it won't show you the revision number.

ver takes no options.

Notes

- Windows Vista is known internally as Windows 6.0.*xxxx*, where *xxxx* is the build/revision number.

See also

"Windows Update," in Chapter 8

---

where

Displays the location of files that match a filename.

Usage

```
where /r /q [dir] /f /t [filename]
```

Description

where will show you the location of files for which you're searching. It searches along your default path, although you can add directories to the default with the use of /r. It accepts wildcards such as * and ?. You can use the following commands with where:

/r   Searches for and displays the file, starting with the specified directory

/q   Quiet mode (no output, but it sets the exit code in %ERRORLEVEL%)

/f   Displays the matched filename in double quotes

/t   Displays the file size and last modified date and time for all matched files

Examples

Display the location of all files named *eula.txt* along the default path:

```
where eula.txt
```

Display the location and file size, and last modified date and time, for all *.doc* files in the directory *latest*:

```
where /r \latest /t *.doc
```

Notes

- where is new to Windows Vista.

---

whoami

Gets username and group information, security identifiers (SIDs), privileges, and logon identifier (logon ID) for the current user.

Usage

```
whoami /upn /fqdn /user /groups /priv /logonid /all /fo format /nh
```

Description

You use whoami to get a variety of information about the currently logged-in user. You can use the following options with the whoami command:

/upn
> Displays the username in User Principal Name (UPN) format. (Works only when the user is connected to a domain.)

/fqdn
> Displays the username in Fully Qualified Distinguished Name (FQDN) format. (Works only when the user is connected to a domain.)

/user
> Displays information about the current user along with the SID.

/groups
> Displays group membership for the current user, the type of account, SIDs, and attributes.

/priv
> Displays the security privileges of the current user.

/logonid
> Displays the logon ID of the current user.

/all
> Displays the current username and the groups the user belongs to, along with the SID and privileges for the current user.

/fo format
> Specifies the output format to be displayed. Valid values are TABLE, LIST, and CSV. Column headings are not displayed with the CSV format. The default format is TABLE.

/nh
> Specifies that the column header should not be displayed in the output. This is valid only for the TABLE and CSV formats.

Examples

Display login ID and security privileges of the current user:

```
whoami /logonid
```

Display the current username, the groups the user belongs to, and the SID and privileges for the current user, in CSV output format, with no header displayed:

```
whoami /all /fo CSV /nh
```

Notes

- whoami is new to Windows Vista.
- whoami is in essence the equivalent of the whoami Unix command.

---

xcopy
\windows\system32\xcopy.exe

Copy files and directory trees (directories, subdirectories, and their contents).

Usage

```
xcopy source [destination] [/a | /m] [/d[:date]] [/p] [/s [/e]]
  [/v] [/w] [/c] [/i] [/q] [/f] [/l] [/g] [/h] [/r] [/t] [/u]
  [/k] [/n] [/o] [/x] [/y] [/-y] [/z] [/b] [/exclude:filenames]
```

Description

xcopy works like copy but provides more options and is often faster.

The xcopy32 options are:

source
: Specifies the file(s) to copy; source must include the full path.

destination
: Specifies the location and/or name of new files. If omitted, files are copied to the current directory.

/a
: Copies files with the archive attribute set but doesn't change the attribute of the source file (similar to /m).

/c
: Continues copying even if errors occur.

/d:date
: Copies only files changed on or after the specified date. If no date is given, copies only those source files that are newer than existing destination files.

/e
: Copies all directories and subdirectories (everything), including empty ones (similar to /s). May be used to modify /t.

/exclude:filenames
: Specifies a file (or a list of files) containing strings of text (each on its own line). When any of the strings match any part of the absolute path of the file to be copied, that file will be excluded from being copied. Contrary to what you might expect, *filenames* does not actually list the filenames to exclude.

/f
: Displays full source and destination filenames while copying (unless /q is specified); normally, only filenames are displayed.

/g
: Allows the copying of encrypted files to a destination that does not support encryption; otherwise, such files are skipped.

/h
: Copies hidden and system files also; normally files with the hidden or system attributes are skipped (see "Attrib," earlier in this chapter, for details).

/i   If a destination is not supplied and you are copying more than one file, assumes that the destination must be a directory. (By default, xcopy asks if the destination is a file or directory.)

/k   Duplicates the attributes of the source files; by default, xcopy turns off the read-only attributes (see "Attrib," earlier in this chapter, for details).

/l   Displays files that would be copied given other options, but does not actually copy the files.

/m   Copies files with the archive attribute set, then turns off the archive attribute of the source file (similar to /a).

/n   Copies files using short (8.3) file- and directory names (for example, *PROGRA~1* instead of *Program Files*). Use this feature to convert an entire branch of files and folders to their short names.

/o   Copies file ownership and ACL information.

/p   Prompts you before creating each destination file.

/q   Quiet mode; does not display filenames while copying.

/r   Overwrites read-only files.

/s   Copies directories and subdirectories, except empty ones (similar to /e).

/t   Creates the directory structure but does not copy files; does not include empty directories unless /e is specified.

/u   Copies from the source-only files that already exist on destination; used to update files.

/v   Verifies copied files by comparing them to the originals.

/w   Prompts you to press a key before copying (useful in batch files).

/x   Copies file audit settings (implies /o).

/y, /-y
      Turns off or on (respectively) the prompt for overwriting existing files.

/z   Copies networked files in restartable mode.

/b   When copying a symbolic link (see "mklink," earlier in this chapter), copies the file as a link rather than making a couple of the source file (the default behavior).

The following are exit codes generated by xcopy. They can be tested in a batch file with ERRORLEVEL to determine whether the xcopy operation was successful.

0   All files were copied without errors.

1   No files were found to copy.

2   xcopy was terminated by Ctrl-C before copying was complete.

4   An initialization error occurred. Such an error would generally be caused by insufficient memory or disk space, or an invalid drive name or syntax.

5   A disk-write error occurred.

Examples

Copy all the files and subdirectories, including any empty subdirectories and hidden files, from *c:\foobar* to the root directory of *d:*:

```
C:\>xcopy \foobar d: /s /e /h
```

Notes

- copy, move, and xcopy will prompt you before overwriting an existing file, unless you specify a command-line parameter instructing them to do otherwise. To change the default, set the copycmd environment variable to /y. To restore the default behavior, set copycmd to /-y. See "set," earlier in this chapter, for details.

- In some earlier versions of Windows, there were two versions of xcopy: *xcopy.exe* and *xcopy32.exe*. In Windows Vista, the xcopy command is equivalent to the 32-bit *xcopy32.exe* utility; there's no equivalent to the old 16-bit *xcopy.exe*, however.

- Use caution when using the /s or /e option in conjunction with /d or /u, as the results may be unpredictable.

See also

"copy" and "robocopy"

Batch Files

Most Windows books treat batch files as though they are some kind of skeleton in the closet or a crazy aunt you wouldn't want anyone to meet. Although it's true that batch files are much less important than they were in DOS and earlier versions of Windows, they can still provide useful functionality.

A batch file is a text file containing a series of commands, each on its own line, that will be executed one line at a time. The filename of the batch file becomes a command that can be executed at the Command Prompt, executed from another batch file, or even run from a Windows shortcut.

Although any commands you can type at the command line can be used in a batch file, several additional commands can be used only in a batch file. These commands are used for loops, conditionals, and other programming functions within the batch file and are explained in detail later in this chapter.

Creating Batch Files

You can create batch files with any text editor or word processor that can save plain-text files, such as Notepad. In fact, by default, you can right-click any batch file and select Edit to open that file in Notepad.

When naming a batch file, make sure you don't use a name that is already used by a Command Prompt internal command (such as *dir*, *copy*, or *cd*) or by a *.com* or *.exe* file in your search path. The reason for this is that when the Command Prompt executes programs, it first looks for the *.com* extension and then the *.exe* extension before finally executing a file with the *.bat* extension. For instance, if you have a file called *work.exe* and you create *work.bat* in the same directory, your batch file will not execute unless you type the filename extension as well.

You can create and execute batch files from the current directory or any directory in your search path, or by specifying their complete pathname, as with any other command. But if you're going to use batch files a lot, it makes sense to keep them all in one place. Create a directory called \Batch and add it to your search path. See "path," earlier in this chapter, for details.

Some Rules of the Road

Here are the basics of batch file programming:

- Each command in a batch file must be on a separate line. The last command line in the file should end with a carriage return. The commands are the same as those you'd type in succession at the Command Prompt.

- The name of the batch file itself is stored in the variable %0. This allows you to do things such as have a temporary batch file that deletes itself when done. The name is stored as it was typed at the command line, so if you had typed myfile.bat, %0 would be *myfile.bat*, but if you had typed c:\batch\myfile, %0 would be *c:\batch\ myfile*.

- A batch file run from the Command Prompt or by double-clicking on its icon will open a Command Prompt window while it is executing; however, a batch file run from an existing Command Prompt window will run inside that window.

- Click the control menu and select Properties (see "Using the Command Line," earlier in this chapter, for details) to control the default look and feel of the Command Prompt window. To change these settings for an individual batch file, create a Windows shortcut to the batch file, right-click the new shortcut, and select Properties.

- The Properties sheet for the shortcut actually adds several options not normally available through the control menu. For example, Shortcut → Start In allows you to choose the initial working directory, and Shortcut → Run allows you to have the batch file run minimized.

- You can stop a running batch file by pressing Ctrl-Break or Ctrl-C; the following message will appear in its DOS window: "Terminate batch job (Y/N)?".

- By default, each command in a batch file is echoed to the Command Prompt window. To execute a command silently, precede it with an @ symbol. Alternatively, you can turn command echo off by issuing @echo off at the beginning of the batch file.

- A batch file can contain any command that you can type at the Command Prompt. However, keep in mind that each line in the batch file is executed sequentially, so there are a couple of gotchas, especially when the batch file runs programs that pop up a separate window. When you run a Windows program and it pops up its own window, control returns immediately to the batch file and the next line is executed. This "race condition" is unfortunately unavoidable with batch files; you'll have to use a WSH script for this type of control.

- You can store temporary data in your batch file using environment variables created with the set command. To use the value of any variable with any other command or program, surround its name with % symbols.

The "Why" and "When" of Using Batch Files

This section gives a few examples of instances when you might want to use batch files.

Batch files are used to automate repetitive tasks, but they can be useful for more than just issuing a sequence of commands. For example, type the names of three applications in a batch file to have them all opened in a single step. Or write a one-line batch file that copies a directory of files onto a removable drive; instead of performing a copy manually every day before you go home from work, just double-click the batch file icon and it will be done for you.

Batch files are particularly powerful for creating and moving files and directories. For example, when starting a new project, an author might always want to create the same directory structure and put some basic files into each directory. Here's the kind of batch file you might create for this kind of housekeeping:

```
@echo off
if "%1"=="" goto skip
mkdir %1\figures
mkdir %1\sources
mkdir %1\old
copy c:\templates\mainfile.doc %1
copy c:\templates\other.doc %1
copy c:\templates\image.tif %1\figures
:skip
```

Create a new folder in the Explorer, and then drag and drop it onto this batch file (or add the batch file to the SendTo menu). Subdirectories called *figures*, *sources*, and *old* will be created inside the target (when you drag and drop something onto a batch file, its name is put into the %1 variable), and three template files are copied into the new directories. *Voilà*—you just saved about a minute of clicking and dragging.

The construct:

```
if "%1"=="" go to skip
```

is a useful error-checking technique. You can use an if statement to test for null arguments (or other similar conditions), and if encountered, either issue an error message or simply quit. (This example will exit after jumping to the :skip label because there are no further commands to be executed.)

You can also use batch files to work around some of the limits of Windows Vista. For example, the Explorer doesn't let you print out a hardcopy listing of the contents of a folder. You can do this from the command line by typing:

```
dir > lpt1:
```

But the following batch file does even better—you can drag and drop a folder icon onto it to get a printed directory listing:

```
@echo off
if "%1"=="" goto skip
dir %1 > lpt1:
:skip
```

If you don't have a parallel printer, you could also replace lpt1: with something such as c:\windows\desktop\dir-list.txt to output the directory listing to a text file instead (and then print it with notepad /p *filename*), or construct a loop so that the batch file could repeat itself automatically for multiple directory name arguments.

Variables

Variables can be used in batch files. In fact, a variable that is assigned in one batch file can be accessed by a different batch file (in the same Command Prompt session), because the Command Prompt environment is used to store all variables. See "set," earlier in this chapter, for more information on setting, modifying, reading, and deleting variables from the environment.

A batch file can take arguments such as filenames or options. Up to nine arguments are stored in the variables %1 through %9. For example, the following line in a batch file:

```
copy %1 %2
```

means that the batch file would copy the filename specified in the first argument to the name specified in the second argument. Use this feature in conjunction with the if statement—for example, to display a help screen when the "user" includes the /? option. The %* variable returns a string with all arguments (e.g., %1 %2 %3 %4 %5 . . .), which can be a convenient way to pass all a batch file's arguments to another batch file or command.

The following variable operators can also be used with variables containing filenames. They don't actually change the contents of the target variable, but they do return an expanded version of it.

%~var

> Expands %var, removing any surrounding quotes.

%~fvar

> Expands %var to a fully qualified pathname (useful if %var references a file in the current directory).

%~dvar

> Expands %var to a drive letter only.

%~pvar

> Expands %var to a path only.

%~nvar

> Expands %var to a filename only.

%~xvar

> Expands %var to a file extension only.

%~svar

> The expanded path contains short names only.

%~avar

> Expands %var to file attributes.

%~tvar

> Expands %var to the date/time of the file.

%~zvar

> Expands %var to the size of the file.

%~$dir:var

> Searches the directories listed in the dir variable and expands %var to the fully qualified name of the first one found. If dir is not defined, or if the file is not found by the search, an empty string is returned. If you specify $PATH for dir, the command search path will be used (see "path," earlier in this chapter).

These operators are most commonly used with command-line arguments; for example, use %~z2 in a batch file to display the size of the file specified by %2. These operators can be combined; for example, %~nx1 expands %1 to the filename and extension only, and %~ftza7 expands %7 to a dir-like output line. If the variable %var is not defined or does not contain the filename of an existing file, an empty string will be returned.

Additional Commands Used in Batch Files

The following list contains descriptions of the commands that are used principally within batch files. You can use these in conjunction with any of the commands listed earlier in this chapter, as well as the filenames of any Command Prompt programs or even Windows applications.

call

Invoke a batch file from within another batch file, returning control to the original when the called file completes.

Usage

```
call [filename] [arguments]
```

Description

The call command lets you invoke a batch file from within another batch file and wait for it to finish before continuing. Once the called file has completed its execution, the control returns to the original batch file.

 If you run another batch file from within a batch file without using call, the control will never be returned to the parent batch file when the child process is finished. The whole thing just quits. Of course, this fact can be put to use; for example, it helps to avoid recursion when a batch file calls itself.

The options for call are as follows:

filename
    Specifies the filename of the batch file to call

arguments
    Specifies any command-line arguments to be passed to the target batch file

Examples

The following *parent.bat* calls *child.bat*, and then returns the control to itself:

parent.bat:

```
@echo off
cls
call child.bat First
set first=%inputvar%
call child.bat Second
set second=%inputvar%
echo You typed %first% and then you typed %second%
```

child.bat:

```
set /p inputvar=Please type the %1 option:
echo Thank you.
```

In this example, *parent.bat* launches *child.bat* twice, which illustrates how you can write modular code in batch files. *child.bat* asks for input and then places what the user types into the environment variable inputvar. When control is returned to *parent.bat*, the variable first stores the input so that *child.bat* can be run again. At the end, *parent.bat* spits out both variables.

The next example illustrates how one of the batch file's limitations can be overcome. The if statement, discussed later in this chapter, is capable of executing only a single command, but the following is a simple workaround:

parent.bat:

```
@echo off
for %%j in (1,2,3,4,5) do call child.bat
```

child.bat:

```
set /p inputvar=Please type option #%j%:
echo You typed %inputvar% - good for you.
```

Notes

- call accepts labels as targets. For details, look in the help by typing **help call** at a command prompt.

choice

\windows\system32\choice.exe

Lets you select an item from a list of choices, then returns the index of that choice.

Usage

```
choice [/c choices] [/n] [/cs] [/t timeout /c choice] [/m text]
```

Description

The options for choice are as follows:

/c *choices*

Specifies the list of choices to be created.

/n

Hides the list of choices in the prompt. The message before the prompt is displayed, however, and the choices are still enabled, even though the list is hidden.

/cs

Enables case-sensitive choices. By default, choice is case-insensitive.

/t *timeout*

The number of seconds to pause before a default choice is made. Acceptable values are between 0 and 9999. If 0 is specified, there will be no pause and the default choice will be selected.

/D *character*

Specifies the default choice after *timeout* seconds. *character* must be in the set of choices specified by the /c option and must also specify *timeout* with /t.

/M text

Specifies the message to be displayed before the prompt. If it is not specified, choice displays only a prompt.

errorlevel

See "if," later in this chapter.

for

Repeat a specified command any number of times.

Usage

```
for [/d] %%variable in (set) do command [arguments]
for /r [path] %%variable in (set) do command [arguments]
for /l %%variable in (start,step,end) do command [arguments]
```

(in and do are not options, but rather are simply part of the syntax; if omitted, an error will occur.)

Description

Use this command to create loops in a batch file. A for loop is a programming construct that allows you to repeat a command for a list of items (such as filenames). You specify an arbitrary variable name and a set of values to be iterated through. For each value in the set, the command is repeated.

for uses the following options:

command [arguments]

> The command to execute or the program filename to run. This can be anything you'd normally type at a command prompt; *arguments* are the options, if any, to pass to the command.

%%variable

> A one-letter variable name that is assigned, one by one, to the elements listed in *set*. Although *variable* is treated like a standard environment variable (see "set," earlier in this chapter), its name is case-sensitive (%%j is different from %%J) and can be only one letter long. Note also the use of two preceding percent signs. If the for command is issued directly from the Command Prompt (and not from within a batch file), use only one percent sign here.

set

> The sequence of elements through which the for command cycles. Elements are separated by spaces and can be files, strings, or numbers. Wildcards can be used when specifying files. See "Examples," discussed next, for details. Use the /l option for the more traditional *start,step,end* format.

/d

> Instructs for to match against directory names instead of filenames if *set* contains wildcards. Can't be used with the /l or /r option.

/l

> Specifies that *set* takes the form of *start,step,end*, allowing you to specify a range of numbers and an increment instead of having to list each element. The /l parameter allows you to mimic the more traditional usage of for found in more advanced programming languages. See "Examples," discussed next, for details.

/r [path]

> Recursively executes *command* for each directory and subdirectory in *path*. If *path* is omitted, the current directory is used. Without /r, files specified in *set* relate only to the current directory. The /r option instructs for to "walk" the directory tree rooted at *path* and repeat the entire loop in each directory of the tree encountered. If *set* is just a single period (.), for will simply list all the directories in the tree.

Examples

for can cycle through an array of strings (remember, if you want to try these from the command line rather than in a batch file, use only one percent sign here):

```
for %%n in (rock paper scissors) do echo %%n
```

Create a set of numbered directories (e.g., *ch1*, *ch2*, *ch3*, *ch4*, and *ch5*):

```
for %%n in (1 2 3 4 5) do md ch%%n
```

Here's an alternate way to accomplish the same thing, using the /l option:

```
for /l %%n in (1,1,5) do md ch%%n
```

Here, the first 1 represents the beginning number, the second 1 represents the increment (or step), and the 5 represents the end. Here are some more examples of this syntax:

```
for /l %%n in (0,5,100) do echo %%n
for /l %%n in (100,-2,0) do echo %%n
```

Because the for loop works only for a single command (and it doesn't work well with goto), you need to do something like this to run multiple commands with for:

```
for %%f in (1 2 3 4 5) do call loop1.bat %%f
echo done!
```

loop1.bat might then look like this:

```
if not exist file%1 goto skip
copy file%1 c:\backup
:skip
```

Note how the %%f variable is passed to *loop1.bat* as a command-line parameter and is then referenced with %1.

The set parameter can also contain filenames:

```
for %%j in (a.txt b.txt c.txt) do copy %%j a:
```

The following statements are equivalent:

```
for %%x in (*.txt) do type %%x
type *.txt
```

Although the second example is simpler, it does illustrate a way to deal with programs or commands that don't normally support wildcards.

List all the directories (with full paths) on your hard disk:

```
for /r c:\ %%i in (.) do echo %%i
```

Copy all *.doc* files in all subdirectories of *c:\Users\%USERNAME%\Documents* to drive *D*:

```
for /r "c:\Users\%USERNAME%\Documents" %%i in (*.doc) do copy %%i d:
```

Notes

- When redirecting the output of a for loop to a file, you'll want to use >> (append to a file) rather than >. Otherwise, you will save only the last iteration of the loop.

- The commands executed by the for statement will be echoed to the screen unless you issue the @echo off command beforehand or precede *command* with @. See "echo," earlier in this chapter, for details.

- The for command also supports the rather arcane /f option; type **for /?** at the Command Prompt for more information.

goto

Branch to a labeled line in a batch program.

Usage

```
goto label
...
:label
GOTO :EOF
```

Description

goto is typically used with the if statement to branch to a particular part of a batch file, depending on the result of the condition or user response.

label, any string of text (no spaces) following a colon, marks the beginning of a section of a batch file and represents a target for the goto command. If you type **goto :eof** (note the colon, not normally used here), it will skip to the end of the batch file (eof = end of file).

If your batch program doesn't contain the label you specify after goto, the batch program stops and displays the message "Label not found." However, you can specify labels that don't appear in goto commands.

Examples

Format a floppy disk in drive *a:* and display an appropriate message of success or failure:

```
@echo off
format a:
if not errorlevel 1 goto skip
echo An error occurred during formatting.
exit /b
:skip
echo Successfully formatted the disk in drive a!
```

See also

"if"

if

Execute a command if certain conditions are met.

Usage

```
if [not] string1==string2 command [arguments]
if [/i] string1 compare-op string2 command [arguments]
if [not] exist filename command [arguments]
if [not] errorlevel n command [arguments]
```

Description

Conditional branching lets your batch file test to see whether a condition is true, and if it is, it instructs the batch file to execute a command or continue execution at another location in the batch file (via the goto command). You can use the following options with the if command:

command [*arguments*]

    The command to execute or the program filename to run. This can be anything you'd normally type at a command prompt; *arguments* are the options, if any, to pass to the command.

not

    Specifies that *command* should be carried out only if the condition is false; not valid with *compare-op*.

string1==string2

    Specifies a true condition if the specified text strings match. *String1* and *string2* must be enclosed in quotation marks or parentheses.

string1 compare-op string2

    Performs a more flexible comparison than *string1==string2*. The *compare-op* term can be one of the following:

    EQU

        Equal to

    NEQ

        Not equal to

    LSS

        Less than

    LEQ

        Less than or equal to

    GTR

        Greater than

    GEQ

        Greater than or equal to

/i

    Specifies a case-insensitive comparison; used only with *compare-op*.

exist *filename*

    Specifies a true condition if the specified file exists.

errorlevel *n*

    Specifies a true condition if the preceding command or program returned an exit code equal to or greater than the number specified. Zero typically means no error; other numbers depend on the command or program.

Examples

Because batch files can accept parameters (stored in %1, %2, %3, and so on), the if statement is vital to interpreting these parameters. The following statements might appear at the beginning of such a batch file:

```
if "%1"=="" echo You didn't specify a parameter
if "%1"=="/?" goto help
if "%1"=="hullabalooza" goto doit
```

The following statements are equivalent:

```
if not "%1"=="" echo You must've typed something.
if "%1" NEQ "" echo You must've typed something.
```

The following batch file checks the current directory for the file *form.bat*. If it finds it, the message "It exists!" is displayed, and if it doesn't, "The file doesn't exist." is displayed:

```
@echo off
if exist form.bat goto jump
goto skip
:jump
echo It exists!
pause
exit /b
:skip
echo The file doesn't exist.
pause
exit /b
```

When a program exits or a command completes, it returns an integer value to the operating system called the errorlevel. Typically, errorlevel is zero (0) if the operation was successful or a higher number if there was a problem. The if errorlevel statement checks whether the errorlevel value is equal to or greater than a specified number:

```
find /i "vista" c:\stuff\tips.txt
if errorlevel 2 goto error
if errorlevel 1 goto nomatch
if errorlevel 0 goto match
:match
echo A match was found!
goto end
:nomatch
echo Sorry, but a match wasn't found.
goto end
:error
echo Ack! An error has occurred!
:end
pause
```

Note that the if errorlevel statements are ordered so that higher numbers are checked first; if the order was reversed, the first one (if errorlevel 0) would always return true because the errorlevel is always greater than or equal to zero.

It's also important to account for the possibility that none of the if statements will encounter a true condition; in the preceding example, if all errorlevel checks failed, execution would simply continue onto the :match section.

The if statement also supports else, but the syntax is very strict. else must be the first word on the line immediately following the if statement, like this:

```
if exist %1 del %1
else echo Sorry, %1 was not found
```

Batch files in Windows Vista also support if...else blocks, like this:

```
if exist %1 (
 echo I'm about to delete %1. Press Control-C to cancel
 pause
 del %1
) else (
 echo I couldn't find %1. Too bad for you.
 exit /b
)
```

The indenting here isn't necessary, but it does make the code easier to read. Note the opening and closing parentheses used to enclose the blocks, and the fact that else must be on the same line as the closing parenthesis of the first block and the opening parenthesis of the second block.

See also
"for" and "goto"

---

pause

Suspends processing of a batch program and prompts the user to press any key to continue.

Description
Include the pause command whenever you want your batch file to stop and wait for user input, giving the user a chance to read the text on the screen, insert a floppy disk, or press Ctrl-C to abort the batch file.

The message "Press any key to continue..." is automatically displayed whenever the pause command is used; it is not affected by the echo off statement.

Examples
Prompt the user to change disks in one of the drives in a batch program:

```
@echo off
echo Insert next disk in drive A, and
pause
```

When this batch file is executed, the following message will appear:

```
Insert next disk in drive A, and
Press any key to continue ...
```

Something like this is also common:

```
@echo off
echo Press Ctrl-C to cancel, or
pause
```

---

rem

Insert comments ("remarks") into a batch file. Lines beginning with rem will be ignored when the batch file is executed.

Usage
```
rem [comment]
```

Description
The comment can say whatever you want. It's a good idea to put comments in your batch file so that others (including you in the distant future) can figure out how it works.

The rem command is also useful for disabling commands. Just add rem right before the command to disable it.

Examples

A batch file that uses remarks for explanations and to disable a command:

```
@echo off
rem This batch program may one day change a directory.
rem But not until I remove the rem before the cd command.
rem It is called mydir.bat.
rem cd \batch\ch2
```

This example, if executed, would do absolutely nothing.

See also

"echo"

---

shift

Delete the variable that holds the first command-line argument (%1) and shifts over the remaining arguments.

Usage

```
shift
```

Description

Use the shift command when you want to cycle through all of the command-line arguments specified when the batch file was run. When a shift statement is encountered, the value stored in %2 is assigned to %1, the value stored in %3 is assigned to %2, and so on. The value stored in %1 before the shift statement is lost. This is particularly useful when processing loops.

Examples

In the following batch file, shift is used so that each of the command-line options becomes option #1 (%1) for processing within the loop. The beauty is that this works regardless of the number of arguments entered:

```
@echo off
rem MTYPE.BAT
rem example: mtype foo.txt bar.txt *.bat
:loop
if "%1"=="" exit /b
for %%f in (%1) do type %%f
shift
pause
goto loop
```

The if statement tests for an empty argument (meaning that shift has exhausted the supply of arguments) and ends the loop when found.

Notes

- Normally, the number of command-line arguments is limited to nine (%1 through %9), but shift makes it possible for a batch file to accommodate more.
- If you use a wildcard on the command line, it is passed to the batch file as a single argument (e.g., *.*), which can be used as is. It isn't expanded first, as with Unix shells, so you can't pick it apart in the script and use each matched filename separately (fortunately, the FOR command does expand wildcards, which is why you can use *.bat as an argument to the batch file just shown).

timeout

Wait for a specified amount of time, or until a key is pressed, before performing the next command.

Usage

```
timeout /t [number] \nobreak
```

Description

In addition to waiting a specified amount of time for a key to be pressed, timeout can also be told to ignore any key presses and wait the specified amount of time before performing the next command. You can use the following options with the timeout command:

/t

Specifies the number of seconds to wait. The valid range is from −1 to 99,999 seconds. A value of ‑1 means to wait indefinitely for a key press.

/nobreak

Ignore key presses and wait the specified amount of time.

Examples

Wait 35 seconds before performing the next command:

```
timeout /t 35
```

Wait 50 seconds and ignore any pressed keys before performing the next command:

```
timeout /t 50 /nobreak
```

Notes

- timeout is new to Windows Vista.

Appendixes

A

Installing Windows Vista

Some of you will be fortunate enough to never have to endure the installation of an operating system. After all, a large number of Windows Vista users will obtain the operating system preinstalled on new PCs. Others, however, may be confronted with one of the scenarios discussed in this appendix.

When you install Windows Vista, you'll either upgrade over your existing operating system, which is the less expensive option, or you'll have to buy a full version and install from scratch. Only PCs with Windows XP or Windows 2000 qualify for upgrades; those with PCs of earlier versions of Windows will have to buy the full version.

If you have Windows XP or Windows 2000 and can upgrade, you'll have two choices for installing Windows Vista. You can either perform an in-place upgrade, or do a clean install. An in-place upgrade installs Windows Vista directly over your previous version of Windows. You'll keep all of your applications, files, and settings, just as they were with your earlier Windows version.

If you can't perform an in place upgrade, you'll have to back up your files, then do a clean install of Vista. When you do that, you'll wipe out your previous operating system, files, and so on. You will then have to install Windows Vista, reinstall your applications, and copy your files to the PC.

Table A-1 summarizes your options for installing Windows Vista.

Table A-1. Upgrade options for Windows Vista

	Home Basic	Home Premium	Business	Ultimate
Windows XP Professional	Clean install	Clean install	In-place installation available	In-place installation available
Windows XP Home	In-place installation available	In-place installation available	In-place installation available	In-place installation available
Windows XP Media Center	Clean install	In-place installation available	Clean install	In-place installation available

	Home Basic	Home Premium	Business	Ultimate
Windows XP Tablet PC	Clean install	Clean install	In-place installation available	In-place installation available
Windows XP Professional 64-bit	Clean install	Clean install	Clean install	Clean install
Windows 2000	Clean install	Clean install	Clean install	Clean install

Performing a Clean Install

The Windows Vista installation DVD is bootable and self-installing, so you need only put it into your DVD drive and reboot, and the installation program will launch. (See Figure A-1.)

To configure your computer to boot off a DVD, you'll need to use your system's BIOS setup utility. When you first power on your machine, you'll see a text screen with a summary of your motherboard, processor, and installed memory. (If you see only a logo, try pressing the Esc or Tab key.) Here, you typically press F2, Delete, or some other key combination to "Enter Setup." (Refer to your PC's documentation for specifics.) Once you've entered the BIOS setup utility, go to the boot section and change the "boot device priority" or "boot sequence" so that your DVD drive appears before your hard disk. (Some computers offer a boot menu, usually accessible by pressing F12, which lets you choose to boot from CD/DVD without having to enter the BIOS.) Exit the BIOS setup screen when you're finished.

You'll be prompted to type in your product key (find it on the DVD case or the retail box). Then you need to accept the license terms. You'll now come to a screen with two options—to upgrade, or to perform a "Custom" install, which is the choice you'll make for a clean install. (See Figure A-2.) If you boot from the install disc, the Upgrade option will be grayed out. (For more details about doing an upgrade rather than a clean install, see the next section.)

The next screen will allow you to choose a drive and partition on which to install Windows; in most cases, you'll have only a single drive and a single partition. Here, you'll have the option of installing onto an existing drive, making changes to your partition table, and formatting or deleting a partition. It's important to note that if you delete a partition that has data on it, all of the data will be erased.

If you're installing on a clean system (with a new, empty hard disk), you'll want to create a new partition using all of the available space (or several partitions, as desired).

If you're installing on a hard disk with data on it and you don't want to erase the data, simply select the desired partition (usually the first one, C:\). Note that if you've backed up your data, you can safely choose to delete your partition, create a new one, and install fresh. Although this does require the additional work involved in restoring your data, it results in a cleaner, usually faster, and more reliable installation.

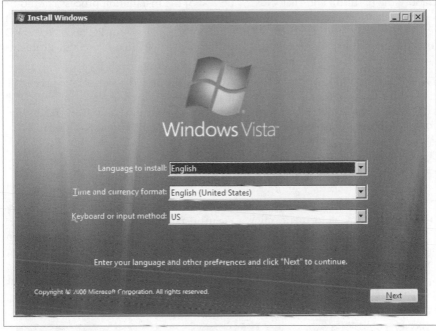

Figure A-1. Choosing your language, time and currency format, and keyboard

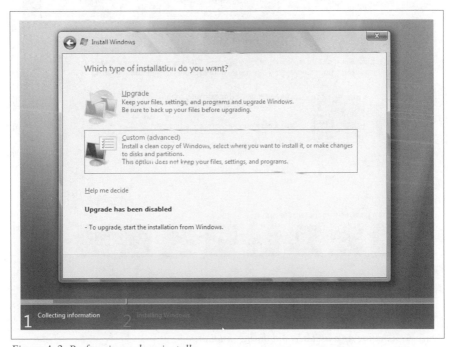

Figure A-2. Performing a clean install

Choose the partition and click Next. The rest of the installation process should be fairly straightforward. Your PC will restart, possibly more than once; don't remove the DVD from the drive when it reboots, because your PC needs the DVD to complete the installation. If you run into a problem, see "Potential Problems During Setup," later in this appendix.

The first time Windows Vista starts, you'll be prompted to choose a username and password to create a user account (Figure A-3), then a name for your PC. You'll also be asked for other information, such as your time and date settings and your computer's current location (home, work, or a public location). Then Windows will finally run for the first time.

Upgrading from a Previous Version of Windows

The initial steps for upgrading from a previous version of Windows to Vista are virtually the same as for performing a clean install. The only differences are that you must insert the Vista DVD while Windows XP is running, and when presented with the Upgrade/Custom screen shown in Figure A-2, you must choose Upgrade, and your files, settings, and programs will be kept intact during the upgrade process. However, just to be safe, it's a good idea to back up your data, in case something goes wrong during the upgrade.

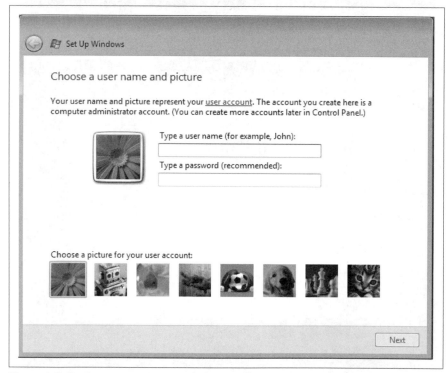

Figure A-3. Setting up a user account during installation

Windows Anytime Upgrade

If you have Windows Vista and you want to upgrade to another version—for example, from Windows Vista Home Basic to Windows Vista Home Premium, or from Windows Vista Home Premium to Windows Vista Ultimate—you don't have to buy a new disc. Each copy of Windows Vista actually has all the available versions on it, and you can unlock any version by paying for it online.

If you're not sure what version of Windows Vista you have, select Control Panel → System and Maintenance, and click Welcome Center. Your version will be displayed at the top of the page. To upgrade to another version of Windows Vista, select Control Panel → System and Maintenance → System, and click Upgrade Windows Vista. Then follow the instructions and pay online. You'll be instructed to insert your Windows Vista disk into your PC, and you can upgrade directly from that disc. You can, of course, also buy an upgrade disc if you would prefer not to pay online.

Potential Problems During Setup

Fully documenting all of the problems that could occur during the installation of Windows Vista would require a book 10 times the size of this one. Here, though, are some of the most common problems you're likely to encounter, and how to solve them:

- An out-of-date BIOS may cause a failed installation. Your motherboard will have a software-upgradeable flash BIOS. Contact the manufacturer of your system or motherboard for any BIOS updates it has available, but don't bother unless a BIOS upgrade is absolutely necessary. (A failed BIOS upgrade will make your motherboard unusable.)

- Another common stumbling block to Windows Vista setup is your video card (display adapter). If setup stops with an unintelligible error message, hangs at a blank screen, or reboots unexpectedly during setup, your video card may be at fault. If replacing the video card permits Windows Vista to install, you should discard your video card.

- If installation stops because files cannot be copied from the DVD, the disc may be scratched or dirty, or there may be a problem with your drive. Remove the disc, clean it with a soft cloth, and try again. Try another DVD with your drive to see if there is a problem with the drive.

- Incompatible hardware may cause your PC to stop responding. If that is the case, exit the installation and then disable any unnecessary hardware. Remove Universal Serial Bus (USB) devices, and remove or disable your network adapters, sound cards, and any other cards, then restart the installation.

- Another cause of your system not responding may be a conflict with your antivirus program. Disable the antivirus program and try installing again, but remember to turn it on after the installation is complete (you may need to upgrade to a Vista-compatible version after the upgrade; Vista will warn you about any incompatible software you have installed if you are upgrading from Windows XP).

B

Keyboard Shortcuts

This appendix lists many useful keyboard accelerators. The listings are organized both by keystroke (alphabetically within groups such as function key, Alt-key combination, and so forth) and by function or context (during startup, in the Recycle Bin, for managing windows, and so forth). The first section lists the key and then the function. The second section lists the desired function and then the required key(s).

Note that in addition to the standard keyboard accelerators, you can define accelerators of your own. For example, you can define a Ctrl-Alt combination to invoke any shortcut, whether it's on the Desktop, in the Start menu, or in any other folder. Right-click any Windows shortcut icon (even those right in your Start menu), select Properties, choose the Shortcut tab, and in the Shortcut key field, type the key (not including Ctrl and Alt) to which the shortcut should be linked. For example, to assign Ctrl-Alt-Z to the current shortcut, simply type **Z** in the field. You can use any key except Esc, Enter, Tab, the Space bar, PrintScreen, Backspace, and Delete. If it conflicts with an accelerator used by any existing application, the accelerator you've just defined will usually override the existing accelerator (test it to make sure). To clear an existing shortcut's accelerator, just empty the Shortcut key field on the shortcut's Properties sheet. These instructions apply to Windows shortcuts only. Internet shortcuts don't support keyboard accelerators.

Keyboard Accelerators Listed by Key

Tables B-1 through B-7 list keystrokes that will work in Windows Explorer and most of the components that come with Windows Vista. However, some applications (including Microsoft applications) don't always follow the rules.

Table B-1. Function keys

Key	Action
F1	Start Help (supported in most applications).
F2	Rename selected icon or file in Windows Explorer or on the Desktop.
F3	Open Search (in Windows Explorer or on the Desktop only).
F4	Open a drop-down list (supported in many dialog boxes)—for example, press F4 in a File Open dialog to drop down the Look In list.
F5	Refresh the view in Windows Explorer, on the Desktop, in the Registry Editor, and some other applications.
F6	Move focus between panes in Windows Explorer.
F10	Send focus to the current application's menu.

Table B-2. Miscellaneous keys

Key	Action
Arrow keys	Basic navigation: move through menus, reposition the text cursor (insertion point), change the file selection, and so on.
Backspace	Move up one level in the folder hierarchy (Windows Explorer only).
Delete	Delete selected item(s) or selected text.
Down arrow	Open a drop-down listbox.
End	Go to end of line when editing text, or to the end of file list.
Enter	Activate highlighted choice in menu or dialog box, or insert a carriage return when editing text.
Esc	Close dialog box, message window, or menu without activating any choice (usually the same as clicking Cancel).
Home	Go to beginning of line (when editing text), or to the beginning of file list.
Page down	Scroll down one screen.
Page up	Scroll up one screen.
PrintScreen	Copy entire screen as a bitmap to the Clipboard.
Space bar	Toggle a checkbox that is selected in a dialog box, activate the command button with the focus, or toggle the selection of files when selecting multiple files with Ctrl.
Tab	Move focus to next control in a dialog box or window (hold Shift to go backward).

Table B-3. Alt key combinations

Key(s)	Action
Alt (by itself)	Send focus to the menu (same as F10). Also turns on the menu in applications where it is no longer used by default, such as Windows Explorer and Internet Explorer.
Alt-x	Activate menu or dialog control, where letter x is underlined (if the underlines are not visible, pressing Alt will display them).
Alt-double-click (on icon)	Display Properties sheet.
Alt-Enter	Display Properties sheet for selected icon in Windows Explorer or on the Desktop. Also switches command prompt between windowed and full-screen display.
Alt-Esc	Drop active window to bottom of pile, which, in effect, activates next open window.
Alt-F4	Close current window; if Taskbar or Desktop has the focus, exit Windows.

Keyboard
Shortcuts

Table B-3. Alt key combinations (continued)

Key(s)	Action
Alt-hyphen	Open the current document's system menu in a multiple document interface (MDI) application.
Alt-*numbers*	When used with the numbers on the numeric keypad only, inserts special characters corresponding to their ASCII codes into many applications. For example, press the Alt key and type **0169** for the copyright symbol. See "Character Map," in Chapter 10, for details.
Alt-PrintScreen	Copy active window as a bitmap to the Clipboard.
Alt-Shift-Tab	Same as Alt-Tab, but in the opposite direction.
Alt-Space bar	Open the current window's system menu.
Alt-Tab	Switch to the next running application—hold Alt while pressing Tab to cycle through running applications.
Alt-M	When the Taskbar has the focus, minimize all windows and move focus to the Desktop.
Alt-S	When the Taskbar has the focus, open the Start menu.

Table B-4. Ctrl key combinations

Keys	Action
Ctrl-A	Select all; in Windows Explorer, selects all files in the current folder. In word processors, selects all text in the current document.
Ctrl-Alt-*x*	User-defined accelerator for a shortcut, in which *x* is any key (discussed at the beginning of this appendix).
Ctrl-Alt-Delete	Show the logon dialog when no user is currently logged on; otherwise, switch to the Windows Security dialog, which provides access to Task Manager and Log Off, as well as switching to another user, allowing you to change your password or lock the computer. Use Ctrl-Alt-Delete to access the Task Manager when Explorer crashes or your computer becomes unresponsive.
Ctrl-arrow key	Scroll without moving selection.
Ctrl-click	Use to select multiple, noncontiguous items in a list or in Windows Explorer.
Ctrl-drag	Copy a file.
Ctrl-End	Move to the end of a document (in many applications).
Ctrl-Esc	Open the Start menu; press Esc and then Tab to move focus to the Taskbar, or press Tab again to move focus to the Taskbar, and then cycle through the toolbars on the Taskbar every time you press Tab.
Ctrl-F4	Close a document window in an MDI application.
Ctrl-F6	Switch between multiple documents in an MDI application. Similar to Ctrl-Tab; hold Shift to go in reverse.
Ctrl-Home	Move to the beginning of a document (in many applications).
Ctrl-Space bar	Select or deselect multiple, noncontiguous items in a listbox or in Windows Explorer.
Ctrl-Tab	Switch among tabs in a tabbed dialog or Internet Explorer; hold Shift to go in reverse.
Ctrl-C	Copy the selected item or selected text to the Clipboard. Also interrupts some command prompt applications.
Ctrl-F	Open Search (in Windows Explorer or on the Desktop only).
Ctrl-V	Paste the contents of the Clipboard.
Ctrl-X	Cut the selected item or selected text to the Clipboard.
Ctrl-Z	Undo; for example, erases text just entered, and repeals the last file operation in Windows Explorer.

Table B-5. Shift key combinations

Key(s)	Action
Shift	While inserting a CD, hold to disable AutoPlay.
Shift-arrow keys	Select text or select multiple items in a listbox or in Windows Explorer.
Shift-click	Select all items between currently selected item and item on which you're clicking; also works when selecting text.
Shift-click Close button	Close current folder and all parent folders (Windows Explorer in single-folder view only).
Shift-Alt-Tab	Same as Alt-Tab, but in reverse.
Shift-Ctrl-Tab	Same as Ctrl-Tab, but in reverse.
Shift-Ctrl-Esc	Open the Task Manager.
Shift-Delete	Delete a file without putting it in the Recycle Bin.
Shift-double-click	Open folder in two-pane Explorer view.
Shift-Tab	Same as Tab, but in reverse.

Table B-6. Windows logo key (WIN) combinations

Key(s)	Action
WIN	Open the Start menu.
WIN-Tab	If the Aero interface is active, this activates Windows Flip 3D.
WIN-Pause/Break	Display System Control Panel applet.
WIN-Space bar	Display the Sidebar.
WIN-D	Minimize all windows and move focus to Desktop.
WIN-E	Start Windows Explorer.
WIN-F	Launch Search.
Ctrl-WIN-F	Search for a computer on your network (requires Active Directory).
WIN-L	Lock computer, requiring password to regain access.[a]
WIN-M	Minimize current window.
Shift-WIN-M	Undo minimize current window.
WIN-R	Display Run dialog.
WIN-U	Open the Ease of Access Center.

a   You can also lock your computer by pressing Ctrl-Alt-Delete and clicking Lock this Computer.

Table B-7. Command Prompt keyboard accelerators

Key(s)	Action
Left/right arrow	Move cursor backward/forward one character.
Ctrl + left/right arrow	Move cursor backward/forward one word.
Home/End	Move cursor to beginning/end of line.
Up/down arrow	Scroll up (and back) through list of stored commands (called the Command Buffer or History). Each press of the up key recalls the previous command and displays it on the command line.
Page Up/Down	Recall oldest/most recent command in buffer.
Insert	Toggle insert/overtype mode (block cursor implies overtype mode).
Esc	Erase current line.

Table B-7. Command Prompt keyboard accelerators (continued)

Key(s)	Action
F1	Repeat text typed in preceding line, one character at a time.
F2 + *key*	Repeat text typed in preceding line, up to first character matching *key*.
F3	Repeat text typed in preceding line.
F5	Change the template for F1, F2, and F3 (described earlier) so that earlier commands are used as the template; press F5 repeatedly to cycle through the entire command buffer.
F6	Place an end-of-file character (^Z) at current position of command line.
F7	Show all entries in Command Buffer (History).
Alt-F7	Clear all entries in Command Buffer (History).
chars + F8	Entering one or more characters *chars* followed by F8 will display the most recent entry in the Command Buffer beginning with *chars*. Pressing F8 again will display the next most recent matching command, and so on. If no characters are specified, F8 simply cycles through existing commands in buffer.
F9 + *command#*	Display designated command on command line; use F7 to obtain numbers.
Ctrl-C	Interrupt the output of most Command Prompt applications.

Keyboard Accelerators Listed by Function

Table B-8 lists keys that operate in most contexts—in other words, on the Desktop, in the Explorer, and within most applications and dialogs. Functions are listed alphabetically, except where a logical order might make more sense.

Note also that there is essentially a limitless combination of keystrokes that you can use to activate any particular feature in a given application, all of which you can form by combining the various keystrokes listed in this appendix. For example, you can press Alt-F to open an application's File menu, then press P to Print, then press Enter to begin printing. Or press Ctrl-Esc to open the Start menu, Alt-Enter to open the Taskbar and Start Menu Properties, Ctrl-Tab to open the Taskbar tab (if necessary), and Alt-L to lock (or unlock) the Taskbar.

Table B-8. Keyboard accelerators listed by function

Key(s)	Action
Space bar	Checkbox, toggle on or off
Ctrl-C	Clipboard, copy
Alt-PrintScreen	Clipboard, copy current window as a bitmap
PrintScreen	Clipboard, copy entire screen as a bitmap
Ctrl-X	Clipboard, cut
Ctrl-V	Clipboard, paste
Ctrl-F4	Close current document
Alt-F4	Close current window
Esc	Close dialog box, message window, or menu
Space bar	Command button, click
Shift-F10, or context menu key on some keyboards	Context menu, open
Tab (hold Shift to go in reverse)	Controls cycle focus on a dialog box
Ctrl-C	Copy selected item or selected text to the Clipboard

Table B-8. Keyboard accelerators listed by function (continued)

Key(s)	Action
Ctrl-X	Cut selected item or selected text to the Clipboard
Windows Logo Key-B, Space bar	Puts you in the notification area (Windows Logo Key-B), then reveals hidden icons (Space bar)
Shift-Delete or Shift-drag item to Recycle Bin	Delete a file without putting it in the Recycle Bin
Delete	Delete selected item
Ctrl-Esc (or Windows Logo Key), then Esc, Tab, Tab, Tab	Desktop, activate
Windows Logo Key-D, or click empty portion of Taskbar and press Alt-M	Desktop, activate by minimizing all windows
Tab (hold Shift to go in reverse)	Dialog box, cycle through controls
Ctrl-Tab (hold Shift to go in reverse)	Dialog box, cycle through tabs
Ctrl-F4	Document, close
Ctrl-Home	Document, move to the beginning
Ctrl-End	Document, move to the end
Ctrl-F6 or Ctrl-Tab	Document, switch between
Down Arrow or F4	Drop-down listbox, open
Alt-F4	Exit an application
Ctrl-Esc, then Alt-F4	Exit Windows
Shift-Delete	File, delete without moving to Recycle Bin
Windows Logo Key-F (or F3 or Ctrl-F in Windows Explorer or on the Desktop)	File, search
Ctrl-Windows Logo Key-F	Find a computer on your network
Windows Logo Key-F (or F3 or Ctrl-F in Windows Explorer or on the Desktop)	Find files or folders
Tab (hold Shift to go in reverse)	Focus, move between controls on a dialog box
Shift-click Close button	Folder, close current and all parents (Windows Explorer in single-folder view only)
Right and left arrows	Folder, expand and collapse folders in tree
Shift-double-click	Folder, open in two-pane Explorer view
Windows Logo Key-F (or F3 or Ctrl-F in Windows Explorer or on the Desktop)	Folder, search
F1	Help (in most applications)
Down arrow or F4	Listbox, drop-down
Ctrl-click	Listbox, select multiple items
Ctrl-Space bar	Listbox, select or deselect items
Windows Logo Key-L (or press Ctrl-Alt-Delete and then Space bar)	Lock computer
Alt-x if menu doesn't have focus, x by itself if menu has focus	Menu, activate specific item with letter x underlined
Arrow keys	Menu, basic navigation
Esc	Menu, close
F10 or Alt (by itself)	Menu, move focus to
Shift-F10, or context menu key on some keyboards	Menu, open context menu
Windows Logo Key-D, or click empty portion of Taskbar and press Alt-M	Minimize all windows and move focus to Desktop

Table B-8. Keyboard accelerators listed by function (continued)

Key(s)	Action
Windows Logo Key-M (hold Shift to undo)	Minimize current window
F6	Panes, move focus between
Backspace	Parent folder, move to (in Windows Explorer)
Ctrl-V	Paste the contents of the Clipboard
Alt-double-click, or select and then press Alt-Enter	Properties, display for an icon
F5	Refresh (in Windows Explorer, on the Desktop, and some other applications)
F2	Rename selected icon or file in Windows Explorer or on the Desktop
Windows Logo Key-R	Run
Alt-PrintScreen	Screenshot, copy current window as a bitmap to the Clipboard
PrintScreen	Screenshot, copy entire screen as a bitmap to the Clipboard
Page Down	Scroll down one screen
Page Up	Scroll up one screen
Ctrl-arrow key	Scroll without moving selection
Windows Logo Key-F	Search for files or folders
F3 or Ctrl-F	Search for files or folders (in Windows Explorer or on the Desktop only)
Ctrl-A	Select all
Alt-drag file	Shortcut, create
Windows Logo Key or Ctrl-Esc	Start menu, open
Alt-Tab or Ctrl-Esc (hold Shift to go in reverse)	Switch to next application
Ctrl-F6 or Ctrl-Tab (hold Shift to go in reverse)	Switch to next document window
Alt-hyphen	System menu, show for current document
Alt-Space bar	System menu, show for current window
Windows Logo Key-Pause/Break	System Properties, open
Ctrl-Tab (hold Shift to go in reverse)	Tabs, switch between tabs
Shift-Ctrl-Esc (or press Ctrl-Alt-Delete and click Task Manager)	Task Manager, open
Ctrl-Esc, then Alt-Enter	Taskbar and Start Menu Properties, open
Windows Logo Key-Tab	Launches Flip 3D
Ctrl-Z	Undo
Alt-Tab (hold Shift to go in reverse)	Window, activate next
Alt-F4	Window, close
Alt-Esc	Window, drop to bottom of pile
Windows Logo Key-M (hold Shift to undo)	Window, minimize
Windows Logo Key-D (hold Shift to undo)	Window, minimize all
Alt-Tab (hold Shift to go in reverse)	Window, switch to
Windows Logo Key-E	Windows Explorer, open
F6	Windows Explorer, switch between panes

C

Keyboard Equivalents for Symbols and International Characters

Among the programs included in Windows Vista is the Character Map utility (described in Chapter 10), which allows you to place special characters and symbols in your documents that can't otherwise by typed from the keyboard. The collection of 1,185 characters and symbols shown in Character Map is the Unicode set, a character encoding standard developed by the Unicode Consortium, intended to represent nearly all of the written languages of the world.

A subset of the Unicode set is the ASCII character set (ASCII stands for American Standard Code for Information Interchange); although only a mere 255 characters, this character set includes the numbers, upper- and lowercase letters, and standard symbols (!, @, #, $, %, [,], and so on) found on any standard keyboard. The symbols and international characters shown in Table C-1 are also part of the ASCII character set.

What sets the members of the ASCII set apart from the larger Unicode set is that you can type every single one of the ASCII characters from the keyboard, even the extended characters shown here. To type a character listed in Table C-1, hold the Alt key and type the four-digit number shown on the right using the numeric keypad, including the initial zero. For example, for the copyright symbol, press the Alt key and type **0169**. Note that the standard number keys (above the alphabet) won't work, so those with abbreviated laptop keyboards may not be able to use these at all.

Table C-1. Common symbols and characters and their keyboard shortcuts

Char	Code	Char	Code	Char	Code	Char	Code
ª	0170	©	0169	À	0192	à	0224
º	0176	®	0174	Á	0193	á	0225
°	0186	™	0153	Â	0194	â	0226
¹	0185	Æ	0198	Ã	0195	ã	0227
²	0178	æ	0230	Ä	0196	ä	0228

Table C-1. Common symbols and characters and their keyboard shortcuts (continued)

Char	Code	Char	Code	Char	Code	Char	Code
³	0179	ß	0223	Å	0197	å	0229
¼	0188	Œ	0140	Ç	0199	ç	0231
½	0189	œ	0156	È	0200	è	0232
¾	0190	Ð	0208	É	0201	é	0233
‰	0137	þ	0254	Ê	0202	ê	0234
±	0177	Þ	0222	Ë	0203	ë	0235
×	0215	?	0259	Ì	0204	ì	0236
÷	0247	µ	0181	Í	0205	í	0237
Ø	0216	…	0133	Î	0206	î	0238
ø	0248	´	0180	Ï	0207	ï	0239
‹	0139	'	0145	Ñ	0209	ñ	0241
›	0155	'	0146	Ò	0210	ò	0242
«	0171	"	0147	Ó	0211	ó	0243
»	0187	"	0148	Ô	0212	ô	0244
¦	0166	•	0149	Õ	0213	õ	0245
€	0128	·	0183	Ö	0214	ö	0246
¢	0162	¤	0164	Š	0138	š	0154
£	0163		0173	Ù	0217	ù	0249
¥	0165	–	0150	Ú	0218	ú	0250
§	0167	—	0151	Û	0219	û	0251
ƒ	0131	¬	0172	Ü	0220	ü	0252
†	0134	¯	0175	Ý	0221	ý	0253
‡	0135	¿	0191	Ÿ	0159	ÿ	0255
¶	0182	¨	0168	Ž	0142	ž	0158

Common Filename Extensions

This appendix lists many of the most common filename extensions that you'll find on your system, that you might download, or that you have received over the Internet.

Extensions were universally used on DOS and Windows 3.1 files, but Microsoft has gone to some difficulty to hide them in Windows Vista. This is unfortunate, because they play a major role in the way Windows decides what application will be used to open a file, as well as which files will be visible when opening files in a given application. Although direct associations are made between some files without extensions and the applications needed to open them, in most cases the association is between an extension and a Registry setting that tells the system what application to use. To enable the display of filename extensions, open Windows Explorer, go to Control Panel → [Appearance and Personalization] → Folder Options → View tab, and turn off the "Hide extensions for known file types" option.

If you double-click on an unknown file type, the Open With dialog box appears, allowing you to make a new association. To subsequently change an association once it has been made, right-click on the file and select Open With, or select Properties and then click Change.

Table D-1 list many system extensions, but third-party applications use literally thousands of file formats. And you might be thrown off by an improperly named file, or by an application using a standard filename extension for a nonstandard purpose. You can open many of these file types only if you have the appropriate application. If all else fails, you can open just about any file in Notepad; although nontext files will look mostly like gibberish, you may get clues in some of the excerpts of readable text you'll see.

If you still can't find a file's type from its extension, there are several more good sources:

- Microsoft has put together a simple "extension finder" web site, intended for use with the "Use the Web service to find the correct program" feature that appears when you try to open a file with an extension that Windows doesn't recognize. The address for this site is:

  http://shell.windows.com/fileassoc/0409/xml/redir.asp?Ext={your extension}

  where *{your extension}* is the filename extension (without the dot) that you want to learn more about. For example, to find out about the *.sit* extension, you'd go to:

  http://shell.windows.com/fileassoc/0409/xml/redir.asp?Ext=sit

- Use an ordinary search engine such as Google (*http://www.google.com*) to search for references to the filename extension. For example, to find out about the *.hqx* extension, try searching for "hqx file" (with the quotes).

Table D-1. Common filename extensions

Extension	Description
.$$$	Temporary file
.1st	ASCII text file (e.g., *READ.1st*)
.3ds	3D Studio file
.3gp, .3gpp	Video clip created on a cell phone or other mobile device
.3gr	Windows Video Grabber datafile
.8m	PageMaker Printer font with Math 8 extended character set
.8u	PageMaker Printer font with Roman 8 extended character set
.abf	Adobe Binary Font
.abm	Photo album
.abs	MPEG audio sound file
.aca	Microsoft Agent Character file
.ace	Ace Archiver compressed file
.acf	Microsoft Agent Character file
.ad	AfterDark screensaver
.adi	AutoCAD graphics
.adx	Archetype designer document
.afi	Truevision bitmap graphics
.afm	ATM Type 1 font metric ASCII data for font installer
.ai	Adobe Illustrator vector graphics
.ans	ANSI graphics; character animation
.aps	Microsoft Visual C++ file
.arc	Compressed file archive
.arf	Automatic Response File
.arj	Compressed file archive created by ARJ
.asc	ASCII text file

Extension	Description
.ascx	Microsoft ASP.NET user control file
.asd	Word for Windows Autosave file
.asm	Assembly source code file
.asmx	Microsoft .NET Web Service file
.asp	Microsoft Active Server Page
.aspx	Microsoft ASP.NET file
.asx	Microsoft Windows Media Active Stream Redirector file
.asx	Windows Media Streaming video shortcut
.atm	Adobe Type Manager data/information
.au	Audio file used on older web pages
.avi	Video for Windows Audio Video Interleaved movie clip
.awm	Animation Works movie
.b3d	3D Builder file
.bak	Backup file (generic)
.bas	Basic source code file
.bat	DOS batch file
.bco	Bitstream Outline font description
.bdr	Microsoft Publisher Border
.bez	Bitstream Outline font description
.bga	Bitmap graphics
.bib	Bibliography (ASCII)
.bin	Binary file
.bit	Bitmap X11
.bkf	Microsoft backup file
.bkw	FontEdit mirror image of font set
.bm	Bitmap graphics
.bmf	Corel image file
.bmp	Windows bitmap
.bsc	Microsoft Fortran Pwbrmake object file
.bup	Backup file (generic)
.c	C source code file
.c++	C++ source code file
.cab	Microsoft installation archive Cabinet file
.cas	Comma-delimited ASCII file
.cc	C++ source code file
.ccb	Visual Basic animated button configuration
.cel	Autodesk Animator—Lumena Graphics
.cfg	Configuration file
.cgi	Common Gateway Interface script
.cgm	Computer Graphics Metafile vector graphics
.chd	FontChameleon Font descriptor

Extension	Description
.chk	ChkDsk recovered data
.cif	Caltech Intermediate Format graphics
.cif	Easy CD Creator CD image file
.class	Compiled Java class file
.cls	C++ class definition file
.cmf	Creative Music File FM-music file
.cnt	Helpfile contents
.col	Microsoft Multiplan spreadsheet
.contact	Windows Contacts contact entry
.cpi	Colorlab Processed Image bitmap graphics
.cpi	DOS Code Page Information file
.cpp	C++ source code file
.cps	Colored PostScript files
.crf	Microsoft MASM—Zortech C++ cross-reference
.cs	C# source code file
.csv	Comma Separated Value text file format (ASCII)
.ctx	Microsoft online guides Course TeXt file
.ctx	Pretty Good Privacy RSA System cipher text file
.cvp	WinFax cover page
.cvs	Canvas graphics
.dat	Datafile (generic)
.dbg	Microsoft C/C++ symbolic debugging information
.dcr	Shockwave file
.dcs	CYMK format bitmap graphics
.ddb	Bitmap graphics
.dev	Device driver (old)
.dib	Device-Independent Bitmap bitmap graphics
.dic	Lotus Notes/Domino dictionary file
.dip	Graphics
.diz	Description In Zip description file
.dlg	Microsoft Windows SDK dialog resource script file
.doc	Microsoft Word document
.dot	Word for Windows template
.drv	Device driver (old)
.dvr-ms	Windows Media Center recorded video file
.dxf	AutoCAD Drawing Interchange File format vector graphics
.emf	Enhanced Metafile graphics
.eml	Microsoft Outlook Express electronic mail
.eps	Adobe Illustrator Encapsulated PostScript vector graphics
.evt	Event log
.exe	Executable program

Extension	Description
.f77	Fortran 77 source code file
.faq	Frequently Asked Questions text file
.fax	Incoming fax
.fd	Microsoft Fortran Declaration file
.ff	Agfa Compugraphics Outline font description
.ffl	Microsoft Fast Find file
.ffo	Microsoft Fast Find file
.ffx	Microsoft Fast Find file
.fhx	Macromedia FreeHand version *x* vector graphics
.fh4	Macromedia FreeHand 4.*x* vector graphics
.fi	Microsoft Fortran Interface file
.fif	Fractal Image Format file
.flc	Autodesk Animator animation
.fli	Autodesk Animator animation
.fm	FrameMaker document
.fm1	Lotus 1-2-3 release 2.*x* spreadsheet
.fm3	Lotus 1-2-3 release 3.*x* spreadsheet
.fmb	WordPerfect for Windows File Manager button bar
.fnt	Font file
.fon	Windows 3.*x* font library font file
.fot	Windows Font Installer installed TrueType font
.frf	FontMonger Font
frm	Visual Basic form
.fts	Windows Help full-text search index file
.fxs	WinFax fax transmit format graphics
.gadget	Windows Gadget
.gcd	Graphics
.gwi	Groupwise file
.gz	GNU ZIP compressed file archive created by GZIP
.h	Header file (used with .c source code)
.h++	C++ header file
.hdf	Help Development Kit help file
.hgl	HP Graphics Language graphics
.hh	C++ header file
.hlp	Help information
.hpf	PageMaker HP LaserJet fonts
.hpj	Microsoft Help Compiler help project
.hqx	Compressed Macintosh file archive created by Binhex
.htm	HyperText Markup Language document
.html	HyperText Markup Language document
.htt	HyperText template

Table D-1. Common filename extensions (continued)

Extension	Description
.hxx	C++ header file
.ical	iCalendar file
.icb	Bitmap graphics
.icn	Icon source code file
.ilk	Microsoft ILink incremental linker outline of program's format
.imp	Lotus Improv spreadsheet
.imz	Compressed floppy image
.inc	Include file (programming)
.inf	Information text file
.inf	Install script/Driver information
.ini	Initialization file
.ion	File description (e.g., *descript.ion*)
.iso	CD or DVD image file
.isr	Microsoft Streets & Trips route file
.jar	Java archive file
.jas	Graphics
.java	Java source code file
.jff	JPEG File Interchange Format bitmap graphics
.jpg	JPEG image file
.jsp	Java Server Page
.jtf	JPEG Tagged Interchange Format bitmap graphics
.kar	MIDI file with karaoke word track
.key	Keyboard macros
.lbm	DeluxePaint bitmap graphics
.ldb	Microsoft Access data
.lex	Lexicon
.lha	Compressed file archive created by LHA/LHARC
.lib	Library file (programming)
.lif	Compressed file archive
.lnk	Windows shortcut
.log	Logfile (text)
.lrf	Microsoft C/C++ Linker response file
.lwz	Microsoft Linguistically Enhanced Sound file
.lzh	Compressed file archive created by LHA/LHARC
.lzs	Compressed file archive created by LARC
.lzx	Compressed file archive
.m3u	Media playlist
.mak	Makefile
.mak	Visual Basic project file
.man	Command manual
.map	Color palette

Extension	Description
.map	Linker map file
.mat	Matlab datafile
.mbx	Eudora mailbox
.mda	Microsoft Access data
.mdb	Microsoft Access database
.mdl	3D Design Plus model
.mdt	Microsoft ILink incremental linker data table
.me	ASCII text file (e.g., *READ.me*)
.mht	Microsoft MHTML document
.mic	Microsoft Image Composer file
.mif	FrameMaker Maker Interchange Format
.mim	MIME file (used for email attachments)
.mk	Makefile
.mke	Microsoft Windows SDK makefile
.mmf	Microsoft Mail mail message file
.mny	Microsoft Money Account book
.mov	QuickTime movie
.mp2	MPEG audio or video file
.mp3	MPEG Layer 3 audio file
.mp4	MPEG-4 movie
.mpc	Microsoft Project Calendar file
.mpe	MPEG movie clip
.mpd	Microsoft Project database file
.mpg	MPEG movie
.mpp	Microsoft Project project file
.mpv	Microsoft Project view file
.mrb	Microsoft C/C++ Multiple Resolution Bitmap graphics
.msc	Microsoft C makefile
.msi	Windows Installer file
.mso	Microsoft FrontPage file
.msp	Microsoft Paint bitmap graphics
.mst	Microsoft Windows SDK setup script
.msw	Microsoft Word text file
.mswmm	Windows Movie Maker project
.mxt	Microsoft C data
.nfo	Info file (ASCII)
.nlm	Netware Loadable Module
.nsf	Lotus Notes/Domino database
.nt	Windows NT Startup files
.ntf	Lotus Notes/Domino template file
.nws	Info text file

Extension	Description
.nxt	NeXT format sound
.ofm	Adobe font
.oft	Microsoft Outlook Item template
.ogg	Ogg Vorbis music file
.old	Backup file (generic)
.one	Microsoft Office OneNote file
.ost	Microsoft Outlook Offline file
.out	Output file (ASCII)
.p65	Adobe PageMaker v6.5
.pab	Microsoft Outlook personal address book
.pak	Compressed file archive created by PAK; also a Quake game file
.pal	Color palette
.pas	Pascal source code file
.pb	WinFax Pro phonebook
.pbi	Microsoft Source Profiler profiler binary input
.pbm	Portable Bit Map graphics
.pbo	Microsoft Source Profiler profiler binary output
.pbt	Microsoft Source Profiler profiler binary table
.pcc	PC Paintbrush Cutout picture vector graphics
.pcd	Kodak PhotoCD graphics
.pcf	Microsoft Source Profiler profiler command file
.pch	Microsoft C/C++ precompiled header
.pcl	HP Printer Control Language HP-PCL graphics data
.pcx	PC Paintbrush bitmap graphics
.pda	Bitmap graphics
.pdb	Palm database
.pdd	Adobe PhotoDeluxe image
.pdf	Adobe Portable Document Format
.pfb	Type 1 font file
.pfm	Type 1 font metric file
.pgm	Portable Grayscale bitmap graphics
.pgp	Pretty Good Privacy RSA System Support file
.ph	Microsoft C/C++ Phrase-table
.ph	Perl header file
.pic	PC Paint bitmap graphics
.pka	Compressed file archive created by PKARC
.pkg	NeXT/Mac OS X Installer archive
.pl	Perl source code file
.pl1	3D Home Architect room plan
.pm3	PageMaker 3 document
.pm4	PageMaker 4 document

Extension	Description
.pm5	PageMaker 5 document
.png	Portable Network Graphics bitmap
.pnm	Graphics file (Portable aNy Map)
.pov	Persistence Of Vision raytraced graphics image
.ppd	Acrobat PostScript Printer Description
.ppm	Portable Pixel Map graphics
.ppt	PowerPoint presentation
.pr2	Adobe Persuasion 2.*x* presentation
.pr3	Adobe Persuasion 3.*x* presentation
.prc	Palm resource file
.prj	Project
.ps	PostScript file
.psd	Photoshop image
.pst	Microsoft Outlook personal folder
.pt3	PageMaker 3 template
.pt4	PageMaker 4 template
.pub	Microsoft Publisher Page template
.pub	Pretty Good Privacy RSA System Public key ring file
.pwl	Password List
.py	Python script file
.pyc	Compiled Python script file
.qbw	QuickBooks for Windows spreadsheet
.qdat	QuickTime Installer cache
.qdb	Quicken datafile
.qdf	Quicken for Windows datafile
.qdt	Quicken datafile
.qfl	Quicken Family Lawyer file
.qfx	QuickLink fax
.qic	Backup set for Microsoft Backup
.qif	Quicken Interchange Format
.qlb	Microsoft C/C++ Quick library
.qlp	QuickLink Printer driver
.qt	QuickTime movie
.qxd	QuarkXPress Document
.qxl	QuarkXPress Element library
.r00, .r01	Compressed file archive created by RAR (supplemental to .rar)
.ra	RealMedia file
.ram	RealMedia shortcut
.rar	Compressed file archive created by RAR
.ras	Sun Rasterfile graphics
.rc	Microsoft C/C++, Borland C++ Resource script

Table D-1. Common filename extensions (continued)

Extension	Description
.rcg	Netscape newsgroup file
.rdp	Remote Desktop Connection Profile
.ref	Cross-reference
.res	Microsoft C/C++, Borland C++ Compiled resource
.rib	3DReality Graphics in Renderman format
.rif	Fractal Design Painter Riff bitmap graphics
.rl4	Bitmap graphics
.rl8	Bitmap graphics
.rlc	Graphics 1-bit/pixel scanner output
.rtf	Windows Word Rich Text Format text file (Word)
.rtf	Windows Help file script
.rvp	Microsoft Scan Configuration file
.sav	Configuration file
.sav	Backup file
.sbi	Creative Labs Sound Blaster Instrument file
.sco	High score
.sdf	System Data Format (ASCII)
.sea	Self-Extracting compressed Macintosh file Archive
.search-ms	Windows Vista saved search folder
.sec	Pretty Good Privacy RSA System Secret key ring file
.sfi	HP LaserJet landscape printer font
.sif	Windows NT Setup Setup Installation Files info
.sit	Compressed Macintosh archive created by STUFFIT
.sng	MIDI sound Song
.spc	Microsoft Multiplan Program
.srp	QuickLink Script
.ssm	RealPlayer Standard Streaming Metafile
.sts	Microsoft C/C++ Project status info
.swf	ShockWave Flash object
.sys	Windows or DOS System file—device driver or hardware configuration info
.tar	Compressed file archive created by TAR
.taz	Compressed file archive created by TAR and COMPRESS (equiv. to .tar.Z)
.tga	Truevision Targa bitmap graphics
.tgz	Compressed file archive created by TAR and GNUzip (equiv. to .tar.gz)
.thm	Microsoft Clipart Gallery database
.tif	Tagged Image File Format bitmap graphics
.tis	MahJongg 3.0 Tile set
.tlb	Visual C++ Type library
.tmp	Temporary file
.toc	Eudora Table Of Contents
.torrent	BitTorrent

Extension	Description
.tpz	Compressed file archive created by TAR and GNUzip (equiv. to .tar.gz)
.ttf	TrueType Font file
.txt	Text file
.tym	PageMaker Time Stamp
.tz	Compressed file archive created by TAR and COMPRESS (equiv. to .tar.Z)
.uhs	Universal Hint System
.uu	Compressed ASCII file archive created by UUEncode/UUDecode
.uue	Compressed ASCII file archive created by UUEncode/UUDecode
.vbs	Visual Basic Script file
.vbx	Visual Basic Visual Basic eXtension (custom control)
.vcf	VCard file
.vcw	Microsoft Visual C++ Visual workbench information
.vda	Bitmap graphics
.vmc	Acrobat reader Virtual Memory Configuration
.vnc	VNC connection profile
.vob	DVD video movie file
.voc	Creative Voice file Digitized samples
.vds	Visio drawing file
.vue	3D Studio animation
.vxd	Virtual device driver
.wab	Outlook (Windows Address Book) file
.wad	Doom game file
.wav	Waveform audio file
.wb1	Quattro Pro Notebook
.wb2	Quattro Pro Spreadsheet
.wba	Winace ZIP file
.wba	WindowBlinds Compressed Skin for Windows XP
.wbk	WordPerfect for Windows document/workbook
.wcm	Microsoft Works Data transmission file
.wdb	Microsoft Works Database
.wdl	Windows XP Watchdog Log file
.wfx	WinFax datafile
.wiz	Microsoft Publisher Page wizard
.wk1	Lotus 1-2-3 version 2.x—Symphony 1.1+ spreadsheet
.wk3	Lotus 1-2-3 version 3.x spreadsheet
.wk4	Lotus 1-2-3 version 3.4 spreadsheet
.wkb	WordPerfect for Windows document
.wkq	Quattro spreadsheet
.wks	Lotus 1-2-3 version 1A—Symphony 1.0— Microsoft Works spreadsheet
.wma	Microsoft Windows Media Active Streaming file
.wmf	Windows MetaFile vector graphics

Table D-1. Common filename extensions (continued)

Extension	Description
.wmv	Microsoft Active Streaming file
.wn	NeXT WriteNow Text
.wp	WordPerfect 4.2 text file
.wp5	WordPerfect 5.x document
.wpm	WordPerfect macros
.wps	Microsoft Works text document
.wq1	Quattro Pro spreadsheet
.wri	Windows Write text file
.wrl	VRML file
.wrml	VRML file
.wsz	WinAmp Skin ZIP file
.xla	Microsoft Excel Add-in macro sheet
.xlb	Microsoft Excel data
.xlc	Microsoft Excel Chart document
.xll	Microsoft Excel Excel Dynamic Link Library
.xlm	MS Excel Macro sheet
.xlr	Microsoft Works file
.xls	Microsoft Excel worksheet
.xlt	Microsoft Excel template
.xlw	Microsoft Excel workbook
.xmi	Compressed extended MIDI music
.xml	XML document
.xnk	Microsoft Exchange Shortcut
.xps	XPS Document (Paper Specification)
.xsl	XSL stylesheet
.xwk	Crosstalk keyboard mapping
.xwp	Crosstalk session
.z	Compressed file archive created by COMPRESS
.z3	Infocom game module
.z5	Inform game module
.zip	Compressed ZIP file archive
.zoo	Compressed file archive created by ZOO

E

Services

Table E-1 lists the background services installed by default in Windows Vista. Note that some of the following may not be present in your system (depending on your Windows edition or installed components), and you may see some services on your own computer that aren't listed here (which may have been added after you installed Windows Vista).

One of the advantages of services over standard applications and drivers is that they are run when Windows starts, but before a user logs in.

Services can be started, stopped, and configured to automatically start with the Services utility (*services.msc*). By default, most of the services listed in Table E-1 will remain dormant (stopped) until started by the user (directly or indirectly by starting a program that depends on these services). For more information on services, see "Microsoft Management Console," in Chapter 10.

If you disable any service, any other services that explicitly depend on it will fail to start. So be careful before disabling services, and if you find that one refuses to start, it may be because a service on which it depends has been disabled. Check the Event Viewer (see Chapter 11) for error messages from services.

Table E-1. Services in Windows Vista

Name	Filename	Description
Application Experience	*svchost.exe*	Processes application compatibility cache requests for applications when they are launched.
Application Information	*svchost.exe*	Helps interactive applications run with additional administrative privileges.
Application Layer Gateway Service	*alg.exe*	Provides support for third-party protocol plug-ins for Internet Connection Sharing and the Windows Firewall.
Application Management	*svchost.exe*	Provides software installation services such as Assign, Publish, and Remove.

Name	Filename	Description
Background Intelligent Transfer Service	*svchost.exe*	Uses idle network bandwidth to transfer data.
Base Filtering Engine	*svchost.exe*	Manages firewall and Internet Protocol security (IPsec) policies and implements user mode filtering. Stopping or disabling the BFE service will reduce system security and cause unpredictable behavior in IPsec management and firewall applications.
Block Level Backup Engine Service	*wbengine.exe*	Performs block-level backup and recovery of data.
Certificate Propagation	*svchost.exe*	Propagates certificates from smart cards.
CNG Key Isolation	*lsass.exe*	Service stores and uses long-lived private keys and associated cryptographic operations in a secure process.
COM+ Event System	*svchost.exe*	Supports System Event Notification Service (SENS), which provides automatic distribution of events to subscribing component object model (COM) components. If the service is stopped, SENS will close and will not be able to provide logon and logoff notifications.
COM+ System Application	*dllhost.exe*	Manages the configuration and tracking of components based on COM+. If the service is stopped, most components based on COM+ will not function properly.
Computer Browser	*svchost.exe*	Maintains an updated list of computers on the network and supplies this list to computers designated as browsers. If this service is stopped, this list will not be updated or maintained.
Cryptographic Services	*svchost.exe*	Provides four management services: Catalog Database Service, which confirms the signatures of Windows files; Protected Root Service, which adds and removes Trusted Root Certification Authority certificates from this computer; Automatic Root Certificate Update Service, which retrieves root certificates from Windows Update; and Key Service, which helps enroll this computer for certificates. If this service is stopped, these management services will not function properly.
DCOM Server Process Launcher	*svchost.exe*	Provides launch functionality for distributed component object model (DCOM) services. DCOM allows COM components to communicate over networks.
Desktop Window Manager Session Manager	*dfsr.exe*	Provides startup and maintenance services for the Desktop Window Manager, which is the windowing system that enables Windows Aero.
DFS Replication	*dfsr.exe*	Replicates files among multiple PCs and keeps them synchronized.
DHCP Client	*svchost.exe*	Manages network configuration by registering and updating Internet Protocol (IP) addresses and Domain Name System (DNS) names.
Diagnostic Policy Service	*svchost.exe*	Enables detection of problems, troubleshooting, and problem resolution for Windows components. If the service is stopped, diagnostics will no longer function.
Diagnostic Service Host	*svchost.exe*	Enables detection of problems, troubleshooting, and problem resolution for Windows components. If the service is stopped, diagnostics will no longer function.
Diagnostic System Host	*svchost.exe*	Enables detection of problems, troubleshooting, and problem resolution for Windows components. If the service is stopped, diagnostics will no longer function.
Distributed Link Tracking Client	*svchost.exe*	Maintains links between NTFS files within a computer or across computers in a network domain.
Distributed Transaction Coordinator	*msdtc.exe*	Coordinates transactions that span multiple resource managers, such as databases, message queues, and filesystems. If this service is stopped, these transactions will not occur.

Name	Filename	Description
DNS Client	*svchost.exe*	Resolves and caches DNS names for this computer. If this service is stopped, this computer will not be able to resolve DNS names and locate Active Directory domain controllers.
Extensible Authentication Protocol	*svchost.exe*	The Extensible Authentication Protocol (EAP) service provides network authentication for 802.1x wired and wireless, Virtual Private Network (VPN), and Network Access Protection (NAP). It also provides APIs used by network access clients, including wireless and VPN clients, during the authentication process. If you disable the service, the PC cannot access networks that require EAP authentication.
Fax	*fxssvc.exe*	Enables you to send and receive faxes, utilizing fax resources available on this computer or on the network.
Function Discovery Provider Host	*svchost.exe*	The Host process for Function Discovery providers, which allows resources to be discovered over the network.
Function Discovery Resource Publication	*svchost.exe*	Make information available to the computer and its attached resources so that they can be discovered over the network. If the service is stopped, network resources will no longer be published and they will not be discovered by other computers on the network.
Group Policy Client	*svchost.exe*	Applies settings configured by administrators for the computer and users through Group Policy. If the service is stopped or disabled, applications and components will not be manageable through Group Policy. Any components or applications that depend on the Group Policy component might not work If the service is stopped or disabled.
Health Key and Certificate Management	*svchost.exe*	Provides X.509 certificate and key management services for the Network Access Protection Agent. Enforcement technologies that use X.509 certificates may not function properly without the service.
Human Interface Device Access	*svchost.exe*	Enables generic input access to Human Interface Devices (HIDs), which activates and maintains the use of predefined hot buttons on keyboards, remote controls, and other multimedia devices. If this service is stopped, hot buttons controlled by this service will no longer function.
IKE and AuthIP IPsec Keying Module	*svchost.exe*	Modules used for authentication and key exchange in Internet Protocol security (IPsec). Stopping or disabling the service will disable IKE and AuthIP key exchange with peer computers.
Interactive Services Detection	*UIODetect.exe*	Enables notification of user input for interactive services. This enables access to dialogs created by interactive services when they appear. If the service is stopped, notifications of new interactive service dialogs will no longer function. If the service is disabled, both notifications of and access to new interactive service dialogs will no longer function.
Internet Connection Sharing (ICS)	*svchost.exe*	Provides Network Address Translation (NAT), addressing, name resolution, and/or intrusion prevention services for a home or small-office network.
IP Helper	*svchost.exe*	Provides automatic IPv6 connectivity over an IPv4 network. If the service is stopped, the PC will only have IPv6 connectivity if it is connected to a native IPv6 network.
IPsec Policy Agent	*svchost.exe*	Enforces IPsec policies created through the IP Security Policies Snap-in or the command-line tool netsh ipsec. If you stop the service, you may experience network connectivity issues if your policy requires that connections use IPsec. Remote management of the Windows Firewall will not be available if the service is stopped.
KtmRm for Distributed Transaction Coordinator	*svchost.exe*	Coordinates transactions between MSDTC and the Kernel Transaction Manager (KTM).

Name	Filename	Description
Link-Layer Topology Discovery Mapper	*svchost.exe*	Creates the Network Map in the Network and Sharing Center. If this service is disabled, the Network Map will not function properly.
Microsoft .NET Framework NGEN	*mscorsvw.exe*	Microsoft .NET Framework native image generator (NGEN).
Microsoft iSCSI Initiator Service	*svchost.exe*	Manages Internet SCSI (iSCSI) sessions from the computer to remote iSCSI target devices. If the service is stopped, this computer will not be able to log in or access iSCSI targets.
Microsoft Software Shadow Copy Provider	*dllhost.exe*	Manages software-based volume shadow copies taken by the Volume Shadow Copy service. If this service is stopped, software-based volume shadow copies cannot be managed.
Multimedia Class Scheduler	*svchost.exe*	Used mainly by multimedia applications, this service enables relative prioritization of work based on system-wide task priorities. If the service is stopped, individual tasks resort to their default priority.
Net.Tcp Port Sharing Service	*SMSvcHost.exe*	Provides ability to share TCP ports over the net.tcp protocol.
Netlogon	*lsass.exe*	Maintains a secure channel between the PC and the domain controller for authenticating users and services. If the service is stopped, the computer may not authenticate users and services and the domain controller cannot register DNS records.
Network Access Protection Agent	*svchost.exe*	Enables NAP functionality, which allows network administrators to set security requirements for computers that want to connect to a network.
Network Connections	*svchost.exe*	Manages objects in the Network and Dial-Up Connections folder.
Network List Service	*svchost.exe*	Identifies the networks to which the computer has connected, collects and stores properties for these networks, and notifies applications when these properties change.
Network Location Awareness	*svchost.exe*	Collects and stores configuration information for the network and notifies programs when the information is modified. If the service is stopped, configuration information might be unavailable.
Network Store Interface Service	*svchost.exe*	Delivers network notifications to clients. Stopping the service will cause loss of network connectivity.
Offline Files	*svchost.exe*	Performs maintenance activities on the Offline Files cache, responds to user logon and logoff events, implements the internals of the public API, and dispatches interesting events to those interested in Offline Files activities and changes in cache state.
Parental Controls	*svchost.exe*	Enables Parental Controls. If the service is not running, Parental Controls will not work.
Peer Name Resolution Protocol	*svchost.exe*	Enables Serverless Peer Name Resolution over the Internet. If disabled, some Peer-to-Peer and Collaborative applications, such as Windows Meetings, may not function.
Peer Networking Grouping	*svchost.exe*	Provides Peer Networking Grouping services.
Peer Networking Identity Manager	*svchost.exe*	Provides Identity service for Peer Networking.
Performance Logs & Alerts	*svchost.exe*	Collects performance data from local or remote computers based on preconfigured schedule parameters, then writes the data to a log or triggers an alert. If this service is stopped, performance information will not be collected.
Plug and Play	*svchost.exe*	Enables a computer to recognize and adapt to hardware changes with little or no user input. Stopping or disabling this service will result in system instability.

Name	Filename	Description
PnP-X IP Bus Enumerator	*svchost.exe*	Manages the virtual network bus. It discovers network-connected devices using the SSDP/WS discovery protocols and gives them presence in PnP. If this service is stopped or disabled, presence of NCD devices will not be maintained in PnP.
PNRP Machine Name Publication Service	*svchost.exe*	Publishes a machine name using the Peer Name Resolution Protocol.
Portable Device Enumerator Service	*svchost.exe*	Enforces group policy for removable mass-storage devices. Enables applications such as Windows Media Player and the Image Import Wizard to transfer and synchronize content using removable mass-storage devices.
Print Spooler	*spoolsv.exe*	Loads files to memory for later printing.
Problem Reports and Solutions Control Panel Support	*svchost.exe*	Provides support for viewing, sending, and deleting system-level problem reports for the Problem Reports and Solutions control panel.
Program Compatibility Assistant Service	*svchost.exe*	Provides support for the Program Compatibility Assistant. If this service is stopped, the Program Compatibility Assistant will not function properly. If this service is disabled, any services that depend on it will fail to start.
Protected Storage	*lsass.exe*	Provides protected storage for sensitive data, such as private keys, to prevent access by unauthorized services, processes, or users.
Quality Windows Audio Video Experience (qWave)	*svchost.exe*	A networking platform for Audio Video (AV) streaming applications on IP home networks. qWave enhances AV streaming performance and reliability by ensuring network quality of service (QoS) for AV applications.
ReadyBoost	*svchost.exe*	Provides support for improving system performance using ReadyBoost.
Remote Access Auto Connection Manager	*svchost.exe*	Creates a connection to a remote network whenever a program references a remote DNS or NetBIOS name or address.
Remote Access Connection Manager	*svchost.exe*	Creates a network connection.
Remote Procedure Call (RPC)	*svchost.exe*	Provides the endpoint mapper and other miscellaneous RPC services.
Remote Procedure Call (RPC) Locator	*locator.exe*	Manages the RPC name service database.
Remote Registry	*svchost.exe*	Enables remote users to modify Registry settings on this computer. If this service is stopped, only users on this computer can modify the Registry.
Routing and Remote Access	*svchost.exe*	Offers routing services to businesses in local- and wide-area network environments.
Secondary Logon	*svchost.exe*	Enables starting processes under alternate credentials. If this service is stopped, this type of logon access will be unavailable.
Security Accounts Manager	*lsass.exe*	Stores security information for local user accounts.
Security Center	*svchost.exe*	Monitors system security settings and configurations.
Server	*svchost.exe*	Supports file, print, and named-pipe sharing over the network for this computer. If this service is stopped, these functions will be unavailable.
Shell Hardware Detection	*svchost.exe*	Provides notifications for AutoPlay hardware events.
SL UI Notification Service	*svchost.exe*	Provides Software Licensing activation and notification.

Name	Filename	Description
Smart Card	*svchost.exe*	Manages access to smart cards read by this computer. If this service is stopped, this computer will be unable to read smart cards.
Smart Card Removal Policy	*svchost.exe*	Allows the system to be configured to lock the user desktop upon smart card removal.
SNMP Trap	*Snmptrap.exe*	Receives trap messages generated by local or remote Simple Network Management Protocol (SNMP) agents and forwards the messages to SNMP management programs running on this computer. If this service is stopped, SNMP-based programs on this computer will not receive SNMP trap messages.
Software Licensing	*slsvc.exe*	Enables the download, installation, and enforcement of digital licenses for Windows and Windows applications. If the service is disabled, the operating system and licensed applications may run in a reduced function mode.
SSDP Discovery Service	*svchost.exe*	Enables discovery of UPnP devices on your home network.
Superfetch	*svchost.exe*	Maintains and improves system performance over time.
System Event Notification	*svchost.exe*	Tracks system events such as Windows logon, network, and power events. Notifies COM+ Event System subscribers of these events.
Tablet PC Input Service	*svchost.exe*	Enables Tablet PC pen and ink functionality.
Task Scheduler	*svchost.exe*	Enables a user to configure and schedule automated tasks on this computer. If this service is stopped, these tasks will not be run at their scheduled times.
TCP/IP NetBIOS Helper	*svchost.exe*	Enables support for NetBIOS over TCP/IP (NetBT) service and NetBIOS name resolution.
Telephony	*svchost.exe*	Provides Telephony API (TAPI) support for programs that control telephony devices and IP-based voice connections on the local computer and, through the LAN, on servers that are also running the service.
Terminal Services	*svchost.exe*	Allows multiple users to be connected interactively to a machine as well as the display of Desktops and applications to remote computers. The underpinning of Remote Desktop (including RD for Administrators), Fast User Switching, Remote Assistance, and Terminal Server.
Terminal Services Configuration	*svchost.exe*	Responsible for all Terminal Services and Remote Desktop–related configuration and session maintenance activities that require SYSTEM context.
Terminal Services User-Mode Port Redirector	*svchost.exe*	Allows the redirection of printers/drives/ports for RDP connections.
Themes	*svchost.exe*	Provides user experience theme management.
Thread Ordering Server	*svchost.exe*	Provides ordered execution for a group of threads within a specific period of time.
TPM Base Services	*svchost.exe*	Enables access to the Trusted Platform Module (TPM), which provides hardware-based cryptographic services to system components and applications. If this service is stopped or disabled, applications will be unable to use keys protected by the TPM.
Universal Plug and Play Device Host	*svchost.exe*	Provides support to host Universal Plug and Play devices.
User Profile Service	*svchost.exe*	Responsible for loading and unloading user profiles. If this service is stopped or disabled, users will no longer be able to successfully log on or log off, applications may have problems getting to users' data, and components registered to receive profile event notifications will not receive them.

Name	Filename	Description
Virtual Disk	*vds.exe*	Provides management services for disks, volumes, filesystems, and hardware array objects such as subsystems, controllers, and so on.
Volume Shadow Copy	*vssvc.exe*	Manages and implements Volume Shadow Copies used for backup and other purposes. If this service is stopped, shadow copies will be unavailable for backup and the backup may fail.
WebClient	*svchost.exe*	Enables Windows-based programs to create, access, and modify Internet-based files. If this service is stopped, these functions will not be available.
Windows Audio	*svchost.exe*	Manages audio devices for Windows-based programs. If this service is stopped, audio devices and effects will not function properly.
Windows Audio Endpoint Builder	*svchost.exe*	Manages audio devices for the Windows Audio service. If this service is stopped, audio devices and effects will not function properly.
Windows Backup	*svchost.exe*	Provides Windows Backup and Restore capabilities.
Windows CardSpace	*infocard.exe*	Securely enables the creation, management, and disclosure of digital identities.
Windows Color System	*svchost.exe*	Hosts third-party Windows Color System color device model and gamut map model plug-in modules.
Windows Connect Now—Config Registrar	*svchost.exe*	Acts as a registrar; issues network credential to enrollee.
Windows Defender	*svchost.exe*	Scans your computer for unwanted software, schedules scans, and gets the latest unwanted software definitions
Windows Driver Foundation—User-mode Driver Framework	*svchost.exe*	Manages user-mode driver host processes.
Windows Error Reporting Service	*svchost.exe*	Allows errors to be reported when programs stop working or responding and allows existing solutions to be delivered. Also allows logs to be generated for diagnostic and repair services. If this service is stopped, error reporting might not work correctly and results of diagnostic services and repairs might not be displayed.
Windows Event Collector	*svchost.exe*	Manages persistent subscriptions to events from remote sources that support the WS-Management protocol. This includes Windows Vista event logs, hardware, and IPMI-enabled event sources. If this service is stopped or disabled, event subscriptions cannot be created and forwarded events cannot be accepted.
Windows Event Log	*svchost.exe*	Manages events and event logs. It supports logging events, querying events, subscribing to events, archiving event logs, and managing event metadata. It can display events in both XML and plain-text formats. Stopping this service may compromise security and reliability of the system.
Windows Firewall	*svchost.exe*	Helps protect your computer by preventing unauthorized users from gaining access to your computer through the Internet or a network.
Windows Image Acquisition (WIA)	*svchost.exe*	Provides image acquisition services for scanners and cameras.
Windows Installer	*msiexec.exe*	Installs, repairs, and removes software according to instructions contained in .*msi* files.
Windows Management Instrumentation	*svchost.exe*	Provides a common interface and object model to access management information about operating systems, devices, applications, and services. If this service is stopped, most Windows-based software will not function properly.

Table E-1. Services in Windows Vista (continued)

Name	Filename	Description
Windows Media Center Receiver Service	*ehrecvr.exe*	Windows Media Center Service for TV and FM broadcast reception.
Windows Media Center Scheduler Service	*ehsched.exe*	Starts and stops recording of TV programs within Windows Media Center.
Windows Media Center Service Launcher	*svchost.exe*	Starts Windows Media Center Scheduler and Windows Media Center Receiver services at startup if TV is enabled within Windows Media Center.
Windows Media Player Network Sharing Service	*wmpnetwk.exe*	Shares Windows Media Player libraries with other networked players and media devices using Universal Plug and Play.
Windows Modules Installer	*trustedinstaller.exe*	Enables installation, modification, and removal of Windows updates and optional components. If this service is disabled, you may not be able to install or uninstall Windows updates.
Windows Presentation Foundation Font Cache	*presentation-fontcache.exe*	Optimizes performance of Windows Presentation Foundation (WPF) applications by caching commonly used font data. WPF applications will start this service if it is not already running. It can be disabled, though doing so will degrade the performance of WPF applications.
Windows Process Activation Service	*svchost.exe*	Provides process activation, resource management, and health management services for message-activated applications.
Windows Remote Management (WS-Management)	*svchost.exe*	Implements the WS-Management protocol for remote management, a standard web services protocol used for remote software and hardware management.
Windows Search	*searchindexer.exe*	Provides content indexing and property caching for file, email, and other content (via extensibility APIs). If the service is stopped or disabled, the Explorer will not be able to display virtual folder views of items, and search in the Explorer will fall back to item-by-item slow search.
Windows Time	*svchost.exe*	Maintains date and time synchronization on all clients and servers in the network. If this service is stopped, date and time synchronization will be unavailable.
Windows Update	*svchost.exe*	Enables the detection, download, and installation of updates for Windows and other programs. If this service is disabled, users of this computer will not be able to use Windows Update or its automatic updating feature, and programs will not be able to use the Windows Update Agent (WUA) API.
WinHTTP Web Proxy Auto-Discovery Service	*svchost.exe*	Implements the client HTTP stack and provides developers with a Win32 API and COM Automation component for sending HTTP requests and receiving responses. In addition, WinHTTP provides support for auto-discovering a proxy configuration via its implementation of the Web Proxy Auto-Discovery (WPAD) protocol.
Wired AutoConfig	*svchost.exe*	Performs IEEE 802.1X authentication on Ethernet interfaces.
WLAN AutoConfig	*svchost.exe*	Enumerates WLAN adapters, and manages WLAN connections and profiles.
WMI Performance Adapter	*wmiapsrv.exe*	Provides performance library information from WMI HiPerf providers.
Workstation	*svchost.exe*	Creates and maintains client network connections to remote servers. If this service is stopped, these connections will be unavailable.
World Wide Web Publishing Service	*svchost.exe*	Provides web connectivity and administration through the Internet Information Services Manager.

Index

We'd like to hear your suggestions for improving our indexes. Send email to *index@oreilly.com*.

About the Author

Preston Gralla is the editor of WindowsDevCenter.com and OnDotNet. He is the author of *Internet Annoyances*, *PC Pest Control*, *Windows XP Power Hound*, and *Windows XP Hacks*, Second Edition, and he is co-author of *Windows XP Cookbook*. He has also authored more than 30 other books. He has written for major national newspapers and magazines, including *PC Magazine*, *Computerworld*, the *Los Angeles Times*, the *Dallas Morning News* (where he was the technology columnist), *USA Today*, and several others. A well-known technology expert, Preston has also appeared on many TV and radio programs and networks, including CNN, MSNBC, and NPR. In addition, he's won a number of awards for his writing, including "Best Feature in a Computer Magazine" from the Computer Press Association. He lives in Cambridge, Massachusetts.

Colophon

The animal on the cover of *Windows Vista in a Nutshell* is a European common frog (*Rana temporaria*), also known as the "brown frog" or "grass frog." This species inhabits Europe from the Pyrenees to the Urals and West Siberia. It can be found in just about any damp habitat within this range, including lowland and mountain forests, meadows, swamps, ponds, lakes, rivers, gardens, backyards, and parks.

The European common frog has a small, squat body and a wide, flat head. The frog is typically brown or grayish in color but can also have yellowish or red hues. The lower segments of its backbone are fused into a stiff rod called the urostyle, which, along with its strong pelvic bones, helps provide strength and firmness to the rear of the body. The frogs have powerful hind legs and webbed feet, which contribute to their excellent jumping and swimming abilities.

The males of the species tend to be slightly smaller than the females and are identifiable by whitish swellings on the inner digits of their front feet. During breeding season, these swellings support dark "nuptial pads" that enable the male to grasp the female more effectively. The male can be very vocal when trying to attract a mate, even croaking underwater. Once he has attracted a female, he climbs on her back and embraces her in a tight, sometimes suffocating grip called amplexus, which can last up to two days. He fertilizes the eggs as the female lays them. In recent years, scientists researching the species in the Pyrenees have discovered a behavior known as "clutch piracy," in which gangs of males search for newly laid eggs to fertilize them again. The researchers have found evidence of fertilization from as many as four males in a single clutch of eggs.

Although huge numbers of eggs are laid, few frogs survive to adulthood. Tadpoles are preyed upon by both terrestrial and aquatic animals, and adult frogs count grass snakes, kingfishers, and herons among their many predators. Additionally, many frogs are caught by humans for the purposes of education, medicine, and science. Overall, however, this particular species is neither declining nor threatened.

The cover image is from Wood's *Reptiles, Fishes, Insects, &c.* The cover font is Adobe ITC Garamond. The text font is Linotype Birka; the heading font is Adobe Myriad Condensed; and the code font is LucasFont's TheSans Mono Condensed.

Better than e-books

Buy *Windows Vista in a Nutshell* and access
the digital edition FREE on Safari for 45 days.

Go to www.oreilly.com/go/safarienabled
and type in coupon code AOFKSAA

Search
thousands of
top tech books

Download
whole chapters

Cut and Paste
code examples

Find
answers fast

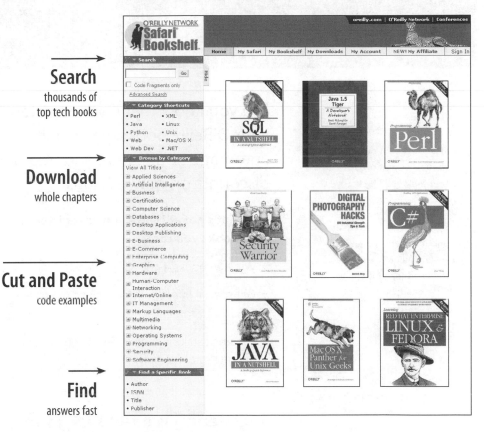

Search Safari! The premier electronic reference
library for programmers and IT professionals.